Java AWT Reference

THE JAVA SERIES™

Exploring Java

Java Threads

Java Network Programming

Java Virtual Machine

Java AWT Reference

Java Language Reference

Java Fundamental Classes Reference

Also from O'Reilly

Java in a Nutshell

Java AWT Reference

John Zukowski

O'REILLY™

Cambridge · Köln · Paris · Sebastopol · Tokyo

Java AWT Reference

by John Zukowski

Published by O'Reilly & Associates, Inc., 101 Morris Street, Sebastopol, CA 95472.

Editor: Mike Loukides

Production Editor: Nancy Crumpton

Printing History:

      March 1997:   First Edition

ISBN: 1-56592-240-9   [8/97]

Table of Contents

Preface

The Abstract Window Tookit (AWT) provides the user interface for Java programs. Unless you want to construct your own GUI or use a crude text-only interface, the AWT provides the tools you will use to communicate with the user. Although we are beginning to see some other APIs for building user interfaces, like Netscape's IFC (Internet Foundation Classes), those alternative APIs will not be in widespread use for some time, and some will be platform specific. Likewise, we are beginning to see automated tools for building GUIs in Java; Sun's JavaBeans effort promises to make such tools much more widespread. (In fact, the biggest changes in Java 1.1 prepare the way for using the various AWT components as JavaBeans.) However, even with automated tools and JavaBeans in the future, an in-depth knowledge of AWT is essential for the practicing Java programmer.

The major problem facing Java developers these days is that AWT is a moving target. Java 1.0.2 is being replaced by Java 1.1, with many significant new features. Java 1.1 was released on February 18, 1997, but it isn't clear how long it will take for 1.1 to be accepted in the market. The problem facing developers is not just learning about the new features and changes in Java 1.1, but also knowing when they can afford to use these new features in their code. In practice, this boils down to one question: when will Netscape Navigator support Java 1.1? Rumor has it that the answer is "as soon as possible"—and we all hope this rumor is correct. But given the realities of maintaining a very complex piece of software, and the fact that Netscape is currently in the beta process for Navigator 4.0, there's a possibility that "as soon as possible" and "soon" aren't the same thing. In other words, you should expect Java 1.0.2 to stick around for a while, especially since Web users won't all replace their browsers as soon as Navigator has 1.1 support.

This state of affairs raises obvious problems for my book. Nothing would have made me happier than to write a book that covered AWT 1.1 only. It would be significantly shorter, for one thing, and I wouldn't have to spend so much effort pointing out which features are present in which release. But that's not the current reality. For the time being, programmers still need to know about 1.0.2. Therefore, this book covers both releases thoroughly. There are many examples using 1.0.2; many more examples that require 1.1; and more examples showing you how to update 1.0.2 code to use 1.1's features.

Sun has done a good job of maintaining compatibility between versions: 1.0 code runs under Java 1.1, with very few exceptions. All of the 1.0 examples in this book have been tested under Java 1.1. However, Java 1.1—and particularly, AWT 1.1—offer many advantages over older releases. If nothing else, I hope this book convinces you that you should be looking forward to the day when you can forget about writing code for Java 1.0.2.

New Features of AWT in Java 1.1

Having spent all this time talking about 1.0.2 and 1.1 and the transitional state we're currently in and having alluded briefly to the advantages of Java 1.1, you deserve a brief summary of what has changed. Of course, you'll find the details in the book.

Improved event handling

Java 1.1 provides a completely new event model. Instead of propagating events to all objects that might possibly have an interest, objects in Java 1.1 register their interest in particular kinds of events and get only the events they're interested in hearing. The old event model is still supported, but the new model is much more efficient.

The new event model is also important in the context of JavaBeans. The old events were pretty much specific to AWT. The new model has been designed as a general purpose feature for communication between software components. Unfortunately, how to use events in this more general sense is beyond the scope of this book, but you should be aware that it's possible.

New components and containers

Java 1.1 provides one new component, the PopupMenu, and one new container, the ScrollPane. Pop-up menus are a staple of modern user interfaces; providing them fixes a serious omission. ScrollPane makes it trivial to implement scrolling; in Java 1.0, you had to do scrolling "by hand." In Java 1.1, you also get menu shortcuts (i.e., the ability to select menu items using the keyboard), another standard feature of modern user interfaces.

Java 1.1 also introduces a `LightweightPeer`, which means that it is possible to create "lightweight components." To do so, you subclass `Component` or `Container` directly; this wasn't possible in earlier releases. For simple operations, lightweight components are much more efficient than full-fledged components.

Clipboards

Java 1.1 lets you read from and write to the system clipboard and create private clipboards for use by your programs. The clipboard facility is a down payment on a larger data transfer facility, which will support drag and drop. (No promises about when drag and drop will appear.)

Printing

Java 1.1 gives components the ability to print.

The rest

There are many other new features, including more flexible use of cursors; the ability to use system color schemes, and thus make your program look like other software in the run-time environment; more image filters to play with; and the ability to prescale an image.

Deprecated Methods and JavaBeans

One of the biggest changes in Java 1.1 doesn't concern the feature set at all. This was the addition of many new methods that differ from a method of Java 1.0 in name only. There are hundreds of these, particularly in AWT. The new method names show an important future direction for the AWT package (in fact, all of Java). The new names obey the naming conventions used by JavaBeans, which means that all AWT classes are potentially Beans. These conventions make it possible for an application builder to analyze what a component does based on its public methods. For example, the method `setFont()` changes the value of the component's `Font` property. In turn, this means that you will eventually be able to build user interfaces and, in some cases, entire applications, inside some other tool, without writing any Java code at all. An application builder will be able to find out what it needs to know about any component by looking at the component itself, and letting you customize the component and its interactions with others.

Comments in the JDK source code indicate that the older method names have been "deprecated," which means that you should consider the old names obsolete and avoid using them; they could disappear in a future release.

Reworking AWT to comply with JavaBeans is both necessary and inevitable. Furthermore, it's a good idea to get into the habit of following the same conventions for your own code; the advantages of JavaBeans are much greater than the inconvenience of changing your coding style.

Other Changes in Java

Other new features are scattered throughout the rest of the Java classes, most notably, improvements in the networking and I/O packages and support for internationalization. Some new features were added to the language itself, of which the most important is "inner classes." For the most part, I don't discuss these changes; in fact, I stay away from them and base non-AWT code on the 1.0.2. release. Though these changes are important, covering the new material in AWT is enough for one book. If I used a new feature at this point, I would feel that I owed you an explanation, and this book is already long enough. A future edition will update the code so that it doesn't rely on any older features.

What This Book Covers

The *Java AWT Reference* is the definitive resource for programmers working with AWT. It covers all aspects of the AWT package, in versions 1.0.2 and 1.1. If there are any changes to AWT after 1.1 (at least two patch releases are expected), we will integrate them as soon as possible. Watch the book's Web site *http://www.ora.com/catalog/javawt/* for details on changes.

Specifically, this book completely covers the following packages:

java.awt (1.0 and 1.1)
java.awt.image (1.0 and 1.1)
java.awt.event (new to 1.1)
java.awt.datatransfer (new to 1.1)
java.awt.peer (1.0 and 1.1)
java.applet (1.0 and 1.1)

The book also covers some aspects of the sun.awt package (some interesting and useful layout managers) and the sun.audio package (some more flexible ways of working with audio files). It also gives a brief overview of the behind-the-scenes machinery for rendering images, much of which is in the sun.awt.image package.

Organization

The *Java AWT Reference* is divided into two large parts. The first part is a thorough guide to using AWT. Although this guide is organized by class, it was designed to flow logically, rather than alphabetically. I know that few people read a book like this from beginning to end, but if you want to, it's possible. With a few exceptions, you should be able to read the early chapters without knowing the material that's covered in the later chapters. You'll want to read this section to find out how any chunk of the AWT package works in detail.

The second part is a set of documentation pages typical of what you find in most reference sets. It is organized alphabetically by package, and within each package, alphabetically by class. It is designed to answer questions like "What are the arguments to the FilteredImageSource constructor?" The reference section provides brief summaries, rather than detailed discussions and examples. When you use a typical reference book, you're usually trying to look up some detail, rather than learn how something works from scratch.

In other words, this book provides two views of AWT: terse summaries designed to help you when you need to look something up quickly, and much more detailed explanations designed to help you understand how to use AWT to the fullest. In doing so, it goes well beyond the standard reference manual. A reference manual alone gives you a great view of hundreds of individual trees; this book gives you the trees, but also gives you the forest that allows you to put the individual pieces in context. There are dozens of complete examples, together with background information, overview material, and other information that doesn't fit into the standard reference manual format.

About the Source Code

The source code for the programs presented in this book is available online. See *http://www.ora.com/catalog/javawt/* for downloading instructions.

Obtaining the Example Programs

The example programs in this book are available electronically in a number of ways: by FTP, Ftpmail, BITFTP, and UUCP. The cheapest, fastest, and easiest ways are listed first. If you read from the top down, the first one that works for you is probably the best. Use FTP if you are directly on the Internet. Use Ftpmail if you are not on the Internet but can send and receive electronic mail to Internet sites (this includes CompuServe users). Use BITFTP if you send electronic mail via BIT-NET. Use UUCP if none of the above works.

FTP

To use FTP, you need a machine with direct access to the Internet. A sample session is shown, with what you should type in **boldface**.

```
% ftp ftp.ora.com
Connected to ftp.ora.com.
220 FTP server (Version 6.21 Tue Mar 10 22:09:55 EST 1992) ready.
Name (ftp.ora.com:yourname): anonymous
331 Guest login ok, send domain style e-mail address as password.
Password: yourname@yourhost.com (use your user name and host here)
230 Guest login ok, access restrictions apply.
ftp> cd /published/oreilly/java/awt
```

```
250 CWD command successful.
ftp> binary (Very important! You must specify binary transfer for compressed files.)
200 Type set to I.
ftp> get examples.tar.gz
200 PORT command successful.
150 Opening BINARY mode data connection for examples.tar.gz.
226 Transfer complete.
ftp> quit
221 Goodbye.
%
```

The file is a compressed *tar* archive; extract the files from the archive by typing:

```
% zcat examples.tar.gz | tar xvf -
```

System V systems require the following *tar* command instead:

```
% zcat examples.tar.gz | tar xof -
```

If *zcat* is not available on your system, use separate *gunzip* and *tar* commands.

```
% gunzip examples.tar.gz
% tar xvf examples.tar
```

Ftpmail

Ftpmail is a mail server available to anyone who can send electronic mail to, and receive it from, Internet sites. This includes any company or service provider that allows email connections to the Internet. Here's how you do it.

You send mail to *ftpmail@online.ora.com*. (Be sure to address the message to *ftpmail* and not to *ftp*.) In the message body, give the FTP commands you want to run. The server will run anonymous FTP for you and mail the files back to you. To get a complete help file, send a message with no subject and the single word "help" in the body. The following is a sample mail session that should get you the examples. This command sends you a listing of the files in the selected directory and the requested example files. The listing is useful if there's a later version of the examples you're interested in.

```
% mail ftpmail@online.ora.com
Subject:
reply-to yourname@yourhost.com        Where you want files mailed
open
cd /published/oreilly/java/awt
dir
mode binary
uuencode
get examples.tar.gz
quit
.
```

A signature at the end of the message is acceptable as long as it appears after "quit."

BITFTP

BITFTP is a mail server for BITNET users. You send it electronic mail messages requesting files, and it sends you back the files by electronic mail. BITFTP currently serves only users who send it mail from nodes that are directly on BITNET, EARN, or NetNorth. BITFTP is a public service of Princeton University. Here's how it works.

To use BITFTP, send mail containing your FTP commands to *BITFTP@PUCC*. For a complete help file, send HELP as the message body.

The following is the message body you send to BITFTP:

```
FTP   ftp.uu.net   NETDATA
USER  anonymous
PASS  yourname@yourhost.edu   Put your Internet email address here (not your BITNET address)
CD    /published/oreilly/java/awt
DIR
BINARY
GET   examples.tar.gz
QUIT
```

Once you've got the desired file, follow the directions under FTP to extract the files from the archive. Since you are probably not on a UNIX system, you may need to get versions of *uudecode, uncompress, atob,* and *tar* for your system. VMS, DOS, and Mac versions are available. The VMS versions are on *gatekeeper.dec.com* in */pub/VMS*.

UUCP

UUCP is standard on virtually all UNIX systems and is available for IBM-compatible PCs and Apple Macintoshes. The examples are available by UUCP via modem from UUNET; UUNET's connect-time charges apply.

If you or your company has an account with UUNET, you have a system somewhere with a direct UUCP connection to UUNET. Find that system, and type:

```
uucp uunet\!~/published/oreilly/java/awt/examples.tar.gz yourhost\!~/yourname/
```

The backslashes can be omitted if you use the Bourne shell (*sh*) instead of *csh*. The file should appear some time later (up to a day or more) in the directory */usr/spool/uucppublic/yourname*. If you don't have an account, but would like one so that you can get electronic mail, contact UUNET at 703-204-8000.

Once you've got the desired file, follow the directions under FTP to extract the files from the archive.

Other Java Books and Resources

This book is part of a series of Java books from O'Reilly & Associates that covers everything you wanted to know, and then some. The *Java AWT Reference* is paired with the *Java Fundamental Class Reference* to document the entire Core Java API. Other books in the series provide an introduction (*Exploring Java*) and document the virtual machine (*Java Virtual Machine*), the language (*Java Language Reference*), multithreaded programming (*Java Threads*), and network programming (*Java Network Programming*), with more to come. *Java in a Nutshell* is another popular Java book in the Nutshell series from O'Reilly. For a complete up-to-date list of the available Java resources, refer to *http://www.ora.com/info/java/*.

In addition to the resources from O'Reilly, Sun's online documentation on Java is maintained at *http://www.javasoft.com/nav/download/index.html*. Information on specific Java-capable browsers can be found at their respective Web sites, which are listed in Table 1. More are sure to be on the way. (Some browsers are platform specific, while others are multi-platform.)

Table 1: Popular Web Browsers that Support Java

Browser	Location
Netscape Navigator	*http://home.netscape.com/comprod/products/navigator/*
Microsoft's Internet Explorer	*http://www.microsoft.com/ie*
Sun's HotJava	*http://www.javasoft.com/HotJava/*
Oracle's PowerBrowser	*http://www.oracle.com/products/websystem/powerbrowser*
Apple's Cyberdog	*http://cyberdog.apple.com/*

Newsgroups also serve as a discussion area for Java-related topics. The *comp.lang.java* group has formally split into several others. The new groups are:

comp.lang.java.advocacy	*comp.lang.java.machine*
comp.lang.java.announce	*comp.lang.java.programmer*
comp.lang.java.beans	*comp.lang.java.security*
comp.lang.java.databases	*comp.lang.java.setup*
comp.lang.java.gui	*comp.lang.java.softwaretools*
comp.lang.java.help	*comp.lang.java.tech*

For folks without time to dig through all the noise, *Digital Espresso* provides a periodic digest of the newsfeed at *http://www.io.org./~mentor/DigitalEspresso.html*. A list of

Java FAQs is at *http://www-net.com/java/faq/*; one of the most interesting is *Cafe Au Lait*, at *http://sunsite.unc.edu/javafaq/*. (*Cafe Au Lait* is written by Elliotte Rusty Harold, author of *Java Network Programming*.)

Local Java user groups are another good resource. (Having founded one myself, I'm biased.) What they offer varies greatly, but unless you look at one, you are potentially leaving out a vast resource for knowledge and experience. Lists of area user groups are available from JavaSoft at *http://www.javasoft.com/Mail/usrgrp.html*; also check out the Sun User Group's Special Interest Group for Users of Java at *http://www.sug.org/Java/groups.html*. In addition to the usual monthly meetings and forums, some maintain a mailing list for technical exchanges.

Security is a major issue with Java. If you are interested in reading more about Java security issues, Princeton University's Safe Internet Programming Web site at *http://www.cs.princeton.edu/sip/News.html* is an excellent resource.

About Java

Java is one of 13,000 islands that makes up Indonesia, whose capital is Jakarta (see Figure 1). It is home to about 120 million people with an area about 50,000 square miles. While on the island, you can hear traditional music such as gamelan or angklung. The island also has a dangerous volcano named Merapi, which makes up part of the Pacific "Ring of Fire." In 1891, fossils from Pithecanthropus erectus, better known as "Java man" (*homo javanensis*) were discovered on the island by Eugene Dubois.

Java's main export is a coffee that is considered spicy and full bodied, with a strong, slightly acidic flavor. O'Reilly has shown good taste in staying away from the pervasive coffee theme in its book titles and cover designs. (However, if you're ever in Sebastopol, check out the coffee at AromaRoasters in Santa Rosa.)

Conventions Used in This Book

Italic is used for:

* Pathnames, filenames, and program names
* Internet addresses, such as domain names and URLs

`Typewriter Font` is used for:

* Anything that might appear in a Java program, including keywords, method names, variables names, class names, and interface names

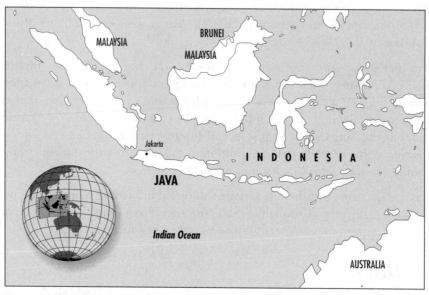

Figure 1: Map of Java, Indonesia

- Command lines and options that should be typed verbatim on the screen

- Tags that might appear in an HTML document

To sort out the potential for confusion between different versions, I use the following dingbats throughout the book:

★   Identifies a method, variable, or constant that is new in Java 1.1.

☆   Identifies a method from Java 1.0 that has been deprecated. Deprecated methods are available for compatibility but may disappear in a future release. These methods are tagged with the @deprecated flag, which causes the Java 1.1 compiler to display a warning message if you use them.

Request for Comments

We invite you to help us improve the book. If you have an idea that could make this a more useful resource, or if you find a bug in an example program or an error in the text, please let us know by sending email to *bookquestions@ora.com*.

As Java continues to evolve, we may find it necessary to issue errata for this book or to release updated examples or reference information. This information will be found at the book's Web site *http://www.ora.com/catalog/javawt/*.

Acknowledgments

I am grateful to many people who helped me along while working on this book, especially my wife, Lisa, and her patience during this whole process. A special thanks goes to our Old English sheep dog, Sir Dudley Fuzzybuns McDuff for gladly sharing the house with me during the entire process. I am grateful to the people at Sun who helped me become involved with Java so early on: Pete Seymour, Anne Pettitt, Tom McGinn, and Jen Sullivan-Volpe. I am also grateful to my employers, Rapid Systems Solutions (when I started) and the MageLang Institute (when I finished), who let me work on the book. Another thanks goes out to Dale Carnegie Training and John Captain, whose human relations class helped me feel comfortable with public speaking, without which I would not have become immersed in Java so quickly.

Particular thanks are owed to the technical reviewers: Yadu Zambre, Andy Cohen, David Flanagan, Jen Sullivan-Volpe, and Dan Jacobs. All of them performed an invaluable service with their thorough reviews and helped spot my errors and omissions. It seemed everyone contributed many bits of text that eventually found their way into the final product.

Random thanks go out to the many people on the Internet who I never met but provided valuable information, from the newsgroups and mailing lists: Simon "FISH" Morris, Mike Gallant, Eric Link, and many others whose names I did not write down.

Bits and pieces of various figures were borrowed from David Flanagan's book, *Java in a Nutshell*, and Patrick Niemeyer's and Joshua Peck's book, *Exploring Java*. The class hierarchy diagrams come from David's book. These diagrams were based on similar diagrams by Charles L. Perkins. His original efforts are available at *http://rendezvous.com/java/*.

For the gang at O'Reilly who gave me the opportunity to write this work, I thank everyone who helped along the way. For series editor, Mike Loukides, thanks for all your time and effort, especially with the early drafts. Best of luck to Mike and Judy with their new bundle of joy, Alexandra. Special thanks to Jonathan Knudsen who updated the reference section for the new release. Thanks to Nancy Crumpton and John Files for book production and project management, and to Trina Jackson, Paula Ferguson, and Andy Oram who helped during the review stages. Thanks also to the O'Reilly Tools group, Ellen Siever, Erik Ray, and Lenny Muellner; to Seth Maislin, the indexer; and David Futato and Danny Marcus who handled the proofreading and QCs.

The final product is much better because of their help.

1

Abstract Window Toolkit Overview

For years, programmers have had to go through the hassles of porting software from BSD-based UNIX to System V Release 4–based UNIX, from OpenWindows to Motif, from PC to UNIX to Macintosh (or some combination thereof), and between various other alternatives, too numerous to mention. Getting an application to work was only part of the problem; you also had to port it to all the platforms you supported, which often took more time than the development effort itself. In the UNIX world, standards like POSIX and X made it easier to move applications between different UNIX platforms. But they only solved part of the problem and didn't provide any help with the PC world. Portability became even more important as the Internet grew. The goal was clear: wouldn't it be great if you could just move applications between different operating environments without worrying about the software breaking because of a different operating system, windowing environment, or internal data representation?

In the spring of 1995, Sun Microsystems announced Java, which claimed to solve this dilemma. What started out as a dancing penguin (or Star Trek communicator) named Duke on remote controls for interactive television has become a new paradigm for programming on the Internet. With Java, you can create a program on one platform and deliver the compilation output (byte-codes/class files) to every other supported environment without recompiling or worrying about the local windowing environment, word size, or byte order. The first generation of Java programs consisted mostly of fancy animation applets that ran in a web browser like Netscape Navigator, Internet Explorer, or HotJava. We're beginning to see the next generation now: powerful distributed applications in areas ranging from commerce to medical imaging to network management. All of these applications require extreme portability: Joe's Online Bait Shop doesn't have the time or energy to port its "Online Bait Buyer" program to every platform on the Internet but doesn't want to limit its market to a specific platform. Java neatly solves their problem.

Windowing systems present the biggest challenges for portability. When you move an application from Windows to the Macintosh, you may be able to salvage most of the computational guts, but you'll have to rewrite the window interface code completely. In Java, this part of the portability challenge is addressed by a package called AWT, which stands for Abstract Window Toolkit (although people have come up with many other expansions). AWT provides the magic of maintaining the local look and feel of the user's environment. Because of AWT, the same application program can look appropriate in any environment. For example, if your program uses a pull-down list, that list will look like a Windows list when you run the program under Windows; a Macintosh list when you run the program on a Mac; and a Motif list when you run the program on a UNIX system under Motif. The same code works on all platforms. In addition to providing a common set of user interface components, AWT provides facilities for manipulating images and generating graphics.

This book is a complete programmer's guide and reference to the `java.awt` package (including `java.awt.image`, `java.awt.event`, `java.awt.datatransfer`, and `java.awt.peer`). It assumes that you're already familiar with the Java language and class libraries. If you aren't, *Exploring Java*, by Pat Niemeyer and Josh Peck, provides a general introduction, and other books in the O'Reilly Java series provide detailed references and tutorials on specific topics. This chapter provides a quick overview of AWT: it introduces you to the various GUI elements contained within the `java.awt` package and gives you pointers to the chapters that provide more specific information about each component. If you're interested in some of the more advanced image manipulation capabilities, head right to Chapter 12, *Image Processing*. The book ends with a reference section that summarizes what you need to know about every class in AWT.

In using this book, you should be aware that it covers two versions of AWT: 1.0.2 and 1.1. The Java 1.1 JDK (Java Developer's Kit) occurred in December 1996. This release includes many improvements and additions to AWT and is a major step forward in Java's overall functionality. It would be nice if I could say, "Forget about 1.0.2, it's obsolete—use this book to learn 1.1." However, I can't; at this point, since browsers (Netscape Navigator in particular) still incorporate 1.0.2, and we have no idea when they will incorporate the new release. As of publication, Navigator 4.0 is in beta test and incorporates 1.0.2. Therefore, Java release 1.0.2 will continue to be important, at least for the foreseeable future.

In this summary, we'll point out new features of Java 1.1 as they come up. However, one feature deserves mention and doesn't fit naturally into an overview. Many of the methods of Java 1.0.2 have been renamed in Java 1.1. The old names still work but are "deprecated." The new names adhere strictly to the design patterns discussed in the JavaBeans documentation:[*] all methods that retrieve the value of an object's property begin with "get," all methods that set the value of a property begin with "set," and all methods that test the value of some property begin with "is." For example, the `size()` method is now called `getSize()`. The Java 1.1 compiler issues warnings whenever you used a deprecated method name.

1.1 Components

Modern user interfaces are built around the idea of "components": reusable gadgets that implement a specific part of the interface. They don't need much introduction: if you have used a computer since 1985 or so, you're already familiar with buttons, menus, windows, checkboxes, scrollbars, and many other similar items. AWT comes with a repertoire of basic user interface components, along with the machinery for creating your own components (often combinations of the basic components) and for communicating between components and the rest of the program.

The next few sections summarize the components that are part of AWT. If you're new to AWT, you may find it helpful to familiarize yourself with what's available before jumping into the more detailed discussions later in this book.

1.1.1 Static Text

The `Label` class provides a means to display a single line of text on the screen. That's about it. They provide visual aids to the user: for example, you might use a label to describe an input field. You have control over the size, font, and color of the text. Labels are discussed in Section 5.2. Figure 1-1 displays several labels with different attributes.

1.1.2 User Input

Java provides several different ways for a user to provide input to an application. The user can type the information or select it from a preset list of available choices. The choice depends primarily on the desired functionality of the program, the user-base, and the amount of back-end processing that you want to do.

---

[*] *http://splash.javasoft.com/beans/spec.html*

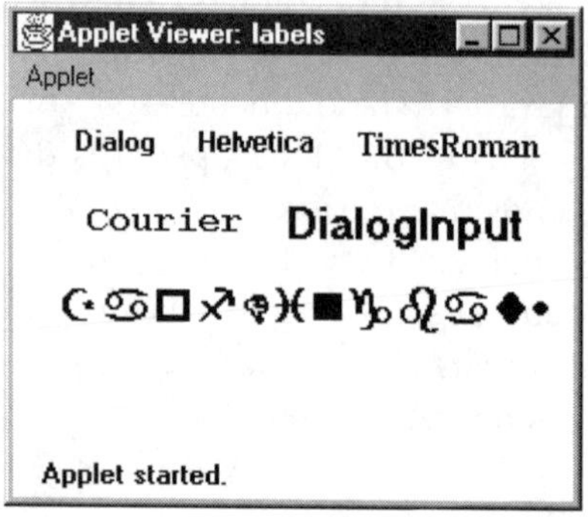

Figure 1–1: Multiple Label instances

1.1.2.1 The TextField and TextArea classes

Two components are available for entering keyboard input: TextField for single
line input and TextArea for multi-line input. They provide the means to do things
from character-level data validation to complex text editing. These are discussed in
much more detail in Chapter 8, *Input Fields*. Figure 1-2 shows a screen that contains various TextField and TextArea components.

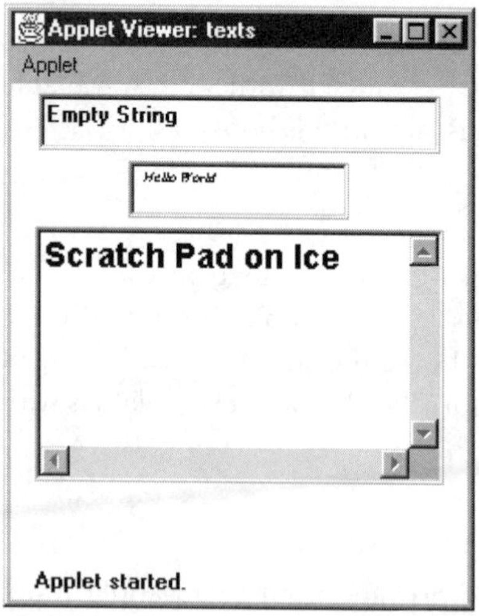

Figure 1–2: TextField and TextArea elements

1.1.2.2 The Checkbox and CheckboxGroup classes

The remaining input-oriented components provide mechanisms for letting the
user select from a list of choices. The first such mechanism is Checkbox, which lets
you select or deselect an option. The left side of the applet in Figure 1-3 shows a
checkbox for a Dialog option. Clicking on the box selects the option and makes

the box change appearance. A second click deselects the option.

The CheckboxGroup class is not a component; it provides a means for grouping checkboxes into a mutual exclusion set, often called a set of radio buttons. Selecting any button in the group automatically deselects the other buttons. This behavior is useful for a set of mutually exclusive choices. For example, the right side of the applet in Figure 1-3 shows a set of checkboxes for selecting a font. It makes sense to select only one font at a time, so these checkboxes have been put in a CheckboxGroup.

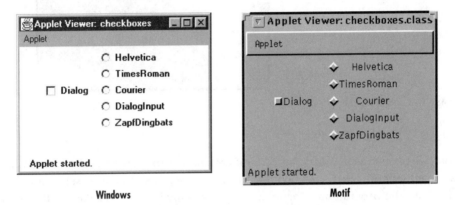

Figure 1–3: Examples of Checkbox and CheckboxGroup

The appearance of a checkbox varies from platform to platform. On the left, Figure 1-3 shows Windows; the right shows Motif. On most platforms, the appearance also changes when a checkbox is put into a CheckboxGroup.

1.1.2.3 The Choice class

Checkbox and CheckboxGroup present a problem when the list of choices becomes long. Every element of a CheckboxGroup uses precious screen real estate, which limits the amount of space available for other components. The Choice class was designed to use screen space more efficiently. When a Choice element is displayed on the screen, it takes up the space of a single item in the list, along with some extra space for decorations. This leaves more space for other components. When the user selects a Choice component, it displays the available options next to or below the Choice. Once the user makes a selection, the choices are removed from the screen, and the Choice displays the selection. At any time, only one item in a Choice may be selected, so selecting an item implicitly deselects everything else. Section 9.1 explores the details of the Choice class. Figure 1-4 shows examples of open (on the right of the screens) and closed (on the left) Choice items in Windows 95 and Motif.

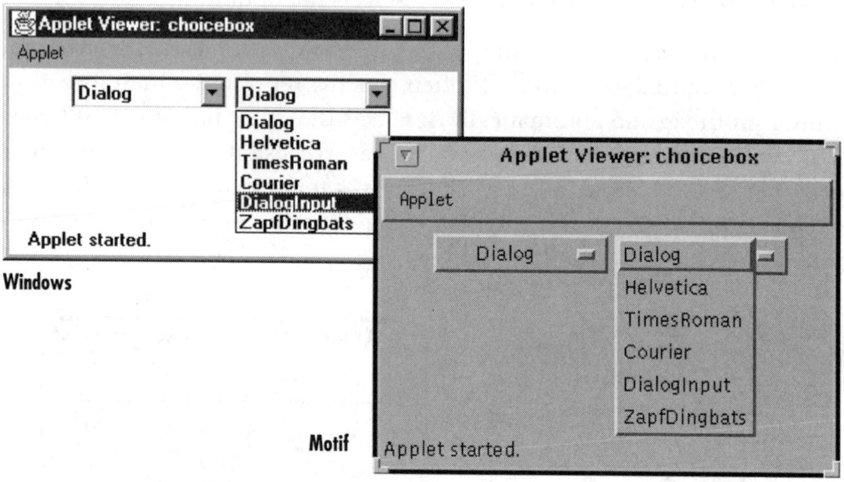

Figure 1–4: Open and closed Choice items

1.1.2.4 The List class

Somewhere between `Choice` and `CheckboxGroup` in the screen real estate business is a component called `List`. With a `List`, the user is still able to select any item. However, the programmer recommends how many items to display on the screen at once. All additional choices are still available, but the user moves an attached scrollbar to access them. Unlike a `Choice`, a `List` allows the user to select multiple items. Section 9.2 covers the `List` component. Figure 1-5 shows `List` components in different states.

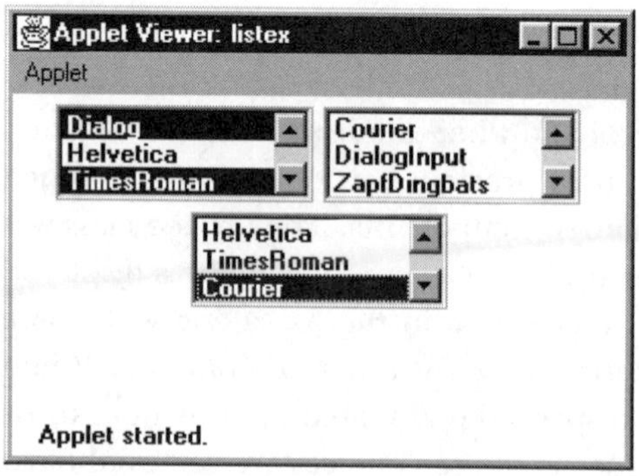

Figure 1–5: List components in different states

1.1.2.5 Menus

Most modern user interfaces use menus heavily; therefore, it's no surprise that Java supports menus. As you'd expect, Java menus look like the menus in the windowing environment under which the program runs. Currently, menus can only appear within a Frame, although this will probably change in the future. A Menu is a fairly complex object, with lots of moving parts: menu bars, menu items, etc. Java 1.1 adds hot keys to menus, allowing users to navigate a menu interface using keyboard shortcuts. The details of Menu are explored in Chapter 10, *Would You Like to Choose from the Menu?* Figure 1-6 shows frames with open menus for both Windows and Motif. Since tear-off menus are available on Motif systems, its menus look and act a little differently. Figure 1-6 also includes a tear-off menu. The shortcuts (Ctrl+F8) are newly supported in Java 1.1.

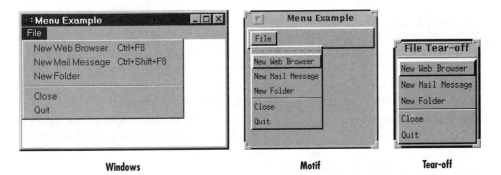

Windows   Motif   Tear-off

Figure 1–6: Examples of menus

1.1.2.6 The PopupMenu class

The PopupMenu class is new to Java 1.1. Pop-up menus can be used for context-sensitive, component-level menus. Associated with each Component can be its own pop-up menu. The details of creating and working with the PopupMenu class and the fun time you have catching their events are covered in Chapter 10, *Would You Like to Choose from the Menu?* Figure 1-7 shows an example of a pop-up menu.

1.1.3 Event Triggers

Java provides two components whose sole purpose is to trigger actions on the screen: Button and Scrollbar. They provide the means for users to signal that they are ready to perform an operation. (Note that all components except labels generate events; I'm singling out buttons and scrollbars because their only purpose is to generate events.)

Figure 1–7: A Pop-up menu

1.1.3.1 The Scrollbar class

Most people are familiar with scrollbars. In a word processor or a web browser, when an image or document is too large to fit on the screen, the scrollbar allows the user to move to another area. With Java, the Scrollbar performs similarly. Selecting or moving the scrollbar triggers an event that allows the program to process the scrollbar movement and respond accordingly. The details of the Scrollbar are covered in Section 11.1. Figure 1-8 shows horizontal and vertical scrollbars.

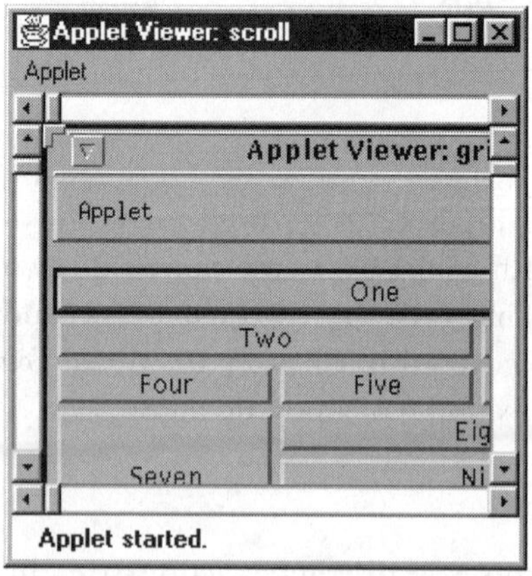

Figure 1–8: Horizontal and vertical scrollbars

Note that a scrollbar is just that. It generates events when the user adjusts it, but the program using the scrollbar is responsible for figuring out what to do with the events, such as displaying a different part of an image or the text, etc. Several of the components we've discussed, like TextArea and List, have built-in scrollbars, saving you the trouble of writing your own code to do the actual scrolling. Java 1.1 has a new container called a ScrollPane that has scrolling built in. By using a scroll pane, you should be able to avoid using scroll bars as a positioning mechanism. An example of ScrollPane appears later in this chapter.

1.1.3.2 The Button class

A button is little more than a label that you can click on. Selecting a button triggers an event telling the program to go to work. Section 5.3 explores the Button component. Figure 1-9 shows Button examples.

Figure 1–9: Various buttons

The Java Management API includes a fancier button (ImageButton) with pictures rather than labels. For the time being, this is a standard extension of Java and not in the Core API. If you don't want to use these extensions, you'll have to implement an image button yourself.

1.1.4 Expansion

1.1.4.1 The Canvas class

The Canvas class is just a blank area; it doesn't have any predefined appearance. You can use Canvas for drawing images, building new kinds of components, or creating super-components that are aggregates of other components. For example, you can build a picture button by drawing a picture on a Canvas and detecting mouse click events within the area of the Canvas. Canvas is discussed in Section 5.5.

1.2 Peers

Java programs always have the look and feel of the platform they are running on. If you create your program on a UNIX platform and deliver it to Microsoft Windows users, your program will have Motif's look and feel while you're developing it, but users will see Microsoft Windows objects when they use it. Java accomplishes this through a peer architecture, shown in Figure 1-10.

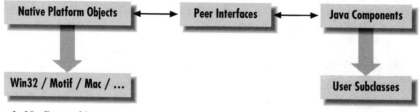

Figure 1–10: Peer architecture

There are several layers of software between your Java program and the actual screen. Let's say you are working with a scrollbar. On your screen, you see the scrollbar that's native to the platform you're using. This system-dependent scrollbar is the "peer" of the Java Scrollbar object. The peer scrollbar deals with events like mouse clicks first, passing along whatever it deems necessary to the corresponding Java component. The peer interface defines the relationship between each Java component and its peer; it is what allows a generic component (like a Scrollbar) to work with scrollbars on different platforms.

Peers are described in Chapter 15, *Toolkit and Peers*. However, you rarely need to worry about them; interaction between a Java program and a peer takes place behind the scenes. On occasion, you need to make sure that a component's peer exists in order to find out about platform-specific sizes. This process usually involves the addNotify() method.

1.3 Layouts

Layouts allow you to format components on the screen in a platform-independent way. Without layouts, you would be forced to place components at explicit locations on the screen, creating obvious problems for programs that need to run on multiple platforms. There's no guarantee that a TextArea or a Scrollbar or any other component will be the same size on each platform; in fact, you can bet they won't be. In an effort to make your Java creations portable across multiple platforms, Sun created a LayoutManager interface that defines methods to reformat the screen based on the current layout and component sizes. Layout managers try to give programs a consistent and reasonable appearance, regardless of the platform, the screen size, or actions the user might take.

The standard JDK provides five classes that implement the LayoutManager interface. They are FlowLayout, GridLayout, BorderLayout, CardLayout, and Grid-BagLayout. All of these layouts are covered in much greater detail in Chapter 7, *Layouts*. This chapter also discusses how to create complex layouts by combining layout managers and how to write your own LayoutManager. The Java 1.1 JDK includes the LayoutManager2 interface. This interface extends the LayoutManager interface for managers that provide constraint-based layouts.

1.3.1 FlowLayout

The FlowLayout is the default layout for the Panel class, which includes its most famous subclass, Applet. When you add components to the screen, they flow left to right (centered within the applet) based upon the order added and the width of the applet. When there are too many components to fit, they "wrap" to a new row, similar to a word processor with word wrap enabled. If you resize an applet, the components' flow will change based upon the new width and height. Figure 1-11 shows an example both before and after resizing. Section 7.2 contains all the FlowLayout details.

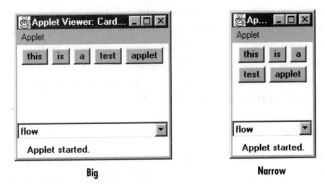

Figure 1–11: A FlowLayout before and after resizing

1.3.2 GridLayout

The GridLayout is widely used for arranging components in rows and columns. As with FlowLayout, the order in which you add components is relevant. You start at row one, column one, move across the row until it's full, then continue on to the next row. However, unlike FlowLayout, the underlying components are resized to fill the row-column area, if possible. GridLayout can reposition or resize objects after adding or removing components. Whenever the area is resized, the components within it are resized. Figure 1-12 shows an example before and after resizing. Section 7.4 contains all the details about GridLayout.

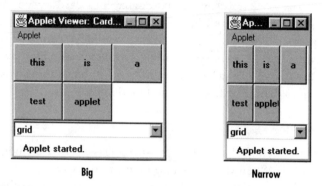

Figure 1–12: A GridLayout before and after resizing

1.3.3 BorderLayout

BorderLayout is one of the more unusual layouts provided. It is the default layout for Window, along with its children, Frame and Dialog. BorderLayout provides five areas to hold components. These areas are named after the four different borders of the screen, North, South, East, and West, with any remaining space going into the Center area. When you add a component to the layout, you must specify which area to place it in. The order in which components are added to the screen is not important, although you can have only one component in each area. Figure 1-13 shows a BorderLayout that has one button in each area, before and after resizing. Section 7.3 covers the details of the BorderLayout.

1.3.4 CardLayout

The CardLayout is a bit on the strange side. A CardLayout usually manages several components, displaying one of them at a time and hiding the rest. All the components are given the same size. Usually, the CardLayout manages a group of Panels (or some other container), and each Panel contains several components of its own. With a little work, you can use the CardLayout to create tabbed dialog boxes or property sheets, which are not currently part of AWT. CardLayout lets you assign names to the components it is managing and lets you jump to a component by name. You can also cycle through components in order. Figure 1-11, Figure 1-12, and Figure 1-13 show multiple cards controlled by a single CardLayout. Selecting the Choice button displays a different card. Section 7.5 discusses the details of CardLayout.

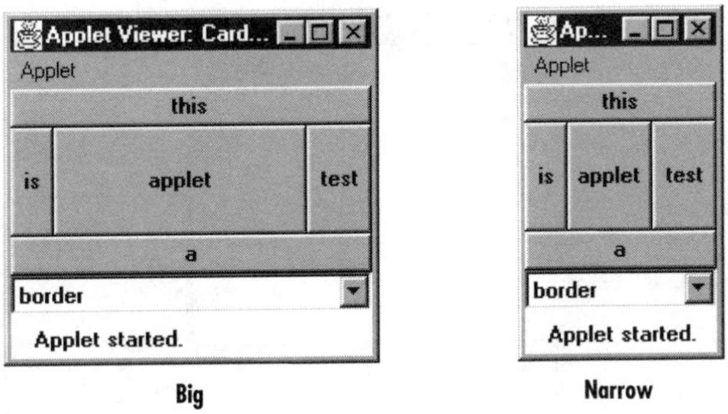

Figure 1–13: A BorderLayout

1.3.5 GridBagLayout

GridBagLayout is the most sophisticated and complex of the layouts provided in the development kit. With the GridBagLayout, you can organize components in multiple rows and columns, stretch specific rows or columns when space is available, and anchor objects in different corners. You provide all the details of each component through instances of the GridBagConstraints class. Figure 1-14 shows an example of a GridBagLayout. GridBagLayout and GridBagConstraints are discussed in Section 7.6 and Section 7.7.

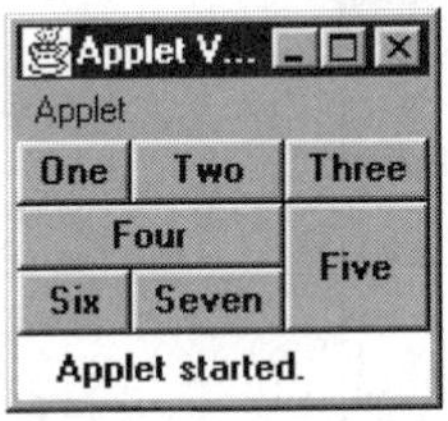

Figure 1–14: A GridBagLayout

1.4 Containers

A Container is a type of component that provides a rectangular area within which other components can be organized by a LayoutManager. Because Container is a subclass of Component, a Container can go inside another Container, which can go inside another Container, and so on, like Russian nesting dolls. Subclassing Container allows you to encapsulate code for the components within it. This allows you to create reusable higher-level objects easily. Figure 1-15 shows the components in a layout built from several nested containers.

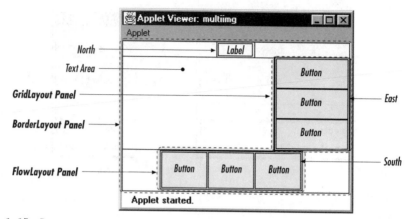

Figure 1–15: Components within containers

1.4.1 Panels

A Panel is the basic building block of an applet. It provides a container with no special features. The default layout for a Panel is FlowLayout. The details of Panel are discussed in Section 6.2. Figure 1-16 shows an applet that contains panels within panels within panels.

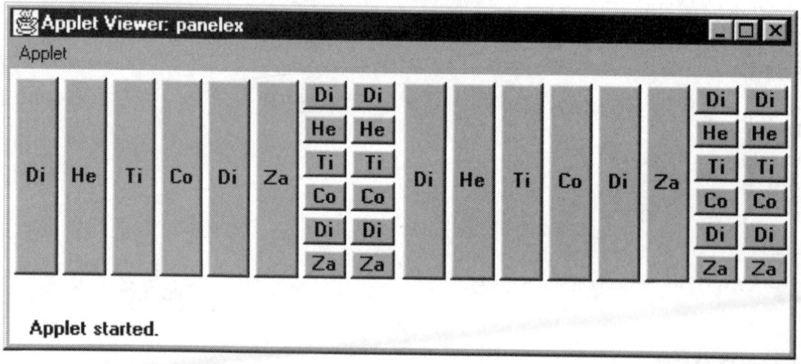

Figure 1–16: A multilevel panel

1.4.2 Windows

A Window provides a top-level window on the screen, with no borders or menu bar. It provides a way to implement pop-up messages, among other things. The default layout for a Window is BorderLayout. Section 6.4 explores the Window class in greater detail. Figure 1-17 shows a pop-up message using a Window in Microsoft Windows and Motif.

Windows

Motif

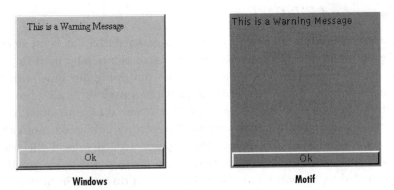

Figure 1–17: Pop-up windows

1.4.3 Frames

A `Frame` is a `Window` with all the window manager's adornments (window title, borders, window minimize/maximize/close functionality) added. It may also include a menu bar. Since `Frame` subclasses `Window`, its default layout is `BorderLayout`. `Frame` provides the basic building block for screen-oriented applications. `Frame` allows you to change the mouse cursor, set an icon image, and have menus. All the details of `Frame` are discussed in Section 6.5. Figure 1-18 shows an example `Frame`.

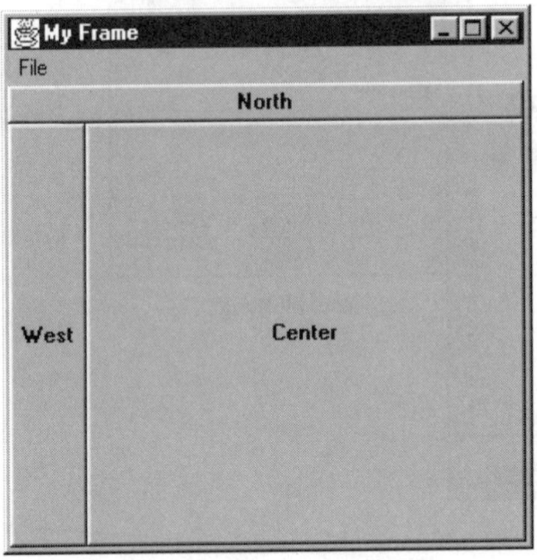

Figure 1–18: A frame

1.4.4 Dialog and FileDialog

A `Dialog` is a `Window` that accepts input from the user. `BorderLayout` is the default layout of `Dialog` because it subclasses `Window`. A `Dialog` is a pop-up used for user interaction; it can be modal to prevent the user from doing anything with the application before responding. A `FileDialog` provides a prebuilt `Dialog` box that interacts with the filesystem. It implements the Open/Save dialog provided by the native windowing system. You will primarily use `FileDialog` with applications since there is no guarantee that an applet can interact with the local filesystem. (Netscape Navigator will throw an exception if you try to use it.) The details of `Dialog` are revealed in Section 6.6, while `FileDialog` is discussed in Section 6.7. Figure 1-19 shows sample `Dialog` and `FileDialog` boxes.

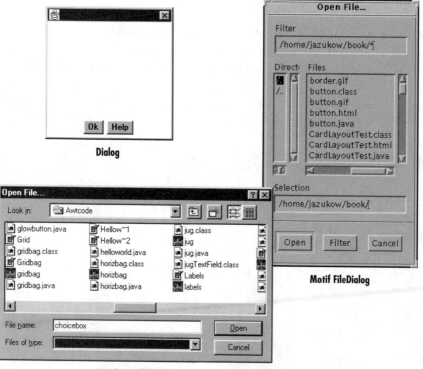

Figure 1–19: Examples of Dialog and FileDialog boxes

1.4.5 ScrollPane

Java 1.1 introduces the ScrollPane container. In version 1.0, if you want to have a scrolling area (for example, to display an image that won't fit onto the screen), you create a panel using BorderLayout that contains scrollbars on the right and bottom, and display part of the image in the rest of the screen. When the user scrolls, you capture the event, figure out what part of the image to display, and update the screen accordingly. Although this works, its performance is poor, and it's inconvenient. With version 1.1 of Java, you can tell the ScrollPane what needs to scroll; it creates the scrollbars and handles all the events automatically. Section 11.4 covers the ScrollPane; Figure 1-20 shows a ScrollPane. Chapter 11, *Scrolling*, covers the Adjustable interface that Scrollbar implements and ScrollPane utilizes.

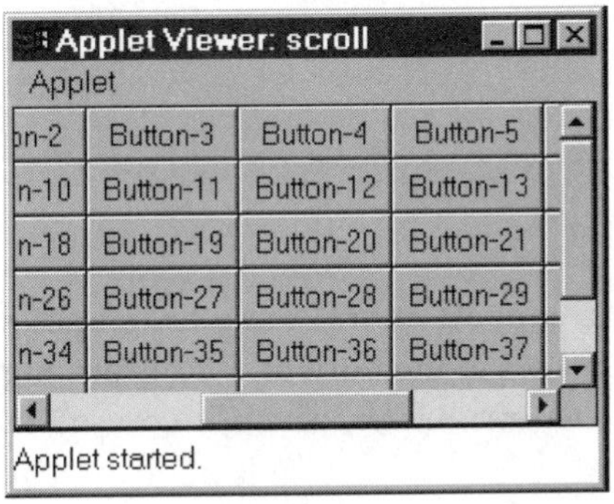

Figure 1–20: A ScrollPane

1.5 And the Rest

Several of the remaining classes within java.awt are important to mention here but did not fit well into a general category. The following sections are a grab bag that summarize the remaining classes.

1.5.1 Drawing and Graphics

Java provides numerous primitives for drawing lines, squares, circles, polygons, and images. Figure 1-21 shows a simple drawing. The drawing components of AWT are discussed in Chapter 2, *Simple Graphics*.

The Font, FontMetrics, Color, and SystemColor classes provide the ability to alter the displayed output. With the Font class, you adjust how displayed text will appear. With FontMetrics, you can find out how large the output will be, for the specific system the user is using. You can use the Color class to set the color of text and graphics. SystemColor is new to Java 1.1; it lets you take advantage of desktop color schemes. These classes are discussed in Chapter 3, *Fonts and Colors*.

Figure 1–21: A simple drawing

AWT also includes a number of classes that support more complex graphics manipulations: displaying images, generating images in memory, and transforming images. These classes make up the package java.awt.image, which is covered in Chapter 12.

1.5.2 Events

Like most windows programming environments, AWT is event driven. When an event occurs (for example, the user presses a key or moves the mouse), the environment generates an event and passes it along to a handler to process the event. If nobody wants to handle the event, the system ignores it. Unlike some windowing environments, you do not have to provide a main loop to catch and process all the events, or an infinite busy-wait loop. AWT does all the event management and passing for you.

Probably the most significant difference between versions 1.0.2 and 1.1 of AWT is the way events work. In older versions of Java, an event is distributed to every component that might conceivably be interested in it, until some component declares that it has handled the event. This event model can still be used in 1.1, but there is also a new event model in which objects listen for particular events. This new model is arguably a little more work for the programmer but promises to be much more efficient, because events are distributed only to objects that want to hear about them. It is also how JavaBeans works.

In this book, examples that are using the older (1.0.2) components use the old event model, unless otherwise indicated. Examples using new components use the new event model. Don't let this mislead you; all components in Java 1.1 support the new event model. The details of Event for both version 1.0.2 and 1.1 can be found in Chapter 4, *Events*.

1.5.3 Applets

Although it is not a part of the java.awt package, the Core Java API provides a framework for applet development. This includes support for getting parameters from HTML files, changing the web page a browser is displaying, and playing audio files. Chapter 14, *And Then There Were Applets*, describes all the details of the java.applet package. Because audio support is part of java.applet, portable audio playing is limited to applets. Chapter 14 also shows a nonportable way to play audio in applications. Additional audio capabilities are coming to the Java Core API in the announced extensions.

1.5.4 Clipboards

In Java 1.1, programs can access the system clipboard. This process makes it easier to transfer (cut, copy, and paste) data between various other sources and your Java programs and introduces developers to the concepts involved with JavaBeans. Chapter 16, *Data Transfer*, describes the java.awt.datatransfer package.

1.5.5 Printing

Java 1.1 adds the ability to print. Adding printing to an existing program is fairly simple: you don't have to do much beside adding a Print menu button. Chapter 17, *Printing*, describes these capabilities.

1.6 Summary

The java.awt package provides a great deal of functionality and flexibility. The package goes well beyond the basics presented in this chapter. Do not be intimidated by the vast libraries available to you in Java. With the help of this book, you should get an excellent grasp of the java.awt, java.awt.image, java.awt.datatransfer, java.awt.event, and java.applet packages, along with some pieces of the proprietary sun.awt and sun.audio packages.

Do not feel the need to read this book cover to cover. Pick the section that interests you most, where you feel you do not fully understand something, or where you have an immediate question to be answered and dive right in.

2

In this chapter:
- *Graphics*
- *Point*
- *Dimension*
- *Shape*
- *Rectangle*
- *Polygon*
- *Image*
- *MediaTracker*

Simple Graphics

This chapter digs into the meat of the AWT classes. After completing this chapter, you will be able to draw strings, images, and shapes via the Graphics class in your Java programs. We discuss geometry-related classes—Polygon, Rectangle, Point, and Dimension, and the Shape interface—you will see these throughout the remaining AWT objects. You will also learn several ways to do smooth animation by using double buffering and the MediaTracker.

After reading this chapter, you should be able to do simple animation and image manipulation with AWT. For most applications, this should be sufficient. If you want to look at AWT's more advanced graphics capabilities, be sure to take a look at Chapter 12, *Image Processing*.

2.1 Graphics

The Graphics class is an abstract class that provides the means to access different graphics devices. It is the class that lets you draw on the screen, display images, and so forth. Graphics is an abstract class because working with graphics requires detailed knowledge of the platform on which the program runs. The actual work is done by concrete classes that are closely tied to a particular platform. Your Java Virtual Machine vendor provides the necessary concrete classes for your environment. You never need to worry about the platform-specific classes; once you have a Graphics object, you can call all the methods of the Graphics class, confident that the platform-specific classes will work correctly wherever your program runs.

You rarely need to create a Graphics object yourself; its constructor is protected and is only called by the subclasses that extend Graphics. How then do you get a

Graphics object to work with? The sole parameter of the Component.paint() and Component.update() methods is the current graphics context. Therefore, a Graphics object is always available when you override a component's paint() and update() methods. You can ask for the graphics context of a Component by calling Component.getGraphics(). However, many components do not have a drawable graphics context. Canvas and Container objects return a valid Graphics object; whether or not any other component has a drawable graphics context depends on the run-time environment. (The latest versions of Netscape Navigator provide a drawable graphics context for any component, but you shouldn't get used to writing platform-specific code.) This restriction isn't as harsh as it sounds. For most components, a drawable graphics context doesn't make much sense; for example, why would you want to draw on a List? If you want to draw on a component, you probably can't. The notable exception is Button, and that may be fixed in future versions of AWT.

2.1.1 Graphics Methods

Constructors

protected Graphics ()

> Because Graphics is an abstract class, it doesn't have a visible constructor. The way to get a Graphics object is to ask for one by calling getGraphics() or to use the one given to you by the Component.paint() or Component.update() method.

The abstract methods of the Graphics class are implemented by some windowing system–specific class. You rarely need to know which subclass of Graphics you are using, but the classes you actually get (if you are using the JDK) are sun.awt.win32.Win32Graphics (JDK1.0), sun.awt.window.WGraphics (JDK1.1), sun.awt.motif.X11Graphics, or sun.awt.macos.MacGraphics.

Pseudo-constructors

In addition to using the graphics contexts given to you by getGraphics() or in Component.paint(), you can get a Graphics object by creating a copy of another Graphics object. Creating new graphics contexts has resource implications. Certain platforms have a limited number of graphics contexts that can be active. For instance, on Windows 95 you cannot have more than four in use at one time. Therefore, it's a good idea to call dispose() as soon as you are done with a Graphics object. Do not rely on the garbage collector to clean up for you.

public abstract Graphics create ()

> This method creates a second reference to the graphics context. It is useful for clipping (reducing the drawable area).

public Graphics create (int x, int y, int width, int height)

> This method creates a second reference to a subset of the drawing area of the graphics context. The new `Graphics` object covers the rectangle from (x, y) through (x+width-1, y+height-1) in the original object. The coordinate space of the new `Graphics` context is translated so that the upper left corner is (0, 0) and the lower right corner is (width, height). Shifting the coordinate system of the new object makes it easier to work within a portion of the drawing area without using offsets.

Drawing strings

These methods let you draw text strings on the screen. The coordinates refer to the left end of the text's baseline.

public abstract void drawString (String text, int x, int y)

> The `drawString()` method draws `text` on the screen in the current font and color, starting at position (x, y). The starting coordinates specify the left end of the `String`'s baseline.

public void drawChars (char text[], int offset, int length, int x, int y)

> The `drawChars()` method creates a `String` from the char array `text` starting at `text[offset]` and continuing for `length` characters. The newly created `String` is then drawn on the screen in the current font and color, starting at position (x, y). The starting coordinates specify the left end of the `String`'s baseline.

public void drawBytes (byte text[], int offset, int length, int x, int y)

> The `drawBytes()` method creates a `String` from the byte array `text` starting at `text[offset]` and continuing for `length` characters. This `String` is then drawn on the screen in the current font and color, starting at position (x, y). The starting coordinates specify the left end of the `String`'s baseline.

public abstract Font getFont ()

> The `getFont()` method returns the current `Font` of the graphics context. See Chapter 3, *Fonts and Colors*, for more on what you can do with fonts. You cannot get meaningful results with `getFont()` until the applet or application is displayed on the screen (generally, not in `init()` of an applet or `main()` of an application).

public abstract void setFont (Font font)

> The `setFont()` method changes the current `Font` to font. If font is not available on the current platform, the system chooses a default. To change the current font to 12 point bold TimesRoman:

```
setFont (new Font ("TimesRoman", Font.BOLD, 12));
```

public FontMetrics getFontMetrics ()

The `getFontMetrics()` method returns the current `FontMetrics` object of the graphics context. You use `FontMetrics` to reveal sizing properties of the current `Font`—for example, how wide the "Hello World" string will be in pixels when displayed on the screen.

public abstract FontMetrics getFontMetrics (Font font)

This version of `getFontMetrics()` returns the `FontMetrics` for the `Font` font instead of the current font. You might use this method to see how much space a new font requires to draw text.

For more information about `Font` and `FontMetrics`, see Chapter 3.

Painting

public abstract Color getColor ()

The `getColor()` method returns the current foreground `Color` of the `Graphics` object. All future drawing operations will use this color. Chapter 3 describes the `Color` class.

public abstract void setColor (Color color)

The `setColor()` method changes the current drawing color to `color`. As you will see in the next chapter, the `Color` class defines some common colors for you. If you can't use one of the predefined colors, you can create a color from its RGB values. To change the current color to red, use any of the following:

```
setColor (Color.red);
setColor (new Color (255, 0, 0));
setColor (new Color (0xff0000));
```

public abstract void clearRect (int x, int y, int width, int height)

The `clearRect()` method sets the rectangular drawing area from (x, y) to (x+width-1, y+height-1) to the current background color. Keep in mind that the second pair of parameters is not the opposite corner of the rectangle, but the width and height of the area to clear.

public abstract void clipRect (int x, int y, int width, int height)

The `clipRect()` method reduces the drawing area to the intersection of the current drawing area and the rectangular area from (x, y) to (x+width-1, y+height-1). Any future drawing operations outside this clipped area will have no effect. Once you clip a drawing area, you cannot increase its size with `clipRect()`; the drawing area can only get smaller. (However, if the `clipRect()` call is in `paint()`, the size of the drawing area will be reset to its original size on subsequent calls to `paint()`.) If you want the ability to draw to the entire area, you must create a second `Graphics` object that contains a copy of the drawing area before calling `clipRect()` or use `setClip()`. The following code is a simple applet that demonstrates clipping; Figure 2-1 shows the result.

```
import java.awt.*;
public class clipping extends java.applet.Applet {
    public void paint (Graphics g) {
        g.setColor (Color.red);
        Graphics clippedGraphics = g.create();
        clippedGraphics.drawRect (0,0,100,100);
        clippedGraphics.clipRect (25, 25, 50, 50);
        clippedGraphics.drawLine (0,0,100,100);
        clippedGraphics.dispose();
        clippedGraphics=null;
        g.drawLine (0,100,100,0);
    }
}
```

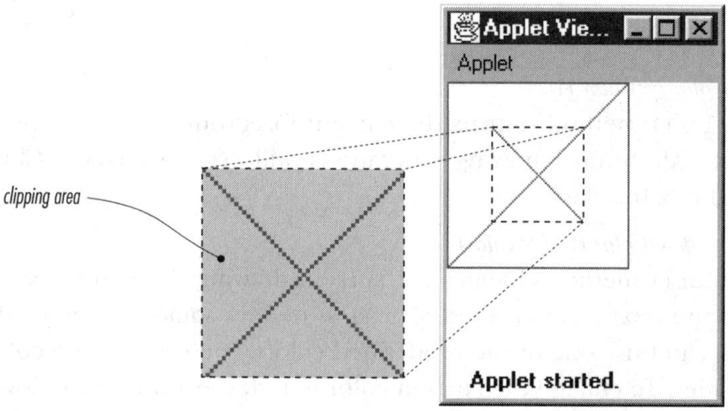

Figure 2–1: Clipping restricts the drawing area

The paint() method for this applet starts by setting the foreground color to red. It then creates a copy of the Graphics context for clipping, saving the original object so it can draw on the entire screen later. The applet then draws a rectangle, sets the clipping area to a smaller region, and draws a diagonal line across the rectangle from upper left to lower right. Because clipping is in effect, only part of the line is displayed. The applet then discards the clipped Graphics object and draws an unclipped line from lower left to upper right using the original object g.

public abstract void setClip(int x, int y, int width, int height) ★

This setClip() method allows you to change the current clipping area based on the parameters provided. setClip() is similar to clipRect(), except that it is not limited to shrinking the clipping area. The current drawing area becomes the rectangular area from (x, y) to (x+width-1, y+height-1); this area may be larger than the previous drawing area.

public abstract void setClip(Shape clip) ★

This `setClip()` method allows you to change the current clipping area based on the `clip` parameter, which may be any object that implements the `Shape` interface. Unfortunately, practice is not as good as theory, and in practice, `clip` must be a `Rectangle`; if you pass `setClip()` a `Polygon`, it throws an `IllegalArgumentException`.[*] (The `Shape` interface is discussed later in this chapter.)

public abstract Rectangle getClipBounds () ★
public abstract Rectangle getClipRect () ☆

The `getClipBounds()` methods returns a `Rectangle` that describes the clipping area of a `Graphics` object. The `Rectangle` gives you the (x, y) coordinates of the top left corner of the clipping area along with its width and height. (`Rectangle` objects are discussed later in this chapter.)

`getClipRect()` is the Java 1.0 name for this method.

public abstract Shape getClip () ★

The `getClip()` method returns a `Shape` that describes the clipping area of a `Graphics` object. That is, it returns the same thing as `getClipBounds()` but as a `Shape`, instead of as a `Rectangle`. By calling `Shape.getBounds()`, you can get the (x, y) coordinates of the top left corner of the clipping area along with its width and height. In the near future, it is hard to imagine the actual object that `getClip()` returns being anything other than a `Rectangle`.

public abstract void copyArea (int x, int y, int width, int height, int delta_x, int delta_y)

The `copyArea()` method copies the rectangular area from (x, y) to (x+width, y+height) to the area with an upper left corner of (x+delta_x, y+delta_y). The `delta_x` and `delta_y` parameters are not the coordinates of the second point but an offset from the first coordinate pair (x, y). The area copied may fall outside of the clipping region. This method is often used to tile an area of the graphics context. `copyArea()` does not save the contents of the area copied.

Painting mode

There are two painting or drawing modes for the `Graphics` class: paint (the default) and XOR mode. In paint mode, anything you draw replaces whatever is already on the screen. If you draw a red square, you get a red square, no matter what was underneath; this is what most programmers have learned to expect.

The behavior of XOR mode is rather strange, at least to people accustomed to modern programming environments. XOR mode is short for eXclusive-OR mode.

---

[*] It should be simple for Sun to fix this bug; one would expect clipping to a `Polygon` to be the same as clipping to the `Polygon`'s bounding rectangle.

The idea behind XOR mode is that drawing the same object twice returns the screen to its original state. This technique was commonly used for simple animations prior to the development of more sophisticated methods and cheaper hardware.

The side effect of XOR mode is that painting operations don't necessarily get the color you request. Instead of replacing the original pixel with the new value, XOR mode merges the original color, the painting color, and an XOR color (usually the background color) to form a new color. The new color is chosen so that if you repaint the pixel with the same color, you get the original pixel back. For example, if you paint a red square in XOR mode, you get a square of some other color on the screen. Painting the same red square again returns the screen to its original state.

public abstract void setXORMode (Color xorColor)

The setXORMode() method changes the drawing mode to XOR mode. In XOR mode, the system uses the xorColor color to determine an alternate color for anything drawn such that drawing the same item twice restores the screen to its original condition. The xorColor is usually the current background color but can be any color. For each pixel, the new color is determined by an exclusive-or of the old pixel color, the painting color, and the xorColor.

For example, if the old pixel is red, the XOR color is blue, and the drawing color is green, the end result would be white. To see why, it is necessary to look at the RGB values of the three colors. Red is (255, 0, 0). Blue is (0, 0, 255). Green is (0, 255, 0). The exclusive-or of these three values is (255, 255, 255), which is white. Drawing another green pixel with a blue XOR color yields red, the pixel's original color, since (255, 255, 255) ^ (0, 0, 255) ^ (0, 255, 0) yields (255, 0, 0).[*] The following code generates the display shown in Figure 2-2.

```
import java.awt.*;
public class xor extends java.applet.Applet {
    public void init () {
        setBackground (Color.red);
    }
    public void paint (Graphics g) {
        g.setColor (Color.green);
        g.setXORMode (Color.blue);
        g.fillRect (10, 10, 100, 100);
        g.fillRect (10, 60, 100, 100);
    }
}
```

Although it's hard to visualize what color XOR mode will pick, there is one important special case. Let's say that there are only two colors: a background color (the

---

* ^ is the Java XOR operator.

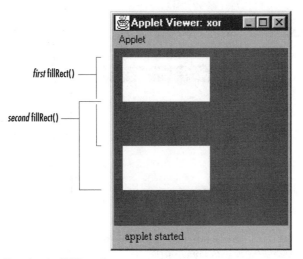

Figure 2–2: Drawing in XOR mode

XOR color) and a foreground color (the painting color). Each pixel must be in one color or the other. Painting "flips" each pixel to the other color. Foreground pixels become background, and vice versa.

public abstract void setPaintMode ()

> The setPaintMode() method puts the system into paint mode. When in paint mode, any drawing operation replaces whatever is underneath it. Call set-PaintMode() to return to normal painting when finished with XOR mode.

Drawing shapes

Most of the drawing methods require you to specify a bounding rectangle for the object you want to draw: the location of the object's upper left corner, plus its width and height. The two exceptions are lines and polygons. For lines, you supply two endpoints; for polygons, you provide a set of points.

Versions 1.0.2 and 1.1 of AWT always draw solid lines that are one pixel wide; there is no support for line width or fill patterns. A future version should support lines with variable widths and patterns.

public abstract void drawLine (int x1, int y1, int x2, int y2)

> The drawLine() method draws a line on the graphics context in the current color from (x1, y1) to (x2, y2). If (x1, y1) and (x2, y2) are the same point, you will draw a point. There is no method specific to drawing a point. The following code generates the display shown in Figure 2-3.

```
g.drawLine (5, 5, 50, 75);    // line
g.drawLine (5, 75, 5, 75);    // point
g.drawLine (50, 5, 50, 5);    // point
```

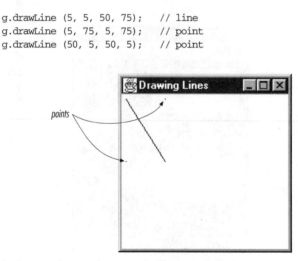

Figure 2–3: Drawing lines and points with drawLine()

public void drawRect (int x, int y, int width, int height)

> The drawRect() method draws a rectangle on the drawing area in the current color from (x, y) to (x+width, y+height). If width or height is negative, nothing is drawn.

public abstract void fillRect (int x, int y, int width, int height)

> The fillRect() method draws a filled rectangle on the drawing area in the current color from (x, y) to (x+width-1, y+height-1). Notice that the filled rectangle is one pixel smaller to the right and bottom than requested. If width or height is negative, nothing is drawn.

public abstract void drawRoundRect (int x, int y, int width, int height, int arcWidth, int arcHeight)

> The drawRoundRect() method draws a rectangle on the drawing area in the current color from (x, y) to (x+width, y+height). However, instead of perpendicular corners, the corners are rounded with a horizontal diameter of arcWidth and a vertical diameter of arcHeight. If width or height is a negative number, nothing is drawn. If width, height, arcWidth, and arcHeight are all equal, you get a circle.

> To help you visualize the arcWidth and arcHeight of a rounded rectangle, Figure 2-4 shows one corner of a rectangle drawn with an arcWidth of 20 and a arcHeight of 40.

public abstract void fillRoundRect (int x, int y, int width, int height, int arcWidth, int arcHeight)

> The fillRoundRect() method draws a filled rectangle on the drawing area in the current color from (x, y) to (x+width-1, y+height-1). However, instead of having perpendicular corners, the corners are rounded with a horizontal

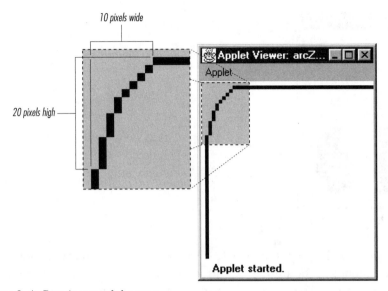

Figure 2–4: Drawing rounded corners

diameter of arcWidth and a vertical diameter of arcHeight for the four corners. Notice that the filled rectangle is one pixel smaller to the right and bottom than requested. If width or height is a negative number, nothing is filled. If width, height, arcWidth, and arcHeight are all equal, you get a filled circle.

Figure 2-4 shows how AWT generates rounded corners. Figure 2-5 shows the collection of rectangles created by the following code. The rectangles in Figure 2-5 are filled and unfilled, with rounded and square corners.

```
g.drawRect (25, 10, 50, 75);
g.fillRect (25, 110, 50, 75);
g.drawRoundRect (100, 10, 50, 75, 60, 50);
g.fillRoundRect (100, 110, 50, 75, 60, 50);
```

public void draw3DRect (int x, int y, int width, int height, boolean raised)

The draw3DRect() method draws a rectangle in the current color from (x, y) to (x+width, y+height); a shadow effect makes the rectangle appear to float slightly above or below the screen. The raised parameter has an effect only if the current color is not black. If raised is true, the rectangle looks like a button waiting to be pushed. If raised is false, the rectangle looks like a depressed button. If width or height is negative, the shadow appears from another direction.

public void fill3DRect (int x, int y, int width, int height, boolean raised)

The fill3DRect() method draws a filled rectangle in the current color from (x, y) to (x+width, y+height); a shadow effect makes the rectangle appear to float slightly above or below the screen. The raised parameter has an effect

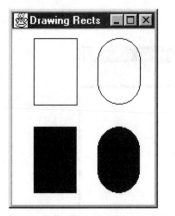

Figure 2–5: Varieties of rectangles

only if the current color is not black. If raised is true, the rectangle looks like
a button waiting to be pushed. If raised is false, the rectangle looks like a
depressed button. To enhance the shadow effect, the depressed area is given a
slightly deeper shade of the drawing color. If width or height is negative, the
shadow appears from another direction, and the rectangle isn't filled. (Different platforms could deal with this differently. Try to ensure the parameters
have positive values.)

Figure 2-6 shows the collection of three-dimensional rectangles created by the
following code. The rectangles in the figure are raised and depressed, filled
and unfilled.

```
g.setColor (Color.gray);
g.draw3DRect (25, 10, 50, 75, true);
g.draw3DRect (25, 110, 50, 75, false);
g.fill3DRect (100, 10, 50, 75, true);
g.fill3DRect (100, 110, 50, 75, false);
```

public abstract void drawOval (int x, int y, int width, int height)
The drawOval() method draws an oval in the current color within an invisible
bounding rectangle from (x, y) to (x+width, y+height). You cannot specify
the oval's center point and radii. If width and height are equal, you get a circle. If width or height is negative, nothing is drawn.

public abstract void fillOval (int x, int y, int width, int height)
The fillOval() method draws a filled oval in the current color within an
invisible bounding rectangle from (x, y) to (x+width-1, y+height-1). You cannot specify the oval's center point and radii. Notice that the filled oval is one
pixel smaller to the right and bottom than requested. If width or height is
negative, nothing is drawn.

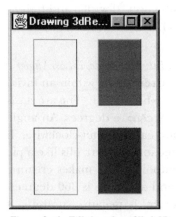

Figure 2–6: Filled and unfilled 3D rectangles

Figure 2-7 shows the collection of ovals, filled and unfilled, that were generated by the following code:

```
g.drawOval (25, 10, 50, 75);
g.fillOval (25, 110, 50, 75);
g.drawOval (100, 10, 50, 50);
g.fillOval (100, 110, 50, 50);
```

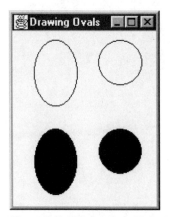

Figure 2–7: Filled and unfilled ovals

public abstract void drawArc (int x, int y, int width, int height, int startAngle, int arcAngle)
The drawArc() method draws an arc in the current color within an invisible
bounding rectangle from (x, y) to (x+width, y+height). The arc starts at
startAngle degrees and goes to startAngle + arcAngle degrees. An angle of 0
degrees is at the 3 o'clock position; angles increase counter-clockwise. If

arcAngle is negative, drawing is in a clockwise direction. If width and height are equal and arcAngle is 360 degrees, drawArc() draws a circle. If width or height is negative, nothing is drawn.

public abstract void fillArc (int x, int y, int width, int height, int startAngle, int arcAngle)

The fillArc() method draws a filled arc in the current color within an invisible bounding rectangle from (x, y) to (x+width-1, y+height-1). The arc starts at startAngle degrees and goes to startAngle + arcAngle degrees. An angle of 0 degrees is at the 3 o'clock position; angles increase counter-clockwise. If arcAngle is negative, drawing is in a clockwise direction. The arc fills like a pie (to the origin), not from arc endpoint to arc endpoint. This makes creating pie charts easier. If width and height are equal and arcAngle is 360 degrees, fillArc() draws a filled circle. If width or height is negative, nothing is drawn.

Figure 2-8 shows a collection of filled and unfilled arcs that were generated by the following code:

```
g.drawArc (25, 10, 50, 75, 0, 360);
g.fillArc (25, 110, 50, 75, 0, 360);
g.drawArc (100, 10, 50, 75, 45, 215);
g.fillArc (100, 110, 50, 75, 45, 215);
```

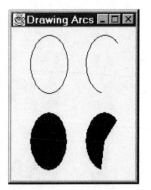

Figure 2–8: Filled and unfilled arcs

public void drawPolygon (Polygon p)

The drawPolygon() method draws a path for the points in polygon p in the current color. Section 2.6 discusses the Polygon class in detail.

The behavior of drawPolygon() changes slightly between Java 1.0.2 and 1.1. With version 1.0.2, if the first and last points of a Polygon are not the same, a call to drawPolygon() results in an open polygon, since the endpoints are not connected for you. Starting with version 1.1, if the first and last points are not the same, the endpoints are connected for you.

public abstract void drawPolygon (int xPoints[], int yPoints[], int numPoints)

The `drawPolygon()` method draws a path of `numPoints` nodes by plucking one element at a time out of `xPoints` and `yPoints` to make each point. The path is drawn in the current color. If either `xPoints` or `yPoints` does not have `numPoints` elements, `drawPolygon()` throws a run-time exception. In 1.0.2, this exception is an `IllegalArgumentException`; in 1.1, it is an `ArrayIndexOutOfBoundsException`. This change shouldn't break older programs, since you are not required to catch run-time exceptions.

public abstract void drawPolyline (int xPoints[], int yPoints[], int numPoints) ★

The `drawPolyline()` method functions like the 1.0 version of `drawPolygon()`. It plays connect the dots with the points in the `xPoints` and `yPoints` arrays and does not connect the endpoints. If either `xPoints` or `yPoints` does not have `numPoints` elements, `drawPolygon()` throws the run-time exception, `ArrayIndexOutOfBoundsException`.

Filling polygons is a complex topic. It is not as easy as filling rectangles or ovals because a polygon may not be closed and its edges may cross. AWT uses an even-odd rule to fill polygons. This algorithm works by counting the number of times each scan line crosses an edge of the polygon. If the total number of crossings to the left of the current point is odd, the point is colored. If it is even, the point is left alone. Figure 2-9 demonstrates this algorithm for a single scan line that intersects the polygon at x values of 25, 75, 125, 175, 225, and 275.

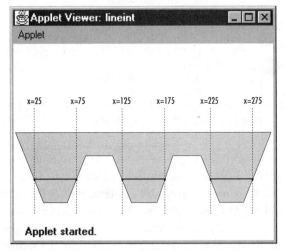

Figure 2–9: Polygon fill algorithm

The scan line starts at the left edge of the screen; at this point there haven't been any crossings, so the pixels are left untouched. The scan line reaches the first crossing when x equals 25. Here, the total number of crossings to the left is one, so the scan line is inside the polygon, and the pixels are colored. At 75, the scan line crosses again; the total number of crossings is two, so coloring stops.

public void fillPolygon (Polygon p)

The `fillPolygon()` method draws a filled polygon for the points in `Polygon p` in the current color. If the polygon is not closed, `fillPolygon()` adds a segment connecting the endpoints. Section 2.6 discusses the `Polygon` class in detail.

public abstract void fillPolygon (int xPoints[], int yPoints[], int nPoints)

The `fillPolygon()` method draws a polygon of `numPoints` nodes by plucking one element at a time out of `xPoints` and `yPoints` to make each point. The polygon is drawn in the current color. If either `xPoints` or `yPoints` does not have `numPoints` elements, `fillPolygon()` throws the run-time exception `IllegalArgumentException`. If the polygon is not closed, `fillPolygon()` adds a segment connecting the endpoints.[*]

Figure 2-10 shows several polygons created by the following code, containing different versions of `drawPolygon()` and `fillPolygon()`:

```
int[] xPoints[] = {{50, 25, 25, 75, 75},
                    {50, 25, 25, 75, 75},
                    {100, 100, 150, 100, 150, 150, 125, 100, 150},
                    {100, 100, 150, 100, 150, 150, 125, 100, 150}};
int[] yPoints[] = {{10, 35, 85, 85, 35, 10},
                    {110, 135, 185, 185, 135},
                    {85, 35, 35, 85, 85, 35, 10, 35, 85},
                    {185, 135, 135, 185, 185, 135, 110, 135, 185}};
int   nPoints[] = {5, 5, 9, 9};
g.drawPolygon (xPoints[0], yPoints[0], nPoints[0]);
g.fillPolygon (xPoints[1], yPoints[1], nPoints[1]);
g.drawPolygon (new Polygon(xPoints[2], yPoints[2], nPoints[2]));
g.fillPolygon (new Polygon(xPoints[3], yPoints[3], nPoints[3]));
```

Drawing images

An `Image` is a displayable object maintained in memory. To get an image on the screen, you must draw it onto a graphics context, using the `drawImage()` method of the `Graphics` class. For example, within a `paint()` method, you would call `g.drawImage(image, ... , this)` to display some image on the screen. In other situations, you might use the `createImage()` method to generate an offscreen `Graphics` object, then use `drawImage()` to draw an image onto this object, for display later.

---

[*] In Java 1.1, this method throws `ArrayIndexOutOfBoundsException`, not `IllegalArgumentException`.

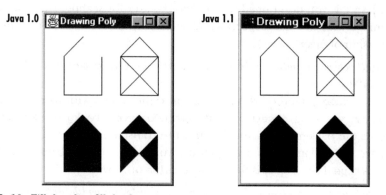

Figure 2–10: Filled and unfilled polygons

This begs the question: where do images come from? We will have more to say about the Image class later in this chapter. For now, it's enough to say that you can call getImage() to load an image from disk or across the Net. There are versions of getImage() in the Applet and Toolkit classes; the latter is for use in applications. You can also call createImage(), a method of the Component class, to generate an image in memory.

What about the last argument to drawImage()? What is this for? The last argument of drawImage() is always an image observer—that is, an object that implements the ImageObserver interface. This interface is discussed in detail in Chapter 12. For the time being, it's enough to say that the call to drawImage() starts a new thread that loads the requested image. An image observer monitors the process of loading an image; the thread that is loading the image notifies the image observer whenever new data has arrived. The Component class implements the ImageObserver interface; when you're writing a paint() method, you're almost certainly overriding some component's paint() method; therefore, it's safe to use this as the image observer in a call to drawImage(). More simply, we could say that any component can serve as an image observer for images that are drawn on it.

public abstract boolean drawImage (Image image, int x, int y, ImageObserver observer)
> The drawImage() method draws image onto the screen with its upper left corner at (x, y), using observer as its ImageObserver. Returns true if the object is fully drawn, false otherwise.

public abstract boolean drawImage (Image image, int x, int y, int width, int height,
ImageObserver observer)
> The drawImage() method draws image onto the screen with its upper left corner at (x, y), using observer as its ImageObserver. The system scales image to fit into a width × height area. The scaling may take time. This method returns true if the object is fully drawn, false otherwise.

With Java 1.1, you don't need to use drawImage() for scaling; you can prescale
the image with the Image.getScaledInstance() method, then use the previous version of drawImage().

public abstract boolean drawImage (Image image, int x, int y, Color backgroundColor, Ima-
geObserver$nbsp;observer)

The drawImage() method draws image onto the screen with its upper left corner at (x, y), using observer as its ImageObserver. backgroundColor is the
color of the background seen through the transparent parts of the image. If
no part of the image is transparent, you will not see backgroundColor.
Returns true if the object is fully drawn, false otherwise.

public abstract boolean drawImage (Image image, int x, int y, int width, int height,
Color backgroundColor, ImageObserver observer)

The drawImage() method draws image onto the screen with its upper left corner at (x, y), using observer as its ImageObserver. backgroundColor is the
color of the background seen through the transparent parts of the image. The
system scales image to fit into a width x height area. The scaling may take
time. This method returns true if the image is fully drawn, false otherwise.

With Java 1.1, you can prescale the image with the AreaAveragingScaleFilter
or ReplicateScaleFilter described in Chapter 12, then use the previous version of drawImage() to display it.

The following code generated the images in Figure 2-11. The images on the left
come from a standard JPEG file. The images on the right come from a file in
GIF89a format, in which the white pixel is "transparent." Therefore, the gray background shows through this pair of images.

```
import java.awt.*;
import java.applet.*;
public class drawingImages extends Applet {
    Image i, j;
    public void init () {
        i = getImage (getDocumentBase(), "rosey.jpg");
        j = getImage (getDocumentBase(), "rosey.gif");
    }
    public void paint (Graphics g) {
        g.drawImage (i, 10, 10, this);
        g.drawImage (i, 10, 85, 150, 200, this);
        g.drawImage (j, 270, 10, Color.lightGray, this);
        g.drawImage (j, 270, 85, 150, 200, Color.lightGray, this);
    }
}
```

public abstract boolean drawImage(Image img, int dx1, int dy1, int dx2, int dy2, int sx1,
int sy1, int sx2, int sy2, ImageObserver observer) ★

The drawImage() method draws a portion of image onto the screen. It takes
the part of the image with corners at (sx1, sy1) and (sx2, sy2); it places this

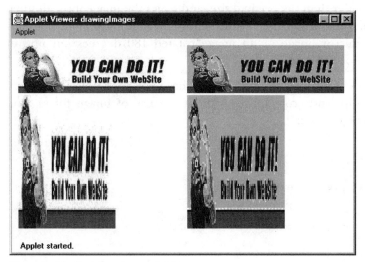

Figure 2–11: Scaled and unscaled images

rectangular

snippet on the screen with one corner at (dx1, dy1) and another at (dx2, dy2), using observer as its ImageObserver. (Think of d for destination location and s for source image.) This method returns true if the object is fully drawn, false otherwise.

drawImage() flips the image if source and destination endpoints are not the same corners, crops the image if the destination is smaller than the original size, and scales the image if the destination is larger than the original size. It does not do rotations, only flips (i.e., it can produce a mirror image or an image rotated 180 degrees but not an image rotated 90 or 270 degrees).

public abstract boolean drawImage(Image img, int dx1, int dy1, int dx2, int dy2, int sx1, int sy1, int sx2, int sy2, Color backgroundColor, ImageObserver observer) ★

The drawImage() method draws a portion of image onto the screen. It takes the part of the image with corners at (sx1, sy1) and (sx2, sy2); it places this rectangular snippet on the screen with one corner at (dx1, dy1) and another at (dx2, dy2), using observer as its ImageObserver. (Think of d for destination location and s for source image.) backgroundColor is the color of the background seen through the transparent parts of the image. If no part of the image is transparent, you will not see backgroundColor. This method returns true if the object is fully drawn, false otherwise.

Like the previous version of drawImage(), this method flips the image if source and destination endpoints are not the same corners, crops the image if the destination is smaller than the original size, and scales the image if the destination is larger than the original size. It does not do rotations, only flips (i.e., it can produce a mirror image or an image rotated 180 degrees but not an image rotated 90 or 270 degrees).

The following code demonstrates the new drawImage() methods in Java 1.1. They allow you to scale, flip, and crop images without the use of image filters. The results are shown in Figure 2-12.

```
// Java 1.1 only
import java.awt.*;
import java.applet.*;
public class drawingImages11 extends Applet {
    Image i, j;
    public void init () {
        i = getImage (getDocumentBase(), "rosey.gif");
    }
    public void paint (Graphics g) {
        g.drawImage (i, 10, 10, this);
        g.drawImage (i, 10, 85,
                        i.getWidth(this)+10, i.getHeight(this)+85,
                        i.getWidth(this), i.getHeight(this), 0, 0, this);
        g.drawImage (i, 270, 10,
                        i.getWidth(this)+270, i.getHeight(this)*2+10, 0, 0,
                        i.getWidth(this), i.getHeight(this), Color.gray, this);
        g.drawImage (i, 10, 170,
                        i.getWidth(this)*2+10, i.getHeight(this)+170, 0,
                        i.getHeight(this)/2, i.getWidth(this)/2, 0, this);
    }
}
```

Miscellaneous methods

public abstract void translate (int x, int y)

The translate() method sets how the system translates the coordinate space for you. The point at the (x, y) coordinates becomes the origin of this graphics context. Any future drawing will be relative to this location. Multiple translations are cumulative. The following code leaves the coordinate system translated by (100, 50).

```
translate (100, 0);
translate (0, 50);
```

Note that each call to paint() provides an entirely new Graphics context with its origin in the upper left corner. Therefore, don't expect translations to persist from one call to paint() to the next.

Figure 2–12: Flipped, mirrored, and cropped images

public abstract void dispose ()

The dispose() method frees any system resources used by the Graphics context. It's a good idea to call dispose() whenever you are finished with a Graphics object, rather than waiting for the garbage collector to call it automatically (through finalize()). Disposing of the Graphics object yourself will help your programs on systems with limited resources. However, you should not dispose the Graphics parameter to Component.paint() or Component.update().

public void finalize ()

The garbage collector calls finalize() when it determines that the Graphics object is no longer needed. finalize() calls dispose(), which frees any resources that the Graphics object has used.

public String toString ()

The toString() method of Graphics returns a string showing the current font and color. However, Graphics is an abstract class, and classes that extend Graphics usually override toString(). For example, on a Windows 95 machine, sun.awt.win32.Win32Graphics is the concrete class that extends Graphics. The class's toString() method displays the current origin of the Graphics object, relative to the original coordinate system:

```
sun.awt.win32.Win32Graphics[0,0]
```

2.2 Point

The Point class encapsulates x and y coordinates within a single object. It is probably one of the most underused classes within Java. Although there are numerous
places within AWT where you would expect to see a Point, its appearances are sur-
prisingly rare. Java 1.1 is starting to use Point more heavily. The Point class is most
often used when a method needs to return a pair of coordinates; it lets the method
return both x and y as a single object. Unfortunately, Point usually is not used
when a method requires x and y coordinates as arguments; for example, you
would expect the Graphics class to have a version of translate() that takes a
point as an argument, but there isn't one.

The Point class does *not* represent a point on the screen. It is not a visual object;
there is no drawPoint() method.

2.2.1 Point Methods

Variables

The two public variables of Point represent a pair of coordinates. They are accessible directly or use the getLocation() method. There is no predefined origin for
the coordinate space.

public int x
> The coordinate that represents the horizontal position.

public int y
> The coordinate that represents the vertical position.

Constructors

public Point ()
> The first constructor creates an instance of Point with an initial x value of 0
> and an initial y value of 0.

public Point (int x, int y)
> The next constructor creates an instance of Point with an initial x value of x
> and an initial y value of y.

public Point (Point p)
> The last constructor creates an instance of Point from another point, the x
> value of p.x and an initial y value of p.y.

Locations

public Point getLocation () ★

> The getLocation() method retrieves the current location of this point as a new Point.

public void setLocation (int x, int y) ★
public void move (int x, int y) ☆

> The setLocation() method changes the point's location to (x, y).
>
> move() is the Java 1.0 name for this method.

public void setLocation (Point p) ★

> This setLocation() method changes the point's location to (p.x, p.y).

public void translate (int x, int y)

> The translate() method moves the point's location by adding the parameters (x, y) to the corresponding fields of the Point. If the original Point p is (3, 4) and you call p.translate(4, -5), the new value of p is (7, -1).

Miscellaneous methods

public int hashCode ()

> The hashCode() method returns a hash code for the point. The system calls this method when a Point is used as the key for a hash table.

public boolean equals (Object object)

> The equals() method overrides the Object.equals() method to define equality for points. Two Point objects are equal if their x and y values are equal.

public String toString ()

> The toString() method of Point displays the current values of the x and y variables. For example:

```
java.awt.Point[x=100,y=200]
```

2.3 Dimension

The Dimension class is similar to the Point class, except it encapsulates a width and height in a single object. Like Point, Dimension is somewhat underused; it is used primarily by methods that need to return a width and a height as a single object; for example, getSize() returns a Dimension object.

2.3.1 Dimension Methods

Variables

A Dimension instance has two variables, one for width and one for height. They are accessible directly or through use of the getSize() method.

public int width

> The width variable represents the size of an object along the x axis (left to right). Width should not be negative; however, there is nothing within the class to prevent this from happening.

public int height

> The height variable represents the size of an object along the y axis (top to bottom). Height should not be negative; however, there is nothing within the class to prevent this from happening.

Constructors

public Dimension ()

> This constructor creates a Dimension instance with a width and height of 0.

public Dimension (Dimension dim)

> This constructor creates a copy of dim. The initial width is dim.width. The initial height is dim.height.

public Dimension (int width, int height)

> This constructor creates a Dimension with an initial width of width and an initial height of height.

Sizing

public Dimension getSize () ★

> The getSize() method retrieves the current size as a new Dimension, even though the instance variables are public.

public void setSize (int width, int height) ★

> The setSize() method changes the dimension's size to width × height.

public void setSize (Dimension d) ★

> The setSize() method changes the dimension's size to d.width × d.height.

Miscellaneous methods

public boolean equals (Object object)

> The equals() method overrides the Object.equals() method to define equality for dimensions. Two Dimension objects are equal if their width and height values are equal.

public String toString ()

> The toString() method of Dimension returns a string showing the current width and height settings. For example:
>
> ```
> java.awt.Dimension[width=0,height=0]
> ```

2.4 Shape

The new Shape interface defines a single method; it requires a geometric object to be able to report its bounding box. Currently, the Rectangle and Polygon classes implement Shape; one would expect other geometric classes to implement Shape in the future. Although Component has the single method defined by the Shape interface, it does not implement the interface.

2.4.1 Shape Method

public abstract Rectangle getBounds() ★

> The getBounds() method returns the shape's bounding Rectangle. Once you have the bounding area, you can use methods like Graphics.copyArea() to copy the shape.

2.5 Rectangle

The Rectangle class encapsulates x and y coordinates and width and height (Point and Dimension information) within a single object. It is often used by methods that return a rectangular boundary as a single object: for example, Polygon.getBounds(), Component.getBounds(), and Graphics.getClipBounds(). Like Point, the Rectangle class is not a visual object and does not represent a rectangle on the screen; ironically, drawRect() and fillRect() don't take Rectangle as an argument.

2.5.1 Rectangle Methods

Variables

The four public variables available for Rectangle have the same names as the public instance variables of Point and Dimension. They are all accessible directly or through use of the getBounds() method.

public int x

> The x coordinate of the upper left corner.

public int y

　　The y coordinate of the upper left corner.

public int width

　　The width variable represents the size of the Rectangle along the horizontal axis (left to right). Width should not be negative; however, there is nothing within the class to prevent this from happening.

public int height

　　The height variable represents the size of the Rectangle along the vertical axis (top to bottom). Height should not be negative; however, there is nothing within the class to prevent this from happening.

Constructors

The following seven constructors create Rectangle objects. When you create a Rectangle, you provide the location of the top left corner, along with the Rectangle's width and height. A Rectangle located at (0,0) with a width and height of 100 has its bottom right corner at (99, 99). The Point (100, 100) lies outside the Rectangle, since that would require a width and height of 101.

public Rectangle ()

　　This Rectangle constructor creates a Rectangle object in which x, y, width, and height are all 0.

public Rectangle (int width, int height)

　　This Rectangle constructor creates a Rectangle with (x, y) coordinates of (0,0) and the specified width and height. Notice that there is no Rectangle(int x, int y) constructor because that would have the same method signature as this one, and the compiler would have no means to differentiate them.

public Rectangle (int x, int y, int width, int height)

　　The Rectangle constructor creates a Rectangle object with an initial x coordinate of x, y coordinate of y, width of width, and height of height. Height and width should be positive, but the constructor does not check for this.

public Rectangle (Rectangle r)

　　This Rectangle constructor creates a Rectangle matching the original. The (x, y) coordinates are (r.x, r.y), with a width of r.width and a height of r.height.

public Rectangle (Point p, Dimension d)

> This Rectangle constructor creates a Rectangle with (x, y) coordinates of (p.x, p.y), a width of d.width, and a height of d.height.

public Rectangle (Point p)

> This Rectangle constructor creates a Rectangle with (x, y) coordinates of (p.x, p.y). The width and height are both zero.

public Rectangle (Dimension d)

> The last Rectangle constructor creates a Rectangle with (x, y) coordinates of (0, 0). The initial Rectangle width is d.width and height is d.height.

Shaping and sizing

public Rectangle getBounds() ★

> The getBounds() method returns a copy of the original Rectangle.

public void setBounds (int x, int y, int width, int height) ★
public void reshape (int x, int y, int width, int height) ☆

> The setBounds() method changes the origin of the Rectangle to (x, y) and changes the dimensions to width by height.
>
> reshape() is the Java 1.0 name for this method.

public void setBounds (Rectangle r) ★

> The setBounds() method changes the origin of the Rectangle to (r.x, r.y) and changes the dimensions to r.width by r.height.

public Point getLocation() ★

> The getLocation() retrieves the current origin of this rectangle as a Point.

public void setLocation (int x, int y) ★
public void move (int x, int y) ☆

> The setLocation() method changes the origin of the Rectangle to (x, y).
>
> move() is the Java 1.0 name for this method.

public void setLocation (Point p) ★

> The setLocation() method changes the Rectangle's origin to (p.x, p.y).

public void translate (int x, int y)

> The translate() method moves the Rectangle's origin by the amount (x, y). If the original Rectangle's location (r) is (3, 4) and you call r.translate (4, 5), then r's location becomes (7, 9). x and y may be negative. translate() has no effect on the Rectangle's width and height.

public Dimension getSize () ★

The getSize() method retrieves the current size of the rectangle as a Dimension.

public void setSize() (int width, int height) ★
public void resize (int width, int height) ☆

The setSize() method changes the Rectangle's dimensions to width x height.

resize() is the Java 1.0 name for this method.

public void setSize() (Dimension d) ★

The setSize() method changes the Rectangle's dimensions to d.width x d.height.

public void grow (int horizontal, int vertical)

The grow() method increases the Rectangle's dimensions by adding the amount horizontal on the left and the right and adding the amount vertical on the top and bottom. Therefore, all four of the rectangle's variables change. If the original location is (x, y), the new location will be (x-horizontal, y-vertical) (moving left and up if both values are positive); if the original size is (width, height), the new size will be (width+2*horizontal, height+2*vertical). Either horizontal or vertical can be negative to decrease the size of the Rectangle. The following code demonstrates the changes:

```
import java.awt.Rectangle;
public class rect {
    public static void main (String[] args) {
        Rectangle r = new Rectangle (100, 100, 200, 200);
        System.out.println (r);
        r.grow (50, 75);
        System.out.println (r);
        r.grow (-25, -50);
        System.out.println (r);
    }
}
```

This program produces the following output:

```
java.awt.Rectangle[x=100,y=100,width=200,height=200]
java.awt.Rectangle[x=50,y=25,width=300,height=350]
java.awt.Rectangle[x=75,y=75,width=250,height=250]
```

public void add (int newX, int newY)

The add() method incorporates the point (newX, newY) into the Rectangle. If this point is already in the Rectangle, there is no change. Otherwise, the size of the Rectangle increases to include (newX, newY) within itself.

public void add (Point p)

> This add() method incorporates the point (p.x, p.y) into the Rectangle. If this point is already in the Rectangle, there is no change. Otherwise, the size of the Rectangle increases to include (p.x, p.y) within itself.

public void add (Rectangle r)

> This add() method incorporates another Rectangle r into this Rectangle. This transforms the current rectangle into the union of the two Rectangles. This method might be useful in a drawing program that lets you select multiple objects on the screen and create a rectangular area from them.

> We will soon encounter a method called union() that is almost identical. add() and union() differ in that add() modifies the current Rectangle, while union() returns a new Rectangle. The resulting rectangles are identical.

Intersections

public boolean contains (int x, int y) ★
public boolean inside (int x, int y) ☆

> The contains() method determines if the point (x, y) is within this Rectangle. If so, true is returned. If not, false is returned.

> inside() is the Java 1.0 name for this method.

public boolean contains (Point p) ★

> The contains() method determines if the point (p.x, p.y) is within this Rectangle. If so, true is returned. If not, false is returned.

public boolean intersects (Rectangle r)

> The intersects() method checks whether Rectangle r crosses this Rectangle at any point. If it does, true is returned. If not, false is returned.

public Rectangle intersection (Rectangle r)

> The intersection() method returns a new Rectangle consisting of all points that are in both the current Rectangle and Rectangle r. For example, if r = new Rectangle (50, 50, 100, 100) and r1 = new Rectangle (100, 100, 75, 75), then r.intersection (r1) is the Rectangle (100, 100, 50, 50), as shown in Figure 2-13.

public Rectangle union (Rectangle r)

> The union() method combines the current Rectangle and Rectangle r to form a new Rectangle. For example, if r = new Rectangle (50, 50, 100, 100) and r1 = new Rectangle (100, 100, 75, 75), then r.union (r1) is the Rectangle (50, 50, 125, 125). The original rectangle is unchanged. Figure 2-14 demonstrates the effect of union(). Because fillRect() fills to width-1

and height-1, the rectangle drawn appears slightly smaller than you would
expect. However, that's an artifact of how rectangles are drawn; the returned
rectangle contains all the points within both.

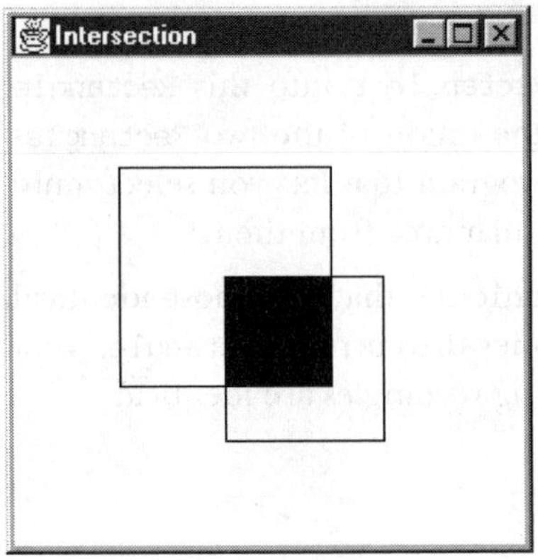

Figure 2–13: Rectangle intersection

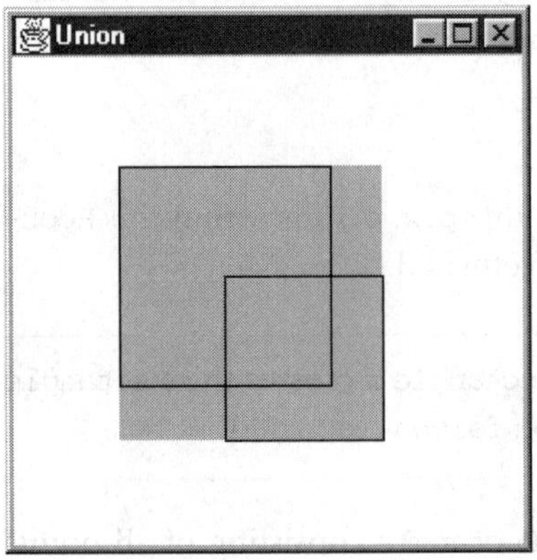

Figure 2–14: Rectangle union

Miscellaneous methods

public boolean isEmpty ()

The isEmpty() method checks whether there are any points within the Rectangle. If the width and height of the Rectangle are both 0 (or less), the Rectangle is empty, and this method returns true. If either width or height is
greater than zero, isEmpty() returns false. This method could be used to
check the results of a call to any method that returns a Rectangle object.

public int hashCode ()

> The hashCode() method returns a hash code for the rectangle. The system calls this method when a Rectangle is used as the key for a hash table.

public boolean equals (Object object)

> The equals() method overrides the Object's equals() method to define what equality means for Rectangle objects. Two Rectangle objects are equal if their x, y, width, and height values are equal.

public String toString ()

> The toString() method of Rectangle displays the current values of the x, y, width, and height variables. For example:

```
java.awt.Rectangle[x=100,y=200,width=300,height=400]
```

2.6 Polygon

A Polygon is a collection of points used to create a series of line segments. Its primary purpose is to draw arbitrary shapes like triangles or pentagons. If the points are sufficiently close, you can create a curve. To display the Polygon, call draw-Polygon() or fillPolygon().

2.6.1 Polygon Methods

Variables

The collection of points maintained by Polygon are stored in three variables:

public int npoints

> The npoints variable stores the number of points.

public int xpoints[]

> The xpoints array holds the x component of each point.

public int ypoints[]

> The ypoints array holds the y component of each point.

You might expect the Polygon class to use an array of points, rather than separate arrays of integers. More important, you might expect the instance variables to be private or protected, which would prevent them from being modified directly. Since the three instance variables are public, there is no guarantee that the array sizes are in sync with each other or with npoints. To avoid trouble, always use add-Points() to modify your polygons, and avoid modifying the instance variables directly.

Constructors

public Polygon ()

This constructor creates an empty `Polygon`.

public Polygon (int xPoints[], int yPoints[], int numPoints)

This constructor creates a `Polygon` that consists of `numPoints` points. Those points are formed from the first `numPoints` elements of the `xPoints` and `yPoints` arrays. If the `xPoints` or `yPoints` arrays are larger than `numPoints`, the additional entries are ignored. If the `xPoints` or `yPoints` arrays do not contain at least `numPoints` elements, the constructor throws the run-time exception `ArrayIndexOutOfBoundsException`.

Miscellaneous methods

public void addPoint (int x, int y)

The `addPoint()` method adds the point (x, y) to the `Polygon` as its last point. If you alter the `xpoints`, `ypoints`, and `npoints` instance variables directly, `add-Point()` could add the new point at a place other than the end, or it could throw the run-time exception `ArrayIndexOutOfBoundsException` with a message showing the position at which it tried to add the point. Again, for safety, don't modify a `Polygon`'s instance variables yourself; always use `addPoint()`.

public Rectangle getBounds () ★
public Rectangle getBoundingBox () ☆

The `getBounds()` method returns the `Polygon`'s bounding `Rectangle` (i.e., the smallest rectangle that contains all the points within the polygon). Once you have the bounding box, it's easy to use methods like `copyArea()` to copy the `Polygon`.

`getBoundingBox()` is the Java 1.0 name for this method.

public boolean contains (int x, int y) ★
public boolean inside (int x, int y) ☆

The `contains()` method checks to see if the (x, y) point is within an area that would be filled if the `Polygon` was drawn with `Graphics.fillPolygon()`. A point may be within the bounding rectangle of the polygon, but `contains()` can still return `false` if not within a closed part of the polygon.

`inside()` is the Java 1.0 name for this method.

public boolean contains (Point p) ★

The `contains()` method checks to see if the point p is within an area that would be filled if the `Polygon` were drawn with `Graphics.fillPolygon()`.

public void translate (int x, int y) ★

> The `translate()` method moves all the `Polygon`'s points by the amount (x, y). This allows you to alter the location of the `Polygon` by shifting the points.

2.7 *Image*

An `Image` is a displayable object maintained in memory. AWT has built-in support for reading files in GIF and JPEG format, including GIF89a animation. Netscape Navigator, Internet Explorer, HotJava, and Sun's JDK also understand the XBM image format. Images are loaded from the filesystem or network by the `getImage()` method of either `Component` or `Toolkit`, drawn onto the screen with `drawImage()` from `Graphics`, and manipulated by several objects within the `java.awt.image` package. Figure 2-15 shows an `Image`.

Figure 2–15: An Image

`Image` is an abstract class implemented by many different platform-specific classes. The system that runs your program will provide an appropriate implementation; you do not need to know anything about the platform-specific classes, because the `Image` class completely defines the API for working with images. If you're curious, the platform-specific packages used by the JDK are:

- `sun.awt.win32.Win32Image` on Java 1.0 Windows NT/95 platforms

- `sun.awt.windows.WImage` on Java 1.1 Windows NT/95 platforms

- `sun.awt.motif.X11Image` on UNIX/Motif platforms

- `sun.awt.macos.MacImage` on the Macintosh

This section covers only the `Image` object itself. AWT also includes a package named `java.awt.image` that includes more advanced image processing utilities. The classes in `java.awt.image` are covered in Chapter 12.

2.7.1 Image Methods

Constants

public static final Object UndefinedProperty

In Java 1.0, the sole constant of `Image` is `UndefinedProperty`. It is used as a return value from the `getProperty()` method to indicate that the requested property is unavailable.

Java 1.1 introduces the `getScaledInstance()` method. The final parameter to the method is a set of hints to tell the method how best to scale the image. The following constants provide possible values for this parameter.

public static final int SCALE_DEFAULT ★

The `SCALE_DEFAULT` hint should be used alone to tell `getScaledInstance()` to use the default scaling algorithm.

public static final int SCALE_FAST ★

The `SCALE_FAST` hint tells `getScaledInstance()` that speed takes priority over smoothness.

public static final int SCALE_SMOOTH ★

The `SCALE_SMOOTH` hint tells `getScaledInstance()` that smoothness takes priority over speed.

public static final int SCALE_REPLICATE ★

The `SCALE_REPLICATE` hint tells `getScaledInstance()` to use `ReplicateScaleFilter` or a reasonable alternative provided by the toolkit. `ReplicateScaleFilter` is discussed in Chapter 12.

public static final int SCALE_AREA_AVERAGING ★

The `SCALE_AREA_AVERAGING` hint tells `getScaledInstance()` to use `AreaAveragingScaleFilter` or a reasonable alternative provided by the toolkit. `AreaAveragingScaleFilter` is discussed in Chapter 12.

Constructors

There are no constructors for `Image`. You get an `Image` object to work with by using the `getImage()` method of `Applet` (in an applet), `Toolkit` (in an application), or the `createImage()` method of `Component` or `Toolkit`. `getImage()` uses a separate thread to fetch the image. The thread starts when you call `drawImage()`, `prepareImage()`, or any other method that requires image information. `getImage()` returns immediately. You can also use the `MediaTracker` class to force an image to load before it is needed. `MediaTracker` is discussed in the next section.

Characteristics

public abstract int getWidth (ImageObserver observer)

The getWidth() method returns the width of the image object. The width may not be available if the image has not started loading; in this case, getWidth() returns –1. An image's size is available long before loading is complete, so it is often useful to call getWidth() while the image is loading.

public abstract int getHeight (ImageObserver observer)

The getHeight() method returns the height of the image object. The height may not be available if the image has not started loading; in this case, the getHeight() method returns –1. An image's size is available long before loading is complete, so it is often useful to call getHeight() while the image is loading.

Miscellaneous methods

public Image getScaledInstance (int width, int height, int hints) ★

The getScaledInstance() method enables you to generate scaled versions of images before they are needed. Prior to Java 1.1, it was necessary to tell the drawImage() method to do the scaling. However, this meant that scaling didn't take place until you actually tried to draw the image. Since scaling takes time, drawing the image required more time; the net result was degraded appearance. With Java 1.1, you can generate scaled copies of images before drawing them; then you can use a version of drawImage() that does not do scaling, and therefore is much quicker.

The width parameter of getScaledInstance() is the new width of the image. The height parameter is the new height of the image. If either is –1, the scaling retains the aspect ratio of the original image. For instance, if the original image size was 241 by 72 pixels, and width and height were 100 and –1, the new image size would be 100 by 29 pixels. If both width and height are –1, the getScaledInstance() method retains the image's original size. The hints parameter is one of the Image class constants.

```
Image i = getImage (getDocumentBase(), "rosey.jpg");
Image j = i.getScaledInstance (100, -1, Image.SCALE_FAST);
```

public abstract ImageProducer getSource ()

The getSource() method returns the image's producer, which is an object of type ImageProducer. This object represents the image's source. Once you have the ImageProducer, you can use it to do additional image processing; for example, you could create a modified version of the original image by using a FilteredImageSource. Image producers and image filters are covered in Chapter 12.

public abstract Graphics getGraphics ()

> The getGraphics() method returns the image's graphics context. The method getGraphics() works only for Image objects created in memory with Component.createImage (int, int). If the image came from a URL or a file (i.e., from getImage()), getGraphics() throws the run-time exception Class-CastException.

public abstract Object getProperty (String name, ImageObserver observer)

> The getProperty() method interacts with the image's property list. An object representing the requested property name will be returned for observer. observer represents the Component on which the image is rendered. If the property name exists but is not available yet, getProperty() returns null. If the property name does not exist, the getProperty() method returns the Image.UndefinedProperty object.

> Each image type has its own property list. A property named comment stores a comment String from the image's creator. The CropImageFilter adds a property named croprect. If you ask getProperty() for an image's croprect property, you get a Rectangle that shows how the original image was cropped.

public abstract void flush()

> The flush() method resets an image to its initial state. Assume you acquire an image over the network with getImage(). The first time you display the image, it will be loaded over the network. If you redisplay the image, AWT normally reuses the original image. However, if you call flush() before redisplaying the image, AWT fetches the image again from its source. (Images created with createImage() aren't affected.) The flush() method is useful if you expect images to change while your program is running. The following program demonstrates flush(). It reloads and displays the file *flush.gif* every time you click the mouse. If you change the file *flush.gif* and click on the mouse, you will see the new file.

```
import java.awt.*;
public class flushMe extends Frame {
    Image im;
    flushMe () {
        super ("Flushing");
        im = Toolkit.getDefaultToolkit().getImage ("flush.gif");
        resize (175, 225);
    }
    public void paint (Graphics g) {
        g.drawImage (im, 0, 0, 175, 225, this);
    }
    public boolean mouseDown (Event e, int x, int y) {
        im.flush();
        repaint();
        return true;
    }
```

```
     public static void main (String [] args) {
         Frame f = new flushMe ();
         f.show();
     }
  }
```

2.7.2 Simple Animation

Creating simple animation sequences in Java is easy. Load a series of images, then display the images one at a time. Example 2-1 is an application that displays a simple animation sequence. Example 2-2 is an applet that uses a thread to run the application. These programs are far from ideal. If you try them, you'll probably notice some flickering or missing images. We discuss how to fix these problems shortly.

Example 2–1: Animation Application

```
import java.awt.*;
public class Animate extends Frame {
    static Image im[];
    static int numImages = 12;
    static int counter=0;
    Animate () {
        super ("Animate");
    }
    public static void main (String[] args) {
        Frame f = new Animate();
        f.resize (225, 225);
        f.show();
        im = new Image[numImages];
        for (int i=0;i<numImages;i++) {
            im[i] = Toolkit.getDefaultToolkit().getImage ("clock"+i+".jpg");
        }
    }
    public synchronized void paint (Graphics g) {
        g.translate (insets().left, insets().top);
        g.drawImage (im[counter], 0, 0, this);
        counter++;
        if (counter == numImages)
            counter = 0;
        repaint (200);
    }
}
```

This application displays images with the name *clock*n.*jpg*, where *n* is a number between 0 and 11. It fetches the images using the getImage() method of the Toolkit class—hence, the call to Toolkit.getDefaultToolkit(), which gets a Toolkit object to work with. The paint() method displays the images in sequence, using drawImage(). paint() ends with a call to repaint(200), which schedules another call to paint() in 200 milliseconds.

The `AnimateApplet`, whose code is shown in Example 2-2, does more or less the same thing. It is able to use the `Applet.getImage()` method. A more significant difference is that the applet creates a new thread to control the animation. This thread calls `sleep(200)`, followed by `repaint()`, to display a new image every 200 milliseconds.

Example 2–2: Multithreaded Animation Applet

```java
import java.awt.*;
import java.applet.*;
public class AnimateApplet extends Applet implements Runnable {
    static Image im[];
    static int numImages = 12;
    static int counter=0;
    Thread animator;
    public void init () {
        im = new Image[numImages];
        for (int i=0;i<numImages;i++)
            im[i] = getImage (getDocumentBase(), "clock"+i+".jpg");
    }
    public void start() {
        if (animator == null) {
            animator = new Thread (this);
            animator.start ();
        }
    }
    public void stop() {
        if ((animator != null) && (animator.isAlive())) {
            animator.stop();
            animator = null;
        }
    }
    public void run () {
        while (animator != null) {
            try {
                animator.sleep(200);
                repaint ();
                counter++;
                if (counter==numImages)
                    counter=0;
            } catch (Exception e) {
                e.printStackTrace ();
            }
        }
    }
    public void paint (Graphics g) {
        g.drawImage (im[counter], 0, 0, this);
    }
}
```

One quick fix will help the flicker problem in both of these examples. The update() method (which is inherited from the Component class) normally clears the drawing area and calls paint(). In our examples, clearing the drawing area is unnecessary and, worse, results in endless flickering; on slow machines, you'll see update() restore the background color between each image. It's a simple matter to override update() so that it doesn't clear the drawing area first. Add the following method to both of the previous examples:

```
public void update (Graphics g) {
    paint (g);
}
```

Overriding update() helps, but the real solution to our problem is double buffering, which we'll turn to next.

2.7.3 Double Buffering

Double buffering means drawing to an offscreen graphics context and then displaying this graphics context to the screen in a single operation. So far, we have done all our drawing directly on the screen—that is, to the graphics context provided by the paint() method. As your programs grow more complex, paint() gets bigger and bigger, and it takes more time and resources to update the entire drawing area. On a slow machine, the user will see the individual drawing operations take place, which will make your program look slow and clunky. By using the double buffering technique, you can take your time drawing to another graphics context that isn't displayed. When you are ready, you tell the system to display the completely new image at once. Doing so eliminates the possibility of seeing partial screen updates and flickering.

The first thing you need to do is create an image as your drawing canvas. To get an image object, call the createImage() method. createImage() is a method of the Component class, which we will discuss in Chapter 5, *Components*. Since Applet extends Component, you can call createImage() within an applet. When creating an application and extending Frame, createImage() returns null until the Frame's peer exists. To make sure that the peer exists, call addNotify() in the constructor, or make sure you call show() before calling createImage(). Here's the call to the createImage() method that we'll use to get an Image object:

```
Image im = createImage (300, 300); // width and height
```

Once you have an Image object, you have an area you can draw on. But how do you draw on it? There are no drawing methods associated with Image; they're all in the Graphics class. So we need to get a Graphics context from the Image. To do so, call the getGraphics() method of the Image class, and use that Graphics context for your drawing:

```
Graphics buf = im.getGraphics();
```

Now you can do all your drawings with buf. To display the drawing, the paint()
method only needs to call drawImage(im, . . .). Note the hidden connection
between the Graphics object, buf, and the Image you are creating, im. You draw
onto buf; then you use drawImage() to render the image on the on-screen Graphics context within paint().

Another feature of buffering is that you do not have redraw the entire image with
each call to paint(). The buffered image you're working on remains in memory,
and you can add to it at will. If you are drawing directly to the screen, you would
have to recreate the entire drawing each time paint() is called; remember,
paint() always hands you a completely new Graphics object. Figure 2-16 shows
how double buffering works.

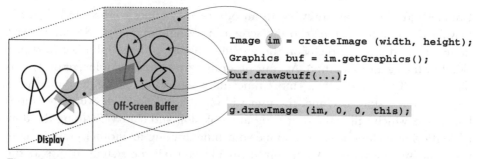

Figure 2–16: Double buffering

Example 2-3 puts it all together for you. It plays a game, with one move drawn to
the screen each cycle. We still do the drawing within paint(), but we draw into an
offscreen buffer; that buffer is copied onto the screen by g.drawImage(im, 0, 0,
this). If we were doing a lot of drawing, it would be a good idea to move the drawing operations into a different thread, but that would be overkill for this simple
applet.

Example 2–3: Double Buffering—Who Won?

```
import java.awt.*;
import java.applet.*;
public class buffering extends Applet {
    Image im;
    Graphics buf;
    int pass=0;
    public void init () {
        // Create buffer
        im = createImage (size().width, size().height);
        // Get its graphics context
        buf = im.getGraphics();
        // Draw Board Once
```

Example 2–3: Double Buffering—Who Won? (continued)

```
        buf.setColor (Color.red);
        buf.drawLine (  0,  50, 150,  50);
        buf.drawLine (  0, 100, 150, 100);
        buf.drawLine ( 50,   0,  50, 150);
        buf.drawLine (100,   0, 100, 150);
        buf.setColor (Color.black);
    }
    public void paint (Graphics g) {
        // Draw image - changes are written onto buf
        g.drawImage (im, 0, 0, this);
        // Make a move
        switch (pass) {
            case 0:
                buf.drawLine (50, 50, 100, 100);
                buf.drawLine (50, 100, 100, 50);
                break;
            case 1:
                buf.drawOval (0, 0, 50, 50);
                break;
            case 2:
                buf.drawLine (100, 0, 150, 50);
                buf.drawLine (150, 0, 100, 50);
                break;
            case 3:
                buf.drawOval (0, 100, 50, 50);
                break;
            case 4:
                buf.drawLine (0, 50, 50, 100);
                buf.drawLine (0, 100, 50, 50);
                break;
            case 5:
                buf.drawOval (100, 50, 50, 50);
                break;
            case 6:
                buf.drawLine (50,   0, 100, 50);
                buf.drawLine (50,  50, 100,  0);
                break;
            case 7:
                buf.drawOval (50, 100, 50, 50);
                break;
            case 8:
                buf.drawLine (100, 100, 150, 150);
                buf.drawLine (150, 100, 100, 150);
                break;
        }
        pass++;
        if (pass <= 9)
            repaint (500);
    }
}
```

2.8 MediaTracker

The MediaTracker class assists in the loading of multimedia objects across the network. Tracking is necessary because Java loads images in separate threads. Calls to getImage() return immediately; image loading starts only when you call the method drawImage(). MediaTracker lets you force images to start loading before you try to display them; it also gives you information about the loading process, so you can wait until an image is fully loaded before displaying it.

Currently, MediaTracker can monitor the loading of images, but not audio, movies, or anything else. Future versions are rumored to be able to monitor other media types.

2.8.1 MediaTracker Methods

Constants

The MediaTracker class defines four constants that are used as return values from the class's methods. These values serve as status indicators.

public static final int LOADING

The LOADING variable indicates that the particular image being checked is still loading.

public static final int ABORTED

The ABORTED variable indicates that the loading process for the image being checked aborted. For example, a timeout could have happened during the download. If something ABORTED during loading, it is possible to flush() the image to force a retry.

public static final int ERRORED

The ERRORED variable indicates that an error occurred during the loading process for the image being checked. For instance, the image file might not be available from the server (invalid URL) or the file format could be invalid. If an image has ERRORED, retrying it will fail.

public static final int COMPLETE

The COMPLETE flag means that the image being checked successfully loaded.

If COMPLETE, ABORTED, or ERRORED is set, the image has stopped loading. If you are checking multiple images, you can OR several of these values together to form a composite. For example, if you are loading several images and want to find out about any malfunctions, call statusAll() and check for a return value of ABORTED | ERRORED.

Constructors

public MediaTracker (Component component)

> The MediaTracker constructor creates a new MediaTracker object to track images to be rendered onto component.

Adding images

The addImage() methods add objects for the MediaTracker to track. When placing an object under a MediaTracker's control, you must provide an identifier for grouping purposes. When multiple images are grouped together, you can perform operations on the entire group with a single request. For example, you might want to wait until all the images in an animation sequence are loaded before starting the animation; in this case, assigning the same ID to all the images makes good sense. However, when multiple images are grouped together, you cannot check on the status of a single image. The moral is: if you care about the status of individual images, put each into a group by itself.

Folklore has it that the identifier also serves as a loading priority, with a lower ID meaning a higher priority. This is not completely true. Current implementations start loading lower IDs first, but at most, this is implementation-specific functionality for the JDK. Furthermore, although an object with a lower identifier might be told to start loading first, the MediaTracker does nothing to ensure that it finishes first.

public synchronized void addImage (Image image, int id, int width, int height)

> The addImage() method tells the MediaTracker instance that it needs to track the loading of image. The id is used as a grouping. Someone will eventually render the image at a scaled size of width × height. If width and height are both –1, the image will be rendered unscaled. If you forget to notify the MediaTracker that the image will be scaled and ask the MediaTracker to waitForID (id), it is possible that the image may not be fully ready when you try to draw it.

public void addImage (Image image, int id)

> The addImage() method tells the MediaTracker instance that it needs to track the loading of image. The id is used as a grouping. The image will be rendered at its actual size, without scaling.

Removing images

Images that have finished loading are still watched by the MediaTracker. The removeImage() methods, added in Java 1.1, allow you to remove objects from the MediaTracker. Once you no longer care about an image (usually after waiting for it to load), you can remove it from the tracker. Getting rid of loaded images results in better performance because the tracker has fewer objects to check. In Java 1.0, you can't remove an image from MediaTracker.

public void removeImage (Image image) ★

The removeImage() method tells the MediaTracker to remove all instances of image from its tracking list.

public void removeImage (Image image, int id) ★

The removeImage() method tells the MediaTracker to remove all instances of image from group id of its tracking list.

public void removeImage (Image image, int id, int width, int height) ★

This removeImage() method tells the MediaTracker to remove all instances of image from group id and scale width × height of its tracking list.

Waiting

A handful of methods let you wait for a particular image, image group, all images, or a particular time period. They enable you to be sure that an image has finished trying to load prior to continuing. The fact that an image has finished loading does not imply it has successfully loaded. It is possible that an error condition arose, which caused loading to stop. You should check the status of the image (or group) for actual success.

public void waitForID (int id) throws InterruptedException

The waitForID() method blocks the current thread from running until the images added with id finish loading. If the wait is interrupted, waitForID() throws an InterruptedException.

public synchronized boolean waitForID (int id, long ms) throws InterruptedException

The waitForID() method blocks the current thread from running until the images added with id finish loading or until ms milliseconds have passed. If all the images have loaded, waitForID() returns true; if the timer has expired, it returns false, and one or more images in the id set have not finished loading. If ms is 0, it waits until all images added with id have loaded, with no timeout. If the wait is interrupted, waitForID() throws an InterruptedException.

public void waitForAll () throws InterruptedException

The waitForAll() method blocks the current thread from running until all images controlled by this MediaTracker finish loading. If the wait is interrupted, waitForAll() throws an InterruptedException.

public synchronized boolean waitForAll (long ms) throws InterruptedException

> The `waitForAll()` method blocks the current thread from running until all images controlled by this `MediaTracker` finish loading or until `ms` milliseconds have passed. If all the images have loaded, `waitForAll()` returns `true`; if the timer has expired, it returns `false`, and one or more images have not finished loading. If `ms` is 0, it waits until all images have loaded, with no timeout. When you interrupt the waiting, `waitForAll()` throws an `InterruptedException`.

Checking status

Several methods are available to check on the status of images loading. None of these methods block, so you can continue working while images are loading.

public boolean checkID (int id)

> The `checkID()` method determines if all the images added with the `id` tag have finished loading. The method returns `true` if all images have completed loading (successfully or unsuccessfully). Since this can return `true` on error, you should also use `isErrorID()` to check for errors. If loading has not completed, `checkID()` returns `false`. This method does not force images to start loading.

public synchronized boolean checkID (int id, boolean load)

> The `checkID()` method determines if all the images added with the `id` tag have finished loading. If the `load` flag is `true`, any images in the `id` group that have not started loading yet will start. The method returns `true` if all images have completed loading (successfully or unsuccessfully). Since this can return `true` on error, you should also use `isErrorID()` to check for errors. If loading has not completed, `checkID()` returns `false`.

public boolean checkAll ()

> The `checkAll()` method determines if all images associated with the `Media-Tracker` have finished loading. The method returns `true` if all images have completed loading (successfully or unsuccessfully). Since this can return `true` on error, you should also use `isErrorAny()` to check for errors. If loading has not completed, `checkAll()` returns `false`. This method does not force images to start loading.

public synchronized boolean checkAll (boolean load)

> The `checkAll()` method determines if all images associated with the `Media-Tracker` have finished loading. If the `load` flag is `true`, any image that has not started loading yet will start. The method returns `true` if all images have completed loading (successfully or unsuccessfully). Since this can return `true` on error, you should also use `isErrorAny()` to check for errors. If loading has not completed, `checkAll()` returns `false`.

public int statusID (int id, boolean load)

> The `statusID()` method checks on the load status of the images in the `id` group. If there are multiple images in the group, the results are ORed together. If the `load` flag is `true`, any image in the `id` group that has not started loading yet will start. The return value is some combination of the class constants `LOADING`, `ABORTED`, `ERRORED`, and `COMPLETE`.

public int statusAll (boolean load)

> The `statusAll()` method determines the load status of all the images associated with the `MediaTracker`. If this `MediaTracker` is watching multiple images, the results are ORed together. If the `load` flag is `true`, any image that has not started loading yet will start. The return value is some combination of the class constants `LOADING`, `ABORTED`, `ERRORED`, and `COMPLETE`.

public synchronized boolean isErrorID (int id)

> The `isErrorId()` method checks whether any media in the `id` group encountered an error while loading. If any image resulted in an error, `isErrorId()` returns `true`; if there were no errors, it returns `false`.

public synchronized boolean isErrorAny ()

> The `isErrorAny()` method checks to see if any image associated with the `MediaTracker` encountered an error. If there was an error, the method returns `true`; if none, `false`.

public synchronized Object[] getErrorsID (int id)

> The `getErrorsID()` method returns an array of the objects that encountered errors in the group ID during loading. If loading caused no errors, the method returns `null`. The return type is an `Object` array instead of an `Image` array because `MediaTracker` will eventually support additional media types.

public synchronized Object[] getErrorsAny ()

> The `getErrorsAny()` method returns an array of all the objects that encountered an error during loading. If there were no errors, the method returns `null`. The return type is an `Object` array instead of an `Image` array because `MediaTracker` will eventually support additional media types.

2.8.2 Using a MediaTracker

The `init()` method improves the `AnimateApplet` from Example 2-2 to ensure that images load before the animation sequence starts. Waiting for images to load is particularly important if there is a slow link between the computer on which the applet is running and the server for the image files. Note that in a few cases, like interlaced GIF files, you might be willing to display an image before it has completely loaded. However, judicious use of `MediaTracker` will give you much more control over your program's behavior.

The new init() method creates a MediaTracker, puts all the images in the animation sequence under the tracker's control, and then calls waitForAll() to wait
until the images are loaded. Once the images are loaded, it calls isErrorsAny() to
make sure that the images loaded successfully.

```
public void init () {
    MediaTracker mt = new MediaTracker (this);
    im = new Image[numImages];
    for (int i=0;i<numImages;i++) {
        im[i] = getImage (getDocumentBase(), "clock"+i+".jpg");
        mt.addImage (im[i], i);
    }
    try {
        mt.waitForAll();
        if (mt.isErrorAny())
            System.out.println ("Error loading images");
    } catch (Exception e) {
        e.printStackTrace ();
    }
}
```

3

Fonts and Colors

This chapter introduces the java.awt classes that are used to work with different fonts and colors. First, we discuss the Font class, which determines the font used to display text strings, whether they are drawn directly on the screen (with draw-String()) or displayed within a component like a text field. The FontMetrics class gives you detailed information about a font, which you can use to position text strings intelligently. Next, the Color class is used to represent colors and can be used to specify the background color of any object, as well as the foreground color used to display a text string or a shape. Finally, the SystemColor class (which is new to Java 1.1) provides access to the desktop color scheme.

3.1 Fonts

An instance of the Font class represents a specific font to the system. Within AWT, a font is specified by its name, style, and point size. Each platform that supports Java provides a basic set of fonts; to find the fonts supported on any platform, call Toolkit.getDefaultToolkit().getFontList(). This method returns a String array of the fonts available. Under Java 1.0, on any platform, the available fonts were: TimesRoman, Helvetica, Courier, Dialog, DialogInput, and ZapfDingbats. For copyright reasons, the list is substantially different in Java 1.1: the available font names are TimesRoman ☆, Serif, Helvetica ☆, SansSerif, Courier ☆, Monospaced, Dialog, and DialogInput. The actual fonts available aren't changing; the deprecated font names are being replaced by non-copyrighted equivalents. Thus, TimesRoman is now Serif, Helvetica is now SansSerif, and Courier is Monospaced. The ZapfDingbats font name has been dropped completely because the characters in this font have official Unicode mappings in the range \u2700 to \u27ff.

NOTE   If you desire non-Latin font support with Java 1.1, use the Unicode mappings for the characters. The actual font used is specified in a set of *font.properties* files in the *lib* subdirectory under *java.home*. These localized font files allow you to remap the "Serif", "SansSerif", and "Monospaced" names to different fonts.

The font's `style` is passed with the help of the class variables `Font.PLAIN`, `Font.BOLD`, and `Font.ITALIC`. The combination `Font.BOLD | Font.ITALIC` specifies bold italics.

A font's `size` is represented as an integer. This integer is commonly thought of as a point size; although that's not strictly correct, this book follows common usage and talks about font sizes in points.

It is possible to add additional font names to the system by setting properties. For example, putting the line below in the properties file or a resource file (resource files are new to Java 1.1) defines the name "AvantGarde" as an alias for the font SansSerif:

```
awt.font.avantgarde=SansSerif
```

With this line in the properties file, a Java program can use "AvantGarde" as a font name; when this font is selected, AWT uses the font SansSerif for display. The property name must be all lowercase. Note that we haven't actually added a new font to the system; we've only created a new name for an old font. See the discussion of `getFont()` and `decode()` for more on font properties.

3.1.1 The Font Class

Constants

There are four styles for displaying fonts in Java: plain, bold, italic, and bold italic. Three class constants are used to represent font styles:

public static final int BOLD
    The `BOLD` constant represents a boldface font.

public static final int ITALIC
    The `ITALIC` constant represents an italic font.

public static final int PLAIN
    The `PLAIN` constant represents a plain or normal font.

The combination `BOLD | ITALIC` represents a bold italic font. `PLAIN` combined with either `BOLD` or `ITALIC` represents bold or italic, respectively.

There is no style for underlined text. If you want underlining, you have to do it manually, with the help of `FontMetrics`.

NOTE   If you are using Microsoft's SDK, the `com.ms.awt.FontX` class includes direct support for underlined, strike through (line through middle), and outline fonts.

Variables

Three protected variables access the font setting. They are initially set through the `Font` constructor. To read these variables, use the `Font` class's "get" methods.

protected String name
    The name of the font.

protected int size
    The size of the font.

protected int style
    The style of the font. The style is some logical combination of the constants listed previously.

Constructors

public Font (String name, int style, int size)
    There is a single constructor for `Font`. It requires a `name`, `style`, and `size`. `name` represents the name of the font to create, case insensitive.

```
setFont (new Font ("TimesRoman", Font.BOLD | Font.ITALIC, 20));
```

Characteristics

public String getName ()
    The `getName()` method returns the font's logical name. This is the name passed to the constructor for the specific instance of the `Font`. Remember that system properties can be used to alias font names, so the name used in the constructor isn't necessarily the actual name of a font on the system.

public String getFamily ()
    The `getFamily()` method returns the actual name of the font that is being used to display characters. If the font has been aliased to another font, the `getFamily()` method returns the name of the platform-specific font, not the alias. For example, if the constructor was `new Font ("AvantGarde", Font.PLAIN, 10)` and the `awt.font.avantgarde=Helvetica` property is set,

then `getName()` returns AvantGarde, and `getFamily()` returns Helvetica. If nobody set the property, both methods return AvantGarde, and the system uses the default font (since AvantGarde is a nonstandard font).

public int getStyle ()

The `getStyle()` method returns the current style of the font as an integer. Compare this value with the constants `Font.BOLD`, `Font.PLAIN`, and `Font.ITALIC` to see which style is meant. It is easier to use the `isPlain()`, `isBold()`, and `isItalic()` methods to find out the current style. `getStyle()` is more useful if you want to copy the style of some font when creating another.

public int getSize ()

The `getSize()` method retrieves the point size of the font, as set by the size parameter in the constructor. The actual displayed size may be different.

public FontPeer getPeer () ★

The `getPeer()` method retrieves the platform-specific peer object. The object `FontPeer` is a platform-specific subclass of `sun.awt.PlatformFont`. For example, on a Windows 95 platform, this would be an instance of `sun.awt.windows.WFontPeer`.

Styles

public boolean isPlain ()

The `isPlain()` method returns `true` if the current font is neither bold nor italic. Otherwise, it returns `false`.

public boolean isBold ()

The `isBold()` method returns `true` if the current font is either bold or bold and italic. Otherwise, it returns `false`.

public boolean isItalic ()

The `isItalic()` method returns `true` if the current font is either italic or bold and italic. Otherwise, it returns `false`.

Font properties

Earlier, you saw how to use system properties to add aliases for fonts. In addition to adding aliases, you can use system properties to specify which fonts your program will use when it runs. This allows your users to customize their environments to their liking; your program reads the font settings at run-time, rather than using hard-coded settings. The format of the settings in a properties file is:

```
propname=fontname-style-size
```

where `propname` is the name of the property being set, `fontname` is any valid font name (including aliases), style is plain, bold, italic, or bolditalic, and size represents the desired size for the font. style and size default to plain and 12 points. Order is important; the font's style must always precede its size.

For example, let's say you have three areas on your screen: one for menus, one for labels, and one for input. In the system properties, you allow users to set three properties: myPackage.myClass.menuFont, myPackage.myClass.labelFont, and myPackage.myClass.inputFont. One user sets two:

```
myPackage.myClass.menuFont=TimesRoman-italic-24
myPackage.myClass.inputFont=Helvetica
```

The user has specified a Times font for menus and Helvetica for other input. The property names are up to the developer. The program uses getFont() to read the properties and set the fonts accordingly.

NOTE   The location of the system properties file depends on the run-time environment and version you are using. Normally, the file goes into a subdirectory of the installation directory, or for environments where users have home directories, in a subdirectory for the user. Sun's HotJava, JDK, and *appletviewer* tools use the *properties* file in the *.hotjava* directory.

Most browsers do not permit modifying properties, so there is no file.

Java 1.1 adds the idea of "resource files," which are syntactically similar to properties files. Resource files are then placed on the server or within a directory found in the CLASSPATH. Updating the properties file is no longer recommended.

---

public static Font getFont (String name)

The getFont() method gets the font specified by the system property name. If name is not a valid system property, null is returned. This method is implemented by a call to the next version of getFont(), with the defaultFont parameter set to null.

Assuming the properties defined in the previous example, if you call the getFont() method with name set to myPackage.myClass.menuFont, the return value is a 24-point, italic, TimesRoman Font object. If called with name set to myPackage.myClass.inputFont, getFont() returns a 12-point, plain Helvetica Font object. If called with myPackage.myClass.labelFont as name, getFont() returns null because this user did not set the property myPackage.myClass.labelFont.

public static Font getFont (String name, Font defaultFont)

The getFont() method gets the font specified by the system property name. If name is not a valid system property, this version of getFont() returns the Font specified by defaultFont. This version allows you to provide defaults in the event the user does not wish to provide his own font settings.

public static Font decode (String name) ★

The decode() method provides an explicit means to decipher font property settings, regardless of where the setting comes from. (The getFont() method can decipher settings, but only if they're in the system properties file.) In particular, you can use decode() to look up font settings in a resource file. The format of name is the same as that used by getFont(). If the contents of name are invalid, a 12-point plain font is returned. To perform the equivalent of getFont("myPackage.myClass.menuFont") without using system properties, see the following example. For a more extensive example using resource files, see Appendix A.

```
// Java 1.1 only
InputStream is = instance.getClass().getResourceAsStream("propfile");
Properties p = new Properties();
try {
    p.load (is);
    Font f = Font.decode(p.getProperty("myPackage.myClass.menuFont"));
} catch (IOException e) {
    System.out.println ("error loading props...");
}
```

Miscellaneous methods

public int hashCode ()

The hashCode() method returns a hash code for the font. This hash code is used whenever a Font object is used as the key in a Hashtable.

public boolean equals (Object o)

The equals() method overrides the equals() method of Object to define equality for Font objects. Two Font objects are equal if their size, style, and name are equal. The following example demonstrates why this is necessary.

```
Font a = new Font ("TimesRoman", Font.PLAIN, 10);
Font b = new Font ("TimesRoman", Font.PLAIN, 10);
// displays false since the objects are different objects
System.out.println (a == b);
// displays true since the objects have equivalent settings
System.out.println (a.equals (b));
```

public String toString ()

The `toString()` method of `Font` returns a string showing the current family, name, style, and size settings. For example:

```
java.awt.Font[family=TimesRoman,name=TimesRoman,style=bolditalic,size=20]
```

3.2 FontMetrics

The abstract `FontMetrics` class provides the tools for calculating the actual width and height of text when displayed on the screen. You can use the results to position objects around text or to provide special effects like shadows and underlining.

Like the `Graphics` class, `FontMetrics` is abstract. The run-time Java platform provides a concrete implementation of `FontMetrics`. You don't have to worry about the actual class; it is guaranteed to implement all the methods of `FontMetrics`. In case you're curious, on a Windows 95 platform, either the class `sun.awt.win32.Win32FontMetrics` (JDK1.0) or the class `sun.awt.windows.WFontMetrics` (JDK1.1) extends `FontMetrics`. On a UNIX/Motif platform, the class is `sun.awt.motif.X11FontMetrics`. With the Macintosh, the class is `sun.awt.macos.MacFontMetrics`. If you're not using the JDK, the class names may be different, but the principle still applies: you don't have to worry about the concrete class.

3.2.1 The FontMetrics Class

Variables

protected Font font

The font whose metrics are contained in this `FontMetrics` object; use the `getFont()` method to get the value.

Constructors

protected FontMetrics (Font font)

There is no visible constructor for `FontMetrics`. Since the class is abstract, you cannot create a `FontMetrics` object. The way to get the `FontMetrics` for a font is to ask for it. Through the current graphics context, call the method `getGraphics().getFontMetrics()` to retrieve the `FontMetrics` for the current font. If a graphics context isn't available, you can get a `FontMetrics` object from the default `Toolkit` by calling the method `Toolkit.getDefaultToolkit().getFontMetrics (aFontObject)`.

Font height

Four variables describe the height of a font: leading (pronounced like the metal), ascent, descent, and height. Leading is the amount of space required between lines of the same font. Ascent is the space above the baseline required by the tallest character in the font. Descent is the space required below the baseline by the lowest descender (the "tail" of a character like "y"). Height is the total of the three: ascent, baseline, and descent. Figure 3-1 shows these values graphically.

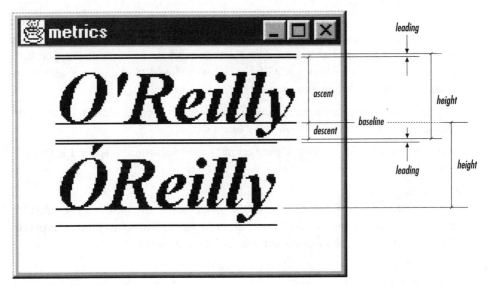

Figure 3–1: Font height metrics

If that were the entire story, it would be simple. Unfortunately, it isn't. Some special characters (for example, capitals with umlauts or accents) are taller than the "tallest" character in the font; so Java defines a value called maxAscent to account for these. Similarly, some characters descend below the "greatest" descent, so Java defines a maxDescent to handle these cases.

NOTE   It seems that on Windows and Macintosh platforms there is no difference between the return values of getMaxAscent() and getAscent(), or between getMaxDescent() and getDescent(). On UNIX platforms, they sometimes differ. For developing truly portable applications, the max methods should be used where necessary.

---

public int getLeading ()

The getLeading() method retrieves the leading required for the FontMetrics of the font. The units for this measurement are pixels.

public int getAscent ()

The getAscent() method retrieves the space above the baseline required for the tallest character in the font. The units for this measurement are pixels. You cannot get the ascent value for a specific character.

public int getMaxAscent ()

getMaxAscent() retrieves the height above the baseline for the character that's really the tallest character in the font, taking into account accents, umlauts, tildes, and other special marks. The units for this measurement are pixels. If you are using only ordinary ASCII characters below 128 (i.e., the English language character set), getMaxAscent() is not necessary.

If you're using getMaxAscent(), avoid getHeight(); getHeight() is based on getAscent() and doesn't account for extra space.

For some fonts and platforms, getAscent() may include the space for the diacritical marks.

public int getDescent ()

The getDescent() method retrieves the space below the baseline required for the deepest character for the font. The units for this measurement are pixels. You cannot get the descent value for a specific character.

public int getMaxDescent ()
public int getMaxDecent ()

Some fonts may have special characters that extend farther below the baseline than the value returned by getDescent(). getMaxDescent() returns the real maximum descent for the font, in pixels. In most cases, you can still use the getDescent() method; visually, it is okay for an occasional character to extend into the space between lines. However, if it is absolutely, positively necessary that the descent space does not overlap with the next line's ascent requirements, use getMaxDescent() and avoid getDescent() and getHeight().

An early beta release of the AWT API included the method getMaxDecent(). It is left for compatibility with early beta code. Avoid using it; it is identical to getMaxDescent() in every way except spelling. Unfortunately, it is not flagged as deprecated.

public int getHeight ()

> The getHeight() method returns the sum of getDescent(), getAscent(), and getLeading(). In most cases, this will be the distance between successive baselines when you are displaying multiple lines of text. The height of a font in pixels is not necessarily the size of a font in points.
>
> Don't use getHeight() if you are displaying characters with accents, umlauts, and other marks that increase the character's height. In this case, compute the height yourself using the getMaxAscent() method. Likewise, you shouldn't use the method getHeight() if you are using getMaxDescent() instead of getDescent().

Character width

In the horizontal dimension, positioning characters is relatively simple: you don't have to worry about ascenders and descenders, you only have to worry about how far ahead to draw the next character after you have drawn the current one. The "how far" is called the *advance width* of a character. For most cases, the advance width is the actual width plus the intercharacter space. However, it's not a good idea to think in these terms; in many cases, the intercharacter space is actually negative (i.e., the bounding boxes for two adjacent characters overlap). For example, consider an italic font. The top right corner of one character probably extends beyond the character's advance width, overlapping the next character's bounding box. (To see this, look back at Figure 3-1; in particular, look at the *ll* in *O'Reilly*.) If you think purely in terms of the advance width (the amount to move horizontally after drawing a character), you won't run into trouble. Obviously, the advance width depends on the character, unless you're using a fixed width font.

public int charWidth (char character)

> This version of the charWidth() method returns the advance width of the given character in pixels.

public int charWidth (int character)

> The charWidth() method returns the advance width of the given character in pixels. Note that the argument has type int rather than char. This version is useful when overriding the Component.keyDown() method, which gets the integer value of the character pressed as a parameter. With the KeyEvent class, you should use the previous version with its getKeyChar() method.

public int stringWidth (String string)

The stringWidth() method calculates the advance width of the entire string
in pixels. Among other things, you can use the results to underline or center
text within an area of the screen. Example 3-1 and Figure 3-2 show an example
that centers several text strings (taken from the command-line arguments) in
a Frame.

Example 3–1: Centering Text in a Frame

```
import java.awt.*;
public class Center extends Frame {
    static String text[];
    private Dimension dim;
    static public void main (String args[]) {
        if (args.length == 0) {
            System.err.println ("Usage: java Center <some text>");
            return;
        }
        text = args;
        Center f = new Center();
        f.show();
    }
    public void addNotify() {
        super.addNotify();
        int maxWidth = 0;
        FontMetrics fm = getToolkit().getFontMetrics(getFont());
        for (int i=0;i<text.length;i++) {
            maxWidth = Math.max (maxWidth, fm.stringWidth(text[i]));
        }
        Insets inset = insets();
        dim = new Dimension (maxWidth + inset.left + inset.right,
            text.length*fm.getHeight() + inset.top + inset.bottom);
        resize (dim);
    }
    public void paint (Graphics g) {
        g.translate(insets().left, insets().top);
        FontMetrics fm = g.getFontMetrics();
        for (int i=0;i<text.length;i++) {
            int x,y;
            x = (size().width - fm.stringWidth(text[i]))/2;
            y = (i+1)*fm.getHeight()-1;
            g.drawString (text[i], x, y);
        }

    }
}
```

This application extends the Frame class. It stores its command-line arguments in
the String array text[]. The addNotify() method sizes the frame appropriately.
It computes the size needed to display the arguments and resizes the Frame accordingly. To compute the width, it takes the longest stringWidth() and adds the left
and right insets. To compute the height, it takes the current font's height,

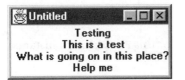

Figure 3–2: Centering text in a frame

multiplies it by the number of lines to display, and adds insets. Then it is up to the paint() method to use stringWidth() and getHeight() to figure out where to put each string.

public int charsWidth (char data[], int offset, int length)

The charsWidth() method allows you to calculate the advance width of the char array data, without first converting data to a String and calling the stringWidth() method. The offset specifies the element of data to start with; length specifies the number of elements to use. The first element of the array has an offset of zero. If offset or length is invalid, charsWidth() throws the run-time exception ArrayIndexOutOfBoundsException.

public int bytesWidth (byte data[], int offset, int length)

The bytesWidth() method allows you to calculate the advance width of the byte array data, without first converting data to a String and calling the stringWidth()method. The offset specifies the element of data to start with; length specifies the number of elements to use. The first element of the array has an offset of zero. If offset or length is invalid, bytesWidth() throws the run-time exception ArrayIndexOutOfBoundsException.

public int[] getWidths ()

The getWidths() method returns an integer array of the advance widths of the first 255 characters in the FontMetrics font. getWidths() is very useful if you are continually looking up the widths of ASCII characters. Obtaining the widths as an array and looking up individual character widths yourself results in less method invocation overhead than making many calls to charWidth().

public int getMaxAdvance ()

The getMaxAdvance() method returns the advance pixel width of the widest character in the font. This allows you to reserve enough space for characters before you know what they are. If you know you are going to display only ASCII characters, you are better off calculating the maximum value returned from getWidths(). When unable to determine the width in advance, the method getMaxAdvance() returns –1.

Miscellaneous methods

public Font getFont ()

    The getFont() method returns the specific font for this FontMetrics instance.

public String toString ()

    The toString() method of FontMetrics returns a string displaying the current font, ascent, descent, and height. For example:

```
sun.awt.win32.Win32FontMetrics[font=java.awt.Font[family=TimesRoman,
name=TimesRoman,style=bolditalic,size=20]ascent=17, descent=6, height=24]
```

Because this is an abstract class, the concrete implementation could return something different.

3.2.2 Font Display Example

Example 3-2 displays all the available fonts in the different styles at 12 points. The code uses the FontMetrics methods to ensure that there is enough space for each line. Figure 3-3 shows the results, using the Java 1.0 font names, on several platforms.

Example 3–2: Font Display

```
import java.awt.*;
public class Display extends Frame {
    static String[] fonts;
    private Dimension dim;
    Display () {
        super ("Font Display");
        fonts = Toolkit.getDefaultToolkit().getFontList();
    }
    public void addNotify() {
        Font f;
        super.addNotify();
        int height  = 0;
        int maxWidth = 0;
        final int vMargin  = 5, hMargin = 5;
        for (int i=0;i<fonts.length;i++) {
            f = new Font (fonts[i], Font.PLAIN, 12);
            height += getHeight (f);
            f = new Font (fonts[i], Font.BOLD, 12);
            height += getHeight (f);
            f = new Font (fonts[i], Font.ITALIC, 12);
            height += getHeight (f);
            f = new Font (fonts[i], Font.BOLD | Font.ITALIC, 12);
            height += getHeight (f);
            maxWidth = Math.max (maxWidth, getWidth (f, fonts[i] + " BOLDITALIC"));
        }
        Insets inset = insets();
        dim = new Dimension (maxWidth + inset.left + inset.right + hMargin,
                    height + inset.top + inset.bottom + vMargin);
```

Example 3–2: Font Display (continued)

```
        resize (dim);
    }
    static public void main (String args[]) {
        Display f = new Display();
        f.show();
    }
    private int getHeight (Font f) {
        FontMetrics fm = Toolkit.getDefaultToolkit().getFontMetrics(f);
        return fm.getHeight();
    }
    private int getWidth (Font f, String s) {
        FontMetrics fm = Toolkit.getDefaultToolkit().getFontMetrics(f);
        return fm.stringWidth(s);
    }
    public void paint (Graphics g) {
        int x = 0;
        int y = 0;
        g.translate(insets().left, insets().top);
        for (int i=0;i<fonts.length;i++) {
            Font plain = new Font (fonts[i], Font.PLAIN, 12);
            Font bold = new Font (fonts[i], Font.BOLD, 12);
            Font italic = new Font (fonts[i], Font.ITALIC, 12);
            Font bolditalic = new Font (fonts[i], Font.BOLD | Font.ITALIC, 12);
            g.setFont (plain);
            y += getHeight (plain);
            g.drawString (fonts[i] + " PLAIN", x, y);
            g.setFont (bold);
            y += getHeight (bold);
            g.drawString (fonts[i] + " BOLD", x, y);
            g.setFont (italic);
            y += getHeight (italic);
            g.drawString (fonts[i] + " ITALIC", x, y);
            g.setFont (bolditalic);
            y += getHeight (bolditalic);
            g.drawString (fonts[i] + " BOLDITALIC", x, y);
        }
        resize (dim);
    }
}
```

3.3 *Color*

Not so long ago, color was a luxury; these days, color is a requirement. A program
that uses only black and white seems hopelessly old fashioned. AWT's Color class
lets you define and work with Color objects. When we discuss the Component class
(see Chapter 5, *Components*), you will see how to use these color objects, and our
discussion of the SystemColor subclass (new to Java 1.1; discussed later in this
chapter) shows you how to control the colors that are painted on the screen.

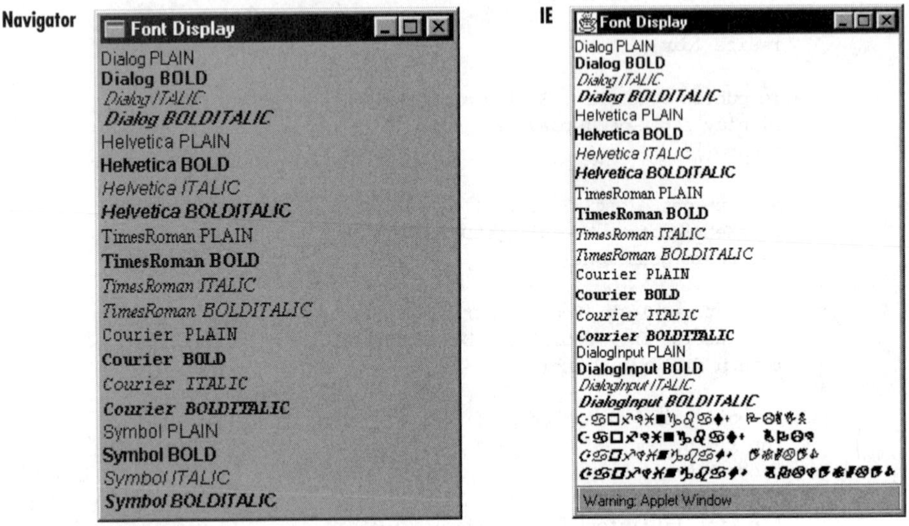

Figure 3–3: Fonts available with the Netscape Navigator 3.0 and Internet Explorer 3.0

A few words of warning: while colors give you the opportunity to make visually pleasing applications, they also let you do things that are incredibly ugly. Resist the urge to go overboard with your use of color; it's easy to make something hideous when you are trying to use every color in the palette. Also, realize that colors are fundamentally platform dependent, and in a very messy way. Java lets you use the same Color objects on any platform, but it can't guarantee that every display will treat the color the same way; the result depends on everything from your software to the age of your monitor. What looks pink on one monitor may be red on another. Furthermore, when running in an environment with a limited palette, AWT picks the available color that is closest to what you requested. If you really care about appearance, there is no substitute for testing.

3.3.1 Color Methods

Constants

The Color class has predefined constants (all of type public static final Color) for frequently used colors. These constants, their RGB values, and their HSB values (hue, saturation, brightness) are given in Table 3-1.

Table 3–1: Comparison of RGB and HSB Colors

Color	Red	Green	Blue	Hue	Saturation	Brightness
black	0	0	0	0	0	0
blue	0	0	255	.666667	1	1
cyan	0	255	255	.5	1	1
darkGray	64	64	64	0	0	.25098
gray	128	128	128	0	0	.501961
green	0	255	0	.333333	1	1
lightGray	192	192	192	0	0	.752941
magenta	255	0	255	.833333	1	1
orange	255	200	0	.130719	1	1
pink	255	175	175	0	.313726	1
red	255	0	0	0	1	1
white	255	255	255	0	0	1
yellow	255	255	0	.166667	1	1

These constants are used like any other class variable: for example, `Color.red` is a constant `Color` object representing the color red. Many other color constants are defined in the `SystemColor` class.

Constructors

When you're not using a predefined constant, you create `Color` objects by specifying the color's red, green, and blue components. Depending on which constructor you use, you can specify the components as integers between 0 and 255 (most intense) or as floating point intensities between 0.0 and 1.0 (most intense). The result is a 24-bit quantity that represents a color. The remaining 8 bits are used to represent transparency: that is, if the color is painted on top of something, does whatever was underneath show through? The `Color` class doesn't let you work with the transparency bits; all `Color` objects are opaque. However, you can use transparency when working with images; this topic is covered in Chapter 12, *Image Processing.*

public Color (int red, int green, int blue)

This constructor is the most commonly used. You provide the specific `red`, `green`, and `blue` values for the color. Valid values for `red`, `green`, and `blue` are between 0 and 255. The constructor examines only the low-order byte of the integer and ignores anything outside the range, including the sign bit.

public Color (int rgb)

This constructor allows you to combine all three variables in one parameter, rgb. Bits 16–23 represent the red component, and bits 8–15 represent the green component. Bits 0–7 represent the blue component. Bits 24–31 are ignored. Going from three bytes to one integer is fairly easy:

```
(((red & 0xFF) << 16 ) | ((green & 0xFF) << 8) | ((blue & 0xFF) << 0))
```

public Color (float red, float green, float blue)

This final constructor allows you to provide floating point values between 0.0 and 1.0 for each of red, green, and blue. Values outside of this range yield unpredictable results.

Settings

public int getRed ()

The getRed() method retrieves the current setting for the red component of the color.

public int getGreen ()

The getGreen() method retrieves the current setting for the green component of the color.

public int getBlue ()

The getBlue() method retrieves the current setting for the blue component of the color.

public int getRGB ()

The getRGB() method retrieves the current settings for red, green, and blue in one combined value. Bits 16–23 represent the red component. Bits 8–15 represent the green component. Bits 0–7 represent the blue component. Bits 24–31 are the transparency bits; they are always 0xff (opaque) when using the default RGB ColorModel.

public Color brighter ()

The brighter() method creates a new Color that is somewhat brighter than the current color. This method is useful if you want to highlight something on the screen.

NOTE   Black does not get any brighter.

---

public Color darker ()

The darker() method returns a new Color that is somewhat darker than the current color. This method is useful if you are trying to de-emphasize an object on the screen. If you are creating your own Component, you can use a `darker()` `Color` to mark it inactive.

Color properties

`Color` properties are very similar to `Font` properties. You can use system properties (or resource files) to allow users to select colors for your programs. The settings have the form `0xRRGGBB`, where `RR` is the red component of the color, `GG` represents the green component, and `BB` represents the blue component. `0x` indicates that the number is in hexadecimal. If you (or your user) are comfortable using decimal values for colors (0x112233 is 1122867 in decimal), you can, but then it is harder to see the values of the different components.

NOTE   The location of the system properties file depends on the run-time environment and version you are using. Ordinarily, the file will go into a subdirectory of the installation directory or, for environment's where users have home directories, in a subdirectory for the user. Sun's HotJava, JDK, and *appletviewer* tools use the *properties* file in the *.hotjava* directory.

Most browsers do not permit modifying properties, so there is no file.

Java 1.1 adds the idea of "resource files," which are syntactically similar to properties files. Resource files are then placed on the server or within a directory found in the `CLASSPATH`. Updating the properties file is no longer recommended.

For example, consider a screen that uses four colors: one each for the foreground, the background, inactive components, and highlighted text. In the system properties file, you allow users to select colors by setting the following properties:

```
myPackage.myClass.foreground
myPackage.myClass.background
myPackage.myClass.inactive
myPackage.myClass.highlight
```

One particular user set two:

```
myPackage.myClass.foreground=0xff00ff        #magenta
myPackage.myClass.background=0xe0e0e0         #light gray
```

These lines tell the program to use magenta as the foreground color and light gray for the background. The program will use its default colors for inactive components and highlighted text.

public static Color getColor (String name)

The getColor() method gets the color specified by the system property name. If name is not a valid system property, getColor() returns null. If the property value does not convert to an integer, getColor() returns null.

For the properties listed above, if you call getColor() with name set to the property myPackage.myClass.foreground, it returns a magenta Color object. If called with name set to myPackage.myClass.inactive, getColor() returns null.

public static Color getColor (String name, Color defaultColor)

The getColor() method gets the color specified by the system property name. This version of the getColor() method returns defaultColor if name is not a valid system property or the property's value does not convert to an integer.

For the previous example, if getColor() is called with name set to myPackage.myClass.inactive,   the getColor() method returns the value of defaultColor. This allows you to provide defaults for properties the user doesn't wish to set explicitly.

public static Color getColor (String name, int defaultColor)

This getColor() method gets the color specified by the system property name. This version of the getColor() method returns defaultColor if name is not a valid system property or the property's value does not convert to an integer. The default color is specified as an integer in which bits 16–23 represent the red component, 8–15 represent the green component, and 0–7 represent the blue component. Bits 24–31 are ignored. If the property value does not convert to an integer, defaultColor is returned.

public static Color decode (String name) ★

The decode() method provides an explicit means to decipher color property settings, regardless of where the setting comes from. (The getColor() method can decipher settings but only if they're in the system properties file.) In particular, you can use decode() to look up color settings in a resource file. The format of name is the same as that used by getColor(). If the contents of name do not translate to a 24-bit integer, the NumberFormatException run-time exception is thrown. To perform the equivalent of get-Color("myPackage.myClass.foreground"), without using system properties, see the following example. For a more extensive example using resource files, see Appendix A.

```
// Java 1.1 only
InputStream is = instance.getClass().getResourceAsStream("propfile");
Properties p = new Properties();
try {
    p.load (is);
    Color c = Color.decode(p.getProperty("myPackage.myClass.foreground"));
```

```
  } catch (IOException e) {
     System.out.println ("error loading props...");
  }
```

Hue, saturation, and brightness

So far, the methods we have seen work with a color's red, green, and blue components. There are many other ways to represent colors. This group of methods allows you to work in terms of the HSB (hue, saturation, brightness) model. Hue represents the base color to work with: working through the colors of the rainbow, red is represented by numbers immediately above 0; magenta is represented by numbers below 1; white is 0; and black is 1. Saturation represents the color's purity, ranging from completely unsaturated (either white or black depending upon brightness) to totally saturated (just the base color present). Brightness is the desired level of luminance, ranging from black (0) to the maximum amount determined by the saturation level.

public static float[] RGBtoHSB (int red, int green, int blue, float[] hsbvalues)

The RGBtoHSB() method allows you to convert a specific red, green, blue value to the hue, saturation, and brightness equivalent. RGBtoHSB() returns the results in two different ways: the parameter hsbvalues and the method's return value. The values of these are the same. If you do not want to pass an hsbvalues array parameter, pass null. In both the parameter and the return value, the three components are placed in the array as follows:

hsbvalues[0]	*contains hue*
hsbvalues[1]	*contains saturation*
hsbvalues[2]	*contains brightness*

public static Color getHSBColor (float hue, float saturation, float brightness)

The getHSBColor() method creates a Color object by using hue, saturation, and brightness instead of red, green, and blue values.

public static int HSBtoRGB (float hue, float saturation, float brightness)

The HSBtoRGB() method converts a specific hue, saturation, and brightness to a Color and returns the red, green, and blue values as an integer. As with the constructor, bits 16–23 represent the red component, 8–15 represent the green component, and 0–7 represent the blue component. Bits 24–31 are ignored.

Miscellaneous methods

public int hashCode ()

>   The hashCode() method returns a hash code for the color. The hash code is
>   used whenever a color is used as a key in a Hashtable.

public boolean equals (Object o)

>   The equals() method overrides the equals() method of the Object to define
>   equality for Color objects. Two Color objects are equivalent if their red, green,
>   and blue values are equal.

public String toString ()

>   The toString() method of Color returns a string showing the color's red,
>   green, and blue settings. For example System.out.println (Color.orange)
>   would result in the following:

```
java.awt.Color[r=255,g=200,b=0]
```

3.4 SystemColor

In Java 1.1, AWT provides access to desktop color schemes, or *themes*. To give you
an idea of how these themes work, with the Windows Standard scheme for the
Windows 95 desktop, buttons have a gray background with black text. If you use
the control panel to change to a High Contrast Black scheme, the button's background becomes black and the text white. Prior to 1.1, Java didn't know anything
about desktop colors: all color values were hard coded. If you asked for a particular shade of gray, you got that shade, and that was it; applets and applications had
no knowledge of the desktop color scheme in effect, and therefore, wouldn't
change in response to changes in the color scheme.

Starting with Java 1.1, you can write programs that react to changes in the color
scheme: for example, a button's color will change automatically when you use the
control panel to change the color scheme. To do so, you use a large number of
constants that are defined in the SystemColor class. Although these constants are
public static final, they actually have a very strange behavior. Your program is
not allowed to modify them (like any other constant). However, their initial values
are loaded at run-time, and their values may change, corresponding to changes in
the color scheme. This has one important consequence for programmers: you
should not use equals() to compare a SystemColor with a "regular" Color; use the
getRGB() methods of the colors you are comparing to ensure that you compare
the current color value.[*] Section 3.6 contains a usage example.

---

[*] The omission of an equals() method that can properly compare a SystemColor with a Color is unfortunate.

Because SystemColor is a subclass of Color, you can use a SystemColor anywhere you can use a Color object. You will never create your own SystemColor objects; there is no public constructor. The only objects in this class are the twenty or so SystemColor constants.

3.4.1 SystemColor Methods

Constants

There are two sets of constants within SystemColor. The first set provides names for indices into the internal system color lookup table; you will probably never need to use these. All of them have corresponding constants in the second set, except SystemColor.NUM_COLORS, which tells you how many SystemColor constants are in the second set.

public final static int ACTIVE_CAPTION ★
public final static int ACTIVE_CAPTION_BORDER ★
public final static int ACTIVE_CAPTION_TEXT ★
public final static int CONTROL ★
public final static int CONTROL_DK_SHADOW ★
public final static int CONTROL_HIGHLIGHT ★
public final static int CONTROL_LT_HIGHLIGHT ★
public final static int CONTROL_SHADOW ★
public final static int CONTROL_TEXT ★
public final static int DESKTOP ★
public final static int INACTIVE_CAPTION ★
public final static int INACTIVE_CAPTION_BORDER ★
public final static int INACTIVE_CAPTION_TEXT ★
public final static int INFO ★
public final static int INFO_TEXT ★
public final static int MENU ★
public final static int MENU_TEXT ★
public final static int NUM_COLORS ★
public final static int SCROLLBAR ★
public final static int TEXT ★
public final static int TEXT_HIGHLIGHT ★
public final static int TEXT_HIGHLIGHT_TEXT ★
public final static int TEXT_INACTIVE_TEXT ★
public final static int TEXT_TEXT ★
public final static int WINDOW ★

public final static int WINDOW_BORDER ★
public final static int WINDOW_TEXT ★

The second set of constants is the set of SystemColors you use when creating Component objects, to ensure they appear similar to other objects in the user's desktop environment. By using these symbolic constants, you can create new objects that are well integrated into the user's desktop environment, making it easier for the user to work with your program.

public final static SystemColor activeCaption ★

The activeCaption color represents the background color for the active window's title area. This is automatically set for you when you use Frame.

public final static SystemColor activeCaptionBorder ★

The activeCaptionBorder color represents the border color for the active window.

public final static SystemColor activeCaptionText ★

The activeCaptionText color represents the text color to use for the active window's title.

public final static SystemColor control ★

The control color represents the background color for the different components. If you are creating your own Component by subclassing Canvas, this should be the background color of the new object.

public final static SystemColor controlDkShadow ★

The controlDkShadow color represents a dark shadow color to be used with control and controlShadow to simulate a three-dimensional appearance. Ordinarily, when not depressed, the controlDkShadow should be used for the object's bottom and right edges. When depressed, controlDkShadow should be used for the top and left edges.

public final static SystemColor controlHighlight ★

The controlHighlight color represents an emphasis color for use in an area or an item of a custom component.

public final static SystemColor controlLtHighlight ★

The controlLtHighlight color represents a lighter emphasis color for use in an area or an item of a custom component.

public final static SystemColor controlShadow ★

The controlShadow color represents a light shadow color to be used with control and controlDkShadow to simulate a three-dimensional appearance. Ordinarily, when not depressed, the controlShadow should be used for the top and left edges. When depressed, controlShadow should be used for the bottom and right edges.

public final static SystemColor controlText ★

The `controlText` color represents the text color of a component. Before drawing any text in your own components, you should change the color to `controlText` with a statement like this:

```
g.setColor(SystemColor.controlText);
```

public final static SystemColor desktop ★

The `desktop` color represents the background color of the desktop workspace.

public final static SystemColor inactiveCaption ★

The `inactiveCaption` color represents the background color for an inactive window's title area.

public final static SystemColor inactiveCaptionBorder ★

The `inactiveCaptionBorder` color represents the border color for an inactive window.

public final static SystemColor inactiveCaptionText ★

The `inactiveCaptionText` color represents the text color to use for each inactive window's title.

public final static SystemColor info ★

The `info` color represents the background color for mouse-over help text. When a mouse dwells over an object, any pop-up help text should be displayed in an area of this color. In the Microsoft Windows world, these are also called "tool tips."

public final static SystemColor infoText ★

The `infoText` color represents the text color for mouse-over help text.

public final static SystemColor menu ★

The `menu` color represents the background color of deselected `MenuItem`-like objects. When the menu is selected, the `textHighlight` color is normally the background color.

public final static SystemColor menuText ★

The `menuText` color represents the color of the text on deselected `MenuItem`-like objects. When a menu is selected, the `textHighlightText` color is normally the text color. If the menu happens to be inactive, `textInactiveText` would be used.

public final static SystemColor scrollbar ★

The `scrollbar` color represents the background color for scrollbars. This color is used by default with `Scrollbar`, `ScrollPane`, `TextArea`, and `List` objects.

public final static SystemColor textHighlight ★

The textHighlight color represents the background color of highlighted text; for example, it is used for the selected area of a TextField or a selected Menu-Item.

public final static SystemColor textHighlightText ★

The textHighlightText color represents the text color of highlighted text.

public final static SystemColor textInactiveText ★

The textInactiveText color represents the text color of an inactive component.

public final static SystemColor textText ★

The textText color represents the color of text in TextComponent objects.

public final static SystemColor window ★

The window color represents the background color of the window's display area. For an applet, this would be the display area specified by the WIDTH and HEIGHT values of the <APPLET> tag (setBackground(SystemColor.window)), although you would probably use it more for the background of a Frame.

public final static SystemColor windowBorder ★

The windowBorder color represents the color of the borders around a window. With AWT, instances of Window do not have borders, but instances of Frame and Dialog do.

public final static SystemColor windowText ★

The windowText color represents the color of the text drawn within the window.

NOTE   Every platform does not fully support every system color. However, on platforms that do not provide natural values for some constants, Java selects reasonable alternate colors.

If you are going to be working only with Java's prefabricated components (Button, List, etc.), you don't have to worry about system colors; the component's default colors will be set appropriately. You are most likely to use system colors if you are creating your own components. In this case, you will use system colors to make your component emulate the behavior of other components; for example, you will use controlText as the color for drawing text, activeCaption as the background for the caption of an active window, and so on.

Constructors

There are no public constructors for SystemColor. If you need to create a new color, use the Color class described previously.

Miscellaneous methods

public int getRGB ()

The getRGB() method retrieves the current settings for red, green, and blue in one combined value, like Color. However, since the color value is dynamic, getRGB() needs to look up the value in an internal table. Therefore, System-Color overrides Color.getRGB().

public String toString ()

The toString() method of SystemColor returns a string showing the system color's index into its internal table. For example, the following string is returned by SystemColor.text.toString():

```
java.awt.SystemColor[i=12]
```

3.5 Displaying Colors

Example 3-3 displays the predefined colors on the screen in a series of filled rectangles. When you press a mouse button, they appear brighter. When you press a key, they appear darker. (Event handling is fully explained in Chapter 4, *Events*.) Figure 3-4 shows the results, although it doesn't look very impressive in black and white.

Example 3–3: Color Display

```
import java.awt.*;
public class ColorDisplay extends Frame {
    int width, height;
    static Color colors[] =
                {Color.black, Color.blue, Color.cyan, Color.darkGray,
                Color.gray, Color.green, Color.lightGray, Color.magenta,
                Color.orange, Color.pink, Color.red, Color.white,
                Color.yellow};
    ColorDisplay () {
        super ("ColorDisplay");
        setBackground (Color.white);
    }
    static public void main (String args[]) {
        ColorDisplay f = new ColorDisplay();
        f.resize (300,300);
        f.show();
    }
    public void paint (Graphics g) {
        g.translate (insets().left, insets().top);
        if (width == 0) {
```

Example 3–3: Color Display (continued)

```
            Insets inset = insets();
            width  = (size().width - inset.right - inset.left) / 3;
            height = (size().height - inset.top - inset.bottom) / 5;
        }
        for (int i = 0; i < 3; i++) {
            for (int j = 0; j < 5; j++) {
                if ((i == 2) && (j >= 3)) break;
                g.setColor (colors[i*5+j]);
                g.fillRect (i*width, j*height, width, height);
            }
        }
    }
    public boolean keyDown (Event e, int c) {
        for (int i=0;i<colors.length;i++)
            colors[i] = colors[i].darker();
        repaint();
        return true;
    }
    public boolean mouseDown (Event e, int x, int y) {
        for (int i=0;i<colors.length;i++)
            colors[i] = colors[i].brighter();
        repaint();
        return true;
    }
}
```

Figure 3–4: A color display

3.6 Using Desktop Colors

Example 3-4 demonstrates how to use the desktop color constants introduced in Java 1.1. If you run this example under an earlier release, an uncatchable class verifier error will occur.

NOTE   Notice that the border lines are drawn from 0 to width-1 or height-1. This is to draw lines of length width and height, respectively.

Example 3–4: Desktop Color Usage

```
// Java 1.1 only
import java.awt.*;
public class TextBox3D extends Canvas {
    String text;
    public TextBox3D (String s, int width, int height) {
        super();
        text=s;
        setSize(width, height);
    }
    public synchronized void paint (Graphics g) {
        FontMetrics fm = g.getFontMetrics();
        Dimension size=getSize();
        int x = (size.width - fm.stringWidth(text))/2;
        int y = (size.height - fm.getHeight())/2;
        g.setColor (SystemColor.control);
        g.fillRect (0, 0, size.width, size.height);
        g.setColor (SystemColor.controlShadow);
        g.drawLine (0, 0, 0, size.height-1);
        g.drawLine (0, 0, size.width-1, 0);
        g.setColor (SystemColor.controlDkShadow);
        g.drawLine (0, size.height-1, size.width-1, size.height-1);
        g.drawLine (size.width-1, 0, size.width-1, size.height-1);
        g.setColor (SystemColor.controlText);
        g.drawString (text, x, y);
    }
}
```

4

In this chapter:
- *Java 1.0 Event Model*
- *The Event Class*
- *The Java 1.1 Event Model*

Events

This chapter covers Java's event-driven programming model. Unlike procedural programs, windows-based programs require an event-driven model in which the underlying environment tells your program when something happens. For example, when the user clicks on the mouse, the environment generates an event that it sends to the program. The program must then figure out what the mouse click means and act accordingly.

This chapter covers two different event models, or ways of handling events. In Java 1.0.2 and earlier, events were passed to all components that could possibly have an interest in them. Events themselves were encapsulated in a single Event class. Java 1.1 implements a "delegation" model, in which events are distributed only to objects that have been registered to receive the event. While this is somewhat more complex, it is much more efficient and also more flexible, because it allows any object to receive the events generated by a component. In turn, this means that you can separate the user interface itself from the event-handling code.

In the Java 1.1 event model, all event functionality is contained in a new package, java.awt.event. Within this package, subclasses of the abstract class AWTEvent represent different kinds of events. The package also includes a number of Event-Listener interfaces that are implemented by classes that want to receive different kinds of events; they define the methods that are called when events of the appropriate type occur. A number of adapter classes are also included; they correspond to the EventListener interfaces and provide null implementations of the methods in the corresponding listener. The adapter classes aren't essential but provide a convenient shortcut for developers; rather than declaring that your class implements a particular EventListener interface, you can declare that your class extends the appropriate adapter.

94

The old and new event models are incompatible. Although Java 1.1 supports both, you should not use both models in the same program.

4.1   Java 1.0 Event Model

The event model used in versions 1.0 through 1.0.2 of Java is fairly simple. Upon receiving a user-initiated event, like a mouse click, the system generates an instance of the Event class and passes it along to the program. The program identifies the event's target (i.e., the component in which the event occurred) and asks that component to handle the event. If the target can't handle this event, an attempt is made to find a component that can, and the process repeats. That is all there is to it. Most of the work takes place behind the scenes; you don't have to worry about identifying potential targets or delivering events, except in a few special circumstances. Most Java programs only need to provide methods that deal with the specific events they care about.

4.1.1   Identifying the Target

All events occur within a Java Component. The program decides which component gets the event by starting at the outermost level and working in. In Figure 4-1, assume that the user clicks at the location (156, 70) within the enclosing Frame's coordinate space. This action results in a call to the Frame's deliverEvent() method, which determines which component within the frame should receive the event and calls that component's deliverEvent() method. In this case, the process continues until it reaches the Button labeled Blood, which occupies the rectangular space from (135, 60) to (181, 80). Blood doesn't contain any internal components, so it must be the component for which the event is intended. Therefore, an action event is delivered to Blood, with its coordinates translated to fit within the button's coordinate space—that is, the button receives an action event with the coordinates (21, 10). If the user clicked at the location (47, 96) within the Frame's coordinate space, the Frame itself would be the target of the event because there is no other component at this location.

To reach Blood, the event follows the component/container hierarchy shown in Figure 4-2.

4.1.2   Dealing With Events

Once deliverEvent() identifies a target, it calls that target's handleEvent() method (in this case, the handleEvent() method of Blood) to deliver the event for processing. If Blood has not overridden handleEvent(), its default implementation would call Blood's action() method. If Blood has not overridden action(), its default implementation (which is inherited from Component) is executed and

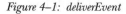

Figure 4–1: deliverEvent

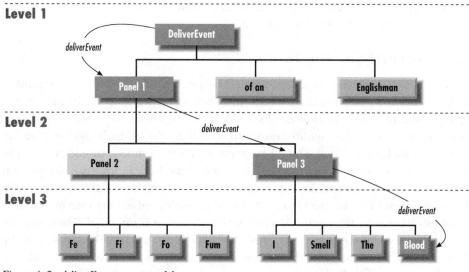

Figure 4–2: deliverEvent screen model

does nothing. For your program to respond to the event, you would have to provide your own implementation of action() or handleEvent().

handleEvent() plays a particularly important role in the overall scheme. It is really a dispatcher, which looks at the type of event and calls an appropriate method to do the actual work: action() for action events, mouseUp() for mouse up events, and so on. Table 4-1 shows the event-handler methods you would have to override when using the default handleEvent() implementation. If you create your own handleEvent(), either to handle an event without a default handler or to process events differently, it is best to leave these naming conventions in place. Whenever you override an event-handler method, it is a good idea to call the overridden method to ensure that you don't lose any functionality. All of the event handler methods return a boolean, which determines whether there is any further event processing; this is described in the next section, "Passing the Buck."

Table 4–1: Event Types and Event Handlers

Event Type	Event Handler
MOUSE_ENTER	mouseEnter()
MOUSE_EXIT	mouseExit()
MOUSE_MOVE	mouseMove()
MOUSE_DRAG	mouseDrag()
MOUSE_DOWN	mouseDown()
MOUSE_UP	mouseUp()
KEY_PRESS	keyDown()
KEY_ACTION	keyDown()
KEY_RELEASE	keyUp()
KEY_ACTION_RELEASE	keyUp()
GOT_FOCUS	gotFocus()
LOST_FOCUS	lostFocus()
ACTION_EVENT	action()

4.1.3 Passing the Buck

In actuality, deliverEvent() does not call handleEvent() directly. It calls the postEvent() method of the target component. In turn, postEvent() manages the calls to handleEvent(). postEvent() provides this additional level of indirection to monitor the return value of handleEvent(). If the event handler returns true, the handler has dealt with the event completely. All processing has been completed, and the system can move on to the next event. If the event handler returns false, the handler has not completely processed the event, and postEvent() will contact the component's Container to finish processing the event. Using the screen in Figure 4-1 as the basis, Example 4-1 traces the calls through deliverEvent(), postEvent(), and handleEvent(). The action starts when the user clicks on the Blood button at coordinates (156, 70). In short, Java dives into the depths of the screen's component hierarchy to find the target of the event (by way of the method deliverEvent()). Once it locates the target, it tries to find something to deal with the event by working its way back out (by way of postEvent(), handleEvent(), and the convenience methods). As you can see, there's a lot of overhead, even in this relatively simple example. When we discuss the Java 1.1 event model, you will see that it has much less overhead, primarily because it doesn't need to go looking for a component to process each event.

Example 4–1: The deliverEvent, postEvent, and handleEvent Methods

```
DeliverEvent.deliverEvent (Event e) called
    DeliverEvent.locate (e.x, e.y)
    Finds Panel1
    Translate Event Coordinates for Panel1
    Panel1.deliverEvent (Event e)
        Panel1.locate (e.x, e.y)
        Finds Panel3
        Translate Event Coordinates for Panel3
        Panel3.deliverEvent (Event e)
            Panel3.locate (e.x, e.y)
            Finds Blood
            Translate Event Coordinates for Blood
            Blood.deliverEvent (Event e)
                Blood.postEvent (Event e)
                    Blood.handleEvent (Event e)
                        Blood.mouseDown    (Event e, e.x, e.y)
                            returns false
                        return false
                    Get parent Container Panel3
                    Translate Event Coordinates for Panel3
                    Panel3.postEvent (Event e)
                        Panel3.handleEvent (Event e)
                            Component.mouseDown (Event e, e.x, e.y)
                                returns false
                            return false
                        Get parent Container Panel1
                        Translate Event Coordinates for Panel1
                        Panel1.postEvent (Event e)
                            Panel1.handleEvent (Event e)
                                Component.action (Event e, e.x, e.y)
                                    return false
                                return false
                            Get parent Container DeliverEvent
                            Translate Event Coordinates for DeliverEvent
                            DeliverEvent.postEvent (Event e)
                                DeliverEvent.handleEvent
                                    DeliverEvent.action (Event e, e.x, e.y)
                                        return true
                                    return true
                                return true
                            return true
                        return true
                    return true
                return true
            return true
        return true
    return true
```

4.1.4 Overriding handleEvent()

In many programs, you only need to override convenience methods like action()
and mouseUp(); you usually don't need to override handleEvent(), which is the
high level event handler that calls the convenience methods. However, convenience methods don't exist for all event types. To act upon an event that doesn't
have a convenience method (for example, LIST_SELECT), you need to override
handleEvent() itself. Unfortunately, this presents a problem. Unlike the convenience methods, for which the default versions don't take any action, han-
dleEvent() does quite a lot: as we've seen, it's the dispatcher that calls the
convenience methods. Therefore, when you override handleEvent(), either you
should reimplement all the features of the method you are overriding (a very bad
idea), or you must make sure that the original handleEvent() is still executed to
ensure that the remaining events get handled properly. The simplest way for you
to do this is for your new handleEvent() method to act on any events that it is
interested in and return true if it has handled those events completely. If the
incoming event is not an event that your handleEvent() is interested in, you
should call super.handleEvent() and return its return value. The following code
shows how you might override handleEvent() to deal with a LIST_SELECT event:

```
public boolean handleEvent (Event e) {
    if (e.id == Event.LIST_SELECT) {   // take care of LIST_SELECT
        System.out.println ("Selected item: " + e.arg);
        return true;     // LIST_SELECT handled completely; no further action
    } else {    // make sure we call the overridden method to ensure
                // that other events are handled correctly
        return super.handleEvent (e);
    }
}
```

4.1.5 Basic Event Handlers

The convenience event handlers like mouseDown(), keyUp(), and lostFocus() are
all implemented by the Component class. The default versions of these methods do
nothing and return false. Because these methods do nothing by default, when
overriding them you do not have to ensure that the overridden method gets
called. This simplifies the programming task, since your method only needs to
return false if it has not completely processed the event. However, if you start to
subclass nonstandard components (for example, if someone has created a fancy
AudioButton, and you're subclassing that, rather than the standard Button), you
probably should explicitly call the overridden method. For example, if you are
overriding mouseDown(), you should include a call to super.mouseDown(), just as
we called super.handleEvent() in the previous example. This call is "good

housekeeping"; most of the time, your program will work without it. However, your program will break as soon as someone changes the behavior of the AudioButton and adds some feature to its mouseDown() method. Calling the super class's event handler helps you write "bulletproof" code.

The code below overrides the mouseDown() method. I'm assuming that we're extending a standard component, rather than extending some custom component, and can therefore dispense with the call to super.mouseDown().

```
public boolean mouseDown (Event e, int x, int y) {
    System.out.println ("Coordinates: " + x + "-" + y);
    if ((x > 100) || (y < 100))
        return false;        // we're not interested in this event; pass it on
    else                     // we're interested;
        ...                  // this is where event-specific processing goes
        return true;         // no further event processing
}
```

Here's a debugging hint: when overriding an event handler, make sure that the parameter types are correct—remember that each convenience method has different parameters. If your overriding method has parameters that don't match the original method, the program will still compile correctly. However, it won't work. Because the parameters don't match, your new method simply overloads the original, rather than overriding it. As a result, your method will never be called.

4.2 The Event Class

An instance of the Event class is a platform-independent representation that encapsulates the specifics of an event that happens within the Java 1.0 model. It contains everything you need to know about an event: who, what, when, where, and why the event happened. Note that the Event class is not used in the Java 1.1 event model; instead, Java 1.1 has an AWTEvent class, with subclasses for different event types.

When an event occurs, you decide whether or not to process the event. If you decide against reacting, the event passes through your program quickly without anything happening. If you decide to handle the event, you must deal with it quickly so the system can process the next event. If handling the event requires a lot of work, you should move the event-handling code into its own thread. That way, the system can process the next event while you go off and process the first. If you do not multithread your event processing, the system becomes slow and unresponsive and could lose events. A slow and unresponsive program frustrates users and may convince them to find another solution for their problems.

4.2.1 Variables

Event contains ten instance variables that offer all the specific information for a particular event.

Instance variables

public Object arg

The arg field contains some data regarding the event, to be interpreted by the recipient. For example, if the user presses Return within a TextField, an Event with an id of ACTION_EVENT is generated with the TextField as the target and the string within it as the arg. See a description of each specific event to find out what its arg means.

public int clickCount

The clickCount field allows you to check for double clicking of the mouse. This field is relevant only for MOUSE_DOWN events. There is no way to specify the time delta used to determine how quick a double-click needs to be, nor is there a maximum value for clickCount. If a user quickly clicks the mouse four times, clickCount is four. Only the passage of a system-specific time delta will reset the value so that the next MOUSE_DOWN is the first click. The incrementing of clickCount does not care which mouse button is pressed.

public Event evt

The evt field does not appear to be used anywhere but is available if you wish to pass around a linked list of events. Then your program can handle this event and tell the system to deal with the next one (as demonstrated in the following code), or you can process the entire chain yourself.

```
public boolean mouseDown (Event e, int x, int y) {
    System.out.println ("Coordinates: " + x + "-" + y);
    if (e.evt != null)
        postEvent (e.evt);
    return true;
}
```

public int id

The id field of Event contains the identifier of the event. The system-generated events are the following Event constants:

WINDOW_DESTROY	MOUSE_ENTER
WINDOW_EXPOSE	MOUSE_EXIT
WINDOW_ICONIFY	MOUSE_DRAG
WINDOW_DEICONIFY	SCROLL_LINE_UP

KEY_PRESS	SCROLL_LINE_DOWN
KEY_RELEASE	SCROLL_PAGE_UP
KEY_ACTION	SCROLL_PAGE_DOWN
KEY_ACTION_RELEASE	SCROLL_ABSOLUTE
MOUSE_DOWN	LIST_SELECT
MOUSE_UP	LIST_DESELECT
MOUSE_MOVE	ACTION_EVENT

As a user, you can create your own event types and store your own unique event ID here. In Java 1.0, there is no formal way to prevent conflicts between your events and system events, but using a negative IO is a good ad-hoc method. It is up to you to check all the user events generated in your program in order to avoid conflicts among user events.

public int key

For keyboard-related events, the key field contains the integer representation of the keyboard element that caused the event. Constants are available for the keypad keys. To examine key as a character, just cast it to a char. For nonkeyboard-related events, the value is zero.

pubic int modifiers

The modifiers field shows the state of the modifier keys when the event happened. A flag is set for each modifier key pressed by the user when the event happened. Modifier keys are Shift, Control, Alt, and Meta. Since the middle and right mouse key are indicated in a Java event by a modifier key, one reason to use the modifiers field is to determine which mouse button triggered an event. See Section 4.2.4 for an example.

public Object target

The target field contains a reference to the object that is the cause of the event. For example, if the user selects a button, the button is the target of the event. If the user moves the mouse into a Frame, the Frame is the target. The target indicates where the event happened, not the component that is dealing with it.

public long when

The when field contains the time of the event in milliseconds. The following code converts this long value to a Date to examine its contents:

```
Date d = new Date (e.when);
```

public int x
public int y

The x and y fields show the coordinates where the event happened. The coordinates are always relative to the top left corner of the target of the event and get translated based on the top left corner of the container as the event gets passed through the containing components. (See the previous Section 4.1.1 for an example of this translation.) It is possible for either or both of these to be outside the coordinate space of the applet (e.g., if user quickly moves the mouse outside the applet).

4.2.2 Constants

Numerous constants are provided with the Event class. Several designate which event happened (the why). Others are available to help in determining the function key a user pressed (the what). And yet more are available to make your life easier.

When the system generates an event, it calls a handler method for it. To deal with the event, you have to override the appropriate method. The different event type sections describe which methods you override.

Key constants

These constants are set when a user presses a key. Most of them correspond to function and keypad keys; since such keys are generally used to invoke an action from the program or the system, Java calls them *action keys* and causes them to generate a different Event type (KEY_ACTION) from regular alphanumeric keys (KEY_PRESS).

Table 4-2 shows the constants used to represent keys and the event type that uses each constant. The values, which are all declared public static final int, appear in the key variable of the event instance. A few keys represent ASCII characters that have string equivalents such as \n. Black stars (★) mark the constants that are new in Java 1.1; they can be used with the 1.0 event model, provided that you are running Java 1.1. Java 1.1 events use a different set of key constants defined in the KeyEvent class.

Table 4–2: Constants for Keys in Java 1.0

Constant	Event Type	Constant	Event Type
HOME	KEY_ACTION	F9	KEY_ACTION
END	KEY_ACTION	F10	KEY_ACTION
PGUP	KEY_ACTION	F11	KEY_ACTION
PGDN	KEY_ACTION	F12	KEY_ACTION
UP	KEY_ACTION	PRINT_SCREEN★	KEY_ACTION
DOWN	KEY_ACTION	SCROLL_LOCK★	KEY_ACTION
LEFT	KEY_ACTION	CAPS_LOCK★	KEY_ACTION
RIGHT	KEY_ACTION	NUM_LOCK★	KEY_ACTION
F1	KEY_ACTION	PAUSE★	KEY_ACTION

Table 4–2: Constants for Keys in Java 1.0 (continued)

Constant	Event Type	Constant	Event Type
F2	KEY_ACTION	INSERT★	KEY_ACTION
F3	KEY_ACTION	ENTER (\n)★	KEY_PRESS
F4	KEY_ACTION	BACK_SPACE (\b)★	KEY_PRESS
F5	KEY_ACTION	TAB (\t)★	KEY_PRESS
F6	KEY_ACTION	ESCAPE★	KEY_PRESS
F7	KEY_ACTION	DELETE★	KEY_PRESS
F8	KEY_ACTION		

Modifiers

Modifiers are keys like Shift, Control, Alt, or Meta. When a user presses any key or mouse button that generates an Event, the modifiers field of the Event instance is set. You can check whether any modifier key was pressed by ANDing its constant with the modifiers field. If multiple modifier keys were down at the time the event occurred, the constants for the different modifiers are ORed together in the field.

```
public static final int ALT_MASK
public static final int CTRL_MASK
public static final int META_MASK
public static final int SHIFT_MASK
```

When reporting a mouse event, the system automatically sets the modifiers field. Since Java is advertised as supporting the single-button mouse model, all buttons generate the same mouse events, and the system uses the modifiers field to differentiate between mouse buttons. That way, a user with a one- or two-button mouse can simulate a three-button mouse by clicking on his mouse while holding down a modifier key. Table 4-3 lists the mouse modifier keys; an applet in Section 4.2.4 demonstrates how to differentiate between mouse buttons.

Table 4–3: Mouse Button Modifier Keys

Mouse Button	Modifier Key
Left mouse button	None
Middle mouse button	ALT_MASK
Right mouse button	META_MASK

For example, if you have a three-button mouse, and click the right button, Java generates some kind of mouse event with the META_MASK set in the modifiers field. If you have a one-button mouse, you can generate the same event by clicking the mouse while depressing the Meta key.

NOTE   If you have a multibutton mouse and do an Alt+right mouse or Meta+left mouse, the results are platform specific. You should get a mouse event with two masks set.

Key events

The component peers deliver separate key events when a user presses and releases nearly any key. KEY_ACTION and KEY_ACTION_RELEASE are for the function and arrow keys, while KEY_PRESS and KEY_RELEASE are for the remaining control and alphanumeric keys.

public static final int KEY_ACTION

> The peers deliver the KEY_ACTION event when the user presses a function or keypad key. The default Component.handleEvent() method calls the keyDown() method for this event. If the user holds down the key, this event is generated multiple times. If you are using the 1.1 event model, the interface method KeyListener.keyPressed() handles this event.

public static final int KEY_ACTION_RELEASE

> The peers deliver the KEY_ACTION_RELEASE event when the user releases a function or keypad key. The default handleEvent() method for Component calls the keyUp() method for this event. If you are using the 1.1 event model, the KeyListener.keyReleased() interface method handles this event.

public static final int KEY_PRESS

> The peers deliver the KEY_PRESS event when the user presses an ordinary key. The default Component.handleEvent() method calls the keyDown() method for this event. Holding down the key causes multiple KEY_PRESS events to be generated. If you are using the 1.1 event model, the interface method KeyListener.keyPressed() handles this event.

public static final int KEY_RELEASE

> The peers deliver KEY_RELEASE events when the user releases an ordinary key. The default handleEvent() method for Component calls the keyUp() method for this event. If you are using the 1.1 event model, the interface method KeyListener.keyReleased() handles this event.

NOTE   If you want to capture arrow and keypad keys under the X Window System, make sure the key codes are set up properly, using the *xmodmap* command.

NOTE   Some platforms generate events for the modifier keys by themselves, whereas other platforms require modifier keys to be pressed with another key. For example, on a Windows 95 platform, if Ctrl+A is pressed, you would expect one KEY_PRESS and one KEY_RELEASE. However, there is a second KEY_RELEASE for the Control key. Under Motif, you get only a single KEY_RELEASE.

Window events

Window events happen only for components that are children of Window. Several of these events are available only on certain platforms. Like other event types, the id variable holds the value of the specific event instance.

public static final int WINDOW_DESTROY

The peers deliver the WINDOW_DESTROY event whenever the system tells a window to destroy itself. This is usually done when the user selects the window manager's Close or Quit window menu option. By default, Frame instances do not deal with this event, and you must remember to catch it yourself. If you are using the 1.1 event model, the WindowListener.windowClosing() interface method handles this event.

public static final int WINDOW_EXPOSE

The peers deliver the WINDOW_EXPOSE event whenever all or part of a window becomes visible. To find out what part of the window has become uncovered, use the getClipRect() method (or getClipBounds() in Java version 1.1) of the Graphics parameter to the paint() method. If you are using the 1.1 event model, the WindowListener.windowOpening() interface method most closely corresponds to the handling of this event.

public static final int WINDOW_ICONIFY

The peers deliver the WINDOW_ICONIFY event when the user iconifies the window. If you are using the 1.1 event model, the interface method WindowListener.windowIconified() handles this event.

public static final int WINDOW_DEICONIFY

The peers deliver the WINDOW_DEICONIFY event when the user de-iconifies the window. If you are using the 1.1 event model, the interface method WindowListener.windowDeiconified() handles this event.

public static final int WINDOW_MOVED

> The WINDOW_MOVED event signifies that the user has moved the window. If you are using the 1.1 event model, the ComponentListener.componentMoved() interface method handles this event.

Mouse events

The component peers deliver mouse events when a user presses or releases a mouse button. Events are also delivered whenever the mouse moves. In order to be platform independent, Java pretends that all mice have a single button. If you press the second or third button, Java generates a regular mouse event but sets the event's modifers field with a flag that indicates which button was pressed. If you press the left button, no modifiers flags are set. Pressing the center button sets the ALT_MASK flag; pressing the right button sets the META_MASK flag. Therefore, you can determine which mouse button was pressed by looking at the Event.modifiers attribute. Furthermore, users with a one-button or two-button mouse can generate the same events by pressing a mouse button while holding down the Alt or Meta keys.

NOTE   Early releases of Java (1.0.2 and earlier) only propagated mouse events from Canvas and Container objects. With the 1.1 event model, the events that different components process are better defined.

---

public static final int MOUSE_DOWN

> The peers deliver the MOUSE_DOWN event when the user presses any mouse button. This action must occur over a component that passes along the MOUSE_DOWN event. The default Component.handleEvent() method calls the mouseDown() method for this event. If you are using the 1.1 event model, the MouseListener.mousePressed() interface method handles this event.

public static final int MOUSE_UP

> The peers deliver the MOUSE_UP event when the user releases the mouse button. This action must occur over a component that passes along the MOUSE_UP event. The default handleEvent() method for Component calls the mouseUp() method for this event. If you are using the 1.1 event model, the interface method MouseListener.mouseReleased() handles this event.

public static final int MOUSE_MOVE

> The peers deliver the MOUSE_MOVE event whenever the user moves the mouse over any part of the applet. This can happen many, many times more than you want to track, so make sure you really want to do something with this event before trying to capture it. (You can also capture MOUSE_MOVE events and

without losing much, choose to deal with only every third or fourth move-ment.) The default `handleEvent()` method calls the `mouseMove()` method for the event. If you are using the 1.1 event model, the interface method `MouseMotionListener.mouseMoved()` handles this event.

public static final int MOUSE_DRAG

The peers deliver the `MOUSE_DRAG` event whenever the user moves the mouse over any part of the applet with a mouse button depressed. The default method `handleEvent()` calls the `mouseDrag()` method for the event. If you are using the 1.1 event model, the interface method `MouseMotionListener.mouseDragged()` handles this event.

public static final int MOUSE_ENTER

The peers deliver the `MOUSE_ENTER` event whenever the cursor enters a compo-nent. The default `handleEvent()` method calls the `mouseEnter()` method for the event. If you are using the 1.1 event model, the interface method `MouseListener.mouseEntered()` handles this event.

public static final int MOUSE_EXIT

The peers deliver the `MOUSE_EXIT` event whenever the cursor leaves a compo-nent. The default `handleEvent()` method calls the `mouseExit()` method for the event. If you are using the 1.1 event model, the interface method `MouseListener.mouseExited()` handles this event.

Scrolling events

The peers deliver scrolling events for the `Scrollbar` component. The objects that have a built-in scrollbar (like `List`, `ScrollPane`, and `TextArea`) do not generate these events. No default methods are called for any of the scrolling events. They must be dealt with in the `handleEvent()` method of the `Container` or a subclass of the `Scrollbar`. You can determine which particular event occurred by checking the `id` variable of the event, and find out the new position of the thumb by looking at the `arg` variable or calling `getValue()` on the scrollbar. See also the description of the `AdjustmentListener` interface later in this chapter.

public static final int SCROLL_LINE_UP

The scrollbar peers deliver the `SCROLL_LINE_UP` event when the user presses the arrow pointing up for the vertical scrollbar or the arrow pointing left for the horizontal scrollbar. This decreases the scrollbar setting by one back toward the minimum value. If you are using the 1.1 event model, the interface method `AdjustmentListener.adjustmentValueChanged()` handles this event.

public static final int SCROLL_LINE_DOWN

> The peers deliver the SCROLL_LINE_DOWN event when the user presses the arrow pointing down for the vertical scrollbar or the arrow pointing right for the horizontal scrollbar. This increases the scrollbar setting by one toward the maximum value. If you are using the 1.1 event model, the interface method AdjustmentListener.adjustmentValueChanged() handles this event.

public static final int SCROLL_PAGE_UP

> The peers deliver the SCROLL_PAGE_UP event when the user presses the mouse with the cursor in the area between the slider and the decrease arrow. This decreases the scrollbar setting by the paging increment, which defaults to 10, back toward the minimum value. If you are using the 1.1 event model, the interface method AdjustmentListener.adjustmentValueChanged() handles this event.

public static final int SCROLL_PAGE_DOWN

> The peers deliver the SCROLL_PAGE_DOWN event when the user presses the mouse with the cursor in the area between the slider and the increase arrow. This increases the scrollbar setting by the paging increment, which defaults to 10, toward the maximum value. If you are using the 1.1 event model, the interface method AdjustmentListener.adjustmentValueChanged() handles this event.

public static final int SCROLL_ABSOLUTE

> The peers deliver the SCROLL_ABSOLUTE event when the user drags the slider part of the scrollbar. There is no set time period or distance between multiple SCROLL_ABSOLUTE events. If you are using the Java version 1.1 event model, the AdjustmentListener.adjustmentValueChanged() interface method handles this event.

public static final int SCROLL_BEGIN ★

> The SCROLL_BEGIN event is not delivered by peers, but you may wish to use it to signify when a user drags the slider at the beginning of a series of SCROLL_ABSOLUTE events. SCROLL_END, described next, would then be used to signify the end of the series.

public static final int SCROLL_END ★

> The SCROLL_END event is not delivered by peers, but you may wish to use it to signify when a user drags the slider at the end of a series of SCROLL_ABSOLUTE events. SCROLL_BEGIN, described previously, would have been used to signify the beginning of the series.

List events

Two events specific to the List class are passed along by the peers. They signify when the user has selected or deselected a specific choice in the List. It is not ordinarily necessary to capture these events, because the peers deliver the ACTION_EVENT when the user double-clicks on a specific item in the List and it is this ACTION_EVENT that triggers something to happen. However, if there is reason to do something when the user has just single-clicked on a choice, these events may be useful. An example of how they would prove useful is if you are displaying a list of filenames with the ability to preview files before loading. Single selection would preview, double-click would load, and deselect would stop previewing.

No default methods are called for any of the list events. They must be dealt with in the handleEvent() method of the Container of the List or a subclass of the List. You can determine which particular event occurred by checking the id variable of the event.

public static final int LIST_SELECT

> The peers deliver the LIST_SELECT event when the user selects an item in a List. If you are using the 1.1 event model, the interface method ItemListener.itemStateChanged() handles this event.

public static final int LIST_DESELECT

> The peers deliver the LIST_DESELECT event when an item in a List has been deselected. This is generated only if the List permits multiple selections. If you are using the 1.1 event model, the ItemListener.itemStateChanged() interface method handles this event.

Focus events

The peers deliver focus events when a component gains (GOT_FOCUS) or loses (LOST_FOCUS) the input focus. No default methods are called for the focus events. They must be dealt with in the handleEvent() method of the Container of the component or a subclass of the component. You can determine which particular event occurred by checking the id variable of the event.

NOTE   Early releases of Java (1.0.2 and before) did not propagate focus events on all platforms. This is fixed in release 1.1 of Java. Still, you should avoid capturing focus events if you want to write portable 1.0 code.

---

public static final int GOT_FOCUS

> The peers deliver the GOT_FOCUS event when a component gets the input focus. If you are using the 1.1 event model, the FocusListener.focusGained() interface method handles this event.

public static final int LOST_FOCUS

> The peers deliver the LOST_FOCUS event when a component loses the input focus. If you are using the 1.1 event model, the FocusListener.focusLost() interface method handles this event.

FileDialog events

The FileDialog events are another set of nonportable events. Ordinarily, the FileDialog events are completely dealt with by the system, and you never see them. Refer to Chapter 6, *Containers* for exactly how to work with the FileDialog object. If you decide to create a generic FileDialog object, you can use these events to indicate file loading and saving. These constants would be used in the id variable of the specific event instance:

public static final int LOAD_FILE
public static final int SAVE_FILE

Miscellaneous events

ACTION_EVENT is probably the event you deal with most frequently. It is generated when the user performs the desired action for a specific component type (e.g., when a user selects a button or toggles a checkbox). This constant would be found in the id variable of the specific event instance.

public static final int ACTION_EVENT

> The circumstances that lead to the peers delivering the ACTION_EVENT event depend upon the component that is the target of the event and the user's platform. Although the event can be passed along differently on different platforms, users will be accustomed to how the peers work on their specific platforms and will not care that it is different on the other platforms. For example, a Java 1.0 List component on a Microsoft Windows platform allows the user to select an item by pressing the first letter of the choice, whereupon the List tries to find an item that starts with the letter. The X Window System List component does not provide this capability. It works like a normal X List, where the user must scroll to locate the item and then select it.
>
> When the ACTION_EVENT is generated, the arg variable of the specific Event instance is set based upon the component type. In Chapters 5–11, which

describe Java's GUI components, the description of each component contains an "Events" subsection that describes the value of the event's arg field. If you are using the 1.1 event model, the `ActionListener.actionPerformed()` and `ItemListener.itemStateChanged()` interface methods handle this event, depending upon the component type.

4.2.3 Event Methods

Constructors

Ordinarily, the peers deliver all your events for you. However, if you are creating your own components or want to communicate across threads, it may be necessary to create your own events. You can also create your own events to notify your component's container of application-specific occurrences. For example, if you were implementing your own tab sequencing for text fields, you could create a "next text field" event to tell your container to move to the next text field. Once you create the event, you send it through the system using the `Component.postEvent()` method.

public Event (Object target, long when, int id, int x, int y, int key, int modifiers, Object arg)
> The first version of the constructor is the most complete and is what the other two call. It initializes all the fields of the Event to the parameters passed and sets `clickCount` to 0. See the descriptions of the instance variables Section 4.2.1 for the meanings of the arguments.

public Event (Object target, long when, int id, int x, int y, int key, int modifiers)
> The second constructor version calls the first with arg set to null.

public Event (Object target, int id, Object arg)
> The final version calls the first constructor with the when, x, y, key, and modifiers parameters set to 0.

Modifier methods

The modifier methods check to see if the different modifier mask values are set. They report the state of each modifier key at the moment an event occurred. It is possible for multiple masks to be set if multiple modifiers are pressed when the event occurs.

There is no `altDown()` method; to check whether the Alt key is pressed you must directly compare the event's `modifiers` against the `Event.ALT_MASK` constant. The `metaDown()` method is helpful when dealing with mouse events to see if the user pressed the right mouse button.

public boolean shiftDown ()

> The `shiftDown()` method returns `true` if the Shift key was pressed and `false` otherwise. There is no way to differentiate left and right shift keys.

public boolean controlDown ()

> The `controlDown()` method returns `true` if the Control key was pressed and `false` otherwise.

public boolean metaDown ()

> The `metaDown()` method returns `true` if the Meta key was pressed and `false` otherwise.

Miscellaneous methods

public void translate (int x, int y)

> The `translate()` method translates the x and y coordinates of the `Event` instance by x and y. The system does this so that the coordinates of the event are relative to the component receiving the event, rather than the container of the component. The system takes care of all this for you when passing the event through the containment hierarchy (not the object hierarchy), so you do not have to bother with translating them yourself. Figure 4-3 shows how this method would change the location of an event from a container down to an internal component.

protected String paramString ()

> When you call the `toString()` method of `Event`, the `paramString()` method is called in turn to build the string to display. In the event you subclass `Event` to add additional information, instead of having to provide a whole new `toString()` method, you need only add the new information to the string already generated by `paramString()`. Assuming the new information is `foo`, this would result in the following method declaration:
>
> ```
> protected String paramString() {
>     return super.paramString() + ",foo=" + foo;
> }
> ```

public String toString ()

> The `toString()` method of `Event` returns a string with numerous components. The only variables that will always be in the output will be the event ID and the x and y coordinates. The others will be present if necessary (i.e., non-null): key (as the integer corresponding to a keyboard event), shift when `shift-Down()` is true; control, when `controlDown()` is true; meta, when `metaDown()` is true; target (if it was a `Component`); and arg (the value depends on the target and ID). `toString()` does not display all pieces of the `Event` information. An event when moving a `Scrollbar` might result in the following:

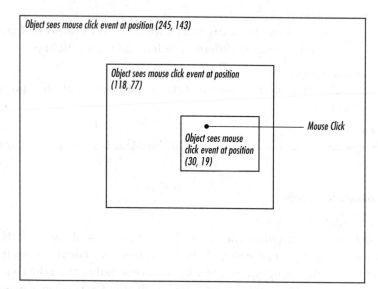

Figure 4–3: Translating an event's location relative to a component

```
java.awt.Event[id=602,x=374,y=110,target=java.awt.Scrollbar[374,
110,15x50,val=1,vis=true,min=0,max=255,vert],arg=1]
```

4.2.4 *Working With Mouse Buttons in Java 1.0*

As stated earlier, the modifiers component of Event can be used to differentiate
the different mouse buttons. If the user has a multibutton mouse, the modifiers
field is set automatically to indicate which button was pressed. If the user does not
own a multibutton mouse, he or she can press the mouse button in combination
with the Alt or Meta keys to simulate a three-button mouse. Example 4-2 is a sample program called mouseEvent that displays the mouse button selected.

Example 4–2: Differentiating Mouse Buttons in Java 1.0

```
import java.awt.*;
import java.applet.*;
public class mouseEvent extends Applet {
    String theString = "Press a Mouse Key";
    public synchronized void setString (String s) {
        theString = s;
    }
    public synchronized String getString () {
        return theString;
    }
    public synchronized void paint (Graphics g) {
        g.drawString (theString, 20, 20);
    }
    public boolean mouseDown (Event e, int x, int y) {
        if (e.modifiers == Event.META_MASK) {
```

Example 4–2: Differentiating Mouse Buttons in Java 1.0 (continued)

```
                setString ("Right Button Pressed");
        } else if (e.modifiers == Event.ALT_MASK) {
            setString ("Middle Button Pressed");
        } else {
            setString ("Left Button Pressed");
        }
        repaint ();
        return true;
    }
    public boolean mouseUp (Event e, int x, int y) {
        setString ("Press a Mouse Key");
        repaint ();
        return true;
    }
}
```

Unfortunately, this technique does not always work. With certain components on some platforms, the peer captures the mouse event and does not pass it along; for example, on Windows, the display-edit menu of a `TextField` appears when you select the right mouse button. Be cautious about relying on multiple mouse buttons; better yet, if you want to ensure absolute portability, stick to a single button.

4.2.5 Comprehensive Event List

Unfortunately, there are many platform-specific differences in the way event handling works. It's not clear whether these differences are bugs or whether vendors think they are somehow improving their product by introducing portability problems. We hope that as Java matures, different platforms will gradually come into synch. Until that happens, you might want your programs to assume the lowest common denominator. If you are willing to take the risk, you can program for a specific browser or platform, but should be aware of the possibility of changes.

Appendix C, *Platform-Specific Event Handling*, includes a table that shows which components pass along which events by default in the most popular environments. This table was developed using an interactive program called compList, which generates a list of supported events for each component. You can find compList on this book's Web site, *http://www.ora.com/catalog/javawt*. If you want to check the behavior of some new platform, or a newer version of one of the platforms in Appendix C, feel free to use compList. It does require a little bit of work on your part. You have to click, toggle, type, and mouse over every object. Hopefully, as Java matures, this program will become unnecessary.

4.3 The Java 1.1 Event Model

Now it's time to discuss the new event model that is implemented by the 1.1 release of the JDK. Although this model can seem much more complex (it does have many more pieces), it is really much simpler and more efficient. The new event model does away with the process of searching for components that are interested in an event—deliverEvent(), postEvent(), handleEvent()—and all that. The new model requires objects be registered to receive events. Then, only those objects that are registered are told when the event actually happens.

This new model is called "delegation"; it implements the Observer-Observable design pattern with events. It is important in many respects. In addition to being much more efficient, it allows for a much cleaner separation between GUI components and event handling. It is important that any object, not just a Component, can receive events. Therefore, you can separate your event-handling code from your GUI code. One set of classes can implement the user interface; another set of classes can respond to the events generated by the interface. This means that if you have designed a good interface, you can reuse it in different applications by changing the event processing. The delegation model is essential to JavaBeans, which allows interaction between Java and other platforms, like OpenDoc or ActiveX. To allow such interaction, it was essential to separate the source of an event from the recipient.[*]

The delegation model has several other important ramifications. First, event handlers no longer need to worry about whether or not they have completely dealt with an event; they do what they need to, and return. Second, events can be broadcast to multiple recipients; any number of classes can be registered to receive an event. In the old model, broadcasting was possible only in a very limited sense, if at all. An event handler could declare that it hadn't completely processed an event, thus letting its container receive the event when it was done, or an event handler could generate a new event and deliver it to some other component. In any case, developers had to plan how to deliver events to other recipients. In Java 1.1, that's no longer necessary. An event will be delivered to every object that is registered as a listener for that event, regardless of what other objects do with the event. Any listener can mark an event "consumed," so it will be ignored by the peer or (if they care) other listeners.

Finally, the 1.1 event model includes the idea of an event queue. Instead of having to override handleEvent() to see all events, you can peek into the system's event queue by using the EventQueue class. The details of this class are discussed at the end of this chapter.

---

* For more information about JavaBeans, see *http://splash.javasoft.com/beans/*.

In Java 1.1, each component is an event *source* that can generate certain types of events, which are all subclasses of AWTEvent. Objects that are interested in an event are called *listeners*. Each event type corresponds to a listener interface that specifies the methods that are called when the event occurs. To receive an event, an object must implement the appropriate listener interface and must be registered with the event's source, by a call to an "add listener" method of the component that generates the event. Who calls the "add listener" method can vary; it is probably the best design for the component to register any listeners for the events that it generates, but it is also possible for the event handler to register itself, or for some third object to handle registration (for example, one object could call the constructor for a component, then call the constructor for an event handler, then register the event handler as a listener for the component's events).

This sounds complicated, but it really isn't that bad. It will help to think in concrete terms. A TextField object can generate action events, which in Java 1.1 are of the class ActionEvent. Let's say we have an object of class TextActionHandler that is called myHandler that is interested in receiving action events from a text field named inputBuffer. This means that our object must implement the ActionListener interface, and this in turn, means that it must include an actionPerformed() method, which is called when an action event occurs. Now, we have to register our object's interest in action events generated by inputBuffer; to do so, we need a call to inputBuffer.addActionListener(myHandler). This call would probably be made by the object that is creating the TextField but could also be made by our event handler itself. The code might be as simple as this:

```
    ...
    public void init(){
        ...
        inputBuffer = new TextField();
        myHandler = new TextActionHandler();
        inputBuffer.addActionListener(myHandler); // register the handler for the
                                                  // buffer's events
        add (inputBuffer);  // add the input buffer to the display
        ...
    }
```

Once our object has been registered, myHandler.actionPerformed() will be called whenever a user does anything in the text field that generates an action event, like typing a carriage return. In a way, actionPerformed() is very similar to the action() method of the old event model—except that it is not tied to the Component hierarchy; it is part of an interface that can be implemented by any object that cares about events.

Of course, there are many other kinds of events. Figure 4-4 shows the event hierarchy for Java 1.1. Figure 4-5 shows the different listener interfaces, which are all subinterfaces of EventListener, along with the related adapter classes.

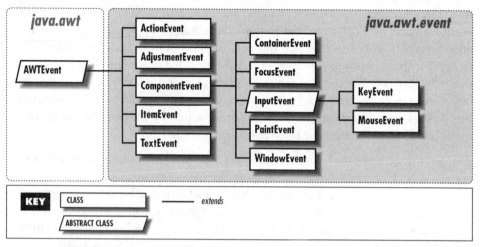

Figure 4–4: AWTEvent class hierarchy

Some of the listener interfaces are constructed to deal with multiple events. For instance, the MouseListener interface declares five methods to handle different kinds of mouse events: mouse down, mouse up, click (both down and up), mouse enter, and mouse exit. Strictly speaking, this means that an object interested in mouse events must implement MouseListener and must therefore implement five methods to deal with all possible mouse actions. This sounds like a waste of the programmer's effort; most of the time, you're only interested in one or two of these events. Why should you have to implement all five methods? Fortunately, you don't. The java.awt.event package also includes a set of *adapter classes*, which are shorthands that make it easier to write event handlers. The adapter class for any listener interface provides a null implementation of all the methods in that interface. For example, the MouseAdapter class provides stub implementations of the methods mouseEntered(), mouseExited(), mousePressed(), mouseReleased(), and mouseClicked(). If you want to write an event-handling class that deals with mouse clicks only, you can declare that your class extends MouseAdapter. It then inherits all five of these methods, and your only programming task is to override the single method you care about: mouseClicked().

A particularly convenient way to use the adapters is to write an anonymous inner class. For example, the following code deals with the MOUSE_PRESSED event without creating a separate listener class:

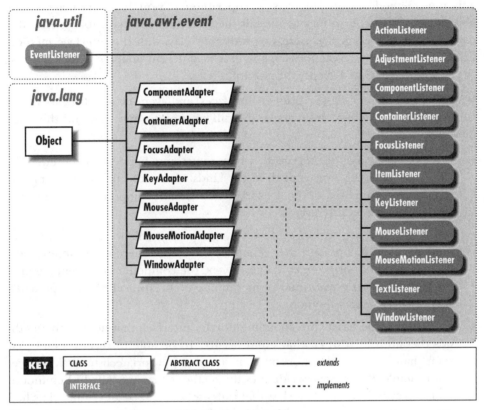

Figure 4–5: AWT EventListener and Adapter class hierarchies

```
addMouseListener (new MouseAdapter()    {
  public void mousePressed (MouseEvent e)   {
    // do what's needed to handle the event
    System.out.println ("Clicked at: " + e.getPoint());
  }
});
```

This code creates a MouseAdapter, overrides its mousePressed() method, and registers the resulting unnamed object as a listener for mouse events. Its mouse-
Pressed() method is called when MOUSE_PRESSED events occur. You can also use
the adapter classes to implement something similar to a callback. For example, you
could override mousePressed() to call one of your own methods, which would
then be called whenever a MOUSE_PRESSED event occurs.

There are adapter classes for most of the listener interfaces; the only exceptions
are the listener interfaces that contain only one method (for example, there's no
ActionAdapter to go with ActionListener). When the listener interface contains

only one method, an adapter class is superfluous. Event handlers may as well implement the listener interface directly, because they will have to override the only method in the interface; creating a dummy class with the interface method stubbed out doesn't accomplish anything. The different adapter classes are discussed with their related EventListener interfaces.

With all these adapter classes, listener interfaces, and event classes, it's easy to get confused. Here's a quick summary of the different pieces involved and the roles they play:

- Components generate AWTEvents when something happens. Different subclasses of AWTEvent represent different kinds of events. For example, mouse events are represented by the MouseEvent class. Each component can generate certain subclasses of AWTEvent.

- Event handlers are registered to receive events by calls to an "add listener" method in the component that generates the event. There is a different "add listener" method for every kind of AWTEvent the component can generate; for example, to declare your interest in a mouse event, you call the component's addMouseListener() method.

- Every event type has a corresponding listener interface that defines the methods that are called when that event occurs. To be able to receive events, an event handler must therefore implement the appropriate listener interface. For example, MouseListener defines the methods that are called when mouse events occur. If you create a class that calls addMouseListener(), that class had better implement the MouseListener interface.

- Most event types also have an adapter class. For example, MouseEvents have a MouseAdapter class. The adapter class implements the corresponding listener interface but provides a stub implementation of each method (i.e., the method just returns without taking any action). Adapter classes are shorthand for programs that only need a few of the methods in the listener interface. For example, instead of implementing all five methods of the MouseListener interface, a class can extend the MouseAdapter class and override the one or two methods that it is interested in.

4.3.1 Using the 1.1 Event Model

Before jumping in and describing all the different pieces in detail, we will look at a simple applet that uses the Java 1.1 event model. Example 4-3 is equivalent to Example 4-2, except that it uses the new event model; when you press a mouse button, it just tells you what button you pressed. Notice how the new class, mouseEvent11, separates the user interface from the actual work. The class mouseEvent11 implements a very simple user interface. The class UpDownCatcher handles the events, figures out what to do, and calls some methods in mouseEvent11 to communicate the results. I added a simple interface that is called GetSetString to define the communications between the user interface and the event handler; strictly speaking, this isn't necessary, but it's a good programming practice.

Example 4–3: Handling Mouse Events in Java 1.1

```
// Java 1.1 only
import java.awt.*;
import java.awt.event.*;
import java.applet.*;
interface GetSetString {
    public void setString (String s);
    public String getString ();
}
```

The UpDownCatcher class is responsible for handling events generated by the user interface. It extends MouseAdapter so that it needs to implement only the MouseListener methods that we care about (such as mousePressed() and mouseReleased()).

```
class UpDownCatcher extends MouseAdapter {
    GetSetString gss;
    public UpDownCatcher (GetSetString s) {
        gss = s;
    }
```

The constructor simply saves a reference to the class that is using this handler.

```
    public void mousePressed (MouseEvent e) {
        int mods = e.getModifiers();
        if ((mods & MouseEvent.BUTTON3_MASK) != 0) {
            gss.setString ("Right Button Pressed");
        } else if ((mods & MouseEvent.BUTTON2_MASK) != 0) {
            gss.setString ("Middle Button Pressed");
        } else {
            gss.setString ("Left Button Pressed");
        }
        e.getComponent().repaint();
    }
```

The mousePressed method overrides one of the methods of the MouseAdapter class. The method mousePressed() is called whenever a user presses any mouse button. This method figures out which button on a three-button mouse was pressed and calls the setString() method in the user interface to inform the user of the result.

```
    public void mouseReleased (MouseEvent e) {
        gss.setString ("Press a Mouse Key");
        e.getComponent().repaint();
    }
}
```

The mouseReleased method overrides another of the methods of the Mouse-Adapter class. When the user releases the mouse button, it calls setString() to restore the user interface to the original message.

```
    public class mouseEvent11 extends Applet implements GetSetString {
        private String theString = "Press a Mouse Key";
        public synchronized void setString (String s) {
            theString = s;
        }
        public synchronized String getString () {
            return theString;
        }
        public synchronized void paint (Graphics g) {
            g.drawString (theString, 20, 20);
        }
        public void init () {
            addMouseListener (new UpDownCatcher(this));
        }
    }
```

mouseEvent11 is a very simple applet that implements our user interface. All it does is draw the desired string on the screen; the event handler tells it what string to draw. The init() method creates an instance of the event handler, which is UpDownCatcher, and registers it as interested in mouse events.

Because the user interface and the event processing are in separate classes, it would be easy to use this user interface for another purpose. You would have to replace only the UpDownCatcher class with something else—perhaps a more complex class that reported when the mouse entered and exited the area.

4.3.2 AWTEvent and Its Children

Under the 1.1 delegation event model, all system events are instances of AWTEvent or its subclasses. The model provides two sets of event types. The first set are fairly raw events, such as those indicating when a component gets focus, a key is pressed, or the mouse is moved. These events exist in ComponentEvent and its subclasses, along with some new events previously available only by overriding non-event-related methods. In addition, higher-level event types (for example, selecting a button) are encapsulated in other subclasses of AWTEvent that are not children of ComponentEvent.

4.3.2.1 AWTEvent

Variables

protected int id ★

> The id field of AWTEvent is protected and is accessible through the getID()
> method. It serves as the identifier of the event type, such as the
> ACTION_PERFORMED type of ActionEvent or the MOUSE_MOVE type of Event. With
> the delegation event model, it is usually not necessary to look at the event id
> unless you are looking in the event queue; just register the appropriate event
> listener.

Constants The constants of AWTEvent are used in conjunction with the internal
method Component.eventEnabled(). They are used to help the program
determine what style of event handling (true/false-containment or
listening-delegation) the program uses and which events a component processes.
If you want to process 1.1 events without providing a listener, you need to set the
mask for the type of event you want to receive. Look in Chapter 5, *Components*, for
more information on the use of these constants:

public final static long ACTION_EVENT_MASK ★
public final static long ADJUSTMENT_EVENT_MASK ★
public final static long COMPONENT_EVENT_MASK ★
public final static long CONTAINER_EVENT_MASK ★
public final static long FOCUS_EVENT_MASK ★
public final static long ITEM_EVENT_MASK ★
public final static long KEY_EVENT_MASK ★
public final static long MOUSE_EVENT_MASK ★
public final static long MOUSE_MOTION_EVENT_MASK ★
public final static long TEXT_EVENT_MASK ★
public final static long WINDOW_EVENT_MASK ★

In addition to the mask constants, the constant RESERVED_ID_MAX is the largest
event ID reserved for "official" events. You may use ID numbers greater than this
value to create your own events, without risk of conflicting with standard events.

public final static long RESERVED_ID_MAX ★

Constructors Since AWTEvent is an abstract class, you cannot call the
constructors directly. They are automatically called when an instance of a child
class is created.

public AWTEvent(Event event) ★

> The first constructor creates an AWTEvent from the parameters of a 1.0 Event. The event.target and event.id are passed along to the second constructor.

public AWTEvent(Object source, int id) ★

> This constructor creates an AWTEvent with the given source; the source is the object generating the event. The id field serves as the identifier of the event type. It is protected and is accessible through the getID() method. With the delegation event model, it is usually not necessary to look at the event id unless you are looking in the event queue or in the processEvent() method of a component; just register the appropriate event listener.

Methods

public int getID() ★

> The getID() method returns the id from the constructor, thus identifying the event type.

protected void consume() ★

> The consume() method is called to tell an event that it has been handled. An event that has been marked "consumed" is still delivered to the source component's peer and to all other registered listeners. However, the peer will ignore the event; other listeners may also choose to ignore it, but that's up to them. It isn't possible for a listener to "unconsume" an event that has already been marked "consumed."

> Noncomponent events cannot be consumed. Only keyboard and mouse event types can be flagged as consumed. Marking an event "consumed" is useful if you are capturing keyboard input and need to reject a character; if you call consume(), the key event never makes it to the peer, and the keystroke isn't displayed. In Java 1.0, you would achieve the same effect by writing an event handler (e.g., keyDown()) that returns true.

> You can assume that an event won't be delivered to the peer until all listeners have had a chance to consume it. However, you should not make any other assumptions about the order in which listeners are called.

protected boolean isConsumed() ★

> The isConsumed() method returns whether the event has been consumed. If the event has been consumed, either by default or through consume(), this method returns true; otherwise, it returns false.

public String paramString() ★

> When you call the `toString()` method of an `AWTEvent`, the `paramString()` method is called in turn to build the string to display. Since you are most frequently dealing with children of `AWTEvent`, the children need only to override `paramString()` to add their specific information.

public String toString() ★

> The `toString()` method of `AWTEvent` returns a string with the name of the event, specific information about the event, and the source. In the method `MouseAdapter.mouseReleased()`, printing the parameter would result in something like the following:

```
java.awt.event.MouseEvent[MOUSE_RELEASED,(69,107),mods=0,clickCount=1] on panel1
```

4.3.2.2 ComponentEvent

Constants

public final static int COMPONENT_FIRST ★
public final static int COMPONENT_LAST ★

> The `COMPONENT_FIRST` and `COMPONENT_LAST` constants hold the endpoints of the range of identifiers for `ComponentEvent` types.

public final static int COMPONENT_HIDDEN ★

> The `COMPONENT_HIDDEN` constant identifies component events that occur because a component was hidden. The interface method `ComponentListener.componentHidden()` handles this event.

public final static int COMPONENT_MOVED ★

> The `COMPONENT_MOVED` constant identifies component events that occur because a component has moved. The `ComponentListener.componentMoved()` interface method handles this event.

public final static int COMPONENT_RESIZED ★

> The `COMPONENT_RESIZED` constant identifies component events that occur because a component has changed size. The interface method `ComponentListener.componentResized()` handles this event.

public final static int COMPONENT_SHOWN ★

> The `COMPONENT_SHOWN` constant identifies component events that occur because a component has been shown (i.e., made visible). The interface method `ComponentListener.componentShown()` handles this event.

Constructors

public ComponentEvent(Component source, int id) ★

> This constructor creates a `ComponentEvent` with the given source; the source is the object generating the event. The `id` field identifies the event type. If

system generated, the id will be one of the last four constants above. However, nothing stops you from creating your own id for your event types.

Methods

public Component getComponent() ★

The getComponent() method returns the source of the event—that is, the component initiating the event.

public String paramString() ★

When you call the toString() method of an AWTEvent, the paramString() method is called in turn to build the string to display. At the ComponentEvent level, paramString() adds a string containing the event id (if available) and the bounding rectangle for the source (if appropriate). For example:

```
java.awt.event.ComponentEvent[COMPONENT_RESIZED (0, 0, 100x100)] on button0
```

4.3.2.3 ContainerEvent

The ContainerEvent class includes events that result from specific container operations.

Constants

public final static int CONTAINER_FIRST ★
public final static int CONTAINER_LAST ★

The CONTAINER_FIRST and CONTAINER_LAST constants hold the endpoints of the range of identifiers for ContainerEvent types.

public final static int COMPONENT_ADDED ★

The COMPONENT_ADDED constant identifies container events that occur because a component has been added to the container. The interface method ContainerListener.componentAdded() handles this event. Listening for this event is useful if a common listener should be attached to all components added to a container.

public final static int COMPONENT_REMOVED ★

The COMPONENT_REMOVED constant identifies container events that occur because a component has been removed from the container. The interface method ContainerListener.componentRemoved() handles this event.

Constructors

public ContainerEvent(Container source, int id, Component child) ★

The constructor creates a ContainerEvent with the given source (the container generating the event), to which the given child has been added or removed. The id field serves as the identifier of the event type. If system generated, the id will be one of the constants described previously. However, nothing stops you from creating your own id for your event types.

Methods

public Container getContainer() ★

The getContainer() method returns the container that generated the event.

public Component getComponent() ★

The getComponent() method returns the component that was added to or removed from the container.

public String paramString() ★

When you call the toString() method of an AWTEvent, the paramString() method is in turn called to build the string to display. At the ContainerEvent level, paramString() adds a string containing the event id (if available) along with the name of the child.

4.3.2.4 FocusEvent

The FocusEvent class contains the events that are generated when a component gets or loses focus. These may be either temporary or permanent focus changes. A temporary focus change is the result of something else happening, like a window appearing in front of you. Once the window is removed, focus is restored. A permanent focus change is usually the result of focus traversal, using the keyboard or the mouse: for example, you clicked in a text field to type in it, or used Tab to move to the next component. More programmatically, permanent focus changes are the result of calls to Component.requestFocus().

Constants

public final static int FOCUS_FIRST ★
public final static int FOCUS_LAST ★

The FOCUS_FIRST and FOCUS_LAST constants hold the endpoints of the range of identifiers for FocusEvent types.

public final static int FOCUS_GAINED ★

The FOCUS_GAINED constant identifies focus events that occur because a component gains input focus. The FocusListener.focusGained() interface method handles this event.

public final static int FOCUS_LOST ★

> The FOCUS_LOST constant identifies focus events that occur because a component loses input focus. The FocusListener.focusLost() interface method handles this event.

Constructors

public FocusEvent(Component source, int id, boolean temporary) ★

> This constructor creates a FocusEvent with the given source; the source is the object generating the event. The id field serves as the identifier of the event type. If system generated, the id will be one of the two constants described previously. However, nothing stops you from creating your own id for your event types. The temporary parameter is true if this event represents a temporary focus change.

public FocusEvent(Component source, int id) ★

> This constructor creates a FocusEvent by calling the first constructor with the temporary parameter set to false; that is, it creates an event for a permanent focus change.

Methods

public boolean isTemporary() ★

> The isTemporary() method returns true if the focus event describes a temporary focus change, false if the event describes a permanent focus change. Once set by the constructor, the setting is permanent.

public String paramString() ★

> When you call the toString() method of an AWTEvent, the paramString() method is in turn called to build the string to display. At the FocusEvent level, paramString() adds a string showing the event id (if available) and whether or not it is temporary.

4.3.2.5 WindowEvent

The WindowEvent class encapsulates the window-oriented events.

Constants

public final static int WINDOW_FIRST ★
public final static int WINDOW_LAST ★

> The WINDOW_FIRST and WINDOW_LAST constants hold the endpoints of the range of identifiers for WindowEvent types.

public final static int WINDOW_ICONIFIED ★

The `WINDOW_ICONIFIED` constant identifies window events that occur because the user iconifies a window. The `WindowListener.windowIconified()` interface method handles this event.

public final static int WINDOW_DEICONIFIED ★

The `WINDOW_DEICONIFIED` constant identifies window events that occur because the user de-iconifies a window. The interface method `WindowListener.windowDeiconified()` handles this event.

public final static int WINDOW_OPENED ★

The `WINDOW_OPENED` constant identifies window events that occur the first time a `Frame` or `Dialog` is made visible with `show()`. The interface method `WindowListener.windowOpened()` handles this event.

public final static int WINDOW_CLOSING ★

The `WINDOW_CLOSING` constant identifies window events that occur because the user wants to close a window. This is similar to the familiar event `Event.WINDOW_DESTROY` dealt with under 1.0 with frames. The `WindowListener.windowClosing()` interface method handles this event.

public final static int WINDOW_CLOSED ★

The `WINDOW_CLOSED` constant identifies window events that occur because a `Frame` or `Dialog` has finally closed, after `hide()` or `destroy()`. This comes after `WINDOW_CLOSING`, which happens when the user wants the window to close. The `WindowListener.windowClosed()` interface method handles this event.

NOTE   If there is a call to `System.exit()` in the `windowClosing()` listener, the window will not be around to call `windowClosed()`, nor will other listeners know.

---

public final static int WINDOW_ACTIVATED ★

The `WINDOW_ACTIVATED` constant identifies window events that occur because the user brings the window to the front, either after showing the window, de-iconifying, or removing whatever was in front. The interface method `WindowListener.windowActivated()` handles this event.

public final static int WINDOW_DEACTIVATED ★

The `WINDOW_DEACTIVATED` constant identifies window events that occur because the user makes another window the active window. The interface method `WindowListener.windowDeactivated()` handles this event.

Constructors

public WindowEvent(Window source, int id) ★

> This constructor creates a WindowEvent with the given source; the source is the object generating the event. The id field serves as the identifier of the event type. If system generated, the id will be one of the seven constants described previously. However, nothing stops you from creating your own id for your event types.

Methods

public Window getWindow() ★

> The getWindow() method returns the Window that generated the event.

public String paramString() ★

> When you call the toString() method of an AWTEvent, the paramString() method is in turn called to build the string to display. At the WindowEvent level, paramString() adds a string containing the event id (if available). In a call to windowClosing(), printing the parameter would yield:

```
java.awt.event.WindowEvent[WINDOW_CLOSING] on frame0
```

4.3.2.6 PaintEvent

The PaintEvent class encapsulates the paint-oriented events. There is no corresponding PaintListener class, so you cannot listen for these events. To process them, override the paint() and update() routines of Component. The PaintEvent class exists to ensure that events are serialized properly through the event queue.

Constants

public final static int PAINT_FIRST ★
public final static int PAINT_LAST ★

> The PAINT_FIRST and PAINT_LAST constants hold the endpoints of the range of identifiers for PaintEvent types.

public final static int PAINT ★

> The PAINT constant identifies paint events that occur because a component needs to be repainted. Override the Component.paint() method to handle this event.

public final static int UPDATE ★

> The UPDATE constant identifies paint events that occur because a component needs to be updated before painting. This usually refreshes the display. Override the Component.update() method to handle this event.

Constructors

public PaintEvent(Component source, int id, Rectangle updateRect) ★

This constructor creates a `PaintEvent` with the given `source`. The source is the object whose display needs to be updated. The `id` field identifies the event type. If system generated, the `id` will be one of the two constants described previously. However, nothing stops you from creating your own `id` for your event types. `updateRect` represents the rectangular area of `source` that needs to be updated.

Methods

public Rectangle getUpdateRect()

The `getUpdateRect()` method returns the rectangular area within the `PaintEvent`'s source component that needs repainting. This area is set by either the constructor or the `setUpdateRect()` method.

public void setUpdateRect(Rectangle updateRect)

The `setUpdateRect()` method changes the area of the `PaintEvent`'s source component that needs repainting.

public String paramString() ★

When you call the `toString()` method of an `AWTEvent`, the `paramString()` method is called in turn to build the string to display. At the `PaintEvent` level, `paramString()` adds a string containing the event `id` (if available) along with the area requiring repainting (a clipping rectangle). If you peek in the event queue, one possible result may yield:

```
java.awt.event.PaintEvent[PAINT,updateRect=java.awt.Rectangle[x=0,y=0,
width=192,height=173]] on frame0
```

4.3.2.7 InputEvent

The `InputEvent` class provides the basis for the key and mouse input and movement routines. `KeyEvent` and `MouseEvent` provide the specifics of each.

Constants   The constants of `InputEvent` help identify which modifiers are present when an input event occurs, as shown in Example 4-3. To examine the event modifiers and test for the presence of these masks, call `getModifiers()` to get the current set of modifiers.

public final static int ALT_MASK ★
public final static int CTRL_MASK ★
public final static int META_MASK ★
public final static int SHIFT_MASK ★

The first set of `InputEvent` masks are for the different modifier keys on the keyboard. They are often set to indicate which button on a multibutton mouse has been pressed.

public final static int BUTTON1_MASK ★
public final static int BUTTON2_MASK ★
public final static int BUTTON3_MASK ★

> The button mask constants are equivalents for the modifier masks, allowing you to write more intelligible code for dealing with button events. BUTTON2_MASK is the same as ALT_MASK, and BUTTON3_MASK is the same as META_MASK; BUTTON1_MASK currently isn't usable and is never set. For example, if you want to check whether the user pressed the second (middle) mouse button, you can test against BUTTON2_MASK rather than ALT_MASK. Example 4-3 demonstrates how to use these constants.

Constructors   InputEvent is an abstract class with no public constructors.

Methods   Unlike the Event class, InputEvent has an isAltDown() method to check the ALT_MASK setting.

public boolean isAltDown() ★

> The isAltDown() method checks to see if ALT_MASK is set. If so, isAltDown() returns true; otherwise, it returns false.

public boolean isControlDown() ★

> The isControlDown() method checks to see if CONTROL_MASK is set. If so, isControlDown() returns true; otherwise, it returns false.

public boolean isMetaDown() ★

> The isMetaDown() method checks to see if META_MASK is set. If so, the method isMetaDown() returns true; otherwise, it returns false.

public boolean isShiftDown() ★

> The isShiftDown() method checks to see if SHIFT_MASK is set. If so, the method isShiftDown() returns true; otherwise, it returns false.

public int getModifiers() ★

> The getModifiers() method returns the current state of the modifier keys. For each modifier key pressed, a different flag is raised in the return argument. To check if a modifier is set, AND the return value with a flag and check for a nonzero value.

```
if ((ie.getModifiers() & MouseEvent.META_MASK) != 0) {
    System.out.println ("Meta is set");
}
```

public long getWhen() ★

> The getWhen() method returns the time at which the event occurred. The return value is in milliseconds. Convert the long value to a Date to examine the contents. For example:

```
Date d = new Date (ie.getWhen());
```

public void consume() ★

This class overrides the `AWTEvent.consume()` method to make it public. Anyone, not just a subclass, can mark an `InputEvent` as consumed.

public boolean isConsumed() ★

This class overrides the `AWTEvent.isconsumed()` method to make it public. Anyone can find out if an `InputEvent` has been consumed.

4.3.2.8 KeyEvent

The `KeyEvent` class is a subclass of `InputEvent` for dealing with keyboard events. There are two fundamental key actions: key presses and key releases. These are represented by `KEY_PRESSED` and `KEY_RELEASED` events. Of course, it's inconvenient to think in terms of all these individual actions, so Java also keeps track of the "logical" keys you type. These are represented by `KEY_TYPED` events. For every keyboard key pressed, a `KeyEvent.KEY_PRESSED` event occurs; the key that was pressed is identified by one of the virtual keycodes from Table 4-4 and is available through the `getKeyCode()` method. For example, if you type an uppercase A, you will get two `KEY_PRESSED` events, one for shift (`VK_SHIFT`) and one for the "a" (`VK_A`). You will also get two `KeyEvent.KEY_RELEASED` events. However, there will only be one `KeyEvent.KEY_TYPED` event; if you call `getKeyChar()` for the `KEY_TYPED` event, the result will be the Unicode character "A" (type `char`). `KEY_TYPED` events do not happen for action-oriented keys like function keys.

Constants   Like the `Event` class, numerous constants help you identify all the keyboard keys. Table 4-4 shows the constants that refer to these keyboard keys. The values are all declared `public static final int`. A few keys represent ASCII characters that have string equivalents like `\n`.

Table 4–4: Key Constants in Java 1.1

VK_ENTER	VK_0	VK_A	VK_F1	VK_ACCEPT
VK_BACK_SPACE	VK_1	VK_B	VK_F2	VK_CONVERT
VK_TAB	VK_2	VK_C	VK_F3	VK_FINAL
VK_CANCEL	VK_3	VK_D	VK_F4	VK_KANA
VK_CLEAR	VK_4	VK_E	VK_F5	VK_KANJI
VK_SHIFT	VK_5	VK_F	VK_F6	VK_MODECHANGE
VK_CONTROL	VK_6	VK_G	VK_F7	VK_NONCONVERT
VK_ALT	VK_7	VK_H	VK_F8	
VK_PAUSE	VK_8	VK_I	VK_F9	

Table 4–4: Key Constants in Java 1.1 (continued)

VK_CAPS_LOCK	VK_9	VK_J	VK_F10
VK_ESCAPE	VK_NUMPAD0	VK_K	VK_F11
VK_SPACE	VK_NUMPAD1	VK_L	VK_F12
VK_PAGE_UP	VK_NUMPAD2	VK_M	VK_DELETE
VK_PAGE_DOWN	VK_NUMPAD3	VK_N	VK_NUM_LOCK
VK_END	VK_NUMPAD4	VK_O	VK_SCROLL_LOCK
VK_HOME	VK_NUMPAD5	VK_P	VK_PRINTSCREEN
VK_LEFT	VK_NUMPAD6	VK_Q	VK_INSERT
VK_UP	VK_NUMPAD7	VK_R	VK_HELP
VK_RIGHT	VK_NUMPAD8	VK_S	VK_META
VK_DOWN	VK_NUMPAD9	VK_T	VK_BACK_QUOTE
VK_COMMA	VK_MULTIPLY	VK_U	VK_QUOTE
VK_PERIOD	VK_ADD	VK_V	VK_OPEN_BRACKET
VK_SLASH	VK_SEPARATER[a]	VK_W	VK_CLOSE_BRACKET
VK_SEMICOLON	VK_SUBTRACT	VK_X	
VK_EQUALS	VK_DECIMAL	VK_Y	
VK_BACK_SLASH	VK_DIVIDE	VK_Z	

[a] Expect VK_SEPARATOR to be added at some future point. This constant represents the numeric separator key on your keyboard.

public final static int VK_UNDEFINED ★

When a KEY_TYPED event happens, there is no keycode. If you ask for it, the getKeyCode() method returns VK_UNDEFINED.

public final static char CHAR_UNDEFINED ★

For KEY_PRESSED and KEY_RELEASED events that do not have a corresponding Unicode character to display (like Shift), the getKeyChar() method returns CHAR_UNDEFINED.

Other constants identify what the user did with a key.

public final static int KEY_FIRST ★
public final static int KEY_LAST ★

The KEY_FIRST and KEY_LAST constants hold the endpoints of the range of identifiers for KeyEvent types.

public final static int KEY_PRESSED ★

The KEY_PRESSED constant identifies key events that occur because a keyboard key has been pressed. To differentiate between action and non-action keys, call the isActionKey() method described later. The KeyListener.keyPressed() interface method handles this event.

public final static int KEY_RELEASED ★

The KEY_RELEASED constant identifies key events that occur because a keyboard key has been released. The KeyListener.keyReleased() interface method handles this event.

public final static int KEY_TYPED ★

The KEY_TYPED constant identifies a combination of a key press followed by a key release for a non-action oriented key. The KeyListener.keyTyped() interface method handles this event.

Constructors

public KeyEvent(Component source, int id, long when, int modifiers, int keyCode, char keyChar) ★

This constructor[*] creates a KeyEvent with the given source; the source is the object generating the event. The id field identifies the event type. If system-generated, the id will be one of the constants above. However, nothing stops you from creating your own id for your event types. The when parameter represents the time the event happened. The modifiers parameter holds the state of the various modifier keys; masks to represent these keys are defined in the InputEvent class. Finally, keyCode is the virtual key that triggered the event, and keyChar is the character that triggered it.

The KeyEvent constructor throws the IllegalArgumentException run-time exception in two situations. First, if the id is KEY_TYPED and keyChar is CHAR_UNDEFINED, it throws an exception because if a key has been typed, it must be associated with a character. Second, if the id is KEY_TYPED and key-Code is not VK_UNDEFINED, it throws an exception because typed keys frequently represent combinations of key codes (for example, Shift struck with "a"). It is legal for a KEY_PRESSED or KEY_RELEASED event to contain both a keyCode and a keyChar, though it's not clear what such an event would represent.

Methods

public char getKeyChar() ★

The getKeyChar() method retrieves the Unicode character associated with the key in this KeyEvent. If there is no character, CHAR_UNDEFINED is returned.

public void setKeyChar(char KeyChar) ★

The setKeyChar() method allows you to change the character for the KeyEvent. You could use this method to convert characters to uppercase.

---

[*] Beta releases of Java 1.1 have an additional constructor that lacks the keyChar parameter. Comments in the code indicate that this constructor will be deleted prior to the 1.1.1 release.

public int getKeyCode() ★

The getKeyCode() method retrieves the virtual keycode (i.e., one of the constants in Table 4-4) of this KeyEvent.

public void setKeyCode(int keyCode) ★

The setKeyCode() method allows you to change the keycode for the KeyEvent. Changes you make to the KeyEvent are seen by subsequent listeners and the component's peer.

public void setModifiers(int modifiers) ★

The setModifiers() method allows you to change the modifier keys associated with a KeyEvent to modifiers. The parent class InputEvent already has a getModifiers() method that is inherited. Since this is your own personal copy of the KeyEvent, no other listener can find out about the change.

public boolean isActionKey() ★

The isActionKey() method allows you to check whether the key associated with the KeyEvent is an action key (e.g., function, arrow, keypad) or not (e.g., an alphanumeric key). For action keys, this method returns true; otherwise, it returns false. For action keys, the keyChar field usually has the value CHAR_UNDEFINED.

public static String getKeyText (int keyCode) ★

The static getKeyText() method returns the localized textual string for key-Code. For each nonalphanumeric virtual key, there is a key name (the "key text"); these names can be changed using the AWT properties. Table 4-5 shows the properties used to redefine the key names and the default name for each key.

Table 4–5: Key Text Properties

Property	Default	Property	Default
AWT.accept	Accept	AWT.f8	F8
AWT.add	NumPad +	AWT.f9	F9
AWT.alt	Alt	AWT.help	Help
AWT.backQuote	Back Quote	AWT.home	Home
AWT.backSpace	Backspace	AWT.insert	Insert
AWT.cancel	Cancel	AWT.kana	Kana
AWT.capsLock	Caps Lock	AWT.kanji	Kanji
AWT.clear	Clear	AWT.left	Left
AWT.control	Control	AWT.meta	Meta
AWT.decimal	NumPad .	AWT.modechange	Mode Change
AWT.delete	Delete	AWT.multiply	NumPad *
AWT.divide	NumPad /	AWT.noconvert	No Convert

Table 4–5: Key Text Properties (continued)

Property	Default	Property	Default
AWT.down	Down	AWT.numLock	Num Lock
AWT.end	End	AWT.numpad	NumPad
AWT.enter	Enter	AWT.pause	Pause
AWT.escape	Escape	AWT.pgdn	Page Down
AWT.final	Final	AWT.pgup	Page Up
AWT.f1	F1	AWT.printScreen	Print Screen
AWT.f10	F10	AWT.quote	Quote
AWT.f11	F11	AWT.right	Right
AWT.f12	F12	AWT.scrollLock	Scroll Lock
AWT.f2	F2	AWT.separator	NumPad ,
AWT.f3	F3	AWT.shift	Shift
AWT.f4	F4	AWT.space	Space
AWT.f5	F5	AWT.subtract	NumPad -
AWT.f6	F6	AWT.tab	Tab
AWT.f7	F7	AWT.unknown	Unknown keyCode
AWT.up	Up		

public static String getKeyModifiersText (int modifiers) ★

The static getKeyModifiersText() method returns the localized textual string for modifiers. The parameter modifiers is a combination of the key masks defined by the InputEvent class. As with the keys themselves, each modifier is associated with a textual name. If multiple modifiers are set, they are concatenated with a plus sign (+) separating them. Similar to getKeyText(), the strings are localized because for each modifier, an awt property is available to redefine the string. Table 4-6 lists the properties and the default modifier names.

Table 4–6: Key Modifiers Text Properties

Property	Default
AWT.alt	Alt
AWT.control	Ctrl
AWT.meta	Meta
AWT.shift	Shift

public String paramString() ★

When you call the toString() method of an AWTEvent, the paramString() method is called in turn to build the string to display. At the KeyEvent level, paramString() adds a textual string for the id (if available), the text for the key (if available from getKeyText()), and modifiers (from getKeyModifiers-Text()). A key press event would result in something like the following:

```
java.awt.event.KeyEvent[KEY_PRESSED,keyCode=118,
F7,modifiers=Ctrl+Shift] on textfield0
```

4.3.2.9 MouseEvent

The MouseEvent class is a subclass of InputEvent for dealing with mouse events.

Constants

public final static int MOUSE_FIRST ★
public final static int MOUSE_LAST ★

The MOUSE_FIRST and MOUSE_LAST constants hold the endpoints of the range of identifiers for MouseEvent types.

public final static int MOUSE_CLICKED ★

The MOUSE_CLICKED constant identifies mouse events that occur when a mouse button is clicked. A mouse click consists of a mouse press and a mouse release. The MouseListener.mouseClicked() interface method handles this event.

public final static int MOUSE_DRAGGED ★

The MOUSE_DRAGGED constant identifies mouse events that occur because the mouse is moved over a component with a mouse button pressed. The interface method MouseMotionListener.mouseDragged() handles this event.

public final static int MOUSE_ENTERED ★

The MOUSE_ENTERED constant identifies mouse events that occur when the mouse first enters a component. The MouseListener.mouseEntered() interface method handles this event.

public final static int MOUSE_EXITED ★

The MOUSE_EXISTED constant identifies mouse events that occur because the mouse leaves a component's space. The MouseListener.mouseExited() interface method handles this event.

public final static int MOUSE_MOVED ★

The MOUSE_MOVED constant identifies mouse events that occur because the mouse is moved without a mouse button down. The interface method Mouse-MotionListener.mouseMoved() handles this event.

public final static int MOUSE_PRESSED ★

The MOUSE_PRESSED constant identifies mouse events that occur because a mouse button has been pressed. The MouseListener.mousePressed() interface method handles this event.

public final static int MOUSE_RELEASED ★

The `MOUSE_RELEASED` constant identifies mouse events that occur because a mouse button has been released. The `MouseListener.mouseReleased()` interface method handles this event.

Constructors

public MouseEvent(Component source, int id, long when, int modifiers, int x, int y,
int clickCount, boolean popupTrigger) ★

This constructor creates a `MouseEvent` with the given `source`; the source is the object generating the event. The `id` field serves as the identifier of the event type. If system-generated, the `id` will be one of the constants described in the previous section. However, nothing stops you from creating your own `id` for your event types. The `when` parameter represents the time the event happened. The `modifiers` parameter holds the state of the various modifier keys, using the masks defined for the `InputEvent` class, and lets you determine which button was pressed. (x, y) represents the coordinates of the event relative to the origin of `source`, while `clickCount` designates the number of consecutive times the mouse button was pressed within an indeterminate time period. Finally, the `popupTrigger` parameter signifies whether this mouse event should trigger the display of a `PopupMenu`, if one is available. (The `PopupMenu` class is discussed in Chapter 10, *Would You Like to Choose from the Menu?*)

Methods

public int getX() ★

The `getX()` method returns the current x coordinate of the event relative to the source.

public int getY() ★

The `getY()` method returns the current y coordinate of the event relative to the source.

public synchronized Point getPoint() ★

The `getPoint()` method returns the current x and y coordinates of the event relative to the event source.

public synchronized void translatePoint(int x, int y) ★

The `translatePoint()` method translates the x and y coordinates of the `MouseEvent` instance by x and y. This method functions similarly to the `Event.translate()` method.

public int getClickCount() ★

   The getClickCount() method retrieves the current clickCount setting for the
   event.

public boolean isPopupTrigger() ★

   The isPopupTrigger() method retrieves the state of the popupTrigger setting
   for the event. If this method returns true and the source of the event has an
   associated PopupMenu, the event should be used to display the menu, as shown
   in the following code. Since the action the user performs to raise a pop-up
   menu is platform specific, this method lets you raise a pop-up menu without
   worrying about what kind of event took place. You only need to call isPopup-
   Trigger() and show the menu if it returns true.

```
public void processMouseEvent(MouseEvent e) {
    if (e.isPopupTrigger())
        aPopup.show(e.getComponent(), e.getX(), e.getY());
    super.processMouseEvent(e);
}
```

public String paramString() ★

   When you call the toString() method of an AWTEvent, the paramString()
   method is called in turn to build the string to display. At the MouseEvent level,
   a textual string for the id (if available) is tacked on to the coordinates, modifiers, and click count. A mouse down event would result in something like the
   following:

```
java.awt.event.MouseEvent[MOUSE_PRESSED,(5,7),mods=0,clickCount=2] on textfield0
```

4.3.2.10 ActionEvent

The ActionEvent class is the first higher-level event class. It encapsulates events
that signify that the user is doing something with a component. When the user
selects a button, list item, or menu item, or presses the Return key in a text field,
an ActionEvent passes through the event queue looking for listeners.

Constants

public final static int ACTION_FIRST ★
public final static int ACTION_LAST ★

   The ACTION_FIRST and ACTION_LAST constants hold the endpoints of the range
   of identifiers for ActionEvent types.

public final static int ACTION_PERFORMED ★

   The ACTION_PERFORMED constant represents when a user activates a component. The ActionListener.actionPerformed() interface method handles this
   event.

public static final int ALT_MASK ★
public static final int CTRL_MASK ★
public static final int META_MASK ★
public static final int SHIFT_MASK ★

Similar to the mouse events, action events have modifiers. However, they are not automatically set by the system, so they don't help you see what modifiers were pressed when the event occurred. You may be able to use these constants if you are generating your own action events. To see the value of an action event's modifiers, call getModifiers().

Constructors

public ActionEvent(Object source, int id, String command) ★

This constructor creates an ActionEvent with the given source; the source is the object generating the event. The id field serves as the identifier of the event type. If system-generated, the id will be ACTION_PERFORMED. However, nothing stops you from creating your own id for your event types. The command parameter is the event's action command. Ideally, the action command should be some locale-independent string identifying the user's action. Most components that generate action events set this field to the selected item's label by default.

public ActionEvent(Object source, int id, String command, int modifiers) ★

This constructor adds modifiers to the settings for an ActionEvent. This allows you to define action-oriented events that occur only if certain modifier keys are pressed.

Methods

public String getActionCommand() ★

The getActionCommand() method retrieves the command field from the event. It represents the command associated with the object that triggered the event. The idea behind the action command is to differentiate the command associated with some event from the displayed content of the event source. For example, the action command for a button may be Help. However, what the user sees on the label of the button could be a string localized for the environment of the user. Instead of having your event handler look for 20 or 30 possible labels, you can test whether an event has the action command Help.

public int getModifiers() ★

The getModifiers() method returns the state of the modifier keys. For each one set, a different flag is raised in the method's return value. To check if a modifier is set, AND the return value with a flag, and check for a nonzero value.

public String paramString() ★

> When you call the toString() method of an AWTEvent, the paramString() method is called in turn to build the string to display. At the ActionEvent level, paramString() adds a textual string for the event id (if available), along with the command from the constructor. When the user selects a Button with the action command Help, printing the resulting event yields:

```
java.awt.event.ActionEvent[ACTION_PERFORMED,cmd=Help] on button0
```

4.3.2.11 AdjustmentEvent

The AdjustmentEvent class is another higher-level event class. It encapsulates events that represent scrollbar motions. When the user moves the slider of a scrollbar or scroll pane, an AdjustmentEvent passes through the event queue looking for listeners. Although there is only one type of adjustment event, there are five subtypes represented by constants UNIT_DECREMENT, UNIT_INCREMENT, and so on.

Constants

public final static int ADJUSTMENT_FIRST ★
public final static int ADJUSTMENT_LAST ★

> The ADJUSTMENT_FIRST and ADJUSTMENT_LAST constants hold the endpoints of the range of identifiers for AdjustmentEvent types.

public final static int ADJUSTMENT_VALUE_CHANGED ★

> The ADJUSTMENT_VALUE_CHANGED constant identifies adjustment events that occur because a user moves the slider of a Scrollbar or ScrollPane. The AdjustmentListener.adjustmentValueChanged() interface method handles this event.

public static final int UNIT_DECREMENT ★

> UNIT_DECREMENT identifies adjustment events that occur because the user selects the increment arrow.

public static final int UNIT_INCREMENT ★

> UNIT_INCREMENT identifies adjustment events that occur because the user selects the decrement arrow.

public static final int BLOCK_DECREMENT ★

> BLOCK_DECREMENT identifies adjustment events that occur because the user selects the block decrement area, between the decrement arrow and the slider.

public static final int BLOCK_INCREMENT ★

> BLOCK_INCREMENT identifies adjustment events that occur because the user selects the block increment area, between the increment arrow and the slider.

public static final int TRACK ★

> TRACK identifies adjustment events that occur because the user selects the slider and drags it. Multiple adjustment events of this subtype usually occur consecutively.

Constructors

public AdjustmentEvent(Adjustable source, int id, int type, int value) ★

> This constructor creates an AdjustmentEvent with the given source; the source is the object generating the event. The id field serves as the identifier of the event type. If system-generated, the id of the AdjustmentEvent will be ADJUSTMENT_VALUE_CHANGED. However, nothing stops you from creating your own id for your event types. The type parameter is normally one of the five subtypes, with value being the current setting of the slider, but is not restricted to that.

Methods

public Adjustable getAdjustable() ★

> The getAdjustable() method retrieves the Adjustable object associated with this event—that is, the event's source.

public int getAdjustmentType() ★

> The getAdjustmentType() method retrieves the type parameter from the constructor. It represents the subtype of the current event and, if system-generated, is one of the following constants: UNIT_DECREMENT, UNIT_INCREMENT, BLOCK_DECREMENT, BLOCK_INCREMENT, or TRACK.

public int getValue() ★

> The getValue() method retrieves the value parameter from the constructor. It represents the current setting of the adjustable object.

public String paramString() ★

> When you call the toString() method of an AWTEvent, the paramString() method is called to help build the string to display. At the AdjustableEvent level, paramString() adds a textual string for the event id (if available), along with a textual string of the type (if available), and value. For example:

```
java.awt.event.AdjustableEvent[ADJUSTMENT_VALUE_CHANGED,
adjType=TRACK,value=27] on scrollbar0
```

4.3.2.12 ItemEvent

The ItemEvent class is another higher-level event class. It encapsulates events that occur when the user selects a component, like ActionEvent. When the user selects a checkbox, choice, list item, or checkbox menu item, an ItemEvent passes through the event queue looking for listeners. Although there is only one type of ItemEvent, there are two subtypes represented by the constants SELECTED and DE-SELECTED.

Constants

public final static int ITEM_FIRST ★
public final static int ITEM_LAST ★

> The ITEM_FIRST and ITEM_LAST constants hold the endpoints of the range of identifiers for ItemEvent types.

public final static int ITEM_STATE_CHANGED ★

> The ITEM_STATE_CHANGED constant identifies item events that occur because a user selects a component, thus changing its state. The interface method Item-Listener.itemStateChanged() handles this event.

public static final int SELECTED ★

> SELECTED indicates that the user selected the item.

public static final int DESELECTED ★

> DESELECTED indicates that the user deselected the item.

Constructors

public ItemEvent(ItemSelectable source, int id, Object item, int stateChange) ★

> This constructor creates a ItemEvent with the given source; the source is the object generating the event. The id field serves as the identifier of the event type. If system-generated, the id will be ITEM_STATE_CHANGE. However, nothing stops you from creating your own id for your event types. The item parameter represents the text of the item selected: for a Checkbox, this would be its label, for a Choice the current selection. For your own events, this parameter could be virtually anything, since its type is Object.

Methods

public ItemSelectable getItemSelectable() ★

> The getItemSelectable() method retrieves the ItemSelectable object associated with this event—that is, the event's source.

public Object getItem() ★

> The getItem() method returns the item that was selected. This usually represents some text to help identify the source but could be nearly anything for user-generated events.

public int getStateChange() ★

The getStateChange() method returns the stateChange parameter from the constructor and, if system generated, is either SELECTED or DESELECTED.

public String paramString() ★

When you call the toString() method of an AWTEvent, the paramString() method is called in turn to build the string to display. At the ItemEvent level, paramString() adds a textual string for the event id (if available), along with a textual string indicating the value of stateChange (if available) and item. For example:

```
java.awt.event.ItemEvent[ITEM_STATE_CHANGED,item=Help,
stateChange=SELECTED] on checkbox1
```

4.3.2.13 TextEvent

The TextEvent class is yet another higher-level event class. It encapsulates events that occur when the contents of a TextComponent have changed, although is not required to have a TextComponent source. When the contents change, either programmatically by a call to setText() or because the user typed something, a TextEvent passes through the event queue looking for listeners.

Constants

public final static int TEXT_FIRST ★
public final static int TEXT_LAST ★

The TEXT_FIRST and TEXT_LAST constants hold the endpoints of the range of identifiers for TextEvent types.

public final static int TEXT_VALUE_CHANGED ★

The TEXT_VALUE_CHANGED constant identifies text events that occur because a user changes the contents of a text component. The interface method TextListener.textValueChanged() handles this event.

Constructors

public TextEvent(Object source, int id) ★

This constructor creates a TextEvent with the given source; the source is the object generating the event. The id field identifies the event type. If system-generated, the id will be TEXT_VALUE_CHANGE. However, nothing stops you from creating your own id for your event types.

Method

public String paramString() ★

When you call the toString() method of an AWTEvent, the paramString() method is called in turn to build the string to display. At the TextEvent level, paramString() adds a textual string for the event id (if available).

4.3.3 Event Listener Interfaces and Adapters

Java 1.1 has 11 event listener interfaces, which specify the methods a class must implement to receive different kinds of events. For example, the ActionListener interface defines the single method that is called when an ActionEvent occurs. These interfaces replace the various event-handling methods of Java 1.0: action() is now the actionPerformed() method of the ActionListener interface, mouseUp() is now the mouseReleased() method of the MouseListener interface, and so on. Most of the listener interfaces have a corresponding adapter class, which is an abstract class that provides a null implementation of all the methods in the interface. (Although an adapter class has no abstract methods, it is declared abstract to remind you that it must be subclassed.) Rather than implementing a listener interface directly, you have the option of extending an adapter class and overriding only the methods you care about. (Much more complex adapters are possible, but the adapters supplied with AWT are very simple.) The adapters are available for the listener interfaces with multiple methods. (If there is only one method in the listener interface, there is no need for an adapter.)

This section describes Java 1.1's listener interfaces and adapter classes. It's worth noting here that Java 1.1 does not allow you to modify the original event when you're writing an event handler.

4.3.3.1 ActionListener

The ActionListener interface contains the one method that is called when an ActionEvent occurs. It has no adapter class. For an object to listen for action events, it is necessary to call the addActionListener() method with the class that implements the ActionListener interface as the parameter. The method addActionListener() is implemented by Button, List, MenuItem, and TextField components. Other components don't generate action events.

public abstract void actionPerformed(ActionEvent e) ★

The actionPerformed() method is called when a component is selected or activated. Every component is activated differently; for a List, activation means that the user has double-clicked on an entry. See the appropriate section for a description of each component.

actionPerformed() is the Java 1.1 equivalent of the action() method in the 1.0 event model.

4.3.3.2 AdjustmentListener

The AdjustmentListener interface contains the one method that is called when an AdjustmentEvent occurs. It has no adapter class. For an object to listen for adjustment events, it is necessary to call addAdjustmentListener() with the class that implements the `AdjustmentListener` interface as the parameter. The `addAdjustmentListener()` method is implemented by the `Scrollbar` component and the `Adjustable` interface. Other components don't generate adjustment events.

public abstract void adjustmentValueChanged(AdjustmentEvent e) ★

The `adjustmentValueChanged()` method is called when a slider is moved. The `Scrollbar` and `ScrollPane` components have sliders, and generate adjustment events when the sliders are moved. (The `TextArea` and `List` components also have sliders, but do not generate adjustment events.) See the appropriate section for a description of each component.

There is no real equivalent to `adjustmentValueChanged()` in Java 1.0; to work with scrolling events, you had to override the `handleEvent()` method.

4.3.3.3 ComponentListener and ComponentAdapter

The `ComponentListener` interface contains four methods that are called when a `ComponentEvent` occurs; component events are used for general actions on components, like moving or resizing a component. The adapter class corresponding to `ComponentListener` is `ComponentAdapter`. If you care only about one or two of the methods in `ComponentListener`, you can subclass the adapter and override only the methods that you are interested in. For an object to listen for component events, it is necessary to call `Component.addComponentListener()` with the class that implements the interface as the parameter.

public abstract void componentResized(ComponentEvent e) ★

The `componentResized()` method is called when a component is resized (for example, by a call to `Component.setSize()`).

public abstract void componentMoved(ComponentEvent e) ★

The `componentMoved()` method is called when a component is moved (for example, by a call to `Component.setLocation()`).

public abstract void componentShown(ComponentEvent e) ★

The `componentShown()` method is called when a component is shown (for example, by a call to `Component.show()`).

public abstract void componentHidden(ComponentEvent e) ★

The `componentHidden()` method is called when a component is hidden (for example, by a call to `Component.hide()`).

4.3.3.4 ContainerListener and ContainerAdapter

The `ContainerListener` interface contains two methods that are called when a `ContainerEvent` occurs; container events are generated when components are added to or removed from a container. The adapter class for `ContainerListener` is `ContainerAdapter`. If you care only about one of the two methods in `Container-Listener`, you can subclass the adapter and override only the method that you are interested in. For a container to listen for container events, it is necessary to call `Container.addContainerListener()` with the class that implements the interface as the parameter.

public abstract void componentAdded(ContainerEvent e) ★

> The `componentAdded()` method is called when a component is added to a container (for example, by a call to `Container.add()`).

public abstract void componentRemoved(ContainerEvent e) ★

> The `componentRemoved()` method is called when a component is removed from a container (for example, by a call to `Container.remove()`).

4.3.3.5 FocusListener and FocusAdapter

The `FocusListener` interface has two methods, which are called when a `Focus-Event` occurs. Its adapter class is `FocusAdapter`. If you care only about one of the methods, you can subclass the adapter and override the method you are interested in. For an object to listen for a `FocusEvent`, it is necessary to call the `Compo-nent.addFocusListener()` method with the class that implements the `FocusLis-tener` interface as the parameter.

public abstract void focusGained(FocusEvent e) ★

> The `focusGained()` method is called when a component receives input focus, usually by the user clicking the mouse in the area of the component.

> This method is the Java 1.1 equivalent of `Component.gotFocus()` in the Java 1.0 event model.

public abstract void focusLost(FocusEvent e) ★

> The `focusLost()` method is called when a component loses the input focus.

> This method is the Java 1.1 equivalent of `Component.lostFocus()` in the Java 1.0 event model.

4.3.3.6 ItemListener

The `ItemListener` interface contains the one method that is called when an `Ite-mEvent` occurs. It has no adapter class. For an object to listen for an `ItemEvent`, it is necessary to call `addItemListener()` with the class that implements the `ItemLis-tener` interface as the parameter. The `addItemListener()` method is implemented by the `Checkbox`, `CheckboxMenuItem`, `Choice`, and `List` components. Other components don't generate item events.

public abstract void itemStateChanged(ItemEvent e) ★

> The `itemStateChanged()` method is called when a component's state is modified. Every component is modified differently; for a `List`, modifying the component means single-clicking on an entry. See the appropriate section for a description of each component.

4.3.3.7 *KeyListener and KeyAdapter*

The `KeyListener` interface contains three methods that are called when a `KeyEvent` occurs; key events are generated when the user presses or releases keys. The adapter class for `KeyListener` is `KeyAdapter`. If you only care about one or two of the methods in `KeyListener`, you can subclass the adapter and only override the methods that you are interested in. For an object to listen for key events, it is necessary to call `Component.addKeyListener()` with the class that implements the interface as the parameter.

public abstract void keyPressed(KeyEvent e) ★

> The `keyPressed()` method is called when a user presses a key. A key press is, literally, just what it says. A key press event is called for every key that is pressed, including keys like Shift and Control. Therefore, a `KEY_PRESSED` event has a virtual key code identifying the physical key that was pressed; but that's not the same as a typed character, which usually consists of several key presses (for example, Shift+A to type an uppercase A). The `keyTyped()` method reports actual characters.
>
> This method is the Java 1.1 equivalent of `Component.keyDown()` in the Java 1.0 event model.

public abstract void keyReleased(KeyEvent e) ★

> The `keyReleased()` method is called when a user releases a key. Like the `keyPressed()` method, when dealing with `keyReleased()`, you must think of virtual key codes, not characters.
>
> This method is the Java 1.1 equivalent of `Component.keyUp()` in the Java 1.0 event model.

public abstract void keyTyped(KeyEvent e) ★

> The `keyTyped()` method is called when a user types a key. The method `keyTyped()` method reports the actual character typed. Action-oriented keys, like function keys, do not trigger this method being called.

4.3.3.8 *MouseListener and MouseAdapter*

The `MouseListener` interface contains five methods that are called when a non-motion oriented `MouseEvent` occurs; mouse events are generated when the user presses or releases a mouse button. (Separate classes, `MouseMotionListener` and

MouseMotionAdapter, are used to handle mouse motion events; this means that you can listen for mouse clicks only, without being bothered by thousands of mouse motion events.) The adapter class for MouseListener is MouseAdapter. If you care about only one or two of the methods in MouseListener, you can subclass the adapter and override only the methods that you are interested in. For an object to listen for mouse events, it is necessary to call the method Window.addWindowListener() with the class that implements the interface as the parameter.

public abstract void mouseEntered(MouseEvent e) ★

The mouseEntered() method is called when the mouse first enters the bounding area of the component.

This method is the Java 1.1 equivalent of Component.mouseEnter() in the Java 1.0 event model.

public abstract void mouseExited(MouseEvent e) ★

The mouseExited() method is called when the mouse leaves the bounding area of the component.

This method is the Java 1.1 equivalent of Component.mouseExit() in the Java 1.0 event model.

public abstract void mousePressed(MouseEvent e) ★

The mousePressed() method is called each time the user presses a mouse button within the component's space.

This method is the Java 1.1 equivalent of Component.mouseDown() in the Java 1.0 event model.

public abstract void mouseReleased(MouseEvent e) ★

The mouseReleased() method is called when the user releases the mouse button after a mouse press. The user does not have to be over the original component any more; the original component (i.e., the component in which the mouse was pressed) is the source of the event.

This method is the Java 1.1 equivalent of Component.mouseUp() in the Java 1.0 event model.

public abstract void mouseClicked(MouseEvent e) ★

The mouseClicked() method is called once each time the user clicks a mouse button; that is, once for each mouse press/mouse release combination.

4.3.3.9 *MouseMotionListener and MouseMotionAdapter*

The MouseMotionListener interface contains two methods that are called when a motion-oriented MouseEvent occurs; mouse motion events are generated when the user moves the mouse, whether or not a button is pressed. (Separate classes, MouseListener and MouseAdapter, are used to handle mouse clicks and entering/exiting components. This makes it easy to ignore mouse motion events, which are very frequent and can hurt performance. You should listen only for mouse motion events if you specifically need them.) MouseMotionAdapter is the adapter class for MouseMotionListener. If you care about only one of the methods in MouseMotionListener, you can subclass the adapter and override only the method that you are interested in. For an object to listen for mouse motion events, it is necessary to call Component.addMouseMotionListener() with the class that implements the interface as the parameter.

public abstract void mouseMoved(MouseEvent e) ★

> The mouseMoved() method is called every time the mouse moves within the bounding area of the component, and no mouse button is pressed.

> This method is the Java 1.1 equivalent of Component.mouseMove() in the Java 1.0 event model.

public abstract void mouseDragged(MouseEvent e) ★

> The mouseDragged() method is called every time the mouse moves while a mouse button is pressed. The source of the MouseEvent is the component that was under the mouse when it was first pressed.

> This method is the Java 1.1 equivalent of Component.mouseDrag() in the Java 1.0 event model.

4.3.3.10 TextListener

The TextListener interface contains the one method that is called when a Text-Event occurs. It has no adapter class. For an object to listen for a TextEvent, it is necessary to call addTextListener() with the class that implements the Text-Listener interface as the parameter. The addTextListener() method is implemented by the TextComponent class, and thus the TextField and TextArea components. Other components don't generate text events.

public abstract void textValueChanged(TextEvent e) ★

> The textValueChanged() method is called when a text component's contents are modified, either by the user (by a keystroke) or programmatically (by the setText() method).

4.3.3.11 WindowListener and WindowAdapter

The WindowListener interface contains seven methods that are called when a Win-dowEvent occurs; window events are generated when something changes the visibility or status of a window. The adapter class for WindowListener is WindowAdapter. If you care about only one or two of the methods in WindowListener, you can subclass the adapter and override only the methods that you are interested in. For an object to listen for window events, it is necessary to call the method `Window.addWindowListener()` or `Dialog.addWindowListener()` with the class that implements the interface as the parameter.

public abstract void windowOpened(WindowEvent e) ★

> The `windowOpened()` method is called when a `Window` is first opened.

public abstract void windowClosing(WindowEvent e) ★

> The `windowClosing()` method is triggered whenever the user tries to close the `Window`.

public abstract void windowClosed(WindowEvent e) ★

> The `windowClosed()` method is called after the `Window` has been closed.

public abstract void windowIconified(WindowEvent e) ★

> The `windowIconified()` method is called whenever a user iconifies a `Window`.

public abstract void windowDeiconified(WindowEvent e) ★

> The `windowDeiconified()` method is called when the user deiconifies the `Window`.

public abstract void windowActivated(WindowEvent e) ★

> The `windowActivated()` method is called whenever a `Window` is brought to the front.

public abstract void windowDeactivated(WindowEvent e) ★

> The `windowDeactivated()` method is called when the `Window` is sent away from the front, either through iconification, closing, or another window becoming active.

4.3.4 AWTEventMulticaster

The `AWTEventMulticaster` class is used by AWT to manage the listener queues for the different events, and for sending events to all interested listeners when they occur (multicasting). Ordinarily, you have no need to work with this class or know about its existence. However, if you wish to create your own components that have their own set of listeners, you can use the class instead of implementing your own event-delivery system. See "Constructor methods" in this section for more on how to use the `AWTEventMulticaster`.

`AWTEventMulticaster` looks like a strange beast, and to some extent, it is. It contains methods to add and remove every possible kind of listener and implements all of the listener interfaces (11 as of Java 1.1). Because it implements all the listener interfaces, you can pass an event multicaster as an argument wherever you expect any kind of listener. However, unlike a class you might implement to listen for a specific kind of event, the multicaster includes machinery for maintaining chains of listeners. This explains the rather odd signatures for the `add()` and `remove()` methods. Let's look at one in particular:

```
public static ActionListener add(ActionListener first, ActionListener second)
```

This method takes two `ActionListeners` and returns another `ActionListener`. The returned listener is actually an event multicaster that contains the two listeners given as arguments in a linked list. However, because it implements the `ActionListener` interface, it is just as much an `ActionListener` as any class you might write; the fact that it contains two (or more) listeners inside it is irrelevant. Furthermore, both arguments can also be event multicasters, containing arbitrarily long chains of action listeners; in this case, the returned listener combines the two chains. Most often, you will use add to add a single listener to a chain that you're building, like this:

```
actionListenerChain=AWTEventMulticaster.add(actionListenerChain,
                                            newActionListener);
```

`actionListenerChain` is an `ActionListener`—but it is also a multicaster holding a chain of action listeners. To start a chain, use `null` for the first argument. You rarely need to call the `AWTEventMulticaster` constructor. `add()` is a static method, so you can use it with either argument set to `null` to start the chain.

Now that you can maintain chains of listeners, how do you use them? Simple; just deliver your event to the appropriate method in the chain. The multicaster takes care of sending the event to all the listeners it contains:

```
actionListenerChain.actionPerformed(new ActionEvent(...));
```

Variables

protected EventListener a; ★
protected EventListener b; ★
> The a and b event listeners each consist of a chain of `EventListeners`.

Constructor methods

protected AWTEventMulticaster(EventListener a, EventListener b) ★
> The constructor is protected. It creates an `AWTEventMulticaster` instance from the two chains of listeners. An instance is automatically created for you when you add your second listener by calling an `add()` method.

Listener methods

These methods implement all of the listener interfaces. Rather than repeating all
the descriptions, the methods are just listed.

public void actionPerformed(ActionEvent e) ★
public void adjustmentValueChanged(AdjustmentEvent e) ★
public void componentAdded(ContainerEvent e) ★
public void componentHidden(ComponentEvent e) ★
public void componentMoved(ComponentEvent e) ★
public void componentRemoved(ContainerEvent e) ★
public void componentResized(ComponentEvent e) ★
public void componentShown(ComponentEvent e) ★
public void focusGained(FocusEvent e) ★
public void focusLost(FocusEvent e) ★
public void itemStateChanged(ItemEvent e) ★
public void keyPressed(KeyEvent e) ★
public void keyReleased(KeyEvent e) ★
public void keyTyped(KeyEvent e) ★
public void mouseClicked(MouseEvent e) ★
public void mouseDragged(MouseEvent e) ★
public void mouseEntered(MouseEvent e) ★
public void mouseExited(MouseEvent e) ★
public void mouseMoved(MouseEvent e) ★
public void mousePressed(MouseEvent e) ★
public void mouseReleased(MouseEvent e) ★
public void textValueChanged(TextEvent e) ★
public void windowActivated(WindowEvent e) ★
public void windowClosed(WindowEvent e) ★
public void windowClosing(WindowEvent e) ★
public void windowDeactivated(WindowEvent e) ★
public void windowDeiconified(WindowEvent e) ★
public void windowIconified(WindowEvent e) ★
public void windowOpened(WindowEvent e) ★

These methods broadcast the event given as an argument to all the listeners.

Support methods

There is an add() method for every listener interface. Again, I've listed them with
a single description.

public static ActionListener add(ActionListener first, ActionListener second) ★
public static AdjustmentListener add(AdjustmentListener first,
AdjustmentListener second) ★

public static ComponentListener add(ComponentListener first, ComponentListener second) ★
public static ContainerListener add(ContainerListener first, ContainerListener second) ★
public static FocusListener add(FocusListener first, FocusListener second) ★
public static ItemListener add(ItemListener first, ItemListener second) ★
public static KeyListener add(KeyListener first, KeyListener second)
public static MouseListener add(MouseListener first, MouseListener second) ★
public static MouseMotionListener add(MouseMotionListener first,
MouseMotionListener second) ★
public static TextListener add(TextListener first, TextListener second) ★
public static WindowListener add(WindowListener first, WindowListener second) ★

These methods combine the listener sets together; they are called by the "add listener" methods of the various components. Usually, the `first` parameter is the initial listener chain, and the `second` parameter is the listener to add. However, nothing forces that. The combined set of listeners is returned.

protected static EventListener addInternal(EventListener first, EventListener second) ★

The `addInternal()` method is a support routine for the various `add()` methods. The combined set of listeners is returned.

Again, there are `remove()` methods for every listener type, and I've economized on the descriptions.

public static ComponentListener remove(ComponentListener list,
ComponentListener oldListener) ★
public static ContainerListener remove(ContainerListener list,
ContainerListener oldListener) ★
public static FocusListener remove(FocusListener list, FocusListener oldListener) ★
public static KeyListener remove(KeyListener list, KeyListener oldListener) ★
public static MouseMotionListener remove(MouseMotionListener list,
MouseMotionListener oldListener) ★
public static MouseListener remove(MouseListener list, MouseListener oldListener) ★
public static WindowListener remove(WindowListener list, WindowListener oldListener) ★
public static ActionListener remove(ActionListener list, ActionListener oldListener) ★
public static ItemListener remove(ItemListener list, ItemListener oldListener) ★
public static AdjustmentListener remove(AdjustmentListener list,
AdjustmentListener oldListener) ★
public static TextListener remove(TextListener list, TextListener oldListener) ★

These methods remove `oldListener` from the list of listeners, `list`. They are called by the "remove listener" methods of the different components. If `oldListener` is not found in the `list`, nothing happens. All these methods return the new list of listeners.

protected static EventListener removeInternal(EventListener list,
EventListener oldListener) ★

The `removeInternal()` method is a support routine for the various `remove()`
methods. It removes `oldListener` from the list of listeners, `list`. Nothing
happens if `oldListener` is not found in the `list`. The new set of listeners is
returned.

protected EventListener remove(EventListener oldListener) ★

This `remove()` method removes `oldListener` from the `AWTEventMulticaster`.
It is a support routine for `removeInternal()`.

protected void saveInternal(ObjectOutputStream s, String k) throws IOException ★

The `saveInternal()` method is a support method for serialization.

4.3.4.1 Using an event multicaster

Example 4-4 shows how to use `AWTEventMulticaster` to create a component that
generates `ItemEvents`. The `AWTEventMulticaster` is used in the `addItemLis-`
`tener()` and `removeItemListener()` methods. When it comes time to generate the
event in `processEvent()`, the `itemStateChanged()` method is called to notify anyone who might be interested. The item event is generated when a mouse button is
clicked; we just count the number of clicks to determine whether an item was
selected or deselected. Since we do not have any mouse listeners, we need to
enable mouse events with `enableEvents()` in the constructor, as shown in the following example.

Example 4–4: Using an AWTEventMulticaster

```
// Java 1.1 only
import java.awt.*;
import java.awt.event.*;
class ItemEventComponent extends Component implements ItemSelectable {
    boolean selected;
    int i = 0;
    ItemListener itemListener = null;
    ItemEventComponent () {
        enableEvents (AWTEvent.MOUSE_EVENT_MASK);
    }
    public Object[] getSelectedObjects() {
        Object o[] = new Object[1];
        o[0] = new Integer (i);
        return o;
    }
    public void addItemListener (ItemListener l) {
        itemListener = AWTEventMulticaster.add (itemListener, l);
    }
    public void removeItemListener (ItemListener l) {
        itemListener = AWTEventMulticaster.remove (itemListener, l);
    }
    public void processEvent (AWTEvent e) {
```

Example 4–4: Using an AWTEventMulticaster (continued)

```
          if (e.getID() == MouseEvent.MOUSE_PRESSED) {
              if (itemListener != null) {
                  selected = !selected;
                  i++;
                  itemListener.itemStateChanged (
                      new ItemEvent (this, ItemEvent.ITEM_STATE_CHANGED,
                          getSelectedObjects(),
                          (selected?ItemEvent.SELECTED:ItemEvent.DESELECTED)));
              }
          }
      }
  }

public class ItemFrame extends Frame implements ItemListener {
    ItemFrame () {
        super ("Listening In");
        ItemEventComponent c = new ItemEventComponent ();
        add (c, "Center");
        c.addItemListener (this);
        c.setBackground (SystemColor.control);
        setSize (200, 200);
    }
    public void itemStateChanged (ItemEvent e) {
        Object[] o = e.getItemSelectable().getSelectedObjects();
        Integer i = (Integer)o[0];
        System.out.println (i);
    }
    public static void main (String args[]) {
        ItemFrame f = new ItemFrame();
        f.show();
    }
}
```

The `ItemFrame` displays just an `ItemEventComponent` and listens for its item events.

The `EventQueue` class lets you manage Java 1.1 events directly. You don't usually need to manage events yourself; the system takes care of event delivery behind the scene. However, should you need to, you can acquire the system's event queue by calling `Toolkit.getSystemEventQueue()`, peek into the event queue by calling `peekEvent()`, or post new events by calling `postEvent()`. All of these operations may be restricted by the `SecurityManager`. You should not remove the events from the queue (i.e., don't call `getNextEvent()`) unless you really mean to.

Constructors

public EventQueue() ★

This constructor creates an `EventQueue` for those rare times when you need to manage your own queue of events. More frequently, you just work with the system event queue acquired through the `Toolkit`.

Methods

public synchronized AWTEvent peekEvent() ★

The peekEvent() method looks into the event queue and returns the first event, without removing that event. If you modify the event, your modifications are reflected in the event still on the queue. The returned object is an instance of AWTEvent. If the queue is empty, peekEvent() returns null.

public synchronized AWTEvent peekEvent(int id) ★

This peekEvent() method looks into the event queue for the first event of the specified type. id is one of the integer constants from an AWTEvent subclass or an integer constant of your own. If there are no events of the appropriate type on the queue, peekEvent() returns null.

Note that a few of the AWTEvent classes have both event types and subtypes; peekEvent() checks event types only and ignores the subtype. For example, to find an ItemEvent, you would call peekEvent(ITEM_STATE_CHANGED). However, a call to peekEvent(SELECTED) would return null, since SELECTED identifies an ItemEvent subtype.

public synchronized void postEvent(AWTEvent theEvent) ★

This version of postEvent() puts a new style (Java1.1) event on the event queue.

public synchronized AWTEvent getNextEvent() throws InterruptedException ★

The getNextEvent() method removes an event from the queue. If the queue is empty, the call waits. The object returned is the item taken from the queue; it is either an Event or an AWTEvent. If the method call is interrupted, the method getNextEvent() throws an InterruptedException.

5

Components

This chapter introduces the generic graphical widget used within the AWT package, Component, along with a trio of specific components: Label, Button, and Canvas. It also covers the Cursor class, new to Java 1.1. (Cursor support was previously part of the Frame class.) Although many objects within AWT don't subclass Component, and though you will never create an instance of Component, anything that provides screen-based user interaction and relies on the system for its layout will be a child of Component. As a subclass of Component, each child inherits a common set of methods and an API for dealing with the different events (i.e., mouse click, keyboard input) that occur within your Java programs.

After discussing the methods in Component classes, this chapter goes into detail about two specific components, Label and Button. A Label is a widget that contains descriptive text, usually next to an input field. A Button is a basic mechanism that lets the user signal the desire to perform an action. You will learn about the Canvas object and how to use a Canvas to create your own component. Finally, we cover the Cursor class, which lets you change the cursor over a Component.

Before going into the mechanics of the Component class, it's necessary to say a little about the relationship between components and containers. A Container is also a component with the ability to contain other components. There are several different kinds of containers; they are discussed in Chapter 6, *Containers*. To display a component, you have to put it in a container by calling the container's add() method. We often call the container that holds a component the component's *parent*; likewise, we call the components a container holds its *children*. Certain operations are legal only if a component has a parent—that is, the component is in a container. Of course, since containers are components, containers can contain other containers, *ad infinitum*.

NOTE   If you think some component is missing a method that should obviously be there, check the methods it inherits. For example, the Label class appears to lack a setFont() method. Obviously, labels ought to be able to change their fonts. The setFont() method really is there; it is inherited from the Component class, and therefore, not documented as part of the Label class. Even if you're familiar with object-oriented techniques, the need to work up a class hierarchy to find all of the class's methods can lead to confusion and frustration. While all Java objects inherit methods from other classes, the potential for confusion is worst with components, which inherit over a hundred methods from Component and may only have a few methods of their own.

5.1 Component

Every GUI-based program consists of a screen with a set of objects. With Java, these objects are called components. Some of the more frequently used components are buttons, text fields, and containers.

A container is a special component that allows you to group different components together within it. You will learn more about containers in the next chapter, but they are in fact just another kind of component. Also, some of the parameters and return types for the methods of Component have not been explained yet and have their own sections in future chapters.

5.1.1 Component Methods

Constants

Prior to Java 1.1, you could not subclass Component or Container. With the introduction of the LightweightPeer, you can now subclass either Component or Container. However, since you no longer have a native peer, you must rely on your container to provide a display area and other services that are normally provided by a full-fledged peer. Because you cannot rely on your peer to determine your alignment, the Component class now has five constants to indicate six possible alignment settings (one constant is used twice). The alignment constants designate where to position a lightweight component; their values range from 0.0 to 1.0. The lower the number, the closer the component will be placed to the origin (top left corner) of the space allotted to it.*

---

* As of Beta 3, these constants appear to be seldom used. The getAlignmentX() and getAlignmentY() methods return these values, but there are no setAlignment methods.

public static final float BOTTOM_ALIGNMENT ★

> The BOTTOM_ALIGNMENT constant indicates that the component should align itself to the bottom of its available space. It is a return value from the method getAlignmentY().

public static final float CENTER_ALIGNMENT ★

> The CENTER_ALIGNMENT constant indicates that the component should align itself to the middle of its available space. It is a return value from either the getAlignmentX() or getAlignmentY() method. This constant represents both the horizontal and vertical center.

public static final float LEFT_ALIGNMENT ★

> The LEFT_ALIGNMENT constant indicates that the component should align itself to the left side of its available space. It is a return value from getAlignmentX().

public static final float RIGHT_ALIGNMENT ★

> The RIGHT_ALIGNMENT constant indicates that the component should align itself to the right side of its available space. It is a return value from the method getAlignmentX().

public static final float TOP_ALIGNMENT ★

> The TOP_ALIGNMENT constant indicates that the component should align itself to the top of its available space. It is a return value from getAlignmentY().

Variables

protected Locale locale ★

> The protected locale variable can be accessed by calling the getLocale() method.

Constructor

Prior to Java 1.1, there was no public or protected constructor for Component. Only package members were able to subclass Component directly. With the introduction of lightweight peers, components can exist without a native peer, so the constructor was made protected, allowing you to create your own Component subclasses.

protected Component() ★

> The constructor for Component creates a new component without a native peer. Since you no longer have a native peer, you must rely on your container to provide a display area. This allows you to create components that require fewer system resources than components that subclass Canvas. The example in the "Using an event multicaster" section of the previous chapter is of a lightweight component. Use the SystemColor class to help you colorize the new component appropriately or make it transparent.

Appearance

public Toolkit getToolkit ()

> The getToolkit() method returns the current Toolkit of the Component. This returns the parent's Toolkit (from a getParent() call) when the Component has not been added to the screen yet or is lightweight. If there is no parent, getToolkit() returns the default Toolkit. Through the Toolkit, you have access to the details of the current platform (like screen resolution, screen size, and available fonts), which you can use to adjust screen real estate requirements or check on the availability of a font.

public Color getForeground ()

> The getForeground() method returns the foreground color of the component. If no foreground color is set for the component, you get its parent's foreground color. If none of the component's parents have a foreground color set, null is returned.

public void setForeground (Color c)

> The setForeground() method changes the current foreground color of the area of the screen occupied by the component to c. After changing the color, it is necessary for the screen to refresh before the change has any effect. To refresh the screen, call repaint().

public Color getBackground ()

> The getBackground() method returns the background color of the component. If no background color is set for the component, its parent's background color is retrieved. If none of the component's parents have a background color set, null is returned.

public void setBackground (Color c)

> The setBackground() method changes the current background color of the area of the screen occupied by the component to c. After changing the color, it is necessary for the screen to refresh before the change has any affect. To refresh the screen, call repaint().

public Font getFont ()

> The getFont() method returns the font of the component. If no font is set for the component, its parent's font is retrieved. If none of the component's parents have a font set, null is returned.

public synchronized void setFont (Font f)

> The setFont() method changes the component's font to f. If the font family (such as TimesRoman) provided within f is not available on the current platform, the system uses a default font family, along with the supplied size and style (plain, bold, italic). Depending upon the platform, it may be necessary to refresh the component/screen before seeing any changes.

Changing the font of a component could have an affect on the layout of the component.

public synchronized ColorModel getColorModel ()

The getColorModel() method returns the ColorModel used to display the current component. If the component is not displayed, the ColorModel from the component's Toolkit is used. The normal ColorModel for a Java program is 8 bits each for red, green, and blue.

public Graphics getGraphics ()

The getGraphics() method gets the component's graphics context. Most noncontainer components do not manage them correctly and therefore throw an InternalError exception when you call this method. The Canvas component is one that does since you can draw on that directly. If the component is not visible, null is returned.

public FontMetrics getFontMetrics (Font f)

The getFontMetrics() method retrieves the component's view of the FontMetrics for the requested font f. Through the FontMetrics, you have access to the platform-specific sizing for the appearance of a character or string.

public Locale getLocale () ★

The getLocale() method retrieves the current Locale of the component, if it has one. Using a Locale allows you to write programs that can adapt themselves to different languages and different regional variants. If no Locale has been set, getLocale() returns the parent's Locale.[*] If the component has no locale of its own and no parent (i.e., it isn't in a container), getLocale() throws the run-time exception IllegalComponentStateException.

public void setLocale (Locale l) ★

The setLocale() method changes the current Locale of the component to l. In order for this change to have any effect, you must localize your components so that they have different labels or list values for different environments. Localization is part of the broad topic of internationalization and is beyond the scope of this book.

public Cursor getCursor () ★

The getCursor() method retrieves the component's current Cursor. If one hasn't been set, the default is Cursor.DEFAULT_CURSOR. The Cursor class is described fully in Section 5.7. Prior to Java 1.1, the ability to associate cursors with components was restricted to frames.

---

* For more on the Locale class, see the *Java Fundamental Classes Reference* from O'Reilly & Associates.

public synchronized void setCursor (Cursor c) ★

> The setCursor() method changes the current Cursor of the component to c. The change takes effect as soon as the cursor is moved. Lightweight components cannot change their cursors.

Positioning/Sizing

Component provides a handful of methods for positioning and sizing objects. Most of these are used behind the scenes by the system. You will also need them if you create your own LayoutManager or need to move or size an object. All of these depend on support for the functionality from the true component's peer.

public Point getLocation () ★
public Point location () ☆

> The getLocation() method returns the current position of the Component in its parent's coordinate space. The Point is the top left corner of the bounding box around the Component.

> location() is the Java 1.0 name for this method.

public Point getLocationOnScreen () ★

> The getLocationOnScreen() method returns the current position of the Component in the screen's coordinate space. The Point is the top left corner of the bounding box around the Component. If the component is not showing, the getLocationOnScreen() method throws the IllegalComponentState-Exception run-time exception.

public void setLocation (int x, int y) ★
public void move (int x, int y) ☆

> The setLocation() method moves the Component to the new position (x, y). The coordinates provided are in the parent container's coordinate space. This method calls setBounds() to move the component. The LayoutManager of the container may make it impossible to change a component's location.

> Calling this method with a new position for the component generates a ComponentEvent with the ID COMPONENT_MOVED.

> move() is the Java 1.0 name for this method.

public void setLocation (Point p) ★

> This setLocation() method moves the component to the position specified by the given Point. It is the same as calling setLocation(p.x, p.y).

> Calling this method with a new position for the component generates a ComponentEvent with the ID COMPONENT_MOVED.

public Dimension getSize () ★
public Dimension size () ☆

> The getSize() method returns the width and height of the component as a Dimension object.
>
> size() is the Java 1.0 name for this method.

public void setSize (int width, int height) ★
public void resize (int width, int height) ☆

> The setSize() method changes the component's width and height to the width and height provided. width and height are specified in pixels. The component is resized by a call to setBounds(). The LayoutManager of the Container that contains the component may make it impossible to change a component's size.
>
> Calling this method with a new size for the component generates a Component-Event with the ID COMPONENT_RESIZED.
>
> resize() is the Java 1.0 name for this method.

public void setSize (Dimension d) ★
public void resize (Dimension d) ☆

> This setSize() method changes the component's width and height to the Dimension d provided. The Dimension object includes the width and height attributes in one object. The component is resized by a call to the setBounds() method. The LayoutManager of the Container that contains the component may make it impossible to change a component's size.
>
> Calling this method with a new size for the component generates a Component-Event with the ID COMPONENT_RESIZED.
>
> resize() is the Java 1.0 name for this method.

public Rectangle getBounds () ★
public Rectangle bounds () ☆

> The getBounds() method returns the bounding rectangle of the object. The fields of the Rectangle that you get back contain the component's position and dimensions.
>
> bounds() is the Java 1.0 name for this method.

public void setBounds (int x, int y, int width, int height) ★
public void reshape (int x, int y, int width, int height) ☆

> The setBounds() method moves and resizes the component to the bounding rectangle with coordinates of (x, y) (top left corner) and width × height. If the size and shape have not changed, no reshaping is done. If the component is resized, it is invalidated, along with its parent container. The LayoutManager

of the Container that contains the component may make it impossible to change the component's size or position. Calling setBounds() invalidates the container, which results in a call to the LayoutManager to rearrange the container's contents. In turn, the LayoutManager calls setBounds() to give the component its new size and position, which will probably be the same size and position it had originally. In short, if a layout manager is in effect, it will probably undo your attempts to change the component's size and position.

Calling this method with a new size for the component generates a Component-Event with the ID COMPONENT_RESIZED. Calling this method with a new position generates a ComponentEvent with the ID COMPONENT_MOVED.

reshape() is the Java 1.0 name for this method.

public void setBounds (Rectangle r) ★

This setBounds() method calls the previous method with parameters of r.x, r.y, r.width, and r.height.

Calling this method with a new size for the component generates a Component-Event with the ID COMPONENT_RESIZED. Calling this method with a new position generates a ComponentEvent with the ID COMPONENT_MOVED.

public Dimension getPreferredSize () ★
public Dimension preferredSize () ☆

The getPreferredSize() method returns the Dimension (width and height) for the preferred size of the component. Each component's peer knows its preferred size. Lightweight objects return getSize().

preferredSize() is the Java 1.0 name for this method.

public Dimension getMinimumSize () ★
public Dimension minimumSize () ☆

The getMinimumSize() method returns the Dimension (width and height) for the minimum size of the component. Each component's peer knows its minimum size. Lightweight objects return getSize(). It is possible that the methods getMinimumSize() and getPreferredSize() will return the same dimensions.

minimumSize() is the Java 1.0 name for this method.

public Dimension getMaximumSize () ★

The getMaximumSize() method returns the Dimension (width and height) for the maximum size of the component. This may be used by a layout manager to prevent a component from growing beyond a predetermined size. None of the java.awt layout managers call this method. By default, the value returned is Short.MAX_VALUE for both dimensions.

public float getAlignmentX () ★

> The getAlignmentX() method returns the alignment of the component along the x axis. The alignment could be used by a layout manager to position this component relative to others. The return value is between 0.0 and 1.0. Values nearer 0 indicate that the component should be placed closer to the left edge of the area available. Values nearer 1 indicate that the component should be placed closer to the right. The value 0.5 means the component should be centered. The default setting is Component.CENTER_ALIGNMENT.

public float getAlignmentY () ★

> The getAlignmentY() method returns the alignment of the component along the y axis. The alignment could be used by a layout manager to position this component relative to others. The return value is between 0.0 and 1.0. Values nearer 0 indicate that the component should be placed closer to the top of the area available. Values nearer 1 indicate that the component should be placed closer to the bottom. The value 0.5 means the component should be centered. The default setting is Component.CENTER_ALIGNMENT.

public void doLayout () ★
public void layout () ☆

> The doLayout() method of Component does absolutely nothing. It is called when the Component is validated (through the validate() method). The Container class overrides this method.

> layout() is the Java 1.0 name for this method.

public boolean contains (int x, int y) ★
public boolean inside (int x, int y) ☆

> The contains() method checks if the x and y coordinates are within the bounding box of the component. If the Component is not rectangular, the method acts as if there is a rectangle around the Component. contains() returns true if the x and y coordinates are within the component, false otherwise.

> inside() is the Java 1.0 name for this method.

public boolean contains (Point p) ★

> This contains() method calls the previous method with parameters of p.x and p.y.

public Component getComponentAt (int x, int y) ★
public Component locate (int x, int y) ☆

> The getComponentAt() method uses contains() to see if the x and y coordinates are within the component. If they are, this method returns the Component. If they aren't, it returns null. getComponentAt() is overridden by Container to provide enhanced functionality.

`locate()` is the Java 1.0 name for this method.

public Component getComponentAt (Point p) ★

This `getComponentAt()` method calls the previous method with parameters of `p.x` and `p.y`.

Painting

The only methods in this section that you call directly are the versions of `repaint()`. The `paint()` and `update()` methods are called by the system when the display area requires refreshing, such as when a user resizes a window. When your program changes the display you should call `repaint()` to trigger a call to `update()` and `paint()`. Otherwise, the system is responsible for updating the display.

public void paint (Graphics g)

The `paint()` method is offered so the system can display whatever you want in a `Component`. In the base `Component` class, this method does absolutely nothing. Ordinarily, it would be overridden in an applet to do something other than the default, which is display a box in the current background color. g is the graphics context of the component being drawn on.

public void update (Graphics g)

The `update()` method is automatically called when you ask to repaint the `Component`. If the component is not lightweight, the default implementation of `update()` clears graphics context g by drawing a filled rectangle in the background color, resetting the color to the current foreground color, and calling `paint()`. If you do not override `update()` when you do animation, you will see some flickering because `Component` clears the screen. Animation is discussed in Chapter 2, *Simple Graphics*.

public void paintAll (Graphics g)

The `paintAll()` method validates the component and paints its peer if it is visible. g represents the graphics context of the component. This method is called when the `paintComponents()` method of `Container` is called.

public void repaint ()

The `repaint()` method requests the scheduler to redraw the component as soon as possible. This will result in `update()` getting called soon thereafter. There is not a one-to-one correlation between `repaint()` and `update()` calls. It is possible that multiple `repaint()` calls can result in a single `update()`.

public void repaint (long tm)

This version of repaint() allows for a delay of tm milliseconds. It says, please update this component within tm milliseconds, which may happen immediately.

public void repaint (int x, int y, int width, int height)

This version of repaint() allows you to select the region of the Component you desire to be updated. (x, y) are the coordinates of the upper left corner of the bounding box of the component with dimensions of width×height. This is similar to creating a clipping area and results in a quicker repaint.

public void repaint (long tm, int x, int y, int width, int height)

This final version of repaint() is what the other three repaint() methods call. tm is the maximum delay in milliseconds before update should be called. (x, y) are the coordinates of the upper left corner of the clipping area of the component with dimensions of width × height.

public void print (Graphics g)

The default implementation of the print() method calls paint().

In Java 1.0, there was no way to print; in Java 1.1, if the graphics parameter implements PrintGraphics, anything drawn on g will be printed. Printing is covered in Chapter 17, *Printing*.

public void printAll (Graphics g)

The printAll() method validates the component and paints its peer if it is visible. g represents the graphics context of the component. This method is called when the printComponents() method of Container is called or when you call it with a PrintGraphics parameter.

The default implementation of printAll() is identical to paintAll(). As with paintAll(), g represents the graphics context of the component; if g implements PrintGraphics, it can be printed.

Imaging

Background information about using images is discussed in Chapter 2 and Chapter 12, *Image Processing*. The imageUpdate() method of Component is the sole method of the ImageObserver interface. Since images are loaded in a separate thread, this method is called whenever additional information about the image becomes available.

public boolean imageUpdate (Image image, int infoflags, int x, int y, int width, int height)

imageUpdate() is the java.awt.image.ImageObserver method implemented by Component. It is an asynchronous update interface for receiving notifications about Image information as image is loaded and is automatically called when additional information becomes available. This method is necessary because image loading is done in a separate thread from the getImage() call. Ordinarily, x and y would be the coordinates of the upper left corner of the image loaded so far, usually (0, 0). However, the method imageUpdate() of the component ignores these parameters. width and height are the image's dimensions, so far, in the loading process.

The infoflags parameter is a bit-mask of information available to you about image. Please see the text about ImageObserver in Chapter 12 for a complete description of the different flags that can be set. When overriding this method, you can wait for some condition to be true by checking a flag in your program and then taking the desired action. To check for a particular flag, perform an AND (&) of infoflags and the constant. For example, to check if the FRAMEBITS flag is set:

```
if ((infoflags & ImageObserver.FRAMEBITS) == ImageObserver.FRAMEBITS)
    System.out.println ("The Flag is set");
```

The return value from a call to imageUpdate() is true if image has changed and false otherwise.

Two system properties let the user control the behavior of updates:

- awt.image.incrementaldraw allows the user to control whether or not partial images are displayed. Initially, the value of incrementaldraw is unset and defaults to true, which means that partial images are drawn. If incrementaldraw is set to false, the image will be drawn only when it is complete or when the screen is resized or refreshed.

- awt.image.redrawrate allows the user to change the delay between successive repaints. If not set, the default redraw rate is 100 milliseconds.

public Image createImage (int width, int height)

The createImage() method creates an empty Image of size width × height. The returned Image is an in-memory image that can be drawn on for double buffering to manipulate an image in the background. If an image of size width × height cannot be created, the call returns null. In order for createImage() to succeed, the peer of the Component must exist; if the component is lightweight, the peer of the component's container must exist.

public Image createImage (ImageProducer producer)

This createImage() method allows you to take an existing image and modify it in some way to produce a new Image. This can be done through ImageFilter and FilteredImageSource or a MemoryImageSource, which accepts an array of pixel information. You can learn more about these classes and this method in Chapter 12.

public boolean prepareImage (Image image, ImageObserver observer)

The prepareImage() method forces image to start loading, asynchronously, in another thread. observer is the Component that image will be rendered on and is notified (via imageUpdate()) as image is being loaded. In the case of an Applet, this would be passed as the ImageObserver. If image has already been fully loaded, prepareImage() returns true. Otherwise, false is returned. Since image is loaded asynchronously, prepareImage() returns immediately. Ordinarily, prepareImage() would be called by the system when image is first needed to be displayed (in drawImage() within paint()). As more information about the image gets loaded, imageUpdate() is called periodically.

If you do not want to go through the trouble of creating a MediaTracker instance to start the loading of the image objects, you can call prepareImage() to trigger the start of image loading prior to a call to drawImage().

If image has already started loading when this is called or if this is an in-memory image, there is no effect.

public boolean prepareImage (Image image, int width, int height, ImageObserver observer)

This version of prepareImage() is identical to the previous one, with the addition of a scaling factor of width×height. As with other width and height parameters, the units for these parameters are pixels. Also, if width and height are −1, no scaling factor is assumed. This method is called by one of the internal MediaTracker methods.

public int checkImage (Image image, ImageObserver observer)

The checkImage() method returns the status of the construction of a screen representation of image, being watched by observer. If image has not started loading yet, this will not start it. The return value is the ImageObserver flags ORed together for the data that is now available. The available ImageObserver flags are: WIDTH, HEIGHT, PROPERTIES, SOMEBITS, FRAMEBITS, ALLBITS, ERROR, and ABORT. See Chapter 12 for a complete description of ImageObserver.

public int checkImage (Image image, int width, int height, ImageObserver observer)

This version of checkImage() is identical to the previous one, with the addition of a scaling factor of width×height. If you are using the drawImage() version with width and height parameters, you should use this version of checkImage() with the same width and height.

Peers

public ComponentPeer getPeer () ☆

The getPeer() method returns a reference to the component's peer as a ComponentPeer object. For example, if you issue this method from a Button object, getPeer() returns an instance of the ComponentPeer subclass ButtonPeer.

This method is flagged as deprecated in comments but not with @deprecated. There is no replacement method for Java 1.1.

public void addNotify ()

The addNotify() method is overridden by each individual component type. When addNotify() is called, the peer of the component gets created, and the Component is invalidated. The addNotify() method is called by the system when it needs to create the peer. The peer needs to be created when a Component is first shown, or when a new Component is added to a Container and the Container is already being shown (in which case it already has a peer, but a new one must be created to take account of the new Component). If you override this method for a specific Component, call super.addNotify() first, then do what you need for the Component. You will then have information available about the newly created peer.

Certain tasks cannot succeed unless the peer has been created. An incomplete list includes finding the size of a component, laying out a container (because it needs the component's size), and creating an Image object. Peers are discussed in more depth in Chapter 15, *Toolkit and Peers*.

public synchronized void removeNotify ()

The removeNotify() method destroys the peer of the component and removes it from the screen. The state information about the Component is retained by the specific subtype. The removeNotify() method is called by the system when it determines the peer is no longer needed. Such times would be when the Component is removed from a Container, when its container changes, or when the Component is disposed. If you override this method for a specific Component, issue the particular commands for you need for this Component, then call super.removeNotify() last.

State Procedures

These methods determine whether the component is ready to be displayed and can be seen by the user. The first requirement is that it be *valid*—that is, whether the system knows its size, and (in the case of a container) whether the layout manager is aware of all its parts and has placed them as requested. A component becomes invalid if the size has changed since it was last displayed. If the component is a container, it becomes invalid when one of the components contained within it becomes invalid.

Next, the component must be *visible*—a possibly confusing term, because components can be considered "visible" without being seen by the user. Frames (because they have their own top-level windows) are not visible until you request that they be shown, but other components are visible as soon as you create them.

Finally, to be seen, a component must be *showing*. You show a component by adding it to its container. For something to be showing, it must be visible and be in a container that is visible and showing.

A subsidiary aspect of state is the *enabled* quality, which determines whether a component can accept input.

public boolean isValid ()

> The isValid() method tells you whether or not the component needs to be laid out.

public void validate ()

> The validate() method sets the component's valid state to true. Ordinarily, this is done for you when the Component is laid out by its Container. Since objects are invalid when they are first drawn on the screen, you should call validate() to tell the system you are finished adding objects so that it can validate the screen and components. One reason you can override validate() is to find out when the container that the component exists in has been resized. The only requirement when overriding is that the original validate() be called. With Java 1.1, instead of overriding, you can listen for resize events.

public void invalidate ()

> The invalidate() method sets the component's valid state to false and propagates the invalidation to its parent. Ordinarily, this is done for you, or should be, whenever anything that affects the layout is changed.

public boolean isVisible ()

> The isVisible() methods tells you if the component is currently visible. Most components are initially visible, except for top-level objects like frames. Any component that is visible will be shown on the screen when the screen is painted.

public boolean isShowing ()

> The isShowing() method tells you if the component is currently shown on the screen. It is possible for isVisible() to return true and isShowing() to return false if the screen has not been painted yet.

Table 5-1 compares possible return values from isVisible() and isShowing(). The first two entries are for objects that have their own Window. These will always return the same values for isVisible() and isShowing(). The next three are for Component objects that exist within a Window, Panel, or Applet. The visible setting is always initially true. However, the showing setting is not true until the object is actually drawn. The last case shows another possibility. If the component exists within an invisible Container, the component will be visible but will not be shown.

Table 5–1: isVisible vs. isShowing

Happenings	isVisible	isShowing
Frame created `Frame f = new Frame ()`	false	false
Frame showing `f.show ()`	true	true
Component created `Button b= new Button ("Help")`	true	false
Button added to screen in init() `add (b)`	true	false
Container laid out with Button in it	true	true
Button within Panel that is not visible	true	false

public void show ()

> The `show()` method displays a component by making it visible and showing its peer. The parent `Container` becomes invalid because the set of children to display has changed. You would call `show()` directly to display a `Frame` or `Dialog`.

> In Java 1.1, you should use `setVisible()` instead.

public void hide ()

> The `hide()` method hides a component by making it invisible and hiding its peer. The parent `Container` becomes invalid because the set of children to display has changed. If you call `hide()` for a `Component` that does not subclass `Window`, the component's `Container` reserves space for the hidden object.

> In Java 1.1, you should use `setVisible()` instead.

public void setVisible(boolean condition) ★
public void show (boolean condition) ☆

> The `setVisible()` method calls either `show()` or `hide()` based on the value of condition. If condition is `true`, `show()` is called. When condition is `false`, `hide()` is called.

> `show()` is the Java 1.0 name for this method.

public boolean isEnabled ()

> The `isEnabled()` method checks to see if the component is currently enabled. An enabled `Component` can be selected and trigger events. A disabled `Component` usually has a slightly lighter font and doesn't permit the user to select or interact with it. Initially, every `Component` is enabled.

public synchronized void enable ()

> The enable() method allows the user to interact with the component. Components are enabled by default but can be disabled by a call to disabled() or setEnabled(false).

> In Java 1.1, you should use setEnabled() instead.

public synchronized void disable ()

> The disable() method disables the component so that it is unresponsive to user interactions.

> In Java 1.1, you should use setEnabled() instead.

public void setEnabled (boolean condition) ★
public void enable (boolean condition) ☆

> The setEnabled() method calls either enable() or disable() based on the value of condition. If condition is true, enable() is called. When condition is false, disable() is called. Enabling and disabling lets you create components that can be operated only under certain conditions—for example, a Button that can be pressed only after the user has typed into a TextArea.

> enable() is the Java 1.0 name for this method.

Focus

Although there was some support for managing input focus in version 1.0, 1.1 improved on this greatly by including support for Tab and Shift+Tab to move input focus to the next or previous component, and by being more consistent across different platforms. This support is provided by the package-private class FocusManager.

public boolean isFocusTraversable() ★

> The isFocusTraversable() method is the support method that tells you whether or not a component is capable of receiving the input focus. Every component asks its peer whether or not it is traversable. If there is no peer, this method returns false.

> If you are creating a component by subclassing Component or Canvas and you want it to be traversable, you should override this method; a Canvas is not traversable by default.

public void requestFocus ()

> The requestFocus() method allows you to request that a component get the input focus. If it can't (isFocusTraversable() returns false), it won't.

public void transferFocus () ★
public void nextFocus () ☆

The `transferFocus()` method moves the focus from the current component to the next one.

`nextFocus()` is the Java 1.0 name for this method.

Miscellaneous methods

public final Object getTreeLock () ★

The `getTreeLock()` method retrieves the synchronization lock for all AWT components. Instead of using `synchronized` methods in Java 1.1, previously synchronized methods lock the tree within a `synchronized` (component.getTreeLock()) {} code block. This results in a more efficient locking mechanism to improve performance.

public String getName () ★

The `getName()` method retrieves the current name of the component. The component's name is useful for object serialization. Components are given a name by default; you can change the name by calling `setName()`.

public void setName (String name) ★

The `setName()` method changes the name of the component to `name`.

public Container getParent ()

The `getParent()` method returns the component's `Container`. The container for anything added to an applet is the applet itself, since it subclasses `Panel`. The container for the applet is the browser. In the case of Netscape Navigator versions 2.0 and 3.0, the return value would be a specific instance of the `netscape.applet.EmbeddedAppletFrame` class. If the applet is running within the *appletviewer*, the return value would be an instance of `sun.applet.AppletViewerPanel`.

public synchronized void add(PopupMenu popup) ★

The `add()` method introduced in Java 1.1 provides the ability to associate a `PopupMenu` with a `Component`. The pop-up menu can be used to provide context-sensitive menus for specific components. (On some platforms for some components, pop-up menus exist already and cannot be overridden.) Interaction with the menu is discussed in Chapter 10, *Would You Like to Choose from the Menu?*

Multiple pop-up menus can be associated with a component. To display the appropriate pop-up menu, call the pop-up menu's `show()` method.

public synchronized void remove(MenuComponent popup) ★

> The remove() method is the MenuContainer interface method to disassociate the popup from the component. (PopupMenu is a subclass of MenuComponent.) If popup is not associated with the Component, nothing happens.

protected String paramString ()

> The paramString() method is a protected method that helps build a String listing the different parameters of the Component. When the toString() method is called for a specific Component, paramString() is called for the lowest level and works its way up the inheritance hierarchy to build a complete parameter string to display. At the Component level, potentially seven (Java1.0) or eight (1.1) items are added. The first five items added are the component's name (if non-null and using Java 1.1), x and y coordinates (as returned by getLocation()), along with its width and height (as returned by getSize()). If the component is not valid, "invalid" is added next. If the component is not visible, "hidden" is added next. Finally, if the component is not enabled, "disabled" is added.

public String toString ()

> The toString() method returns a String representation of the object's values. At the Component level, the class's name is placed before the results of paramString(). This method is called automatically by the system if you try to print an object using System.out.println().

public void list ()

> The list() method prints the contents of the Component (as returned by toString()) to System.out. If c is a type of Component, the two statements System.out.println(c) and c.list() are equivalent. This method is more useful at the Container level, because it prints all the components within the container.

public void list (PrintWriter out) ★
public void list (PrintStream out)

> This version of list() prints the contents of the Component (as returned by toString()) to a different PrintStream, out.

public void list (PrintWriter out, int indentation) ★
public void list (PrintStream out, int indentation)

> These versions of list() are called by the other two. They print the component's contents (as returned by toString()) with the given indentation. This allows you to prepare nicely formatted lists of a container's contents for debugging; you could use the indentation to reflect how deeply the component is nested within the container.

5.1.2 Component Events

Chapter 4, *Events* covers event handling in detail. This section summarizes what Component does for the different event-related methods.

With the Java 1.0 event model, many methods return true to indicate that the program has handled the event and false to indicate that the event was not handled (or only partially handled); when false is returned, the system passes the event up to the parent container. Thus, it is good form to return true only when you have fully handled the event, and no further processing is necessary.

With the Java 1.1 event model, you register a listener for a specific event type. When that type of event happens, the listener is notified. Unlike the 1.0 model, you do not need to override any methods of Component to handle the event.

Controllers

The Java 1.0 event model controllers are deliverEvent(), postEvent(), and handleEvent(). With 1.1, the controller is a method named dispatchEvent().

public void deliverEvent (Event e) ☆

The deliverEvent() method delivers the 1.0 Event e to the Component in which an event occurred. Internally, this method calls postEvent(). The deliverEvent() method is an important enhancement to postEvent() for Container objects since they have to determine which component in the Container gets the event.

public boolean postEvent (Event e) ☆

The postEvent() method tells the Component to deal with 1.0 Event e. It calls handleEvent(), which returns true if some other object handled e and false if no one handles it. If handleEvent() returns false, postEvent() posts the Event to the component's parent. You can use postEvent() to hand any events you generate yourself to some other component for processing. (Creating your own events is a useful technique that few developers take advantage of.) You can also use postEvent() to reflect an event from one component into another.

public boolean handleEvent (Event e) ☆

The handleEvent() method determines the type of event e and passes it along to an appropriate method to deal with it. For example, when a mouse motion event is delivered to postEvent(), it is passed off to handleEvent(), which calls mouseMove(). As shown in the following listing, handleEvent() can be implemented as one big switch statement. Since not all event types have default event handlers, you may need to override this method. If you do, remember to

call the overridden method to ensure that the default behavior still takes
place. To do so, call super.handleEvent(event) for any event your method
does not deal with.

```
public boolean handleEvent(Event event) {
    switch (event.id) {
      case Event.MOUSE_ENTER:
        return mouseEnter (event, event.x, event.y);
      case Event.MOUSE_EXIT:
        return mouseExit (event, event.x, event.y);
      case Event.MOUSE_MOVE:
        return mouseMove (event, event.x, event.y);
      case Event.MOUSE_DOWN:
        return mouseDown (event, event.x, event.y);
      case Event.MOUSE_DRAG:
        return mouseDrag (event, event.x, event.y);
      case Event.MOUSE_UP:
        return mouseUp (event, event.x, event.y);
      case Event.KEY_PRESS:
      case Event.KEY_ACTION:
        return keyDown (event, event.key);
      case Event.KEY_RELEASE:
      case Event.KEY_ACTION_RELEASE:
        return keyUp (event, event.key);
      case Event.ACTION_EVENT:
        return action (event, event.arg);
      case Event.GOT_FOCUS:
        return gotFocus (event, event.arg);
      case Event.LOST_FOCUS:
        return lostFocus (event, event.arg);
    }
    return false;
}
```

public final void dispatchEvent(AWTEvent e) ★

The dispatchEvent() method allows you to post new AWT events to this component's listeners. dispatchEvent() tells the Component to deal with the
AWTEvent e by calling its processEvent() method. This method is similar to
Java 1.0's postEvent() method. Events delivered in this way bypass the system's
event queue. It's not clear why you would want to bypass the event queue,
except possibly to deliver some kind of high priority event.

Action

public boolean action (Event e, Object o) ☆

The action() method is called when the user performs some action in the
Component. e is the 1.0 Event instance for the specific event, while the content
of o varies depending upon the specific Component. The particular action that

triggers a call to action() depends on the Component. For example, with a TextField, action() is called when the user presses the carriage return. This method should not be called directly; to deliver any event you generate, call postEvent(), and let it decide how the event should propagate.

The default implementation of the action() method does nothing and returns false. When you override this method, return true only if you fully handle the event. Your method should always have a default case that returns false or calls super.action(e, o) to ensure that the event propagates to the component's container or component's superclass, respectively.

Keyboard

public boolean keyDown (Event e, int key) ★

The keyDown() method is called whenever the user presses a key. e is the 1.0 Event instance for the specific event, while key is the integer representation of the character pressed. The identifier for the event (e.id) could be either Event.KEY_PRESS for a regular key or Event.KEY_ACTION for an action-oriented key (e.g., arrow or function key). The default keyDown() method does nothing and returns false. If you are doing input validation, return true if the character is invalid; this keeps the event from propagating to a higher component. If you wish to alter the input (i.e., convert to uppercase), return false, but change e.key to the new character.

public boolean keyUp (Event e, int key)

The keyUp() method is called whenever the user releases a key. e is the Event instance for the specific event, while key is the integer representation of the character pressed. The identifier for the event (e.id) could be either Event.KEY_RELEASE for a regular key or Event.KEY_ACTION_RELEASE for an action-oriented key (e.g., arrow or function key). keyUp() may be used to determine how long key has been pressed. The default keyUp() method does nothing and returns false.

Mouse

NOTE   Early releases of Java (1.0.2 and earlier) propagated only mouse events from Canvas and Container objects. However, Netscape Navigator seems to have jumped the gun and corrected the situation with their 3.0 release, which is based on Java release 1.0.2.1. Until other Java releases catch up, use these events with care. For more information on platform dependencies, see Appendix C, *Platform-Specific Event Handling.*

---

public boolean mouseDown (Event e, int x, int y) ☆

The mouseDown() method is called when the user presses a mouse button over the Component. e is the Event instance for the specific event, while x and y are the coordinates where the cursor was located when the event was initiated. It is necessary to examine the modifiers field of e to determine which mouse button the user pressed. The default mouseDown() method does nothing and returns false. When you override this method, return true only if you fully handle the event. Your method should always have a default case that returns false or calls super.mouseDown(e, x, y) to ensure that the event propagates to the component's container or component's superclass, respectively.

public boolean mouseDrag (Event e, int x, int y) ☆

The mouseDrag() method is called when the user is pressing a mouse button and moves the mouse. e is the Event instance for the specific event, while x and y are the coordinates where the cursor was located when the event was initiated. mouseDrag() could be called multiple times as the mouse is moved. The default mouseDrag() method does nothing and returns false. When you override this method, return true only if you fully handle the event. Your method should always have a default case that returns false or calls super.mouseDrag(e, x, y) to ensure that the event propagates to the component's container or component's superclass, respectively.

public boolean mouseEnter (Event e, int x, int y) ☆

The mouseEnter() method is called when the mouse enters the Component. e is the Event instance for the specific event, while x and y are the coordinates where the cursor was located when the event was initiated. The default mouseEnter() method does nothing and returns false. mouseEnter() can be used for implementing balloon help. When you override this method, return true only if you fully handle the event. Your method should always have a default case that returns false or calls super.mouseEnter(e, x, y) to ensure that the event propagates to the component's container or component's superclass, respectively.

public boolean mouseExit (Event e, int x, int y) ☆

The mouseExit() method is called when the mouse exits the Component. e is the Event instance for the specific event, while x and y are the coordinates where the cursor was located when the event was initiated. The default method mouseExit() does nothing and returns false. When you override this method, return true only if you fully handle the event. Your method should always have a default case that returns false or calls super.mouseExit(e, x, y) to ensure that the event propagates to the component's container or component's superclass, respectively.

public boolean mouseMove (Event e, int x, int y) ☆

The mouseMove() method is called when the user moves the mouse without pressing a mouse button. e is the Event instance for the specific event, while x and y are the coordinates where the cursor was located when the event was initiated. mouseMove() will be called numerous times as the mouse is moved. The default mouseMove() method does nothing and returns false. When you override this method, return true only if you fully handle the event. Your method should always have a default case that returns false or calls super.mouseMove(e, x, y) to ensure that the event propagates to the component's container or component's superclass, respectively.

public boolean mouseUp (Event e, int x, int y) ☆

The mouseUp() method is called when the user releases a mouse button over the Component. e is the Event instance for the specific event, while x and y are the coordinates where the cursor was located when the event was initiated. The default mouseUp() method does nothing and returns false. When you override this method, return true only if you fully handle the event. Your method should always have a default case that returns false or calls super.mouseUp(e, x, y) to ensure that the event propagates to the component's container or component's superclass, respectively.

Focus

Focus events indicate whether a component can get keyboard input. Not all components can get focus (e.g., Label cannot). Precisely which components can get the focus is platform specific.

Ordinarily, the item with the focus has a light gray rectangle around it, though the actual display depends on the platform and the component. Figure 5-1 displays the effect of focus for buttons in Windows 95.

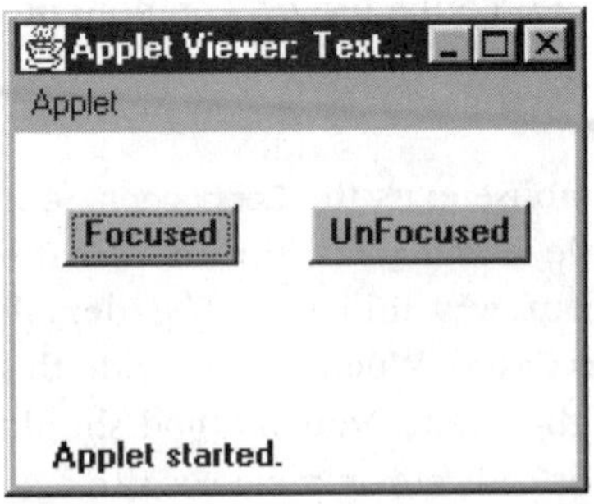

Figure 5–1: Focused and UnFocused buttons

NOTE   Early releases of Java (1.0.2 and earlier) do not propagate all focus events on all platforms. Java 1.1 seems to propagate them properly. For more information on platform dependencies, see Appendix C.

---

public boolean gotFocus (Event e, Object o) ☆

The gotFocus() method is triggered when the Component gets the input focus. e is the 1.0 Event instance for the specific event, while the content of o varies depending upon the specific Component. The default gotFocus() method does nothing and returns false. For a TextField, when the cursor becomes active, it has the focus. When you override this method, return true to indicate that you have handled the event completely or false if you want the event to propagate to the component's container.

public boolean lostFocus (Event e, Object o) ☆

The lostFocus() method is triggered when the input focus leaves the Component. e is the Event instance for the specific event, while the content of o varies depending upon the specific Component. The default lostFocus() method does nothing and returns false. When you override this method, return true to indicate that you have handled the event completely or false if you want the event to propagate to the component's container.

Listeners and 1.1 Event Handling

With the 1.1 event model, you receive events by registering event listeners, which are told when the event happens. Components don't have to receive and handle their own events; you can cleanly separate the event-handling code from the user interface itself. This section covers the methods used to add and remove event listeners, which are part of the Component class. There is a pair of methods to add and remove listeners for each event type that is appropriate for a Component: ComponentEvent, FocusEvent, KeyEvent, MouseEvent, and MouseMotionEvent. Subclasses of Component may have additional event types and therefore will have additional methods for adding and removing listeners. For example, Button, List, MenuItem, and TextField each generate action events and therefore have methods to add and remove action listeners. These additional listeners are covered with their respective components.

public void addComponentListener(ComponentListener listener) ★

The addComponentListener() method registers listener as an object interested in being notified when a ComponentEvent passes through the EventQueue with this Component as its target. When such an event occurs, a method in the ComponentListener interface is called. Multiple listeners can be registered.

public void removeComponentListener(ComponentListener listener) ★

The `removeComponentListener()` method removes `listener` as a interested listener. If `listener` is not registered, nothing happens.

public void addFocusListener(FocusListener listener) ★

The `addFocusListener()` method registers `listener` as an object interested in being notified when a `FocusEvent` passes through the `EventQueue` with this `Component` as its target. When such an event occurs, a method in the `Focus-Listener` interface is called. Multiple listeners can be registered.

public void removeFocusListener(FocusListener listener) ★

The `removeFocusListener()` method removes `listener` as a interested listener. If `listener` is not registered, nothing happens.

public void addKeyListener(KeyListener listener) ★

The `addKeyListener()` method registers `listener` as an object interested in being notified when a `KeyEvent` passes through the `EventQueue` with this `Component` as its target. When such an event occurs, a method in the `KeyListener` interface is called. Multiple listeners can be registered.

public void removeKeyListener(KeyListener listener) ★

The `removeKeyListener()` method removes `listener` as a interested listener. If listener is not registered, nothing happens.

public void addMouseListener(MouseListener listener) ★

The `addMouseListener()` method registers `listener` as an object interested in being notified when a nonmotion-oriented `MouseEvent` passes through the `EventQueue` with this `Component` as its target. When such an event occurs, a method in the `MouseListener` interface is called. Multiple listeners can be registered.

public void removeMouseListener(MouseListener listener) ★

The `removeMouseListener()` method removes `listener` as a interested listener. If listener is not registered, nothing happens.

public void addMouseMotionListener(MouseMotionListener listener) ★

The `addMouseMotionListener()` method registers `listener` as an object interested in being notified when a motion-oriented `MouseEvent` passes through the `EventQueue` with this `Component` as its target. When such an event occurs, a method in the `MouseMotionListener` interface is called. Multiple listeners can be registered.

The mouse motion–oriented events are separate from the other mouse events because of their frequency of generation. If they do not have to propagate around, resources can be saved.

public void removeMouseMotionListener(MouseMotionListener listener) ★

The `removeMouseMotionListener()` method removes `listener` as a interested listener. If `listener` is not registered, nothing happens.

Handling your own events

Under the 1.1 event model, it is still possible for components to receive their own events, simulating the old event mechanism. If you want to write components that process their own events but are also compatible with the new model, you can override `processEvent()` or one of its related methods. `processEvent()` is logically similar to `handleEvent()` in the old model; it receives all the component's events and sees that they are forwarded to the appropriate listeners. Therefore, by overriding `processEvent()`, you get access to every event the component generates. If you want only a specific type of event, you can override `processComponentEvent()`, `processKeyEvent()`, or one of the other event-specific methods.

However, there is one problem. In Java 1.1, events aren't normally generated if there are no listeners. Therefore, if you want to receive your own events without registering a listener, you should first enable event processing (by a call to `enableEvent()`) to make sure that the events you are interested in are generated.

protected final void enableEvents(long eventsToEnable) ★

The `enableEvents()` method allows you to configure a component to listen for events without having any active listeners. Under normal circumstances (i.e., if you are not subclassing a component), it is not necessary to call this method.

The `eventsToEnable` parameter contains a mask specifying which event types you want to enable. The `AWTEvent` class (covered in Chapter 4) contains constants for the following types of events:

COMPONENT_EVENT_MASK
CONTAINER_EVENT_MASK
FOCUS_EVENT_MASK
KEY_EVENT_MASK
MOUSE_EVENT_MASK
MOUSE_MOTION_EVENT_MASK
WINDOW_EVENT_MASK
ACTION_EVENT_MASK
ADJUSTMENT_EVENT_MASK
ITEM_EVENT_MASK
TEXT_EVENT_MASK

OR the masks for the events you want; for example, call
enableEvents(MOUSE_EVENT_MASK | MOUSE_MOTION_EVENT_MASK) to enable all
mouse events. Any previous event mask settings are retained.

protected final void disableEvents(long eventsToDisable) ★

The disableEvents() method allows you to stop the delivery of events when
they are no longer needed. eventsToDisable is similar to the eventsToEnable
parameter but instead contains a mask specifying which event types to stop. A
disabled event would still be delivered if someone were listening.

protected void processEvent(AWTEvent e) ★

The processEvent() method receives all AWTEvent with this Component as its
target. processEvent() then passes them along to one of the event-specific
processing methods (e.g., processKeyEvent()). When you subclass Component, overriding processEvent() allows you to process all events without providing listeners. Remember to call super.processEvent(e) last to ensure that
normal event processing still occurs; if you don't, events won't get distributed
to any registered listeners. Overriding processEvent() is like overriding the
handleEvent() method using the 1.0 event model.

protected void processComponentEvent(ComponentEvent e) ★

The processComponentEvent() method receives ComponentEvent with this
Component as its target. If any listeners are registered, they are then notified.
When you subclass Component, overriding processComponentEvent() allows
you to process component events without providing listeners. Remember to
call super.processComponentEvent(e) last to ensure that normal event processing still occurs; if you don't, events won't get distributed to any registered
listeners. Overriding processComponentEvent() is roughly similar to overriding resize(), move(), show(), and hide() to add additional functionality
when those methods are called.

protected void processFocusEvent(FocusEvent e) ★

The processFocusEvent() method receives FocusEvent with this Component as
its target. If any listeners are registered, they are then notified. When you subclass Component, overriding processFocusEvent() allows you to process the
focus event without providing listeners. Remember to call
super.processFocusEvent(e) last to ensure that normal event processing still
occurs; if you don't, events won't get distributed to any registered listeners.
Overriding processFocusEvent() is like overriding the methods gotFocus()
and lostFocus() using the 1.0 event model.

protected void processKeyEvent(KeyEvent e) ★

> The `processKeyEvent()` method receives `KeyEvent` with this `Component` as its target. If any listeners are registered, they are then notified. When you subclass `Component`, overriding `processKeyEvent()` allows you to process key events without providing listeners. Be sure to remember to call `super.processKeyEvent(e)` last to ensure that normal event processing still occurs; if you don't, events won't get distributed to any registered listeners. Overriding `processKeyEvent()` is roughly similar to overriding `keyDown()` and `keyUp()` with one method using the 1.0 event model.

protected void processMouseEvent(MouseEvent e) ★

> This `processMouseEvent()` method receives all nonmotion-oriented `MouseEvents` with this `Component` as its target. If any listeners are registered, they are then notified. When you subclass `Component`, overriding the method `processMouseEvent()` allows you to process mouse events without providing listeners. Remember to call `super.processMouseEvent(e)` last to ensure that normal event processing still occurs; if you don't, events won't get distributed to any registered listeners. Overriding the method `processMouseEvent()` is roughly similar to overriding `mouseDown()`, `mouseUp()`, `mouseEnter()`, and `mouseExit()` with one method using the 1.0 event model.

protected void processMouseMotionEvent(MouseEvent e) ★

> The `processMouseMotionEvent()` method receives all motion-oriented `MouseEvents` with this `Component` as its target. If there are any listeners registered, they are then notified. When you subclass `Component`, overriding `processMouseMotionEvent()` allows you to process mouse motion events without providing listeners. Remember to call `super.processMouseMotionEvent(e)` last to ensure that normal event processing still occurs; if you don't, events won't get distributed to any registered listeners. Overriding the method `processMouseMotionEvent()` is roughly similar to overriding `mouseMove()` and `mouseDrag()` with one method using the 1.0 event model.

5.2 *Labels*

Having covered the features of the `Component` class, we can now look at some of the simplest components. The first component introduced here is a `Label`. A label is a `Component` that displays a single line of static text.[*] It is useful for putting a title or message next to another component. The text can be centered or justified to the left or right. Labels react to all events they receive. However, they do not get any events from their peers.

---

[*] *Java in A Nutshell* (from O'Reilly & Associates) includes a multiline `Label` component.

5.2.1 Label Methods

Constants

There are three alignment specifiers for labels. The alignment tells the Label where to position its text within the space allotted. Setting an alignment for a Label might not do anything noticeable if the LayoutManager being used does not resize the Label to give it more space. With FlowLayout, the alignment is barely noticeable. See Chapter 7, *Layouts*, for more information.

public final static int LEFT

LEFT is the constant for left alignment. If no alignment is specified in the constructor, left alignment is the default.

public final static int CENTER

CENTER is the constant for center alignment.

public final static int RIGHT

RIGHT is the constant for right alignment.

Constructors

public Label ()

This constructor creates an empty Label. By default, the label's text is left justified.

public Label (String label)

This constructor creates a Label whose initial text is label. By default, the label's text is left justified.

public Label (String label, int alignment)

This constructor creates a Label whose initial text is label. The alignment of the label is alignment. If alignment is invalid (not LEFT, RIGHT, or CENTER), the constructor throws the run-time exception IllegalArgumentException.

Text

public String getText ()

The getText() method returns the current value of Label.

public void setText (String label)

The setText() method changes the text of the Label to label. If the new label is a different size from the old one, you should revalidate the display to ensure the label's entire contents will be seen.

Alignment

public int getAlignment ()

> The getAlignment() method returns the current alignment of the Label.

public void setAlignment (int alignment)

> The setAlignment() method changes the alignment of the Label to alignment. If alignment is invalid (not LEFT, RIGHT, or CENTER), setAlignment() throws the run-time exception IllegalArgumentException. Figure 5-2 shows all three alignments.

Figure 5–2: Labels with different alignments

Miscellaneous methods

public synchronized void addNotify ()

> The addNotify() method creates the Label peer. If you override this method, first call super.addNotify(), then put in your customizations. Then you will be able to do everything you need with the information about the newly created peer.

protected String paramString ()

> The paramString() method overrides Component's paramString() method. It is a protected method that calls the overridden paramString() to build a String from the different parameters of the Component. When the method paramString() is called for a Label, the alignment and label's text are added. Thus, for the Label created by the constructor new Label ("ZapfDingbats", Label.RIGHT), the results displayed from a call to toString() would be:

```
java.awt.Label[0,0,0x0,invalid,align=right,label=ZapfDingbats]
```

5.2.2 Label Events

The Label component can react to any event it receives, though the Label peer normally does not send any. However, there is nothing to stop you from posting an event yourself.

5.3 Buttons

The Button component provides one of the most frequently used objects in graphical applications. When the user selects a button, it signals the program that something needs to be done by sending an action event. The program responds in its handleEvent() method (for Java 1.0) or its actionPerformed() method (defined by Java 1.1's ActionListener interface). Next to Label, which does nothing, Button is the simplest component to understand. Because it is so simple, we will use a lot of buttons in our examples for the next few chapters.

5.3.1 Button Methods

Constructors

public Button ()

> This constructor creates an empty Button. You can set the label later with setLabel().

public Button (String label)

> This constructor creates a Button whose initial text is label.

Button Labels

public String getLabel ()

> The getLabel() method retrieves the current text of the label on the Button and returns it as a String.

public synchronized void setLabel (String label)

> The setLabel() method changes the text of the label on the Button to label. If the new text is a different size from the old, it is necessary to revalidate the screen to ensure that the button size is correct.

Action Commands

With Java 1.1, every button can have two names. One is what the user sees (the button's label); the other is what the programmer sees and is called the button's *action command*. Distinguishing between the label and the action command is a major help to internationalization. The label can be localized for the user's environment.

However, this means that labels can vary at run-time and are therefore useless for comparisons within the program. For example, you can't test whether the user pushed the Yes button if that button might read Oui or Ja, depending on some run-time environment setting. To give the programmer something reliable for comparisons, Java 1.1 introduces the action command. The action command for our button might be Yes, regardless of the button's actual label.

By default, the action command is equivalent to the button's label. Java 1.0 code, which only relies on the label, will continue to work. Furthermore, you can continue to write in the Java 1.0 style as long as you're sure that your program will never have to account for other languages. These days, that's a bad bet. Even if you aren't implementing multiple locales now, get in the habit of testing a button's action command rather than its label; you will have less work to do when internationalization does become an issue.

public String getActionCommand () ★

> The getActionCommand() method returns the button's current action command. If no action command was explicitly set, this method returns the label.

public void setActionCommand (String command) ★

> The setActionCommand() method changes the button's action command to command.

Miscellaneous methods

public synchronized void addNotify ()

> The addNotify() method creates the Button peer. If you override this method, first call super.addNotify(), then add your customizations. Then you can do everything you need with the information about the newly created peer.

protected String paramString ()

> The paramString() method overrides the component's paramString() method. It is a protected method that calls the overridden paramString() to build a String from the different parameters of the Component. When the method paramString() is called for a Button, the button's label is added. Thus, for the Button created by the constructor new Button ("ZapfDingbats"), the results displayed from a call to toString() could be:

```
java.awt.Button[77,5,91x21,label=ZapfDingbats]
```

5.3.2 Button Events

With the 1.0 event model, Button components generate an ACTION_EVENT when the user selects the button.

With the version 1.1 event model, you register an ActionListener with the method addActionListener(). When the user selects the Button, the method ActionListener.actionPerformed() is called through the protected Button.processActionEvent() method. Key, mouse, and focus listeners are registered through the Component methods of addKeyListener(), addMouseListener(), or addMouseMotionListener(), and addFocusListener(), respectively.

Action

public boolean action (Event e, Object o)

The action() method for a Button is called when the user presses and releases the button. e is the Event instance for the specific event, while o is the button's label. The default implementation of action() does nothing and returns false, passing the event to the button's container for processing. For a button to do something useful, you should override either this method or the container's action() method. Example 5-1 is a simple applet called Button-Test that demonstrates the first approach; it creates a Button subclass called TheButton, which overrides action(). This simple subclass doesn't do much; it just labels the button and prints a message when the button is pressed. Figure 5-3 shows what ButtonTest looks like.

Example 5–1: Button Event Handling

```
import java.awt.*;
import java.applet.*;

class TheButton extends Button {
    TheButton (String s) {
        super (s);
    }
    public boolean action (Event e, Object o) {
        if ("One".equals(o)) {
            System.out.println ("Do something for One");
        } else if ("Two".equals(o)) {
            System.out.println ("Ignore Two");
        } else if ("Three".equals(o)) {
            System.out.println ("Reverse Three");
        } else if ("Four".equals(o)) {
            System.out.println ("Four is the one");
        } else {
            return false;
        }
        return true;
    }
}
```

Example 5–1: Button Event Handling (continued)

```
      }
    public class ButtonTest extends Applet {
      public void init () {
          add (new TheButton ("One"));
          add (new TheButton ("Two"));
          add (new TheButton ("Three"));
          add (new TheButton ("Four"));
      }
    }
```

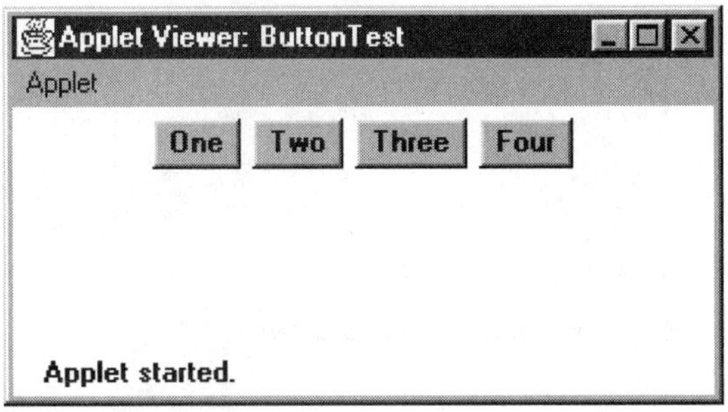

Figure 5–3: The ButtonTest applet

Keyboard

Buttons are able to capture keyboard-related events once the button has the input focus. In order to give a Button the input focus without triggering the action event, call requestFocus(). The button also gets the focus if the user selects it and drags the mouse off of it without releasing the mouse.

public boolean keyDown (Event e, int key) ☆

The keyDown() method is called whenever the user presses a key while the Button has the input focus. e is the Event instance for the specific event, while key is the integer representation of the character pressed. The identifier for the event (e.id) could be either Event.KEY_PRESS for a regular key or Event.KEY_ACTION for an action-oriented key (i.e., an arrow or a function key). There is no visible indication that the user has pressed a key over the button.

public boolean keyUp (Event e, int key) ☆

The keyUp() method is called whenever the user releases a key while the Button has the input focus. e is the Event instance for the specific event, while key is the integer representation of the character pressed. The identifier for the event (e.id) could be either Event.KEY_RELEASE for a regular key or Event.KEY_ACTION_RELEASE for an action-oriented key (i.e., an arrow or a function key). keyUp() may be used to determine how long key has been pressed.

Listeners and 1.1 event handling

With the 1.1 event model, you register listeners, which are told when the event happens.

public void addActionListener(ActionListener listener) ★

The `addActionListener()` method registers `listener` as an object interested in receiving notifications when an `ActionEvent` passes through the `EventQueue` with this `Button` as its target. The `listener.actionPerformed()` method is called when these events occur. Multiple listeners can be registered. The following code demonstrates how to use an `ActionListener` to handle the events that occur when the user selects a button. This applet has the same display as the previous one, shown in Figure 5-3.

```
// Java 1.1 only
import java.awt.*;
import java.applet.*;
import java.awt.event.*;

public class ButtonTest11 extends Applet implements ActionListener {
    Button b;
    public void init () {
        add (b = new Button ("One"));
        b.addActionListener (this);
        add (b = new Button ("Two"));
        b.addActionListener (this);
        add (b = new Button ("Three"));
        b.addActionListener (this);
        add (b = new Button ("Four"));
        b.addActionListener (this);
    }
    public void actionPerformed (ActionEvent e) {
        String s = e.getActionCommand();
        if ("One".equals(s)) {
            System.out.println ("Do something for One");
        } else if ("Two".equals(s)) {
            System.out.println ("Ignore Two");
        } else if ("Three".equals(s)) {
            System.out.println ("Reverse Three");
        } else if ("Four".equals(s)) {
            System.out.println ("Four is the one");
        }
    }
}
```

public void removeActionListener(ActionListener listener) ★

The `removeActionListener()` method removes `listener` as an interested listener. If `listener` is not registered, nothing happens.

protected void processEvent(AWTEvent e) ★

> The `processEvent()` method receives `AWTEvent` with this `Button` as its target. `processEvent()` then passes them along to any listeners for processing. When you subclass `Button`, overriding `processEvent()` allows you to process all events yourself, before sending them to any listeners. In a way, overriding `processEvent()` is like overriding `handleEvent()` using the 1.0 event model.
>
> If you override `processEvent()`, remember to call `super.processEvent(e)` last to ensure that regular event processing can occur. If you want to process your own events, it's a good idea to call `enableEvents()` (inherited from `Component`) to ensure that events are delivered even in the absence of registered listeners.

protected void processActionEvent(ActionEvent e) ★

> The `processActionEvent()` method receives `ActionEvent` with this `Button` as its target. `processActionEvent()` then passes them along to any listeners for processing. When you subclass `Button`, overriding `processActionEvent()` allows you to process all action events yourself, before sending them to any listeners. In a way, overriding `processActionEvent()` is like overriding `action()` using the 1.0 event model.
>
> If you override the `processActionEvent()` method, you must remember to call `super.processActionEvent(e)` last to ensure that regular event processing can occur. If you want to process your own events, it's a good idea to call `enableEvents()` (inherited from `Component`) to ensure that events are delivered even in the absence of registered listeners.

5.4 A Simple Calculator

It is always helpful to see complete and somewhat useful examples after learning something new. Example 5-2 shows a working calculator that performs floating point addition, subtraction, multiplication, and division. Figure 5-4 shows the calculator in operation. The button in the lower left corner is a decimal point. This applet uses a number of classes that will be discussed later in the book (most notably, some layout managers and a `Panel`); try to ignore them for now. Focus on the `action()` and `compute()` methods; `action()` figures out which button was pressed, converting it to a digit (0–9 plus the decimal point) or an operator (=, +, −, *, /). As you build a number, it is displayed in the label `lab`, which conveniently serves to store the number in string form. The `compute()` method reads the label's text, converts it to a floating point number, does the computation, and displays the result in the label. The `addButtons()` method is a helper method to create a group of `Button` objects at one time.

Example 5–2: Calculator Source Code

```
import java.awt.*;
import java.applet.*;

public class JavaCalc extends Applet {
    Label lab;
    boolean firstDigit = true;
    float savedValue = 0.0f;      // Initial value
    String operator = "=";  // Initial operator
    public void addButtons (Panel p, String labels) {
        int count = labels.length();
        for (int i=0;i<count;i++)
            p.add (new Button (labels.substring(i,i+1)));
    }
    public void init () {
        setLayout (new BorderLayout());
        add ("North", lab = new Label ("0", Label.RIGHT));
        Panel p = new Panel();
        p.setLayout (new GridLayout (4, 4));
        addButtons (p, "789/");
        addButtons (p, "456*");
        addButtons (p, "123-");
        addButtons (p, ".0=+");
        add ("Center", p);
    }
    public boolean action (Event e, Object o) {
        if (e.target instanceof Button) {
            String s = (String)o;
            if ("0123456789.".indexOf (s) != -1) { // isDigit
                if (firstDigit) {
                    firstDigit = false;
                    lab.setText (s);
                } else {
                    lab.setText (lab.getText() + s);
                }
            } else { // isOperator
                if (!firstDigit) {
                    compute (lab.getText());
                    firstDigit = true;
                }
                operator = s;
            }
            return true;
        }
        return false;
    }
    public void compute (String s) {
        float sValue = new Float (s).floatValue();
        char c = operator.charAt (0);
        switch (c) {
            case '=':   savedValue  = sValue;
                        break;
            case '+':   savedValue += sValue;
```

Example 5–2: Calculator Source Code (continued)

```
                              break;
                  case '-':   savedValue -= sValue;
                              break;
                  case '*':   savedValue *= sValue;
                              break;
                  case '/':   savedValue /= sValue;
                              break;
            }
            lab.setText (String.valueOf(savedValue));
      }
   }
```

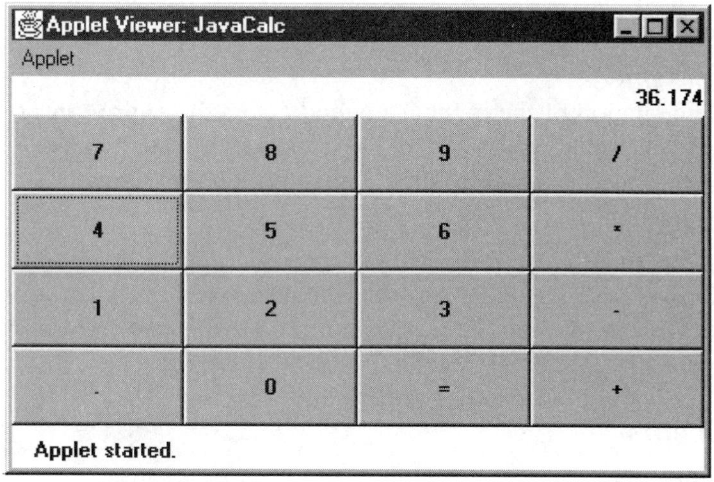

Figure 5–4: Calculator applet

5.5 Canvas

A Canvas is a class just waiting to be subclassed. Through Canvas, you can create additional AWT objects that are not provided by the base classes. Canvas is also useful as a drawing area, particularly when additional components are on the screen. It is tempting to draw directly onto a Container, but this often isn't a good idea. Anything you draw might disappear underneath the components you add to the container. When you are drawing on a container, you are essentially drawing on the background. The container's layout manager doesn't know anything about what you have drawn and won't arrange components with your artwork in mind. To be safe, do your drawing onto a Canvas and place that Canvas in a Container.

5.5.1 Canvas Methods

Constructors

public Canvas () ★

> The constructor creates a new Canvas with no default size. If you place the canvas in a container, the container's layout manager sizes the canvas for you. If you aren't placing the canvas in a container, call setBounds() to specify the canvas's size.
>
> Java 1.0 used the default constructor for Canvas; there was no explicit constructor.

Miscellaneous methods

public void paint (Graphics g) ★

> The default implementation of the paint() method colors the entire Canvas with the current background color. When you subclass this method, your paint() method needs to draw whatever should be shown on the canvas.

public synchronized void addNotify ()

> The addNotify() method creates the Canvas peer. If you override this method, first call super.addNotify(), then add your customizations. Then you can do everything you need with the information about the newly created peer.

5.5.2 Canvas Events

The Canvas peer passes all events to you, which is why it's well suited to creating your own components.

5.6 Creating Your Own Component

If you find that no AWT component satisfies your needs, you can create your own. This is usually done either by extending an existing component or by starting from scratch. When extending an existing component, you start with the base functionality of an existing object and add to it. The users will not see anything new or different about the object until they start to interact with it, since it is not a new component. For example, a TextField could be subclassed to convert all letters input to uppercase. On the other hand, if you create a new component from scratch, it will appear the same on all platforms (regardless of what the platform's native components look like), and you have to make sure the user can fairly easily figure out how to work with it. Example 5-3 shows how to create your own Component by creating a Label that displays vertically, as opposed to the standard Label Component that displays horizontally. The whole process is fairly easy.

The third possibility for creating your own components involves adding functionality to containers. This is fairly easy to do and can be useful if you are constantly grouping components together. For example, if you are always adding a TextField or Label to go with a Scrollbar to display the value, do it once, and call it something meaningful like LabeledScrollbarPanel. Then whenever you need it again, reuse your LabeledScrollbarPanel. Think about reusability whenever you can.

With Java 1.1, the colors for these new components should be set to color values consistent to the user's platform. This is done through color constants provided in the SystemColor class introduced in Chapter 2.

5.6.1 VerticalLabel

When you create new components, they must meet three requirements:

- In Java 1.0, you must extend a subclass of Component, usually Canvas. In Java 1.1, you can extend Component itself, creating a lightweight component. In many cases, this alternative is more efficient.

- You must provide a constructor for the new component so that you can create new instances of it; if you really don't need a constructor, you can use the default constructor that you inherit from Canvas or Component.

- You must provide a way to draw the object on the screen by overriding the paint() method.

If initializing the component requires information about display characteristics (for example, you need to know the default Font), you must wait until the object is displayed on the screen before you initialize it. This is done by overriding the addNotify() method. First, call super.addNotify() to create the peer; you can now ask for platform-dependent information and initialize your component accordingly. Remember to override getPreferredSize() and getMinimumSize() (the Java 1.0 names are preferredSize() and minimumSize()) to return the proper dimensions for the new component, so that layout management works properly. There can be other support methods, depending upon the requirements of the object. For example, it is helpful, but not required, to provide a toString() or paramString() method.

Creating a new component sounds a lot harder than it is. Example 5-3 contains the source for a new component called VerticalLabel. It displays a label that reads from top to bottom, instead of from left to right, and can be configured to display its text right or left justified or centered. Figure 5-5 displays the new component VerticalLabel in action.

Example 5–3: Source for VerticalLabel Component

```java
import java.awt.*;

public class VerticalLabel extends Canvas {
    public static final int LEFT = 0;
    public static final int CENTER = 1;
    public static final int RIGHT = 2;
    private String text;
    private int     vgap;
    private int     alignment;
    Dimension       mySize;
    int             textLength;
    char            chars[];
    // constructors
    public VerticalLabel () {
        this (null, 0, CENTER);
    }
    public VerticalLabel (String text) {
        this (text, 0, CENTER);
    }
    public VerticalLabel (String text, int vgap, int alignment) {
        this.text = text;
        this.vgap = vgap;
        this.alignment = alignment;
    }
    void init () {
        textLength = text.length();
        chars = new char[textLength];
        text.getChars (0, textLength, chars, 0);
        Font f = getFont();
        FontMetrics fm = getFontMetrics (f);
        mySize = new Dimension(0,0);
        mySize.height = (fm.getHeight() * textLength) + (vgap * 2);
        for (int i=0; i < textLength; i++) {
            mySize.width = Math.max (mySize.width, fm.charsWidth(chars, i, 1));
        }
    }
    public int getAlignment () {
        return alignment;
    }
    public void addNotify () {
        super.addNotify();
        init();  // Component must be visible for init to work
    }
    public void setText (String text)    {this.text = text; init();}
    public String getText ()             {return text; }
    public void setVgap (int vgap)       {this.vgap = vgap; init();}
    public int getVgap ()                {return vgap; }
    public Dimension preferredSize ()    {return mySize; }
    public Dimension minimumSize ()      {return mySize; }
    public void paint (Graphics g) {
        int x,y;
        int xPositions[];
```

Example 5–3: Source for VerticalLabel Component (continued)

```
        int yPositions[];
// Must redo this each time since font/screen area might change
// Use actual width for alignment
        Font f = getFont();
        FontMetrics fm = getFontMetrics (f);
        xPositions = new int[textLength];
        for (int i=0; i < textLength; i++) {
            if (alignment == RIGHT) {
                xPositions[i] = size().width - fm.charWidth (chars[i]);
            } else if (alignment == LEFT) {
                xPositions[i] = 0;
            } else {// CENTER
                xPositions[i] = (size().width - fm.charWidth (chars[i])) / 2;
            }
        }
        yPositions = new int[textLength];
        for (int i=0; i < textLength; i++) {
            yPositions[i] = (fm.getHeight() * (i+1)) + vgap;
        }
        for (int i = 0; i < textLength; i++) {
            x = xPositions[i];
            y = yPositions[i];
            g.drawChars (chars, i, 1, x, y);
        }
    }
    protected String paramString () {
        String str=",align=";
        switch (alignment) {
            case LEFT:    str += "left"; break;
            case CENTER:  str += "center"; break;
            case RIGHT:   str += "right"; break;
        }
        if (vgap!=0) str+= ",vgap=" + vgap;
        return super.paramString() + str + ",label=" + text;
    }
}
```

The following code is a simple applet using the VerticalLabel. It creates five instances of VerticalLabel within a BorderLayout panel, with gaps (see Chapter 7 for more on BorderLayout). The top and bottom labels are justified to the left and right, respectively, to demonstrate justification.

```
import java.awt.*;
import java.applet.*;
public class vlabels extends Applet {
    public void init () {
        setLayout (new BorderLayout (10, 10));
        setFont (new Font ("TimesRoman", Font.BOLD, 12));
        add ("North",  new VerticalLabel ("One", 10, VerticalLabel.LEFT));
        add ("South",  new VerticalLabel ("Two", 10, VerticalLabel.RIGHT));
        add ("West",   new VerticalLabel ("Three"));
        add ("East",   new VerticalLabel ("Four"));
```

Figure 5–5: Using VerticalLabel

```
        add ("Center", new VerticalLabel ("Five"));
        resize (preferredSize());
    }
}
```

5.6.2 Lightweight VerticalLabel

The VerticalLabel in Example 5-3 works in both Java 1.0 and 1.1 but is relatively inefficient. When you create one, the system must create a Canvas and the peer of the Canvas. This work doesn't gain you anything; since this is a new component, it doesn't have to match the native appearance of any other component.

In Java 1.1, there's a way to avoid the overhead if you are creating a component that doesn't have to match a native object. This is called a *lightweight component*. To create one, you just subclass Component itself. To make a lightweight version of our VerticalLabel, we have to change only one line of code.

```
// Java 1.1 only
public class VerticalLabel extends Component
```

Everything else remains unchanged.

5.7 Cursor

Introduced in Java 1.1, the Cursor class provides the different cursors that can be associated with a Component. Previously, cursors could only be associated with a whole Frame. Now any component can use fancy cursors when the user is interacting with the system.

To change the cursor, a component calls its setCursor() method; its argument is a Cursor object, which is defined by this class.

NOTE There is still no way to assign a user-defined cursor to a Component. You are restricted to the 14 predefined cursors.

5.7.1 Cursor Constants

The following is a list of Cursor constants. The cursors corresponding to the constants are shown in Figure 5-6.

public final static int DEFAULT_CURSOR
public final static int CROSSHAIR_CURSOR
public final static int TEXT_CURSOR
public final static int WAIT_CURSOR
public final static int HAND_CURSOR
public final static int MOVE_CURSOR
public final static int N_RESIZE_CURSOR
public final static int S_RESIZE_CURSOR
public final static int E_RESIZE_CURSOR
public final static int W_RESIZE_CURSOR
public final static int NE_RESIZE_CURSOR
public final static int NW_RESIZE_CURSOR
public final static int SE_RESIZE_CURSOR
public final static int SW_RESIZE_CURSOR

5.7.2 Cursor Methods

public Cursor (int type) ★

> The sole constructor creates a Cursor of the specified type. type must be one of the Cursor class constants. If type is not one of the class constants, the constructor throws the run-time exception IllegalArgumentException.

> This constructor exists primarily to support object serialization; you don't need to call it in your code. It is more efficient to call getPredefinedCursor(), discussed later in this section.

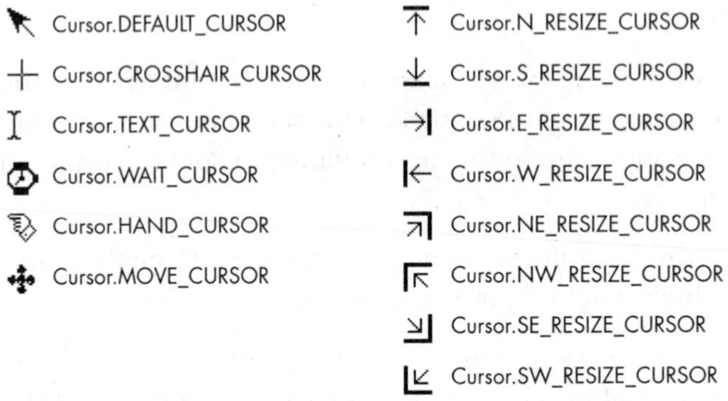

Cursor.DEFAULT_CURSOR   Cursor.N_RESIZE_CURSOR

Cursor.CROSSHAIR_CURSOR   Cursor.S_RESIZE_CURSOR

Cursor.TEXT_CURSOR   Cursor.E_RESIZE_CURSOR

Cursor.WAIT_CURSOR   Cursor.W_RESIZE_CURSOR

Cursor.HAND_CURSOR   Cursor.NE_RESIZE_CURSOR

Cursor.MOVE_CURSOR   Cursor.NW_RESIZE_CURSOR

                               Cursor.SE_RESIZE_CURSOR

                               Cursor.SW_RESIZE_CURSOR

Figure 5–6: Standard Java cursors

Miscellaneous methods

public int getType() ★

The getType() method returns the cursor type. The value returned is one of the class constants.

static public Cursor getPredefinedCursor(int type) ★

The getPredefinedCursor() method returns the predefined Cursor of the given type. If type is not one of the class constants, this method throws the run-time exception IllegalArgumentException. This method checks what Cursor objects already exist and gives you a reference to a preexisting Cursor if it can find one with the appropriate type. Otherwise, it creates a new Cursor for you. This is more efficient than calling the Cursor constructor whenever you need one.

static public Cursor getDefaultCursor() ★

The getDefaultCursor() method returns the predefined Cursor for the DEFAULT_CURSOR type.

6

Containers

This chapter covers a special type of Component called Container. A Container is a subclass of Component that can contain other components, including other containers. Container allows you to create groupings of objects on the screen. This chapter covers the methods in the Container class and its subclasses: Panel, Window, Frame, Dialog, and FileDialog. It also covers the Insets class, which provides an internal border area for the Container classes.

Every container has a layout associated with it that controls how the container organizes the components in it. The layouts are described in Chapter 7, *Layouts*.

Java 1.1 introduces a special Container called ScrollPane. Because of the similarities between scrolling and ScrollPane, the new ScrollPane container is covered with the Scrollbar class in Chapter 11, *Scrolling*.

6.1 Container

Container is an abstract class that serves as a general purpose holder of other Component objects. The Container class holds the methods for grouping the components together, laying out the components inside it, and dealing with events occurring within it. Because Container is an abstract class, you never see a pure Container object; you only see subclasses that add specific behaviors to a generic container.

6.1.1 Container Methods

Constructors

The abstract Container class contains a single constructor to be called by its children. Prior to Java 1.1, the constructor was package private.

protected Container() ★

> The constructor for Container creates a new component without a native peer. Since you no longer have a native peer, you must rely on your container to provide a display area. This allows you to create containers that require fewer system resources. For example, if you are creating panels purely for layout management, you might consider creating a LightweightPanel class to let you assign a layout manager to a component group. Using LightweightPanel will speed things up since events do not have to propagate through the panel and you do not have to get a peer from the native environment. The following code creates the LightweightPanel class:

```
import java.awt.*;
public class LightweightPanel extends Container {
    LightweightPanel () {}
    LightweightPanel (LayoutManager lm) {
        setLayout(lm);
    }
}
```

Grouping

A Container holds a set of objects within itself. This set of methods describes how to examine and add components to the set.

public int getComponentCount () ★
public int countComponents () ☆

> The getComponentCount() method returns the number of components within the container at this level. getComponentCount() does not count components in any child Container (i.e., containers within the current container).
>
> countComponents() is the Java 1.0 name for this method.

public Component getComponent (int position)

> The getComponent() method returns the component at the specific position within it. If position is invalid, this method throws the run-time exception ArrayIndexOutOfBoundsException.

public Component[] getComponents ()

getComponents() returns an array of all the components held within the container. Since these are references to the actual objects on the screen, any changes made to the components returned will be reflected on the display.

public Component add (Component component, int position)

The add() method adds component to the container at position. If position is -1, add() inserts component as the last object within the container. What the container does with position depends upon the LayoutManager of the container. If position is invalid, the add() method throws the run-time exception IllegalArgumentException. If you try to add component's container to itself (anywhere in the containment tree), this method throws an IllegalArgumentException. In Java 1.1, if you try to add a Window to a container, add() throws the run-time exception IllegalArgumentException. If you try to add component to a container that already contains it, the container is removed and re-added, probably at a different position.

Assuming that nothing goes wrong, the parent of component is set to the container, and the container is invalidated. add() returns the component just added.

Calling this method generates a ContainerEvent with the id COMPONENT_ADDED.

public Component add (Component component)

The add() method adds component to the container as the last object within the container. This is done by calling the earlier version of add() with a position of -1. If you try to add component's container to itself (anywhere in the containment tree), this method throws the run-time exception IllegalArgumentException. In Java 1.1, if you try to add a Window to a container, add() throws the run-time exception IllegalArgumentException.

Calling this method generates a ContainerEvent with the id COMPONENT_ADDED.

public void add (Component component, Object constraints) ★
public Component add (String name, Component component)

This next version of add() is necessary for layouts that require additional information in order to place components. The additional information is provided by the constraints parameter. This version of the add() method calls the addLayoutComponent() method of the LayoutManager. What the container does with constraints depends upon the actual LayoutManager. It can be used for naming containers within a CardLayout, specifying a screen area for BorderLayout, or providing a set of GridBagConstraints for a GridBagLayout. In the event that this add() is called and the current LayoutManager does not take advantage of constraints, component is added at the end with a position of -1. If you try to add component's container to itself (anywhere in the containment tree), this method throws the run-time exception IllegalArgumentException. In Java 1.1, if you try to add a Window to a container, add() throws the run-time exception IllegalArgumentException.

The add(String, Component) method was changed to add(component, object) in Java 1.1 to accommodate the LayoutManager2 interface (discussed in Chapter 7) and to provide greater flexibility. In all cases, you can just flip the parameters to bring the code up to 1.1 specs. The string used as an identifier in Java 1.0 is just treated as a particular kind of constraint.

Calling this method generates a ContainerEvent with the id COMPONENT_ADDED.

public void add (Component component, Object constraints, int index) ★

This final version of add() is necessary for layouts that require an index and need additional information to place components. The additional information is provided by the constraints parameter. This version of add() also calls the addLayoutComponent() method of the LayoutManager. component is added with a position of index. If you try to add component's container to itself (anywhere in the containment tree), this method throws the run-time exception IllegalArgumentException. In Java 1.1, if you try to add a Window to a Container, add() throws the run-time exception IllegalArgumentException.

Some layout managers ignore any index. For example, if you call add(aButton, BorderLayout.NORTH, 3) to add a Button to a BorderLayout panel, the Button appears in the north region of the layout, no matter what the index.

Calling this method generates a ContainerEvent with the id COMPONENT_ADDED.

protected void addImpl(Component comp, Object constraints, int index) ★

The protected addImpl() method is the helper method that all the others call. It deals with synchronization and enforces all the restrictions on adding components to containers.

The addImpl() method tracks the container's components in an internal list. The index with which each component is added determines its position in the list. The lower the component's index, the higher it appears in the stacking order. In turn, the stacking order determines how components are displayed when sufficient space isn't available to display all of them. Components that are added without indices are placed at the end of the list (i.e., at the end of the stacking order) and therefore displayed behind other components. If all components are added without indices, the first component added to the container is first in the stacking order and therefore displayed in front.

You could override addImpl() to track when components are added to a container. However, the proper way to find out when components are added is to register a ContainerListener and watch for the COMPONENT_ADDED and the COMPONENT_REMOVED events.

public void remove (int index) ★

The remove() method deletes the component at position index from the container. If index is invalid, the remove() method throws the run-time exception IllegalArgumentException. This method calls the removeLayoutComponent() method of the container's LayoutManager.

removeAll() generates a ContainerEvent with the id COMPONENT_REMOVED.

public void remove (Component component)

The remove() method deletes component from the container, if the container directly contains component. remove() does not look through nested containers trying to find component. This method calls the removeLayoutComponent() method of the container's LayoutManager.

When you call this method, it generates a ContainerEvent with the id COMPONENT_REMOVED.

public void removeAll ()

The removeAll() method removes all components from the container. This is done by looping through all the components, setting each component's parent to null, setting the container's reference to the component to null, and invalidating the container.

When you call this method, it generates a ContainerEvent with the id COMPONENT_REMOVED for each component removed.

public boolean isAncestorOf(Component component) ★

The isAncestorOf() method checks to see if component is a parent (or grandparent or great grandparent) of this container. It could be used as a helper method for addImpl() but is not. If component is an ancestor of the container, isAncestorOf() returns true; otherwise, it returns false.

Layout and sizing

Every container has a LayoutManager. The LayoutManager is responsible for positioning the components inside the container. The Container methods listed here are used in sizing the objects within the container and specifying a layout.

public LayoutManager getLayout ()

The getLayout() method returns the container's current LayoutManager.

public void setLayout (LayoutManager manager)

> The `setLayout()` method changes the container's `LayoutManager` to `manager` and invalidates the container. This causes the components contained inside to be repositioned based upon `manager`'s rules. If `manager` is `null`, there is no layout manager, and you are responsible for controlling the size and position of all the components within the container yourself.

public Dimension getPreferredSize () ★
public Dimension preferredSize () ☆

> The `getPreferredSize()` method returns the `Dimension` (width and height) for the preferred size of the components within the container. The container determines its preferred size by calling the `preferredLayoutSize()` method of the current `LayoutManager`, which says how much space the layout manager needs to arrange the components. If you override this method, you are overriding the default preferred size.
>
> `preferredSize()` is the Java 1.0 name for this method.

public Dimension getMinimumSize () ★
public Dimension minimumSize () ☆

> The `getMinimumSize()` method returns the minimum `Dimension` (width and height) for the size of the components within the container. This container determines its minimum size by calling the `minimumLayoutSize()` method of the current `LayoutManager`, which computes the minimum amount of space the layout manager needs to arrange the components. It is possible for `get-MinimumSize()` and `getPreferredSize()` to return the same dimensions. There is no guarantee that you will get this amount of space for the layout.
>
> `minimumSize()` is the Java 1.0 name for this method.

public Dimension getMaximumSize () ★

> The `getMaximumSize()` method returns the maximum `Dimension` (width and height) for the size of the components within the container. This container determines its maximum size by calling the `maximumLayoutSize()` method of the current `LayoutManager2`, which computes the maximum amount of space the layout manager needs to arrange the components. If the layout manager is not an instance of `LayoutManager2`, this method calls the `getMaximumSize()` method of the `Component`, which returns `Integer.MAX_VALUE` for both dimensions. None of the `java.awt` layout managers use the concept of maximum size yet.

public float getAlignmentX () ★

> The getAlignmentX() method returns the alignment of the components within the container along the x axis. This container determines its alignment by calling the current LayoutManager2's getLayoutAlignmentX() method, which computes it based upon its children. The return value is between 0.0 and 1.0. Values nearer 0 indicate that the component should be placed closer to the left edge of the area available. Values nearer 1 indicate that the component should be placed closer to the right. The value 0.5 means the component should be centered. If the layout manager is not an instance of LayoutManager2, this method calls Component's getAlignmentX() method, which returns the constant Component.CENTER_ALIGNMENT. None of the java.awt layout managers use the concept of alignment yet.

public float getAlignmentY () ★

> The getAlignmentY() method returns the alignment of the components within the container along the y axis. This container determines its alignment by calling the current LayoutManager2's getLayoutAlignmentY() method, which computes it based upon its children. The return value is between 0.0 and 1.0. Values nearer 0 indicate that the component should be placed closer to the top of the area available. Values nearer 1 indicate that the component should be placed closer to the bottom. The value 0.5 means the component should be centered. If the layout manager is not an instance of LayoutManager2, this method calls Component's getAlignmentY() method, which returns the constant Component.CENTER_ALIGNMENT. None of the java.awt layout managers use the concept of alignment yet.

public void doLayout () ★
public void layout () ☆

> The doLayout() method of Container instructs the LayoutManager to lay out the container. This is done by calling the layoutContainer() method of the current LayoutManager.

> layout() is the Java 1.0 name for this method.

public void validate ()

> The validate() method sets the container's valid state to true and recursively validates all of its children. If a child is a Container, its children are in turn validated. Some components are not completely initialized until they are validated. For example, you cannot ask a Button for its display dimensions or position until it is validated.

protected void validateTree () ★

    The validateTree() method is a helper for validate() that does all the work.

public void invalidate () ★

    The invalidate() method invalidates the container and recursively invalidates the children. If the layout manager is an instance of LayoutManager2, its invalidateLayout() method is called to invalidate any cached values.

Event delivery

The event model for Java is described in Chapter 4, *Events*. These methods help in the handling of the various system events at the container level.

public void deliverEvent (Event e) ☆

    The deliverEvent() method is called by the system when the Java 1.0 Event e happens. deliverEvent() tries to locate a component contained in the container that should receive it. If one is found, the x and y coordinates of e are translated for the new target, and Event e is delivered to this by calling its deliverEvent(). If getComponentAt() fails to find an appropriate target, the event is just posted to the container with postEvent().

public Component getComponentAt (int x, int y) ★
public Component locate (int x, int y) ☆

    The container's getComponentAt() method calls each component's contains() method to see if the x and y coordinates are within it. If they are, that component is returned. If the coordinates are not in any child component of this container, the container is returned. It is possible for getComponentAt() to return null if the x and y coordinates are not within the container. The method getComponentAt() can return another Container or a lightweight component.

    locate()is the Java 1.0 name for this method.

public Component getComponentAt (Point p) ★

    This getComponentAt() method is identical to the previous method, with the exception that the location is passed as a single point, rather than as separate x and y coordinates.

Listeners and 1.1 event handling

With the 1.1 event model, you register listeners, which are told when events occur. Container events occur when a component is added or removed.

public synchronized void addContainerListener(ContainerListener listener) ★

    The addContainerListener() method registers listener as an object interested in receiving notifications when an ContainerEvent passes through the EventQueue with this Container as its target. The listener.componentAdded() or listener.componentRemoved() method is called when these events occur. Multiple listeners can be registered. The following code demonstrates how to use a ContainerListener to register action listeners for all buttons added to an applet. It is similar to the ButtonTest11 example in Section 5.3.2. The trick that makes this code work is the call to enableEvents() in init(). This method makes sure that container events are delivered in the absence of listeners. In this applet, we know there won't be any container listeners, so we must enable container events explicitly before adding any components.

```
// Java 1.1 only
import java.awt.*;
import java.applet.*;
import java.awt.event.*;
public class NewButtonTest11 extends Applet implements ActionListener {
        Button b;
        public void init () {
                enableEvents (AWTEvent.CONTAINER_EVENT_MASK);
                add (b = new Button ("One"));
                add (b = new Button ("Two"));
                add (b = new Button ("Three"));
                add (b = new Button ("Four"));
        }
        protected void processContainerEvent (ContainerEvent e) {
                if (e.getID() == ContainerEvent.COMPONENT_ADDED) {
                        if (e.getChild() instanceof Button) {
                                Button b = (Button)e.getChild();
                                b.addActionListener (this);
                        }
                }
        }
        public void actionPerformed (ActionEvent e) {
                System.out.println ("Selected: " + e.getActionCommand());
        }
}
```

public void removeContainerListener(ContainerListener listener) ★

The removeContainerListener() method removes listener as an interested listener. If listener is not registered, nothing happens.

protected void processEvent(AWTEvent e) ★

The processEvent() method receives all AWTEvents with this Container as its target. processEvent() then passes them along to any listeners for processing. When you subclass Container, overriding processEvent() allows you to process all events yourself, before sending them to any listeners. There is no equivalent under the 1.0 event model.

If you override processEvent(), remember to call super.processEvent(e) last to ensure that regular event processing can occur. If you want to process your own events, it's a good idea to call enableEvents() (inherited from Component) to ensure that events are delivered even in the absence of registered listeners.

protected void processContainerEvent(ContainerEvent e) ★

The processContainerEvent() method receives all ContainerEvents with this Container as its target. processContainerEvent() then passes them along to any listeners for processing. When you subclass Container, overriding the processContainerEvent() method allows you to process all container events yourself, before sending them to any listeners. There is no equivalent under the 1.0 event model.

If you override the processContainerEvent() method, remember to call super.processContainerEvent(e) last to ensure that regular event processing can occur. If you want to process your own events, it's a good idea to call enableEvents() (inherited from Component) to ensure that events are delivered even in the absence of registered listeners.

Painting

The following methods are early vestiges of an approach to painting and printing. They are not responsible for anything that couldn't be done with a call to paintAll() or printAll(). However, they are available if you wish to call them.

public void paintComponents (Graphics g)

The paintComponents() method of Container paints the different components it contains. It calls each component's paintAll() method with a clipped graphics context g, which is eventually passed to paint().

public void printComponents (Graphics g)

The printComponents() method of Container prints the different components it contains. It calls each component's printAll() method with a clipped graphics context g, which is passed to print(), and eventually works its way to paint().

Since it is the container's responsibility to deal with painting lightweight peers, the paint() and print() methods are overridden in Java 1.1.

public void paint(Graphics g) ★

The paint() method of Container paints the different lightweight components it contains.

public void print(Graphics g) ★

> The print() method of Container prints the different lightweight compo-
> nents it contains.

NOTE   If you override paint() or print() in your containers (especially
           applets), call super.paint(g) or super.print(g), respectively, to
           make sure that lightweight components are rendered. This is a good
           practice even if you don't currently use any lightweight components;
           you don't want your code to break mysteriously if you add a
           lightweight component later.

Peers

The container is responsible for creating and destroying all the peers of the components within it.

public void addNotify ()

> The addNotify() method of Container creates the peer of all the components
> within it. After addNotify() is called, the Container is invalid. It is useful for
> top-level containers to call this method explicitly before calling the method
> setVisible(true) to guarantee that the container is laid out before it is dis-
> played.

public void removeNotify ()

> The removeNotify() method destroys the peer of all the top-level objects con-
> tained within it. This in effect destroys the peers of all the components within
> the container.

Miscellaneous methods

protected String paramString ()

> When you call the toString() method of a container, the default toString()
> method of Component is called. This in turn calls paramString() which builds
> up the string to display. At the Container level, paramString() appends the
> layout manager name, like layout=java.awt.BorderLayout, to the output.

public Insets getInsets () ★
public Insets insets () ☆

> The getInsets() method gets the container's current insets. An inset is the
> amount of space reserved for the container to use between its edge and the
> area actually available to hold components. For example, in a Frame, the inset
> for the top would be the space required for the title bar and menu bar. Insets
> exist for top, bottom, right, and left. When you override this method, you are
> providing an area within the container that is reserved for free space. If the
> container has insets, they would be the default. If not, the default values are

all zeroes.

The following code shows how to override insets() to provide values other than the default. The top and bottom have 20 pixels of inset. The left and right have 50. Section 6.3 describes the Insets class in more detail.

```
public Insets insets () {                // getInsets() for Java 1.1
        return new Insets (20, 50, 20, 50);
}
```

To find out the current value, just call the method and look at the results. For instance, for a Frame the results could be the following in the format used by toString():

```
java.awt.Insets[top=42,left=4,right=4,bottom=4]
```

The 42 is the space required for the title and menu bar, while the 4 around the edges are for the window decorations. These results are platform specific and allow you to position items based upon the user's run-time environment.

When drawing directly onto the graphics context of a container with a large inset such as Frame, remember to work around the insets. If you do something like g.drawString("Hello World", 5, 5) onto a Frame, the user won't see the text. It will be under the title bar and menu bar.

insets() is the Java 1.0 name for this method.

public void list (PrintWriter output, int indentation) ★
public void list (PrintStream output, int indentation)

The list() method is very helpful if you need to find out what is inside a container. It recursively calls itself for each container level of objects inside it, increasing the indentation at each level. The results are written to the PrintStream or PrintWriter output.

6.2 *Panel*

The Panel class provides a generic container within an existing display area. It is the simplest of all the containers. When you load an applet into Netscape Navigator or an *appletviewer*, you have a Panel to work with at the highest level.

A Panel has no physical appearance. It is just a rectangular display area. The default LayoutManager of Panel is FlowLayout; FlowLayout is described in Section 7.2.

6.2.1 Panel Methods

Constructors

public Panel ()

The first constructor creates a Panel with a LayoutManager of FlowLayout.

public Panel (LayoutManager layout) ★

This constructor allows you to set the initial LayoutManager of the new Panel to layout. If layout is null, there is no LayoutManager, and you must shape and position the components within the Panel yourself.

Miscellaneous methods

public void addNotify ()

The addNotify() method creates the Panel peer. If you override this method, first call super.addNotify(), then add your customizations for the new class. Then you can do everything you need with the information about the newly created peer.

6.2.2 Panel Events

In Java 1.0, a Panel peer generates all the events that are generated by the Component class; it does not generate events that are specific to a particular type of component. That is, it generates key events, mouse events, and focus events; it doesn't generate action events or list events. If an event happens within a child component of a Panel, the target of the event is the child component, not the Panel. There's one exception to this rule: if a component uses the LightweightPeer (new to Java 1.1), it cannot be the target of an event.

With Java 1.1, events are delivered to whatever listener is associated with a contained component. The fact that the component is within a Panel has no relevance.

6.3 Insets

The Insets class provides a way to encapsulate the layout margins of the four different sides of a container. The class helps in laying out containers. The Container can retrieve their values through the getInsets() method, then analyze the settings to position components. The different inset values are measured in pixels. The space reserved by insets can still be used for drawing directly within paint(). Also, if the LayoutManager associated with the container does not look at the insets, the request will be completely ignored.

6.3.1 Insets Methods

Variables

There are four variables for insets, one for each border.

public int top

This variable contains the border width in pixels for the top of a container.

public int bottom

This variable contains the border width in pixels for the bottom of a container.

public int left

This variable contains the border width in pixels for the left edge of a container.

public int right

This variable contains the border width in pixels for the right edge of a container.

Constructors

public Insets (int top, int left, int bottom, int right)

The constructor creates an `Insets` object with `top`, `left`, `bottom`, and `right` being the size of the insets in pixels. If this object was the return object from the `getInsets()` method of a container, these values represent the size of a border inside that container.

Miscellaneous methods

public Object clone ()

The `clone()` method creates a clone of the `Insets` so the same `Insets` object can be associated with multiple containers.

public boolean equals(Object object) ★

The `equals()` method defines equality for insets. Two `Insets` objects are equal if the four settings for the different values are equal.

public String toString ()

The `toString()` method of `Insets` returns the current settings. Using the new `Insets (10, 20, 30, 40)` constructor, the results would be:

```
java.awt.Insets[top=10,left=20,bottom=30,right=40]
```

6.3.2 Insets Example

The following source code demonstrates the use of insets within an applet's Panel.
The applet displays a button that takes up the entire area of the Panel, less the
insets, then draws a rectangle around that area. This is shown visually in Figure 6-1.
The example demonstrates that if you add components to a container, the Layout-
Manager deals with the insets for you in positioning them. But if you are drawing
directly to the Panel, you must look at the insets if you want to avoid the requested
area within the container.

```
import java.awt.*;
import java.applet.*;
public class myInsets extends Applet {
    public Insets insets () {
        return new Insets (50, 50, 50, 50);
    }
    public void init () {
        setLayout (new BorderLayout ());
        add ("Center", new Button ("Insets"));
    }
    public void paint (Graphics g) {
        Insets i = insets();
        int width  = size().width - i.left - i.right;
        int height = size().height - i.top - i.bottom;
        g.drawRect (i.left-2, i.top-2, width+4, height+4);
        g.drawString ("Insets Example", 25, size().height - 25);
    }
}
```

To change the applet's insets from the default, we override the insets() method
to return a new Insets object, with the new values.

6.4 Window

A Window is a top-level display area that exists outside the browser or applet area
you are working in. It has no adornments, such as the borders, window title, or
menu bar that a typical window manager might provide. A Frame is a subclass of
Window that adds these parts (borders, window title). Normally you will work with
the children of Window and not Window directly. However, you might use a Window
to create your own pop-up menu or some other GUI component that requires its
own window and isn't provided by AWT. This technique isn't as necessary in Java
1.1, which has a PopupMenu component.

The default LayoutManager for Window is BorderLayout, which is described in Section 7.3.

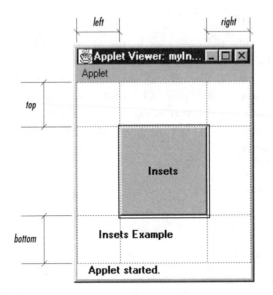

Figure 6–1: Insets

6.4.1 Window Methods

Constructors

public Window (Frame parent)

There is one public constructor for Window. It has one parameter, which specifies the parent of the Window. When the parent is minimized, so is the Window. In an application, you must therefore create a Frame before you can create a Window; this isn't much of an inconvenience since you usually need a Frame in which to build your user interface. In an applet, you often do not have access to a Frame to use as the parent, so you can pass null as the argument.

Figure 6-2 shows a simple Window on the left. Notice that there are no borders or window management adornments present. The Window on the right was created by an applet loaded over the network. Notice the warning message you get in the status bar at the bottom of the screen. This is to warn users that the Window was created by an applet that comes from an untrusted source, and you can't necessarily trust it to do what it says. The warning is particularly appropriate for windows, since a user can't necessarily tell whether a window was created by an applet or any other application. It is therefore possible to write applets that mimic windows from well-known applications, to trick the user into giving away passwords, credit card numbers, or other sensitive information.

In some environments, you can get the browser's Frame to use with the Window's constructor. This is one way to create a Dialog, as we shall see. By

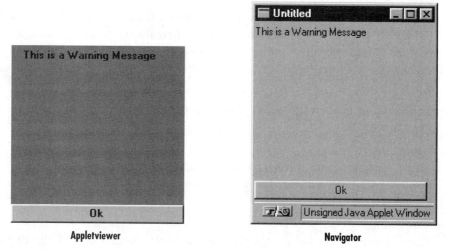

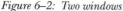

Figure 6–2: Two windows

repeatedly calling `getParent()` until there are no more parents, you can discover an applet's top-level parent, which should be the browser's `Frame`. Example 6-1 contains the code you would write to do this. You should then check the return value to see if you got a `Frame` or `null`. This code is completely nonportable, but you may happen to be in an environment where it works.

Example 6–1: Finding a Parent Frame

```
import java.awt.*;
public class ComponentUtilities {
    public static Frame getTopLevelParent (Component component) {
        Component c = component;
        while (c.getParent() != null)
            c = c.getParent();
        if (c instanceof Frame)
            return (Frame)c;
        else
            return null;
    }
}
```

Appearance methods

A handful of methods assist with the appearance of the `Window`.

public void pack ()

The `pack()` method resizes the `Window` to the preferred size of the components it contains and validates the `Window`.

public void show ()

> The show() method displays the Window. When a Window is initially created it is hidden. If the window is already showing when this method is called, it calls toFront() to bring the window to the foreground. To hide the window, just call the hide() method of Component. After you show() a window, it is validated for you.

> The first call to show() for any Window generates a WindowEvent with the ID WINDOW_OPENED.

public void dispose ()

> The dispose() method releases the resources of the Window by hiding it and removing its peer. Calling this method generates a WindowEvent with the ID WINDOW_CLOSED.

public void toFront ()

> The toFront() method brings the Window to the foreground of the display. This is automatically called if you call show() and the Window is already shown.

public void toBack ()

> The toBack() method puts the Window in the background of the display.

public boolean isShowing() ★

> The isShowing() method returns true if the Window is visible on the screen.

Miscellaneous methods

public Toolkit getToolkit ()

> The getToolkit() method returns the current Toolkit of the window. The Toolkit provides you with information about the native platform. This will allow you to size the Window based upon the current screen resolution and get images for an application. See Section 6.5.5 for a usage example.

public Locale getLocale () ★

> The getLocale() method retrieves the current Locale of the window, if it has one. Using a Locale allows you to write programs that can adapt themselves to different languages and different regional variants. If no Locale has been set, getLocale() returns the default Locale. The default Locale has a user language of English and no region. To change the default Locale, set the system properties user.language and user.region or call Locale.setDefault() (setDefault() verifies access rights with the security manager).[*]

---

[*] For more on the Locale class, see the *Java Fundamental Classes Reference* from O'Reilly & Associates.

public final String getWarningString ()

> The getWarningString() method returns null or a string that is displayed on the bottom of insecure Window instances. If the SecurityManager says that top-level windows do not get a warning message, this method returns null. If a message is required, the default text is "Warning: Applet Window". However, Java allows the user to change the warning by setting the system property awt.appletWarning. (Netscape Navigator and Internet Explorer do not allow the warning message to be changed. Netscape Navigator's current (V3.0) warning string is "Unsigned Java Applet Window.") The purpose of this string is to warn users that the Window was created by an untrusted source, as opposed to a standard application, and should be used with caution.

public Component getFocusOwner () ★

> The getFocusOwner() method allows you to ask the Window which of its components currently has the input focus. This is useful if you are cutting and pasting from the system clipboard; asking who has the input focus tells you where to put the data you get from the clipboard. The system clipboard is covered in Chapter 16, *Data Transfer*. If no component in the Window has the focus, getFocusOwner() returns null.

public synchronized void addNotify ()

> The addNotify() method creates the Window peer. This is automatically done when you call the show() method of the Window. If you override this method, first call super.addNotify(), then add your customizations for the new class. Then you can do everything you need to with the information about the newly created peer.

6.4.2 Window Events

In Java 1.0, a Window peer generates all the events that are generated by the Component class; it does not generate events that are specific to a particular type of component. That is, it generates key events, mouse events, and focus events; it doesn't generate action events or list events. If an event occurs within a child component of a Window, the target of the event is the child component, not the Window.

In addition to the Component events, five events are specific to windows, none of which are passed on by the window's peer. These events happen at the Frame and Dialog level. The events are WINDOW_DESTROY, WINDOW_EXPOSE, WINDOW_ICONIFY, WINDOW_DEICONIFY, and WINDOW_MOVED. The default event handler, handleEvent(), doesn't call a convenience method to handle any of these events. If you want to work with them, you must override handleEvent(). See Section 6.5.4 for an example that catches the WINDOW_DESTROY event.

public boolean postEvent (Event e) ☆

The postEvent() method tells the Window to deal with Event e. It calls the handleEvent() method, which returns true if somebody handled e and false if no one handles it. This method, which overrides Component.postEvent(), is necessary because a Window is, by definition, an outermost container, and therefore does not need to post the event to its parent.

Listeners and 1.1 event handling

With the 1.1 event model, you register listeners for different event types; the listeners are told when the event happens. These methods register listeners and let the Window component inspect its own events.

public void addWindowListener(WindowListener listener) ★

The addWindowListener() method registers listener as an object interested in being notified when an WindowEvent passes through the EventQueue with this Window as its target. When such an event occurs, one of the methods in the WindowListener interface is called. Multiple listeners can be registered.

public void removeWindowListener(WindowListener listener) ★

The removeWindowListener() method removes listener as an interested listener. If listener is not registered, nothing happens.

protected void processEvent(AWTEvent e) ★

The processEvent() method receives every AWTEvent with this Window as its target. processEvent() then passes them along to any listeners for processing. When you subclass Window, overriding processEvent() allows you to process all events yourself, before sending them to any listeners. In a way, overriding processEvent() is like overriding handleEvent() using the 1.0 event model.

If you override processEvent(), remember to call super.processEvent(e) last to ensure that regular event processing can occur. If you want to process your own events, it's a good idea to call enableEvents() (inherited from Component) to ensure that events are delivered even in the absence of registered listeners.

protected void processWindowEvent(WindowEvent e) ★

The processWindowEvent() method receives every WindowEvent with this Window as its target. processWindowEvent() then passes them along to any listeners for processing. When you subclass Window, overriding processWindowEvent() allows you to process all events yourself, before sending them to any listeners. In a way, overriding processWindowEvent() is like overriding handleEvent() using the 1.0 event model.

If you override `processWindowEvent()`, you must remember to call
`super.processWindowEvent(e)` last to ensure that regular event processing
can occur. If you want to process your own events, it's a good idea to call
`enableEvents()` (inherited from `Component`) to ensure that events are delivered even in the absence of registered listeners.

6.5 Frames

The `Frame` is a special type of `Window` that looks like other high level programs in
your windowing environment. It adds a `MenuBar`, window title, and window gadgets
(like resize, maximize, minimize, window menu) to the basic `Window` object. All the
menu-related pieces are discussed in Chapter 10, *Would You Like to Choose from the
Menu?*

The default layout manager for a `Frame` is `BorderLayout`.

6.5.1 Frame Constants

The `Frame` class includes a number of constants used to specify cursors. These constants are left over from Java 1.0 and maintained for compatibility. In Java 1.1, you
should use the new `Cursor` class, introduced in the previous chapter, and the `Com-
ponent.setCursor()` method to change the cursor over a frame. Avoid using the
`Frame` constants for new code. To see these cursors, refer to Figure 5-6.

public final static int DEFAULT_CURSOR
public final static int CROSSHAIR_CURSOR
public final static int TEXT_CURSOR
public final static int WAIT_CURSOR
public final static int SW_RESIZE_CURSOR
public final static int SE_RESIZE_CURSOR
public final static int NW_RESIZE_CURSOR
public final static int NE_RESIZE_CURSOR
public final static int N_RESIZE_CURSOR
public final static int S_RESIZE_CURSOR
public final static int W_RESIZE_CURSOR
public final static int E_RESIZE_CURSOR
public final static int HAND_CURSOR
public final static int MOVE_CURSOR

NOTE   HAND_CURSOR and MOVE_CURSOR are not available on Windows platforms with Java 1.0. If you ask to use these and they are not available,
you get DEFAULT_CURSOR.

6.5.2 Frame Constructors

public Frame ()

The constructor for `Frame` creates a hidden window with a window title of "Untitled" (Java1.0) or an empty string (Java1.1). Like `Window`, the default `LayoutManager` of a `Frame` is `BorderLayout`. `DEFAULT_CURSOR` is the initial cursor. To position the `Frame` on the screen, call `Component.move()`. Since the `Frame` is initially hidden, you need to call the `show()` method before the user sees the `Frame`.

public Frame (String title)

This version of `Frame`'s constructor is identical to the first but sets the window title to `title`. Figure 6-3 shows the results of a call to `new Frame("My Frame")` followed by `resize()` and `show()`.

Figure 6–3: A typical Frame

6.5.3 Frame Methods

public String getTitle ()

The `getTitle()` method returns the current title for the `Frame`. If there is no title, this method returns `null`.

public void setTitle (String title)

The `setTitle()` method changes the `Frame`'s title to `title`.

public Image getIconImage ()

The `getIconImage()` method returns the image used as the icon. Initially, this returns `null`. For some platforms, the method should not be used because the platform does not support the concept.

public void setIconImage (Image image)

> The setIconImage() method changes the image to display when the Frame is iconified to image. Not all platforms utilize this resource.

public MenuBar getMenuBar ()

> The getMenuBar() method retrieves the Frame's current menu bar.

public synchronized void setMenuBar (MenuBar bar)

> The setMenuBar() method changes the menu bar of the Frame to bar. If bar is null, it removes the menu bar so that none is available. It is possible to have multiple menu bars based upon the context of the application. However, the same menu bar cannot appear on multiple frames and only one can appear at a time. The MenuBar class, and everything to do with menus, is covered in Chapter 10.

public synchronized void remove (MenuComponent component)

> The remove() method removes component from Frame if component is the frame's menu bar. This is equivalent to calling setMenuBar() with a parameter of null and in actuality is what remove() calls.

public synchronized void dispose ()

> The dispose() method frees up the system resources used by the Frame. If any Dialogs or Windows are associated with this Frame, their resources are freed, too. Some people like to call Component.hide() before calling the dispose() method so users do not see the frame decomposing.

public boolean isResizable ()

> The isResizable() method will tell you if the current Frame is resizable.

public void setResizable (boolean resizable)

> The setResizable() method changes the resize state of the Frame. A resizable value of true means the user can resize the Frame, false means the user cannot. This must be set before the Frame is shown or the peer created.

public void setCursor (int cursorType)

> The setCursor() method changes the cursor of the Frame to cursorType. cursorType must be one of the cursor constants provided with the Frame class. You cannot create your own cursor image yet. When changing from the DEFAULT_CURSOR to another cursor, the mouse must be moved for the cursor icon to change to the new cursor. If cursorType is not one of the predefined cursor types, setCursor() throws the IllegalArgumentException run-time exception.
>
> This method has been replaced by the Component.setCursor() method. Both function equivalently, but this method is being phased out.

public int getCursorType ()

>   The getCursorType() method retrieves the current cursor.

>   This method has been replaced by the Component.getCursor() method. Both function equivalently, but this method is being phased out.

Miscellaneous methods

public synchronized void addNotify ()

>   The addNotify() method creates the Frame peer. This is automatically done when you call the show() method of the Frame. If you override this method, first call super.addNotify(), then add your customizations for the new class. Then you can do everything you need to do with the information about the newly created peer.

protected String paramString ()

>   When you call the toString() method of Frame, the default toString() method of Component is called. This in turn calls paramString(), which builds up the string to display. At the Frame level, paramString() appends resizable (if true) and the title (if present). Using the default Frame constructor, the results would be:

>   ```
>   java.awt.Frame[0,0,0x0,invalid,hidden,layout=java.awt.BorderLayout,
>   resizable,title=]
>   ```

Until the Frame is shown, via show(), the position and size are not known and therefore appear as zeros. After showing the Frame, you might see:

```
java.awt.Frame[44,44,300x300,layout=java.awt.BorderLayout,
resizable,title=]
```

6.5.4 Frame Events

In Java 1.0, a Frame peer generates all the events that are generated by the Component class; it does not generate events that are specific to a particular type of component. That is, it generates key events, mouse events, and focus events; it doesn't generate action events or list events. If an event happens within a child component of a Frame, the target of the event is the child component, not the Frame.

Window

In addition to the Component events, Frame generates the WINDOW events. These events are WINDOW_DESTROY, WINDOW_EXPOSE, WINDOW_ICONIFY, WINDOW_DEICONIFY, and WINDOW_MOVED.

One common event, WINDOW_DESTROY, is generated when the user tries to close the Frame by selecting Quit, Close, or Exit (depending on your windowing environment) from the window manager's menu. By default, this event does nothing. You must provide an event handler that explicitly closes the Frame. If you do not, your Frame will close only when the Java Virtual Machine exits—for example, when you quit Netscape Navigator. The handleEvent() method in the following example, or one like it, should therefore be included in all classes that extend Frame. If a WINDOW_DESTROY event occurs, it gets rid of the Frame and exits the program. Make sure your method calls super.handleEvent() to process the other events.

```
public boolean handleEvent (Event e) {
    if (e.id == Event.WINDOW_DESTROY) {
        hide();
        dispose();
        System.exit(0);
        return true;              // boolean method, must return something
    } else {
                                  // handle other events we find interesting
    }

                                  // make sure normal event processing happens
    return super.handleEvent (e);
}
```

Listeners and 1.1 event handling

With the 1.1 event model, you register listeners for different event types; the listeners are told when the event happens. The Frame class inherits all its listener handling from Window.

Here's the Java 1.1 code necessary to handle WINDOW_CLOSING events; it is equivalent to the handleEvent() method in the previous example. First, you must add the following line to the Frame's constructor:

```
enableEvents (AWTEvent.WINDOW_EVENT_MASK);
```

This line guarantees that we will receive window events, even if there is no listener. The processWindowEvent() method in the following code does the actual work of closing things down:

```
// Java 1.1 only
protected void processWindowEvent(WindowEvent e) {
    if (e.getID() == WindowEvent.WINDOW_CLOSING) {
        // Notify others we are closing
        if (windowListener != null)
            windowListener.windowClosing(e);
        System.exit(0);
    } else {
        super.processEvent(e);
    }
}
```

If you forget to enable events, processWindowEvent() may never be called, and your windows will not shut down until the Java Virtual Machine exits. All subclasses of Frame should include code like this to make sure they terminate gracefully.

6.5.5 Building a New Component from a Window

Now that we have discussed the Frame and Window objects, we can briefly investigate some ways to use them together. Previously I said that you can use a Window to build your own pop-up menu. That's no longer necessary in Java 1.1, but the same techniques apply to plenty of other objects. In the following example, we build a set of pop-up buttons; it also uses the Toolkit of a Frame to load images within an application. The pop-up button set appears when the user presses the right mouse button over the image. It is positioned at the coordinates of the mouseDown() event; to do so, we add the current location() of the Frame to the mouse's x and y coordinates. Figure 6-4 shows what this application looks like when the pop-up button set is on the screen.

```java
import java.awt.*;
public class PopupButtonFrame extends Frame {
    Image im;
    Window w = new PopupWindow (this);
    PopupButtonFrame () {
        super ("PopupButton Example");
        resize (250, 100);
        show();
        im = getToolkit().getImage ("rosey.jpg");
        MediaTracker mt = new MediaTracker (this);
        mt.addImage (im, 0);
        try {
            mt.waitForAll();
        } catch (Exception e) {e.printStackTrace(); }
    }
    public static void main (String args[]) {
        Frame f = new PopupMenuFrame ();
    }
    public void paint (Graphics g) {
        if (im != null)
            g.drawImage (im, 20, 20, this);
    }
    public boolean mouseDown (Event e, int x, int y) {
        if (e.modifiers == Event.META_MASK) {
            w.move (location().x+x, location().y+y);
            w.show();
            return true;
        }
        return false;
    }
}
class PopupWindow extends Window {
    PopupWindow (Frame f) {
```

```
            super (f);
            Panel p = new Panel ();
            p.add (new Button ("About"));
            p.add (new Button ("Save"));
            p.add (new Button ("Quit"));
            add ("North", p);
            setBackground (Color.gray);
            pack();
        }
        public boolean action (Event e, Object o) {
            if ("About".equals (o))
                System.out.println ("About");
            else if ("Save".equals (o))
                System.out.println ("Save Me");
            else if ("Quit".equals (o))
                System.exit (0);
            hide();
            return true;
        }
    }
```

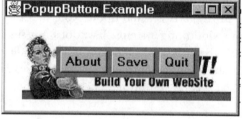

Figure 6–4: Pop-up buttons

The most interesting method in this application is mouseDown(). When the user clicks on the mouse, mouseDown() checks whether the META_MASK is set in the event modifiers; this indicates that the user pressed the right mouse button, or pressed the left button while pressing the Meta key. If this is true, mouseDown() moves the window to the location of the mouse click, calls show() to display the window, and returns true to indicate that the event was handled completely. If mouseDown were called with any other kind of mouse event, we return false to let the event propagate to any other object that might be interested. Remember that the coordinates passed with the mouse event are the coordinates of the mouse click relative to the Frame; to find out where to position the pop-up window, we need an absolute location and therefore ask the Frame for its location.

PopupWindow itself is a simple class. Its constructor simply creates a display with three buttons. The call to pack() sizes the window so that it provides a nice border around the buttons but isn't excessively large; you can change the border by playing with the window's insets if you want, but that usually isn't necessary. The class PopupWindow has an action() method that is called when the user clicks one of the buttons. When the user clicks on a button, action() prints a message and hides the window.

6.6 Dialogs

The Dialog class provides a special type of display window that is normally used for pop-up messages or input from the user. It should be associated with a Frame (a required parameter for the constructor), and whenever anything happens to this Frame, the same thing will happen to the Dialog. For instance, if the parent Frame is iconified, the Dialog disappears until the Frame is de-iconified. If the Frame is destroyed, so are all the associated dialogs. Figure 6-5 and Figure 6-6 show typical dialog boxes.

In addition to being associated with a Frame, Dialog is either modeless or modal. A modeless Dialog means a user can interact with both the Frame and the Dialog at the same time. A modal Dialog is one that blocks input to the remainder of the application, including the Frame, until the Dialog box is acted upon. Note that the parent Frame is still executing; unlike some windowing systems, Java does not suspend the entire application for a modal Dialog. Normally, blocking access would be done to get input from the user or to show a warning message. Example 6-2 shows how to create and use a modal Dialog box, as we will see later in the chapter.

Since Dialog subclasses Window, its default LayoutManager is BorderLayout.

In applets, when you create a Dialog, you need to provide a reference to the browser's Frame, not the applet. In order to get this, you can try to go up the container hierarchy of the Applet with getParent() until it returns null. (You cannot specify a null parent as you can with a Window.) See Example 6-1 for a utility method to do this. Simple include a line like the following in your applet:

```
Frame top = ComponentUtilities.getTopLevelParent (this);
```

Then pass top to the Dialog constructor. Another alternative is to create a new Frame to associate with your dialog.

6.6.1 Dialog Constructors and Methods

Constructors

If any constructor is passed a null parent, the constructor throws the run-time exception IllegalArgumentException.

public Dialog (Frame parent) ★

> This constructor creates an instance of Dialog with no title and with parent as the Frame owning it. It is not modal and is initially resizable.

public Dialog (Frame parent, boolean modal) ☆

> This constructor creates an instance of Dialog with no title and with parent as the Frame owning it. If modal is true, the Dialog grabs all the user input of the program until it is closed. If modal is false, there is no special behavior associated with the Dialog. Initially, the Dialog will be resizable. This constructor is comment-flagged as deprecated.

public Dialog (Frame parent, String title) ★

> This version of the constructor creates an instance of Dialog with parent as the Frame owning it and a window title of title. It is not modal and is initially resizable.

public Dialog (Frame parent, String title, boolean modal)

> This version of the constructor creates an instance of Dialog with parent as the Frame owning it and a window title of title. If mode is true, the Dialog grabs all the user input of the program until it is closed. If modal is false, there is no special behavior associated with the Dialog. Initially, the Dialog will be resizable.

NOTE   In some 1.0 versions of Java, modal dialogs were not supported properly. You needed to create some multithreaded contraption that simulated modality. Modal dialogs work properly in 1.1.

Appearance methods

public String getTitle ()

> The getTitle() method returns the current title for the Dialog. If there is no title for the Dialog, getTitle() returns null.

public void setTitle (String title)

> The setTitle() method changes the current title of the Dialog to title. To turn off any title for the Dialog, use null for title.

Figure 6–5: A Dialog in an application or local applet

Figure 6–6: The same Dialog in an applet that came across the network

public boolean isResizable ()

> The isResizable() method tells you if the current Dialog is resizable.

public void setResizable (boolean resizable)

> The setResizable() method changes the resize state of the Dialog. A resizable value of true means the user can resize the Dialog, while false means the user cannot. This must be set before the Dialog is shown or the peer created.

Modal methods

public boolean isModal ()

> The isModal() method returns the current mode of the Dialog. true indicates the dialog traps all user input.

public void setModal (boolean mode) ★

> The setModal() method changes the current mode of the Dialog to mode. The next time the dialog is displayed via show(), it will be modal. If the dialog is currently displayed, setModal() has no immediate effect. The change will take place the next time show() is called.

public void show () ★

> The show() method brings the Dialog to the front and displays it. If the dialog is modal, show() takes care of blocking events so that they don't reach the parent Frame.

Miscellaneous methods

public synchronized void addNotify ()

> The addNotify() method creates the Dialog peer. The peer is created automatically when you call the dialog's show() method. If you override the method addNotify(), first call super.addNotify(), then add your customizations for the new class. You will then be able to do everything you need with the information about the newly created peer.

protected String paramString ()

> When you call the toString() method of Dialog, the default toString() method of Component is called. This in turn calls paramString() which builds up the string to display. At the Dialog level, paramString() appends the current mode (modal/modeless) and title (if present). Using the constructor Dialog (top, "Help", true), the results would be as follows:

```
java.awt.Dialog[0,0,0x0,invalid,hidden,layout=java.awt.BorderLayout,
    modal,title=Help]
```

6.6.2 Dialog Events

In Java 1.0, a Dialog peer generates all the events that are generated by the Component class; it does not generate events that are specific to a particular type of component. That is, it generates key events, mouse events, and focus events; it doesn't generate action events or list events. If an event happens within a child component of a Dialog, the target of the event is the child component, not the Dialog.

Window

In addition to the Component events, Dialog generates the WINDOW events. These events are WINDOW_DESTROY, WINDOW_EXPOSE, WINDOW_ICONIFY, WINDOW_DEICONIFY, and WINDOW_MOVED.

Listeners and 1.1 event handling

With the 1.1 event model, you register listeners for different event types; the listeners are told when the event happens. The `Dialog` class inherits all its listener handling from `Window`.

6.6.3 Dialog Example

Example 6-2 demonstrates how a modal `Dialog` tries to work in Java 1.0. In some windowing systems, "modal" means that the calling application, and sometimes the entire system stops, and input to anything other than the `Dialog` is blocked. With Java 1.0, a modal `Dialog` acts only on the parent frame and simply prevents it from getting screen-oriented input by disabling all components within the frame. The Java program as a whole continues to execute.

Example 6-2 displays a `Dialog` window with username and password fields, and an Okay button. When the user selects the Okay button, a realistic application would validate the username and password; in this case, they are just displayed on a `Frame`. Since the `Frame` must wait for the `Dialog` to finish before looking at the values of the two fields, the `Dialog` must tell the `Frame` when it can look. This is done through a custom interface implemented by the parent `Frame` and invoked by the `Dialog` in its action method.

Figure 6-7 is the initial `Dialog`; Figure 6-8 shows the result after you click Okay. Example 6-2 contains the source code.

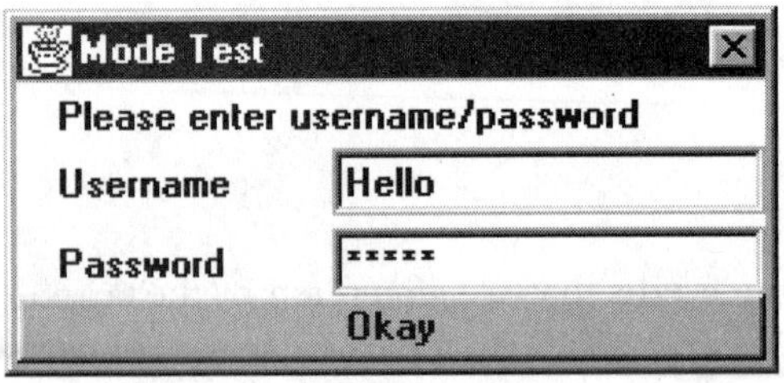

Figure 6–7: Username and password Dialog

Notice the use of the newly created `DialogHandler` interface when the user selects the Okay button. Also, see how the pre– and post–event-handling methods are separated. All the pre-event processing takes place before the `Dialog` is shown. The post-event processing is called by the `Dialog` through the new `DialogHandler` interface method, `dialogDoer()`. The interface provides a common method name for all your `Dialog` boxes to call.

Figure 6–8: Resulting Frame

Example 6–2: Modal Dialog Usage

```
import java.awt.*;
interface DialogHandler {
    void dialogDoer (Object o);
}
class modeTest extends Dialog {
    TextField user;
    TextField pass;
    modeTest (DialogHandler parent) {
        super ((Frame)parent, "Mode Test", true);
        add ("North", new Label ("Please enter username/password"));
        Panel left = new Panel ();
        left.setLayout (new BorderLayout ());
        left.add ("North", new Label ("Username"));
        left.add ("South", new Label ("Password"));
        add ("West", left);
        Panel right = new Panel ();
        right.setLayout (new BorderLayout ());
        user = new TextField (15);
        pass = new TextField (15);
        pass.setEchoCharacter ('*');
        right.add ("North", user);
        right.add ("South", pass);
        add ("East", right);
        add ("South", new Button ("Okay"));
        resize (250, 125);
    }
    public boolean handleEvent (Event e) {
        if (e.id == Event.WINDOW_DESTROY) {
            dispose();
            return true;
        } else if ((e.target instanceof Button) &&
            (e.id == Event.ACTION_EVENT)) {
            ((DialogHandler)getParent ()).dialogDoer(e.arg);
        }
        return super.handleEvent (e);
    }
}

public class modeFrame extends Frame implements DialogHandler {
    modeTest d;
    modeFrame (String s) {
        super (s);
```

Example 6–2: Modal Dialog Usage (continued)

```
            resize (100, 100);
            d = new modeTest (this);
            d.show ();
    }
    public static void main (String []args) {
        Frame f = new modeFrame ("Frame");
    }
    public boolean handleEvent (Event e) {
        if (e.id == Event.WINDOW_DESTROY) {
            hide();
            dispose();
            System.exit (0);
        }
        return super.handleEvent (e);
    }
    public void dialogDoer(Object o) {
        d.dispose();
        add ("North", new Label (d.user.getText()));
        add ("South", new Label (d.pass.getText()));
        show ();
    }
}
```

Since the Java 1.1 modal `Dialog` blocks the calling `Frame` appropriately, the overhead of the `DialogHandler` interface is not necessary and all the work can be combined into the `main()` method, as shown in the following:

```
// only reliable in Java 1.1
import java.awt.*;
class modeTest11 extends Dialog {
    TextField user;
    TextField pass;
    modeTest11 (Frame parent) {
        super (parent, "Mode Test", true);
        add ("North", new Label ("Please enter username/password"));
        Panel left = new Panel ();
        left.setLayout (new BorderLayout ());
        left.add ("North", new Label ("Username"));
        left.add ("South", new Label ("Password"));
        add ("West", left);
        Panel right = new Panel ();
        right.setLayout (new BorderLayout ());
        user = new TextField (15);
        pass = new TextField (15);
        pass.setEchoCharacter ('*');
        right.add ("North", user);
        right.add ("South", pass);
        add ("East", right);
        add ("South", new Button ("Okay"));
        resize (250, 125);
    }
    public boolean handleEvent (Event e) {
```

```
                if (e.id == Event.WINDOW_DESTROY) {
                    dispose();
                    return true;
                } else if ((e.target instanceof Button) &&
                    (e.id == Event.ACTION_EVENT)) {
                    hide();
                }
                return super.handleEvent (e);
            }
        }


public class modeFrame11 extends Frame {
    modeFrame11 (String s) {
        super (s);
        resize (100, 100);
    }
    public static void main (String []args) {
        Frame f = new modeFrame11 ("Frame");
        modeTest11 d;
        d = new modeTest11 (f);
        d.show ();
        d.dispose();
        f.add ("North", new Label (d.user.getText()));
        f.add ("South", new Label (d.pass.getText()));
        f.show ();
    }
    public boolean handleEvent (Event e) {
        if (e.id == Event.WINDOW_DESTROY) {
            hide();
            dispose();
            System.exit (0);
        }
        return super.handleEvent (e);
    }
}
```

The remainder of the code is virtually identical. The most significant difference is that the dialog's handleEvent() method just hides the dialog, rather than calling DialogHandler.dialogDoer().

6.7 *FileDialog*

FileDialog is a subclass of Dialog that lets the user select files for opening or saving. You must load or save any files yourself. If used in an application or *applet-viewer*, the FileDialog always looks like the local system's file dialog. The FileDialog is always a modal Dialog, meaning that the calling program is blocked from continuing (and cannot accept input) until the user responds to the File-Dialog. Figure 6-9 shows the FileDialog component in Motif, Windows NT/95, and the Macintosh.

Unlike the other `Window` subclasses, there is no `LayoutManager` for `FileDialog`, since you are creating the environment's actual file dialog. This means you cannot subclass `FileDialog` to alter its behavior or appearance. However, the class is not "final."

NOTE Netscape Navigator throws an `AWTError` when you try to create a `FileDialog` because Navigator does not permit local file system access.

6.7.1 *FileDialog Methods*

Constants

A `FileDialog` has two modes: one for loading a file (input) and one for saving (output). The following variables provide the mode to the constructor. The `FileDialog` functions the same way in both modes. The only visible difference is whether a button on the screen is labeled Load or Save. You must load or save the requested file yourself. On certain platforms there may be functional differences: in `SAVE` mode, the `FileDialog` may ask if you want to replace a file if it already exists; in `LOAD` mode, the `FileDialog` may not accept a filename that does not exist.

public final static int LOAD

    `LOAD` is the constant for load mode. It is the default mode.

public final static int SAVE

    `SAVE` is the constant for save mode.

Constructors

public FileDialog (Frame parent) ★

    The first constructor creates a `FileDialog` for loading with a parent `Frame` of parent. The window title is initially empty.

public FileDialog (Frame parent, String title)

    This constructor creates a `FileDialog` for loading with a parent `Frame` of parent. The window title is title.

public FileDialog (Frame parent, String title, int mode)

    The final constructor creates a `FileDialog` with an initial mode of mode. If mode is neither `LOAD` nor `SAVE`, the `FileDialog` is in `SAVE` mode.

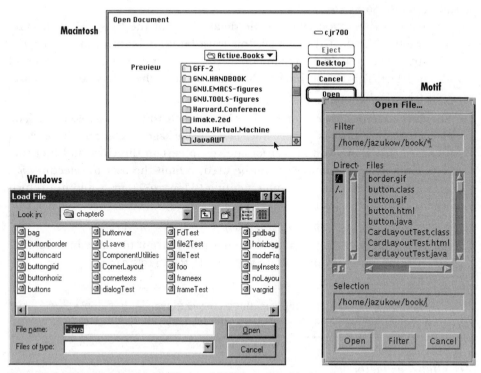

Figure 6–9: FileDialogs for Motif, Windows NT/95, and the Macintosh

Appearance methods

public String getDirectory ()

> getDirectory() returns the current directory for the FileDialog. Normally, you check this when FileDialog returns after a show() and a call to getFile() returns something other than null.

public void setDirectory (String directory)

> The setDirectory() method changes the initial directory displayed in the FileDialog to directory. You must call setDirectory() prior to displaying the FileDialog.

public String getFile ()

> The getFile() method returns the current file selection from the FileDialog. If the user pressed the Cancel button on the FileDialog, getFile() returns null. This is the only way to determine if the user pressed Cancel.

NOTE   On some platforms in Java 1.0 getFile() returns a string that ends in .*.* (two periods and two asterisks) if the file does not exist. You need to remove the extra characters before you can create the file.

---

public void setFile (String file)

The setFile() method changes the default file for the FileDialog to file. Because the FileDialog is modal, this must be done before you call show(). The string may contain a filename filter like *.java* to show a preliminary list of files to select. This has nothing to do with the use of the FilenameFilter class.

public FilenameFilter getFilenameFilter ()

The getFilenameFilter() method returns the current FilenameFilter. The FilenameFilter class is part of the java.io package. FilenameFilter is an interface that allows you to restrict choices to certain directory and filename combinations. For example, it can be used to limit the user to selecting *.jpg*, *.gif*, and *.xbm* files. The class implementing FilenameFilter would not return other possibilities as choices.

public void setFilenameFilter (FilenameFilter filter)

The setFilenameFilter() method changes the current filename filter to filter. This needs to be done before you show() the FileDialog.

NOTE   The JDK does not support the FilenameFilter with FileDialog boxes. FilenameFilter works but can't be used with FileDialog.

Miscellaneous methods

public int getMode ()

The getMode() method returns the current mode of the FileDialog. If an invalid mode was used in the constructor, this method returns an invalid mode here. No error checking is performed.

public void setMode (int mode) ★

The setMode() method changes the current mode of the FileDialog to mode. If mode is not one of the class constants LOAD or SAVE, setMode() throws the run-time exception IllegalArgumentException.

public synchronized void addNotify ()

The addNotify() method creates the FileDialog peer. This is automatically done when you call the show() method of the FileDialog. If you override this method, first call super.addNotify(), then add your customizations for the new class. Then you can do everything you need with the information about the newly created peer.

protected String paramString ()

> When you call the `toString()` method of `FileDialog`, the default `toString()` method of `Component` is called. This in turn calls `paramString()`, which builds up the string to display. At the `FileDialog` level, `paramString()` appends the directory (if not `null`) and current mode to the return value. Using the constructor `FileDialog(top, "Load Me")`, the results would be as follows:

```
java.awt.FileDialog[0,0,0x0,invalid,hidden,modal,title=Load Me,load]
```

6.7.2 A FileDialog Example

To get a better grasp of how the `FileDialog` works, the following application uses a `FileDialog` to select a file for display in a `TextArea`. You can also use `FileDialog` to save the file back to disk. Figure 6-10 shows the application, with a file displayed in the text area; the `FileDialog` itself looks like any other file dialog on the runtime system. Example 6-3 shows the code.

CAUTION   This example can overwrite an existing file.

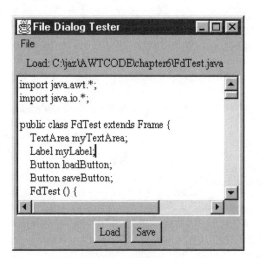

Figure 6–10: FileDialog test program

Example 6–3: Complete FileDialog

```
import java.awt.*;
import java.io.*;

public class FdTest extends Frame {
    TextArea myTextArea;
    Label myLabel;
```

Example 6–3: Complete FileDialog (continued)

```
        Button loadButton;
        Button saveButton;
        FdTest () {
            super ("File Dialog Tester");
            Panel p = new Panel ();
            p.add (loadButton = new Button ("Load"));
            p.add (saveButton = new Button ("Save"));
            add ("North", myLabel = new Label ());
            add ("South", p);
            add ("Center", myTextArea = new TextArea (10, 40));
            Menu m = new Menu ("File");
            m.add (new MenuItem ("Quit"));
            MenuBar mb = new MenuBar();
            mb.add (m);
            setMenuBar (mb);
            pack();
        }
        public static void main (String args[]) {
            FdTest f = new FdTest();
                f.show();
        }
        public boolean handleEvent (Event e) {
            if (e.id == Event.WINDOW_DESTROY) {
                hide();
                dispose ();
                System.exit(0);
                return true;  // never gets here
            }
            return super.handleEvent (e);
        }
        public boolean action (Event e, Object o) {
            if (e.target instanceof MenuItem) {
                hide();
                dispose ();
                System.exit(0);
                return true;  // never gets here
            } else if (e.target instanceof Button) {
                int state;
                String msg;
                if (e.target == loadButton) {
                    state = FileDialog.LOAD;
                    msg = "Load File";
                } else {// if (e.target == saveButton)
                    state = FileDialog.SAVE;
                    msg = "Save File";
                }
                FileDialog file = new FileDialog (this, msg, state);
                file.setFile ("*.java");  // set initial filename filter
                file.show(); // Blocks
                String curFile;
                if ((curFile = file.getFile()) != null) {
                    String filename = file.getDirectory() + curFile;
```

Example 6–3:   Complete FileDialog   (continued)

```
                    // curFile ends in .*.* if file does not exist
                    byte[] data;
                    setCursor (Frame.WAIT_CURSOR);
                    if (state == FileDialog.LOAD) {
                        File f = new File (filename);
                        try {
                            FileInputStream fin = new FileInputStream (f);
                            int filesize = (int)f.length();
                            data = new byte[filesize];
                            fin.read (data, 0, filesize);
                        } catch (FileNotFoundException exc) {
                            String errorString = "File Not Found: " + filename;
                            data = new byte[errorString.length()];
                            errorString.getBytes (0, errorString.length(), data, 0);
                        } catch (IOException exc) {
                            String errorString = "IOException: " + filename;
                            data = new byte[errorString.length()];
                            errorString.getBytes (0, errorString.length(), data, 0);
                        }
                        myLabel.setText ("Load: " + filename);
                    } else {
// Remove trailing ".*.*" if present - signifies file does not exist
                        if (filename.indexOf (".*.*") != -1) {
                            filename = filename.substring (0, filename.length()-4);
                        }
                        File f = new File (filename);
                        try {
                            FileOutputStream fon = new FileOutputStream (f);
                            String text = myTextArea.getText();
                            int textsize = text.length();
                            data = new byte[textsize];
                            text.getBytes (0, textsize, data, 0);
                            fon.write (data);
                            fon.close ();
                        } catch (IOException exc) {
                            String errorString = "IOException: " + filename;
                            data = new byte[errorString.length()];
                            errorString.getBytes (0, errorString.length(), data, 0);
                        }
                        myLabel.setText ("Save: " + filename);
                    }
                    // Note - on successful save, text is redisplayed
                    myTextArea.setText (new String (data, 0));
                    setCursor (Frame.DEFAULT_CURSOR);
                }
                return true;
            }
        return false;
    }
}
```

Most of this application is one long action() method that handles all the action events that take place within the Frame. The constructor doesn't do much besides arrange the display; it includes code to create a File menu with one item, Quit. This menu is visible in the upper left corner of the Frame; we'll see more about working with menus in Chapter 10 We provide a main() method to display the Frame and a handleEvent() method to shut the application down if the event WIN-DOW_DESTROY occurs.

But the heart of this program is clearly its action() method. action() starts by checking whether the user selected a menu item; if so, it shuts down the application because the only item on our menu is Quit. It then checks whether the user clicked on one of the buttons and sets the FileDialog mode to LOAD or SAVE accordingly. It then sets a default filename, *.java, which limits the display to filenames ending in .java. Next, action() shows the dialog. Because file dialogs are modal, show() blocks until the user selects a file or clicks Cancel.

The next line detects whether or not getFile() returns null. A null return indicates that the user selected Cancel; in this case, the dialog disappears, but nothing else happens. We then build a complete filename from the directory name and the name the user selected. If the dialog's state is LOAD, we read the file and display it in the text area. Otherwise, the dialog's state must be SAVE, so we save the contents of the text area under the given filename. Note that we first check for the string *.* and remove it if it is present. In Java 1.1, these two lines are unnecessary, but they don't hurt, either.

7

Layouts

This chapter expands upon the idea of a layout manager, which was mentioned briefly in the previous chapter. Every container has a LayoutManager that is responsible for positioning the component objects within it, regardless of the platform or the screen size. Layout managers eliminate the need to compute component placement on your own, which would be a losing proposition since the size required for any component depends on the platform on which it is displayed. Even for a simple layout, the code required to discover component sizes and compute absolute positions could be hundreds of lines, particularly if you concern yourself with what happens when the user resizes a window. A layout manager takes care of this for you. It asks each component in the layout how much space it requires, then arranges the components on the screen as best it can, based on the component sizes on the platform in use and the space available, resizing the components as needed.

To find out how much space a component needs, a layout manager calls the component's getMinimumSize() and getPreferredSize() methods. (Java 1.1 also has a getMaximumSize() method; the existing layout managers don't take advantage of it.) These methods report the minimum space that a component requires to be displayed correctly and the optimal size at which it looks best. Thus, each component must know its space requirements; the layout manager uses these to arrange the screen; and your Java program never has to worry about platform-dependent positioning.

The java.awt package provides five layout managers: FlowLayout, BorderLayout, GridLayout, CardLayout, and GridBagLayout. Four additional layouts are provided in the sun.awt package: HorizBagLayout, VerticalBagLayout, Orientable-FlowLayout, and VariableGridLayout. OrientableFlowLayout is new to Java 1.1. Of the 1.0 layouts, all are available in the JDK and Internet Explorer. The VariableGridLayout is also available with Netscape Navigator. This chapter discusses all of them, along with the LayoutManager and LayoutManager2 interfaces; we'll pay particular attention to how each layout manager computes positions for its components. We will also discuss how to combine layouts to generate more complex screens and how to create your own LayoutManager for special situations.

7.1 The LayoutManager Interface

The LayoutManager interface defines the responsibilities of something that wants to lay out Components within a Container. It is the LayoutManager's duty to determine the position and size of each component within the Container. You will never directly call the methods of the LayoutManager interface; for the most part, layout managers do their work behind the scenes. Once you have created a LayoutManager object and told the container to use it (by calling setLayout()), you're finished with it. The system calls the appropriate methods in the layout manager when necessary.

Therefore, the LayoutManager interface is most important when you are writing a new layout manager; we'll discuss it here because it's the scaffolding on which all layout managers are based. Like any interface, LayoutManager specifies the methods a layout manager must implement but says nothing about how the LayoutManager does its job. Therefore, we'll make a few observations before proceeding. First, a layout manager is free to ignore some of its components; there is no requirement that a layout manager display everything. For example, a Container using a BorderLayout might include thirty or forty components. However, the BorderLayout will display at most five of them (the last component placed in each of its five named areas). Likewise, a CardLayout may manage many components but displays only one at a time.

Second, a layout manager can do anything it wants with the components' minimum and preferred sizes. It is free to ignore either. It makes sense that a layout manager can ignore a preferred size; after all, "preferred" means "give me this if it's available." However, a layout manager can also ignore a minimum size. At times, there is no reasonable alternative: the container may not have enough room to display a component at its minimum size. How to handle this situation is left to the layout manager's discretion. All layout managers currently ignore a component's maximum size, though this may change in the future.

7.1.1 Methods of the LayoutManager Interface

Five methods make up the LayoutManager interface. If you create your own class that implements LayoutManager, you must define all five. As you will see, many of the methods do not have to do anything, but there must still be a stub with the appropriate method signature.

public abstract void addLayoutComponent (String name, Component component)
>   The addLayoutComponent() method is called only when the program assigns a name to the component when adding it to the layout (i.e., the program calls add(String, Component) rather than simply calling add(Component) or the Java 1.1 add(Component, Object)). It is up to the layout manager to decide what, if anything, to do with the name. For example, BorderLayout uses name to specify an area on the screen in which to display the component. Most layout managers don't require a name and will only implement a stub.

public abstract void removeLayoutComponent (Component component)
>   The removeLayoutComponent() method's responsibility is to remove component from any internal storage used by the layout manager. This method will probably be stubbed out for your own layouts and do nothing. However, it may need to do something if your layout manager associates components with names.

public abstract Dimension preferredLayoutSize (Container parent)
>   The preferredLayoutSize() method is called to determine the preferred size of the components within the Container. It returns a Dimension object that contains the required height and width. parent is the object whose components need to be laid out. Usually, the LayoutManager determines how to size parent by calculating the sizes of the components within it and calculating the dimensions required to display them. On other occasions, it may just return parent.setSize().

public abstract Dimension minimumLayoutSize (Container parent)
>   The minimumLayoutSize() method is called to determine the minimum size of the components within the Container. It returns a Dimension object that contains the required height and width. parent is the object whose components need to be laid out.

public abstract void layoutContainer (Container parent)

> The `layoutContainer()` method is where a `LayoutManager` does most of its work. The `layoutContainer()` method is responsible for the positioning of all the `Components` of parent. Each specific layout positions the enclosed components based upon its own rules.

7.1.2 The LayoutManager2 Interface

Numerous changes were introduced in Java 1.1 to make it conform to various design patterns. These patterns provide consistency in usage and make Java programming easier. The `LayoutManager2` interface was introduced for this reason. This new interface solves a problem that occurs when working with the `GridBagLayout`. While the `addLayoutComponent(String, Component)` method of `LayoutManager` works great for `BorderLayout` and `CardLayout`, you can't use it for a `GridBagLayout`. The position of a component in a `GridBagLayout` is controlled by a number of constraints, which are encapsulated in a `GridBagConstraints` object. To associate constraints with a component, you needed to call a `setConstraints()` method. Although this works, it is not consistent with the way you add components to other layouts. Furthermore, as more and more people create their own layout managers, the number of ways to associate positioning information with a component could grow endlessly. `LayoutManager2` defines a version of `addLayoutComponent()` that can be used by all constraint-based layout managers, including older managers like `BorderLayout` and `CardLayout`. This method lets you pass an arbitrary object to the layout manager to provide positioning information. Layout managers that need additional information (like the `GridBagConstraints` object) now implement `LayoutManager2` instead of `LayoutManager`.

In addition to swapping the parameters to the `addLayoutComponent(Component, Object)`, the new `LayoutManager2` interface also defines several methods that aren't really needed now but will facilitate the introduction of "peerless components" in a later release.

Methods of the LayoutManager2 interface

public abstract void addLayoutComponent(Component comp, Object constraints) ★

> The `addLayoutComponent()` method is called when a program assigns constraints to the component `comp` when adding it to the layout. In practice, this means that the program added the component by calling the new method `add(Component component, Object constraints)` rather than the older methods `add(Component component)` or `add(String name, Component component))`. It is up to the layout manager to decide what, if anything, to do with the constraints. For example, `GridBagLayout` uses constraints to associate a `GridBagConstraints` object to the component `comp`. `BorderLayout` uses constraints to associate a location string (like "Center") with the component.

public abstract Dimension maximumLayoutSize(Container target) ★

The `maximumLayoutSize()` method must return the maximum size of the `tar-get` container under this layout manager. Previously, only minimum and pre-ferred sizes were available. Now a container can have a maximum size. Once layout managers support the concept of maximum sizes, containers will not grow without bounds when additional space is available. If there is no actual maximum, the `Dimension` should have a width and height of the constant `Integer.MAX_VALUE`.

public abstract float getLayoutAlignmentX(Container target) ★

The `getLayoutAlignmentX()` method must return the alignment of `target` along the x axis. The return value should be between 0.0 and 1.0. Values nearer 0 mean that the container will be positioned closer to the left edge of the area available. Values nearer 1 mean that the container will be positioned closer to the right. The value 0.5 means the container should be centered.

public abstract float getLayoutAlignmentY(Container target) ★

The `getLayoutAlignmentY()` method must return the alignment of `target` along the y axis. The return value should be between 0.0 and 1.0. Values nearer 0 mean that the container will be positioned closer to the top of the area available. Values nearer 1 mean that the container will be positioned closer to the bottom. The value 0.5 means the container should be centered.

public abstract void invalidateLayout(Container target) ★

The `invalidateLayout()` method tells the layout manager that any layout information it has for `target` is invalid. This method will usually be imple-mented as a stub (i.e., {}). However, if the layout manager caches any infor-mation about `target` when this method is called, the manager should consider that information invalid and discard it.

7.2 *FlowLayout*

`FlowLayout` is the default `LayoutManager` for a `Panel`. A `FlowLayout` adds compo-nents to the container in rows, working from left to right. When it can't fit any more components in a row, it starts a new row—not unlike a word processor with word wrap enabled. When the container gets resized, the components within it get repositioned based on the container's new size. If sufficient space is available, com-ponents within `FlowLayout` containers are given their preferred size. If there is insufficient space, you do not see the components in their entirety.

7.2.1 FlowLayout Methods

Constants

FlowLayout defines three constants, all of which are used to specify alignment. The alignment tells FlowLayout where to start positioning the components on each row. Each component is still added from left to right, no matter what the alignment setting is.

public final static int LEFT

   LEFT is the constant for left alignment.

public final static int CENTER

   CENTER is the constant for center alignment and is the default.

public final static int RIGHT

   RIGHT is the constant for right alignment.

Constructors

public FlowLayout ()

   This constructor creates a FlowLayout using default settings: center alignment with a horizontal and vertical gap of five pixels. The gap is the space between the different components in the different directions. By default, there will be five pixels between components. The constructor is usually called within a call to setLayout(): setLayout (new FlowLayout()). Figure 7-1 shows how the default FlowLayout behaves with different screen sizes. As the screen C shows, if the screen is too small, the components will *not* be shrunk so that they can fit better.

public FlowLayout (int alignment)

   This version of the constructor creates a FlowLayout using the specified alignment and a horizontal and vertical gap of five pixels. Valid alignments are the FlowLayout constants, although there is no verification. Figure 7-2 shows the effect of different alignments: FlowLayout.LEFT (screen A), FlowLayout.CENTER (B), and FlowLayout.RIGHT (C).

public FlowLayout (int alignment, int hgap, int vgap)

   The final version of the constructor is called by the other two. It requires you to explicitly specify the alignment, horizontal gap (hgap), and vertical gap (vgap). This creates a FlowLayout with an alignment of alignment, horizontal gap of hgap, and vertical gap of vgap. The units for gaps are pixels. It is possible to have negative gaps if you want components to be placed on top of one another. Figure 7-3 shows the effect of changing the gap sizes.

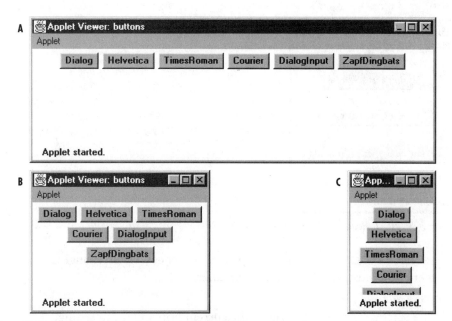

Figure 7–1: FlowLayout with six buttons and three different screen sizes

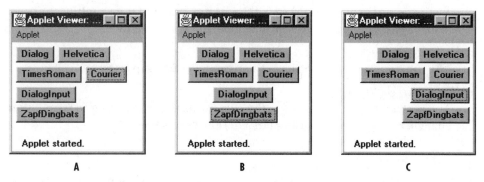

Figure 7–2: FlowLayout with three different alignments

Informational methods

public int getAlignment () ★

> The getAlignment() method retrieves the current alignment of the FlowLayout. The return value should equal one of the class constants LEFT, CENTER, or RIGHT.

public void setAlignment (int alignment) ★

> The setAlignment() method changes the FlowLayout alignment to alignment. The alignment value should equal one of the class constants LEFT,

Figure 7–3: FlowLayout with hgap of 0 and vgap of 20

CENTER, or RIGHT, but this method does not check. After changing the alignment, you must validate() the Container.

public int getHgap () ★

The getHgap() method retrieves the current horizontal gap setting.

public void setHgap (int hgap) ★

The setHgap() method changes the current horizontal gap setting to hgap. After changing the gaps, you must validate() the Container.

public int getVgap () ★

The getVgap() method retrieves the current vertical gap setting.

public void setVgap (int hgap) ★

The setVgap() method changes the current vertical gap setting to vgap. After changing the gaps, you must validate() the Container.

LayoutManager methods

public void addLayoutComponent (String name, Component component)

The addLayoutComponent() method of FlowLayout does nothing.

public void removeLayoutComponent (Component component)

The removeLayoutComponent() method of FlowLayout does nothing.

public Dimension preferredLayoutSize (Container target)

The preferredLayoutSize() method of FlowLayout calculates the preferred dimensions for the target container. The FlowLayout computes the preferred size by placing all the components in one row and adding their individual preferred sizes along with gaps and insets.

public Dimension minimumLayoutSize (Container target)

> The `minimumLayoutSize()` method of `FlowLayout` calculates the minimum dimensions for the container by adding up the sizes of the components. The `FlowLayout` computes the minimum size by placing all the components in one row and adding their individual minimum sizes along with gaps and insets.

public void layoutContainer (Container target)

> The `layoutContainer()` method draws `target`'s components on the screen, starting with the first row of the display, going left to right across the screen, based on the current alignment setting. When it reaches the right margin of the container, it skips down to the next row, and continues drawing additional components.

Miscellaneous methods

public String toString ()

> The `toString()` method of `FlowLayout` returns the current horizontal and vertical gap settings along with the alignment (left, center, right). For a `FlowLayout` that uses all the defaults, `toString()` produces:

```
java.awt.FlowLayout[hgap=5,vgap=5,align=center]
```

7.3 BorderLayout

`BorderLayout` is the default `LayoutManager` for a `Window`. It provides a very flexible way of positioning components along the edges of the window. The following call to `setLayout()` changes the `LayoutManager` of the current container to the default `BorderLayout`: `setLayout(new BorderLayout())`. Figure 7-4 shows a typical `BorderLayout`.

`BorderLayout` is the only layout provided that requires you to name components when you add them to the layout; if you're using a `BorderLayout`, you must use `add(String name, Component component)` in Java 1.0 or `add(Component component, String name)` in Java 1.1 (parameter order switched). (The `CardLayout` can use these versions of `add()`, but does not require it.) The `name` parameter of `add()` specifies the region to which the component should be added. The five different regions are "North", "South", "East", and "West" for the edges of the window, and "Center" for any remaining interior space. These names are case sensitive. It is not necessary that a container use all five regions. If a region is not used, it relinquishes its space to the regions around it. If you `add()` multiple objects to a single region, the layout manager only displays the last one. If you want to display multiple objects within a region, group them within a `Panel` first, then `add()` the `Panel`.

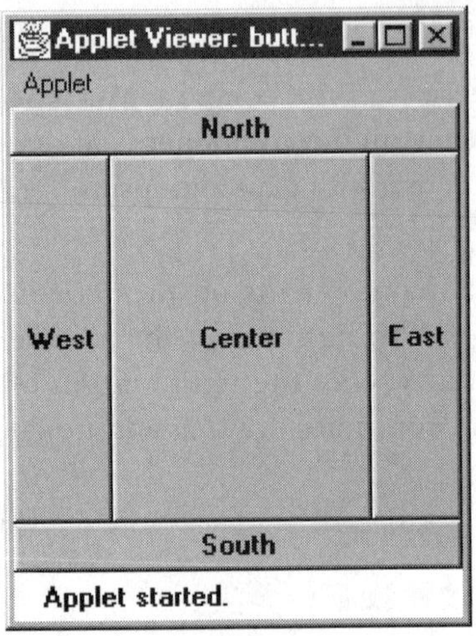

Figure 7–4: BorderLayout

NOTE   In Java 1.1, if you do not provide a name, the component is placed in
              the "Center" region.

7.3.1 BorderLayout Methods

Constants

Prior to Java 1.1, you had to use string constants to specify the constraints when adding a component to a container whose layout is BorderLayout. With Java 1.1, you can use class constants, instead of a literal string, in the following list.

public static final String CENTER ★

> The CENTER constant represents the "Center" string and indicates that a component should be added to the center region.

public static final String EAST ★

> The EAST constant represents the "East" string and indicates that a component should be added to the east region.

public static final String NORTH ★

> The NORTH constant represents the "North" string and indicates that a component should be added to the north region.

public static final String SOUTH ★

> The SOUTH constant represents the "South" string and indicates that a component should be added to the south region.

public static final String WEST ★

> The WEST constant represents the "West" string and indicates that a component should be added to the west region.

Constructors

public BorderLayout ()

> This constructor creates a BorderLayout using a default setting of zero pixels for the horizontal and vertical gaps. The gap specifies the space between adjacent components. With horizontal and vertical gaps of zero, components in adjacent regions will touch each other. As Figure 7-4 shows, each component within a BorderLayout will be resized to fill an entire region.

public BorderLayout (int hgap, int vgap)

> This version of the constructor allows you to create a BorderLayout with a horizontal gap of hgap and vertical gap of vgap, putting some space between the different components. The units for gaps are pixels. It is possible to have negative gaps if you want components to overlap.

Informational methods

public int getHgap () ★

> The getHgap() method retrieves the current horizontal gap setting.

public void setHgap (int hgap) ★

> The setHgap() method changes the current horizontal gap setting to hgap. After changing the gaps, you must validate() the Container.

public int getVgap () ★

> The getVgap() method retrieves the current vertical gap setting.

public void setVgap (int hgap) ★

> The setVgap() method changes the current vertical gap setting to vgap. After changing the gaps, you must validate() the Container.

LayoutManager methods

public void addLayoutComponent (String name, Component component) ☆

> This version of addLayoutComponent() has been deprecated and replaced by the addLayoutComponent(Component, Object) method of the LayoutManager2 interface.

public void removeLayoutComponent (Component component)

The removeLayoutComponent() method of BorderLayout removes component from the container, if it is in one of the five regions. If component is not in the container already, nothing happens.

public Dimension preferredLayoutSize (Container target)

The preferredLayoutSize() method of BorderLayout calculates the preferred dimensions for the components in target. To compute the preferred height, a BorderLayout adds the height of the getPreferredSize() of the north and south components to the maximum getPreferredSize() height of the east, west, and center components. The vertical gaps are added in for the north and south components, if present. The top and bottom insets are also added into the height. To compute the preferred width, a BorderLayout adds the width of the getPreferredSize() of east, west, and center components, along with the horizontal gap for the east and west regions. It compares this value to the preferred widths of the north and south components. The BorderLayout takes the maximum of these three and then adds the left and right insets, plus twice the horizontal gap. The result is the preferred width for the container.

public Dimension minimumLayoutSize (Container target)

The minimumLayoutSize() method of BorderLayout calculates the minimum dimensions for the components in target. To compute the minimum height, a BorderLayout adds the height of the getMinimumSize() of the north and south components to the maximum of the minimum heights of the east, west, and center components. The vertical gaps are added in for the north and south components, if present, along with the container's top and bottom insets. To compute the minimum width, a BorderLayout adds the width of the getMinimumSize() of east, west, and center components, along with the horizontal gap for the east and west regions. The BorderLayout takes the maximum of these three and then adds the left and right insets, plus twice the horizontal gap. The result is the minimum width for the container.

public void layoutContainer (Container target)

The layoutContainer() method draws target's components on the screen in the appropriate regions. The north region takes up the entire width of the container along the top. South does the same along the bottom. The heights of north and south will be the heights of the components they contain. The east and west regions are given the widths of the components they contain. For height, east and west are given whatever is left in the container after satisfying north's and south's height requirements. If there is any extra vertical space, the east and west components are resized accordingly. Any space left in the middle of the screen is assigned to the center region. If there is insufficient space for all the components, space is allocated according to the following priority: north, south, west, east, and center. Unlike `FlowLayout`, `BorderLayout` reshapes the internal components of the container to fit within their region. Figure 7-5 shows what happens if the east and south regions are not present and the gaps are nonzero.

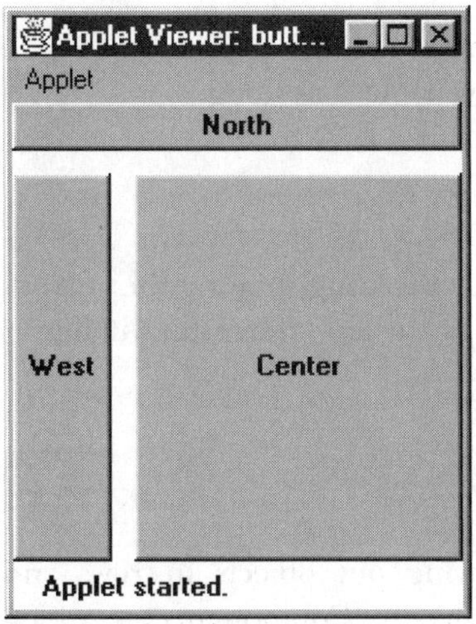

Figure 7–5: BorderLayout with missing regions

LayoutManager2 methods

public void addLayoutComponent (Component component, Object name) ★

This `addLayoutComponent()` method puts `component` in the `name` region of the container. In Java 1.1, if `name` is null, `component` is added to the center. If the name is not "North", "South", "East", "West", or "Center", the component is added to the container but won't be displayed. Otherwise, it is displayed in the appropriate region.

There can only be one component in any region, so any component already in the named region is removed. To get multiple components in one region of a `BorderLayout`, group the components in another container, and add the container as a whole to the layout.

If `name` is not a `String`, `addLayoutComponent()` throws the run-time exception `IllegalArgumentException`.

public abstract Dimension maximumLayoutSize(Container target) ★

The `maximumLayoutSize()` method returns a `Dimension` object with a width and height of `Integer.MAX_VALUE`. In effect, this means that `BorderLayout` does not support the concept of maximum size.

public abstract float getLayoutAlignmentX(Container target) ★

The `getLayoutAlignmentX()` method says that `BorderLayout` containers should be centered horizontally within the area available.

public abstract float getLayoutAlignmentY(Container target) ★

The `getLayoutAlignmentY()` method says that `BorderLayout` containers should centered vertically within the area available.

public abstract void invalidateLayout(Container target) ★

The `invalidateLayout()` method of `BorderLayout` does nothing.

Miscellaneous methods

public String toString ()

The `toString()` method of `BorderLayout` returns a string showing the current horizontal and vertical gap settings. If both gaps are zero, the result will be:

```
java.awt.BorderLayout[hgap=0,vgap=0]
```

7.4 GridLayout

The `GridLayout` layout manager is ideal for laying out objects in rows and columns, where each cell in the layout has the same size. Components are added to the layout from left to right, top to bottom. `setLayout(new GridLayout(2,3))` changes the `LayoutManager` of the current container to a 2 row by 3 column `Grid-Layout`. Figure 7-6 shows an applet using this layout.

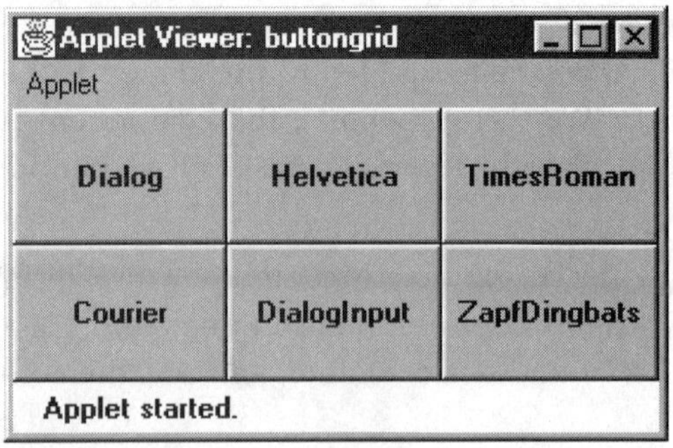

Figure 7–6: Applet using GridLayout

7.4.1 GridLayout Methods

Constructors

public GridLayout () ★

This constructor creates a GridLayout initially configured to have one row, an infinite number of columns, and no gaps. A gap is the space between adjacent components in the horizontal or vertical direction. With a gap of zero, components in adjacent cells will have no space between them.

public GridLayout (int rows, int columns)

This constructor creates a GridLayout initially configured to be rows × columns in size. The default setting for horizontal and vertical gaps is zero pixels. The gap is the space between adjacent components in the horizontal and vertical directions. With a gap of zero, components in adjacent cells will have no space between them.

You can set the number of rows or columns to zero; this means that the layout will grow without bounds in that direction. If both rows and columns are zero, the run-time exception IllegalArgumentException will be thrown.

NOTE   The rows and columns passed to the GridLayout constructor are only recommended values. It is possible that the system will pick other values if the number of objects you add to the layout is sufficiently different from the size you requested; for example, you placed nine objects in a six-element grid.

---

public GridLayout (int rows, int columns, int hgap, int vgap)

This version of the constructor is called by the previous one. It creates a Grid-Layout with an initial configuration of rows × columns, with a horizontal gap of hgap and vertical gap of vgap. The gap is the space between the different components in the different directions, measured in pixels. It is possible to have negative gaps if you want components to overlap.

You can set the number of rows or columns to zero; this means that the layout will grow without bounds in that direction. If both rows and columns are zero, the run-time exception IllegalArgumentException will be thrown.

Informational methods

public int getColumns () ★

The getColumns() method retrieves the current column setting, which may differ from the number of columns displayed.

public void setColumns (int columns) ★

The setColumns() method changes the current column setting to columns. After changing the setting, you must validate() the Container. If you try to set the number of rows and the number of columns to zero, this method throws the run-time exception IllegalArgumentException.

public int getRows () ★

The getRows() method retrieves the current row setting; this may differ from the number of rows displayed.

public void setRows (int rows) ★

The setRows() method changes the current row setting to rows. After changing the setting, you must validate() the Container. If you try to set the number of rows and the number of columns to zero, this method throws the run-time exception IllegalArgumentException.

public int getHgap () ★

The getHgap() method retrieves the current horizontal gap setting.

public void setHgap (int hgap) ★

The setHgap() method changes the current horizontal gap setting to hgap. After changing the gaps, you must validate() the Container.

public int getVgap () ★

The getVgap() method retrieves the current vertical gap setting.

public void setVgap (int hgap) ★

The setVgap() method changes the current vertical gap setting to vgap. After changing the gaps, you must validate() the Container.

LayoutManager methods

public void addLayoutComponent (String name, Component component)

The addLayoutComponent() method of GridLayout does nothing.

public void removeLayoutComponent (Component component)

The removeLayoutComponent() method of GridLayout does nothing.

public Dimension preferredLayoutSize (Container target)

The preferredLayoutSize() method of GridLayout calculates the preferred dimensions for the components in target. The preferred size depends on the size of the grid, which may not be the size requested by the constructor; the GridLayout treats the constructor's arguments as recommendations and may ignore them if appropriate.

The actual number of rows and columns is based upon the number of components within the Container. The GridLayout tries to observe the number of rows requested first, calculating the number of columns. If the requested number of rows is nonzero, the number of columns is determined by (# components + rows − 1) / rows. If request is for zero rows, the number of rows to use is determined by a similar formula: (# components + columns − 1) / columns. Table 7-1 demonstrates this calculation. The last entry in this table is of special interest: if you request a 3×3 grid but only place four components in the layout, you get a 2×2 layout as a result. If you do not want to be surprised, size the GridLayout based on the number of objects you plan to put into the display.

Table 7–1: GridLayout Row/Column Calculation

Rows	Columns	# Components	Display Rows	Display Columns
0	1	10	10	1
0	2	10	5	2
1	0	10	1	10
2	0	10	2	5
2	3	10	2	5
2	3	20	2	10
3	2	10	3	4
3	3	3	3	1
3	3	4	2	2

Once we know the dimensions of the grid, it's easy to compute the preferred size for the layout. The GridLayout takes the maximum height and maximum width of the preferred sizes for all the components in the layout. (Note that the maximum width and maximum height aren't necessarily from the same component.) This becomes the preferred size of each cell within the layout. The preferred size of the layout as a whole is computed using the preferred size of a cell and adding gaps and insets as appropriate.

public Dimension minimumLayoutSize (Container target)

The minimumLayoutSize() method of GridLayout calculates the minimum dimensions for the components in target. First it determines the actual number of rows and columns in the final layout, using the method described previously. The minimumLayoutSize() method then determines the widest and tallest getMinimumSize() of a component, and this becomes the minimum size of a cell within the layout. The minimum size of the layout as a whole is computed using the minimum size of a cell and adding gaps and insets as appropriate.

public void layoutContainer (Container target)

> The `layoutContainer()` method draws `target`'s components on the screen in a series of rows and columns. Each component within a `GridLayout` will be the same size, if it is possible. If there is insufficient space for all the components, the size of each is reduced proportionally.

Miscellaneous methods

public String toString ()

> The `toString()` method of `GridLayout` returns a string including the current horizontal and vertical gap settings, along with the rows and columns settings. For a `GridLayout` created with 2 rows and 3 columns, the result would be:

```
java.awt.GridLayout[hgap=0,vgap=0,rows=2,cols=3]
```

7.5 CardLayout

The `CardLayout` layout manager is significantly different from the other layouts. Whereas the other layout managers attempt to display all the components within the container at once, a `CardLayout` displays only one component at a time. (That component could be a `Component` or another `Container`.) The result is similar to Netscape Navigator's Property sheets or a tabbed Dialog, without the tabs. You can flip through the cards (components) in the layout in order or jump to a specific card if you know its name. The following call to `setLayout()` changes the Layout-Manager of the current container to `CardLayout`:

```
lm = new CardLayout();
setLayout (lm);
```

Unlike most other layout managers, `CardLayout` has a number of instance methods that programs have to call. Therefore, you usually have to retain a reference to the layout manager. In addition, you usually have some other component to control the `CardLayout` (i.e., select which card to view). Most simply, you could put some buttons in a panel and stick this panel in the north region of a `BorderLayout`; then make another panel with a `CardLayout`, and place that in the center. A more complex task would be to build a set of tabs to control the Card-Layout.

A `CardLayout` allows you to assign names to the components it manages. You can use the name to jump to an arbitrary component by calling the manager's `show()` method. In Java 1.0, naming was optional; you could call `add(Component)` to put a component in the layout with a null name. A null name meant only that you couldn't flip to the component at will; you could only display the component by calling next() or previous() (or first() or last()), which cycle through all the components in order. In Java 1.1, all components added to a CardLayout must be named.

7.5.1 CardLayout Methods

Constructors

public CardLayout ()

This constructor creates a CardLayout using a horizontal and vertical gap of zero pixels. With CardLayout, there is no space between components because only one component is visible at a time; think of the gaps as insets.

public CardLayout (int hgap, int vgap)

This version of the constructor allows you to create a CardLayout with a horizontal gap of hgap and vertical gap of vgap to add some space around the outside of the component that is displayed. The units for gaps are pixels. Using negative gaps chops off components at the edges of the container.

Informational methods

public int getHgap () ★

The getHgap() method retrieves the current horizontal gap setting.

public void setHgap (int hgap) ★

The setHgap() method changes the current horizontal gap setting to hgap. After changing the gaps, you must validate() the Container.

public int getVgap () ★

The getVgap() method retrieves the current vertical gap setting.

public void setVgap (int hgap) ★

The setVgap() method changes the current vertical gap setting to vgap. After changing the gaps, you must validate() the Container.

LayoutManager methods

public void addLayoutComponent (String name, Component component) ☆

This version of addLayoutComponent() has been deprecated and replaced by the addLayoutComponent(Component, Object) method of the LayoutManager2 interface.

public void removeLayoutComponent (Component component)

The removeLayoutComponent() method of CardLayout removes component from the container. If component is not in the container already, nothing happens.

public Dimension preferredLayoutSize (Container target)

The `preferredLayoutSize()` method of `CardLayout` retrieves the preferred size for all the components within it. The `preferredLayoutSize()` method then determines the widest and tallest size of all components (not necessarily from the same one), adds the appropriate insets and gaps, and uses that as the preferred size for the layout.

public Dimension minimumLayoutSize (Container target)

The `minimumLayoutSize()` method of `CardLayout` calculates the minimum size for all the components within it. The `minimumLayoutSize()` method then determines the widest and tallest minimum size of all components (not necessarily from the same one), adds the appropriate insets and gaps, and uses that as the minimum size for the layout.

public void layoutContainer (Container target)

The `layoutContainer()` method draws `target`'s visible components one on top of another. Initially, all components are visible. Components do not become invisible until you select one for display, by calling the `first()`, `last()`, `next()`, `previous()`, or `show()` methods. Where possible, `CardLayout` reshapes all components to fit the target container.

LayoutManager2 methods

public void addLayoutComponent (Component component, Object name) ★

This `addLayoutComponent()` method of `CardLayout` puts `component` into an internal table with a key of `name`. The `name` comes from the version of `add()` that has a constraints object as a parameter. The name allows you to refer to the component when you call other card layout methods, like `show()`. If you call the version of `add()` that only takes a `Component` parameter, you cannot call the `show()` method to flip to the specific component.

If `name` is not a `String`, the run-time exception `IllegalArgumentException` is thrown.

public abstract Dimension maximumLayoutSize(Container target) ★

The `maximumLayoutSize()` method returns a `Dimension` object with a width and height of `Integer.MAX_VALUE`. In practice, this means that `CardLayout` doesn't support the concept of maximum size.

public abstract float getLayoutAlignmentX(Container target) ★

The `getLayoutAlignmentX()` method says that `CardLayout` containers should be centered horizontally within the area available.

public abstract float getLayoutAlignmentY(Container target) ★

> The `getLayoutAlignmentY()` method says that `CardLayout` containers should be centered vertically within the area available.

public abstract void invalidateLayout(Container target) ★

> The `invalidateLayout()` method of `CardLayout` does nothing.

CardLayout methods

This group of methods controls which component the `CardLayout` displays. The `show()` is only usable if you assigned components names when adding them to the container. The others can be used even if the components are unnamed; they cycle through the components in the order in which they were added. All of these methods require the parent `Container` (i.e., the container being managed by this layout manager) as an argument. If the layout manager of the `parent` parameter is anything other than the container using this instance of the `CardLayout`, the method throws the run-time exception `IllegalArgumentException`.

public void first (Container parent)

> The `first()` method flips to the initial component in `parent`.

public void next (Container parent)

> The `next()` method flips to the following component in `parent`, wrapping back to the beginning if the current component is the last.

public void previous (Container parent)

> The `previous()` method flips to the prior component in `parent`, wrapping to the end if the current component is the first.

public void last (Container parent)

> The `last()` method flips to the final component in `parent`.

public void show (Container parent, String name)

> The `show()` method displays the component in parent that was assigned the given `name` when it was added to the container. If there is no component with `name` contained within `parent`, nothing happens.

Miscellaneous methods

public String toString ()

> The `toString()` method of `CardLayout` returns the a string showing the current horizontal and vertical gap settings. The result for a typical `CardLayout` would be:

```
java.awt.CardLayout[hgap=0,vgap=0]
```

7.5.2 CardLayout Example

Figure 7-7 shows a simple CardLayout. This layout has three cards that cycle when
you make a selection. The first card (A) contains some Checkbox items within a
Panel, the second card (B) contains a single Button, and the third (C) contains a
List and a Choice within another Panel.

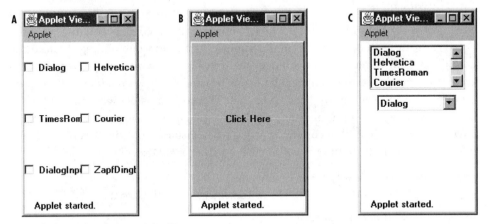

Figure 7–7: Different views of CardLayout

Example 7-1 is the code that generated Figure 7-7.

Example 7–1: The CardExample Class

```
import java.awt.*;
import java.applet.*;
public class CardExample extends Applet {
    CardLayout cl = new CardLayout();
    public void init () {
        String fonts[] = Toolkit.getDefaultToolkit().getFontList();
        setLayout (cl);
        Panel pA = new Panel();
        Panel pC = new Panel ();
        pl.setLayout (new GridLayout (3, 2));
        List l = new List(4, false);
        Choice c = new Choice ();
        for (int i=0;i<fonts.length;i++) {
            pA.add (new Checkbox (fonts[i]));
            l.addItem (fonts[i]);
            c.addItem (fonts[i]);
        }
        pC.add (l);
        pC.add (c);
        add ("One", pA);
        add ("Two", new Button ("Click Here"));
        add ("Three", pC);
    }
}
```

Example 7–1: The CardExample Class (continued)

```
        public boolean action (Event e, Object o) {
            cl.next(this);
            return true;
        }
    }
```

Each panel within the CardLayout has its own layout manager. Panel A uses a GridLayout; panel C uses its default layout manager, which is a FlowLayout. When the user takes any action (i.e., clicking on a checkbox or button, or selecting an item from the List or Choice components), the system generates a call to action(), which calls the CardLayout's next() method, thus displaying the next card in the sequence.

7.6 GridBagLayout

The GridBagLayout is the most complex and flexible of the standard layout managers. Although it sounds like it should be a subclass of GridLayout, it's a different animal entirely. With GridLayout, elements are arranged in a rectangular grid, and each element in the container is sized identically (where possible). With GridBagLayout, elements can have different sizes and can occupy multiple rows or columns. The position and behavior of each element is specified by an instance of the GridBagConstraints class. By properly constraining the elements, you can specify the number of rows and columns an element occupies, which element grows when additional screen real estate is available, and various other restrictions. The actual grid size is based upon the number of components within the GridBagLayout and the GridBagConstraints of those objects. For example, Figure 7-8 shows a GridBagLayout with seven components, arranged on a 3×3 grid. The maximum capacity of a screen using GridBagLayout in Java 1.0 is 128×128 cells; in Java 1.1, the maximum size is 512×512 cells.

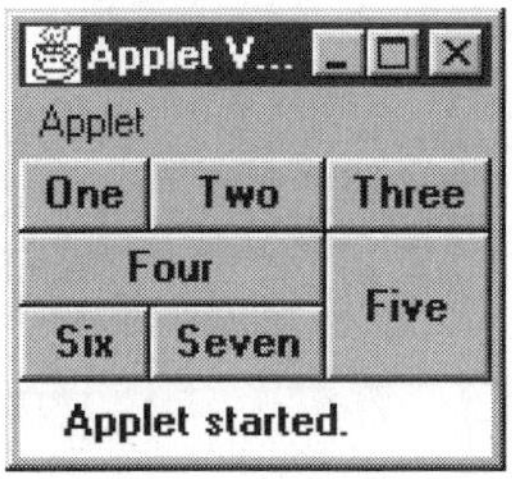

Figure 7–8: GridBagLayout with seven components on a 3×3 grid

With the other layout managers, adding a component to the container requires only a call to add(). In Java 1.0, the GridBagLayout also requires you to call set-Constraints() to tell the layout manager how to position the component. With Java 1.1, you use the new add() method that permits you to pass the component and its constraints in a single method call (add(Component, Object)). If no components are added with constraints (thus all using the defaults), the GridBagLay-out places the components in a single row at the center of the screen and sizes them to their getPreferredSize(). This is a nice way to place a single object in the center of the screen without stretching it to take up the available space, as BorderLayout does. Figure 7-9 compares the default GridBagLayout with a BorderLayout displaying the same object in the center region.

Figure 7–9: Centering a component: GridBagLayout vs. BorderLayout

When designing a container that will use GridBagLayout, it is easiest to plan what you want on graph paper, and then determine how the constraints should be set. The alternative, adding the components to the layout and then tweaking the constraints until you have something you like, could lead to premature baldness. Seriously, a trial-and-error approach to getting the constraints right will certainly be frustrating and will probably fail. Figure 7-10, using the same GridBagLayout used in Figure 7-8, indicates how the layout manager counts cells. The partial code used to create the screen follows in Example 7-2.

Example 7–2: Creating a GridBagLayout

```
public void init() {
    Button b;
    GridBagLayout gb = new GridBagLayout();
    GridBagConstraints gbc = new GridBagConstraints();
    setLayout(gb);
    try {
/* Row One - Three button */
        b = new Button ("One");
        addComponent (this, b, 0, 0, 1, 1,
                GridBagConstraints.NONE, GridBagConstraints.CENTER);
        b = new Button ("Two");
        addComponent (this, b, 1, 0, 1, 1,
                GridBagConstraints.NONE, GridBagConstraints.CENTER);
```

Example 7–2: Creating a GridBagLayout (continued)

```
            b = new Button ("Three");
            addComponent (this, b, 2, 0, 1, 1,
                    GridBagConstraints.NONE, GridBagConstraints.CENTER);
/* Row Two - Two buttons */
            b = new Button ("Four");
            addComponent (this, b, 0, 1, 2, 1,
                    GridBagConstraints.NONE, GridBagConstraints.CENTER);
            b = new Button ("Five");
            addComponent (this, b, 2, 1, 1, 2,
                    GridBagConstraints.NONE, GridBagConstraints.CENTER);
/* Row Three - Two buttons */
            b = new Button ("Six");
            addComponent (this, b, 0, 2, 1, 1,
                    GridBagConstraints.NONE, GridBagConstraints.CENTER);
            b = new Button ("Seven");
            addComponent (this, b, 1, 2, 1, 1,
                    GridBagConstraints.NONE, GridBagConstraints.CENTER);
        } catch (Exception e) {
            e.printStackTrace();
        }
    }
```

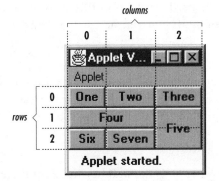

Figure 7–10: How GridBagLayout counts rows and columns

Most of the work in Example 7-2 is done by the helper method addComponent(), which creates a set of constraints, applies them to a component, and adds the component to a container. The code for addComponent() appears in Section 7.7; its signature is:

```
public static void addComponent (Container container, Component component,
        int gridx, int gridy, int gridwidth, int gridheight, int fill,
        int anchor) throws AWTException ;
```

The top left cell in the layout has location (0,0). There's nothing very surprising about buttons one, two, three, six, and seven. They occupy a 1×1 area on the layout's 3×3 grid. Button four occupies a 2×1 area; it is placed at location (0,1), and thus occupies this cell plus the cell at (1,1). Likewise, button five occupies a 1×2 area, and takes up the cells at (2,1) and (2,2). The total size of the layout is determined entirely by the components that are placed in it and their constraints.

7.6.1 GridBagLayout Methods

Variables

There are a handful of instance variables for GridBagLayout. They are not initialized until the container whose layout is GridBagLayout has been validated.

public int columnWidths[]

> The columnWidths[] array contains the widths of the components in the row with the most elements. The values of this array are returned by the getLayoutDimensions() method. You can access the array directly, but it is not recommended.

public int rowHeights[]

> The rowHeights[] array contains the heights of the components in the column with the most elements. The values of this array are returned by the getLayoutDimensions() method. You can access the array directly, but it is not recommended.

public double columnWeights[]

> The columnWeights[] array contains the weightx values of the components in the row with the most elements. The values of this array are returned by the getLayoutWeights() method. You can access the array directly, but it is not recommended.

public double rowWeights[]

> The rowWeights[] array contains the weighty values of the components in the column with the most elements. The values of this array are returned by the getLayoutWeights() method. You can access the array directly, but it is not recommended.

Constructors

public GridBagLayout ()

> The constructor for GridBagLayout creates an instance of GridBagLayout with default GridBagConstraints behavior. An internal table is used to keep track of the components added to the layout.

LayoutManager methods

public void addLayoutComponent (String name, Component component)

The addLayoutComponent() method of GridBagLayout does nothing. This method is not deprecated, unlike the similarly named methods in the other layout managers that implement LayoutManager2.

public void removeLayoutComponent (Component component)

The removeLayoutComponent() method of GridBagLayout does nothing.

public Dimension preferredLayoutSize (Container target)

The preferredLayoutSize() method calculates the preferred dimensions of the components of target. Sizing is based on the constraints of the various components. This task is definitely better off left to the computer.

public Dimension minimumLayoutSize (Container target)

The minimumLayoutSize() method calculates the minimum dimensions required to position the components of target. Sizing is based on the constraints of the various components.

public void layoutContainer (Container target)

The layoutContainer() method positions the components within target based upon the constraints of each component. If a component's anchor constraints are invalid, layoutContainer() throws the run-time exception IllegalArgumentException. The process of arranging the components is very complicated and beyond the scope of this book.

LayoutManager2 methods

public void addLayoutComponent (Component component, Object constraints) ★

This addLayoutComponent() method of GridBagLayout associates the component with the given constraints object. It calls the setConstraints() method.

If name is not a GridBagConstraints, addLayoutComponent() throws the run-time exception IllegalArgumentException.

public abstract Dimension maximumLayoutSize(Container target) ★

The maximumLayoutSize() method returns a Dimension object with a width and height of Integer.MAX_VALUE. In practice, this means that GridBagLayout doesn't support the concept of maximum size.

public abstract float getLayoutAlignmentX(Container target) ★

The getLayoutAlignmentX() method says that GridBagLayout containers should be centered horizontally within the area available.

public abstract float getLayoutAlignmentY(Container target) ★

The `getLayoutAlignmentY()` method says that `GridBagLayout` containers should be centered vertically within the area available.

public abstract void invalidateLayout(Container target) ★

The `invalidateLayout()` method of `GridBagLayout` does nothing.

Constraints

public GridBagConstraints getConstraints (Component component)

The `getConstraints()` method returns a clone of the current constraints for `component`. This makes it easier to generate constraints for a component based on another component.

public void setConstraints (Component component, GridBagConstraints constraints)

The `setConstraints()` method changes the constraints on `component` to a clone of `constraints`. The system creates a `clone()` of `constraints` so you can change the original constraints without affecting `component`.

Layout

public Point getLayoutOrigin ()

The `getLayoutOrigin()` method returns the origin for the `GridBagLayout`. The origin is the top left point within the container at which the components are drawn. Before the container is validated, `getLayoutOrigin()` returns the `Point` (0,0). After validation, `getLayoutOrigin()` returns the actual origin of the layout. The space used by the components within a `GridBagLayout` may not fill the entire container. You can use the results of `getLayoutOrigin()` and `getLayoutDimensions()` to find the layout's actual size and draw a `Rectangle` around the objects.

public int[][] getLayoutDimensions ()

The `getLayoutDimensions()` method returns two one-dimensional arrays as a single two-dimensional array. Index 0 is an array of widths (`columnWidths` instance variable), while index 1 is an array of heights (`rowHeights` instance variable). Until the layout is validated, these will be empty. After validation, the first array contains the widths of the components in the row with the most elements. The second contains the heights of the components in the column with the most elements. For Figure 7-10, the results would be (38, 51, 48) for widths since the first row has three elements and (21, 21, 21) for the heights since the first (and second) column has three elements in it.

public double[][] getLayoutWeights ()

> The getLayoutWeights() method returns two one-dimensional arrays as a single two-dimensional array. Index 0 is an array of column weights (column-Weights instance variable), while index 1 is an array of row weights (rowWeights instance variable). Until the layout is validated, these will be empty. After validation, the first dimension contains all the weightx values of the components in the row with the most elements. The second dimension contains all the weighty values of the components in the column with the most elements. For Figure 7-10, the results would be (0, 0, 0) for weightx since the first row has three elements and (0, 0, 0) for weighty since the first column has three elements in it.

Miscellaneous methods

public Point location (int x, int y)

> The location() method returns the Point (0,0) until the container is validated. After validation, this method returns the grid element under the location (x, y), where x and y are in pixels. The results could be used as the gridx and gridy constraints when adding another component.

public String toString ()

> The toString() method of GridBagLayout returns the name of the class:

```
java.awt.GridBagLayout
```

7.7 *GridBagConstraints*

GridBagConstraints are the meat behind the GridBagLayout; they specify how to display components. Unlike other layout managers, which have a built-in idea about what to do with their display, the GridBagLayout is a blank slate. The constraints attached to each component tell the layout manager how to build its display.

Every Component added to a GridBagLayout has a GridBagConstraints object associated with it. When an object is first added to the layout, it is given a default set of constraints (described later in this section). Calling setConstraints() (or add(Component, GridBagConstraints)) applies a new set of constraints to the object. Most people create a helper method to make the setConstraints() calls, passing constraint information as parameters. The helper method used in Example 7-2 follows:

```
public static void addComponent (Container container, Component component,
    int gridx, int gridy, int gridwidth, int gridheight, int fill,
    int anchor) throws AWTException {
    LayoutManager lm = container.getLayout();
    if (!(lm instanceof GridBagLayout)) {
```

```
            throw new AWTException ("Invalid layout" + lm);
        } else {
            GridBagConstraints gbc = new GridBagConstraints ();
            gbc.gridx = gridx;
            gbc.gridy = gridy;
            gbc.gridwidth = gridwidth;
            gbc.gridheight = gridheight;
            gbc.fill = fill;
            gbc.anchor = anchor;
            ((GridBagLayout)lm).setConstraints(component, gbc);
            container.add (component);
        }
    }
```

In Java 1.1, you can make this method slightly cleaner by adding the component
and applying the constraints in the same call to add(). To do so, replace the lines
calling setConstraints() and add() with this line:

```
        // Java 1.1 only
        container.add(component, gbc);
```

7.7.1 GridBagConstraints Methods

Constants and variables

public int anchor

The anchor specifies the direction in which the component will drift in the
event that it is smaller than the space available for it. CENTER is the default.
Others available are NORTH, SOUTH, EAST, WEST, NORTHEAST, NORTHWEST, SOUTH-
EAST, and SOUTHWEST.

public final static int CENTER
public final static int EAST
public final static int NORTH
public final static int NORTHEAST
public final static int NORTHWEST
public final static int SOUTH
public final static int SOUTHEAST
public final static int SOUTHWEST
public final static int WEST

Constants used to set the anchor.

public int fill

The value of fill controls the component's resize policy. If fill is NONE (the
default), the layout manager tries to give the component its preferred size. If
fill is VERTICAL, it resizes in height if additional space is available. If fill is
HORIZONTAL, it resizes in width. If fill is BOTH, the layout manager takes

advantage of all the space available in either direction. Figure 7-11 demonstrates VERTICAL (A), HORIZONTAL (B), and NONE (C) values; Figure 7-8 demonstrated the use of BOTH.

public final static int NONE
public final static int BOTH
public final static int HORIZONTAL
public final static int VERTICAL

Constants used to set fill.

A   B   C

Figure 7–11: GridBagLayout with fill values of VERTICAL, HORIZONTAL, and NONE

public int gridx
public int gridy

The gridx and gridy variables specify the grid position where this component
will be placed. (0,0) specifies the cell at the origin of the screen. Table 7-2
shows the gridx and gridy values for the screen in Figure 7-8.

It isn't necessary to set gridx and gridy to a specific location; if you set these
fields to RELATIVE (the default), the system calculates the location for you.
According to the comments in the source code, if gridx is RELATIVE, the component appears to the right of the last component added to the layout. If
gridy is RELATIVE, the component appears below the last component added to
the layout. However, this is misleadingly simple. RELATIVE placement works
best if you are adding components along a row or a column. In this case,
there are four possibilities to consider:

- gridx and gridy RELATIVE: components are placed in one row.

- gridx RELATIVE, gridy constant: components are placed in one row, each to
  the right of the previous component.

- gridx constant, gridy RELATIVE: components are placed in one column, each
  below the previous component.

- Varying gridx or gridy while setting the other field to RELATIVE appears to start a new row, placing the component as the first element in the row.

public int gridwidth
public int gridheight

gridwidth and gridheight set the number of rows (gridwidth) and columns (gridheight) a particular component occupies. If gridwidth or gridheight is set to REMAINDER, the component will be the last element of the row or column occupying any space that's remaining. Table 7-2 shows the gridwidth and gridheight values for the screen in Figure 7-8. For the components in the last column, the gridwidth values could be REMAINDER. Likewise, gridheight could be set to REMAINDER for the components in the last row.

gridwidth and gridheight may also have the value RELATIVE, which forces the component to be the next to last component in the row or column. Looking back to Figure 7-8: if button six has a gridwidth of RELATIVE, button seven won't appear because button five is the last item in the row, and six is already next to last. If button five has a gridheight of RELATIVE, the layout manager will reserve space below it, so the button can be the next to last item in the column.

public final static int RELATIVE

Constant used for gridx and gridy to request relative placement, and by gridheight and gridwidth to specify the next to last component in a column or row. The behavior of RELATIVE placement can be very counter intuitive; in most cases, you will be better off specifying gridx, gridy, gridheight, and gridwidth explicitly.

public final static int REMAINDER

Constant used for gridwidth and gridheight, to specify that a component should fill the rest of the row or column.

Table 7–2: Demonstrating gridx/gridy/gridwidth/gridheight

Component	gridx	gridy	gridwidth	gridheight
One	0	0	1	1
Two	1	0	1	1
Three	2	0	1	1
Four	0	1	2	1
Five	2	1	1	2
Six	0	2	1	1
Seven	1	2	1	3

public Insets insets

The insets field specifies the external padding in pixels around the component (i.e., between the component and the edge of the cell, or cells, allotted to it). An Insets object can specify different padding for the top, bottom, left, and right sides of the component.

public int ipadx
public int ipady

ipadx and ipady specify the internal padding within the component. ipadx specifies the extra space to the right and left of the component (so the minimum width increases by 2*ipadx pixels). ipady specifies the extra space above and below the component (so the minimum height increases by 2*ipady pixels).

The difference between insets (external padding) and the ipadx, ipady variables (internal padding) is confusing. The insets don't add space to the component itself; they are external to the component. ipadx and ipady change the component's minimum size, so they do add space to the component itself.

public double weightx
public double weighty

The weightx and weighty variables describe how to distribute any additional space within the container. They allow you to control how components grow (or shrink) when the user resizes the container. If weightx is 0, the component won't get any additional space available in its row. If one or more components in a row have weightx values greater than 0, any extra space is distributed proportionally between them. For example, if one component has a weightx value of 1 and the others are all 0, that one component will get all the additional space. If four components in a row each have weightx values of 1 and the other components have weightx values of 0, the four components each get one quarter of the additional space. weighty behaves similarly. Because weightx and weighty control the distribution of extra space in any row or column, setting either for one component may affect the position of other components.

Constructors

public GridBagConstraints ()

The constructor creates a `GridBagConstraints` object in which all the fields have their default values. These defaults are shown in the Table 7-3.

Table 7–3: GridBagConstraints Defaults.

Variable	Value	Description
anchor	CENTER	If the component is smaller than the space available, it will be centered within its region.
fill	NONE	The component should not resize itself if extra space is available within its region.
gridx	RELATIVE	The component associated with this constraint will be positioned relative to the last item added. If all components have `gridx` and `gridy` RELATIVE, they will be placed in a single row.
gridy	RELATIVE	The component associated with this constraint will be positioned relative to the last item added.
gridwidth	1	The component will occupy a single cell within the layout.
gridheight	1	The component will occupy a single cell within the layout.
insets	0×0×0×0	No extra space is added around the edges of the component.
ipadx	0	There is no internal padding for the component.
ipady	0	There is no internal padding for the component.
weightx	0	The component will not get any extra space, if it is available.
weighty	0	The component will not get any extra space, if it is available.

Miscellaneous methods

public Object clone ()

The `clone()` method creates a clone of the `GridBagConstraints` so the same `GridBagConstraints` object can be associated with multiple components.

7.8 Combining Layouts

If you can't create the display you want with any of the standard layout managers, or you are unable to figure out `GridBagLayout`, you may want to try combining several different layouts. This technique can often help you build the display you want. Figure 7-12 shows a display that uses three panels and three different layouts.

Here's the source code to generate the display in Figure 7-12:

```
import java.awt.*;
public class multi extends java.applet.Applet {
    public void init() {
        Panel s = new Panel();
        Panel e = new Panel();
        setLayout (new BorderLayout ());
        add ("North", new Label ("Enter text", Label.CENTER));
        add ("Center", new TextArea ());
        e.setLayout (new GridLayout (0,1));
        e.add (new Button ("Reformat"));
        e.add (new Button ("Spell Check"));
        e.add (new Button ("Options"));
        add ("East", e);
        s.setLayout (new FlowLayout ());
        s.add (new Button ("Save"));
        s.add (new Button ("Cancel"));
        s.add (new Button ("Help"));
        add ("South", s);
    }
}
```

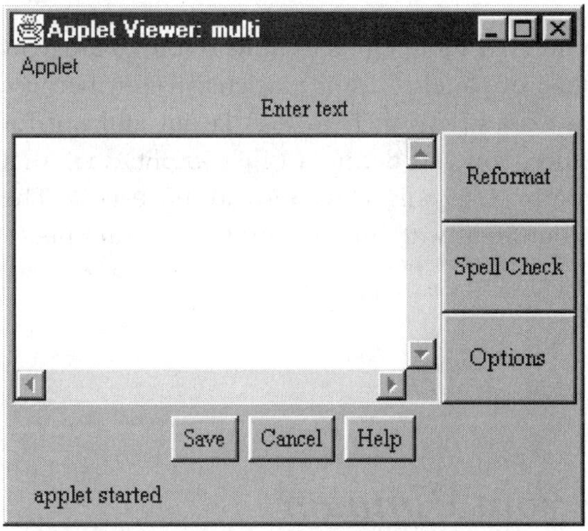

Figure 7–12: Multipanel screen using several layouts

The display in Figure 7-12 is created by adding four sections to a single
BorderLayout. The north region contains a panel with a single Label in it. The
panel uses its default LayoutManager, which is a FlowLayout. Why bother with this
panel? Why not just add a label at the north position in the BorderLayout? Our
strategy gives the label the position and size we want: the label is centered and displayed at its preferred size. If we had added the label directly to the BorderLayout,
it would have been left justified and resized to fill the region.

The TextArea has no special requirements, so we added it directly to the center of the BorderLayout.

The three buttons on the right of the screen were arranged in a panel with a Grid-Layout; then this panel was placed in the east region of the BorderLayout.

To create the buttons at the bottom of the screen, we used another Panel with a FlowLayout. It centers the three buttons and displays them at their preferred size, with a gap between them.

With a little work, we could have created this display using a single Panel with a GridBagLayout. The result would have been more efficient; placing panels within panels has performance implications. Each container in the display has its own peer object, which uses up system resources. Furthermore, in the 1.0 version of AWT, nesting containers complicates event handling. However, using a Grid-BagLayout would have required much more work: figuring out the right GridBag-Constraints for each component would be time consuming and result in code that is harder to understand. Sometimes, it's best to settle for the easy solution: a hybrid layout composed of several simple panels, rather than a single very complex panel.

In Java 1.1, you can make this program even more efficient in its resource usage by using a lightweight component instead of panels. This is particularly easy because the panels in the multipanel screen exist strictly to help with layout and not for partitioning event handling. Therefore, you can define a LightweightPanel that extends Container, with no methods. Use this class instead of Panel. The LightweightPanel allows you to lay out areas without creating unnecessary peers. Here's all the code for the LightweightPanel:

```
// Java 1.1 only
import java.awt.*;
public class LightweightPanel extends Container {
}
```

7.9 Disabling the LayoutManager

To create a container with no layout manager, use null as the argument to set-Layout(). If you do this, you must size and position every component individually. In most cases, disabling the LayoutManager is a bad idea because what might look great on one platform could look really bad on another, due to differences in fonts, native components, and other display characteristics. Figure 7-13 displays a container with a disabled LayoutManager; both buttons were positioned by specifying their size and location explicitly.

Here's the code that produces Figure 7-13:

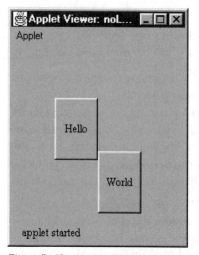

Figure 7–13: Applet with disabled layout manager

```
import java.awt.Button;
import java.applet.Applet;
public class noLayout extends Applet {
    public void init () {
        setLayout (null);
        Button x = new Button ("Hello");
        add (x);
        x.reshape (50, 60, 50, 70);
        Button y = new Button ("World");
        add (y);
        y.reshape (100, 120, 50, 70);
    }
}
```

7.10 Designing Your Own LayoutManager

What if you can't find a LayoutManager that fits your requirements, or you find yourself repeatedly building the same multipanel display? In cases like these, you can build your own layout manager. It's really not that difficult; you only need to implement the five methods of the LayoutManager interface, plus a constructor and any additional methods your design requires. In this section, we'll review the LayoutManager interface and then construct a custom LayoutManager called CornerLayout.

7.10.1 LayoutManager Methods

A custom LayoutManager must implement the following five methods (ten methods if you implement LayoutManager2). For many layout managers, several of these methods can be stubs that don't do anything.

public void addLayoutComponent (String name, Component component)

The addLayoutComponent() method is called by the add(name, component) method of Container. If your new LayoutManager does not have named component areas or does not pass generic positioning information via name, this method will be a stub with no code; you can let the container keep track of the components for you. Otherwise, this method must keep track of the component added, along with the information in name.

How would you implement this method? For layouts that have named component areas (like BorderLayout), you could use a private instance variable to hold the component for each area. For layouts like CardLayout, which lets you refer to individual components by name, you might want to store the components and their names in an internal Hashtable.

public void removeLayoutComponent (Component component)

This method is called by the remove() and removeAll() methods of Container. If you are storing information in internal instance variables or tables, you can remove the information about the given Component from the tables at this point. If you're not keeping track of the components yourself, this method can be a stub that does nothing.

public Dimension preferredLayoutSize (Container target)

This method is called by preferredSize() to calculate the desired size of target.[*] Obviously, the preferred size of the container depends on the layout strategy that you implement. To compute the preferred size, you usually need to call the preferredSize() method of every component in the container.

Computing the preferred size can be messy. However, some layout strategies let you take a shortcut. If your layout policy is "I'm going to cram all the components into the space given to me, whether they fit or not," you can compute the preferred size of your layout simply by calling target.size() or (in Java 1.1) target.getSize().

public Dimension minimumLayoutSize (Container target)

This method is called by minimumSize() to calculate the minimum size of target. The minimum size of the container depends on the layout strategy that you implement. To compute the minimum size, you usually need to call the

---

[*] This is still true in Java 1.1; the new method, getPreferredSize(), just calls the deprecated method, preferredSize().

minimumSize() method of every component in the container.

As with preferredLayoutSize(), you can sometimes save a lot of work by returning target.size().

public void layoutContainer (Container target)

This method is called when target is first displayed and whenever it is resized. It is responsible for arranging the components within the container. Depending upon the type of LayoutManager you are creating, you will either loop through all the components in the container with the getComponent() method or use the named components that you saved in the addLayoutComponent() method. To position and size the components, call their reshape() or set-Bounds() methods.

7.10.2 A New LayoutManager: CornerLayout

CornerLayout is a simple but useful layout manager that is similar in many respects to BorderLayout. Like BorderLayout, it positions components in five named regions: "Northeast", "Northwest", "Southeast", "Southwest", and "Center". These regions correspond to the four corners of the container, plus the center. The "Center" region has three modes. NORMAL, the default mode, places the "Center" component in the center of the container, with its corners at the inner corner of the other four regions. FULL_WIDTH lets the center region occupy the full width of the container. FULL_HEIGHT lets the center region occupy the full height of the container. You cannot specify both FULL_HEIGHT and FULL_WIDTH; if you did, the "Center" component would overlap the corner components and take over the container. Figure 7-14 shows a CornerLayout in each of these modes.

Not all regions are required. If a complete side is missing, the required space for the container decreases. Ordinarily, the other components would grow to fill this vacated space. However, if the container is sized to its preferred size, so are the components. Figure 7-15 shows this behavior.

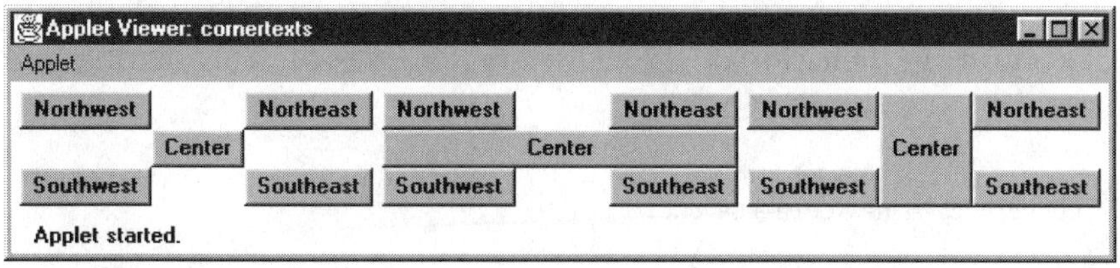

Figure 7–14: CornerLayout

Example 7-3 is the code for the CornerLayout. It shows the Java 1.0 version of the layout manager. At the end of this section, I show the simple change needed to adapt this manager to Java 1.1.

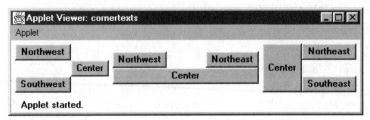

Figure 7–15: CornerLayout with missing regions

Example 7–3: The CornerLayout LayoutManager

```
import java.awt.*;
/**
 * An 'educational' layout. CornerLayout will layout a container
 * using members named "Northeast", "Northwest", "Southeast",
 * "Southwest", and "Center".
 *
 * The "Northeast", "Northwest", "Southeast" and "Southwest" components
 * get sized relative to the adjacent corner's components and
 * the constraints of the container's size. The "Center" component will
 * get any space left over.
 */

public class CornerLayout implements LayoutManager {
    int hgap;
    int vgap;
    int mode;
    public final static int NORMAL = 0;
    public final static int FULL_WIDTH = 1;
    public final static int FULL_HEIGHT = 2;
    Component northwest;
    Component southwest;
    Component northeast;
    Component southeast;
    Component center;
```

The CornerLayout class starts by defining instance variables to hold the gaps and mode and the components for each corner of the screen. It also defines three constants that control the behavior of the center region: NORMAL, FULL_WIDTH, and FULL_HEIGHT.

```
    /**
     * Constructs a new CornerLayout.
     */
    public CornerLayout() {
        this (0, 0, CornerLayout.NORMAL);
    }
    public CornerLayout(int mode) {
        this (0, 0, mode);
    }
    public CornerLayout(int hgap, int vgap) {
```

```
            this (hgap, vgap, CornerLayout.NORMAL);
    }
    public CornerLayout(int hgap, int vgap, int mode) {
        this.hgap = hgap;
        this.vgap = vgap;
        this.mode = mode;
    }
```

The constructors for CornerLayout are simple. The default (no arguments) constructor creates a CornerLayout with no gaps; the "Center" region is NORMAL mode. The last constructor, which is called by the other three, stores the gaps and the mode in instance variables.

```
    public void addLayoutComponent (String name, Component comp) {
        if ("Center".equals(name)) {
            center = comp;
        } else if ("Northwest".equals(name)) {
            northwest = comp;
        } else if ("Southeast".equals(name)) {
            southeast = comp;
        } else if ("Northeast".equals(name)) {
            northeast = comp;
        } else if ("Southwest".equals(name)) {
            southwest = comp;
        }
    }
```

addLayoutComponent() figures out which region a component has been assigned to, and saves the component in the corresponding instance variable. If the name of the component isn't "Northeast", "Northwest", Southeast", "Southwest", or "Center", the component is ignored.

```
    public void removeLayoutComponent (Component comp) {
        if (comp == center) {
            center = null;
        } else if (comp == northwest) {
            northwest = null;
        } else if (comp == southeast) {
            southeast = null;
        } else if (comp == northeast) {
            northeast = null;
        } else if (comp == southwest) {
            southwest = null;
        }
    }
```

removeLayoutComponent() searches for a given component in each region; if it finds the component, removeLayoutComponent() discards it by setting the instance variable to null.

```
public Dimension minimumLayoutSize (Container target) {
    Dimension dim = new Dimension(0, 0);
    Dimension northeastDim = new Dimension (0,0);
    Dimension northwestDim = new Dimension (0,0);
    Dimension southeastDim = new Dimension (0,0);
    Dimension southwestDim = new Dimension (0,0);
    Dimension centerDim    = new Dimension (0,0);
    if ((northeast != null) && northeast.isVisible ()) {
        northeastDim = northeast.minimumSize ();
    }
    if ((southwest != null) && southwest.isVisible ()) {
        southwestDim = southwest.minimumSize ();
    }
    if ((center != null) && center.isVisible ()) {
        centerDim = center.minimumSize ();
    }
    if ((northwest != null) && northwest.isVisible ()) {
        northwestDim = northwest.minimumSize ();
    }
    if ((southeast != null) && southeast.isVisible ()) {
        southeastDim = southeast.minimumSize ();
    }
    dim.width = Math.max (northwestDim.width, southwestDim.width) +
                    hgap + centerDim.width + hgap +
                    Math.max (northeastDim.width, southeastDim.width);
    dim.height = Math.max (northwestDim.height, northeastDim.height) +
                    + vgap + centerDim.height + vgap +
                    Math.max (southeastDim.height, southwestDim.height);
    Insets insets = target.insets();
    dim.width += insets.left + insets.right;
    dim.height += insets.top + insets.bottom;
    return dim;
}
```

minimumLayoutSize() computes the minimum size of the layout by finding the minimum sizes of all components. To compute the minimum width, minimumLayoutSize() adds the width of the center, plus the greater of the widths of the western regions (northwest and southwest), plus the greater of the widths of the eastern regions (northeast and southeast), then adds the appropriate gaps and insets. The minimum height is computed similarly; the method takes the greater of the minimum heights of the northern regions, the greater of the minimum heights of the southern regions, and adds them to the minimum height of the center region, together with the appropriate gaps and insets.

```
public Dimension preferredLayoutSize (Container target) {
    Dimension dim = new Dimension(0, 0);
    Dimension northeastDim = new Dimension (0,0);
    Dimension northwestDim = new Dimension (0,0);
    Dimension southeastDim = new Dimension (0,0);
    Dimension southwestDim = new Dimension (0,0);
    Dimension centerDim    = new Dimension (0,0);
    if ((northeast != null) && northeast.isVisible ()) {
```

```
                    northeastDim = northeast.preferredSize ();
            }
            if ((southwest != null) && southwest.isVisible ()) {
                southwestDim = southwest.preferredSize ();
            }
            if ((center != null) && center.isVisible ()) {
                centerDim = center.preferredSize ();
            }
            if ((northwest != null) && northwest.isVisible ()) {
                northwestDim = northwest.preferredSize ();
            }
            if ((southeast != null) && southeast.isVisible ()) {
                southeastDim = southeast.preferredSize ();
            }
            dim.width = Math.max (northwestDim.width, southwestDim.width) +
                            hgap + centerDim.width + hgap +
                            Math.max (northeastDim.width, southeastDim.width);
            dim.height = Math.max (northwestDim.height, northeastDim.height) +
                            + vgap + centerDim.height + vgap +
                            Math.max (southeastDim.height, southwestDim.height);
            Insets insets = target.insets();
            dim.width += insets.left + insets.right;
            dim.height += insets.top + insets.bottom;
            return dim;
        }
```

preferredLayoutSize() computes the preferred size of the layout. The method is almost identical to minimumLayoutSize(), except that it uses the preferred dimensions of each component.

```
        public void layoutContainer (Container target) {
            Insets insets = target.insets();
            int top = insets.top;
            int bottom = target.size ().height - insets.bottom;
            int left = insets.left;
            int right = target.size ().width - insets.right;
            Dimension northeastDim = new Dimension (0,0);
            Dimension northwestDim = new Dimension (0,0);
            Dimension southeastDim = new Dimension (0,0);
            Dimension southwestDim = new Dimension (0,0);
            Dimension centerDim    = new Dimension (0,0);
            Point topLeftCorner, topRightCorner, bottomLeftCorner,
                        bottomRightCorner;
            if ((northeast != null) && northeast.isVisible ()) {
                northeastDim = northeast.preferredSize ();
            }
            if ((southwest != null) && southwest.isVisible ()) {
                southwestDim = southwest.preferredSize ();
            }
            if ((center != null) && center.isVisible ()) {
                centerDim = center.preferredSize ();
            }
            if ((northwest != null) && northwest.isVisible ()) {
                northwestDim = northwest.preferredSize ();
```

```
    }
    if ((southeast != null) && southeast.isVisible ()) {
        southeastDim = southeast.preferredSize ();
    }
    topLeftCorner = new Point (left +
                    Math.max (northwestDim.width, southwestDim.width),
                    top +
                    Math.max (northwestDim.height, northeastDim.height));
    topRightCorner = new Point (right -
                    Math.max (northeastDim.width, southeastDim.width),
                    top +
                    Math.max (northwestDim.height, northeastDim.height));
    bottomLeftCorner = new Point (left +
                    Math.max (northwestDim.width, southwestDim.width),
                    bottom -
                    Math.max (southwestDim.height, southeastDim.height));
    bottomRightCorner = new Point (right  -
                    Math.max (northeastDim.width, southeastDim.width),
                    bottom -
                    Math.max (southwestDim.height, southeastDim.height));
    if ((northwest != null) && northwest.isVisible ()) {
        northwest.reshape (left, top,
                        left + topLeftCorner.x,
                        top + topLeftCorner.y);
    }
    if ((southwest != null) && southwest.isVisible ()) {
        southwest.reshape (left, bottomLeftCorner.y,
                        bottomLeftCorner.x - left,
                        bottom - bottomLeftCorner.y);
    }
    if ((southeast != null) && southeast.isVisible ()) {
        southeast.reshape (bottomRightCorner.x,
                    bottomRightCorner.y,
                    right - bottomRightCorner.x,
                    bottom - bottomRightCorner.y);
    }
    if ((northeast != null) && northeast.isVisible ()) {
        northeast.reshape (topRightCorner.x, top,
                        right - topRightCorner.x,
                        topRightCorner.y);
    }
    if ((center != null) && center.isVisible ()) {
        int x = topLeftCorner.x + hgap;
        int y = topLeftCorner.y + vgap;
        int width = bottomRightCorner.x - topLeftCorner.x - hgap * 2;
        int height = bottomRightCorner.y - topLeftCorner.y - vgap * 2;
        if (mode == CornerLayout.FULL_WIDTH) {
            x = left;
            width = right - left;
        } else if (mode == CornerLayout.FULL_HEIGHT) {
            y = top;
            height = bottom - top;
        }
        center.reshape (x, y, width, height);
```

```
        }
    }
```

`layoutContainer()` does the real work: it positions and sizes the components in our layout. It starts by computing the region of the target container that we have to work with, which is essentially the size of the container minus the insets. The boundaries of the working area are stored in the variables top, bottom, left, and right. Next, we get the preferred sizes of all visible components and use them to compute the corners of the "Center" region; these are stored in the variables topLeftCorner, topRightCorner, bottomLeftCorner, and bottomRightCorner.

Once we've computed the location of the "Center" region, we can start placing the components in their respective corners. To do so, we simply check whether the component is visible; if it is, we call its reshape() method. After dealing with the corner components, we place the "Center" component, taking into account any gaps (hgap and vgap) and the layout's mode. If the mode is NORMAL, the center component occupies the region between the inner corners of the other components. If the mode is FULL_HEIGHT, it occupies the full height of the screen. If it is FULL_WIDTH, it occupies the full width of the screen.

```
    public String toString() {
        Sting str;
        switch (mode) {
            case FULL_HEIGHT: str = "tall"; break;
            case FULL_WIDTH: str = "wide"; break;
            default: str = "normal"; break;
        }
        return getClass().getName () + "[hgap=" + hgap + ",vgap=" + vgap +
            ",mode="+str+"]";
    }
}
```

`toString()` simply returns a string describing the layout.

Strictly speaking, there's no reason to update the CornerLayout for Java 1.1. Nothing about Java 1.1 says that new layout managers have to implement the Layout-Manager2 interface. However, implementing LayoutManager2 isn't a bad idea, particularly since CornerLayout works with constraints; like BorderLayout, it has named regions. To extend CornerLayout so that it implements LayoutManager2, add the following code; we'll create a new CornerLayout2:

```
// Java 1.1 only
import java.awt.*;
public class CornerLayout2 extends CornerLayout implements LayoutManager2 {

    public void addLayoutComponent(Component comp, Object constraints) {
        if ((constraints == null) || (constraints instanceof String)) {
            addLayoutComponent((String)constraints, comp);
        } else {
```

```
                    throw new IllegalArgumentException(
                        "cannot add to layout: constraint must be a string (or null)");
            }
        }
    }
    public Dimension maximumLayoutSize(Container target) {
        return new Dimension(Integer.MAX_VALUE, Integer.MAX_VALUE);
    }
    public float getLayoutAlignmentX(Container parent) {
        return Component.CENTER_ALIGNMENT;
    }
    public float getLayoutAlignmentY(Container parent) {
        return Component.CENTER_ALIGNMENT;
    }
    public void invalidateLayout(Container target) {
    }
}
```

7.11 The sun.awt Layout Collection

The sun.awt package defines four additional layouts. The first two, HorizBagLayout and VerticalBagLayout, are available only when used with Sun's JDK or Internet Explorer, since they are not provided with Netscape Navigator and may not be available from other vendors. Therefore, these layout managers should be used selectively within applets. The third layout manager, VariableGridLayout, is available with Netscape Navigator 2.0 or 3.0 and Internet Explorer. Usage of this layout manager is safer within applets but is still at your own risk. The final layout manager is introduced in Java 1.1, OrientableFlowLayout. Only time will tell where that one will be available. Any of these layout managers could be moved into a future version of java.awt if there is enough interest.

7.11.1 HorizBagLayout

In a HorizBagLayout, the components are all arranged in a single row, from left to right. The height of each component is the height of the container; the width of each component is its preferred width. Figure 7-16 shows HorizBagLayout in use.

Constructors

public HorizBagLayout ()
> This constructor creates a HorizBagLayout with a horizontal gap of zero pixels. The gap is the space between the different components in the horizontal direction.

public HorizBagLayout (int hgap)
> This constructor creates a HorizBagLayout using a horizontal gap of hgap pixels.

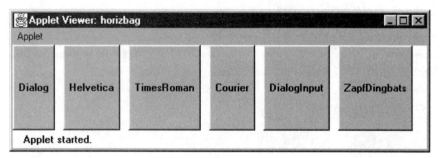

Figure 7–16: HorizBagLayout

LayoutManager methods

public void addLayoutComponent (String name, Component component)

> The addLayoutComponent() method of HorizBagLayout does nothing.

public void removeLayoutComponent (Component component)

> The removeLayoutComponent() method of HorizBagLayout does nothing.

public Dimension preferredLayoutSize (Container target)

> The preferredLayoutSize() method of HorizBagLayout sums up the preferred widths of all the components in target, along with the hgap and right and left insets to get the width of the target. The height returned will be the preferred height of the tallest component.

public Dimension minimumLayoutSize (Container target)

> The minimumLayoutSize() method of HorizBagLayout sums up the minimum widths of all the components in target, along with the hgap and right and left insets to get the width of the target. The height returned will be the minimum height of the tallest component.

public void layoutContainer (Container target)

> The layoutContainer() method draws target's components on the screen in one row. The height of each component is the height of the container. Each component's width is its preferred width, if enough space is available.

Miscellaneous methods

public String toString ()

> The toString() method of HorizBagLayout returns a string with the current horizontal gap setting—for example:

```
sun.awt.HorizBagLayout[hgap=0]
```

7.11.2 VerticalBagLayout

The VerticalBagLayout places all the components in a single column. The width of each component is the width of the container; each component is given its preferred height. Figure 7-17 shows VerticalBagLayout in use.

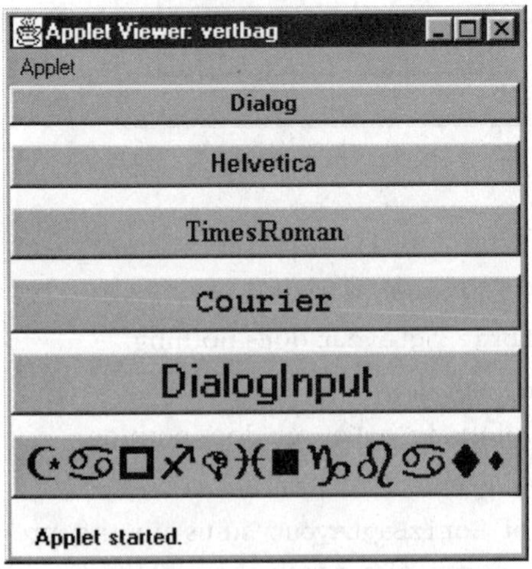

Figure 7–17: VerticalBagLayout

Constructors

public VerticalBagLayout ()

This constructor creates a VerticalBagLayout with a vertical gap of zero pixels. The gap is the space between components in the vertical direction. With a gap of 0, adjacent components will touch each other.

public VerticalBagLayout (int vgap)

This constructor creates a VerticalBagLayout with a vertical gap of vgap pixels.

LayoutManager methods

public void addLayoutComponent (String name, Component component)

The addLayoutComponent() method of VerticalBagLayout does nothing.

public void removeLayoutComponent (Component component)

The removeLayoutComponent() method of VerticalBagLayout does nothing.

public Dimension preferredLayoutSize (Container target)

To get the preferred height of the layout, the `preferredLayoutSize()` method sums up the preferred height of all the components in `target` along with the vgap and top and bottom insets. For the preferred width, `preferredLayout-Size()` returns the preferred width of the widest component.

public Dimension minimumLayoutSize (Container target)

To get the minimum height of the layout, the `minimumLayoutSize()` method sums up the minimum height of all the components in `target` along with the vgap and top and bottom insets. For the minimum width, `minimumLayout-Size()` returns the minimum width of the widest component.

public void layoutContainer (Container target)

The `layoutContainer()` method draws `target`'s components on the screen in one column. The width of each component is the width of the container. Each component's height is its `preferredSize()` height, if available.

Miscellaneous methods

public String toString ()

The `toString()` method of `VerticalBagLayout` returns a string with the current vertical gap setting. For example:

```
sun.awt.VerticalBagLayout[vgap=0]
```

7.11.3 VariableGridLayout

The `VariableGridLayout` builds upon the `GridLayout`. It arranges components on a grid of rows and columns. However, instead of giving all components the same size, the `VariableGridLayout` allows you to size rows and columns fractionally. Another difference between `VariableGridLayout` and `GridBagLayout` is that a `VariableGridLayout` has a fixed size. If you ask for a 3x3 grid, you will get exactly that. The layout manager throws the `ArrayIndexOutOfBoundsException` run-time exception if you try to add too many components.

Figure 7-18 shows a `VariableGridLayout` in which row one takes up 50 percent of the screen, and rows two and three take up 25 percent of the screen each. Column one takes up 50 percent of the screen; columns two and three take 25 percent each.

Here is the code that creates Figure 7-18:

```
import java.awt.*;
java.applet.Applet;
import sun.awt.VariableGridLayout;
public class vargrid extends Applet {
    public void init () {
        VariableGridLayout vgl;
```

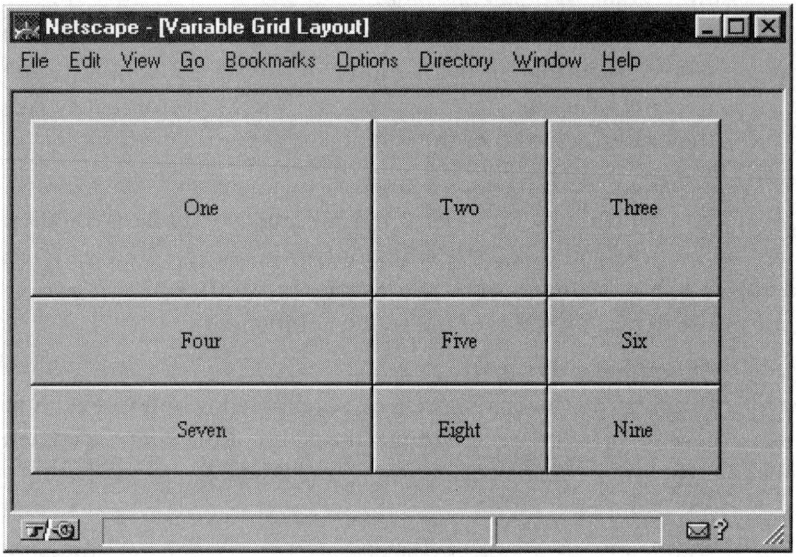

Figure 7–18: VariableGridLayout in Netscape Navigator

```
setLayout (vgl = new VariableGridLayout (3,3));
vgl.setRowFraction (0, 1.0/2.0);
vgl.setRowFraction (1, 1.0/4.0);
vgl.setRowFraction (2, 1.0/4.0);
vgl.setColFraction (0, 1.0/2.0);
vgl.setColFraction (1, 1.0/4.0);
vgl.setColFraction (2, 1.0/4.0);
add (new Button ("One"));
add (new Button ("Two"));
add (new Button ("Three"));
add (new Button ("Four"));
add (new Button ("Five"));
add (new Button ("Six"));
add (new Button ("Seven"));
add (new Button ("Eight"));
add (new Button ("Nine"));
   }
 }
```

Constructors

public VariableGridLayout (int rows, int columns)

This constructor creates a VariableGridLayout with the specified number of
rows and columns. You cannot specify zero for one dimension. If either rows
or columns is zero, the constructor throws the NullPointerException run-time
exception. This constructor uses the default values for horizontal and vertical
gaps (zero pixels), which means that components in adjacent cells will touch
each other.

public VariableGridLayout (int rows, int columns, int hgap, int vgap)

> This version of the constructor is called by the previous one. It creates a Vari-ableGridLayout with the specified number of rows and columns, a horizontal gap of hgap, and a vertical gap of vgap. The gaps specify in pixels the space between adjacent components in the horizontal and vertical directions. It is possible to have negative gaps if you want components to overlap. You cannot specify zero for the number of rows or columns. If either rows or columns is zero, the constructor throws the run-time exception NullPointerException.

Support methods

The distinguishing feature of a VariableGridLayout is that you can tell a particular row or column to take up a certain fraction of the display. By default, the horizontal space available is split evenly among the grid's columns; vertical space is split evenly among the rows. This group of methods lets you find out how much space is allotted to each row or column and lets you change that allocation. The sum of the fractional amounts for each direction should add up to one. If greater than one, part of the display will be drawn offscreen. If less than one, additional screen real estate will be unused.

public void setRowFraction (int rowNumber, double fraction)

> This method sets the percentage of space available for row rowNumber to fraction.

public void setColFraction (int colNumber, double fraction)

> This method sets the percentage of space available for column colNumber to fraction.

public double getRowFraction (int rowNumber)

> This method returns the current fractional setting for row rowNumber.

public double getColFraction (int colNumber)

> This method returns the current fractional setting for column colNumber.

LayoutManager methods

The only method from GridLayout that is overridden is the layoutContainer() method.

public void layoutContainer (Container target)

> The layoutContainer() method draws target's components on the screen in a series of rows and columns. The size of each component within a Variable-GridLayout is determined by the RowFraction and ColFraction settings for its row and column.

Miscellaneous methods

public String toString ()

The toString() method of VariableGridLayout returns a string with the current horizontal and vertical gap settings, the number of rows and columns, and the row and column fractional amounts. For example, the string produced by Figure 7-19 would be:

```
sun.awt.VariableGridLayout[hgap=0,vgap=0,rows=3,cols=3,
    rowFracs=[3]<0.50><0.25><0.25>,colFracs=[3]<0.50><0.25><0.25>]
```

7.11.4 OrientableFlowLayout

The OrientableFlowLayout is available for those who want something like a FlowLayout that lets you arrange components from top to bottom. Figure 7-19 shows OrientableFlowLayout in use.

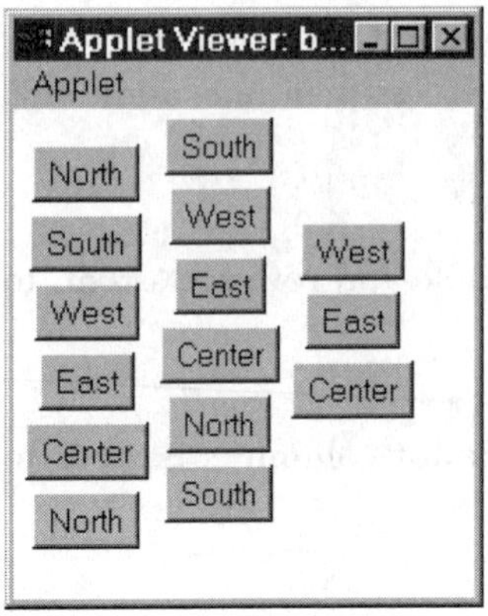

Figure 7–19: OrientableFlowLayout

Constants

Since OrientableFlowLayout subclasses FlowLayout, the FlowLayout constants of LEFT, RIGHT, and CENTER are still available.

public static final int HORIZONTAL ★

The HORIZONTAL constant tells the layout manager to arrange components from left to right, like the FlowLayout manager.

public static final int VERTICAL ★

The VERTICAL constant tells the layout manager to arrange components from top to bottom.

public static final int TOP ★

> The TOP constant tells the layout manager to align the first component at the top of the screen (top justification).

public static final int BOTTOM ★

> The BOTTOM constant tells the layout manager to align the first component at the bottom of the screen (bottom justification).

Constructors

public OrientableFlowLayout () ★

> This constructor creates a OrientableFlowLayout that acts like the default FlowLayout. The objects flow from left to right and have an hgap and vgap of 5.

public OrientableFlowLayout (int direction) ★

> This constructor creates a OrientableFlowLayout in the given direction. Valid values are OrientableFlowLayout.HORIZONTAL or OrientableFlowLayout.VERTICAL.

public OrientableFlowLayout (int direction, int horizAlignment, int vertAlignment) ★

> This constructor creates a OrientableFlowLayout in the given direction. Valid values are OrientableFlowLayout.HORIZONTAL or OrientableFlowLayout.VERTICAL. horizAlignment provides the horizontal alignment setting. vertAlignment provides a vertical alignment setting; it may be OrientableFlowLayout.TOP, FlowLayout.CENTER, or OrientableFlowLayout.BOTTOM. If direction is HORIZONTAL, the vertical alignment is ignored. If direction is VERTICAL, the horizontal alignment is ignored.

public OrientableFlowLayout (int direction, int horizAlignment, int vertAlignment, int horizHgap, int horizVgap, int vertHgap, int vertVgap) ★

> The final constructor adds separate horizontal and vertical gaps to the settings of OrientableFlowLayout. The horizHgap and horizVgap parameters are the gaps when horizontally aligned. The vertHgap and vertVgap parameters are the gaps when vertically aligned.

LayoutManager methods

public Dimension preferredLayoutSize (Container target) ★

> The preferredLayoutSize() method of OrientableFlowLayout calculates the preferred dimensions for the target container. The OrientableFlowLayout computes the preferred size by placing all the components in one row or column, depending upon the current orientation, and adding their individual preferred sizes along with gaps and insets.

public Dimension minimumLayoutSize (Container target) ★

> The `minimumLayoutSize()` method of `OrientableFlowLayout` calculates the minimum dimensions for the container by adding up the sizes of the components. The `OrientableFlowLayout` computes the minimum size by placing all the components in one row or column, depending upon the current orientation, and adding their individual minimum sizes along with gaps and insets.

public void layoutContainer (Container target) ★

> The `layoutContainer()` method draws `target`'s `Components` on the screen, starting with the first row or column of the display, and going from left to right across the screen, or from top to bottom, based on the current orientation. When it reaches the margin of the container, it skips to the next row or column and continues drawing additional components.

Miscellaneous methods

public void orientHorizontally () ★

> The `orientHorizontally()` method allows you to change the orientation of the `LayoutManager` to horizontal. The container must be validated before you see the effect of the change.

public void orientVertically () ★

> The `orientVertically()` method allows you to change the orientation of the `LayoutManager` to vertical. The container must be validated before you see the effect of the change.

public String toString () ★

> The `toString()` method of `OrientableFlowLayout` returns a string with the current orientation setting, along with the entire `FlowLayout.toString()` results. For example:

```
sun.awt.OrientableFlowLayout[orientation=vertical,
sun.awt.OrientableFlowLayout[hgap=5,vgap=5,align=center]]
```

7.12 Other Layouts Available on the Net

Many custom layout managers are available on the Internet. Many of these duplicate the layout behavior of other environments. For example, the `Fractional-Layout` is based on Smalltalk's positioning mechanism; it is located at *http://www.mcs.net/˜elunt/Java/FractionalLayoutDescription.html*. The `RelativeLayout` allows you to position components relative to others, similar to an X Window form; you can find it at *http://www-elec.enst.fr/java/RelativeLayout.java*. If you like the way Tcl/Tk arranges widgets, try the `PackerLayout`; it is available at *http://www.geom.umn.edu/˜daeron/apps/ui/pack/gui.html.* If none of these suit you, you can find a collection of links to custom layout managers at *http://www.softbear.com/people/larry/javalm.htm.* Gamelan (*http://www.gamelan.com/*) is always a good source for Java classes; try searching for `LayoutManager`.

8

In this chapter:
- *Text Component*
- *TextField*
- *TextArea*
- *Extending TextField*

Input Fields

There are two fundamental ways for users to provide input to a program: they can type on a keyboard, or they can select something (a button, a menu item, etc.) using a mouse. When you want a user to provide input to your program, you can display a list of choices to choose from or allow the user to interact with your program by typing with the keyboard. Presenting choices to the user is covered in Chapter 9, *Pick Me*. As far as keyboard input goes, the java.awt package provides two options. The TextField class is a single line input field, while the TextArea class is a multiline one. Both TextField and TextArea are subclasses of the class TextComponent, which contains all the common functionality of the two. TextComponent is a subclass of Component, which is a subclass of Object. So you inherit all of these methods when you work with either TextField or TextArea.

8.1 Text Component

By themselves, the TextField and TextArea classes are fairly robust. However, in order to reduce duplication between the classes, they both inherit a number of methods from the TextComponent class. The constructor for TextComponent is package private, so you cannot create an instance of it yourself. Some of the activities shared by TextField and TextArea through the TextComponent methods include setting the text, getting the text, selecting the text, and making it read-only.

8.1.1 TextComponent Methods

Contents

Both `TextField` and `TextArea` contain a set of characters whose content determines the current value of the `TextComponent`. The following methods are usually called in response to an external event.

public String getText ()

> The `getText()` method returns the current contents of the `TextComponent` as a `String` object.

public void setText (String text)

> The `setText()` method sets the content of the `TextComponent` to text. If the `TextComponent` is a `TextArea`, you can embed newline characters (`\n`) in the text so that it will appear on multiple lines.

Text selection

Users can select text in `TextComponents` by pressing a mouse button at a starting point and dragging the cursor across the text. The selected text is displayed in reverse video. Only one block of text can be selected at any given time within a single `TextComponent`. Once selected, this block could be used to provide the user with some text-related operation such as cut and paste (on a `PopupMenu`).

Depending on the platform, you might or might not be able to get selected text when a `TextComponent` does not have the input focus. In general, the component with selected text must have input focus in order for you to retrieve any information about the selection. However, in some environments, the text remains selected when the component no longer has the input focus.

public int getSelectionStart ()

> The `getSelectionStart()` method returns the initial position of any selected text. The position can be considered the number of characters preceding the first selected character. If there is no selected text, `getSelectionStart()` returns the current cursor position. If the start of the selection is at beginning of the text, the return value is 0.

public int getSelectionEnd ()

> The `getSelectionEnd()` method returns the ending cursor position of any selected text—that is, the number of characters preceding the end of the selection. If there is no selected text, `getSelectionEnd()` returns the current cursor position.

public String getSelectedText ()

> The getSelectedText() method returns the currently selected text of the TextComponent as a String. If nothing is selected, getSelectedText() returns an empty String, not null.

public void setSelectionStart (int position) ★

> The setSelectionStart() method changes the beginning of the current selection to position. If position is after getSelectionEnd(), the cursor position moves to getSelectionEnd(), and nothing is selected.

public void setSelectionEnd (int position) ★

> The setSelectionEnd() method changes the end of the current selection to position. If position is before getSelectionStart(), the cursor position moves to position, and nothing is selected.

public void select (int selectionStart, int selectionEnd)

> The select() method selects the text in the TextComponent from selectionStart to selectionEnd. If selectionStart is after selectionEnd, the cursor position moves to selectionEnd. Some platforms allow you to use select() to ensure that a particular position is visible on the screen.

public void selectAll ()

> The selectAll() method selects all the text in the TextComponent. It basically does a select() call with a selectionStart position of 0 and a selectionEnd position of the length of the contents.

Carets

Introduced in Java 1.1 is the ability to set and get the current insertion position within the text object.

public int getCaretPosition () ★

> The getCaretPosition() method returns the current text insertion position (often called the "cursor") of the TextComponent. You can use this position to paste text from the clipboard with the java.awt.datatransfer package described in Chapter 16, *Data Transfer*.

public void setCaretPosition (int position) ★

> The setCaretPosition() method moves the current text insertion location of the TextComponent to position. If the TextComponent does not have a peer yet, setCaretPosition() throws the IllegalComponentStateException run-time exception. If position < 0, this method throws the run-time exception IllegalArgumentException. If position is too big, the text insertion point is positioned at the end.

Prior to Java version 1.1, the insertion location was usually set by calling select(position, position).

Read-only text

By default, a TextComponent is editable. If a user types while the component has input focus, its contents will change. A TextComponent can also be used in an output-only (read-only) mode.

public void setEditable (boolean state)

The setEditable() method allows you to change the current editable state of the TextComponent to state. true means the component is editable; false means read-only.

public boolean isEditable ()

The isEditable() method tells you if the TextComponent is editable (true) or read-only (false).

The following listing is an applet that toggles the editable status for a TextArea and sets a label to show the current status. As you can see in Figure 8-1, platforms can change the display characteristics of the TextComponent to reflect whether the component is editable. (Windows 95 darkens the background. Motif and Windows NT do nothing.)

```
import java.awt.*;
import java.applet.*;
public class readonly extends Applet {
    TextArea area;
    Label label;
    public void init () {
        setLayout (new BorderLayout (10, 10));
        add ("South", new Button ("toggleState"));
        add ("Center", area = new TextArea ("Help Me", 5, 10));
        add ("North", label = new Label ("Editable", Label.CENTER));
    }
    public boolean action (Event e, Object o) {
        if (e.target instanceof Button) {
            if ("toggleState".equals(o)) {
                area.setEditable (!area.isEditable ());
                label.setText ((area.isEditable () ? "Editable" : "Read-only"));
                return true;
            }
        }
        return false;
    }
}
```

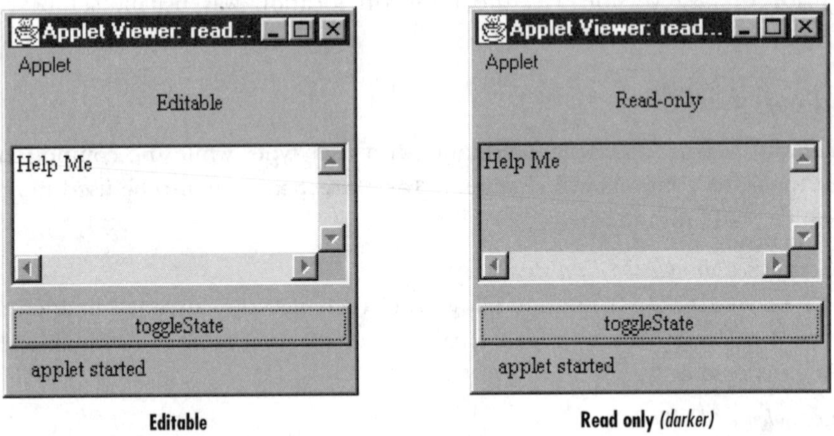

Editable   **Read only** *(darker)*

Figure 8–1: Editable and read-only TextAreas

Miscellaneous methods

public synchronized void removeNotify ()

> The removeNotify() method destroys the peer of the TextComponent and removes it from the screen. Prior to the TextComponent peer's destruction, the current state is saved so that a subsequent call to addNotify() will put it back. (TextArea and TextField each have their own addNotify() methods.) These methods deal with the peer object, which hides the native platform's implementation of the component. If you override this method for a specific TextComponent, put in the customizations for your new class first, and call super.removeNotify() last.

protected String paramString ()

> When you call the toString() method of a TextField or TextArea, the default toString() method of Component is called. This in turn calls paramString(), which builds up the string to display. The TextComponent level potentially adds four items. The first is the current contents of the TextComponent (getText()). If the text is editable, paramString() adds the word *editable* to the string. The last two items included are the current selection range (getSelectionStart() and getSelectionEnd()).

8.1.2 TextComponent Events

With the 1.1 event model, you can register listeners for text events. A text event occurs when the component's content changes, either because the user typed something or because the program called a method like setText(). Listeners are

registered with the addTextListener() method. When the content changes, the
TextListener.textValueChanges() method is called through the protected
method processTextEvent(). There is no equivalent to TextEvent in Java 1.0; you
would have to direct keyboard changes and all programmatic changes to a common method yourself.

In addition to TextEvent listeners, Key, mouse, and focus listeners are registered
through the Component methods addKeyListener(), addMouseListener(),
addMouseMotionListener(), and addFocusListener(), respectively.

Listeners and 1.1 event handling

public synchronized void addTextListener(TextListener listener) ★

The addTextListener() method registers listener as an object interested in
receiving notifications when a TextEvent passes through the EventQueue with
this TextComponent as its target. The listener.textValueChanged() method is
called when these events occur. Multiple listeners can be registered.

The following applet, text13, demonstrates how to use a TextListener to handle the events that occur when a TextField is changed. Whenever the user
types into the TextField, a TextEvent is delivered to the textValueChanged()
method, which prints a message on the Java console. The applet includes a
button that, when pressed, modifies the text field tf by calling setText().
These changes also generate a TextEvent.

```
// Java 1.1 only
import java.applet.*;
import java.awt.*;
import java.awt.event.*;
class TextFieldSetter implements ActionListener {
    TextField tf;
    TextFieldSetter (TextField tf) {
        this.tf = tf;
    }
    public void actionPerformed(ActionEvent e) {
        if (e.getActionCommand().equals ("Set")) {
            tf.setText ("Hello");
        }
    }
}
public class text13 extends Applet implements TextListener {
    TextField tf;
    int i=0;
    public void init () {
        Button b;
        tf = new TextField ("Help Text", 20);
        add (tf);
        tf.addTextListener (this);
        add (b = new Button ("Set"));
        b.addActionListener (new TextFieldSetter (tf));
```

```
        }
        public void textValueChanged(TextEvent e) {
            System.out.println (++i + ": " + e);
        }
    }
```

public void removeTextListener(TextListener listener) ★

The removeTextListener() method removes listener as an interested listener. If listener is not registered, nothing happens.

protected void processEvent(AWTEvent e) ★

The processEvent() method receives all AWTEvents with this TextComponent as its target. processEvent() then passes the events along to any listeners for processing. When you subclass TextComponent, overriding processEvent() allows you to process all events yourself, before sending them to any listeners. In a way, overriding processEvent() is like overriding handleEvent() using the 1.0 event model.

If you override processEvent(), remember to call super.processEvent(e) last to ensure that regular event processing can occur. If you want to process your own events, it's a good idea to call enableEvents() (inherited from Component) to ensure that events are delivered even in the absence of registered listeners.

protected void processTextEvent(TextEvent e) ★

The processTextEvent() method receives all TextEvents with this TextComponent as its target. processTextEvent() then passes them along to any listeners for processing. When you subclass TextField or TextArea, overriding the processTextEvent() method allows you to process all text events yourself, before sending them to any listeners. There is no equivalent to processTextEvent() within the 1.0 event model.

If you override processTextEvent(), remember to call the method super.processTextEvent(e) last to ensure that regular event processing can occur. If you want to process your own events, it's a good idea to call enableEvents() (inherited from Component) to ensure that events are delivered even in the absence of registered listeners.

8.2 *TextField*

TextField is the TextComponent for single-line input. Some constructors permit you to set the width of the TextField on the screen, but the current LayoutManager may change it. The text in the TextField is left justified, and the justification is not customizable. To change the font and size of text within the TextField, call setFont() as shown in Chapter 3, *Fonts and Colors*.

The width of the field does not limit the number of characters that the user can type into the field. It merely suggests how wide the field should be. To limit the number of characters, it is necessary to override the keyDown() method for the Component. Section 8.4 contains an example showing how to do this.

8.2.1 TextField Methods

Constructors

public TextField ()

This constructor creates an empty TextField. The width of the TextField is zero columns, but it will be made wide enough to display just about one character, depending on the current font and size.

public TextField (int columns)

This constructor creates an empty TextField. The TextField width is columns. The TextField will try to be wide enough to display columns characters in the current font and size. As I mentioned previously, the layout manager may change the size.

public TextField (String text)

This constructor creates a TextField with text as its content. In Java 1.0 systems, the TextField is 0 columns wide (the getColumns() result), but the system will size it to fit the length of text. With Java 1.1, getColumns() actually returns text.length.

public TextField (String text, int columns)

This constructor creates a TextField with text as its content and a width of columns.

The following example uses all four constructors; the results are shown in Figure 8-2. With the third constructor, you see that the TextField is not quite wide enough for our text. The system uses an average width per character to try to determine how wide the field should be. If you want to be on the safe side, specify the field's length explicitly, and add a few extra characters to ensure that there is enough room on the screen for the entire text.

```
import java.awt.TextField;
public class texts extends java.applet.Applet {
    public void init () {
        add (new TextField ());                   // A
        add (new TextField (15));                  // B
        add (new TextField ("Empty String"));      // C
        add (new TextField ("Empty String", 20)); // D
    }
}
```

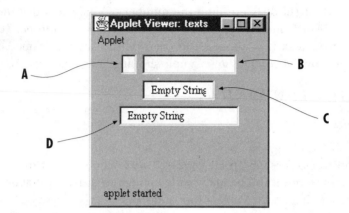

Figure 8–2: Using the TextField constructors

Sizing

public int getColumns ()

> The getColumns() method returns the number of columns set with the constructor or a later call to setColumns(). This could be different from the displayed width of the TextField, depending upon the current LayoutManager.

public void setColumns (int columns) ★

> The setColumns() method changes the preferred number of columns for the TextField to display to columns. Because the current LayoutManager will do what it wants, the new setting may be completely ignored. If columns < 0, set-Columns() throws the run-time exception IllegalArgumentException.

public Dimension getPreferredSize (int columns) ★
public Dimension preferredSize (int columns) ☆

> The getPreferredSize() method returns the Dimension (width and height) for the preferred size of a TextField with a width of columns. The columns specified may be different from the number of columns designated in the constructor.
>
> preferredSize() is the Java 1.0 name for this method.

public Dimension getPreferredSize () ★
public Dimension preferredSize () ☆

> The getPreferredSize() method returns the Dimension (width and height) for the preferred size of the TextField. Without the columns parameter, this getPreferredSize() uses the constructor's number of columns (or the value from a subsequent call to setColumns()) to calculate the TextField's preferred size.

`preferredSize()` is the Java 1.0 name for this method.

public Dimension getMinimumSize (int columns) ★
public Dimension minimumSize (int columns) ☆

> The `getMinimumSize()` method returns the minimum `Dimension` (width and height) for the size of a `TextField` with a width of `columns`. The `columns` specified may be different from the columns designated in the constructor.
>
> `minimumSize()` is the Java 1.0 name for this method.

public Dimension getMinimumSize () ★
public Dimension minimumSize ()

> The `getMinimumSize()` method returns the minimum `Dimension` (width and height) for the size of the `TextField`. Without the columns parameter, this `getMinimumSize()` uses the constructor's number of columns (or the value from a subsequent call to `setColumns()`) to calculate the `TextField`'s minimum size.
>
> `minimumSize()` is the Java 1.0 name for this method.

Echoing character

It is possible to change the character echoed back to the user when he or she types. This is extremely useful for implementing password entry fields.

public char getEchoChar ()

> The `getEchoChar()` method returns the currently echoed character. If the `TextField` is echoing normally, `getEchoChar()` returns zero.

public void setEchoChar (char c) ★
public void setEchoCharacter (char c) ☆

> The `setEchoChar()` method changes the character that is displayed to the user to c for every character in the `TextField`. It is possible to change the echo character on the fly so that existing characters will be replaced. A c of zero, `(char)0`, effectively turns off any change and makes the `TextField` behave normally.
>
> `setEchoCharacter()` is the Java 1.0 name for this method.

public boolean echoCharIsSet ()

> The `echoCharIsSet()` method returns `true` if the echo character is set to a nonzero value. If the `TextField` is displaying input normally, this method returns `false`.

Miscellaneous methods

public synchronized void addNotify ()

> The addNotify() method creates the TextField peer. If you override this method, first call super.addNotify(), then add your customizations for the new class. Then you will be able to do everything you need with the information about the newly created peer.

protected String paramString ()

> When you call the toString() method of TextField, the default toString() method of Component is called. This in turn calls paramString(), which builds up the string to display. The TextField level can add only one item. If the echo character is nonzero, the current echo character is added (the method getEchoChar()). Using new TextField ("Empty String", 20), the results displayed could be:

```
java.awt.TextField[0,0,0x0,invalid,text="Empty String",editable,selection=0-0]
```

8.2.2 TextField Events

With the 1.0 event model, TextField components can generate KEY_PRESS and KEY_ACTION (which calls keyDown()), KEY_RELEASE and KEY_ACTION_RELEASE (which calls keyUp()), and ACTION_EVENT (which calls action()).

With the 1.1 event model, you register an ActionListener with the method addActionListener(). Then when the user presses Return within the TextField the ActionListener.actionPerformed() method is called through the protected TextField.processActionEvent() method. Key, mouse, and focus listeners are registered through the three Component methods of addKeyListener(), addMouseListener(), and addFocusListener(), respectively.

Action

public boolean action (Event e, Object o)

> The action() method for a TextField is called when the input focus is in the TextField and the user presses the Return key. e is the Event instance for the specific event, while o is a String representing the current contents (the getText() method).

Keyboard

public boolean keyDown (Event e, int key)

> The keyDown() method is called whenever the user presses a key. keyDown() may be called many times in succession if the key remains pressed. e is the Event instance for the specific event, while key is the integer representation of the character pressed. The identifier for the event (e.id) for keyDown() could

be either Event.KEY_PRESS for a regular key or Event.KEY_ACTION for an action-oriented key (i.e., an arrow or function key). Some of the things you can do through this method are validate input, convert each character to uppercase, and limit the number or type of characters entered. The technique is simple: you just need to remember that the user's keystroke is actually displayed by the TextField peer, which receives the event after the TextField itself. Therefore, a TextField subclass can modify the character displayed by modifying the key field (e.key) of the Event and returning false, which passes the Event on down the chain; remember that returning false indicates that the Event has not been completely processed. The following method uses this technique to convert all input to uppercase.

```
public boolean keyDown (Event e, int key) {
    e.key = Character.toUpperCase (char(key));
    return false;
}
```

If keyDown() returns true, it indicates that the Event has been completely processed. In this case, the Event never propagates to the peer, and the keystroke is never displayed.

public boolean keyUp (Event e, int key)

The keyUp() method is called whenever the user releases a key. e is the Event instance for the specific event, while key is the integer representation of the character pressed. The identifier for the event (e.id) for keyUp() could be either Event.KEY_RELEASE for a regular key or Event.KEY_ACTION_RELEASE for an action-oriented key (i.e., an arrow or function key). Among other things, keyUp() may be used to determine how long the key has been pressed.

Mouse

Ordinarily, the TextField component does not trigger any mouse events.

NOTE   Mouse events are not generated for TextField with JDK 1.0.2. Your
           run-time environment may behave differently. See Appendix C for
           more information about platform dependencies.

Focus

The TextField component does not reliably generate focus events.

NOTE   The GOT_FOCUS and LOST_FOCUS events can be generated by TextFields, but these events are not reliable across platforms. With Java 1.0, they are generated on most UNIX platforms but not on Windows NT/95 platforms. They are generated on all platforms under Java 1.1. See Appendix C for more information about platform dependencies.

---

public boolean gotFocus (Event e, Object o)

The gotFocus() method is triggered when the TextField gets the input focus. e is the Event instance for the specific event, while o is a String representation of the current contents (getText()).

public boolean lostFocus (Event e, Object o)

The lostFocus() method is triggered when the input focus leaves the TextField. e is the Event instance for the specific event, while o is a String representation of the current contents (getText()).

Listeners and 1.1 event handling

With the 1.1 event model, you register event listeners that are told when an event occurs. You can register text event listeners by calling the method TextComponent.addTextListener().

public void addActionListener(ActionListener listener) ★

The addActionListener() method registers listener as an object interested in receiving notifications when an ActionEvent passes through the EventQueue with this TextField as its target. The listener.actionPerformed() method is called when these events occur. Multiple listeners can be registered. The following code demonstrates how to use an ActionListener to reverse the text in the TextField.

```
// Java 1.1 only
import java.applet.*;
import java.awt.*;
import java.awt.event.*;

class MyAL implements ActionListener {
    public void actionPerformed(ActionEvent e) {
        System.out.println ("The current text is: " +
            e.getActionCommand());
        if (e.getSource() instanceof TextField) {
            TextField tf = (TextField)e.getSource();
            StringBuffer sb = new StringBuffer (e.getActionCommand());
            tf.setText (sb.reverse().toString());
        }
    }
}
```

```
public class text11 extends Applet {
    public void init () {
        TextField tf = new TextField ("Help Text", 20);
        add (tf);
        tf.addActionListener (new MyAL());
    }
}
```

public void removeActionListener(ActionListener listener) ★

The `removeActionListener()` method removes `listener` as a interested listener. If `listener` is not registered, nothing happens.

protected void processEvent(AWTEvent e) ★

The `processEvent()` method receives all `AWTEvents` with this `TextField` as its target. `processEvent()` then passes them along to any listeners for processing. When you subclass `TextField`, overriding `processEvent()` allows you to process all events yourself, before sending them to any listeners. In a way, overriding `processEvent()` is like overriding `handleEvent()` using the 1.0 event model.

If you override `processEvent()`, remember to call `super.processEvent(e)` last to ensure that regular event processing can occur. If you want to process your own events, it's a good idea to call `enableEvents()` (inherited from `Component`) to ensure that events are delivered even in the absence of registered listeners.

protected void processActionEvent(ActionEvent e) ★

The `processActionEvent()` method receives all `ActionEvents` with this `TextField` as its target. `processActionEvent()` then passes them along to any listeners for processing. When you subclass `TextField`, overriding the method `processActionEvent()` allows you to process all action events yourself, before sending them to any listeners. In a way, overriding `processActionEvent()` is like overriding `action()` using the 1.0 event model.

If you override the `processActionEvent()` method, remember to call `super.processActionEvent(e)` last to ensure that regular event processing can occur. If you want to process your own events, it's a good idea to call `enableEvents()` (inherited from `Component`) to ensure that events are delivered even in the absence of registered listeners.

The following applet is equivalent to the previous example, except that it overrides `processActionEvent()` to receive events, eliminating the need for an `ActionListener`. The constructor calls `enableEvents()` to make sure that events are delivered, even if no listeners are registered.

```
// Java 1.1 only
import java.applet.*;
import java.awt.*;
```

```
import java.awt.event.*;

class MyTextField extends TextField {
    public MyTextField (String s, int len) {
        super (s, len);
        enableEvents (AWTEvent.ACTION_EVENT_MASK);
    }
    protected void processActionEvent(ActionEvent e) {
        System.out.println ("The current text is: " +
            e.getActionCommand());
        TextField tf = (TextField)e.getSource();
        StringBuffer sb = new StringBuffer (e.getActionCommand());
        tf.setText (sb.reverse().toString());
        super.processActionEvent(e)
    }
}
public class text12 extends Applet {
    public void init () {
        TextField tf = new MyTextField ("Help Text", 20);
        add (tf);
    }
}
```

8.3 TextArea

TextArea is the TextComponent for multiline input. Some constructors permit you to set the rows and columns of the TextArea on the screen. However, the Layout-Manager may change your settings. As with TextField, the only way to limit the number of characters that a user can enter is to override the keyDown() method. The text in a TextArea appears left justified, and the justification is not customizable.

In Java 1.1, you can control the appearance of a TextArea scrollbar; earlier versions gave you no control over the scrollbars. When visible, the vertical scrollbar is on the right of the TextArea, and the horizontal scrollbar is on the bottom. You can remove either scrollbar with the help of several new TextArea constants; you can't move them to another side. When the horizontal scrollbar is not present, the text wraps automatically when the user reaches the right side of the TextArea. Prior to Java 1.1, there was no way to enable word wrap.

8.3.1 TextArea Variables

Constants

The constants for TextArea are new to Java 1.1; they allow you to control the visibility and word wrap policy of a TextArea scrollbar. There is no way to listen for the events when a user scrolls a TextArea.

public static final int SCROLLBARS_BOTH ★

> The SCROLLBARS_BOTH mode is the default for TextArea. It shows both scrollbars all the time and does no word wrap.

public static final int SCROLLBARS_HORIZONTAL_ONLY ★

> The SCROLLBARS_HORIZONTAL_ONLY mode displays a scrollbar along the bottom of the TextArea. When this scrollbar is present, word wrap is disabled.

public static final int SCROLLBARS_NONE ★

> The SCROLLBARS_NONE mode displays no scrollbars around the TextArea and enables word wrap. If the text is too long, the TextArea displays the lines surrounding the cursor. You can use the cursor to move up and down within the TextArea, but you cannot use a scrollbar to navigate. Because this mode has no horizontal scrollbar, word wrap is enabled.

public static final int SCROLLBARS_VERTICAL_ONLY ★

> The SCROLLBARS_VERTICAL_ONLY mode displays a scrollbar along the right edge of the TextArea. If the text is too long to display, you can scroll within the area. Because this mode has no horizontal scrollbar, word wrap is enabled.

8.3.2 *TextArea Methods*

Constructors

public TextArea ()

> This constructor creates an empty TextArea with both scrollbars. The TextArea is 0 rows high and 0 columns wide. Depending upon the platform, the TextArea could be really small (and useless) or rather large. It is a good idea to use one of the other constructors to control the size of the TextArea.

public TextArea (int rows, int columns)

> This constructor creates an empty TextArea with both scrollbars. The TextArea is rows high and columns wide.

public TextArea (String text)

> This constructor creates a TextArea with an initial content of text and both scrollbars. The TextArea is 0 rows high and 0 columns wide. Depending upon the platform, the TextArea could be really small (and useless) or rather large. It is a good idea to use one of the other constructors to control the size of the TextArea.

public TextArea (String text, int rows, int columns)

> This constructor creates a TextArea with an initial content of text. The TextArea is rows high and columns wide and has both scrollbars.

The following example uses the first four constructors. The results are shown in Figure 8-3. With the size-less constructors, notice that Windows 95 creates a rather large TextArea. UNIX systems create a much smaller area. Depending upon the LayoutManager, the TextAreas could be resized automatically.

```
import java.awt.TextArea;
public class textas extends java.applet.Applet {
    public void init () {
        add (new TextArea ());                           // A
        add (new TextArea (3, 10));                       // B
        add (new TextArea ("Empty Area"));               // C
        add (new TextArea ("Empty Area", 3, 10));        // D
    }
}
```

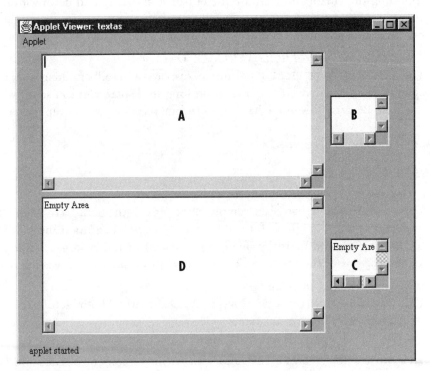

Figure 8–3: TextArea constructor

public TextArea (String text, int rows, int columns, int scrollbarPolicy) ★

The final constructor creates a TextArea with an initial content of text. The TextArea is rows high and columns wide. The initial scrollbar display policy is designated by the scrollbarPolicy parameter and is one of the TextArea constants in the previous example. This constructor is the only way provided to change the scrollbar visibility; there is no setScrollbarVisibility() method. Figure 8-4 displays the different settings.

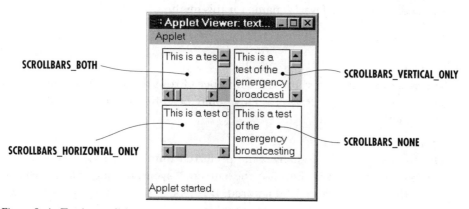

Figure 8–4: TextArea policies

Setting text

The text-setting methods are usually called in response to an external event. When you handle the insertion position, you must translate it from the visual row and column to a one-dimensional position. It is easier to position the insertion point based upon the beginning, end, or current selection (getSelectionStart() and getSelectionEnd()).

public void insert (String string, int position) ★
public void insertText (String string, int position) ☆

> The insert() method inserts string at position into the TextArea. If position is beyond the end of the TextArea, string is appended to the end of the TextArea.
>
> insertText() is the Java 1.0 name for this method.

public void append (String string) ★
public void appendText (String string) ☆

> The append() method inserts string at the end of the TextArea.
>
> appendText() is the Java 1.0 name for this method.

public void replaceRange (String string, int startPosition, int endPosition) ★
public void replaceText (String string, int startPosition, int endPosition) ☆

> The replaceRange() method replaces the text in the current TextArea from startPosition to endPosition with string. If endPosition is before startPosition, it may or may not work as expected. (For instance, on a Windows 95 platform, it works fine when the TextArea is displayed on the screen. However, when the TextArea is not showing, unexpected results happen. Other platforms may vary.) If startPosition is 0 and endPosition is the length of the contents, this method functions the same as TextComponent.setText().

replaceText() is the Java 1.0 name for this method.

Sizing

public int getRows ()

The getRows() method returns the number of rows set by the constructor or a subsequent call to setRows(). This could be different from the displayed height of the TextArea.

public void setRows (int rows) ★

The setRows() method changes the preferred number of rows to display for the TextField to rows. Because the current LayoutManager will do what it wants, the new setting may be ignored. If rows < 0, setRows() throws the run-time exception IllegalArgumentException.

public int getColumns ()

The getColumns() method returns the number of columns set by the constructor or a subsequent call to setColumns(). This could be different from the displayed width of the TextArea.

public void setColumns (int columns) ★

The setColumns() method changes the preferred number of columns to display for the TextArea to columns. Because the current LayoutManager will do what it wants, the new setting may be ignored. If columns < 0, setColumns() throws the run-time exception IllegalArgumentException.

public Dimension getPreferredSize (int rows, int columns) ★
public Dimension preferredSize (int rows, int columns) ☆

The getPreferredSize() method returns the Dimension (width and height) for the preferred size of the TextArea with a preferred height of rows and width of columns. The rows and columns specified may be different from the current settings.

preferredSize() is the Java 1.0 name for this method.

public Dimension getPreferredSize (int rows, int columns) ★
public Dimension preferredSize () ☆

The getPreferredSize() method returns the Dimension (width and height) for the preferred size of the TextArea. Without the rows and columns parameters, this getPreferredSize() uses the constructor's number of rows and columns to calculate the TextArea's preferred size.

preferredSize() is the Java 1.0 name for this method.

public Dimension getMinimumSize (int rows, int columns) ★
public Dimension minimumSize (int rows, int columns) ☆

> The getMinimumSize() method returns the minimum Dimension (width and height) for the size of the TextArea with a height of rows and width of columns. The rows and columns specified may be different from the current settings.
>
> minimumSize() is the Java 1.0 name for this method.

public Dimension getMinimumSize () ★
public Dimension minimumSize () ☆

> The getMinimumSize() method returns the minimum Dimension (width and height) for the size of the TextArea. Without the rows and columns parameters, this getMinimumSize() uses the current settings for rows and columns to calculate the TextArea's minimum size.
>
> minimumSize() is the Java 1.0 name for this method.

Miscellaneous methods

public synchronized void addNotify ()

> The addNotify() method creates the TextArea peer. If you override this method, call super.addNotify() first, then add your customizations for the new class. You will then be able to do everything you need with the information about the newly created peer.

public int getScrollbarVisibility() ★

> The getScrollbarVisibility() method retrieves the scrollbar visibility setting, which is set by the constructor. There is no setScollbarVisibility() method to change the setting. The return value is one of the TextArea constants: SCROLLBARS_BOTH, SCROLLBARS_HORIZONTAL_ONLY, SCROLLBARS_NONE, or SCROLLBARS_VERTICAL_ONLY.

protected String paramString ()

> When you call the toString() method of TextArea, the default toString() method of Component is called. This in turn calls paramString(), which builds up the string to display. The TextArea level adds the number of rows and columns for the TextArea, and Java 1.1 adds the scrollbar visibility policy. Using new TextArea("Empty Area", 3, 10), the results displayed could be:

```
java.awt.TextArea[text0,0,0,0x0,invalid,text="Empty Area",
editable,selection=0-0, rows=3,columns=10, scrollbarVisibility=both]
```

8.3.3 TextArea Events

With the 1.0 event model, the TextArea component can generate KEY_PRESS and
KEY_ACTION (which calls keyDown()) along with KEY_RELEASE and
KEY_ACTION_RELEASE (which called keyUp()). There is no ACTION_EVENT generated
for TextArea.

NOTE   The GOT_FOCUS and LOST_FOCUS events can be generated by this com-
              ponent but not reliably across platforms. Currently, they are gener-
              ated on most UNIX platforms but not on Microsoft Windows NT/95
              under Java 1.0. These events are generated under Java 1.1.

              Similarly, the mouse events are not generated with JDK 1.0.2. See
              Appendix C for more information about platform dependencies.

With the Java 1.1 event model, there are no listeners specific to TextArea. You
can register key, mouse, and focus listeners through the Component methods of
addKeyListener(), addMouseListener(), and addFocusListener(), respectively.
To register listeners for text events, call TextComponent.addTextListener().

Action

The TextArea component has no way to trigger the action event, since carriage
return is a valid character. You would need to put something like a Button on the
screen to cause an action for a TextArea. The following Rot13 program demonstrates this technique. The user enters text in the TextArea and selects the Rotate
Me button to rotate the text. If the user selects Rotate Me again, it rotates again,
back to the original position. Without the button, there would be no way to trigger
the event. Figure 8-5 shows this example in action.

```
import java.awt.*;

public class Rot13 extends Frame {
    TextArea ta;
    Component rotate, done;
    public Rot13 () {
        super ("Rot-13 Example");
        add ("North", new Label ("Enter Text to Rotate:"));
        ta = (TextArea)(add ("Center", new TextArea (5, 40)));
        Panel p = new Panel ();
        rotate = p.add (new Button ("Rotate Me"));
        done = p.add (new Button ("Done"));
        add ("South", p);
    }
    public static void main (String args[]) {
        Rot13 rot = new Rot13 ();
        rot.pack ();
```

```
        rot.show();
    }
    public boolean handleEvent (Event e) {
        if (e.id == Event.WINDOW_DESTROY) {
            hide();
            dispose();
            System.exit (0);
            return true;
        }
        return super.handleEvent (e);
    }
    public boolean action (Event e, Object o) {
        if (e.target == rotate) {
            ta.setText (rot13Text (ta.getText()));
            return true;
        } else if (e.target == done) {
            hide();
            dispose();
            System.exit (0);
        }
        return false;
    }
    String rot13Text (String s) {
        int len = s.length();
        StringBuffer returnString = new StringBuffer (len);
        char c;
        for (int i=0;i<len;i++) {
            c = s.charAt (i);
            if (((c >= 'A') && (c <= 'M')) ||
                ((c >= 'a') && (c <= 'm')))
                c += 13;
            else if (((c >= 'N') && (c <= 'Z')) ||
                ((c >= 'n') && (c <= 'z')))
                c -= 13;
            returnString.append (c);
        }
        return returnString.toString();
    }
}
```

Keyboard

Ordinarily, the TextArea component generates all the key events.

public boolean keyDown (Event e, int key)

The keyDown() method is called whenever the user presses a key. keyDown() may be called many times in succession if the key remains pressed. e is the Event instance for the specific event, while key is the integer representation of the character pressed. The identifier for the event (e.id) for keyDown() could be either Event.KEY_PRESS for a regular key or Event.KEY_ACTION for an action-oriented key (i.e., an arrow or function key). Some of the things you can do through this method are validate input, convert each character to

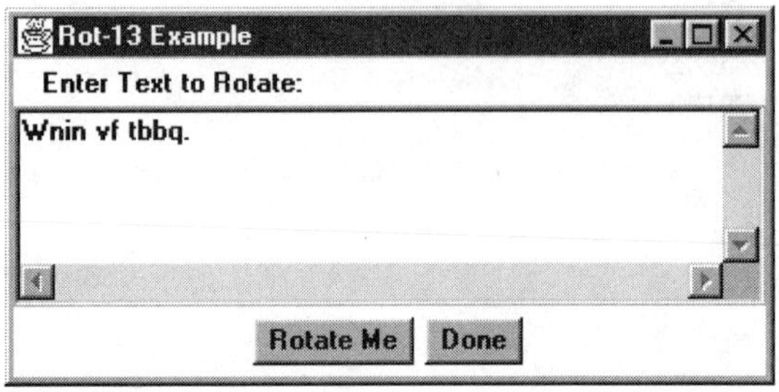

Figure 8–5: TextArea with activator button

uppercase, and limit the number or type of characters entered. The technique is simple: you just need to remember that the user's keystroke is actually displayed by the TextArea peer, which receives the event after the TextArea itself. Therefore, a TextArea subclass can modify the character displayed by modifying the key field (e.key) of the Event and returning false, which passes the Event on down the chain; remember that returning false indicates that the Event has not been completely processed. The following method uses this technique to convert all alphabetic characters to the opposite case:

```
public boolean keyDown (Event e, int key) {
    if (Character.isUpperCase ((char)key)) {
        e.key = Character.toLowerCase ((char)key);
    } else if (Character.isLowerCase ((char)key)) {
        e.key = Character.toUpperCase ((char)key);
    }
    return false;
}
```

If keyDown() returns true, it indicates that the Event has been completely processed. In this case, the Event never propagates to the peer, and the keystroke is never displayed.

public boolean keyUp (Event e, int key)

The keyUp() method is called whenever the user releases a key. e is the Event instance for the specific event, while key is the integer representation of the character pressed. The identifier for the event (e.id) for keyUp() could be either Event.KEY_RELEASE for a regular key, or Event.KEY_ACTION_RELEASE for an action-oriented key (i.e., an arrow or function key).

Mouse

Ordinarily, the TextArea component does not trigger any mouse events.

NOTE	Mouse events are not generated for TextArea with JDK 1.0.2. See Appendix C for more information about platform dependencies.

Focus

The TextArea component does not reliably generate focus events.

NOTE	The GOT_FOCUS and LOST_FOCUS events can be generated by this component but not reliably across platforms. With the JDK, they are generated on most UNIX platforms but not on Microsoft Windows NT/95 under JDK 1.0. These events are generated with JDK 1.1. See Appendix C for more information about platform dependencies.

---

public boolean gotFocus (Event e, Object o)

The gotFocus() method is triggered when the TextArea gets the input focus. e is the Event instance for the specific event, while o is a String representation of the current contents (getText()).

public boolean lostFocus (Event e, Object o)

The lostFocus() method is triggered when the input focus leaves the TextArea. e is the Event instance for the specific event, while o is a String representation of the current contents (getText()).

Listeners and 1.1 event handling

There are no listeners specific to the TextArea class. You can register Key, mouse, and focus listeners through the Component methods of addKeyListener(), addMouseListener(), and addFocusListener(), respectively. Also, you register listeners for text events by calling TextComponent.addTextListener().

8.4 Extending TextField

To extend what you learned so far, Example 8-1 creates a sub-class of TextField that limits the number of characters a user can type into it. Other than the six constructors, all the work is in the keyDown() method. The entire class follows.

Example 8–1: The SizedTextField Class Limits the Number of Characters a User can Type

```
import java.awt.*;
public class SizedTextField extends TextField {
    private int size;  // size = 0 is unlimited
    public SizedTextField () {
        super ("");
        this.size = 0;
    }
    public SizedTextField (int columns) {
        super (columns);
        this.size = 0;
    }
    public SizedTextField (int columns, int size) {
        super (columns);
        this.size = Math.max (0, size);
    }
    public SizedTextField (String text) {
        super (text);
        this.size = 0;
    }
    public SizedTextField (String text, int columns) {
        super (text, columns);
        this.size = 0;
    }
    public SizedTextField (String text, int columns, int size) {
        super (text, columns);
        this.size = Math.max (0, size);
    }
    public boolean keyDown (Event e, int key) {
        if ((e.id == Event.KEY_PRESS) && (this.size > 0) &&
            (((TextField)(e.target)).getText ().length () >= this.size)) {
            // Check for backspace / delete / tab-let these pass through
            if ((key == 127) || (key == 8) || (key == 9)) {
                return false;
            }
            return true;
        }
        return false;
    }
    protected String paramString () {
        String str = super.paramString ();
        if (size != 0) {
            str += ",size=" + size;
        }
        return str;
    }
}
```

Most of the SizedTextField class consists of constructors; you really don't need to provide an equivalent to all the superclass's constructors, but it's not a bad idea.

The `keyDown()` method looks at what the user types before it reaches the screen and acts accordingly. It checks the length of the `TextField` and compares it to the maximum length. It then does another check to see if the user typed a Backspace, Delete, or Tab, all of which we want to allow: if the field has gotten too long, we want to allow the user to shorten it. We also want to allow tab under all circumstances, so that focus traversal works properly. The rest of the logic is simple:

- If the user typed Backspace, Delete, or Tab, return `false` to propagate the event.

- If the field is too long, return `true` to prevent the event from reaching the peer. This effectively ignores the character.

9

Pick Me

Three AWT components let you present a list of choices to users: Choice, List, and Checkbox. All three components implement the ItemSelectable interface (Java1.1). These components are comparable to selection mechanisms in modern GUIs so most readers will be able to learn them easily, but I'll point out some special enhancements that they provide.

Choice and List are similar; both offer a list of choices for the user to select. Choice provides a pull-down list that offers one selection at a time, whereas List is a scrollable list that allows a user to make one or multiple selections. From a design standpoint, which you choose depends at least partially on screen real estate; if you want the user to select from a large group of alternatives, Choice requires the least space, List requires somewhat more, while Checkbox requires the most. Choice is the only component in this group that does not allow multiple selections. A List allows multiple or single selection; because each Checkbox is a separate component, checkboxes inherently allow multiple selection. In order to create a list of mutually exclusive checkboxes, in which only one box can be selected at a time (commonly known as radio buttons), you can put several checkboxes together into a CheckboxGroup, which is discussed at the end of this chapter.

9.1 Choice

The Choice component provides pop-up/pull-down lists. It is the equivalent of Motif's OptionMenu or Windows MFC's ComboBox. (Java 1.1 departs from the MFC world.) With the Choice component, you can provide a short list of choices to the user, while taking up the space of a single item on the screen. When the component is selected, the complete list of available choices appears on the screen. After the user has selected an option, the list is removed from the screen and the selected item is displayed. Selecting any item automatically deselects the previous selection.

9.1.1 Component Methods

Constructors

public Choice ()

> There is only one constructor for Choice. When you call it, a new instance of Choice is created. The component is initially empty, with no items to select. Once you add some items using addItem() (version 1.0) or add() (version 1.1) and display the Choice on the screen, it will look something like the leftmost component in Figure 9-1. The center component shows what a Choice looks like when it is selected, while the one on the right shows what a Choice looks like before any items have been added to it.

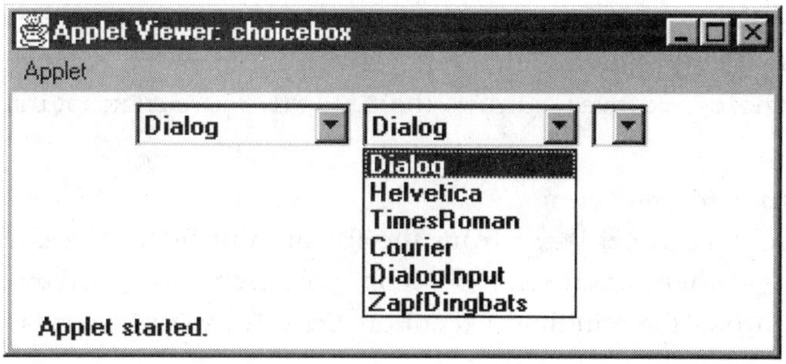

Figure 9–1: How Choices are displayed

Items

public int getItemCount () ★
public int countItems () ☆

> The getItemCount() method returns the number of selectable items in the Choice object. In Figure 9-1, getItemCount() would return 6.
>
> countItems() is the Java 1.0 name for this method.

public String getItem (int index)

> The getItem() method returns the text for the item at position index in the Choice. If index is invalid—either index < 0 or index >= getItem-Count()—the getItem() method throws the ArrayIndexOutOfBoundsException run-time exception.

public synchronized void add (String item) ★
public synchronized void addItem (String item) ☆

> add() adds item to the list of available choices. If item is already an option in the Choice, this method adds it again. If item is null, add() throws the run-time exception NullPointerException. The first item added to a Choice becomes the initial (default) selection.

> addItem() is the Java 1.0 name for this method.

public synchronized void insert (String item, int index) ★

> insert() adds item to the list of available choices at position index. An index of 0 adds the item at the beginning. An index larger than the number of choices adds the item at the end. If item is null, insert() throws the run-time exception NullPointerException. If index is negative, insert() throws the run-time exception IllegalArgumentException.

public synchronized void remove (String item) ★

> remove() removes item from the list of available choices. If item is present in Choice multiple times, a call to remove() removes the first instance. If item is null, remove() throws the run-time exception NullPointerException. If item is not found in the Choice, remove() throws the IllegalArgumentException run-time exception.

public synchronized void remove (int position) ★

> remove() removes the item at position from the list of available choices. If position is invalid—either position < 0 or position >= getItem-Count()—remove() throws the run-time exception ArrayIndexOutOfBounds-Exception.

public synchronized void removeAll () ★

> The removeAll() method removes every option from the Choice. This allows you to refresh the list from scratch, rather than creating a new Choice and repopulating it.

Selection

The Choice has one item selected at a time. Initially, it is the first item that was added to the Choice.

public String getSelectedItem ()

> The getSelectedItem() method returns the currently selected item as a String. The text returned is the parameter used in the addItem() or add() call that put the option in the Choice. If Choice is empty, getSelectedItem() returns null.

public Object[] getSelectedObjects () ★

> The getSelectedObjects() method returns the currently selected item as an Object array, instead of a String. The array will either be a one-element array, or null if there are no items. This method is required by the ItemSelectable interface and allows you to use the same method to look at the items selected by a Choice, List, or Checkbox.

public int getSelectedIndex ()

> The getSelectedIndex() method returns the position of the currently selected item. The Choice list uses zero-based indexing, so the position of the first item is zero. The position of the last item is the value of countItems()-1. If the list is empty, this method returns -1.

public synchronized void select (int position)

> This version of the select() method makes the item at position the selected item in the Choice. If position is too big, select() throws the run-time exception IllegalArgumentException. If position is negative, nothing happens.

public void select (String string)

> This version of select() makes the item with the label string the selected item. If string is in the Choice multiple times, this method selects the first. If string is not in the Choice, nothing happens.

Miscellaneous methods

public synchronized void addNotify ()

> The addNotify() method creates the Choice's peer. If you override this method, call super.addNotify() first, then add your customizations for the new class. You will then be able to do everything you need with the information about the newly created peer.

protected String paramString ()

> When you call the toString() method of a Choice, the default toString() method of Component gets called. This in turn calls paramString() which builds up the string to display. At the Choice level, paramString() appends the currently selected item (the result of getSelectedItem()) to the output. Using the first Choice instance in Figure 9-1, the results would be:

```
java.awt.Choice[139,5,92x27,current=Dialog]
```

9.1.2 Choice Events

The primary event for a Choice occurs when the user selects an item in the list. With the 1.0 event model, selecting an item generates an ACTION_EVENT, which triggers a call to the action() method. Once the Choice has the input focus, the user can change the selection by using the arrow or keyboard keys. The arrow keys scroll through the list of choices, triggering the KEY_ACTION, ACTION_EVENT, and KEY_ACTION_RELEASE event sequence, which in turn invokes the keyDown(), action(), and keyUp() methods, respectively. If the mouse is used to choose an item, no mouse events are triggered as you scroll over each item, and an ACTION_EVENT occurs only when a specific choice is selected.

With the 1.1 event model, you register ItemListener with addItemListener(). Then when the user selects the Choice, the ItemListener.itemStateChanged() method is called through the protected Choice.processItemEvent() method. Key, mouse, and focus listeners are registered through the Component methods of add-KeyListener(), addMouseListener(), and addFocusListener(), respectively.

Action

public boolean action (Event e, Object o)

> The action() method for a choice signifies that the user selected an item. e is the Event instance for the specific event, while o is the String from the call to addItem() or add() that represents the current selection. Here's a trivial implementation of the method:

```
public boolean action (Event e, Object o) {
    if (e.target instanceof Choice) {
        System.out.println ("Choice is now set to " + o);
    }
    return false;
}
```

Keyboard

The keyboard events for a Choice can be generated once the Choice has the input focus. In addition to the KEY_ACTION and KEY_ACTION_RELEASE events you get with the arrow keys, an ACTION_EVENT is generated over each entry.

public boolean keyDown (Event e, int key)

> The keyDown() method is called whenever the user presses a key and the Choice has the input focus. e is the Event instance for the specific event, while key is the integer representation of the character pressed. The identifier for the event (e.id) for keyDown() could be either Event.KEY_PRESS for a regular

key or Event.KEY_ACTION for an action-oriented key (i.e., arrow or function key). If you check the current selection in this method through the method getSelectedItem() or getSelectedIndex(), you will be given the previously selected item because the Choice's selection has not changed yet. keyDown() is not called when the Choice is changed by using the mouse.

public boolean keyUp (Event e, int key)

The keyUp() method is called whenever the user releases a key. e is the Event instance for the specific event, while key is the integer representation of the character pressed. The identifier for the event (e.id) for keyUp() could be either KEY_RELEASE for a regular key or KEY_ACTION_RELEASE for an action oriented key (i.e., arrow or function key).

Mouse

Ordinarily, the Choice component does not trigger any mouse events.

Focus

Ordinarily, the Choice component does not trigger any focus events.

Listeners and 1.1 event handling

With the 1.1 event model, you register listeners for different event types; the listeners are told when the event happens. These methods register listeners, and let the Choice component inspect its own events.

public void addItemListener(ItemListener listener) ★

The addItemListener() method registers listener as an object interested in being notified when an ItemEvent passes through the EventQueue with this Choice as its target. The listener.itemStateChanged() method is called when an event occurs. Multiple listeners can be registered.

public void removeItemListener(ItemListener listener) ★

The removeItemListener() method removes listener as a interested listener. If listener is not registered, nothing happens.

protected void processEvent(AWTEvent e) ★

The processEvent() method receives all AWTEvents with this Choice as its target. processEvent() then passes them along to any listeners for processing. When you subclass Choice, overriding processEvent() allows you to process all events yourself, before sending them to any listeners. In a way, overriding processEvent() is like overriding handleEvent() using the 1.0 event model.

If you override processEvent(), remember to call super.processEvent(e) last to ensure that regular event processing can occur. If you want to process your own events, it's a good idea to call enableEvents() (inherited from Component) to ensure that events are delivered even in the absence of registered listeners.

protected void processItemEvent(ItemEvent e) ★

The processItemEvent() method receives all ItemEvents with this Choice as its target. processItemEvent() then passes them along to any listeners for processing. When you subclass Choice, overriding processItemEvent() allows you to process all events yourself, before sending them to any listeners. In a way, overriding processItemEvent() is like overriding handleEvent() using the 1.0 event model.

If you override processItemEvent(), remember to call the method super.processItemEvent(e) last to ensure that regular event processing can occur. If you want to process your own events, it's a good idea to call enableEvents() (inherited from Component) to ensure that events are delivered even in the absence of registered listeners.

The following simple applet below demonstrates how a component can receive its own events by overriding processItemEvent(), while still allowing other objects to register as listeners. MyChoice11 is a subclass of Choice that processes its own item events. choice11 is an applet that uses the MyChoice11 component and registers itself as a listener for item events.

```java
// Java 1.1 only
import java.awt.*;
import java.applet.*;
import java.awt.event.*;
class MyChoice11 extends Choice {
    MyChoice11 () {
        super ();
        enableEvents (AWTEvent.ITEM_EVENT_MASK);
    }
    protected void processItemEvent(ItemEvent e) {
        ItemSelectable ie = e.getItemSelectable();
        System.out.println ("Item Selected: " + ie.getSelectedObjects()[0]);
        // If you do not call super.processItemEvent()
        // no listener will be notified
        super.processItemEvent (e);
    }
}

public class choice11 extends Applet implements ItemListener {
    Choice c;
    public void init () {
        String []fonts;
        fonts = Toolkit.getDefaultToolkit().getFontList();
```

```
        c = new MyChoice11();
        for (int i = 0; i < fonts.length; i++) {
            c.add (fonts[i]);
        }
        add (c);
        c.addItemListener (this);
    }
    public void itemStateChanged(ItemEvent e)  {
        ItemSelectable ie = e.getItemSelectable();
        System.out.println ("State Change: " + ie.getSelectedObjects()[0]);
    }
}
```

A few things are worth noticing. MyChoice11 calls enableEvents() in its constructor to make sure that item events are delivered, even if nobody registers as a listener: MyChoice11 needs to make sure that it receives events, even in the absence of listeners. Its processItemEvent() method ends by calling the superclass's processItemEvent() method, with the original item event. This call ensures that normal item event processing occurs; super.processItemEvent() is responsible for distributing the event to any registered listeners. The alternative would be to implement the whole registration and event distribution mechanism inside myChoice11, which is precisely what object-oriented programming is supposed to avoid, or being absolutely sure that you will only use MyChoice11 in situations in which there won't be any listeners, drastically limiting the usefulness of this class.

choice11 doesn't contain many surprises. It implements ItemListener, the listener interface for item events; provides the required itemStateChanged() method, which is called whenever an item event occurs; and calls MyChoice11's method addItemListener() to register as a listener for item events. (MyChoice11 inherits this method from the Choice class.)

9.2 Lists

Like the Choice component, the List provides a way to present your user with a fixed sequence of choices to select. However, with List, several items can be displayed at a time on the screen. A List can also allow multiple selection, so that more than one choice can be selected.

Normally, a scrollbar is associated with the List to enable the user to move to the items that do not fit on the screen. On some platforms, the List may not display the scrollbar if there is enough room to display all choices. A List can be resized by the LayoutManager according to the space available. Figure 9-2 shows two lists, one of which has no items to display.

9.2.1 List Methods

Constructors

public List ()

> This constructor creates an empty List with four visible lines. You must rely on the current LayoutManager to resize the List or override the preferredSize() (version 1.0) or getPreferredSize() (version 1.1) method to affect the size of the displayed List. A List created with this constructor is in single-selection mode, so the user can select only one item at a time.

public List (int rows)

> This constructor creates a List that has rows visible lines. This is just a request; the LayoutManager is free to adjust the height of the List to some other amount based upon available space. A List created with this constructor is in single-selection mode, so the user will be able to select only one item at a time.

public List (int rows, boolean multipleSelections)

> The final constructor for List creates a List that has rows visible lines. This is just a request; the LayoutManager is free to adjust the height of the List to some other amount based upon available space. If multipleSelections is true, this List permits multiple items to be selected. If false, this is a single-selection list.

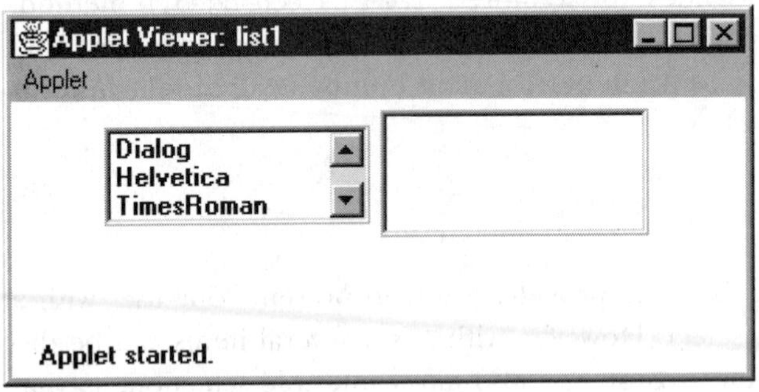

Figure 9–2: Two lists; the list on the right is empty

Content control

public int getItemCount () ★
public int countItems () ☆

> The getItemCount() method returns the length of the list. The length of the list is the number of items in the list, not the number of visible rows.

countItems() is the Java 1.0 name for this method.

public String getItem (int index)

The getItem() method returns the String representation for the item at position index. The String is the parameter passed to the addItem() or add() method.

public String[] getItems () ★

The getItems() method returns a String array that contains all the elements in the List. This method does not care if an item is selected or not.

public synchronized void add (String item) ★
public synchronized void addItem (String item) ☆

The add() method adds item as the last entry in the List. If item already exists in the list, this method adds it again.

addItem() is the Java 1.0 name for this method.

public synchronized void add (String item, int index) ★
public synchronized void addItem (String item, int index) ☆

This version of the add() method has an additional parameter, index, which specifies where to add item to the List. If index < 0 or index >= getItem-Count(), item is added to the end of the List. The position count is zero based, so if index is 0, it will be added as the first item.

addItem() is the Java 1.0 name for this method.

public synchronized void replaceItem (String newItem, int index)

The replaceItem() method replaces the contents at position index with newItem. If the item at index has been selected, newItem will not be selected.

public synchronized void removeAll () ★
public synchronized void clear () ☆

The removeAll() method clears out all the items in the list.

clear() is the Java 1.0 name for this method.

NOTE Early versions (Java1.0) of the clear() method did not work reliably across platforms. You were better off calling the method listVar.delItems(0, listVar.countItems()-1), where listVar is your List instance.

---

public synchronized void remove (String item) ★

The remove() method removes item from the list of available choices. If item appears in the List several times, only the first instance is removed. If item is

null, remove() throws the run-time exception NullPointerException. If item
is not found in the List, remove() throws the IllegalArgumentException run-
time exception.

public synchronized void remove (int position) ★
public synchronized void delItem (int position) ☆

> The remove() method removes the entry at position from the List. If posi-
> tion is invalid—either position < 0 or position >= getItem-
> Count()—remove() throws the ArrayIndexOutOfBoundsException run-time
> exception with a message indicating that position was invalid.
>
> delItem() is the Java 1.0 name for this method.

public synchronized void delItems (int start, int end) ☆

> The delItems() method removes entries from position start to position end
> from the List. If either parameter is invalid—either start < 0 or end >=
> getItemCount()—delItems() throws the ArrayIndexOutOfBoundsException
> run-time exception with a message indicating which position was invalid. If
> start is greater than end, nothing happens.

Selection and positioning

public synchronized int getSelectedIndex ()

> The getSelectedIndex() method returns the position of the selected item. If
> nothing is selected in the List, getSelectedIndex() returns -1. The value -1 is
> also returned if the List is in multiselect mode and multiple items are
> selected. For multiselection lists, use getSelectedIndexes() instead.

public synchronized int[] getSelectedIndexes ()

> The getSelectedIndexes() method returns an integer array of the selected
> items. If nothing is selected, the array will be empty.

public synchronized String getSelectedItem ()

> The getSelectedItem() method returns the label of the selected item. The
> label is the string used in the add() or addItem() call. If nothing is selected in
> the List, getSelectedItem() returns null. The return value is also null if
> List is in multiselect mode and multiple items are selected. For multiselection
> lists, use getSelectedItems() instead.

public synchronized String[] getSelectedItems ()

> The getSelectedItems() method returns a String array of the selected items.
> If nothing is selected, the array is empty.

public synchronized Object[] getSelectedObjects ()

> The getSelectedObjects() method returns the results of the method getSe-lectedItems() as an Object array instead of a String array, to conform to the ItemSelectable interface. If nothing is selected, the returned array is empty.

public synchronized void select (int index)

> The select() method selects the item at position index, which is zero based. If the List is in single-selection mode, any other selected item is deselected. If the List is in multiple-selection mode, calling this method has no effect on the other selections. The item at position index is made visible.

NOTE   A negative index seems to select everything within the List. This
        seems more like an irregularity than a feature to rely upon.

---

public synchronized void deselect (int index)

> The deselect() method deselects the item at position index, which is zero based. deselect() does not reposition the visible elements.

public boolean isIndexSelected (int index) ★
public boolean isSelected (int index) ☆

> The isIndexSelected() method checks whether index is currently selected. If it is, isIndexSelected() returns true; otherwise, it returns false.
>
> isSelected() is the Java 1.0 name for this method.

public boolean isMultipleMode () ★
public boolean allowsMultipleSelections () ☆

> The isMultipleMode() method returns the current state of the List. If the List is in multiselection mode, isMultipleMode() returns true; otherwise, it returns false.
>
> allowsMultipleSelections() is the Java 1.0 name for this method.

public void setMultipleMode (boolean value) ★
public void setMultipleSelections (boolean value) ☆

> The setMultipleMode() method allows you to change the current state of a List from one selection mode to the other. The currently selected items change when this happens. If value is true and the List is going from single- to multiple-selection mode, the selected item gets deselected. If value is false and the List is going from multiple to single, the last item physically selected remains selected (the last item clicked on in the list, not the item with the highest index). If there was no selected item, the first item in the list becomes

selected, or the last item that was deselected becomes selected. If staying within the same mode, setMultipleMode() has no effect on the selected items.

setMultipleSelections() is the Java 1.0 name for this method.

public void makeVisible (int index)

The makeVisible() method ensures that the item at position index is displayed on the screen. This is useful if you want to make sure a certain entry is displayed when another action happens on the screen.

public int getVisibleIndex ()

The getVisibleIndex() method returns the last index from a call to the method makeVisible(). If makeVisible() was never called, -1 is returned.

Sizing

public int getRows ()

The getRows() method returns the number of rows passed to the constructor of the List. It does not return the number of visible rows. To get a rough idea of the number of visible rows, compare the getSize() of the component with the results of getPreferredSize(getRows()).

public Dimension getPreferredSize (int rows) ★
public Dimension preferredSize (int rows) ☆

The getPreferredSize() method returns the preferable Dimension (width and height) for the size of a List with a height of rows. The rows specified may be different from the rows designated in the constructor.

preferredSize() is the Java 1.0 name for this method.

public Dimension getPreferredSize () ★
public Dimension preferredSize () ☆

The getPreferredSize() method returns the Dimension (width and height) for the preferred size of the List. Without the rows parameter, this version of getPreferredSize() uses the constructor's number of rows to calculate the List's preferred size.

preferredSize() is the Java 1.0 name for this method.

public Dimension getMiminumSize (int rows) ★
public Dimension minimumSize (int rows) ☆

The getMinimumSize() method returns the minimum Dimension (width and height) for the size of a List with a height of rows. The rows specified may be different from the rows designated in the constructor. For a List, getMinimumSize() and getPreferredSize() should return the same dimensions.

minimumSize() is the Java 1.0 name for this method.

public Dimension getMiminumSize () ★

public Dimension minimumSize () ☆

> The getMinimumSize() method returns the minimum Dimension (width and height) for the size of the List. Without the rows parameter, this getMinimum-Size() uses the constructor's number of rows to calculate the List's minimum size.
>
> minimumSize() is the Java 1.0 name for this method.

Miscellaneous methods

public synchronized void addNotify ()

> The addNotify() method creates the List peer. If you override this method, call super.addNotify() first, then add your customizations for the new class. You will then be able to do everything you need with the information about the newly created peer.

public synchronized void removeNotify ()

> The removeNotify() method destroys the peer of the List and removes it from the screen. Prior to the List peer's destruction, the last selected entry is saved. If you override this method for a specific List, issue the particular commands that you need for your new object, then call super.removeNotify() last.

protected String paramString ()

> When you call the toString() method of List, the default toString() method of Component is called. This in turn calls paramString(), which builds up the string to display. At the List level, the currently selected item (getSe-lectedItem()) is appended to the output. Using Figure 9-2 as an example, the results would be the following:
>
> ```
> java.awt.List[0,34,107x54,selected=null]
> ```

9.2.2 List Events

The primary event for a List occurs when the user selects an item in the list. With the 1.0 event model, double-clicking a selection causes an ACTION_EVENT and triggers the action() method, while single-clicking causes a LIST_SELECT or LIST_DESELECT event. Once the List has the input focus, it is possible to change the selection by using the arrow or keyboard keys. The arrow keys scroll through the list of choices, triggering the KEY_ACTION, LIST_SELECT, LIST_DESELECT, and KEY_ACTION_RELEASE events, and thus the keyDown(), handleEvent(), and keyUp() methods (no specific method gets called for LIST_SELECT and LIST_DESELECT). action() is called only when the user double-clicks on an item with the mouse. If the mouse is used to scroll through the list, no mouse events are triggered; ACTION_EVENT is generated only when the user double-clicks on an item.

With the 1.1 event model, you register an `ItemListener` with `addItemListener()` or an `ActionListener` with the `addActionListener()` method. When the user selects the `List`, either the `ItemListener.itemStateChanged()` method or the `ActionListener.actionPerformed()` method is called through the protected `List.processItemEvent()` method or `List.processActionEvent()` method. Key, mouse, and focus listeners are registered through the three `Component` methods of `addKeyListener()`, `addMouseListener()`, and `addFocusListener()`, respectively.

Action

public boolean action (Event e, Object o)

The `action()` method for a `List` is called when the user double-clicks on any item in the `List`. e is the `Event` instance for the specific event, while o is the label for the item selected, from the `add()` or `addItem()` call. If `List` is in multiple-selection mode, you might not wish to catch this event because it's not clear whether the user wanted to choose the item just selected or all of the items selected. You can solve this problem by putting a multi-selecting list next to a `Button` that the user presses when the selection process is finished. Capture the event generated by the `Button`. The following example shows how to set up and handle a list in this manner, with the display shown in Figure 9-3. In this example, I just print out the selections to prove that I captured them.

```
import java.awt.*;
import java.applet.*;
public class list3 extends Applet {
    List l;
    public void init () {
        String fonts[];
        fonts = Toolkit.getDefaultToolkit().getFontList();
        l = new List(4, true);
        for (int i = 0; i < fonts.length; i++) {
            l.addItem (fonts[i]);
        }
        setLayout (new BorderLayout (10, 10));
        add ("North", new Label ("Pick Font Set"));
        add ("Center", l);
        add ("South", new Button ("Submit"));
        resize (preferredSize());
        validate();
    }
    public boolean action (Event e, Object o) {
        if (e.target instanceof Button) {
            String chosen[] = l.getSelectedItems();
            for (int i=0;i<chosen.length;i++)
                System.out.println (chosen[i]);
        }
        return false;
    }
}
```

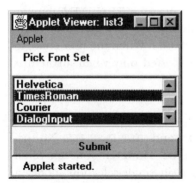

Figure 9–3: Multiselect List

Keyboard

Ordinarily, List generates all the KEY events once it has the input focus. But the way it handles keyboard input differs slightly depending upon the selection mode of the list. Furthermore, each platform offers slightly different behavior, so code that depends on keyboard events in List is not portable. One strategy is to take advantage of the keyboard events when they are available but allow for another way of managing the list in case they are not.

public boolean keyDown (Event e, int key)

The keyDown() method is called whenever the user presses a key while the List has the input focus. e is the Event instance for the specific event, while key is the integer representation of the character pressed. The identifier for the event (e.id) for keyDown() could be either KEY_PRESS for a regular key or KEY_ACTION for an action-oriented key (i.e., arrow or function key). If you check the current selection in this method through getSelectedItem() or getSelectedIndex(), you will actually be told the previously selected item because the List's selection has not changed yet. keyDown() is not called when the user selects items with the mouse.

public boolean keyUp (Event e, int key)

The keyUp() method is called whenever the user releases a key while the List has the input focus. e is the Event instance for the specific event, while key is the integer representation of the character pressed. The identifier for the event (e.id) for keyUp() could be either KEY_RELEASE for a regular key or KEY_ACTION_RELEASE for an action-oriented key (i.e., arrow or function key).

Mouse

Ordinarily, the List component does not trigger any mouse events. Double-clicking the mouse over any element in the list generates an ACTION_EVENT. Single-clicking could result in either a LIST_SELECT or LIST_DESELECT, depending on the mode of the List and the current state of the item chosen. When the user changes the selection with the mouse, the ACTION_EVENT is posted only when an item is double-clicked.

List

There is a special pair of events for lists: LIST_SELECT and LIST_DESELECT. No special method is called when these events are triggered. However, you can catch them in the handleEvent() method. If the List is in single-selection mode, a LIST_SELECT event is generated whenever the user selects one of the items in the List. In multiple-selection mode, you will get a LIST_SELECT event when an element gets selected and a LIST_DESELECT event when it is deselected. The following code shows how to use this event type.

```
public boolean handleEvent (Event e) {
    if (e.id == Event.LIST_SELECT) {
        System.out.println ("Selected item: " + e.arg);
        return true;
    } else {
        return super.handleEvent (e);
    }
}
```

Focus

Normally, the List component does not reliably trigger any focus events.

Listeners and 1.1 event handling

With the 1.1 event model, you register listeners, and they are told when the event happens.

public void addItemListener(ItemListener listener) ★

The addItemListener() method registers listener as an object interested in being notified when an ItemEvent passes through the EventQueue with this List as its target. The listener.itemStateChanged() method is called when these events occur. Multiple listeners can be registered.

public void removeItemListener(ItemListener listener) ★

The removeItemListener() method removes listener as an interested listener. If listener is not registered, nothing happens.

public void addActionListener(ActionListener listener) ★

The addActionListener() method registers listener as an object interested in being notified when an ActionEvent passes through the EventQueue with this List as its target. The listener.actionPerformed() method is called when these events occur. Multiple listeners can be registered.

public void removeActionListener(ActionListener listener) ★

The removeActionListener() method removes listener as a interested listener. If listener is not registered, nothing happens.

protected void processEvent(AWTEvent e) ★

The processEvent() method receives all AWTEvents with this List as its target. processEvent() then passes them along to any listeners for processing. When you subclass List, overriding processEvent() allows you to process all events yourself, before sending them to any listeners. In a way, overriding the method processEvent() is like overriding handleEvent() using the 1.0 event model.

If you override processEvent(), remember to call super.processEvent(e) last to ensure that regular event processing can occur. If you want to process your own events, it's a good idea to call enableEvents() (inherited from Component) to ensure that events are delivered even in the absence of registered listeners.

protected void processItemEvent(ItemEvent e) ★

The processItemEvent() method receives all ItemEvents with this List as its target. processItemEvent() then passes them along to any listeners for processing. When you subclass List, overriding processItemEvent() allows you to process all events yourself, before sending them to any listeners. In a way, overriding processItemEvent() is like overriding handleEvent() to deal with LIST_SELECT and LIST_DESELECT using the 1.0 event model.

If you override processItemEvent(), remember to call the method super.processItemEvent(e) last to ensure that regular event processing can occur. If you want to process your own events, it's a good idea to call enableEvents() (inherited from Component) to ensure that events are delivered even in the absence of registered listeners.

protected void processActionEvent(ActionEvent e) ★

The processActionEvent() method receives all ActionEvents with this List as its target. processActionEvent() then passes them along to any listeners for processing. When you subclass List, overriding processActionEvent() allows you to process all action events yourself, before sending them to any listeners. In a way, overriding processActionEvent() is like overriding action() using the 1.0 event model.

If you override `processActionEvent()`, remember to call the method `super.processActionEvent(e)` last to ensure that regular event processing can occur. If you want to process your own events, it's a good idea to call `enableEvents()` (inherited from `Component`) to ensure that events are delivered even in the absence of registered listeners.

9.3 Checkbox

The `Checkbox` is a general purpose way to record a `true` or `false` state. When several checkboxes are associated in a `CheckboxGroup` (Section 9.4), only one can be selected at a time; selecting each `Checkbox` causes the previous selection to become deselected. The `CheckboxGroup` is Java's way of offering the interface element known as radio buttons or a radio box. When you create a `Checkbox`, you decide whether to place it into a `CheckboxGroup` by setting the proper argument in its constructor.

Every `Checkbox` has both a label and a state, although the label could be empty. You can change the label based on the state of the `Checkbox`. Figure 9-4 shows what several `Checkbox` components might look like. The two on the left are independent, while the five on the right are in a `CheckboxGroup`. Note that the appearance of a `Checkbox` varies quite a bit from platform to platform. However, the appearance of a `CheckboxGroup` is always different from the appearance of an ungrouped `Checkbox`, and the appearance of a checked `Checkbox` is different from an unchecked `Checkbox`.

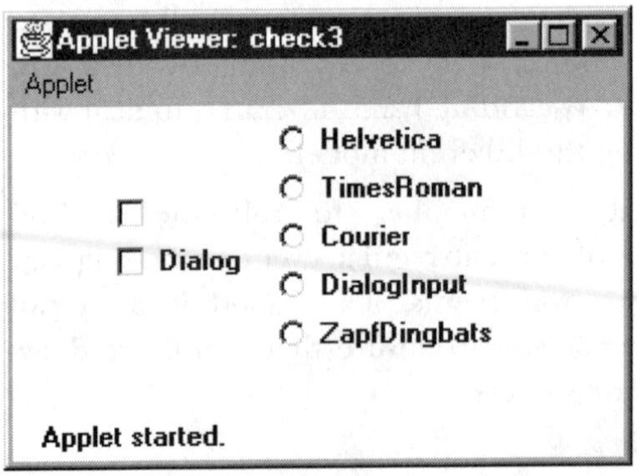

Figure 9–4: Two separate checkboxes and a CheckboxGroup

9.3.1 Checkbox Methods

Constructors

public Checkbox ()

This constructor for Checkbox creates a new instance with no label or grouping. The initial state of the item is false. A checkbox doesn't necessarily need a label; however, a checkbox without a label might be confusing, unless it is being used as a column in a table or a spreadsheet.

public Checkbox (String label)

The second constructor creates a new Checkbox with a label of label and no grouping. The initial state of the item is false. If you want a simple yes/no choice and plan to make no the default, use this constructor. If the Checkbox will be in a group or you want its initial value to be true, use the next constructor.

public Checkbox (String label, boolean state) ★

This constructor allows you to specify the Checkbox's initial state. With it you create a Checkbox with a label of label and an initial state of state.

public Checkbox (String label, boolean state, CheckboxGroup group) ★
public Checkbox (String label, CheckboxGroup group, boolean state)

The final constructor for Checkbox is the most flexible. With this constructor you create a Checkbox with a label of label, a CheckboxGroup of group, and an initial state of state. If group is null, the Checkbox is independent.

In Java 1.0, you created an independent Checkbox with an initial value of true by using null as the group:

```
Checkbox cb = new Checkbox ("Help", null, true)
```

The shape of the Checkbox reflects whether it's in a CheckboxGroup or independent. On Microsoft Windows, grouped checkboxes are represented as circles. On a UNIX system, they are diamonds. On both systems, independent checkboxes are squares.

Label

public String getLabel ()

The getLabel() method retrieves the current label on the Checkbox and returns it as a String object.

public synchronized void setLabel (String label)

> The setLabel() method changes the label of the Checkbox to label. If the new label is a different size than the old one, you have to validate() the container after the change to ensure the entire label will be seen.

State

A state of true means the Checkbox is selected. A state of false means that the Checkbox is not selected.

public boolean getState ()

> The getState() method retrieves the current state of the Checkbox and returns it as a boolean.

public void setState (boolean state)

> The setState() method changes the state of the Checkbox to state. If the Checkbox is in a CheckboxGroup and state is true, the other items in the group become false.

ItemSelectable method

public Objects[] getSelectedObjects () ★

> The getSelectedObjects() method returns the Checkbox label as a one-element Object array if it is currently selected, or null if the Checkbox is not selected. Because this method is part of the ItemSelectable interface, you can use it to look at the selected items in a Choice, List, or Checkbox.

CheckboxGroup

This section lists methods that you issue to Checkbox to affect its relationship to a CheckboxGroup. Methods provided by the CheckboxGroup itself can be found later in this chapter.

public CheckboxGroup getCheckboxGroup ()

> The getCheckboxGroup() method returns the current CheckboxGroup for the Checkbox. If the Checkbox is not in a group, this method returns null.

public void setCheckboxGroup (CheckboxGroup group)

> The setCheckboxGroup() method allows you to insert a Checkbox into a different CheckboxGroup. To make the Checkbox independent, pass a group argument of null. The method sets every Checkbox in the original CheckboxGroup to false (cb.getCheckboxGroup().setCurrent(null)), then the Checkbox is added to the new group without changing any values in the new group.

Checkbox components take on a different shape when they are in a Checkbox-Group. If the checkbox was originally not in a CheckboxGroup, the shape of the checkbox does not change automatically when you put it in one with setCheckboxGroup(). (This also holds when you remove a Checkbox from a CheckboxGroup and make it independent or vice versa.) In order for the Checkbox to look right once added to group, you need to destroy and create (removeNotify() and addNotify(), respectively) the Checkbox peer to correct the shape. Also, it is possible to get multiple true Checkbox components in group this way, since the new CheckboxGroup's current selection does not get adjusted. To avoid this problem, make sure it is grouped properly the first time, or be sure to clear the selections with a call to getCheckbox-Group().setCurrent(null).

Miscellaneous methods

public synchronized void addNotify ()

The addNotify() method will create the Checkbox peer in the appropriate shape. If you override this method, call super.addNotify() first, then add your customizations for the new class. You will then be able to do everything you need with the information about the newly created peer.

protected String paramString ()

When you call the toString() method of Checkbox, the default toString() method of Component is called. This in turn calls paramString() which builds up the string to display. At the Checkbox level, the label (if non-null) and the state of the item are appended. Assuming the Dialog Checkbox in Figure 9-4 was selected, the results would be:

```
java.awt.Checkbox[85,34,344x32,label=Dialog,state=true]
```

9.3.2 Checkbox Events

The primary event for a Checkbox occurs when the user selects it. With the 1.0 event model, this generates an ACTION_EVENT and triggers the action() method. Once the Checkbox has the input focus, the various keyboard events can be generated, but they do not serve any useful purpose because the Checkbox doesn't change. The sole key of value for a Checkbox is the spacebar. This may generate the ACTION_EVENT after KEY_PRESS and KEY_RELEASE; thus the sequence of method calls would be keyDown(), keyUp(), and then action().

With the version 1.1 event model, you register an ItemListener with the method addItemListener(). Then when the user selects the Checkbox, the method Item-Listener.itemStateChanged() is called through the protected

Checkbox.processItemEvent() method. Key, mouse, and focus listeners are registered through the Component methods of addKeyListener(), addMouseListener(), and addFocusListener(), respectively.

Action

public boolean action (Event e, Object o)

The action() method for a Checkbox is called when the user selects it. e is the Event instance for the specific event, while o is the opposite of the old state of the toggle. If the Checkbox was true when it was selected, o will be false. Likewise, if it was false, o will be true. This incantation sounds unnecessarily complex, and for a single Checkbox, it is: o is just the new state of the Checkbox. The following code uses action() with a single Checkbox.

```
public boolean action (Event e, Object o) {
    if (e.target instanceof Checkbox) {
        System.out.println ("Checkbox is now " + o);
    }
    return false;
}
```

On the other hand, if the Checkbox is in a CheckboxGroup, o is still the opposite of the old state of the toggle, which may or may not be the new state of the Checkbox. If the Checkbox is initially false, o will be true, and the Checkbox's new state will be true. However, if the Checkbox is initially true, selecting the Checkbox doesn't change anything because one Checkbox in the group must always be true. In this case, o is false (the opposite of the old state), though the Checkbox's state remains true.

Therefore, if you're working with a CheckboxGroup and need to do something once when the selection changes, perform your action only when o is true. To find out which Checkbox was actually chosen, you need to call the getLabel() method for the target of event e. (It would be nice if o gave us the label of the Checkbox that was selected, but it doesn't.) An example of this follows:

```
public boolean action (Event e, Object o) {
    if (e.target instanceof Checkbox) {
        System.out.println ((((Checkbox)(e.target)).getLabel() +
            " was selected.");
        if (new Boolean (o.toString()).booleanValue()) {
            System.out.println ("New option chosen");
        } else {
            System.out.println ("Use re-selected option");
        }
    }
    return false;
}
```

One other unfortunate twist of CheckboxGroup: it would be nice if there was some easy way to find out about checkboxes that change state without selection—for example, if you could find out which Checkbox was deselected when a new Checkbox was selected. Unfortunately, you can't, except by keeping track of the state of all your checkboxes at all times. When a Checkbox state becomes false because another Checkbox was selected, no additional event is generated, in either Java 1.0 or 1.1.

Keyboard

Checkboxes are able to capture keyboard-related events once the Checkbox has the input focus, which happens when it is selected. If you can find a use for this, you can use keyDown() and keyUp(). For most interface designs I can think of, action() is sufficient. A possible use for keyboard events is to jump to other Checkbox options in a CheckboxGroup, but I think that is more apt to confuse users than help.

public boolean keyDown (Event e, int key)

> The keyDown() method is called whenever the user presses a key while the Checkbox has the input focus. e is the Event instance for the specific event, while key is the integer representation of the character pressed. The identifier for the event (e.id) for keyDown() could be either KEY_PRESS for a regular key or KEY_ACTION for an action-oriented key (i.e., arrow or function key). There is no visible indication that the user has pressed a key over the checkbox.

public boolean keyUp (Event e, int key)

> The keyUp() method is called whenever the user releases a key while the Checkbox has the input focus. e is the Event instance for the specific event, while key is the integer representation of the character pressed. The identifier for the event (e.id) for keyUp() could be either KEY_RELEASE for a regular key or KEY_ACTION_RELEASE for an action-oriented key (i.e., arrow or function key). keyUp() may be used to determine how long key has been pressed.

Mouse

Ordinarily, the Checkbox component does not reliably trigger any mouse events.

Focus

Ordinarily, the Checkbox component does not reliably trigger any focus events.

Listeners and 1.1 event handling

With the 1.1 event model, you register listeners, and they are told when the event happens.

public void addItemListener(ItemListener listener) ★

The addItemListener() method registers listener as an object interested in being notified when an ItemEvent passes through the EventQueue with this Checkbox as its target. Then, the listener.itemStateChanged() method will be called. Multiple listeners can be registered.

public void removeItemListener(ItemListener listener) ★

The removeItemListener() method removes listener as a interested listener. If listener is not registered, nothing happens.

protected void processEvent(AWTEvent e) ★

The processEvent() method receives every AWTEvent with this Checkbox as its target. processEvent() then passes it along to any listeners for processing. When you subclass Checkbox, overriding processEvent() allows you to process all events yourself, before sending them to any listeners. In a way, overriding processEvent() is like overriding handleEvent() using the 1.0 event model.

If you override processEvent(), remember to call super.processEvent(e) last to ensure that regular event processing can occur. If you want to process your own events, it's a good idea to call enableEvents() (inherited from Component) to ensure that events are delivered even in the absence of registered listeners.

protected void processItemEvent(ItemEvent e) ★

The processItemEvent() method receives every ItemEvent with this Checkbox as its target. processItemEvent() then passes it along to any listeners for processing. When you subclass Checkbox, overriding processItemEvent() allows you to process all events yourself, before sending them to any listeners. In a way, overriding processItemEvent() is like overriding action() using the 1.0 event model.

If you override processItemEvent(), remember to call the method super.processItemEvent(e) last to ensure that regular event processing can occur. If you want to process your own events, it's a good idea to call enableEvents() (inherited from Component) to ensure that events are delivered even in the absence of registered listeners.

9.4 CheckboxGroup

The CheckboxGroup lets multiple checkboxes work together to provide a mutually exclusion choice (at most one Checkbox can be selected at a time). Because the CheckboxGroup is neither a Component nor a Container, you should normally put all the Checkbox components associated with a CheckboxGroup in their own Panel (or other Container). The LayoutManager of the Panel should be GridLayout (0, 1) if you want them in one column. Figure 9-5 shows both a good way and bad way of positioning a set of Checkbox items in a CheckboxGroup. The image on the left is preferred because the user can sense that the items are grouped; the image on the right suggests three levels of different checkboxes and can therefore surprise the user when checkboxes are deselected.

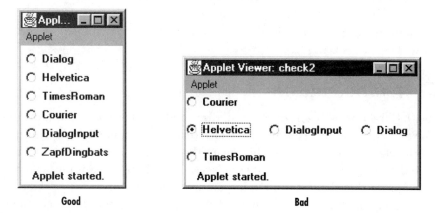

Figure 9–5: Straightforward and confusing layouts of Checkbox components

9.4.1 CheckboxGroup Methods

Constructors

public CheckboxGroup ()

This constructor creates an instance of CheckboxGroup.

Miscellaneous methods

public int getSelectedCheckbox () ★
public Checkbox getCurrent () ☆

The getSelectedCheckbox() method returns the Checkbox within the CheckboxGroup whose value is true. If no item is selected, null is returned.

getCurrent() is the Java 1.0 name for this method.

public synchronized void setSelectedCheckbox (Checkbox checkbox) ★
public synchronized void setCurrent (Checkbox checkbox) ☆

> The `setSelectedCheckbox()` method makes `checkbox` the currently selected `Checkbox` within the `CheckboxGroup`. If `checkbox`is `null`, the method deselects all the items in the `CheckboxGroup`. If `checkbox` is not within the `Checkbox-Group`, nothing happens.
>
> `setCurrent()` is the Java 1.0 name for this method.

public String toString ()

> The `toString()` method of `CheckboxGroup` creates a `String` representation of the current choice (as returned by `getSelectedCheckbox()`). Using the "straightforward" layout in Figure 9-5 as an example, the results would be:

```
java.awt.CheckboxGroup[current=java.awt.Checkbox[0,31,85x21,
    label=Helvetica,state=true]]
```

> If there is no currently selected item, the results within the square brackets would be `current=null`.

9.5 *ItemSelectable*

In Java 1.1, the classes `Checkbox`, `Choice`, `List`, and `CheckboxMenuItem` (covered in the next chapter) share a common interface that defines a method for getting the currently selected item or items. This means that you can use the same methods to retrieve the selection from any of these classes. More important, it means that you can write code that doesn't know what kind of selectable item it's working with. For example, you could write a method that returns the selectable component from some user interface. This method might have the signature:

```
public ItemSelectable getChooser();
```

After you call this method, you can read selections from the user interface without knowing exactly what you're dealing with.

9.5.1 *Methods*

public Object[] getSelectedObjects () ★

> The `getSelectedObjects()` method returns the currently selected item or items as an `Object` array. The return value is `null` if there is nothing selected.

10

Would You Like to Choose from the Menu?

In Chapter 6, *Containers,* I mentioned that a Frame can have a menu. Indeed, to offer a menu in the AWT, you have to attach it to a Frame. With versions 1.0.2 and 1.1, Java does not support menu bars within an applet or any other container. We hope that future versions of Java will allow menus to be used with other containers. Java 1.1 goes partway toward solving this problem by introducing a PopupMenu that lets you attach context menus to any Component. Java 1.1 also adds MenuShortcut events, which represent keyboard accelerator events for menus.

Implementing a menu in a Frame involves connections among a number of different objects: MenuBar, Menu, MenuItem, and the optional CheckboxMenuItem. Several of these classes implement the MenuContainer interface. Once you've created a few menus, you'll probably find the process quite natural, but it's hard to describe until you see what all the objects are. So this chapter describes most of the menu classes first and then shows an example demonstrating their use.

All the components covered in previous chapters were subclasses of Component. Most of the objects in this chapter subclass MenuComponent, which encapsulates the common functionality of menu objects. The MenuComponent class hierarchy is shown in Figure 10-1.

To display a Menu, you must first put it in a MenuBar, which you add to a Frame. (Pop-up menus are different in that they don't need a Frame.) A Menu can contain MenuItem as well as other menus that form submenus. CheckboxMenuItem is a specialized MenuItem that (as you might guess) the user can toggle like a Checkbox. One way to visualize how all these things work together is to imagine a set of curtains. The different MenuItem components are the fabrics and panels that make up the curtains. The Menus are the curtains. They get hung from the MenuBar, which is

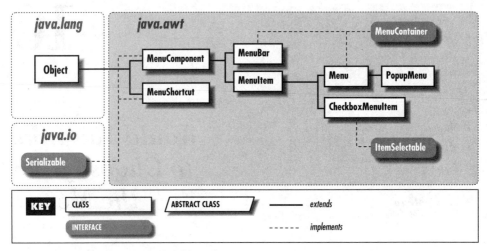

Figure 10–1: MenuComponent class hierarchy

like a curtain rod. Then you place the `MenuBar` curtain rod into the `Frame` (the window, in our metaphor), curtains and all.

It might puzzle you that a `Menu` is a subclass of `MenuItem`, not the other way around. This is because a `Menu` can appear on a `Menu` just like another `MenuItem`, which would not be possible if the hierarchy was the other way around. Figure 10-2 points out the different pieces involved in the creation of a menu: the `MenuBar` and various kinds of menu items, including a submenu.

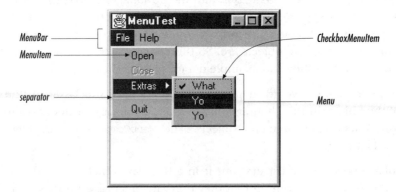

Figure 10–2: The pieces that make up a Menu

10.1 MenuComponent

MenuComponent is an abstract class that is the parent of all menu-related objects. You will never create an instance of the object. Nor are you likely to subclass it yourself—to make the subclass work, you'd have to provide your own peer on every platform where you want the application to run.

10.1.1 MenuComponent Methods

Constructor

public MenuComponent ()—cannot be called directly

Since MenuComponent is an abstract class, you cannot create an instance of the object. This method is called when you create an instance of one of its children.

Fonts

public Font getFont ()

The getFont() method retrieves the font associated with the MenuComponent from setFont(). If the current object's font has not been set, the parent menu's font is retrieved. If there is no parent and the current object's font has not been set, getFont() returns null.

public void setFont (Font f)

The setFont() method allows you to change the font of the particular menu-related component to f. When a MenuComponent is first created, the initial font is null, so the parent menu's font is used.

NOTE   Some platforms do not support changing the fonts of menu items.
          Where supported, it can make some pretty ugly menus.

Names

The name serves as an alternative, nonlocalized reference identifier for menu components. If your event handlers compare menu label strings to an expected value and labels are localized for a new environment, the approach fails.

public String getName ()

The getName() method retrieves the name of the menu component. Every instance of a subclass of MenuComponent is named when it is created.

public void setName (String name)

The setName() method changes the current name of the component to name.

Peers

public MenuComponentPeer getPeer () ☆

The getPeer() method returns a reference to the MenuComponent peer as a MenuComponentPeer.

public synchronized void removeNotify ()

The removeNotify() method destroys the peer of the MenuComponent and removes it from the screen. addNotify() will be specific to the subclass.

Events

Event handling is slightly different between versions. If using the 1.0 event model, use postEvent(). Otherwise, use dispatchEvent() to post an event to this Menu-Component or processEvent() to receive and handle an event. Remember not to mix versions within your programs.

public boolean postEvent (Event e) ☆

The postEvent() method posts Event e to the MenuComponent. The event is delivered to the Frame at the top of the object hierarchy that contains the selected MenuComponent. The only way to capture this event before it gets handed to the Frame is to override this method. There are no helper functions as there are for Components. Find out which MenuComponent triggered the event by checking e.arg, which contains its label, or ((Menu-Item)e.target).getName() for the nonlocalized name of the target.

```
public boolean postEvent (Event e) {
    // Use getName() vs. e.arg for localization possibility
    if ("About".equals (((MenuItem)e.target).getName()))
        playLaughingSound(); // Help request
    return super.postEvent (e);
}
```

If you override this method, in order for this Event to propagate to the Frame that contains the MenuComponent, you must call the original postEvent() method (super.postEvent(e)).

The actual value returned by postEvent() is irrelevant.

public final void dispatchEvent(AWTEvent e) ★

The dispatchEvent() method allows you to post new AWT events to this menu component's listeners. dispatchEvent() tells the MenuComponent to deal with the AWTEvent e by calling its processEvent() method. This method is similar to Java 1.0's postEvent() method. Events delivered in this way bypass the system's event queue. It's not clear why you would want to bypass the event queue, except possibly to deliver some kind of high priority event.

protected void processEvent(AWTEvent e) ★

The processEvent() method receives all AWTEvents with a subclass of Menu-Component as its target. processEvent() then passes them along for processing. When you subclass a child class, overriding processEvent() allows you to process all events without having to provide listeners. However, remember to call super.processEvent(e) last to ensure regular functionality is still executed. This is like overriding postEvent() using the 1.0 event model.

Miscellaneous methods

public MenuContainer getParent ()

The getParent() method returns the parent MenuContainer for the MenuComponent. MenuContainer is an interface that is implemented by Component (in 1.1 only), Frame, Menu, and MenuBar. This means that getParent() could return any one of the four.

protected String paramString ()

The paramString() method of MenuComponent helps build up the string to display when toString() is called for a subclass. At the MenuComponent level, the current name of the object is appended to the output.

public String toString ()—can be called by user for subclass

The toString() method at the MenuComponent level cannot be called directly. This toString() method is called when you call a subclass's toString() and the specifics of the subclass is added between the brackets ([and]). At this level, the results would be:

```
java.awt.MenuComponent[aname1]
```

10.2 *MenuContainer*

MenuContainer is an interface implemented by the three menu containers: Frame, Menu, and MenuBar; Java 1.1 adds a fourth, Component. You should never need to worry about the interface since it does all its work behind the scenes for you. You will notice that the interface does not define an add() method. Each type of Menu-Container defines its own add() method to add menus to itself.

10.2.1 MenuContainer Methods

public abstract Font getFont ()

> The getFont() method should provide an object's font. MenuItem implements this method, so all of its subclasses inherit it. MenuBar implements it, too, while Frame gets the method from Component.

public abstract boolean postEvent (Event e) ☆

> The postEvent() method should post Event e to the object. MenuComponent implements this method, so all of its subclasses inherit it. (Frame gets the method from Component.)

public abstract void remove (MenuComponent component)

> The remove() method should remove the MenuComponent component from the object. If component was not contained within the object, nothing should happen.

10.3 MenuShortcut

MenuShortcut is a class used to represent a keyboard shortcut for a MenuItem. When these events occur, an action event is generated that triggers the menu component. When a shortcut is associated with a MenuItem, the MenuItem automatically displays a visual clue, which indicates that a keyboard accelerator is available.

10.3.1 MenuShortcut Methods

Constructors

public MenuShortcut (int key) ★

> The first MenuShortcut constructor creates a MenuShortcut with key as its designated hot key. The key parameter can be any of the virtual key codes from the KeyEvent class (e.g., VK_A, VK_B, etc.). These constants are listed in Table 4-4. To use the shortcut, the user must combine the given key with a platform-specific modifier key. On Windows and Motif platforms, the modifier is the Control key; on the Macintosh, it is the Command key. For example, if the shortcut key is F1 (VK_F1) and you're using Windows, you would press Ctrl+F1 to execute the shortcut. To find out the platform's modifier key, call the Toolkit.getMenuShortcutKeyMask() method.

public MenuShortcut(int key, boolean useShiftModifier) ★

> This MenuShortcut constructor creates a MenuShortcut with key as its designated hot key. If useShiftModifier is true, the Shift key must be depressed for this shortcut to trigger the action event (in addition to the shortcut key).

The key parameter represents the integer value of a KEY_PRESS event, so in addition to ASCII values, possible values include the various Event keyboard constants (listed in Table 4-2) like Event.F1, Event.HOME, and Event.PAUSE. For example, if key is the ASCII value for A and useShiftModifier is true, the shortcut key is Shift+Ctrl+A on a Windows/Motif platform.

Miscellaneous methods

public int getKey () ★

The getKey() method retrieves the virtual key code for the key that triggered this MenuShortcut. The virtual key codes are the VK constants defined by the KeyEvent class (see Table 4-4).

public boolean usesShiftModifier() ★

The usesShiftModifier() method returns true if this MenuShortcut requires the Shift key be pressed, false otherwise.

public boolean equals(MenuShortcut s) ★

The equals() method overrides Object's equals() method to define equality for menu shortcuts. Two MenuShortcut objects are equal if their key and useShiftModifier values are equal.

protected String paramString () ★

The paramString() method of MenuShortcut helps build up a string describing the shortcut; it appends the shortcut key and a shift modifier indicator to the string under construction. Oddly, this method is not currently used, nor can you call it; MenuShortcut has its own toString() method that does the job itself.

public String toString() ★

The toString() method of MenuShortcut builds a String to display the contents of the MenuShortcut.

10.4 MenuItem

A MenuItem is the basic item that goes on a Menu. Menus themselves are menu items, allowing submenus to be nested inside of menus. MenuItem is a subclass of MenuComponent.

10.4.1 MenuItem Methods

Constructors

public MenuItem () ★

> The first MenuItem constructor creates a MenuItem with an empty label and no keyboard shortcut. To set the label at later time, use setLabel().

public MenuItem (String label)

> This MenuItem constructor creates a MenuItem with a label of label and no keyboard shortcut. A label of "–" represents a separator.

public MenuItem (String label, MenuShortcut shortcut) ★

> The final MenuItem constructor creates a MenuItem with a label of label and a MenuShortcut of shortcut. Pressing the shortcut key is the same as selecting the menu item.

Menu labels

Each MenuItem has a label. This is the text that is displayed on the menu.

NOTE   Prior to Java 1.1, there was no portable way to associate a hot key with a MenuItem. However, in Java 1.0, if you precede a character with an & on a Windows platform, it will appear underlined, and that key will act as the menu's mnemonic key (a different type of shortcut from MenuShortcut). Unfortunately, on a Motif platform, the user will see the &. Because the & is part of the label, even if it is not displayed, you must include it explicitly whenever you compare the label to a string.

---

public String getLabel ()

> The getLabel() method retrieves the label associated with the MenuItem.

public void setLabel (String label)

> The setLabel() method changes the label of the MenuItem to label.

Shortcuts

public MenuShortcut getMenuShortcut () ★

> The getMenuShortcut() method retrieves the shortcut associated with this MenuItem.

public void setShortcut (MenuShortcut shortcut) ★

> The setShortcut() method allows you to change the shortcut associated with a MenuItem to shortcut after the MenuItem has been created.

public void deleteMenuShortcut () ★

The deleteMenuShortcut() method removes any associated MenuShortcut from the MenuItem. If there was no shortcut, nothing happens.

Enabling

public boolean isEnabled ()

The isEnabled() method checks to see if the MenuItem is currently enabled. An enabled MenuItem can be selected by the user. A disabled MenuItem, by convention, appears grayed out on the Menu. Initially, each MenuItem is enabled.

public synchronized void setEnabled(boolean b) ★
public void enable (boolean condition) ☆

The setEnabled() method either enables or disables the MenuItem based on the value of condition. If condition is true, the MenuItem is enabled. If condition is false, it is disabled. When enabled, the user can select it, generating ACTION_EVENT or notifying the ActionListener. When disabled, the peer does not generate an ACTION_EVENT if the user tries to select the MenuItem. A disabled MenuItem is usually grayed out to signify its state. The way that disabling is signified is platform specific.

enable() is the Java 1.0 name for this method.

public synchronized void enable () ☆

The enable() method enables the MenuItem. In Java 1.1, it is better to use setEnabled().

public synchronized void disable () ☆

The disable() method disables the component so that the user cannot select it. In Java 1.1, it is better to use setEnabled().

Miscellaneous methods

public synchronized void addNotify ()

The addNotify() method creates the MenuItem peer.

public String paramString ()

The paramString() method of MenuItem should be protected like other paramString() methods. However, it is public so you have access to it. When you call the toString() method of a MenuItem, the default toString() method of MenuComponent is called. This in turn calls paramString() which builds up the string to display. At the MenuItem level, the current label of the object and the shortcut (if present) is appended to the output. If the constructor for the MenuItem was new MenuItem("File"), the results of toString() would be:

```
java.awt.MenuItem[label=File]
```

10.4.2 MenuItem Events

Event handling

With 1.0 event handing, a `MenuItem` generates an `ACTION_EVENT` when it is selected. The argument to `action()` will be the label of the `MenuItem`. But the target of the `ACTION_EVENT` is the `Frame` containing the menu. You cannot subclass `MenuItem` and catch the `Event` within it with `action()`, but you can with `postEvent()`. No other events are generated for `MenuItem` instances.

public boolean action (Event e, Object o)—overridden by user, called by system

The `action()` method for a `MenuItem` signifies that the user selected it. e is the `Event` instance for the specific event, while o is the label of the `MenuItem`.

Listeners and 1.1 event handling

With the 1.1 event model, you register listeners, and they are told when the event happens.

public String getActionCommand() ★

The `getActionCommand()` method retrieves the command associated with this `MenuItem`. By default, it is the label. However, the default can be changed by using the `setActionCommand()` method (described next). The command acts like the second parameter to the `action()` method in the 1.0 event model.

public void setActionCommand(String command) ★

The `setActionCommand()` method changes the command associated with a `MenuItem`. When an `ActionEvent` happens, the command is part of the event. By default, this would be the label of the `MenuItem`. However, you can change the action command by calling this method. Using action commands is a good idea, particularly if you expect your code to run in a multilingual environment.

public void addActionListener(ItemListener listener) ★

The `addActionListener()` method registers `listener` as an object interested in being notified when an `ActionEvent` passes through the `EventQueue` with this `MenuItem` as its target. The `listener.actionPerformed()` method is called whenever these events occur. Multiple listeners can be registered.

public void removeActionListener(ItemListener listener) ★

The `removeActionListener()` method removes `listener` as an interested listener. If `listener` is not registered, nothing happens.

protected final void enableEvents(long eventsToEnable) ★

Using the `enableEvents()` method is usually not necessary. When you register an action listener, the `MenuItem` listens for action events. However, if you wish to listen for events when listeners are not registered, you must enable the events explicitly by calling this method. The settings for the `eventsToEnable` parameter are found in the `AWTEvent` class; you can use any of the `EVENT_MASK` constants like `COMPONENT_EVENT_MASK`, `MOUSE_EVENT_MASK`, and `WIN-DOW_EVENT_MASK` ORed together for the events you care about. For instance, to listen for action events, call:

```
enableEvents (AWTEvent.ACTION_EVENT_MASK);
```

protected final void disableEvents(long eventsToDisable) ★

Using the `disableEvents()` method is usually not necessary. When you remove an action listener, the `MenuItem` stops listening for action events if there are no more listeners. However, if you need to, you can disable events explicitly by calling `disableEvents()`. The settings for the `eventsToDisable` parameter are found in the `AWTEvent` class; you can use any of the `EVENT_MASK` constants such as `FOCUS_EVENT_MASK`, `MOUSE_MOTION_EVENT_MASK`, and `ACTION_EVENT_MASK` ORed together for the events you no longer care about.

protected void processEvent(AWTEvent e) ★

The `processEvent()` method receives all `AWTEvents` with this `MenuItem` as its target. `processEvent()` then passes them along to any listeners for processing. When you subclass `MenuItem`, overriding `processEvent()` allows you to process all events yourself, before sending them to any listeners. In a way, overriding `processEvent()` is like overriding `postEvent()` using the 1.0 event model.

If you override `processEvent()`, remember to call `super.processEvent(e)` last to ensure that regular event processing can occur. If you want to process your own events, it's a good idea to call `enableEvents()` to ensure that events are delivered even in the absence of registered listeners.

protected void processActionEvent(ItemEvent e) ★

The `processActionEvent()` method receives all `ActionEvents` with this `MenuItem` as its target. `processActionEvent()` then passes them along to any listeners for processing. When you subclass `MenuItem`, overriding `processAction-Event()` allows you to process all action events yourself, before sending them to any listeners. In a way, overriding `processActionEvent()` is like overriding `action()` using the 1.0 event model.

If you override `processActionEvent()`, remember to call the method `super.processActionEvent(e)` last to ensure that regular event processing can occur. If you want to process your own events, it's a good idea to call `enableEvents()` to ensure that events are delivered even in the absence of registered listeners.

10.5 Menu

Menus are the pull-down objects that appear on the MenuBar of a Frame or within other menus. They contain MenuItems or CheckboxMenuItems for the user to select. The Menu class subclasses MenuItem (so it can appear on a Menu, too) and implements MenuContainer. Tear-off menus are menus that can be dragged, placed elsewhere on the screen, and remain on the screen when the input focus moves to something else. Java supports tear-off menus if the underlying platform does. Motif (UNIX) supports tear-off menus; Microsoft Windows platforms do not.

10.5.1 Menu Methods

Constructors

public Menu () ★

The first constructor for Menu creates a menu that has no label and cannot be torn off. To set the label at a later time, use setLabel().

public Menu (String label)

This constructor for Menu creates a Menu with label displayed on it. The Menu cannot be torn off.

public Menu (String label, boolean tearOff)

This constructor for Menu creates a Menu with label displayed on it. The handling of tearOff is platform dependent.

Figure 10-3 shows a tear-off menu for Windows NT/95 and Motif. Since Windows does not support tear-off menus, the Windows menu looks and acts like a regular menu.

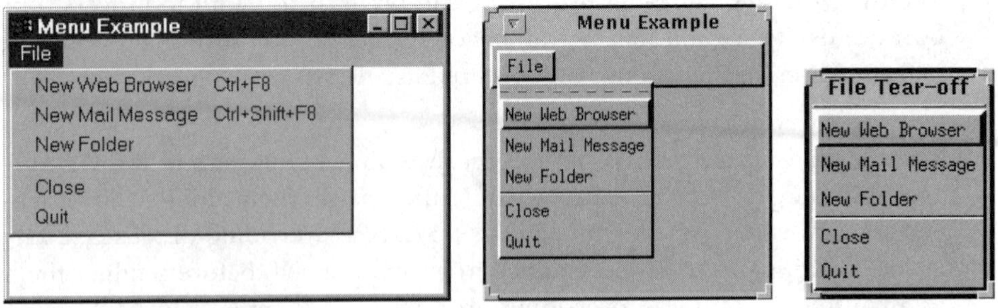

Figure 10–3: Tear-off menu

Items

public int getItemCount() ★
public int countItems () ☆

> The getItemCount() method returns the number of items within the Menu. Only top-level items are counted: if an item is a submenu, this method doesn't include the items on it.

> countItems() is the Java 1.0 name for this method.

public MenuItem getItem (int index)

> The getItem() method returns the MenuItem at position index. If index is invalid, getItem() throws the ArrayIndexOutOfBoundsException run-time exception.

public synchronized MenuItem add (MenuItem item)

> The add() method puts item on the menu. The label assigned to item when it was created is displayed on the menu. If item is already in another menu, it is removed from that menu. If item is a Menu, it creates a submenu. (Remember that Menu subclasses MenuItem.)

public void add (String label)

> This version of add() creates a MenuItem with label as the text and adds that to the menu. If label is the String "-", a separator bar is added to the Menu.

public synchronized void insert(MenuItem item, int index) ★

> The insert() method puts item on the menu at position index. The label assigned to item when it was created is displayed on the menu. Positions are zero based, and if index < 0, insert() throws the IllegalArgumentException run-time exception.

public synchronized void insert(String label, int index) ★

> This version of insert() method creates a MenuItem with label as the text and adds that to the menu at position index. If label is the String "-", a separator bar is added to the Menu. Positions are zero based, and if index < 0, this method throws the IllegalArgumentException run-time exception.

public void addSeparator ()

> The addSeparator() method creates a separator MenuItem and adds that to the menu. Separator menu items are strictly cosmetic and do not generate events when selected.

public void insertSeparator(int index) ★

> The insertSeparator() method creates a separator MenuItem and adds that to the menu at position index. Separator menu items are strictly cosmetic and do not generate events when selected. Positions are zero based. If index < 0, insertSeparator() throws the IllegalArgumentException run-time exception.

public synchronized void remove (int index)

The remove() method removes the MenuItem at position index from the Menu. If index is invalid, remove() throws the ArrayIndexOutOfBoundsException run-time exception. index is zero based, so it can range from 0 to getItem-Count()-1.

public synchronized void remove (MenuComponent component)

This version of remove() removes the menu item component from the Menu. If component is not in the Menu, nothing happens.

public synchronized void removeAll()

The removeAll() removes all MenuItems from the Menu.

Peers

public synchronized void addNotify ()

The addNotify() method creates the Menu peer with all the MenuItems on it.

public synchronized void removeNotify ()

The removeNotify() method destroys the peer of the MenuComponent and removes it from the screen. The peers of the items on the menu are also destroyed.

Miscellaneous methods

public boolean isTearOff ()

The isTearOff() method returns true if this Menu is a tear-off menu, and false otherwise. Once a menu is created, there is no way to change the tear-off setting. This method can return true even on platforms that do not support tear-off menus.

public String paramString () ★

The paramString() method of Menu should be protected like other param-String() methods. However, it is public so you have access to it. When you call the toString() method of a Menu, the default toString() method of MenuComponent is called. This in turn calls paramString(), which builds up the string to display. At the Menu level, the setting for TearOff (from constructor) and whether or not it is the help menu (from MenuBar.setHelpMenu()) for the menu bar are added. If the constructor for the Menu was new Menu ("File"), the results of toString() would be:

```
java.awt.Menu [menu0,label=File,tearOff=false,isHelpMenu=false]
```

10.5.2 Menu Events

A Menu does not generate any event when it is selected. An event is generated when a MenuItem on the menu is selected, as long as it is not another Menu. You can capture all the events that happen on a Menu by overriding postEvent().

10.6 CheckboxMenuItem

The CheckboxMenuItem is a subclass of MenuItem that can be toggled. It is similar to a Checkbox but appears on a Menu. The appearance depends upon the platform. There may or may not be a visual indicator next to the choice. However, when the MenuItem is selected (true), a checkmark or some similar graphic will be displayed next to the label.

There is no way to put CheckboxMenuItem components into a CheckboxGroup to form a radio menu group.

An example of a CheckboxMenuItem is the Show Java Console menu item in Netscape Navigator.

10.6.1 CheckboxMenuItem Methods

Constructors

public CheckboxMenuItem (String label)

> The first CheckboxMenuItem constructor creates a CheckboxMenuItem with no label displayed next to the check toggle. The initial value of the Checkbox-MenuItem is false. To set the label at a later time, use setLabel().

public CheckboxMenuItem (String label)

> The next CheckboxMenuItem constructor creates a CheckboxMenuItem with label displayed next to the check toggle. The initial value of the Checkbox-MenuItem is false.

public CheckboxMenuItem (String label, boolean state)

> The final CheckboxMenuItem constructor creates a CheckboxMenuItem with label displayed next to the check toggle. The initial value of the Checkbox-MenuItem is state.

Selection

public boolean getState ()

> The getState() method retrieves the current state of the CheckboxMenuItem.

public void setState (boolean condition)

> The setState() method changes the current state of the CheckboxMenuItem to condition. When true, the CheckboxMenuItem will have the toggle checked.

public Object[] getSelectedObjects () ★

> The getSelectedItems() method returns the currently selected item as an Object array. This method, which is required by the ItemSelectable interface, allows you to use the same methods to retrieve the selected items of any Checkbox, Choice, or List. The array has at most one element, which contains the label of the selected item; if no item is selected, getSelectedItems() returns null.

Miscellaneous methods

public synchronized void addNotify ()

> The addNotify() method creates the CheckboxMenuItem peer.

public String paramString ()

> The paramString() method of CheckboxMenuItem should be protected like other paramString() methods. However, it is public, so you have access to it. When you call the toString() method of a CheckboxMenuItem, the default toString() method of MenuComponent is called. This in turn calls paramString() which builds up the string to display. At the CheckboxMenuItem level, the current state of the object is appended to the output. If the constructor for the CheckboxMenuItem was new CheckboxMenuItem("File") the results would be:

```
java.awt.CheckboxMenuItem[label=File,state=false]
```

10.6.2 CheckboxMenuItem Events

Event handling

A CheckboxMenuItem generates an ACTION_EVENT when it is selected. The argument to action() is the label of the CheckboxMenuItem, like the method provided by MenuItem, not the state of the CheckboxMenuItem as used in Checkbox. The target of the ACTION_EVENT is the Frame containing the menu. You cannot subclass CheckboxMenuItem and handle the Event within the subclass unless you override postEvent().

Listeners and 1.1 event handling

With the Java 1.1 event model, you register listeners, which are told when the event happens.

public void addItemListener(ItemListener listener) ★

> The addItemListener() method registers listener as an object that is interested in being notified when an ItemEvent passes through the EventQueue with this CheckboxMenuItem as its target. When these item events occur, the listener.itemStateChanged() method is called. Multiple listeners can be registered.

public void removeItemListener(ItemListener listener) ★

> The removeItemListener() method removes listener as a interested listener. If listener is not registered, nothing happens.

protected void processEvent(AWTEvent e) ★

> The processEvent() method receives every AWTEvent with this Checkbox-MenuItem as its target. processEvent() then passes it along to any listeners for processing. When you subclass CheckboxMenuItem, overriding processEvent() allows you to process all events yourself, before sending them to any listeners. In a way, overriding processEvent() is like overriding postEvent() using the 1.0 event model.

> If you override processEvent(), remember to call super.processEvent(e) last to ensure that regular event processing can occur. If you want to process your own events, it's a good idea to call enableEvents() to ensure that events are delivered, even in the absence of registered listeners.

protected void processItemEvent(ItemEvent e) ★

> The processItemEvent() method receives every ItemEvent with this CheckboxMenuItem as its target. processItemEvent() then passes it along to any listeners for processing. When you subclass CheckboxMenuItem, overriding processItemEvent() allows you to process all item events yourself, before sending them to any listeners. In a way, overriding processItemEvent() is like overriding action() using the 1.0 event model.

> If you override processItemEvent(), remember to call the method super.processItemEvent(e) last to ensure that regular event processing can occur. If you want to process your own events, it's a good idea to call enableEvents() to ensure that events are delivered even in the absence of registered listeners.

10.7 *MenuBar*

The MenuBar is the component you add to the Frame that is displayed on the top line of the Frame; the MenuBar contains menus. A Frame can display only one MenuBar at a time. However, you can change the MenuBar based on the state of the program so that different menus can appear at different points. The MenuBar class extends MenuComponent and implements the MenuContainer interface.

A MenuBar can be used only as a child component of a Frame. An applet cannot have a MenuBar attached to it, unless you implement the whole thing yourself. Normally, you cannot modify the MenuBar of the applet holder (the browser), unless it is Java based. In other words, you cannot affect the menus of Netscape Navigator, but you can customize *appletviewer* and HotJava, as shown in the following code with the result shown in Figure 10-4. The getTopLevelParent() method was introduced in Section 6.4 with Window.

```
import java.awt.*;
public class ChangeMenu extends java.applet.Applet {
    public void init ()  {
        Frame f = ComponentUtilities.getTopLevelParent(this);
        if (f != null) {
            MenuBar mb = f.getMenuBar();
            Menu m = new Menu ("Cool");
            mb.add (m);
        }
    }
}
```

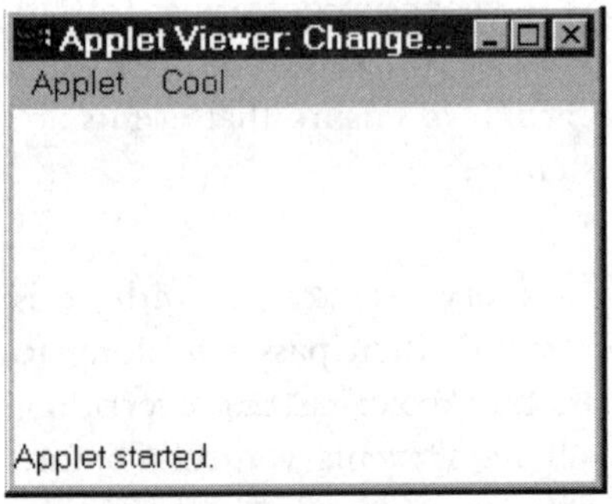

Figure 10–4: Customizing appletviewer's MenuBar

NOTE   When you add a MenuBar to a Frame, it takes up space that is part of
            the drawing area. You need to get the top insets to find out how
            much space is occupied by the MenuBar and be careful not to draw
            under it. If you do, the MenuBar will cover what you draw.

10.7.1 MenuBar Methods

Constructors

public MenuBar()

The MenuBar constructor creates an empty MenuBar. To add menus to the MenuBar, use the add() method.

Menus

public int getMenuCount () ★
public int countMenus () ☆

> The getMenuCount() method returns the number of top-level menus within the MenuBar.

> countMenus() is the Java 1.0 name for this method.

public Menu getMenu (int index)

> The getMenu() method returns the Menu at position index. If index is invalid, getMenu() throws the run-time exception ArrayIndexOutOfBoundsException.

public synchronized Menu add (Menu m)

> The add() method puts choice m on the MenuBar. The label used to create m is displayed on the MenuBar. If m is already in another MenuBar, it is removed from it. The order of items added determines the order displayed on the MenuBar, with one exception: if a menu is designated as a help menu by setHelpMenu(), it is placed at the right end of the menu bar. Only a Menu can be added to a MenuBar; you can't add a MenuItem. In other words, a MenuItem has to lie under at least one menu.

public synchronized void remove (int index)

> The remove() method removes the Menu at position index from the MenuBar. If index is invalid, remove() throws the ArrayIndexOutOfBoundsException run-time exception. index is zero based.

public synchronized void remove (MenuComponent component)

> This version of remove() removes the menu component from the MenuBar. If component is not in MenuBar, nothing happens. The system calls this method when you add a new Menu to make sure it does not exist on another MenuBar.

Shortcuts

public MenuItem getShortcutMenuItem (MenuShortcut shortcut) ★

> The getShortcutMenuItem() method retrieves the MenuItem associated with the MenuShortcut shortcut. If MenuShortcut does not exist for this Menu, the method returns null. getShortcutMenuItem() walks through the all submenus recursively to try to find shortcut.

public synchronized Enumeration shortcuts() ★

> The shortcuts() method retrieves an Enumeration of all the MenuShortcut objects associated with this MenuBar.

public void deleteShortcut (MenuShortcut shortcut) ★

The deleteShortcut() method removes MenuShortcut from the associated MenuItem in the MenuBar. If the shortcut is not associated with any menu item, nothing happens.

Help menus

It is the convention on many platforms to display help menus as the last menu on the MenuBar. The MenuBar class lets you designate one of the menus as this special menu. The physical position of a help menu depends on the platform, but those giving special treatment to help menus place them on the right. A Menu designated as a help menu doesn't have to bear the label "Help"; the label is up to you.

public Menu getHelpMenu ()

The getHelpMenu() method returns the Menu that has been designated as the help menu with setHelpMenu(). If the menu bar doesn't have a help menu, getHelpMenu() returns null.

public synchronized void setHelpMenu (Menu m)

The setHelpMenu() method sets the menu bar's help menu to m. This makes m the rightmost menu on the MenuBar, possibly right justified. If m is not already on the MenuBar, nothing happens.

Peers

public synchronized void addNotify ()

The addNotify() method creates the MenuBar peer with all the menus on it, and in turn their menu items.

public synchronized void removeNotify ()

The removeNotify() method destroys the peer of the MenuBar and removes it from the screen. The peers of the items on the MenuBar are also destroyed.

10.7.2 MenuBar Events

A MenuBar does not generate any events.

10.8 Putting It All Together

Now that you know about all the different menu classes, it is time to show an example. Example 10-1 contains the code to put up a functional MenuBar attached to a Frame, using the 1.0 event model. Figure 10-2 (earlier in the chapter) displays the resulting screen. The key parts to examine are how the menus are put together in the MenuTest constructor and how their actions are handled within action(). I implement one real action in the example: the one that terminates the application when the user chooses Quit. Any other action just displays the label of the item and (if it was a CheckBoxMenuItem) the item's state, to give you an idea of how you can use the information returned in the event.

Example 10–1: MenuTest 1.0 Source Code

```java
import java.awt.*;
public class MenuTest extends Frame {
    MenuTest () {
        super ("MenuTest");
        MenuItem mi;
        Menu file = new Menu ("File", true);
        file.add ("Open");
        file.add (mi = new MenuItem ("Close"));
        mi.disable ();
        Menu extras = new Menu ("Extras", false);
        extras.add (new CheckboxMenuItem ("What"));
        extras.add ("Yo");
        extras.add ("Yo");
        file.add (extras);
        file.addSeparator ();
        file.add ("Quit");
        Menu help = new Menu("Help");
        help.add ("About");
        MenuBar mb = new MenuBar();
        mb.add (file);
        mb.add (help);
        mb.setHelpMenu (help);
        setMenuBar (mb);
        resize (200, 200);
    }
    public boolean handleEvent (Event e) {
        if (e.id == Event.WINDOW_DESTROY) {
            System.exit(0);
        }
        return super.handleEvent (e);
    }
    public boolean action (Event e, Object o) {
        if (e.target instanceof MenuItem) {
            if ("Quit".equals (o)) {
                dispose();
                System.exit(1);
            } else {
                System.out.println ("User selected " + o);
                if (e.target instanceof CheckboxMenuItem) {
                    CheckboxMenuItem cb = (CheckboxMenuItem)e.target;
                    System.out.println ("The value is: " + cb.getState());
                }
            }
            return true;
        }
        return false;
```

Example 10–1: MenuTest 1.0 Source Code (continued)

```
    }
    public static void main (String []args) {
        MenuTest f = new MenuTest ();
        f.show();
    }
}
```

The MenuTest constructor builds all the menus, creates a menu bar, adds the menus to the menu bar, and adds the menu bar to the Frame. To show what is possible, I've included a submenu, a separator bar, a disabled item, and a help menu.

The handleEvent() method exists to take care of WINDOW_DESTROY events, which are generated if the user uses a native command to exit from the window.

The action() method does the work; it received the action events generated whenever the user selects a menu. We ignore most of them, but a real application would need to do more work figuring out the user's selection. As it is, action() is fairly simple. If the user selected a menu item, we check to see whether the item's label was "Quit"; if it was, we exit. If the user selected anything else, we print the selection and return true to indicate that we handled the event.

10.8.1 Using Java 1.1 Events

Example 10-2 uses the Java 1.1 event model but is otherwise very similar to Example 10-1. Take a close look at the differences and similarities. Although the code that builds the GUI is basically the same in both examples, the event handling is completely different. The helper class MyMenuItem is necessary to simplify event handling. In Java 1.1, every menu item can be an event source, so you have to register a listener for each item. Rather than calling addActionListener() explicitly for each item, we create a subclass of MenuItem that registers a listener automatically. The listener is specified in the constructor to MyMenuItem; in this example, the object that creates the menus (MenuTest12) always registers itself as the listener. An alternative would be to override processActionEvent() in MyMenuItem, but then we'd also need to write a subclass for CheckboxMenuItem.

Having said all that, the code is relatively simple. MenuTest12 implements ActionListener so it can receive action events from the menus. As I noted previously, it registers itself as the listener for every menu item when it builds the interface. The actionPerformed() method is called whenever the user selects a menu item; the logic of this method is virtually the same as it was in Example 10-1. Notice, though, that we use getActionCommand() to read the label of the menu item. (Note also that getActionCommand() doesn't necessarily return the label; you can change the command associated with the menu item by calling setActionCommand().) Similarly, we call the event's getSource() method to get the menu item that actually generated the event; we need this to figure out whether the user selected a CheckboxMenuItem (which implements ItemSelectable).

We override processWindowEvent() so that we can receive WINDOW_CLOSING events without registering a listener. Window closings occur when the user uses the native display manager to close the application. If one of these events arrives, we shut down cleanly. To make sure that we receive window events even if there are no listeners, the MenuTest12 constructor calls enableEvents(WINDOW_EVENT_MASK).

Example 10–2: MenuTest12 Source Code, Using Java 1.1 Event Handling

```
// Java 1.1 only
import java.awt.*;
import java.awt.event.*;
public class MenuTest12 extends Frame implements ActionListener {
    class MyMenuItem extends MenuItem {
        public MyMenuItem (String s, ActionListener al) {
            super (s);
            addActionListener (al);
        }
    }
    public MenuTest12 () {
        super ("MenuTest");
        MenuItem mi;
        Menu file = new Menu ("File", true);
        file.add (new MyMenuItem ("Open", this));
        mi = file.add (new MyMenuItem ("Close", this));
        mi.setEnabled (false);
        Menu extras = new Menu ("Extras", false);
        mi = extras.add (new CheckboxMenuItem ("What"));
        mi.addActionListener(this);
        mi = extras.add (new MyMenuItem ("Yo", this));
        mi.setActionCommand ("Yo1");
        mi = extras.add (new MyMenuItem ("Yo", this));
        mi.setActionCommand ("Yo2");
        file.add (extras);
        file.addSeparator();
        file.add (new MyMenuItem ("Quit", this));
        Menu help = new Menu("Help");
        help.add (new MyMenuItem ("About", this));
        MenuBar mb = new MenuBar();
        mb.add (file);
        mb.add (help);
        mb.setHelpMenu (help);
        setMenuBar (mb);
        setSize (200, 200);
        enableEvents (AWTEvent.WINDOW_EVENT_MASK);
    }
    // Cannot override processActionEvent since method of MenuItem
    // Would have to subclass both MenuItem and CheckboxMenuItem
```

Example 10–2: MenuTest12 Source Code, Using Java 1.1 Event Handling (continued)

```java
    public void actionPerformed(ActionEvent e) {
        if (e.getActionCommand().equals("Quit")) {
            System.exit(0);
        }
        System.out.println ("User selected " + e.getActionCommand());
        if (e.getSource() instanceof ItemSelectable) {
            ItemSelectable is = (ItemSelectable)e.getSource();
            System.out.println ("The value is: " +
                (is.getSelectedObjects().length != 0)));
        }
    }
    protected void processWindowEvent(WindowEvent e) {
        if (e.getID() == WindowEvent.WINDOW_CLOSING) {
            // Notify others we are closing
            super.processWindowEvent(e);
            System.exit(0);
        } else {
            super.processWindowEvent(e);
        }
    }
    public static void main (String []args) {
        MenuTest12 f = new MenuTest12 ();
        f.show();
    }
}
```

I took the opportunity when writing the 1.1 code to make one additional improvement to the program. By using action commands, you can easily differentiate between the two Yo menu items. Just call setActionCommand() to assign a different command to each item. (I used "Yo1" and "Yo2".) You could also differentiate between the items by saving a reference to each menu item, calling getSource() in the event handler, and comparing the result to the saved references. However, if the ActionListener is another class, it would need access to those references. Using action commands is simpler and results in a cleaner event handler.

The intent of the setActionCommand() and getActionCommand() methods is more for internationalization support. For example, you could use setActionCommand() to associate the command Quit with a menu item, then set the item's label to the appropriate text for the user's locality.

10.9 PopupMenu

The PopupMenu class is new to Java 1.1; it allows you to associate context-sensitive menus with Java components. To associate a pop-up menu with a component, create the menu, and add it to the component using the add(PopupMenu) method, which all components inherit from the Component class.

In principle, any GUI object can have a pop-up menu. In practice, there are a few exceptions. If the component's peer has its own pop-up menu (i.e., a pop-up menu provided by the run-time platform), that pop-up menu effectively overrides the pop-up menu provided by Java. For example, under Windows NT/95, a TextArea has a pop-up menu provided by the Windows NT/95 platforms. Java can't override this menu; although you can add a pop-up menu to a TextArea, you can't display that menu under Windows NT/95 with the usual mouse sequence.

10.9.1 *PopupMenu Methods*

Constructors

public PopupMenu() ★

The first PopupMenu constructor creates an untitled PopupMenu. Once created, the menu can be populated with menu items like any other menu.

public PopupMenu(String label) ★

This constructor creates a PopupMenu with a title of label. The title appears only on platforms that support titles for context menus. Once created, the menu can be populated with menu items like any other menu.

Miscellaneous methods

public void show(Component origin, int x, int y) ★

Call the show() method to display the PopupMenu. x and y specify the location at which the pop-up menu should appear; origin specifies the Component whose coordinate system is used to locate x and y. In most cases, you'll want the menu to appear at the point where the user clicked the mouse; to do this, set origin to the Component that received the mouse event, and set x and y to the location of the mouse click. It is easy to extract this information from an old-style (1.0) Event or a Java 1.1 MouseEvent. In Java 1.1, the platform-independent way to say "give me the mouse events that are supposed to trigger pop-up menus" is to call MouseEvent.isPopupTrigger(). If this method returns true, you should show the pop-up menu if one is associated with the event source. (Note that the mouse event could also be used for some other purpose.)

If the PopupMenu is not associated with a Component, show() throws the run-time exception NullPointerException. If origin is not the MenuContainer for the PopupMenu and origin is not within the Container that the pop-up menu belongs to, show() throws the run-time exception IllegalArgumentException. Finally, if the Container of origin does not exist or is not showing, show() throws a run-time exception.

public synchronized void addNotify () ★

The addNotify() method creates the PopupMenu peer with all the MenuItems on it.

Example 10-3 is a simple applet that raises a pop-up menu if the user clicks the appropriate mouse button anywhere within the applet. Although the program could use the 1.0 event model, under the 1.0 model, it is impossible to tell which mouse event is appropriate to display the pop-up menu.

Example 10–3: Using a PopupMenu

```java
// Java 1.1 only
import java.awt.*;
import java.applet.*;
import java.awt.event.*;

public class PopupTest extends Applet implements ActionListener {
    PopupMenu popup;
    public void init() {
        MenuItem mi;
        popup = new PopupMenu("Title Goes Here");
        popup.add(mi = new MenuItem ("Undo"));
        mi.addActionListener (this);
        popup.addSeparator();
        popup.add(mi = new MenuItem("Cut")).setEnabled(false);
        mi.addActionListener (this);
        popup.add(mi = new MenuItem("Copy")).setEnabled(false);
        mi.addActionListener (this);
        popup.add(mi = new MenuItem ("Paste"));
        mi.addActionListener (this);
        popup.add(mi = new MenuItem("Delete")).setEnabled(false);
        mi.addActionListener (this);
        popup.addSeparator();
        popup.add(mi = new MenuItem ("Select All"));
        mi.addActionListener (this);
        add (popup);
        resize(200, 200);
        enableEvents (AWTEvent.MOUSE_EVENT_MASK);
    }
    protected void processMouseEvent (MouseEvent e) {
        if (e.isPopupTrigger())
            popup.show(e.getComponent(), e.getX(), e.getY());
        super.processMouseEvent (e);
    }
    public void actionPerformed(ActionEvent e) {
        System.out.println (e);
    }
}
```

11

Scrolling

This chapter describes how Java deals with scrolling. AWT provides two means for scrolling. The first is the fairly primitive Scrollbar object. It really provides only the means to read a value from a slider setting. Anything else is your responsibility: if you want to display the value of the setting (for example, if you're using the scrollbar as a volume control) or want to change the display (if you're using scrollbars to control an area that's too large to display), you have to do it yourself. The Scrollbar reports scrolling actions through the standard event mechanisms; it is up to the programmer to handle those events and perform the scrolling.

Unlike other components, which generate an ACTION_EVENT when something exciting happens, the Scrollbar generates five events: SCROLL_LINE_UP, SCROLL_LINE_DOWN, SCROLL_PAGE_UP, SCROLL_PAGE_DOWN, and SCROLL_ABSOLUTE. In Java 1.0, none of these events trigger a default event handler like the action() method. To work with them, you must override the handleEvent() method. With Java 1.1, you handle scrolling events by registering an AdjustmentListener with the Scrollbar.addAdjustmentListener() method; when adjustment events occur, the listener's adjustmentValueChanged() method is called.

Release 1.1 of AWT also includes a ScrollPane container object; it is a response to one of the limitations of AWT 1.0. A ScrollPane is like a Panel, but it has scrollbars and scrolling built in. In this sense, it's like TextArea, which contains its own scrollbars. You could use a ScrollPane to implement a drawing pad that could cover an arbitrarily large area. This saves you the burden of implementing scrolling yourself: generating scrollbars, handling their events, and figuring out how to redisplay the screen accordingly.

Both `Scrollbar` and `ScrollPane` take advantage of the `Adjustable` interface. `Adjustable` defines the common scrolling activities of the two classes. The `Scrollbar` class implements `Adjustable`; a `ScrollPane` has two methods that return an `Adjustable` object, one for each scrollbar. Currently, you can use the `ScrollPane`'s "adjustables" to find out the scrollbar settings in each direction. You can't change the settings or register `AdjustmentListeners`; the appropriate methods exist, but they don't do anything. It's not clear whether this is appropriate behavior or a bug (remember, an interface only lists methods that must be present but doesn't require them to do anything); it may change in a later release.

11.1 Scrollbar

Scrollbars come in two flavors: horizontal and vertical. Although there are several methods for setting the page size, scrollbar range (minimum and maximum values), and so on, basically all you can do is get and set the scrollbar's value. Scrollbars don't contain any area to display their value, though if you want one, you could easily attach a label.

To work with a `Scrollbar`, you need to understand the pieces from which it is built. Figure 11-1 identifies each of the pieces. At both ends are arrows, which are used to change the `Scrollbar` value the default amount (one unit) in the direction selected. The paging areas are used to change the `Scrollbar` value one page (ten units by default) at a time in the direction selected. The slider can be moved to set the scrollbar to an arbitrary value within the available range.

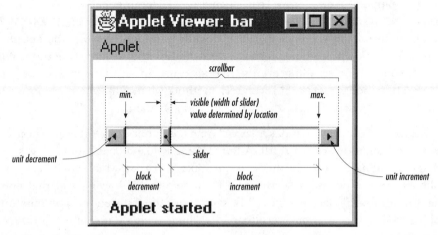

Figure 11–1: Scrollbar elements

11.1.1 Scrollbar Methods

Constants

There are two direction specifiers for Scrollbar. The direction tells the Scrollbar which way to orient itself. They are used in the constructors, as a parameter to setOrientation(), and as the return value for the getOrientation() method.

public final static int HORIZONTAL

HORIZONTAL is the constant for horizontal orientation.

public final static int VERTICAL

VERTICAL is the constant for vertical orientation.

Constructors

public Scrollbar (int orientation, int value, int visible, int minimum, int maximum)

The Scrollbar constructor creates a Scrollbar with a direction of orientation and initial value of value. visible is the size of the slider. minimum and maximum are the range of values that the Scrollbar can be. If orientation is not HORIZONTAL or VERTICAL, the constructor throws the run-time exception IllegalArgumentException. If maximum is below the value of minimum, the scrollbar's minimum and maximum values are both set to minimum. If value is outside the range of the scrollbar, it is set to the limit it exceeded. The default line scrolling amount is one. The default paging amount is ten.

If you are using the scrollbar to control a visual object, visible should be set to the amount of a displayed object that is on the screen at one time, relative to the entire size of the object (i.e., relative to the scrollbar's range: maximum - minimum). Some platforms ignore this parameter and set the scrollbar to a fixed size.

public Scrollbar (int orientation)

This constructor for Scrollbar creates a Scrollbar with the direction of orientation. In Java 1.0, the initial settings for value, visible, minimum, and maximum are 0. In Java 1.1, the default value for visible is 10, and the default for maximum is 100; the other values default to 0. If orientation is not HORIZONTAL or VERTICAL, the constructor throws the run-time exception IllegalArgumentException. This constructor is helpful if you want to reserve space for the Scrollbar on the screen, to be configured later. You would then use the setValues() method to configure the scrollbar.

public Scrollbar ()

> This constructor creates a VERTICAL Scrollbar. In Java 1.0, the initial settings
> for value, visible, minimum, and maximum are 0. In Java 1.1, the default value
> for visible is 10, and the default for maximum is 100; the other values default
> to 0. You would then use the setValues() method to configure the scrollbar.

Figure 11-2 shows both vertical and horizontal scrollbars. It also demonstrates a
problem you'll run into if you're not careful. If not constrained by the LayoutManager, scrollbars can get very fat. The result is rarely pleasing. The solution is to
place scrollbars in layout managers that restrict width for vertical scrollbars or
height for horizontal ones. The side regions (i.e., everything except the center) of
a border layout are ideal. In the long term, the solution will be scrollbars that give
you their maximum size and layout managers that observe the maximum size.

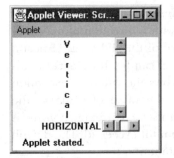

Figure 11–2: Vertical and horizontal scrollbars

Adjustable Methods

public int getOrientation ()

> The getOrientation() method returns the current orientation of the scroll-
> bar: either Scrollbar.HORIZONTAL or Scrollbar.VERTICAL.

public synchronized void setOrientation (int orientation) ★

> The setOrientation() method changes the orientation of the scrollbar to
> orientation, which must be either Scrollbar.HORIZONTAL or Scroll-
> bar.VERTICAL. If orientation is not HORIZONTAL or VERTICAL, this method
> throws the run-time exception IllegalArgumentException. It was not possible
> to change the orientation of a scrollbar prior to Java 1.1.

public int getVisibleAmount () ★
public int getVisible () ☆

> The getVisibleAmount() method gets the visible setting of the Scrollbar. If
> the scrollbar's Container is resized, the visible setting is not automatically
> changed. getVisible() is the Java 1.0 name for this method.

public synchronized void setVisibleAmount (int amount) ★

>   The setVisibleAmount() method changes the current visible setting of the
>   Scrollbar to amount.

public int getValue ()

>   The getValue() method is probably the most frequently called method of
>   Scrollbar. It returns the current value of the scrollbar queried.

public synchronized void setValue (int value)

>   The setValue() method changes the value of the scrollbar to value. If value
>   exceeds a scrollbar limit, the scrollbar's new value is set to that limit. In Java
>   1.1, this method is synchronized; it was not in earlier versions.

public int getMinimum ()

>   The getMinimum() method returns the current minimum setting for the
>   scrollbar.

public synchronized void setMinimum (int minimum) ★

>   The setMinimum() method changes the Scrollbar's minimum value to mini-
>   mum. The current setting for the Scrollbar may change to minimum if minimum
>   increases above getValue().

public int getMaximum ()

>   The getMaximum() method returns the current maximum setting for the
>   scrollbar.

public synchronized void setMaximum (int maximum) ★

>   The setMaximum() method changes the maximum value of the Scrollbar to
>   maximum. The current setting for the Scrollbar may change to maximum if max-
>   imum decreases below getValue().

public synchronized void setValues (int value, int visible, int minimum, int maximum)

>   The setValues() method changes the value, visible, minimum, and maximum
>   settings all at once. In Java 1.0.2, separate methods do not exist for changing
>   visible, minimum, or maximum. The scrollbar's value is set to value, visible to
>   visible, minimum to minimum, and maximum to maximum. If maximum is below
>   the value of minimum, it is set to minimum. If value is outside the range of the
>   scrollbar, it is set to the limit it exceeded. In Java 1.1, this method is synchro-
>   nized; it was not in earlier versions.

public int getUnitIncrement () ★
public int getLineIncrement () ☆

>   The getUnitIncrement() method returns the current line increment. This is
>   the amount the scrollbar will scroll if the user clicks on one of the scrollbar's
>   arrows.

`getLineIncrement()` is the Java 1.0 name for this method.

public void setUnitIncrement (int amount) ★
public void setLineIncrement (int amount) ☆

The `setUnitIncrement()` method changes the line increment amount to `amount`.

`setLineIncrement()` is the Java 1.0 name for this method.

Changing the line increment amount was not possible in Java 1.0.2. This method acted like it returned successfully, and `getLineIncrement()` returned the new value, but the `Scrollbar` changed its value by only one (the default) when you clicked on one of the arrows. However, you could work around this defect by explicitly handling the `SCROLL_LINE_UP` and `SCROLL_LINE_DOWN` events: get the correct line increment, adjust the display appropriately, and then set call `setValue()` to correct the scrollbar's value. This workaround is not needed in Java 1.1.

public int getBlockIncrement () ★
public int getPageIncrement () ☆

The `getBlockIncrement()` method returns the current paging increment. This is the amount the scrollbar will scroll if the user clicks between the slider and one of the scrollbar's arrows.

`getPageIncrement()` is the Java 1.0 name for this method.

public void setBlockIncrement (int amount) ★
public void setPageIncrement (int amount) ☆

The `setBlockIncrement()` method changes the paging increment amount to `amount`.

`setPageIncrement()` is the Java 1.0 name for this method.

Changing the paging increment amount was not possible in Java 1.0.2. This method acts like it returns successfully, and `getPageIncrement()` returns the new value, but the `Scrollbar` changes its value only by 10 (the default) when you click on one of the paging areas. However, you can work around this defect by explicitly handling the `SCROLL_PAGE_UP` and `SCROLL_PAGE_DOWN` events: get the correct page increment, adjust the display appropriately, and then set call `setValue()` to correct the scrollbar's value. This workaround is not necessary in Java 1.1.

Miscellaneous methods

public synchronized void addNotify ()

The `addNotify()` method creates the `Scrollbar`'s peer. If you override this method, call `super.addNotify()` first. You will then be able to do everything you need with the information about the newly created peer.

protected String paramString ()

> `Scrollbar` doesn't have its own `toString()` method; when you call the `toString()` method of a `Scrollbar`, you are actually calling the method `Component.toString()`. This in turn calls `paramString()`, which builds the string to display. For a `Scrollbar`, `paramString()` puts the scrollbar's value, visibility, minimum, maximum, and direction into the string. In Java 1.0, there is a minor bug in the output. Instead of displaying the scrollbar's `visible` setting (an integer), `paramString()` displays the component's `visible` setting (a boolean). (This is corrected in Java 1.1.) The following `String` is the result of calling `toString()` for a horizontal `Scrollbar` that hasn't been configured yet:

```
java.awt.Scrollbar[0,0,0x0,invalid,val=0,vis=true,min=0,max=0,horz]
```

11.1.2 Scrollbar Events

With the 1.0 event model, scrollbars generate five kinds of events in response to user interaction: `SCROLL_LINE_UP`, `SCROLL_LINE_DOWN`, `SCROLL_PAGE_UP`, `SCROLL_PAGE_DOWN`, and `SCROLL_ABSOLUTE`. The event that occurs depends on what the user did, as shown in Table 11-1; the event type is specified in the `id` field of the `Event` object passed to `handleEvent()`. However, as a programmer, you often do not care which of these five events happened. You care only about the scrollbar's new value, which is always passed as the `arg` field of the `Event` object.

Table 11–1: Scrollbar Events

Event Type (Event.id)	Event Meaning
SCROLL_ABSOLUTE	User drags slider.
SCROLL_LINE_DOWN	User presses down arrow.
SCROLL_LINE_UP	User presses up arrow.
SCROLL_PAGE_DOWN	User selects down paging area.
SCROLL_PAGE_UP	User selects up paging area.

Because scrollbar events do not trigger any default event handlers (like `action()`), it is necessary to override the `handleEvent()` method to deal with them. Unless your version of `handleEvent()` deals with all conceivable events, you must ensure that the original `handleEvent()` method is called. The simplest way is to have the return statement call `super.handleEvent()`.

Most `handleEvent()` methods first identify the type of event that occurred. The following two code blocks demonstrate different ways of checking for the `Scrollbar` events.

```
if ((e.id == Event.SCROLL_LINE_UP) ||
    (e.id == Event.SCROLL_LINE_DOWN) ||
    (e.id == Event.SCROLL_PAGE_UP) ||
    (e.id == Event.SCROLL_PAGE_DOWN) ||
    (e.id == Event.SCROLL_ABSOLUTE)) {
    // Then determine which Scrollbar was selected and act upon it
}
```

Or more simply:

```
if (e.target instanceof Scrollbar) {
    // Then determine which Scrollbar was selected and act upon it.
}
```

Although the second code block is simpler, the first is the better choice because it is more precise. For example, what would happen if mouse events are passed to scrollbars? Different Java platforms differ most in the types of events passed to different objects; Netscape Navigator 3.0 for Windows 95 sends MOUSE_ENTER, MOUSE_EXIT, and MOUSE_MOVE events to the Scrollbar.* The second code block executes for all the mouse events—in fact, any event coming from a Scrollbar. Therefore, it executes much more frequently (there can be many MOUSE_MOVE events), leading to poor interactive performance.

Another platform-specific issue is the way the system generates SCROLL_ABSOLUTE events. Some platforms generate many events while the user drags the scrollbar. Others don't generate the event until the user stops dragging the scrollbar. Some implementations wait until the user stops dragging the scrollbar and then generate a flood of SCROLL_ABSOLUTE events for you to handle. In theory, it does not matter which is happening, as long as your event-processing code is tight. If your event-processing code is time consuming, you may wish to start another thread to perform the work. If the thread is still alive when the next event comes along, flag it down, and restart the operation.

Listeners and 1.1 event handling

With the 1.1 event model, you register an AdjustmentListener by calling the addAdjustmentListener() method. Then when the user moves the Scrollbar slider, the AdjustmentListener.adjustmentValueChanged() method is called through the protected Scrollbar.processAdjustmentEvent() method. Key, mouse, and focus listeners are registered through the three Component methods of addKeyListener(), addMouseListener(), and addFocusListener(), respectively. Because you need to register a separate listener for mouse events, you no longer have the problem of distinguishing between mouse events and slider events. An adjustment listener will never receive mouse events.

---

* MOUSE_UP, MOUSE_DOWN, and MOUSE_DRAG are not generated since these operations generate SCROLL events.

public void addAdjustmentListener(AdjustmentListener listener) ★

The addAdjustmentListener() method registers listener as an object inter-ested in being notified when an AdjustmentEvent passes through the Event-Queue with this Scrollbar as its target. The method lis-tener.adjustmentValueChanged() is called when an event occurs. Multiple lis-teners can be registered.

public void removeAdjustmentListener(ItemListener listener) ★

The removeAdjustmentListener() method removes listener as a interested listener. If listener is not registered, nothing happens.

protected void processEvent(AWTEvent e) ★

The processEvent() method receives every AWTEvent with this Scrollbar as its target. processEvent() then passes it along to any listeners for processing. When you subclass Scrollbar, overriding processEvent() allows you to pro-cess all events yourself, before sending them to any listeners. In a way, overrid-ing processEvent() is like overriding handleEvent() using the 1.0 event model.

If you override the processEvent() method, remember to call the super.processEvent(e) method last to ensure that regular event processing can occur. If you want to process your own events, it's a good idea to call enableEvents() (inherited from Component) to ensure that events are deliv-ered even in the absence of registered listeners.

protected void processAdjustmentEvent(ItemEvent e) ★

The processAdjustmentEvent() method receives all AdjustmentEvents with this Scrollbar as its target. processAdjustmentEvent() then passes them along to any listeners for processing. When you subclass Scrollbar, overriding processAdjustmentEvent() allows you to process all events yourself, before sending them to any listeners.

If you override processAdjustmentEvent(), you must remember to call super.processAdjustmentEvent(e) last to ensure that regular event process-ing can occur. If you want to process your own events, it's a good idea to call enableEvents() (inherited from Component) to ensure that events are deliv-ered even in the absence of registered listeners.

11.2 Scrolling An Image

Example 11-1 is a Java application that displays any image in the current directory in a viewing area. The viewing area scrolls to accommodate larger images; the user can use the scrollbars or keypad keys to scroll the image. In Java 1.1, it is trivial to implement this example with a `ScrollPane`; however, if you're using 1.0, you don't have this luxury. Even if you're using 1.1, this example shows a lot about how to use scrollbars.

Our application uses a `Dialog` to select which file to display; a `FilenameFilter` limits the list to image files. We use a menu to let the user request a file list or exit the program. After the user picks a file, the application loads it into the display area. Figure 11-3 shows the main scrolling window.

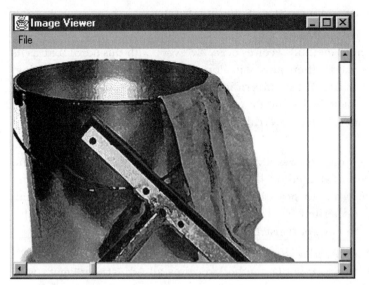

Figure 11–3: Scrolling an image

The code for the scrolling image consists of a `ScrollingImage` class, plus several helper classes. It places everything into the file *ScrollingImage.java* for compilation.

Example 11–1: Source Code for Scrolling an Image

```
import java.awt.*;
import java.io.FilenameFilter;
import java.io.File;
```

The first class contains the `FilenameFilter` used to select relevant filenames: that is, files that are likely to contain GIF, JPEG, or XBM images. If the filename has an appropriate ending, the `accept()` method returns `true`; otherwise, it returns `false`.

```
// True for files ending in jpeg/jpg/gif/xbm
class ImageFileFilter implements FilenameFilter {
    public boolean accept (File dir, String name) {
        String tempname = name.toLowerCase();
        return (tempname.endsWith ("jpg") || tempname.endsWith ("jpeg") ||
```

```
                        tempname.endsWith ("gif") || tempname.endsWith ("xbm"));
        }
    }
```

The `ImageListDialog` class displays a list of files from which the user can select. Instead of using `FileDialog`, we created a customized `List` to prevent the user from roaming around the entire hard drive; choices are limited to appropriate files in the current directory. When the user selects an entry (by double-clicking), the image is then displayed in the scrolling area.

```
class ImageListDialog extends Dialog {
    private String name = null;
    private String entries[];
    private List list;
    ImageListDialog (Frame f) {
        super (f, "Image List", true);
        File dir = new File (System.getProperty("user.dir"));
        entries = dir.list (new ImageFileFilter());
        list = new List (10, false);
        for (int i=0;i<entries.length;i++) {
            list.addItem (entries[i]);
        }
        add ("Center", list);
        pack();
    }
    public String getName () {
        return name;
    }
    public boolean action (Event e, Object o) {
        name = (String)e.arg;
        ((ScrollingImage)getParent()).processImage();
        dispose();
        return true;
    }
}
```

The code in this class is straightforward. The constructor reads the current directory from the system property list, uses the `list()` method of the `File` class to create a list of files that match our filename filter, and then creates a `List` object that lists these files. `getName()` returns the name of the selected file. `action()` is called when the user selects a file; it sets the name of the selected file from the `arg` field of the `Event` and then calls the `processImage()` method of its parent container. The parent container of our `ImageListDialog` is the `ScrollingImage` class we are defining; its `processImage()` method displays a scrollable image.

The next class, `ImageCanvas`, is the `Canvas` that the image is drawn onto. We use a separate `Canvas` rather than drawing directly onto the `Frame` so that the scrollbars do not overlap the edges of the image. You will notice that the `paint()` method uses negative x and y values. This starts the drawing outside the Canvas area; as a result, the Canvas displays only part of the image. This is how we do the actual scrolling. (xPos, yPos) are the values given to us from the scrollbars; by positioning the image at (-xPos, -yPos), we ensure that the point (xPos, yPos) appears in the upper left corner of the canvas.

```
class ImageCanvas extends Canvas {
    Image image;
    int xPos, yPos;
    public void redraw (int xPos, int yPos, Image image) {
        this.xPos = xPos;
        this.yPos = yPos;
        this.image = image;
        repaint();
    }
    public void paint (Graphics g) {
        if (image != null)
            g.drawImage (image, -xPos, -yPos, this);
    }
}
```

ScrollingImage provides the framework for the rest of the program. It provides a menu to bring up the Dialog to choose the file, the scrollbars to scroll the scrolling canvas, and the image canvas area. This class also implements event handling methods to capture the scrollbar events, paging keys, and menu events.

```
public class ScrollingImage extends Frame {
    static Scrollbar horizontal, vertical;
    ImageCanvas center;
    int xPos, yPos;
    Image image;
    ImageListDialog ild;
    ScrollingImage () {
        super ("Image Viewer");
        add ("Center", center = new ImageCanvas ());
        add ("South",  horizontal = new Scrollbar (Scrollbar.HORIZONTAL));
        add ("East", vertical = new Scrollbar (Scrollbar.VERTICAL));
        Menu m = new Menu ("File", true);
        m.add ("Open");
        m.add ("Close");
        m.add ("-");
        m.add ("Quit");
        MenuBar mb = new MenuBar();
        mb.add (m);
        setMenuBar (mb);
        resize (400, 300);
    }
    public static void main (String args[]) {
        ScrollingImage si = new ScrollingImage ();
        si.show();
    }
    public boolean handleEvent (Event e) {
```

```
        if (e.id == Event.WINDOW_DESTROY) {
           System.exit(0);
        } else if (e.target instanceof Scrollbar) {
           if (e.target == horizontal) {
               xPos = ((Integer)e.arg).intValue();
           } else if (e.target == vertical) {
               yPos = ((Integer)e.arg).intValue();
           }
           center.redraw (xPos, yPos, image);
        }
        return super.handleEvent (e);
   }
```

This `handleEvent()` method kills the program if the user used the windowing system to exit from it (`WINDOW_DESTROY`). More to the point, if a `Scrollbar` generated the event, `handleEvent()` figures out if it was the horizontal or vertical scrollbar, saves its value as the x or y position, and redraws the image in the new location. Finally, it calls `super.handleEvent()`; as we will see in the following code, other events that we care about (key events and menu events) we don't want to handle here—we would rather handle them normally, in `action()` and `keyDown()` methods.

```
public void processImage () {
    image = getToolkit().getImage (ild.getName());
    MediaTracker tracker = new MediaTracker (this);
    tracker.addImage (image, 0);
    try {
        tracker.waitForAll();
    } catch (InterruptedException ie) {
    }
    xPos = 0;
    yPos = 0;
    int imageHeight = image.getHeight (this);
    int imageWidth = image.getWidth (this);
    vertical.setValues (0, 5, 0, imageHeight);
    horizontal.setValues (0, 5, 0, imageWidth);
    center.redraw (xPos, yPos, image);
}
```

`processImage()` reads the image's filename, calls `getImage()`, and sets up a `Media-Tracker` to wait for the image to load. Once the image has loaded, it reads the height and width, and uses these to set the maximum values for the vertical and horizontal scrollbars by calling `setValues()`. The scrollbars' minimum and initial values are both 0. The size of the scrollbar "handle" is set to 5, rather than trying to indicate the visible portion of the image.

```
public boolean action (Event e, Object o) {
    if (e.target instanceof MenuItem) {
        if ("Open".equals (o)) {
            // If showing already, do not show again
            if ((ild == null) || (!ild.isShowing())) {
```

```
                        ild = new ImageListDialog (this);
                        ild.show();
                    }
                } else if ("Close".equals(o)) {
                    image = null;
                    center.redraw (xPos, yPos, image);
                } else if ("Quit".equals(o)) {
                    System.exit(0);
                }
                return true;
            }
            return false;
        }
```

action() handles menu events. If the user selected Open, it displays the dialog box that selects a file. Close redraws the canvas with a null image; Quit exits the program. If any of these events occurred, action() returns true, indicating that the event was fully handled. If any other event occurred, action() returns false, so that the system will deliver the event to any other methods that might be interested in it.

```
        public boolean keyDown (Event e, int key) {
            if (e.id == Event.KEY_ACTION) {
                Scrollbar target = null;
                switch (key) {
                    case Event.HOME:
                        target = vertical;
                        vertical.setValue(vertical.getMinimum());
                        break;
                    case Event.END:
                        target = vertical;
                        vertical.setValue(vertical.getMaximum());
                        break;
                    case Event.PGUP:
                        target = vertical;
                        vertical.setValue(vertical.getValue()
                                - vertical.getPageIncrement());
                        break;
                    case Event.PGDN:
                        target = vertical;
                        vertical.setValue(vertical.getValue()
                                + vertical.getPageIncrement());
                        break;
                    case Event.UP:
                        target = vertical;
                        vertical.setValue(vertical.getValue()
                                - vertical.getLineIncrement());
                        break;
                    case Event.DOWN:
                        target = vertical;
                        vertical.setValue(vertical.getValue()
                                + vertical.getLineIncrement());
                        break;
```

```
            case Event.LEFT:
                target = horizontal;
                if (e.controlDown())
                    horizontal.setValue(horizontal.getValue() -
                        horizontal.getPageIncrement());
                else
                    horizontal.setValue(horizontal.getValue() -
                        horizontal.getLineIncrement());
                break;
            case Event.RIGHT:
                target = horizontal;
                if (e.controlDown())
                    horizontal.setValue(horizontal.getValue() +
                        horizontal.getPageIncrement());
                else
                    horizontal.setValue(horizontal.getValue() +
                        horizontal.getLineIncrement());
                break;
            default:
                return false;
            }
            Integer value = new Integer (target.getValue());
            postEvent (new Event ((Object)target,
                    Event.SCROLL_ABSOLUTE, (Object)value));
            return true;
        }
        return false;
    }
}
```

keyDown() isn't really necessary, but it adds a nice extension to our scrollbars: in
addition to using the mouse, the user can scroll with the arrow keys. Pressing an
arrow key generates a KEY_ACTION event. If we have one of these events, we check
what kind of key it was, then compute a new scrollbar value, then call setValue()
to set the appropriate scrollbar to this value. For example, if the user presses the
page up key, we read the page increment, add it to the current value of the vertical
scrollbar, and then set the vertical scrollbar accordingly. (Note that this works even
though nondefault page and line increments aren't implemented correctly.) The
one trick here is that we have to get the rest of the program to realize that the
scrollbar values have changed. To do so, we create a new SCROLL_ABSOLUTE event,
and call postEvent() to deliver it.

11.3 The Adjustable Interface

The Adjustable interface is new to Java 1.1. It provides the method signatures
required for an object that lets you adjust a bounded integer value. It is currently
implemented by Scrollbar and returned by two methods within ScrollPane.

11.3.1 Constants of the Adjustable Interface

There are two direction specifiers for `Adjustable`.

public final static int HORIZONTAL ★

   `HORIZONTAL` is the constant for horizontal orientation.

public final static int VERTICAL ★

   `VERTICAL` is the constant for vertical orientation.

11.3.2 Methods of the Adjustable Interface

public abstract int getOrientation () ★

   The `getOrientation()` method is for returning the current orientation of the
   adjustable object, either `Adjustable.HORIZONTAL` or `Adjustable.VERTICAL`.

   `setOrientation()` is not part of the interface. Not all adjustable objects need
   to be able to alter orientation. For example, `Scrollbar` instances can change
   their orientation, but each `Adjustable` instance associated with a `ScrollPane`
   has a fixed, unchangeable orientation.

public abstract int getVisibleAmount () ★

   The `getVisibleAmount()` method lets you retrieve the size of the visible slider
   of the adjustable object.

public abstract void setVisibleAmount (int amount) ★

   The `setVisibleAmount()` method lets you change the size of the visible slider
   to `amount`.

public abstract int getValue () ★

   The `getValue()` method lets you retrieve the current value of the adjustable
   object.

public abstract void setValue (int value) ★

   The `setValue()` method lets you change the value of the adjustable object to
   `value`.

public abstract int getMinimum ()

   The `getMinimum()` method lets you retrieve the current minimum setting for
   the object.

public abstract void setMinimum (int minimum) ★

   The `setMinimum()` method lets you change the minimum value of the
   adjustable object to `minimum`.

public abstract int getMaximum () ★

> The getMaximum() method lets you retrieve the current maximum setting for the object.

public abstract void setMaximum (int maximum) ★

> The setMaximum() method lets you change the maximum value of the adjustable object to maximum.

public abstract int getUnitIncrement () ★

> The getUnitIncrement() method lets you retrieve the current line increment.

public abstract void setUnitIncrement (int amount) ★

> The setUnitIncrement() method lets you change the line increment amount of the adjustable object to amount.

public abstract int getBlockIncrement () ★

> The getBlockIncrement() method lets you retrieve the current page increment.

public abstract void setBlockIncrement (int amount) ★

> The setBlockIncrement() method lets you change the paging increment amount of the adjustable object to amount.

public abstract void addAdjustmentListener(AdjustmentListener listener) ★

> The addAdjustmentListener() method lets you register listener as an object interested in being notified when an AdjustmentEvent passes through the EventQueue with this Adjustable object as its target.

public abstract void removeAdjustmentListener(ItemListener listener) ★

> The removeAdjustmentListener() method removes listener as a interested listener. If listener is not registered, nothing happens.

11.4 ScrollPane

A ScrollPane is a Container with built-in scrollbars that can be used to scroll its contents. In the current implementation, a ScrollPane can hold only one Component and has no layout manager. The component within a ScrollPane is always given its preferred size. While the scrollpane's inability to hold multiple components sounds like a deficiency, it isn't; there's no reason you can't put a Panel inside a ScrollPane, put as many components as you like inside the Panel, and give the Panel any layout manager you wish.

Scrolling is handled by the ScrollPane peer, so processing is extremely fast. In Example 11-1, the user moves a Scrollbar to trigger a scrolling event, and the peer sends the event to the Java program to find someone to deal with it. Once it identifies the target, it posts the event, then tries to find a handler. Eventually, the applet's `handleEvent()` method is called to reposition the `ImageCanvas`. The new position is then given to the peer, which finally redisplays the `Canvas`. Although most of the real work is behind the scenes, it is still happening. With `ScrollPane`, the peer generates and handles the event itself, which is much more efficient.

11.4.1 ScrollPane Methods

Constants

The `ScrollPane` class contains three constants that can be used to control its scrollbar display policy. The constants are fairly self-explanatory. The constants are used in the constructor for a `ScrollPane` instance.

public static final int SCROLLBARS_AS_NEEDED ★

> `SCROLLBARS_AS_NEEDED` is the default scrollbar display policy. With this policy, the `ScrollPane` displays each scrollbar only if the `Component` is too large in the scrollbar's direction.

public static final int SCROLLBARS_ ALWAYS ★

> With the `SCROLLBARS_ALWAYS` display policy, the `ScrollPane` should always display both scrollbars, whether or not they are needed.

public static final int SCROLLBARS_ NEVER ★

> With the `SCROLLBARS_NEVER` display policy, the `ScrollPane` should never display scrollbars, even when the object is bigger than the `ScrollPane`'s area. When using this mode, you should provide some means for the user to scroll, either through a button outside the container or by listening for events happening within the container.

Constructors

public ScrollPane () ★

> The first constructor creates an instance of `ScrollPane` with the default scrollbar display policy setting, `SCROLLBARS_AS_NEEDED`.

public ScrollPane (int scrollbarDisplayPolicy) ★

> The other constructor creates an instance of `ScrollPane` with a scrollbar setting of `scrollbarDisplayPolicy`. If `scrollbarDisplayPolicy` is not one of the class constants, this constructor throws the `IllegalArgumentException` run-time exception.

Layout methods

public final void setLayout(LayoutManager mgr) ★

The setLayout() method of ScrollPane throws an AWTError. It overrides the setLayout() method of Container to prevent you from changing a Scroll-Pane's layout manager.

public void doLayout () ★
public void layout () ☆

The doLayout() method of ScrollPane shapes the contained object to its preferred size.

layout() is another name for this method.

public final void addImpl(Component comp, Object constraints, int index) ★

The addImpl() method of ScrollPane permits only one object to be added to the ScrollPane. It overides the addImpl() method of Container to enforce the ScrollPane's limitations on adding components. If index > 0, addImpl() throws the run-time exception IllegalArgumentException. If a component is already within the ScrollPane, it is removed before comp is added. The constraints parameter is ignored.

Scrolling methods

public int getScrollbarDisplayPolicy() ★

The getScrollbarDisplayPolicy() method retrieves the current display policy, as set by the constructor. You cannot change the policy once it has been set. The return value is one of the class constants: SCROLLBARS_AS_NEEDED, SCROLLBARS_ALWAYS, or SCROLLBARS_NEVER.

public Dimension getViewportSize() ★

The getViewportSize() method returns the current size of the ScrollPane, less any Insets, as a Dimension object. The size is given in pixels and has an initial value of 100 x 100.

public int getHScrollbarHeight() ★

The getHScrollbarHeight() method retrieves the height in pixels of a horizontal scrollbar. The value returned is without regard to the display policy; that is, you may be given a height even if the scrollbar is not displayed. This method may return 0 if the scrollbar's height cannot be calculated at this time (no peer) or if you are using the SCROLLBARS_NEVER display policy.

The width of a horizontal scrollbar is just getViewportSize().width.

public int getVScrollbarWidth() ★

The getVScrollbarWidth() method retrieves the width in pixels of a vertical scrollbar. The value returned is without regard to the display policy; that is, you may be given a width even if the scrollbar is not displayed. This method may return 0 if the scrollbar's width cannot be calculated at this time (no peer) or if you are using the SCROLLBARS_NEVER display policy.

The height of a vertical scrollbar is just getViewportSize().height.

public Adjustable getHAdjustable() ★

The getHAdjustable() method returns the adjustable object representing the horizontal scrollbar (or null if it is not present). Through the methods of Adjustable, you can get the different settings of the scrollbar.

The object that this method returns is an instance of the package private class ScrollPaneAdjustable, which implements the Adjustable interface. this class allows you to register listeners for the scrollpane's events and inquire about various properties of the pane's scrollbars. It does not let you set some scrollbar properties; the setMinimum(), setMaximum(), and setVisibleAmount() methods throw an AWTError when called.

public Adjustable getVAdjustable() ★

The getVAdjustable() method returns the adjustable object representing the vertical scrollbar (or null if it is not present). Through the methods of Adjustable, you can get the different settings of the scrollbar.

The object that this method returns is an instance of the package private class ScrollPaneAdjustable, which implements the Adjustable interface. this class allows you to register listeners for the scrollpane's events and inquire about various properties of the pane's scrollbars. It does not let you set some scrollbar properties; the setMinimum(), setMaximum(), and setVisibleAmount() methods throw an AWTError when called.

public void setScrollPosition(int x, int y) ★

This setScrollPosition() method moves the ScrollPane to the designated location if possible. The x and y arguments are scrollbar settings, which should be interpreted in terms of the minimum and maximum values given to you by the horizontal and vertical Adjustable objects (returned by the previous two methods). If the ScrollPane does not have a child component, this method throws the run-time exception NullPointerException. You can also move the ScrollPane by calling the Adjustable.setValue() method of one of the scrollpane's Adjustable objects.

public void setScrollPosition(Point p) ★

    This `setScrollPosition()` method calls the previous with parameters of `p.x`, and `p.y`.

public Point getScrollPosition() ★

    The `getScrollPosition()` method returns the current position of both the scrollpane's `Adjustable` objects as a `Point`. If there is no component within the `ScrollPane`, `getScrollPosition()` throws the `NullPointerException` runtime exception. Another way to get this information is by calling the `Adjustable.getValue()` method of each `Adjustable` object.

Miscellaneous methods

public void printComponents (Graphics g) ★

    The `printComponents()` method of `ScrollPane` prints the single component it contains. This is done by clipping the context g to the size of the display area and calling the contained component's `printAll()` method.

public synchronized void addNotify () ★

    The `addNotify()` method creates the `ScrollPane` peer. If you override this method, call `super.addNotify()` first, then add your customizations for the new class. You will then be able to do everything you need with the information about the newly created peer.

protected String paramString () ★

    `ScrollPane` doesn't have its own `toString()` method; so when you call the `toString()` method of a `ScrollPane`, you are actually calling the `Component.toString()` method. This in turn calls `paramString()`, which builds the string to display. For a `ScrollPane`, `paramString()` adds the current scroll position, insets, and scrollbar display policy. For example:

```
java.awt.ScrollPane[scrollpane0,0,0,0x0,invalid,ScrollPosition=(0,0),
        Insets=(0,0,0,0),ScrollbarDisplayPolicy=always]
```

11.4.2 ScrollPane Events

The `ScrollPane` peer deals with the scrolling events for you. It is not necessary to catch or listen for these events. As with any other `Container`, you can handle the 1.0 events of the object you contain or listen for 1.1 events that happen within you.

11.4.3 Using a ScrollPane

The following applet demonstrates one way to use a `ScrollPane`. Basically, you place the object you want to scroll in the `ScrollPane` by calling the `add()` method.

This can be a Panel with many objects on it or a Canvas with an image drawn on it. You then add as many objects as you want to the Panel or scribble on the Canvas to your heart's delight. No scrolling event handling is necessary. That is all there is to it. To make this example a little more interesting, whenever you select a button, the ScrollPane scrolls to a randomly selected position. Figure 11-4 displays the screen.

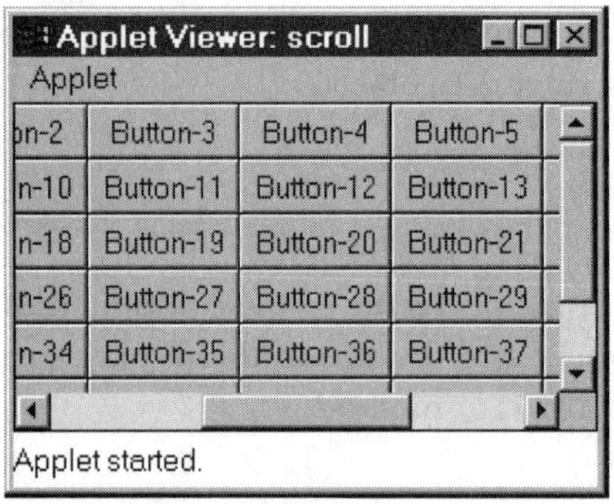

Figure 11–4: A ScrollPane containing many buttons

Here's the code:

```
// Java 1.1 only
import java.awt.*;
import java.awt.event.*;
import java.applet.*;
public class scroll extends Applet implements ActionListener, ContainerListener {
    ScrollPane sp = new ScrollPane (ScrollPane.SCROLLBARS_ALWAYS);
    public void init () {
        setLayout (new BorderLayout ());
        Panel p = new Panel(new GridLayout (7, 8));
        p.addContainerListener (this);
        for (int j=0;j<50;j++)
            p.add (new Button ("Button-" + j));
        sp.add (p);
        add (sp, "Center");
    }
    public void componentAdded(ContainerEvent e) {
        if (e.getID() == ContainerEvent.COMPONENT_ADDED) {
            if (e.getChild() instanceof Button) {
                Button b = (Button)e.getChild();
                b.addActionListener(this);
            }
        }
    }
    public void componentRemoved(ContainerEvent e) {
    }
    public void actionPerformed (ActionEvent e) {
        Component c = sp.getComponent();
```

```
            Dimension d = c.getSize();
            sp.setScrollPosition ((int)(Math.random()*d.width),
                (int)(Math.random()*d.height));
        }
    }
```

Working with the ScrollPane itself is easy; we just create one, add a Panel to it, set the Panel's layout manager to GridLayout, and add a lot of buttons to the Panel. The applet itself is the action listener for all the buttons; when anybody clicks a button, actionPerformed() is called, which generates a new random position based on the viewport size and sets the new scrolling position accordingly by calling setScrollPosition().

The more interesting part of this applet is the way it works with buttons. Instead of directly adding a listener for each button, we add a ContainerListener to the containing panel and let it add listeners. Although this may seem like extra work here, it demonstrates how you can use container events to take actions whenever someone adds or removes a component. At first glance, you might ask why I didn't just call enableEvents(AWTEvent.CONTAINER_EVENT_MASK) and override the applet's processContainerEvent() to attach the listeners. If we were only adding our components to the applet, that would work great. Unfortunately, the applet is not notified when buttons are added to an unrelated panel. It would be notified only when the panel was added to the applet.

12

In this chapter:
- *ImageObserver*
- *ColorModel*
- *ImageProducer*
- *ImageConsumer*
- *ImageFilter*

Image Processing

The image processing parts of Java are buried within the `java.awt.image` package. The package consists of three interfaces and eleven classes, two of which are abstract. They are as follows:

- The `ImageObserver` interface provides the single method necessary to support the asynchronous loading of images. The interface implementers watch the production of an image and can react when certain conditions arise. We briefly touched on `ImageObserver` when we discussed the `Component` class (in Chapter 5, *Components*), because `Component` implements the interface.

- The `ImageConsumer` and `ImageProducer` interfaces provide the means for low level image creation. The `ImageProducer` provides the source of the pixel data that is used by the `ImageConsumer` to create an `Image`.

- The `PixelGrabber` and `ImageFilter` classes, along with the `AreaAveragingScaleFilter`, `CropImageFilter`, `RGBImageFilter`, and `ReplicateScaleFilter` subclasses, provide the tools for working with images. `PixelGrabber` consumes pixels from an `Image` into an array. The `ImageFilter` classes modify an existing image to produce another `Image` instance. `CropImageFilter` makes smaller images; `RGBImageFilter` alters pixel colors, while `AreaAveragingScaleFilter` and `ReplicateScaleFilter` scale images up and down using different algorithms. All of these classes implement `ImageConsumer` because they take pixel data as input.

- `MemoryImageSource` and `FilteredImageSource` produce new images. `MemoryImageSource` takes an array and creates an image from it. `FilteredImageSource` uses an `ImageFilter` to read and modify data from another image and produces the new image based on the original. Both `MemoryImageSource` and `FilteredImageSource` implement `ImageProducer` because they produce new pixel data.

- `ColorModel` and its subclasses, `DirectColorModel` and `IndexColorModel`, provide the palette of colors available when creating an image or tell you the palette used when using `PixelGrabber`.

The classes in the `java.awt.image` package let you create `Image` objects at runtime. These classes can be used to rotate images, make images transparent, create image viewers for unsupported graphics formats, and more.

12.1 *ImageObserver*

As you may recall from Chapter 2, *Simple Graphics*, the last parameter to the `draw-Image()` method is the image's `ImageObserver`. However, in Chapter 2 I also said that you can use `this` as the image observer and forget about it. Now it's time to ask the obvious questions: what is an image observer, and what is it for?

Because `getImage()` acquires an image asynchronously, the entire `Image` object might not be fully loaded when `drawImage()` is called. The `ImageObserver` interface provides the means for a component to be told asynchronously when additional information about the image is available. The `Component` class implements the `imageUpdate()` method (the sole method of the `ImageObserver` interface), so that method is inherited by any component that renders an image. Therefore, when you call `drawImage()`, you can pass `this` as the final argument; the component on which you are drawing serves as the `ImageObserver` for the drawing process. The communication between the image observer and the image consumer happens behind the scenes; you never have to worry about it, unless you want to write your own `imageUpdate()` method that does something special as the image is being loaded.

If you call `drawImage()` to display an image created in local memory (either for double buffering or from a `MemoryImageSource`), you can set the `ImageObserver` parameter of `drawImage()` to `null` because no asynchrony is involved; the entire image is available immediately, so an `ImageObserver` isn't needed.

12.1.1 *ImageObserver Interface*

Constants

The various flags associated with the `ImageObserver` are used for the `infoflags` argument to `imageUpdate()`. The flags indicate what kind of information is available and how to interpret the other arguments to `imageUpdate()`. Two or more flags are often combined (by an OR operation) to show that several kinds of information are available.

public static final int WIDTH

When the WIDTH flag is set, the width argument to imageUpdate() correctly indicates the image's width. Subsequent calls to getWidth() for the Image return the valid image width. If you call getWidth() before this flag is set, expect it to return -1.

public static final int HEIGHT

When the HEIGHT flag is set, the height argument to imageUpdate() correctly indicates the image's height. Subsequent calls to getHeight() for the Image return the valid image height. If you call getHeight() before this flag is set, expect it to return -1.

public static final int PROPERTIES

When the PROPERTIES flag is set, the image's properties are available. Subsequent calls to getProperty() return valid image properties.

public static final int SOMEBITS

When the SOMEBITS flag of infoflags (from imageUpdate()) is set, the image has started loading and at least some of its content are available for display. When this flag is set, the x, y, width, and height arguments to imageUpdate() indicate the bounding rectangle for the portion of the image that has been delivered so far.

public static final int FRAMEBITS

When the FRAMEBITS flag of infoflags is set, a complete frame of a multi-frame image has been loaded and can be drawn. The remaining parameters to imageUpdate() should be ignored (x, y, width, height).

public static final int ALLBITS

When the ALLBITS flag of infoflags is set, the image has been completely loaded and can be drawn. The remaining parameters to imageUpdate() should be ignored (x, y, width, height).

public static final int ERROR

When the ERROR flag is set, the production of the image has stopped prior to completion because of a severe problem. ABORT may or may not be set when ERROR is set. Attempts to reload the image will fail. You might get an ERROR because the URL of the Image is invalid (file not found) or the image file itself is invalid (invalid size/content).

public static final int ABORT

When the ABORT flag is set, the production of the image has aborted prior to completion. If ERROR is not set, a subsequent attempt to draw the image may succeed. For example, an image would abort without an error if a network error occurred (e.g., a timeout on the HTTP connection).

Method

public boolean imageUpdate (Image image, int infoflags, int x, int y, int width, int height)

The `imageUpdate()` method is the sole method in the `ImageObserver` interface. It is called whenever information about an image becomes available. To register an image observer for an image, pass an object that implements the `ImageObserver` interface to `getWidth()`, `getHeight()`, `getProperty()`, `prepareImage()`, or `drawImage()`.

The `image` parameter to `imageUpdate()` is the image being rendered on the observer. The `infoflags` parameter is a set of `ImageObserver` flags ORed together to signify the current information available about `image`. The meaning of the `x`, `y`, `width`, and `height` parameters depends on the current `infoflags` settings.   .

Implementations of `imageUpdate()` should return `true` if additional information about the image is desired; returning `false` means that you don't want any additional information, and consequently, `imageUpdate()` should not be called in the future for this image. The default `imageUpdate()` method returns `true` if neither `ABORT` nor `ALLBITS` are set in the `infoflags`—that is, the method `imageUpdate()` is interested in further information if no errors have occurred and the image is not complete. If either flag is set, `imageUpdate()` returns `false`.

You should not call `imageUpdate()` directly—unless you are developing an `ImageConsumer`, in which case you may find it worthwhile to override the default `imageUpdate()` method, which all components inherit from the `Component` class.

12.1.2 Overriding imageUpdate

Instead of bothering with the `MediaTracker` class, you can override the `imageUpdate()` method and use it to notify you when an image is completely loaded. Example 12-1 demonstrates the use of `imageUpdate()`, along with a way to force your images to load immediately. Here's how it works: the `init()` method calls `getImage()` to request image loading at some time in the future. Instead of waiting for `drawImage()` to trigger the loading process, `init()` forces loading to start by calling `prepareImage()`, which also registers an image observer. `prepareImage()` is a method of the `Component` class discussed in Chapter 5.

The `paint()` method doesn't attempt to draw the image until the variable `loaded` is set to `true`. The `imageUpdate()` method checks the `infoflags` argument to see whether `ALLBITS` is set; when it is set, `imageUpdate()` sets `loaded` to `true`, and schedules a call to `paint()`. Thus, `paint()` doesn't call `drawImage()` until the method `imageUpdate()` has discovered that the image is fully loaded.

Example 12–1: imageUpdate Override.

```
import java.applet.*;
import java.awt.*;
import java.awt.image.ImageObserver;
public class imageUpdateOver extends Applet {
    Image image;
    boolean loaded = false;
    public void init () {
        image = getImage (getDocumentBase(), "rosey.jpg");
        prepareImage (image, -1, -1, this);
    }
    public void paint (Graphics g) {
        if (loaded)
            g.drawImage (image, 0, 0, this);
    }
    public void update (Graphics g) {
        paint (g);
    }
    public synchronized boolean imageUpdate (Image image, int infoFlags,
                        int x, int y, int width, int height) {
        if ((infoFlags & ImageObserver.ALLBITS) != 0) {
            loaded = true;
            repaint();
            return false;
        } else {
            return true;
        }
    }
}
```

Note that the call to prepareImage() is absolutely crucial. It is needed both to start image loading and to register the image observer. If prepareImage() were omitted, imageUpdate() would never be called, loaded would not be set, and paint() would never attempt to draw the image. As an alternative, you could use the Media-Tracker class to force loading to start and monitor the loading process; that approach might give you some additional flexibility.

12.2 ColorModel

A color model determines how colors are represented within AWT. ColorModel is an abstract class that you can subclass to specify your own representation for colors. AWT provides two concrete subclasses of ColorModel that you can use to build your own color model; they are DirectColorModel and IndexColorModel. These two correspond to the two ways computers represent colors internally.

Most modern computer systems use 24 bits to represent each pixel. These 24 bits contain 8 bits for each primary color (red, green, blue); each set of 8 bits represents the intensity of that color for the particular pixel. This arrangement yields the familiar "16 million colors" that you see in advertisements. It corresponds closely to Java's direct color model.

However, 24 bits per pixel, with something like a million pixels on the screen, adds up to a lot of memory. In the dark ages, memory was expensive, and devoting this much memory to a screen buffer cost too much. Therefore, designers used fewer bits—possibly as few as three, but more often eight—for each pixel. Instead of representing the colors directly in these bits, the bits were an index into a color map. Graphics programs would load the color map with the colors they were interested in and then represent each pixel by using the index of the appropriate color in the map. For example, the value 1 might represent fuschia; the value 2 might represent puce. Full information about how to display each color (the red, green, and blue components that make up fuschia or puce) is contained only in the color map. This arrangement corresponds closely to Java's indexed color model.

Because Java is platform-independent, you don't need to worry about how your computer or the user's computer represents colors. Your programs can use an indexed or direct color map as appropriate. Java will do the best it can to render the colors you request. Of course, if you use 5,000 colors on a computer that can only display 256, Java is going to have to make compromises. It will decide which colors to put in the color map and which colors are close enough to the colors in the color map, but that's done behind your back.

Java's default color model uses 8 bits per pixel for red, green, and blue, along with another 8 bits for alpha (transparency) level. However, as I said earlier, you can create your own ColorModel if you want to work in some other scheme. For example, you could create a grayscale color model for black and white pictures, or an HSB (hue, saturation, brightness) color model if you are more comfortable working with this system. Your color model's job will be to take a pixel value in your representation and translate that value into the corresponding alpha, red, green, and blue values. If you are working with a grayscale image, your image producer could deliver grayscale values to the image consumer, plus a ColorModel that tells the consumer how to render these gray values in terms of ARGB components.

12.2.1 ColorModel Methods

Constructors

public ColorModel (int bits)

There is a single constructor for ColorModel. It has one parameter, bits, which describes the number of bits required per pixel of an image. Since this is an abstract class, you cannot call this constructor directly. Since each pixel value must be stored within an integer, the maximum value for bits is 32. If you request more, you get 32.

Pseudo-constructors

public static ColorModel getRGBdefault()

> The getRGBdefault() method returns the default ColorModel, which has 8
> bits for each of the components alpha, red, green, and blue. The order the
> pixels are stored in an integer is 0xAARRGGBB, or alpha in highest order
> byte, down to blue in the lowest.

Other methods

public int getPixelSize ()

> The getPixelSize() method returns the number of bits required for each
> pixel as described by this color model. That is, it returns the number of bits
> passed to the constructor.

public abstract int getAlpha (int pixel)

> The getAlpha() method returns the alpha component of pixel for a color
> model. Its range must be between 0 and 255, inclusive. A value of 0 means the
> pixel is completely transparent and the background will appear through the
> pixel. A value of 255 means the pixel is opaque and you cannot see the back-
> ground behind it.

public abstract int getRed (int pixel)

> The getRed() method returns the red component of pixel for a color model.
> Its range must be between 0 and 255, inclusive. A value of 0 means the pixel
> has no red in it. A value of 255 means red is at maximum intensity.

public abstract int getGreen (int pixel)

> The getGreen() method returns the green component of pixel for a color
> model. Its range must be between 0 and 255, inclusive. A value of 0 means the
> pixel has no green in it. A value of 255 means green is at maximum intensity.

public abstract int getBlue (int pixel)

> The getBlue() method returns the blue component of pixel for a color
> model. Its range must be between 0 and 255, inclusive. A value of 0 means the
> pixel has no blue in it. A value of 255 means blue is at maximum intensity.

public int getRGB(int pixel)

> The getRGB() method returns the color of pixel in the default RGB color
> model. If a subclass has changed the ordering or size of the different color
> components, getRGB() will return the pixel in the RGB color model (0xAAR-
> RGGBB order). In theory, the subclass does not need to override this method,
> unless it wants to make it final. Making this method final may yield a signifi-
> cant performance improvement.

public void finalize ()

>   The garbage collector calls `finalize()` when it determines that the Color-Model object is no longer needed. `finalize()` frees any internal resources that the `ColorModel` object has used.

12.2.2 DirectColorModel

The `DirectColorModel` class is a concrete subclass of `ColorModel`. It specifies a color model in which each pixel contains all the color information (alpha, red, green, and blue values) explicitly. Pixels are represented by 32-bit (`int`) quantities; the constructor lets you change which bits are allotted to each component.

All of the methods in this class, except constructors, are final, because of assumptions made by the implementation. You can create subclasses of `DirectColor-Model`, but you can't override any of its methods. However, you should not need to develop your own subclass. Just create an instance of `DirectColorModel` with the appropriate constructor. Any subclassing results in serious performance degradation, because you are going from fast, static final method calls to dynamic method lookups.

Constructors

public DirectColorModel (int bits, int redMask, int greenMask, int blueMask,
int alphaMask)

>   This constructor creates a `DirectColorModel` in which bits represents the total number of bits used to represent a pixel; it must be less than or equal to 32. The `redMask`, `greenMask`, `blueMask`, and `alphaMask` specify where in a pixel each color component exists. Each of the bit masks must be contiguous (e.g., red cannot be the first, fourth, and seventh bits of the pixel), must be smaller than 2^{bits}, and should not exceed 8 bits. (You cannot display more than 8 bits of data for any color component, but the mask can be larger.) Combined, the masks together should be bits in length. The default RGB color model is:
>
>   ```
>   new DirectColorModel (32, 0x00ff0000, 0x0000ff00, 0x000000ff, 0xff000000)
>   ```
>
>   The run-time exception `IllegalArgumentException` is thrown if any of the following occur:
>
>   •   The bits that are set in a mask are not contiguous.
>
>   •   Mask bits overlap (i.e., the same bit is set in two or more masks).
>
>   •   The number of mask bits exceeds bits.

public DirectColorModel (int bits, int redMask, int greenMask, int blueMask)

This constructor for `DirectColorModel` calls the first with an alpha mask of 0, which means that colors in this color model have no transparency component. All colors will be fully opaque with an alpha value of 255. The same restrictions for the red, green, and blue masks apply.

Methods

final public int getAlpha (int pixel)

The `getAlpha()` method returns the alpha component of `pixel` for the color model as a number from 0 to 255, inclusive. A value of 0 means the pixel is completely transparent, and the background will appear through the pixel. A value of 255 means the pixel is opaque, and you cannot see the background behind it.

final public int getRed (int pixel)

The `getRed()` method returns the red component of `pixel` for the color model. Its range is from 0 to 255. A value of 0 means the pixel has no red in it. A value of 255 means red is at maximum intensity.

final public int getGreen (int pixel)

The `getGreen()` method returns the green component of `pixel` for the color model. Its range is from 0 to 255. A value of 0 means the pixel has no green in it. A value of 255 means green is at maximum intensity.

final public int getBlue (int pixel)

The `getBlue()` method returns the blue component of `pixel` for the color model. Its range is from 0 to 255. A value of 0 means the pixel has no blue in it. A value of 255 means blue is at maximum intensity.

final public int getRGB (int pixel)

The `getRGB()` method returns the color of `pixel` in the default RGB color model. If a subclass has changed the ordering or size of the different color components, `getRGB()` will return the pixel in the RGB color model (0xAARRGGBB order). The `getRGB()` method in this subclass is identical to the method in `ColorModel` but overrides it to make it final.

Other methods

final public int getAlphaMask ()

The `getAlphaMask()` method returns the `alphaMask` from the `DirectColorModel` constructor (or 0 if constructor did not have `alphaMask`). The `alphaMask` specifies which bits in the pixel represent the alpha transparency component of the color model.

final public int getRedMask ()

>The getRedMask() method returns the redMask from the DirectColorModel constructor. The redMask specifies which bits in the pixel represent the red component of the color model.

final public int getGreenMask ()

>The getGreenMask() method returns the greenMask from the DirectColor-Model constructor. The greenMask specifies which bits in the pixel represent the green component of the color model.

final public int getBlueMask ()

>The getBlueMask() method returns the blueMask from the DirectColorModel constructor. The blueMask specifies which bits in the pixel represent the blue component of the color model.

12.2.3 IndexColorModel

The IndexColorModel is another concrete subclass of ColorModel. It specifies a ColorModel that uses a color map lookup table (with a maximum size of 256), rather than storing color information in the pixels themselves. Pixels are represented by an index into the color map, which is at most an 8-bit quantity. Each entry in the color map gives the alpha, red, green, and blue components of some color. One entry in the map can be designated "transparent." This is called the "transparent pixel"; the alpha component of this map entry is ignored.

All of the methods in this class, except constructors, are final because of assumptions made by the implementation. You shouldn't need to create subclasses; you can if necessary, but you can't override any of the IndexColorModel methods. Example 12-2 (later in this chapter) uses an IndexColorModel.

Constructors

There are two sets of constructors for IndexColorModel. The first two constructors use a single-byte array for the color map. The second group implements the color map with separate byte arrays for each color component.

public IndexColorModel (int bits, int size, byte colorMap[], int start, boolean hasalpha, int transparent)

>This constructor creates an IndexColorModel. bits is the number of bits used to represent each pixel and must not exceed 8. size is the number of elements in the map; it must be less than 2^{bits}. hasalpha should be true if the color map includes alpha (transparency) components and false if it doesn't. transparent is the location of the transparent pixel in the map (i.e., the pixel value that is considered transparent). If there is no transparent pixel, set transparent to -1.

The `colorMap` describes the colors used to paint pixels. `start` is the index within the `colorMap` array at which the map begins; prior elements of the array are ignored. An entry in the map consists of three or four consecutive bytes, representing the red, green, blue, and (optionally) alpha components. If `hasalpha` is `false`, a map entry consists of three bytes, and no alpha components are present; if `hasalpha` is `true`, map entries consist of four bytes, and all four components must be present.

For example, consider a pixel whose value is `p`, and a color map with a `hasalpha` set to `false`. Therefore, each element in the color map occupies three consecutive array elements. The red component of that pixel will be located at `colorMap[start + 3*p]`; the green component will be at `colorMap[start + 3*p + 1]`; and so on. The value of size may be smaller than 2^{bits}, meaning that there may be pixel values with no corresponding entry in the color map. These pixel values (i.e., `size` $\le$ `p` $< 2^{bits}$) are painted with the color components set to 0; they are transparent if `hasalpha` is `true`, opaque otherwise.

If `bits` is too large (greater than 8), `size` is too large (greater than 2^{bits}), or the `colorMap` array is too small to hold the map, the run-time exception `ArrayIndexOutOfBoundsException` will be thrown.

public IndexColorModel (int bits, int size, byte colorMap[], int start, boolean hasalpha)
This version of the `IndexColorModel` constructor calls the previous constructor with a `transparent` index of -1; that is, there is no transparent pixel. If `bits` is too large (greater than 8), or `size` is too large (greater than 2^{bits}), or the `colorMap` array is too small to hold the map, the run-time exception, `ArrayIndexOutOfBoundsException` will be thrown.

public IndexColorModel (int bits, int size, byte red[], byte green[], byte blue[], int transparent)
The second set of constructors for `IndexColorModel` is similar to the first group, with the exception that these constructors use three or four separate arrays (one per color component) to represent the color map, instead of a single array.

The `bits` parameter still represents the number of bits in a pixel. `size` represents the number of elements in the color map. `transparent` is the location of the transparent pixel in the map (i.e., the pixel value that is considered transparent). If there is no transparent pixel, set `transparent` to -1.

The `red`, `green`, and `blue` arrays contain the color map itself. These arrays must have at least `size` elements. They contain the red, green, and blue components of the colors in the map. For example, if a pixel is at position `p`, `red[p]` contains the pixel's red component; `green[p]` contains the green component; and blue[p] contains the blue component. The value of size may be smaller than 2^{bits}, meaning that there may be pixel values with no corresponding entry in the color map. These pixel values (i.e., size $\leq$ p $< 2^{bits}$) are painted with the color components set to 0.

If bits is too large (greater than 8), size is too large (greater than 2^{bits}), or the red, green, and blue arrays are too small to hold the map, the run-time exception ArrayIndexOutOfBoundsException will be thrown.

public IndexColorModel (int bits, int size, byte red[], byte green[], byte blue[])

This version of the IndexColorModel constructor calls the previous one with a transparent index of -1; that is, there is no transparent pixel. If bits is too large (greater than 8), size is too large (greater than 2^{bits}), or the red, green, and blue arrays are too small to hold the map, the run-time exception ArrayIndexOutOfBoundsException will be thrown.

public IndexColorModel (int bits, int size, byte red[], byte green[], byte blue[], byte alpha[])

Like the previous constructor, this version creates an IndexColorModel with no transparent pixel. It differs from the previous constructor in that it supports transparency; the array alpha contains the map's transparency values. If bits is too large (greater than 8), size is too large (greater than 2^{bits}), or the red, green, blue, and alpha arrays are too small to hold the map, the run-time exception ArrayIndexOutOfBoundsException will be thrown.

Methods

final public int getAlpha (int pixel)

The getAlpha() method returns the alpha component of pixel for a color model, which is a number between 0 and 255, inclusive. A value of 0 means the pixel is completely transparent and the background will appear through the pixel. A value of 255 means the pixel is opaque and you cannot see the background behind it.

final public int getRed (int pixel)

The getRed() method returns the red component of pixel for a color model, which is a number between 0 and 255, inclusive. A value of 0 means the pixel has no red in it. A value of 255 means red is at maximum intensity.

final public int getGreen (int pixel)

The getGreen() method returns the green component of pixel for a color model, which is a number between 0 and 255, inclusive. A value of 0 means the pixel has no green in it. A value of 255 means green is at maximum intensity.

final public int getBlue (int pixel)

> The getBlue() method returns the blue component of pixel for a color model, which is a number between 0 and 255, inclusive. A value of 0 means the pixel has no blue in it. A value of 255 means blue is at maximum intensity.

final public int getRGB (int pixel)

> The getRGB() method returns the color of pixel in the default RGB color model. If a subclass has changed the ordering or size of the different color components, getRGB() will return the pixel in the RGB color model (0xAAR-RGGBB order). This version of getRGB is identical to the version in the Color-Model class but overrides it to make it final.

Other methods

final public int getMapSize()

> The getMapSize() method returns the size of the color map (i.e., the number of distinct colors).

final public int getTransparentPixel ()

> The getTransparentPixel() method returns the color map index for the transparent pixel in the color model. If no transparent pixel exists, it returns -1. It is not possible to change the transparent pixel after the color model has been created.

final public void getAlphas (byte alphas[])

> The getAlphas() method copies the alpha components of the ColorModel into elements 0 through getMapSize()-1 of the alphas array. Space must already be allocated in the alphas array.

final public void getReds (byte reds[])

> The getReds() method copies the red components of the ColorModel into elements 0 through getMapSize()-1 of the reds array. Space must already be allocated in the reds array.

final public void getGreens (byte greens[])

> The getGreens() method copies the green components of the ColorModel into elements 0 through getMapSize()-1 of the greens array. Space must already be allocated in the greens array.

final public void getBlues (byte blues[])

> The getBlues() method copies the blue components of the ColorModel into elements 0 through getMapSize()-1 of the blues array. Space must already be allocated in the blues array.

12.3 ImageProducer

The ImageProducer interface defines the methods that ImageProducer objects must implement. Image producers serve as sources for pixel data; they may compute the data themselves or interpret data from some external source, like a GIF file. No matter how it generates the data, an image producer's job is to hand that data to an image consumer, which usually renders the data on the screen. The methods in the ImageProducer interface let ImageConsumer objects register their interest in an image. The business end of an ImageProducer—that is, the methods it uses to deliver pixel data to an image consumer—are defined by the ImageConsumer interface. Therefore, we can summarize the way an image producer works as follows:

* It waits for image consumers to register their interest in an image.

* As image consumers register, it stores them in a Hashtable, Vector, or some other collection mechanism.

* As image data becomes available, it loops through all the registered consumers and calls their methods to transfer the data.

There's a sense in which you have to take this process on faith; image consumers are usually well hidden. If you call createImage(), an image consumer will eventually show up.

Every Image has an ImageProducer associated with it; to acquire a reference to the producer, use the getSource() method of Image.

Because an ImageProducer must call methods in the ImageConsumer interface, we won't show an example of a full-fledged producer until we have discussed Image-Consumer.

12.3.1 ImageProducer Interface

Methods

public void addConsumer (ImageConsumer ic)

The addConsumer() method registers ic as an ImageConsumer interested in the Image information. Once an ImageConsumer is registered, the ImageProducer can deliver Image pixels immediately or wait until startProduction() has been called.

Note that one image may have many consumers; therefore, addConsumer() usually stores image consumers in a collection like a Vector or Hashtable. There is one notable exception: if the producer has the image data in memory, `addConsumer()` can deliver the image to the consumer immediately. When `addConsumer()` returns, it has finished with the consumer. In this case, you don't need to manage a list of consumers, because there is only one image consumer at a time. (In this case, `addConsumer()` should be implemented as a synchronized method.)

public boolean isConsumer (ImageConsumer ic)

The `isConsumer()` method checks to see if `ic` is a registered `ImageConsumer` for this `ImageProducer`. If `ic` is registered, `true` is returned. If `ic` is not registered, `false` is returned.

public void removeConsumer (ImageConsumer ic)

The `removeConsumer()` method removes `ic` as a registered `ImageConsumer` for this `ImageProducer`. If `ic` was not a registered `ImageConsumer`, nothing should happen. This is not an error that should throw an exception. Once `ic` has been removed from the registry, the `ImageProducer` should no longer send data to it.

public void startProduction (ImageConsumer ic)

The `startProduction()` method registers `ic` as an `ImageConsumer` interested in the `Image` information and tells the `ImageProducer` to start sending the `Image` data immediately. The `ImageProducer` sends the image data to `ic` and all other registered `ImageConsumer` objects, through `addConsumer()`.

public void requestTopDownLeftRightResend (ImageConsumer ic)

The `requestTopDownLeftRightResend()` method is called by the `ImageConsumer` `ic` requesting that the `ImageProducer` retransmit the `Image` data in top-down, left-to-right order. If the `ImageProducer` is unable to send the data in that order or always sends the data in that order (like with `MemoryImageSource`), it can ignore the call.

12.3.2 *FilteredImageSource*

The `FilteredImageSource` class combines an `ImageProducer` and an `ImageFilter` to create a new `Image`. The image producer generates pixel data for an original image. The `FilteredImageSource` takes this data and uses an `ImageFilter` to produce a modified version: the image may be scaled, clipped, or rotated, or the colors shifted, etc. The `FilteredImageSource` is the image producer for the new image. The `ImageFilter` object transforms the original image's data to yield the new image; it implements the `ImageConsumer` interface. We cover the `ImageConsumer` interface in Section 12.4 and the `ImageFilter` class in Section 12.5. Figure 12-1 shows the relationship between an `ImageProducer`, `FilteredImageSource`, `ImageFilter`, and the `ImageConsumer`.

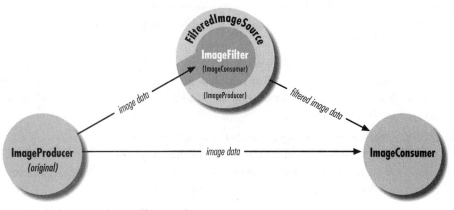

Figure 12–1: Image producers, filters, and consumers

Constructors

public FilteredImageSource (ImageProducer original, ImageFilter filter)

> The `FilteredImageSource` constructor creates an image producer that combines an image, `original`, and a filter, `filter`, to create a new image. The `ImageProducer` of the original image is the constructor's first parameter; given an `Image`, you can acquire its `ImageProducer` by using the `getSource()` method. The following code shows how to create a new image from an original. Section 12.5 shows several extensive examples of image filters.

```
Image image = getImage (new URL
    ("http://www.ora.com/graphics/headers/homepage.gif"));
Image newOne = createImage (new FilteredImageSource
    (image.getSource(), new SomeImageFilter()));
```

ImageProducer interface methods

The `ImageProducer` interface methods maintain an internal table for the image consumers. Since this is private, you do not have direct access to it.

public synchronized void addConsumer (ImageConsumer ic)

> The `addConsumer()` method adds `ic` as an `ImageConsumer` interested in the pixels for this image.

public synchronized boolean isConsumer (ImageConsumer ic)

> The `isConsumer()` method checks to see if `ic` is a registered `ImageConsumer` for this `ImageProducer`. If `ic` is registered, `true` is returned. If not registered, `false` is returned.

public synchronized void removeConsumer (ImageConsumer ic)

   The `removeConsumer()` method removes ic as a registered `ImageConsumer` for this `ImageProducer`.

public void startProduction (ImageConsumer ic)

   The `startProduction()` method registers ic as an `ImageConsumer` interested in the `Image` information and tells the `ImageProducer` to start sending the `Image` data immediately.

public void requestTopDownLeftRightResend (ImageConsumer ic)

   The `requestTopDownLeftRightResend()` method registers ic as an `ImageCon-sumer` interested in the `Image` information and requests the `ImageProducer` to retransmit the `Image` data in top-down, left-to-right order.

12.3.3 MemoryImageSource

The `MemoryImageSource` class allows you to create images completely in memory; you generate pixel data, place it in an array, and hand that array and a `ColorModel` to the `MemoryImageSource` constructor. The `MemoryImageSource` is an image producer that can be used with a consumer to display the image on the screen. For example, you might use a `MemoryImageSource` to display a Mandelbrot image or some other image generated by your program. You could also use a `MemoryImage-Source` to modify a pre-existing image; use `PixelGrabber` to get the image's pixel data, modify that data, and then use a `MemoryImageSource` as the producer for the modified image. Finally, you can use `MemoryImageSource` to simplify implementation of a new image type; you can develop a class that reads an image in some unsupported format from a local file or the network; interprets the image file and puts pixel data into an array; and uses a `MemoryImageSource` to serve as an image producer. This is simpler than implementing an image producer yourself, but it isn't quite as flexible; you lose the ability to display partial images as the data becomes available.

In Java 1.1, `MemoryImageSource` supports multiframe images to animate a sequence. In earlier versions, it was necessary to create a dynamic `ImageFilter` to animate the image.

Constructors

There are six constructors for `MemoryImageSource`, each with slightly different parameters. They all create an image producer that delivers some array of data to an image consumer. The constructors are:

public MemoryImageSource (int w, int h, ColorModel cm, byte pix[], int off, int scan)
public MemoryImageSource (int w, int h, ColorModel cm, byte pix[], int off, int scan,
Hashtable props)

public MemoryImageSource (int w, int h, ColorModel cm, int pix[],
int off, int scan)
public MemoryImageSource (int w, int h, ColorModel cm, int pix[],
int off, int scan, Hashtable props)
public MemoryImageSource (int w, int h, int pix[], int off, int scan)
public MemoryImageSource (int w, int h, int pix[], int off, int scan,
Hashtable props)

The parameters that might be present are:

w   Width of the image being created, in pixels.

h   Height of the image being created, in pixels.

cm The ColorModel that describes the color representation used in the pixel data.
If this parameter is not present, the MemoryImageSource uses the default RGB
color model (ColorModel.getRGBDefault()).

pix[]

> The array of pixel information to be converted into an image. This may be
> either a byte array or an int array, depending on the color model. If you're
> using a direct color model (including the default RGB color model), pix is
> usually an int array; if it isn't, it won't be able to represent all 16 million possi-
> ble colors. If you're using an indexed color model, the array should be a byte
> array. However, if you use an int array with an indexed color model, the Memo-
> ryImageSource ignores the three high-order bytes because an indexed color
> model has at most 256 entries in the color map. In general: if your color
> model requires more than 8 bits of data per pixel, use an int array; if it
> requires 8 bits or less, use a byte array.

off

> The first pixel used in the array (usually 0); prior pixels are ignored.

scan

> The number of pixels per line in the array (usually equal to w). The number of
> pixels per scan line in the array may be larger than the number of pixels in the
> scan line. Extra pixels in the array are ignored.

props

> A Hashtable of the properties associated with the image. If this argument isn't
> present, the constructor assumes there are no properties.

The pixel at location (x, y) in the image is located at pix[y * scan + x + off].

ImageProducer interface methods

In Java 1.0, the ImageProducer interface methods maintain a single internal variable for the image consumer because the image is delivered immediately and synchronously. There is no need to worry about multiple consumers; as soon as one registers, you give it the image, and you're done. These methods keep track of this single ImageConsumer.

In Java 1.1, MemoryImageSource supports animation. One consequence of this new feature is that it isn't always possible to deliver all the image's data immediately. Therefore, the class maintains a list of image consumers that are notified when each frame is generated. Since this list is private, you do not have direct access to it.

public synchronized void addConsumer (ImageConsumer ic)
> The addConsumer() method adds ic as an ImageConsumer interested in the pixels for this image.

public synchronized boolean isConsumer (ImageConsumer ic)
> The isConsumer() method checks to see if ic is a registered ImageConsumer for this ImageProducer. If ic is registered, true is returned. If ic is not registered, false is returned.

public synchronized void removeConsumer (ImageConsumer ic)
> The removeConsumer() method removes ic as a registered ImageConsumer for this ImageProducer.

public void startProduction (ImageConsumer ic)
> The startProduction() method calls addConsumer().

public void requestTopDownLeftRightResend (ImageConsumer ic)
> The requestTopDownLeftRightResend() method does nothing since in-memory images are already in this format or are multiframed, with each frame in this format.

Animation methods

In Java 1.1, MemoryImageSource supports animation; it can now pass multiple frames to interested image consumers. This feature mimics GIF89a's multiframe functionality. (If you have GIF89a animations, you can display them using getImage() and drawImage(); you don't have to build a complicated creature using MemoryImageSource.) . An animation example follows in Example 12-3 (later in this chapter).

public synchronized void setAnimated(boolean animated) ★
> The setAnimated() method notifies the MemoryImageSource if it will be in animation mode (animated is true) or not (animated is false). By default, animation is disabled; you must call this method to generate an image sequence.

To prevent losing data, call this method immediately after calling the Memory-
ImageSource constructor.

public synchronized void setFullBufferUpdates(boolean fullBuffers) ★

The setFullBufferUpdates() method controls how image updates are done
during an animation. It is ignored if you are not creating an animation. If
fullBuffers is true, this method tells the MemoryImageSource that it should
always send all of an image's data to the consumers whenever it received new
data (by a call to newPixels()). If fullBuffers is false, the MemoryImage-
Source sends only the changed portion of the image and notifies consumers
(by a call to ImageConsumer.setHints()) that frames sent will be complete.

Like setAnimated(), setFullBufferUpdates() should be called immediately
after calling the MemoryImageSource constructor, before the animation is
started.

To do the actual animation, you update the image array pix[] that was specified in
the constructor and call one of the overloaded newPixels() methods to tell the
MemoryImageSource that you have changed the image data. The parameters to
newPixels() determine whether you are animating the entire image or just a portion of the image. You can also supply a new array to take pixel data from, replacing pix[]. In any case, pix[] supplies the initial image data (i.e., the first frame of
the animation).

If you have not called setAnimated(true), calls to any version of newPixels() are
ignored.

public void newPixels() ★

The version of newPixels() with no parameters tells the MemoryImageSource
to send the entire pixel data (frame) to all the registered image consumers
again. Data is taken from the original array pix[]. After the data is sent, the
MemoryImageSource notifies consumers that a frame is complete by calling
imageComplete(ImageConsumer.SINGLEFRAMEDONE), thus updating the display
when the image is redisplayed. Remember that in many cases, you don't need
to update the entire image; updating part of the image saves CPU time, which
may be crucial for your application. To update part of the image, call one of
the other versions of newPixels().

public synchronized void newPixels(int x, int y, int w, int h) ★

This newPixels() method sends part of the image in the array pix[] to the
consumers. The portion of the image sent has its upper left corner at the
point (x, y), width w and height h, all in pixels. Changing part of the image
rather than the whole thing saves considerably on system resources. Obviously,
it is appropriate only if most of the image is still. For example, you could use

this method to animate the steam rising from a cup of hot coffee, while leaving the cup itself static (an image that should be familiar to anyone reading JavaSoft's Web site). After the data is sent, consumers are notified that a frame is complete by a call to `imageComplete(ImageConsumer.SINGLEFRAMEDONE)`, thus updating the display when the image is redisplayed.

If `setFullBufferUpdates()` was called, the entire image is sent, and the dimensions of the bounding box are ignored.

public synchronized void newPixels(int x, int y, int w, int h, boolean frameNotify) ★

This `newPixels()` method is identical to the last, with one exception: consumers are notified that new image data is available only when `frameNotify` is true. This method allows you to generate new image data in pieces, updating the consumers only once when you are finished.

If `setFullBufferUpdates()` was called, the entire image is sent, and the dimensions of the bounding box are ignored.

public synchronized void newPixels(byte[] newpix, ColorModel newmodel, int offset,
int scansize) ★
public synchronized void newPixels(int[] newpix, ColorModel newmodel, int offset,
int scansize) ★

These `newPixels()` methods change the source of the animation to the `byte` or int array `newpix[]`, with a `ColorModel` of `newmodel`. `offset` marks the beginning of the data in `newpix` to use, while `scansize` states the number of pixels in `newpix` per line of `Image` data. Future calls to other versions of `newPixels()` should modify `newpix[]` rather than `pix[]`.

Using MemoryImageSource to create a static image

You can create an image by generating an integer or byte array in memory and converting it to an image with `MemoryImageSource`. The following `MemoryImage` applet generates two identical images that display a series of color bars from left to right. Although the images look the same, they were generated differently: the image on the left uses the default `DirectColorModel`; the image on the right uses an `IndexColorModel`.

Because the image on the left uses a `DirectColorModel`, it stores the actual color value of each pixel in an array of integers (`rgbPixels[]`). The image on the right can use a byte array (`indPixels[]`) because the `IndexColorModel` puts the color information in its color map instead of the pixel array; elements of the pixel array need to be large enough only to address the entries in this map. Images that are based on `IndexColorModel` are generally more efficient in their use of space (integer vs. byte arrays, although `IndexColorModel` requires small support arrays) and in performance (if you filter the image).

The output from this example is shown in Figure 12-2. The source is shown in Example 12-2.

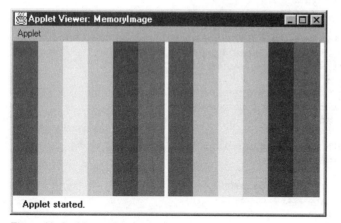

Figure 12–2: MemoryImage applet output

Example 12–2: MemoryImage Test Program

```
import java.applet.*;
import java.awt.*;
import java.awt.image.*;
public class MemoryImage extends Applet {
    Image i, j;
    int width = 200;
    int height = 200;
    public void init () {
        int rgbPixels[] = new int [width*height];
        byte indPixels[] = new byte [width*height];
        int index = 0;
        Color colorArray[] = {Color.red, Color.orange, Color.yellow,
                Color.green, Color.blue, Color.magenta};
        int rangeSize = width / colorArray.length;
        int colorRGB;
        byte colorIndex;
        byte reds[]   = new byte[colorArray.length];
        byte greens[] = new byte[colorArray.length];
        byte blues[]  = new byte[colorArray.length];
        for (int i=0;i<colorArray.length;i++) {
            reds[i]   = (byte)colorArray[i].getRed();
            greens[i] = (byte)colorArray[i].getGreen();
            blues[i]  = (byte)colorArray[i].getBlue();
        }
        for (int y=0;y<height;y++) {
            for (int x=0;x<width;x++) {
                if (x < rangeSize) {
                    colorRGB = Color.red.getRGB();
                    colorIndex = 0;
                } else if (x < (rangeSize*2)) {
```

Example 12–2: MemoryImage Test Program (continued)

```
                    colorRGB = Color.orange.getRGB();
                    colorIndex = 1;
                } else if (x < (rangeSize*3)) {
                    colorRGB = Color.yellow.getRGB();
                    colorIndex = 2;
                } else if (x < (rangeSize*4)) {
                    colorRGB = Color.green.getRGB();
                    colorIndex = 3;
                } else if (x < (rangeSize*5)) {
                    colorRGB = Color.blue.getRGB();
                    colorIndex = 4;
                } else {
                    colorRGB = Color.magenta.getRGB();
                    colorIndex = 5;
                }
                rgbPixels[index] = colorRGB;
                indPixels[index] = colorIndex;
                index++;
            }
        }
        i = createImage (new MemoryImageSource (width, height, rgbPixels,
            0, width));
        j = createImage (new MemoryImageSource (width, height,
            new IndexColorModel (8, colorArray.length, reds, greens, blues),
            indPixels, 0, width));
    }
    public void paint (Graphics g) {
        g.drawImage (i, 0, 0, this);
        g.drawImage (j, width+5, 0, this);
    }
}
```

Almost all of the work is done in init() (which, in a real applet, isn't a terribly good idea; ideally init() should be lightweight). Previously, we explained the color model's use for the images on the left and the right. Toward the end of init(), we create the images i and j by calling createImage() with a MemoryImageSource as the image producer. For image i, we used the simplest MemoryImageSource constructor, which uses the default RGB color model. For j, we called the IndexColorModel constructor within the MemoryImageSource constructor, to create a color map that has only six entries: one for each of the colors we use.

Using MemoryImageSource for animation

As we've seen, Java 1.1 gives you the ability to create an animation using a MemoryImageSource by updating the image data in memory; whenever you have finished an update, you can send the resulting frame to the consumers. This technique gives you a way to do animations that consume very little memory, since you keep overwriting the original image. The applet in Example 12-3 demonstrates Memory-ImageSource's animation capability by creating a Mandelbrot image in memory, updating the image as new points are added. Figure 12-3 shows the results, using four consumers to display the image four times.

Example 12–3: Mandelbrot Program

```
// Java 1.1 only
import java.awt.*;
import java.awt.image.*;
import java.applet.*;

public class Mandelbrot extends Applet implements Runnable {
    Thread animator;
    Image im1, im2, im3, im4;
    public void start() {
        animator = new Thread(this);
        animator.start();
    }
    public synchronized void stop() {
        animator = null;
    }
    public void paint(Graphics g) {
        if (im1 != null)
            g.drawImage(im1, 0, 0, null);
        if (im2 != null)
            g.drawImage(im2, 0, getSize().height / 2, null);
        if (im3 != null)
            g.drawImage(im3, getSize().width / 2, 0, null);
        if (im4 != null)
            g.drawImage(im4, getSize().width / 2, getSize().height / 2, null);
    }
    public void update (Graphics g) {
        paint (g);
    }
    public synchronized void run() {
        Thread.currentThread().setPriority(Thread.MIN_PRIORITY);
        int width = getSize().width / 2;
        int height = getSize().height / 2;
        byte[] pixels = new byte[width * height];
        int index = 0;
        int iteration=0;
        double a, b, p, q, psq, qsq, pnew, qnew;
        byte[] colorMap = {(byte)255, (byte)255, (byte)255, // white
                           (byte)0, (byte)0, (byte)0};       // black
        MemoryImageSource mis = new MemoryImageSource(
            width, height,
            new IndexColorModel (8, 2, colorMap, 0, false, -1),
            pixels, 0, width);
        mis.setAnimated(true);
        im1 = createImage(mis);
        im2 = createImage(mis);
        im3 = createImage(mis);
```

Example 12–3: Mandelbrot Program (continued)

```
            im4 = createImage(mis);
            // Generate Mandelbrot
            final int ITERATIONS = 16;
            for (int y=0; y<height; y++) {
                b = ((double)(y-64))/32;
                for (int x=0; x<width; x++) {
                    a = ((double)(x-64))/32;
                    p=q=0;
                    iteration = 0;
                    while (iteration < ITERATIONS) {
                        psq = p*p;
                        qsq = q*q;
                        if ((psq + qsq) >= 4.0)
                            break;
                        pnew = psq - qsq + a;
                        qnew = 2*p*q+b;
                        p = pnew;
                        q = qnew;
                        iteration++;
                    }
                    if (iteration == ITERATIONS) {
                        pixels[index] = 1;
                        mis.newPixels(x, y, 1, 1);
                        repaint();
                    }
                    index++;
                }
            }
        }
    }
```

Most of the applet in Example 12-3 should be self-explanatory. The init() method starts the thread in which we do our computation. paint() just displays the four images we create. All the work, including the computation, is done in the thread's run() method. run() starts by setting up a color map, creating a MemoryImage-Source with animation enabled and creating four images using that source as the producer. It then does the computation, which I won't explain; for our purposes, the interesting part is what happens when we've computed a pixel. We set the appropriate byte in our data array, pixels[], and then call newPixels(), giving the location of the new pixel and its size (1 by 1) as arguments. Thus, we redraw the images for every new pixel. In a real application, you would probably compute a somewhat larger chunk of new data before updating the screen, but the same principles apply.

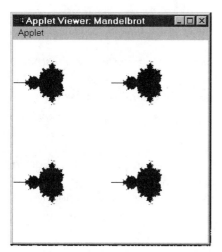

Figure 12–3: Mandelbrot output

12.4 *ImageConsumer*

The ImageConsumer interface specifies the methods that must be implemented to receive data from an ImageProducer. For the most part, that is the only context in which you need to know about the ImageConsumer interface. If you write an image producer, it will be handed a number of obscure objects, about which you know nothing except that they implement ImageConsumer, and that you can therefore call the methods discussed in this section to deliver your data. The chances that you will ever implement an image consumer are rather remote, unless you are porting Java to a new environment. It is more likely that you will want to subclass ImageFilter, in which case you may need to implement some of these methods. But most of the time, you will just need to know how to hand your data off to the next element in the chain.

The java.awt.image package includes two classes that implement ImageConsumer: PixelGrabber and ImageFilter (and its subclasses). These classes are unique in that they don't display anything on the screen. PixelGrabber takes the image data and stores it in a pixel array; you can use this array to save the image in a file, generate a new image, etc. ImageFilter, which is used in conjunction with Filtered-ImageSource, modifies the image data; the FilteredImageSource sends the modified image to another consumer, which can further modify or display the new image. When you draw an image on the screen, the JDK's ImageRepresentation class is probably doing the real work. This class is part of the sun.awt.image package. You really don't need to know anything about it, although you may see ImageRepresentation mentioned in a stack trace if you try to filter beyond the end of a pixel array.

12.4.1 ImageConsumer Interface

Constants

There are two sets of constants for ImageConsumer. One set represents those that can be used for the imageComplete() method. The other is used with the setHints() method. See the descriptions of those methods on how to use them.

The first set of flags is for the imageComplete() method:

public static final int IMAGEABORTED

> The IMAGEABORTED flag signifies that the image creation process was aborted and the image is not complete. In the image production process, an abort could mean multiple things. It is possible that retrying the production would succeed.

public static final int IMAGEERROR

> The IMAGEERROR flag signifies that an error was encountered during the image creation process and the image is not complete. In the image production process, an error could mean multiple things. More than likely, the image file or pixel data is invalid, and retrying won't succeed.

public static final int SINGLEFRAMEDONE

> The SINGLEFRAMEDONE flag signifies that a frame other than the last has completed loading. There are additional frames to display, but a new frame is available and is complete. For an example of this flag in use, see the dynamic ImageFilter example in Example 12-8.

public static final int STATICIMAGEDONE

> The STATICIMAGEDONE flag signifies that the image has completed loading. If this is a multiframe image, all frames have been generated. For an example of this flag in use, see the dynamic ImageFilter example in Example 12-8.

The following set of flags can be ORed together to form the single parameter to the setHints() method. Certain flags do not make sense set together, but it is the responsibility of the concrete ImageConsumer to enforce this.

public static final int COMPLETESCANLINES

> The COMPLETESCANLINES flag signifies that each call to setPixels() will deliver at least one complete scan line of pixels to this consumer.

public static final int RANDOMPIXELORDER

> The RANDOMPIXELORDER flag tells the consumer that pixels are not provided in any particular order. Therefore, the consumer cannot perform optimization that depends on pixel delivery order. In the absence of both COMPLETESCAN-LINES and RANDOMPIXELORDER, the ImageConsumer should assume pixels will arrive in RANDOMPIXELORDER.

public static final int SINGLEFRAME

> The SINGLEFRAME flag tells the consumer that this image contains a single non-changing frame. This is the case with most image formats. An example of an image that does not contain a single frame is the multiframe GIF89a image.

public static final int SINGLEPASS

> The SINGLEPASS flag tells the consumer to expect each pixel once and only once. Certain image formats, like progressive JPEG images, deliver a single image several times, with each pass yielding a sharper image.

public static final int TOPDOWNLEFTRIGHT

> The final setHints() flag, TOPDOWNLEFTRIGHT, tells the consumer to expect the pixels in a top-down, left-right order. This flag will almost always be set.

Methods

The interface methods are presented in the order in which they are normally called by an ImageProducer.

void setDimensions (int width, int height)

> The setDimensions() method should be called once the ImageProducer knows the width and height of the image. This is the actual width and height, not necessarily the scaled size. It is the consumer's responsibility to do the scaling and resizing.

void setProperties (Hashtable properties)

> The setProperties() method should only be called by the ImageProducer if the image has any properties that should be stored for later retrieval with the getProperty() method of Image. Every image format has its own property set. One property that tends to be common is the "comment" property. properties represents the Hashtable of properties for the image; the name of each property is used as the Hashtable key.

void setColorModel (ColorModel model)

> The setColorModel() method gives the ImageProducer the opportunity to tell the ImageConsumer that the ColorModel model will be used for the majority of pixels in the image. The ImageConsumer may use this information for optimization. However, each call to setPixels() contains its own ColorModel, which isn't necessarily the same as the color model given here. In other words, setColorModel() is only advisory; it does not guarantee that all (or any) of the pixels in the image will use this model. Using different color models for different parts of an image is possible, but not recommended.

void setHints (int hints)

An ImageProducer should call the setHints() method prior to any setPixels() calls. The hints are formed by ORing the constants COMPLETESCANLINES, RANDOMPIXELORDER, SINGLEFRAME, SINGLEPASS, and TOPDOWNLEFTRIGHT. These hints give the image consumer information about the order in which the producer will deliver pixels. When the ImageConsumer is receiving pixels, it can take advantage of these hints for optimization.

void setPixels (int x, int y, int width, int height, ColorModel model, byte pixels[],
int offset, int scansize)

An ImageProducer calls the setPixels() method to deliver the image pixel data to the ImageConsumer. The bytes are delivered a rectangle at a time. (x, y) represents the top left corner of the rectangle; its dimensions are width × height. model is the ColorModel used for this set of pixels; different calls to setPixels() may use different color models. The pixels themselves are taken from the byte array pixels. offset is the first element of the pixel array that will be used. scansize is the length of the scan lines in the array. In most cases, you want the consumer to render all the pixels on the scan line; in this case, scansize will equal width. However, there are cases in which you want the consumer to ignore part of the scan line; you may be clipping an image, and the ends of the scan line fall outside the clipping region. In this case, rather than copying the pixels you want into a new array, you can specify a width that is smaller than scansize.

That's a lot of information, but it's easy to summarize. A pixel located at point (x1, y1) within the rectangle being delivered to the consumer is located at position ((y1 - y) * scansize + (x1 - x) + offset) within the array pixels[]. Figure 12-4 shows how the pixels delivered by setPixels() fit into the complete image; Figure 12-5 shows how pixels are stored within the array.

void setPixels (int x, int y, int width, int height, ColorModel model, int pixels[],
int offset, int scansize)

The second setPixels() method is similar to the first. pixels[] is an array of ints; this is necessary when you have more than eight bits of data per pixel.

void imageComplete (int status)

The ImageProducer calls imageComplete() to tell an ImageConsumer that it has transferred a complete image. The status argument is a flag that describes exactly why the ImageProducer has finished. It may have one of the following values: IMAGEABORTED (if the image production was aborted); IMAGEERROR (if an error in producing the image occurred); SINGLEFRAMEDONE (if a single frame of a multiframe image has been completed); or STATICIMAGEDONE (if all pixels have been delivered). When imageComplete() gets called, the ImageConsumer should call the image producer's removeConsumer() method, unless it wants to receive additional frames (status of SINGLEFRAMEDONE).

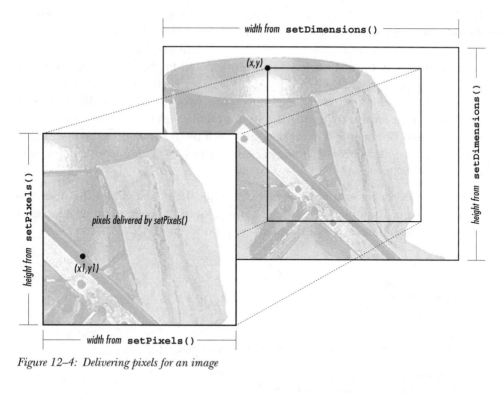

Figure 12–4: Delivering pixels for an image

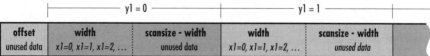

Figure 12–5: Storing pixels in an array

PPMImageDecoder

Now that we have discussed the ImageConsumer interface, we're finally ready to give an example of a full-fledged ImageProducer. This producer uses the methods of the ImageConsumer interface to communicate with image consumers; image consumers use the ImageProducer interface to register themselves with this producer.

Our image producer will interpret images in the PPM format.[*] PPM is a simple image format developed by Jef Poskanzer as part of the *pbmplus* image conversion package. A PPM file starts with a header consisting of the image type, the image's width and height in pixels, and the maximum value of any RGB component. The

---

[*] For more information about PPM and the *pbmplus* package, see *Encyclopedia of Graphics File Formats*, by James D. Murray and William VanRyper (from O'Reilly & Associates). See also *http://www.acme.com/*.

header is entirely in ASCII. The pixel data follows the header; it is either in binary (if the image type is P6) or ASCII (if the image type is P3). The pixel data is simply a series of bytes describing the color of each pixel, moving left to right and top to bottom. In binary format, each pixel is represented by three bytes: one for red, one for green, and one for blue. In ASCII format, each pixel is represented by three numeric values, separated by white space (space, tab, or newline). A comment may occur anywhere in the file, but it would be surprising to see one outside of the header. Comments start with # and continue to the end of the line. ASCII format files are obviously much larger than binary files. There is no compression on either file type.

The PPMImageDecoder source is listed in Example 12-4. The applet that uses this class is shown in Example 12-5. You can reuse a lot of the code in the PPMImageDecoder when you implement your own image producers.

Example 12–4: PPMImageDecoder Source

```
import java.awt.*;
import java.awt.image.*;
import java.util.*;
import java.io.*;

public class PPMImageDecoder implements ImageProducer {

/* Since done in-memory, only one consumer */
    private ImageConsumer consumer;
    boolean loadError = false;
    int width;
    int height;
    int store[][];
    Hashtable props = new Hashtable();
/* Format of Ppm file is single pass/frame, w/ complete scan lines in order */
    private static int PpmHints = (ImageConsumer.TOPDOWNLEFTRIGHT |
                                   ImageConsumer.COMPLETESCANLINES |
                                   ImageConsumer.SINGLEPASS |
                                   ImageConsumer.SINGLEFRAME);
```

The class starts by declaring class variables and constants. We will use the variable PpmHints when we call setHints(). Here, we set this variable to a collection of "hint" constants that indicate we will produce pixel data in top-down, left-right order; we will always send complete scan lines; we will make only one pass over the pixel data (we will send each pixel once); and there is one frame per image (i.e., we aren't producing a multiframe sequence).

The next chunk of code implements the ImageProducer interface; consumers use it to request image data:

```
/* There is only a single consumer. When it registers, produce image. */
/* On error, notify consumer. */

    public synchronized void addConsumer (ImageConsumer ic) {
        consumer = ic;
        try {
            produce();
        }catch (Exception e) {
            if (consumer != null)
                consumer.imageComplete (ImageConsumer.IMAGEERROR);
        }
        consumer = null;
    }

/* If consumer passed to routine is single consumer, return true, else false. */

    public synchronized boolean isConsumer (ImageConsumer ic) {
        return (ic == consumer);
    }

/* Disables consumer if currently consuming. */

    public synchronized void removeConsumer (ImageConsumer ic) {
        if (consumer == ic)
            consumer = null;
    }

/* Production is done by adding consumer. */

    public void startProduction (ImageConsumer ic) {
        addConsumer (ic);
    }

    public void requestTopDownLeftRightResend (ImageConsumer ic) {
        // Not needed.  The data is always in this format.
    }
```

The previous group of methods implements the ImageProducer interface. They are quite simple, largely because of the way this ImageProducer generates images. It builds the image in memory before delivering it to the consumer; you must call the readImage() method (discussed shortly) before you can create an image with this consumer. Because the image is in memory before any consumers can register their interest, we can write an addConsumer() method that registers a consumer and delivers all the data to that consumer before returning. Therefore, we don't need to manage a list of consumers in a Hashtable or some other collection object. We can store the current consumer in an instance variable ic and forget about any others: only one consumer exists at a time. To make sure that only one consumer exists at a time, we synchronize the addConsumer(), isConsumer(), and removeConsumer() methods. Synchronization prevents another consumer from registering itself before the current consumer has finished. If you write an Image-Producer that builds the image in memory before delivering it, you can probably use this code verbatim.

addConsumer() is little more than a call to the method produce(), which handles "consumer relations": it delivers the pixels to the consumer using the methods in the ImageConsumer interface. If produce() throws an exception, addConsumer() calls imageComplete() with an IMAGEERROR status code. Here's the code for the produce() method:

```
/* Production Process:
        Prerequisite: Image already read into store array. (readImage)
                      props / width / height already set (readImage)
        Assumes RGB Color Model - would need to filter to change.
        Sends Ppm Image data to consumer.
        Pixels sent one row at a time.
*/

    private void produce () {
        ColorModel cm = ColorModel.getRGBdefault();
        if (consumer != null) {
            if (loadError) {
                consumer.imageComplete (ImageConsumer.IMAGEERROR);
            } else {
                consumer.setDimensions (width, height);
                consumer.setProperties (props);
                consumer.setColorModel (cm);
                consumer.setHints (PpmHints);
                for (int j=0;j<height;j++)
                    consumer.setPixels (0, j, width, 1, cm, store[j], 0, width);
                consumer.imageComplete (ImageConsumer.STATICIMAGEDONE);
            }
        }
    }
```

produce() just calls the ImageConsumer methods in order: it sets the image's dimensions, hands off an empty Hashtable of properties, sets the color model (the default RGB model) and the hints, and then calls setPixels() once for each row of pixel data. The data is in the integer array store[][], which has already been loaded by the readImage() method (defined in the following code). When the data is delivered, the method setPixels() calls imageComplete() to indicate that the image has been finished successfully.

```
/* Allows reading to be from internal byte array, in addition to disk/socket */

    public void readImage (byte b[]) {
        readImage (new ByteArrayInputStream (b));
    }

/* readImage reads image data from Stream */
/* parses data for PPM format            */
```

```
/* closes inputstream when done            */

    public void readImage (InputStream is) {
        long tm = System.currentTimeMillis();
        boolean raw=false;
        DataInputStream dis = null;
        BufferedInputStream bis = null;
        try {
            bis = new BufferedInputStream (is);
            dis = new DataInputStream (bis);
            String word;
            word = readWord (dis);
            if ("P6".equals (word)) {
                raw = true;
            } else if ("P3".equals (word)) {
                raw = false;
            } else {
                throw (new AWTException ("Invalid Format " + word));
            }
            width = Integer.parseInt (readWord (dis));
            height = Integer.parseInt (readWord (dis));
            // Could put comments in props - makes readWord more complex
            int maxColors = Integer.parseInt (readWord (dis));
            if ((maxColors < 0) || (maxColors > 255)) {
                throw (new AWTException ("Invalid Colors " + maxColors));
            }
            store = new int[height][width];
            if (raw) {                          // binary format (raw) pixel data
                byte row[] = new byte [width*3];
                for (int i=0;i<height;i++){
                    dis.readFully (row);
                    for (int j=0,k=0;j<width;j++,k+=3) {
                        int red = row[k];
                        int green = row[k+1];
                        int blue = row[k+2];
                        if (red < 0)
                            red +=256;
                        if (green < 0)
                            green +=256;
                        if (blue < 0)
                            blue +=256;
                        store[i][j] = (0xff<< 24) | (red << 16) |
                                        (green << 8) | blue;
                    }
                }
            } else {                            // ASCII pixel data
                for (int i=0;i<height;i++) {
                    for (int j=0;j<width;j++) {
                        int red = Integer.parseInt (readWord (dis));
                        int green = Integer.parseInt (readWord (dis));
                        int blue = Integer.parseInt (readWord (dis));
                        store[i][j] = (0xff<< 24) | (red << 16) |
                                        (green << 8) | blue;
                    }
```

```
                    }
                }
            } catch (IOException io) {
                loadError = true;
                System.out.println ("IO Exception " + io.getMessage());
            } catch (AWTException awt) {
                loadError = true;
                System.out.println ("AWT Exception " + awt.getMessage());
            } catch (NoSuchElementException nse) {
                loadError = true;
                System.out.println ("No Such Element Exception " + nse.getMessage());
            } finally {
                try {
                    if (dis != null)
                        dis.close();
                    if (bis != null)
                        bis.close();
                    if (is != null)
                        is.close();
                } catch (IOException io) {
                    System.out.println ("IO Exception " + io.getMessage());
                }
            }
            System.out.println ("Done in " + (System.currentTimeMillis() - tm)
                                + " ms");
        }
```

readImage() reads the image data from an InputStream and converts it into the array of pixel data that produce() transfers to the consumer. Code using this class must call readImage() to process the data before calling createImage(); we'll see how this works shortly. Although there is a lot of code in readImage(), it's fairly simple. (It would be much more complex if we were dealing with an image format that compressed the data.) It makes heavy use of readWord(), a utility method that we'll discuss next; readWord() returns a word of ASCII text as a string.

readImage() starts by converting the InputStream into a DataInputStream. It uses readWord() to get the first word from the stream. This should be either "P6" or "P3", depending on whether the data is in binary or ASCII. It then uses read-Word() to save the image's width and height and the maximum value of any color component. Next, it reads the color data into the store[][] array. The ASCII case is simple because we can use readWord() to read ASCII words conveniently; we read red, green, and blue words, convert them into ints, and pack the three into one element (one pixel) of store[][]. For binary data, we read an entire scan line into the byte array row[], using readFully(); then we start a loop that packs this scan line into one row of store[][]. A little additional complexity is in the inner loop because we must keep track of two arrays (row[] and store[][]). We read red, green, and blue components from row[], converting Java's signed bytes to unsigned data by adding 256 to any negative values; finally, we pack these components into one element of store[][].

```
/* readWord returns a word of text from stream       */
/* Ignores PPM comment lines.                         */
/* word defined to be something wrapped by whitespace  */

    private String readWord (InputStream is) throws IOException {
        StringBuffer buf = new StringBuffer();
        int b;
        do {// get rid of leading whitespace
            if ((b=is.read()) == -1)
                throw new EOFException();
            if ((char)b == '#') { // read to end of line - ppm comment
                DataInputStream dis = new DataInputStream (is);
                dis.readLine();
                b = ' ';  // ensure more reading
            }
        }while (Character.isSpace ((char)b));
        do {
            buf.append ((char)(b));
            if ((b=is.read()) == -1)
                throw new EOFException();
        } while (!Character.isSpace ((char)b));  // reads first space
        return buf.toString();
    }
}
```

readWord() is a utility method that reads one ASCII word from an InputStream. A word is a sequence of characters that aren't spaces; space characters include newlines and tabs in addition to spaces. This method also throws out any comments (anything between # and the end of the line). It collects the characters into a StringBuffer, converting the StringBuffer into a String when it returns.

Example 12–5: PPMImageDecoder Test Program

```
import java.awt.Graphics;
import java.awt.Color;
import java.awt.image.ImageConsumer;
import java.awt.Image;
import java.awt.MediaTracker;
import java.net.URL;
import java.net.MalformedURLException;
import java.io.InputStream;
import java.io.IOException;
import java.applet.Applet;
public class ppmViewer extends Applet {
    Image image = null;
    public void init () {
        try {
            String file = getParameter ("file");
            if (file != null) {
                URL imageurl = new URL (getDocumentBase(), file);
                InputStream is = imageurl.openStream();
                PPMImageDecoder ppm = new PPMImageDecoder ();
                ppm.readImage (is);
```

Example 12–5: PPMImageDecoder Test Program (continued)

```
                    image = createImage (ppm);
                    repaint();
                }
            } catch (MalformedURLException me) {
                System.out.println ("Bad URL");
             } catch (IOException io) {
                System.out.println ("Bad File");
            }
        }
    }
    public void paint (Graphics g) {
        g.drawImage (image, 0, 0, this);
    }
}
```

The applet we use to test our `ImageProducer` is very simple. It creates a URL that points to an appropriate PPM file and gets an `InputStream` from that URL. It then creates an instance of our `PPMImageDecoder`; calls `readImage()` to load the image and generate pixel data; and finally, calls `createImage()` with our `ImageProducer` as an argument to create an `Image` object, which we draw in `paint()`.

12.4.2 PixelGrabber

The `PixelGrabber` class is a utility for converting an image into an array of pixels. This is useful in many situations. If you are writing a drawing utility that lets users create their own graphics, you probably want some way to save a drawing to a file. Likewise, if you're implementing a shared whiteboard, you'll want some way to transmit images across the Net. If you're doing some kind of image processing, you may want to read and alter individual pixels in an image. The `PixelGrabber` class is an `ImageConsumer` that can capture a subset of the current pixels of an `Image`. Once you have the pixels, you can easily save the image in a file, send it across the Net, or work with individual points in the array. To recreate the `Image` (or a modified version), you can pass the pixel array to a `MemoryImageSource`.

Prior to Java 1.1, `PixelGrabber` saves an array of pixels but doesn't save the image's width and height—that's your responsibility. You may want to put the width and height in the first two elements of the pixel array and use an offset of 2 when you store (or reproduce) the image.

Starting with Java 1.1, the grabbing process changes in several ways. You can ask the `PixelGrabber` for the image's size or color model. You can grab pixels asynchronously and abort the grabbing process before it is completed. Finally, you don't have to preallocate the pixel data array.

Constructors

public PixelGrabber (ImageProducer ip, int x, int y, int width, int height, int pixels[],
int offset, int scansize)

> The first `PixelGrabber` constructor creates a new `PixelGrabber` instance. The `PixelGrabber` uses `ImageProducer` ip to store the unscaled cropped rectangle at position (x, y) of size width × height into the `pixels` array, starting at off-set within `pixels`, and each row starting at increments of `scansize` from that.
>
> As shown in Figure 12-5, the position (x1, y1) would be stored in `pixels[]` at position (y1 - y) * scansize + (x1 - x) + offset. Calling `grabPixels()` starts the process of writing pixels into the array.
>
> The `ColorModel` for the pixels copied into the array is always the default RGB model: that is, 32 bits per pixel, with 8 bits for alpha, red, green, and blue components.

public PixelGrabber (Image image, int x, int y, int width, int height, int pixels[], int offset,
int scansize)

> This version of the `PixelGrabber` constructor gets the `ImageProducer` of the `Image` image through `getSource()`; it then calls the previous constructor to create the `PixelGrabber`.

public PixelGrabber (Image image, int x, int y, int width, int height, boolean forceRGB) ★

> This version of the constructor does not require you to preallocate the pixel array and lets you preserve the color model of the original image. If `forceRGB` is `true`, the pixels of `image` are converted to the default RGB model when grabbed. If `forceRGB` is `false` and all the pixels of image use one `ColorModel`, the original color model of `image` is preserved.
>
> As with the other constructors, the x, y, width, and height values define the bounding box to grab. However, there's one special case to consider. Setting width or height to -1 tells the `PixelGrabber` to take the width and height from the image itself. In this case, the grabber stores all the pixels below and to the right of the point (x, y). If (x, y) is outside of the image, you get an empty array.
>
> Once the pixels have been grabbed, you get the pixel data via the `getPixels()` method described in "Other methods." To get the `ColorModel`, see the get-`ColorModel()` method.

ImageConsumer interface methods

public void setDimensions (int width, int height)

> In Java 1.0, the `setDimensions()` method of `PixelGrabber` ignores the width and height, since this was set by the constructor.

With Java 1.1, setDimensions() is called by the image producer to give it the dimensions of the original image. This is how the PixelGrabber finds out the image's size if the constructor specified -1 for the image's width or height.

public void setHints (int hints)

The setHints() method ignores the hints.

public void setProperties (Hashtable properties)

The setProperties() method ignores the properties.

public void setColorModel (ColorModel model)

The setColorModel() method ignores the model.

public void setPixels (int x, int y, int w, int h, ColorModel model, byte pixels[],
int offset, int scansize)

The setPixels() method is called by the ImageProducer to deliver pixel data for some image. If the pixels fall within the portion of the image that the PixelGrabber is interested in, they are stored within the array passed to the PixelGrabber constructor. If necessary, the ColorModel is used to convert each pixel from its original representation to the default RGB representation. This method is called when each pixel coming from the image producer is represented by a byte.

public void setPixels (int x, int y, int w, int h, ColorModel model, int pixels[],
int offset, int scansize)

The second setPixels() method is almost identical to the first; it is used when each pixel coming from the image producer is represented by an int.

public synchronized void imageComplete (int status)

The imageComplete() method uses status to determine if the pixels were successfully delivered. The PixelGrabber then notifies anyone waiting for the pixels from a grabPixels() call.

Grabbing methods

public synchronized boolean grabPixels (long ms) throws InterruptedException

The grabPixels() method starts storing pixel data from the image. It doesn't return until all pixels have been loaded into the pixels array or until ms milliseconds have passed. The return value is true if all pixels were successfully acquired. Otherwise, it returns false for the abort, error, or timeout condition encountered. The exception InterruptedException is thrown if another thread interrupts this one while waiting for pixel data.

public boolean grabPixels () throws InterruptedException

> This `grabPixels()` method starts storing pixel data from the image. It doesn't return until all pixels have been loaded into the pixels array. The return value is `true` if all pixels were successfully acquired. It returns `false` if it encountered an abort or error condition. The exception `InterruptedException` is thrown if another thread interrupts this one while waiting for pixel data.

public synchronized void startGrabbing() ★

> The `startGrabbing()` method provides an asynchronous means of grabbing the pixels. This method returns immediately; it does not block like the `grabPixels()` methods described previously. To find out when the `PixelGrab`-ber has finished, call `getStatus()`.

public synchronized void abortGrabbing() ★

> The `abortGrabbing()` method allows you to stop grabbing pixel data from the image. If a thread is waiting for pixel data from a `grabPixels()` call, it is interrupted and `grabPixels()` throws an `InterruptedException`.

Other methods

public synchronized int getStatus() ★
public synchronized int status () ☆

> Call the `getStatus()` method to find out whether a `PixelGrabber` succeeded in grabbing the pixels you want. The return value is a set of `ImageObserver` flags ORed together. `ALLBITS` and `FRAMEBITS` indicate success; which of the two you get depends on how the image was created. `ABORT` and `ERROR` indicate that problems occurred while the image was being produced.
>
> `status()` is the Java 1.0 name for this method.

public synchronized int getWidth() ★

> The `getWidth()` method reports the width of the image data stored in the destination buffer. If you set width to -1 when you called the `PixelGrabber` constructor, this information will be available only after the grabber has received the information from the image producer (`setDimensions()`). If the width is not available yet, `getWidth()` returns -1.
>
> The width of the resulting image depends on several factors. If you specified the width explicitly in the constructor, the resulting image has that width, no questions asked—even if the position at which you start grabbing is outside the image. If you specified -1 for the width, the resulting width will be the difference between the x position at which you start grabbing (set in the constructor) and the actual image width; for example, if you start grabbing at x=50 and the original image width is 100, the width of the resulting image is 50. If x falls outside the image, the resulting width is 0.

public synchronized int getHeight() ★

The `getHeight()` method reports the height of the image data stored in the destination buffer. If you set height to -1 when you called the `PixelGrabber` constructor, this information will be available only after the grabber has received the information from the image producer (`setDimensions()`). If the height is not available yet, `getHeight()` returns -1.

The height of the resulting image depends on several factors. If you specified the height explicitly in the constructor, the resulting image has that height, no questions asked—even if the position at which you start grabbing is outside the image. If you specified -1 for the height, the resulting height will be the difference between the y position at which you start grabbing (set in the constructor) and the actual image height; for example, if you start grabbing at y=50 and the original image height is 100, the height of the resulting image is 50. If y falls outside the image, the resulting height is 0.

public synchronized Object getPixels() ★

The `getPixels()` method returns an array of pixel data. If you passed a pixel array to the constructor, you get back your original array object, with the data filled in. If, however, the array was not previously allocated, you get back a new array. The size of this array depends on the image you are grabbing and the portion of that image you want. If size and image format are not known yet, this method returns `null`. If the `PixelGrabber` is still grabbing pixels, this method returns an array that may change based upon the rest of the image. The type of the array you get is either `int[]` or `byte[]`, depending on the color model of the image. To find out if the `PixelGrabber` has finished, call `getStatus()`.

public synchronized ColorModel getColorModel() ★

The `getColorModel()` method returns the color model of the image. This could be the default RGB `ColorModel` if a pixel buffer was explicitly provided, `null` if the color model is not known yet, or a varying color model until all the pixel data has been grabbed. After all the pixels have been grabbed, `getColorModel()` returns the actual color model used for the `getPixels()` array. It is best to wait until grabbing has finished before you ask for the `ColorModel`; to find out, call `getStatus()`.

Using PixelGrabber to modify an image

You can modify images by combining a `PixelGrabber` with `MemoryImageSource`. Use `getImage()` to load an image from the Net; then use `PixelGrabber` to convert the image into an array. Modify the data in the array any way you please; then use `MemoryImageSource` as an image producer to display the new image.

Example 12-6 demonstrates the use of the `PixelGrabber` and `MemoryImageSource` to rotate, flip, and mirror an image. (We could also do the rotations with a subclass of `ImageFilter`, which we will discuss next.) The output is shown in Figure 12-6. When working with an image that is loaded from a local disk or the network, remember to wait until the image is loaded before grabbing its pixels. In this example, we use a `MediaTracker` to wait for the image to load.

Example 12–6: Flip Source

```
import java.applet.*;
import java.awt.*;
import java.awt.image.*;
public class flip extends Applet {
        Image i, j, k, l;
        public void init () {
                MediaTracker mt = new MediaTracker (this);
                i = getImage (getDocumentBase(), "ora-icon.gif");
                mt.addImage (i, 0);
        try {
                mt.waitForAll();
                int width = i.getWidth(this);
                int height = i.getHeight(this);
                int pixels[] = new int [width * height];
                PixelGrabber pg = new PixelGrabber
                (i, 0, 0, width, height, pixels, 0, width);
                if (pg.grabPixels() && ((pg.status() &
                        ImageObserver.ALLBITS) !=0)) {
                        j = createImage (new MemoryImageSource (width, height,
                            rowFlipPixels (pixels, width, height), 0, width));
                        k = createImage (new MemoryImageSource (width, height,
                             colFlipPixels (pixels, width, height), 0, width));
                        l = createImage (new MemoryImageSource (height, width,
                             rot90Pixels (pixels, width, height), 0, height));
                }
        } catch (InterruptedException e) {
                e.printStackTrace();
        }
    }
}
```

The `try` block in Example 12-6 does all the interesting work. It uses a `PixelGrab`-ber to grab the entire image into the array `pixels[]`. After calling `grabPixels()`, it checks the `PixelGrabber` status to make sure that the image was stored correctly. It then generates three new images based on the first by calling `createImage()` with a `MemoryImageSource` object as an argument. Instead of using the original array, the `MemoryImageSource` objects call several utility methods to manipulate the array: `rowFlipPixels()`, `colFlipPixels()`, and `rot90Pixels()`. These methods all return integer arrays.

```
public void paint (Graphics g) {
        g.drawImage (i, 10, 10, this); // regular
        if (j != null)
```

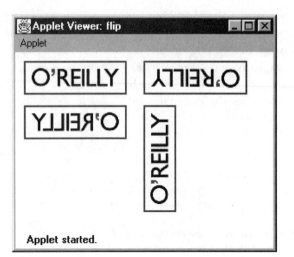

Figure 12–6: Flip output

```
                g.drawImage (j, 150, 10, this); // rowFlip
        if (k != null)
                g.drawImage (k, 10, 60, this); // colFlip
        if (l != null)
                g.drawImage (l, 150, 60, this); // rot90
    }
    private int[] rowFlipPixels (int pixels[], int width, int height) {
        int newPixels[] = null;
        if ((width*height) == pixels.length) {
            newPixels = new int [width*height];
            int newIndex=0;
            for (int y=height-1;y>=0;y--)
                    for (int x=width-1;x>=0;x--)
                            newPixels[newIndex++]=pixels[y*width+x];
        }
        return newPixels;
    }
}
```

rowFlipPixels() creates a mirror image of the original, flipped horizontally. It is
nothing more than a nested loop that copies the original array into a new array.

```
    private int[] colFlipPixels (int pixels[], int width, int height) {
        ...
    }
    private int[] rot90Pixels (int pixels[], int width, int height) {
        ...
    }
}
```

colFlipPixels()   and   rot90Pixels()   are   fundamentally   similar   to rowFlipPixels(); they just copy the original pixel array into another array, and return the result. colFlipPixels() generates a vertical mirror image; rot90Pixels() rotates the image by 90 degrees counterclockwise.

Grabbing data asynchronously

To demonstrate the new methods introduced by Java 1.1 for PixelGrabber, the following program grabs the pixels and reports information about the original image on mouse clicks. It takes its data from the image used in Figure 12-6.

```java
// Java 1.1 only
import java.applet.*;
import java.awt.*;
import java.awt.image.*;
import java.awt.event.*;
public class grab extends Applet {
    Image i;
    PixelGrabber pg;
    public void init () {
        i = getImage (getDocumentBase(), "ora-icon.gif");
        pg = new PixelGrabber (i, 0, 0, -1, -1, false);
        pg.startGrabbing();
        enableEvents (AWTEvent.MOUSE_EVENT_MASK);
    }
    public void paint (Graphics g) {
        g.drawImage (i, 10, 10, this);
    }
    protected void processMouseEvent(MouseEvent e) {
        if (e.getID() == MouseEvent.MOUSE_CLICKED) {
            System.out.println ("Status: " + pg.getStatus());
            System.out.println ("Width:  " + pg.getWidth());
            System.out.println ("Height: " + pg.getHeight());
            System.out.println ("Pixels: " +
                (pg.getPixels() instanceof byte[] ? "bytes" : "ints"));
            System.out.println ("Model:  " + pg.getColorModel());
        }
        super.processMouseEvent (e);
    }
}
```

This applet creates a PixelGrabber without specifying an array, then starts grabbing pixels. The grabber allocates its own array, but we never bother to ask for it since we don't do anything with the data itself: we only report the grabber's status. (If we wanted the data, we'd call getPixels().) Sample output from a single mouse click, after the image loaded, would appear something like the following:

```
Status: 27
Width:  120
Height: 38
Pixels: bytes
Model:  java.awt.image.IndexColorModel@1ed34
```

You need to convert the status value manually to the corresponding meaning by looking up the status codes in ImageObserver. The value 27 indicates that the 1, 2, 8, and 16 flags are set, which translates to the WIDTH, HEIGHT, SOMEBITS, and FRAMEBITS flags, respectively.

12.5 *ImageFilter*

Image filters provide another way to modify images. An ImageFilter is used in conjunction with a FilteredImageSource object. The ImageFilter, which implements ImageConsumer (and Cloneable), receives data from an ImageProducer and modifies it; the FilteredImageSource, which implements ImageProducer, sends the modified data to the new consumer. As Figure 12-1 shows, an image filter sits between the original ImageProducer and the ultimate ImageConsumer.

The ImageFilter class implements a "null" filter that does nothing to the image. To modify an image, you must use a subclass of ImageFilter, by either writing one yourself or using a subclass provided with AWT, like the CropImageFilter. Another ImageFilter subclass provided with AWT is the RGBImageFilter; it is useful for filtering an image on the basis of a pixel's color. Unlike the CropImageFilter, RGBImageFilter is an abstract class, so you need to create your own subclass to use it. Java 1.1 introduces two more image filters, AreaAveragingScaleFilter and ReplicateScaleFilter. Other filters must be created by subclassing ImageFilter and providing the necessary methods to modify the image as necessary.

ImageFilters tend to work on a pixel-by-pixel basis, so large Image objects can take a considerable amount of time to filter, depending on the complexity of the filtering algorithm. In the simplest case, filters generate new pixels based upon the color value and location of the original pixel. Such filters can start delivering data before they have loaded the entire image. More complex filters may use internal buffers to store an intermediate copy of the image so the filter can use adjacent pixel values to smooth or blend pixels together. These filters may need to load the entire image before they can deliver any data to the ultimate consumer.

To use an ImageFilter, you pass it to the FilteredImageSource constructor, which serves as an ImageProducer to pass the new pixels to their consumer. The following code runs the image *logo.jpg* through an image filter, SomeImageFilter, to produce a new image. The constructor for SomeImageFilter is called within the constructor for FilteredImageSource, which in turn is the only argument to createImage().

```
Image image = getImage (new URL (
        "http://www.ora.com/images/logo.jpg"));
Image newOne = createImage (new FilteredImageSource (image.getSource (),
                            new SomeImageFilter ()));
```

12.5.1 ImageFilter Methods

Variables

protected ImageConsumer consumer;

The actual `ImageConsumer` for the image. It is initialized automatically for you by the `getFilterInstance()` method.

Constructor

public ImageFilter ()

The only constructor for `ImageFilter` is the default one, which takes no arguments. Subclasses can provide their own constructors if they need additional information.

ImageConsumer interface methods

public void setDimensions (int width, int height)

The `setDimensions()` method of `ImageFilter` is called when the `width` and height of the original image are known. It calls `consumer.setDimensions()` to tell the next consumer the dimensions of the filtered image. If you subclass `ImageFilter` and your filter changes the image's dimensions, you should override this method to compute and report the new dimensions.

public void setProperties (Hashtable properties)

The `setProperties()` method is called to provide the image filter with the property list for the original image. The image filter adds the property `filters` to the list and passes it along to the next consumer. The value given for the `filters` property is the result of the image filter's `toString()` method; that is, the `String` representation of the current filter. If `filters` is already set, information about this `ImageFilter` is appended to the end. Subclasses of `ImageFilter` may add other properties.

public void setColorModel (ColorModel model)

The `setColorModel()` method is called to give the `ImageFilter` the color model used for most of the pixels in the original image. It passes this color model on to the next consumer. Subclasses may override this method if they change the color model.

public void setHints (int hints)

The `setHints()` method is called to give the `ImageFilter` hints about how the producer will deliver pixels. This method passes the same set of hints to the next consumer. Subclasses must override this method if they need to provide different hints; for example, if they are delivering pixels in a different order.

public void setPixels (int x, int y, int width, int height, ColorModel model, byte pixels[],
int offset, int scansize)
public void setPixels (int x, int y, int width, int height, ColorModel model, int pixels[],
int offset, int scansize)

The setPixels() method receives pixel data from the ImageProducer and passes all the information on to the ImageConsumer. (x, y) is the top left corner of the bounding rectangle for the pixels. The bounding rectangle has size width × height. The ColorModel for the new image is model. pixels is the byte or integer array of the pixel information, starting at offset (usually 0), with scan lines of size scansize (usually width).

public void imageComplete (int status)

The imageComplete() method receives the completion status from the ImageProducer and passes it along to the ImageConsumer.

If you subclass ImageFilter, you will probably override the setPixels() methods. For simple filters, you may be able to modify the pixel array and deliver the result to consumer.setPixels() immediately. For more complex filters, you will have to build a buffer containing the entire image; in this case, the call to imageComplete() will probably trigger filtering and pixel delivery.

Cloneable interface methods

public Object clone ()

The clone() method creates a clone of the ImageFilter. The getFilterInstance() function uses this method to create a copy of the ImageFilter. Cloning allows the same filter instance to be used with multiple Image objects.

Other methods

public ImageFilter getFilterInstance (ImageConsumer ic)

FilteredImageSource calls getFilterInstance() to register ic as the ImageConsumer for an instance of this filter; to do so, it sets the instance variable consumer. In effect, this method inserts the ImageFilter between the image's producer and the consumer. You have to override this method only if there are special requirements for the insertion process. This default implementation just calls clone().

public void resendTopDownLeftRight (ImageProducer ip)

The resendTopDownLeftRight() method tells the ImageProducer ip to try to resend the image data in the top-down, left-to-right order. If you override this method and your ImageFilter has saved the image data internally, you may want your ImageFilter to resend the data itself, rather than asking the ImageProducer. Otherwise, your subclass may ignore the request or pass it along to the ImageProducer ip.

Subclassing ImageFilter: A blurring filter

When you subclass ImageFilter, there are very few restrictions on what you can do. We will create a few subclasses that show some of the possibilities. This Image-Filter generates a new pixel by averaging the pixels around it. The result is a blurred version of the original. To implement this filter, we have to save all the pixel data into a buffer; we can't start delivering pixels until the entire image is in hand. Therefore, we override setPixels() to build the buffer; we override image-Complete() to produce the new pixels and deliver them.

Before looking at the code, here are a few hints about how the filter works; it uses a few tricks that may be helpful in other situations. We need to provide two versions of setPixels(): one for integer arrays, and the other for byte arrays. To avoid duplicating code, both versions call a single method, setThePixels(), which takes an Object as an argument, instead of a pixel array; thus it can be called with either kind of pixel array. Within the method, we check whether the pixels argument is an instance of byte[] or int[]. The body of this method uses another trick: when it reads the byte[] version of the pixel array, it ANDs the value with 0xff. This prevents the byte value, which is signed, from being converted to a negative int when used as an argument to cm.getRGB().

The logic inside of imageComplete() gets a bit hairy. This method does the actual filtering, after all the data has arrived. Its job is basically simple: compute an average value of the pixel and the eight pixels surrounding it (i.e., a 3×3 rectangle with the current pixel in the center). The problem lies in taking care of the edge conditions. We don't always want to average nine pixels; in fact, we may want to average as few as four. The if statements figure out which surrounding pixels should be included in the average. The pixels we care about are placed in sumArray[], which has nine elements. We keep track of the number of elements that have been saved in the variable sumIndex and use a helper method, avgPixels(), to compute the average. The code might be a little cleaner if we used a Vector, which automatically counts the number of elements it contains, but it would probably be much slower.

Example 12-7 shows the code for the blurring filter.

Example 12–7: Blur Filter Source

```
import java.awt.*;
import java.awt.image.*;

public class BlurFilter extends ImageFilter {
    private int savedWidth, savedHeight, savedPixels[];
    private static ColorModel defaultCM = ColorModel.getRGBdefault();

    public void setDimensions (int width, int height) {
        savedWidth=width;
```

Example 12–7: Blur Filter Source (continued)

```
        savedHeight=height;
        savedPixels=new int [width*height];
        consumer.setDimensions (width, height);
    }
```

We override setDimensions() to save the original image's height and width, which
we use later.

```
    public void setColorModel (ColorModel model) {
    // Change color model to model you are generating
        consumer.setColorModel (defaultCM);
    }

    public void setHints (int hintflags) {
    // Set new hints, but preserve SINGLEFRAME setting
        consumer.setHints (TOPDOWNLEFTRIGHT | COMPLETESCANLINES |
                        SINGLEPASS | (hintflags & SINGLEFRAME));
    }
```

This filter always generates pixels in the same order, so it sends the hint flags TOP-
DOWNLEFTRIGHT, COMPLETESCANLINES, and SINGLEPASS to the consumer, regardless
of what the image producer says. It sends the SINGLEFRAME hint only if the producer has sent it.

```
    private void setThePixels (int x, int y, int width, int height,
            ColorModel cm, Object pixels, int offset, int scansize) {
        int sourceOffset = offset;
        int destinationOffset = y * savedWidth + x;
        boolean bytearray = (pixels instanceof byte[]);
        for (int yy=0;yy<height;yy++) {
            for (int xx=0;xx<width;xx++)
                if (bytearray)
                    savedPixels[destinationOffset++]=
                        cm.getRGB(((byte[])pixels)[sourceOffset++]&0xff);
                else
                    savedPixels[destinationOffset++]=
                        cm.getRGB(((int[])pixels)[sourceOffset++]);
            sourceOffset += (scansize - width);
            destinationOffset += (savedWidth - width);
        }
    }
```

setThePixels() saves the pixel data for the image in the array savedPixels[].
Both versions of setPixels() call this method. It doesn't pass the pixels along to
the image consumer, since this filter can't process the pixels until the entire image
is available.

```
    public void setPixels (int x, int y, int width, int height,
            ColorModel cm, byte pixels[], int offset, int scansize) {
        setThePixels (x, y, width, height, cm, pixels, offset, scansize);
    }
```

```
public void setPixels (int x, int y, int width, int height,
        ColorModel cm, int pixels[], int offset, int scansize) {
    setThePixels (x, y, width, height, cm, pixels, offset, scansize);
}

public void imageComplete (int status) {
    if ((status == IMAGEABORTED) || (status == IMAGEERROR)) {
        consumer.imageComplete (status);
        return;
    } else {
        int pixels[] = new int [savedWidth];
        int position, sumArray[], sumIndex;
        sumArray = new int [9]; // maxsize - vs. Vector for performance
        for (int yy=0;yy<savedHeight;yy++) {
            position=0;
            int start = yy * savedWidth;
            for (int xx=0;xx<savedWidth;xx++) {
                sumIndex=0;
                                                                    //  xx     yy
                sumArray[sumIndex++] = savedPixels[start+xx];   // center center
                if (yy != (savedHeight-1))                          // center bottom
                    sumArray[sumIndex++] = savedPixels[start+xx+savedWidth];
                if (yy != 0)                                        // center top
                    sumArray[sumIndex++] = savedPixels[start+xx-savedWidth];
                if (xx != (savedWidth-1))                           // right  center
                    sumArray[sumIndex++] = savedPixels[start+xx+1];
                if (xx != 0)                                        // left   center
                    sumArray[sumIndex++] = savedPixels[start+xx-1];
                if ((yy != 0) && (xx != 0))                         // left   top
                    sumArray[sumIndex++] = savedPixels[start+xx-savedWidth-1];
                if ((yy != (savedHeight-1)) && (xx != (savedWidth-1)))
                    //                                          right  bottom
                    sumArray[sumIndex++] = savedPixels[start+xx+savedWidth+1];
                if ((yy != 0) && (xx != (savedWidth-1)))            //right  top
                    sumArray[sumIndex++] = savedPixels[start+xx-savedWidth+1];
                if ((yy != (savedHeight-1)) && (xx != 0))           //left   bottom
                    sumArray[sumIndex++] = savedPixels[start+xx+savedWidth-1];
                pixels[position++] = avgPixels(sumArray, sumIndex);
            }
            consumer.setPixels (0, yy, savedWidth, 1, defaultCM,
                                pixels, 0, savedWidth);
        }
        consumer.imageComplete (status);
    }
}
```

imageComplete() does the actual filtering after the pixels have been delivered and saved. If the producer reports that an error occurred, this method passes the error flags to the consumer and returns. If not, it builds a new array, pixels[], which contains the filtered pixels, and delivers these to the consumer.

Previously, we gave an overview of how the filtering process works. Here are some details. (xx, yy) represents the current point's x and y coordinates. The point (xx, yy) must always fall within the image; otherwise, our loops are constructed incorrectly. Therefore, we can copy (xx, yy) into the sumArray[] for averaging without any tests. For the point's eight neighbors, we check whether the neighbor falls in the image; if so, we add it to sumArray[]. For example, the point just below (xx, yy) is at the bottom center of the 3×3 rectangle of points we are averaging. We know that xx falls within the image; yy falls within the image if it doesn't equal savedHeight-1. We do similar tests for the other points.

Even though we're working with a rectangular image, our arrays are all one-dimensional so we have to convert a coordinate pair (xx, yy) into a single array index. To help us do the bookkeeping, we use the local variable start to keep track of the start of the current scan line. Then start + xx is the current point; start + xx + savedWidth is the point immediately below; start + xx + saved-Width-1 is the point below and to the left; and so on.

avgPixels() is our helper method for computing the average value that we assign to the new pixel. For each pixel in the pixels[] array, it extracts the red, blue, green, and alpha components; averages them separately, and returns a new ARGB value.

```
private int avgPixels (int pixels[], int size) {
    float redSum=0, greenSum=0, blueSum=0, alphaSum=0;
    for (int i=0;i<size;i++)
        try {
            int pixel = pixels[i];
            redSum   += defaultCM.getRed   (pixel);
            greenSum += defaultCM.getGreen (pixel);
            blueSum  += defaultCM.getBlue  (pixel);
            alphaSum += defaultCM.getAlpha (pixel);
        } catch (ArrayIndexOutOfBoundsException e) {
            System.out.println ("Ooops");
        }
    int redAvg   = (int)(redSum   / size);
    int greenAvg = (int)(greenSum / size);
    int blueAvg  = (int)(blueSum  / size);
    int alphaAvg = (int)(alphaSum / size);
    return ((0xff << 24) | (redAvg << 16) |
            (greenAvg << 8)  | (blueAvg << 0));
    }
}
```

Producing many images from one: dynamic ImageFilter

The ImageFilter framework is flexible enough to allow you to return a sequence of images based on an original. You can send back one frame at a time, calling the following when you are finished with each frame:

```
consumer.imageComplete(ImageConsumer.SINGLEFRAMEDONE);
```

After you have generated all the frames, you can tell the consumer that the sequence is finished with the STATICIMAGEDONE constant. In fact, this is exactly what the new animation capabilities of MemoryImageSource use.

In Example 12-8, the DynamicFilter lets the consumer display an image. After the image has been displayed, the filter gradually overwrites the image with a specified color by sending additional image frames. The end result is a solid colored rectangle. Not too exciting, but it's easy to imagine interesting extensions: you could use this technique to implement a fade from one image into another. The key points to understand are:

- This filter does not override setPixels(), so it is extremely fast. In this case, we want the original image to reach the consumer, and there is no reason to save the image in a buffer.

- Filtering takes place in the image-fetching thread, so it is safe to put the filter-processing thread to sleep if the image is coming from disk. If the image is in memory, filtering should not sleep because there will be a noticeable performance lag in your program if it does. The DynamicFilter class has a delay parameter to its constructor that lets you control this behavior.

- This subclass overrides setDimensions() to save the image's dimensions for its own use. It needs to override setHints() because it sends pixels to the consumer in a nonstandard order: it sends the original image, then goes back and starts sending overlays. Likewise, this subclass overrides resendTopDownLeft-Right() to do nothing because there is no way the original ImageProducer can replace all the changes with the original Image.

- imageComplete() is where all the fun happens. Take a special look at the status flags that are returned.

Example 12–8: DynamicFilter Source

```
import java.awt.*;
import java.awt.image.*;
public class DynamicFilter extends ImageFilter {
    Color overlapColor;
    int    delay;
    int    imageWidth;
    int    imageHeight;
    int    iterations;
    DynamicFilter (int delay, int iterations, Color color) {
        this.delay      = delay;
        this.iterations = iterations;
        overlapColor    = color;
    }
    public void setDimensions (int width, int height) {
        imageWidth  = width;
```

Example 12–8: DynamicFilter Source (continued)

```
            imageHeight = height;
            consumer.setDimensions (width, height);
    }
    public void setHints (int hints) {
            consumer.setHints (ImageConsumer.RANDOMPIXELORDER);
    }
    public void resendTopDownLeftRight (ImageProducer ip) {
    }
    public void imageComplete (int status) {
            if ((status == IMAGEERROR) || (status == IMAGEABORTED)) {
                consumer.imageComplete (status);
                return;
            } else {
                int xWidth = imageWidth / iterations;
                if (xWidth <= 0)
                    xWidth = 1;
                int newPixels[] = new int [xWidth*imageHeight];
                int iColor = overlapColor.getRGB();
                for (int x=0;x<(xWidth*imageHeight);x++)
                    newPixels[x] = iColor;
                int t=0;
                for (;t<(imageWidth-xWidth);t+=xWidth) {
                    consumer.setPixels(t, 0, xWidth, imageHeight,
                            ColorModel.getRGBdefault(), newPixels, 0, xWidth);
                    consumer.imageComplete (ImageConsumer.SINGLEFRAMEDONE);
                    try {
                        Thread.sleep (delay);
                    } catch (InterruptedException e) {
                        e.printStackTrace();
                    }
                }
                int left = imageWidth-t;
                if (left > 0) {
                    consumer.setPixels(imageWidth-left, 0, left, imageHeight,
                            ColorModel.getRGBdefault(), newPixels, 0, xWidth);
                    consumer.imageComplete (ImageConsumer.SINGLEFRAMEDONE);
                }
                consumer.imageComplete (STATICIMAGEDONE);
            }
    }
}
```

The DynamicFilter relies on the default setPixels() method to send the original image to the consumer. When the original image has been transferred, the image producer calls this filter's imageComplete() method, which does the real work. Instead of relaying the completion status to the consumer, imageComplete() starts generating its own data: solid rectangles that are all in the overlapColor specified in the constructor. It sends these rectangles to the consumer by calling consumer.setPixels(). After each rectangle, it calls consumer.imageComplete() with the SINGLEFRAMEDONE flag, meaning that it has just finished one frame of a multi-frame sequence. When the rectangles have completely covered the image, the method imageComplete() finally notifies the consumer that the entire image sequence has been transferred by sending the STATICIMAGEDONE flag.

The following code is a simple applet that uses this image filter to produce a new image:

```
import java.applet.*;
import java.awt.*;
import java.awt.image.*;
public class DynamicImages extends Applet {
    Image i, j;
    public void init () {
        i = getImage (getDocumentBase(), "rosey.jpg");
        j = createImage (new FilteredImageSource (i.getSource(),
                    new DynamicFilter(250, 10, Color.red)));
    }
    public void paint (Graphics g) {
        g.drawImage (j, 10, 10, this);
    }
}
```

One final curiosity: the DynamicFilter doesn't make any assumptions about the color model used for the original image. It sends its overlays with the default RGB color model. Therefore, this is one case in which an ImageConsumer may see calls to setPixels() that use different color models.

12.5.2 RGBImageFilter

RGBImageFilter is an abstract subclass of ImageFilter that provides a shortcut for building the most common kind of image filters: filters that independently modify the pixels of an existing image, based only on the pixel's position and color. Because RGBImageFilter is an abstract class, you must subclass it before you can do anything. The only method your subclass must provide is filterRGB(), which produces a new pixel value based on the original pixel and its location. A handful of additional methods are in this class; most of them provide the behind-the-scenes framework for funneling each pixel through the filterRGB() method.

If the filtering algorithm you are using does not rely on pixel position (i.e., the new pixel is based only on the old pixel's color), AWT can apply an optimization for images that use an IndexColorModel: rather than filtering individual pixels, it can filter the image's color map. In order to tell AWT that this optimization is okay, add a constructor to the class definition that sets the canFilter-IndexColorModel variable to true. If canFilterIndexColorModel is false (the default) and an IndexColorModel image is sent through the filter, nothing happens to the image.

Variables

protected boolean canFilterIndexColorModel

Setting the canFilterIndexColorModel variable permits the ImageFilter to filter IndexColorModel images. The default value is false. When this variable is false, IndexColorModel images are not filtered. When this variable is true, the ImageFilter filters the colormap instead of the individual pixel values.

protected ColorModel newmodel

The newmodel variable is used to store the new ColorModel when canFilter-IndexColorModel is true and the ColorModel actually is of type IndexColor-Model. Normally, you do not need to access this variable, even in subclasses.

protected ColorModel origmodel

The origmodel variable stores the original color model when filtering an IndexColorModel. Normally, you do not need to access this variable, even in subclasses.

Constructors

public RGBImageFilter () —called by subclass

The only constructor for RGBImageFilter is the implied constructor with no parameters. In most subclasses of RGBImageFilter, the constructor has to initialize only the canFilterIndexColorModel variable.

ImageConsumer interface methods

public void setColorModel (ColorModel model)

The setColorModel() method changes the ColorModel of the filter to model. If canFilterIndexColorModel is true and model is of type IndexColorModel, a filtered version of model is used instead.

public void setPixels (int x, int y, int w, int h, ColorModel model, byte pixels[],
int off, int scansize)
public void setPixels (int x, int y, int w, int h, ColorModel model, int pixels[],
int off, int scansize)

If necessary, the setPixels() method converts the pixels buffer to the default RGB ColorModel and then filters them with filterRGBPixels(). If model has already been converted, this method just passes the pixels along to the consumer's setPixels().

Other methods

The only method you care about here is filterRGB(). All subclasses of RGBImage-Filter *must* override this method. It is very difficult to imagine situations in which you would override (or even call) the other methods in this group. They are helper methods that funnel pixels through filterRGB().

public void substituteColorModel (ColorModel oldModel, ColorModel newModel)

substituteColorModel() is a helper method for setColorModel(). It initializes the protected variables of RGBImageFilter. The origmodel variable is set to oldModel and the newmodel variable is set to newModel.

public IndexColorModel filterIndexColorModel (IndexColorModel icm)

filterIndexColorModel() is another helper method for setColorModel(). It runs the entire color table of icm through filterRGB() and returns the filtered ColorModel for use by setColorModel().

public void filterRGBPixels (int x, int y, int width, int height, int pixels[], int off, int scansize)

filterRGBPixels() is a helper method for setPixels(). It filters each element of the pixels buffer through filterRGB(), converting pixels to the default RGB ColorModel first. This method changes the values in the pixels array.

public abstract int filterRGB (int x, int y, int rgb)

filterRGB() is the one method that RGBImageFilter subclasses must implement. The method takes the rgb pixel value at position (x, y) and returns the converted pixel value in the default RGB ColorModel. Coordinates of (-1, -1) signify that a color table entry is being filtered instead of a pixel.

A transparent image filter that extends RGBImageFilter

Creating your own RGBImageFilter is fairly easy. One of the more common applications for an RGBImageFilter is to make images transparent by setting the alpha component of each pixel. To do so, we extend the abstract RGBImageFilter class. The filter in Example 12-9 makes the entire image translucent, based on a percentage passed to the class constructor. Filtering is independent of position, so the constructor can set the canFilterIndexColorModel variable. A constructor with no arguments uses a default alpha value of 0.75.

Example 12–9: TransparentImageFilter Source

```
import java.awt.image.*;
class TransparentImageFilter extends RGBImageFilter {
    float alphaPercent;
    public TransparentImageFilter () {
        this (0.75f);
    }
    public TransparentImageFilter (float aPercent)
            throws IllegalArgumentException {
        if ((aPercent < 0.0) || (aPercent > 1.0))
            throw new IllegalArgumentException();
        alphaPercent = aPercent;
        canFilterIndexColorModel = true;
    }
```

Example 12–9: TransparentImageFilter Source (continued)

```
    public int filterRGB (int x, int y, int rgb) {
        int a = (rgb >> 24) & 0xff;
        a *= alphaPercent;
        return ((rgb & 0x00ffffff) | (a << 24));
    }
}
```

12.5.3 CropImageFilter

The `CropImageFilter` is an `ImageFilter` that crops an image to a rectangular region. When used with `FilteredImageSource`, it produces a new image that consists of a portion of the original image. The cropped region must be completely within the original image. It is never necessary to subclass this class. Also, using the 10 or 11 argument version of `Graphics.drawImage()` introduced in Java 1.1 precludes the need to use this filter, unless you need to save the resulting cropped image.

If you crop an image and then send the result through a second `ImageFilter`, the pixel array received by the filter will be the size of the original `Image`, with the offset and `scansize` set accordingly. The `width` and `height` are set to the cropped values; the result is a smaller `Image` with the same amount of data. `CropImage-Filter` keeps the full pixel array around, partially empty.

Constructors

public CropImageFilter (int x, int y, int width, int height) ★

The constructor for `CropImageFilter` specifies the rectangular area of the old image that makes up the new image. The (x, y) coordinates specify the top left corner for the cropped image; `width` and `height` must be positive or the resulting image will be empty. If the (x, y) coordinates are outside the original image area, the resulting image is empty. If (x, y) starts within the image but the rectangular area of size `width` × `height` goes beyond the original image, the part that extends outside will be black. (Remember the color black has pixel values of 0 for red, green, and blue.)

ImageConsumer interface methods

public void setProperties (Hashtable properties) ★

The `setProperties()` method adds the `croprect` image property to the properties list. The bounding `Rectangle`, specified by the (x, y) coordinates and `width` × `height` size, is associated with this property. After updating properties, this method sets the properties list of the consumer.

public void setDimensions (int width, int height) ★

The `setDimensions()` method of `CropImageFilter` ignores the `width` and `height` parameters to the function call. Instead, it relies on the size parameters in the constructor.

public void setPixels (int x, int y, int w, int h, ColorModel model, byte pixels[], int offset, int scansize) ★

public void setPixels (int x, int y, int w, int h, ColorModel model, int pixels[], int offset, int scansize) ★

These `setPixels()` methods check to see what portion of the `pixels` array falls within the cropped area and pass those pixels along.

Cropping an image with CropImageFilter

Example 12-10 uses a `CropImageFilter` to extract the center third of a larger image. No subclassing is needed; the `CropImageFilter` is complete in itself. The output is displayed in Figure 12-7.

Example 12–10: Crop Applet Source

```
import java.applet.*;
import java.awt.*;
import java.awt.image.*;
public class Crop extends Applet {
    Image i, j;
    public void init () {
        MediaTracker mt = new MediaTracker (this);
        i = getImage (getDocumentBase(), "rosey.jpg");
        mt.addImage (i, 0);
        try {
            mt.waitForAll();
            int width    = i.getWidth(this);
            int height   = i. getHeight(this);
            j = createImage (new FilteredImageSource (i.getSource(),
                        new CropImageFilter (width/3, height/3,
                                             width/3, height/3)));
        } catch (InterruptedException e) {
            e.printStackTrace();
        }
    }
    public void paint (Graphics g) {
        g.drawImage (i, 10, 10, this);                  // regular
        if (j != null) {
            g.drawImage (j, 10, 90, this);              // cropped
        }
    }
}
```

Figure 12–7: Image cropping example output.

TIP　　　You can use CropImageFilter to help improve your animation performance or just the general download time of images. Without
CropImageFilter, you can use Graphics.clipRect() to clip each
image of an image strip when drawing. Instead of clipping each
Image (each time), you can use CropImageFilter to create a new
Image for each cell of the strip. Or for times when an image strip is
inappropriate, you can put all your images within one image file (in
any order whatsoever), and use CropImageFilter to get each out as
an Image .

12.5.4 ReplicateScaleFilter

Back in Chapter 2 we introduced you to the getScaledInstance() method. This
method uses a new image filter that is provided with Java 1.1. The ReplicateScaleFilter and its subclass, AreaAveragingScaleFilter, allow you to scale
images before calling drawImage(). This can greatly speed your programs because
you don't have to wait for the call to drawImage() before performing scaling.

The ReplicateScaleFilter is an ImageFilter that scales by duplicating or removing rows and columns. When used with FilteredImageSource, it produces a new
image that is a scaled version of the original. As you can guess, ReplicateScale-
Filter is very fast, but the results aren't particularly pleasing aesthetically. It is
great if you want to magnify a checkerboard but not that useful if you want to scale
an image of your Aunt Polly. Its subclass, AreaAveragingScaleFilter, implements
a more time-consuming algorithm that is more suitable when image quality is a
concern.

Constructor

public ReplicateScaleFilter (int width, int height)

> The constructor for `ReplicateScaleFilter` specifies the size of the resulting image. If either parameter is -1, the resulting image maintains the same aspect ratio as the original image.

ImageConsumer interface methods

public void setProperties (Hashtable properties)

> The `setProperties()` method adds the `rescale` image property to the properties list. The value of the rescale property is a quoted string showing the image's new width and height, in the form `"<width>x<height>"`, where the width and height are taken from the constructor. After updating `properties`, this method sets the properties list of the consumer.

public void setDimensions (int width, int height)

> The `setDimensions()` method of `ReplicateScaleFilter` passes the new width and height from the constructor along to the consumer. If either of the constructor's parameters are negative, the size is recalculated proportionally. If both are negative, the size becomes `width × height`.

public void setPixels (int x, int y, int w, int h, ColorModel model, int pixels[], int offset, int scansize)

public void setPixels (int x, int y, int w, int h, ColorModel model, byte pixels[], int offset, int scansize)

> The `setPixels()` method of `ReplicateScaleFilter` checks to see which rows and columns of `pixels` to pass along.

12.5.5 AreaAveragingScaleFilter

The `AreaAveragingScaleFilter` subclasses `ReplicateScaleFilter` to provide a better scaling algorithm. Instead of just dropping or adding rows and columns, `AreaAveragingScaleFilter` tries to blend pixel values when creating new rows and columns. The filter works by replicating rows and columns to generate an image that is a multiple of the original size. Then the image is resized back down by an algorithm that blends the pixels around each destination pixel.

AreaAveragingScaleFilter methods

Because this filter subclasses `ReplicateScaleFilter`, the only methods it includes are those that override methods of `ReplicateScaleFilter`.

Constructors

public AreaAveragingScaleFilter (int width, int height) ★

The constructor for `AreaAveragingScaleFilter` specifies the size of the resulting image. If either parameter is -1, the resulting image maintains the same aspect ratio as the original image.

ImageConsumer interface methods

public void setHints (int hints) ★

The `setHints()` method of `AreaAveragingScaleFilter` checks to see if some optimizations can be performed based upon the value of the `hints` parameter. If they can't, the image filter has to cache the pixel data until it receives the entire image.

public void setPixels (int x, int y, int w, int h, ColorModel model, byte pixels[], int offset, int scansize) ★
public void setPixels (int x, int y, int w, int h, ColorModel model, int pixels[], int offset, int scansize) ★

The `setPixels()` method of `AreaAveragingScaleFilter` accumulates the pixels or passes them along based upon the available hints. If `setPixels()` accumulates the pixels, this filter passes them along to the consumer when appropriate.

12.5.6 Cascading Filters

It is often a good idea to perform complex filtering operations by using several filters in a chain. This technique requires the system to perform several passes through the image array, so it may be slower than using a single complex filter; however, cascading filters yield code that is easier to understand and quicker to write—particularly if you already have a collection of image filters from other projects.

For example, assume you want to make a color image transparent and then render the image in black and white. The easy way to do this task is to apply a filter that converts color to a gray value and then apply the `TransparentImageFilter` we developed in Example 12-9. Using this strategy, we have to develop only one very simple filter. Example 12-11 shows the source for the `GrayImageFilter`; Example 12-12 shows the applet that applies the two filters in a daisy chain.

Example 12–11: GrayImageFilter Source

```
import java.awt.image.*;
public class GrayImageFilter extends RGBImageFilter {
    public GrayImageFilter () {
        canFilterIndexColorModel = true;
    }
```

Example 12–11: GrayImageFilter Source (continued)

```
    public int filterRGB (int x, int y, int rgb) {
        int gray  = (((rgb & 0xff0000) >> 16) +
                      ((rgb & 0x00ff00) >> 8) +
                      (rgb & 0x0000ff)) / 3;
        return (0xff000000 | (gray << 16) | (gray <<  8) |  gray);
    }
}
```

Example 12–12: DrawingImages Source

```
import java.applet.*;
import java.awt.*;
import java.awt.image.*;
public class DrawingImages extends Applet {
    Image i, j, k, l;
    public void init () {
        i = getImage (getDocumentBase(), "rosey.jpg");
        GrayImageFilter gif = new GrayImageFilter ();
        j = createImage (new FilteredImageSource (i.getSource(), gif));
        TransparentImageFilter tf = new TransparentImageFilter (.5f);
        k = createImage (new FilteredImageSource (j.getSource(), tf));
        l = createImage (new FilteredImageSource (i.getSource(), tf));
    }
    public void paint (Graphics g) {
        g.drawImage (i, 10, 10, this);                  // regular
        g.drawImage (j, 270, 10, this);                 // gray
        g.drawImage (k, 10, 110, Color.red, this);      // gray - transparent
        g.drawImage (l, 270, 110, Color.red, this);     // transparent
    }
}
```

Granted, neither the `GrayImageFilter` or the `TransparentImageFilter` are very complex, but consider the savings you would get if you wanted to blur an image, crop it, and then render the result in grayscale. Writing a filter that does all three is not a task for the faint of heart; remember, you can't subclass `RGBImageFilter` or `CropImageFilter` because the result does not depend purely on each pixel's color and position. However, you can solve the problem easily by cascading the filters developed in this chapter.

13

AWT Exceptions and Errors

This chapter describes AWTException, IllegalComponentStateException, and AWTError. AWTException is a subclass of Exception. It is not used by any of the public classes in java.awt; you may, however, find it convenient to throw AWTException within your own code. IllegalComponentStateException is another Exception subclass, which is new to Java 1.1. This exception is used when you try to do something with a Component that is not yet appropriate. AWTError is a subclass of Error that is thrown when a serious problem occurs in AWT—for example, the environment is unable to get the platform's Toolkit.

13.1 AWTException

AWTException is a generic exception that can be thrown when an exceptional condition has occurred within AWT. None of the AWT classes throw this. If you subclass any of the AWT classes, you can throw an AWTException to indicate a problem. Using AWTException is slightly preferable to creating your own Exception subclass because you do not have to generate another class file. Since it is a part of Java, AWTException is guaranteed to exist on the run-time platform.

If you throw an instance of AWTException, like any other Exception, it must be caught in a catch clause or declared in the throws clause of the method.

13.1.1 AWTException Method

Constructor

public AWTException (String message)

    The sole constructor creates an AWTException with a detailed message of message. This message can be retrieved using getMessage(), which it inherits from Exception (and which is required by the Throwable interface). If you do not want a detailed message, message may be null.

13.1.2 Throwing an AWTException

An AWTException is used the same way as any other Throwable object. Here's an example:

```
if (someProblem) {
    throw new AWTException ("Problem Encountered While Initializing");
}
```

13.2 IllegalComponentStateException

IllegalComponentStateException is a subclass of IllegalStateException; both are new to Java 1.1. This exception is used when you try to do something with a Component that is not yet appropriate. With the standard AWT components, this can happen only in three instances:

- If you call setCaretPosition() to set the cursor position of a text component before the component's peer exists.

- If you call getLocale() to get the locale of a component that does not have one and is not in a container that has one.

- If you call getLocationOnScreen() for a component that is not showing.

In these cases, the operation isn't fundamentally illegal; you are just trying to perform it before the component is ready. When you create your own components, you should consider using this exception for similar cases.

Since IllegalComponentStateException is a subclass of Run-TimeException, you do not have to enclose method calls that might throw this exception within try/catch blocks. However, catching this exception isn't a bad idea, since it should be fairly easy to correct the problem and retry the operation.

13.2.1 IllegalComponentStateException Method

Constructor

public IllegalComponentStateException () ★

The first constructor creates an IllegalComponentStateException instance with no detail message.

public IllegalComponentStateException (String message) ★

> This constructor creates an `IllegalComponentStateException` with a detail message of `message`. This message can be retrieved using `getMessage()`, which it inherits from `Exception` (and is required by the `Throwable` interface).

13.2.2 *IllegalComponentStateException Example*

The following code throws an `IllegalComponentStateException`. The `Exception` occurs because the `TextField` peer does not exist when `setCaretPosition()` is called. `setCaretPosition()` throws an `IllegalComponentStateException`, and the next statement never executes.

```
import java.awt.TextField;
public class illegal {
    public static void main (String[] args) {
        new TextField().setCaretPosition (24);
        System.out.println ("Never gets here");
    }
}
```

13.3 *AWTError*

`AWTError` is a subclass of `Error` that is used when a serious run-time error has occurred within AWT. For example, an `AWTError` is thrown if the default `Toolkit` cannot be initialized or if you try to create a `FileDialog` within Netscape Navigator (since that program does not permit local file system access). When an `AWTError` is thrown and not caught, the virtual machine stops your program. You may throw this `Error` to indicate a serious run-time problem in any subclass of the AWT classes. Using `AWTError` is slightly preferable to creating your own `Error` because you don't have to provide another class file. Since it is part of Java, `AWTError` is guaranteed to exist on the run-time platform.

Methods are not required to declare that they throw `AWTError`. If you throw an error that is not caught, it will eventually propagate to the top level of the system.

13.3.1 *AWTError Method*

Constructor

public AWTError (String message)

> The sole constructor creates an `AWTError` with a detail message of `message`. This message can be retrieved using `getMessage()`, which it inherits from `Error` (and is required by the `Throwable` interface). If you do not want a detailed message, `message` may be `null`.

13.3.2 Throwing an AWTError

The code in Example 13-1 throws an AWTError if it is executed with this command:

```
java -Dawt.toolkit=foo throwme
```

The error occurs because the Java interpreter tries to use the toolkit foo, which does not exist (assuming that class foo does not exist in your CLASSPATH). Therefore, getDefaultToolkit() throws an AWTError, and the next statement never executes.

Example 13–1: The throwme class

```
import java.awt.Toolkit;
public class throwme {
    public static void main (String[] args) {
        System.out.println (Toolkit.getDefaultToolkit());
        System.out.println ("Never Gets Here");
    }
}
```

14

In this chapter:
- *What's a Java Applet?*
- *AudioClip Interface*
- *AppletContext Interface*
- *AppletStub Interface*
- *Audio in Applications*

And Then There Were Applets

Although it is not part of the `java.awt` package, the `java.applet` package is closely related. The `java.applet` package provides support for running an applet in the context of a World Wide Web browser. It consists of one class (`Applet`) and three interfaces (`AppletContext`, `AudioClip`, and `AppletStub`). The `Applet` class supports the "applet life cycle" methods (`init()`, `start()`, `stop()`, `destroy()`) that you override to write an applet. `AudioClip` provides support for audio within applets. (Applications use the `sun.audio` package for audio support; `sun.audio` is also covered in this chapter.) The `AppletStub` and `AppletContext` interfaces provide a way for the applet to interact with its run-time environment. Many of the methods of `AppletStub` and `AppletContext` are duplicated in the `Applet` class.

14.1 *What's a Java Applet?*

Much of the initial excitement about Java centered around applets. Applets are small Java programs that can be embedded within HTML pages and downloaded and executed by a web browser. Because executing code from random Internet sites presents a security risk, Java goes to great lengths to ensure the integrity of the program executing and to prevent it from performing any unauthorized tasks.

An applet is a specific type of Java `Container`. The class hierarchy of an applet is shown in Figure 14-1.

When you are writing an applet, remember that you can use the features of its ancestors. In particular, remember to check the methods of the `Component`, `Container`, and `Panel` classes, which are inherited by the `Applet` class.

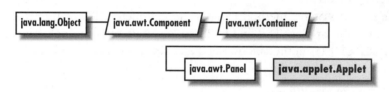

Figure 14–1: Applet class hierarchy

14.1.1 Applet Methods

All the methods of `Applet`, except `setStub()`, either need to be overridden or are methods based on one of the `java.applet` interfaces. The system calls `setStub()` to set up the context of the interfaces. The browser implements the `AppletContext` and `AppletStub` interfaces.

Constructor

public Applet ()

> The system calls the `Applet` constructor when the applet is loaded and before it calls `setStub()`, which sets up the applet's stub and context. When you subclass `Applet`, you usually do not provide a constructor. If you do provide a constructor, you do not have access to the `AppletStub` or `AppletContext` and, therefore, may not call any of their methods.

AppletStub setup

public final void setStub (AppletStub stub)

> The `setStub()` method of `Applet` is called by the browser when the applet is loaded into the system. It sets the `AppletStub` of the applet to stub. In turn, the `AppletStub` contains the applet's `AppletContext`.

Applet information methods

Several methods of `Applet` provide information that can be used while the applet is running.

public AppletContext getAppletContext ()

> The `getAppletContext()` method returns the current `AppletContext`. This is part of the applet's stub, which is set by the system when `setStub()` is called.

public URL getCodeBase ()

The `getCodeBase()` method returns the complete URL of the *.class* file that contains the applet. This method can be used with the `getImage()` or the `getAudioClip()` methods, described later in this chapter, to load an image or audio file relative to the *.class* file location.

public URL getDocumentBase ()

The `getDocumentBase()` method returns the complete URL of the *.html* file that loaded the applet. This can be used with the `getImage()` or `getAudio-Clip()` methods, described later in this chapter, to load an image or audio file relative to the *.html* file.

public String getParameter (String name)

The `getParameter()` method allows you to get run-time parameters from within the <APPLET> tag of the *.html* file that loaded the applet. Parameters are defined by HTML <PARAM> tags, which have the form:

```
<PARAM name="parameter" value="value">
```

If the `name` parameter of `getParameter()` matches the `name` string of a <PARAM> tag, `getParameter()` returns the tag's `value` as a string. If `name` is not found within the <PARAM> tags of the <APPLET>, `getParameter()` returns `null`. The argument `name` is not case sensitive; that is, it matches parameter names regardless of case. Remember that `getParameter()` always returns a string, even though the parameter values might appear as integers or floating point numbers in the HTML file. In some situations, it makes sense to pass multiple values in a single parameter; if you do this, you have to parse the parameter string manually. Using a `StringTokenizer` will make the job easier.

Enabling your applets to accept parameters allows them to be customized at run-time by the HTML author, without providing the source code. This provides greater flexibility on the Web without requiring any recoding. Example 14-1 shows how an applet reads parameters from an HTML file. It contains three parts: the HTML file that loads the applet, the applet source code, and the output from the applet.

Example 14–1: Getting Parameters from an HTML File

```
<APPLET CODE=ParamApplet WIDTH=100 HEIGHT=100>
<PARAM NAME=one VALUE=1.0>
<PARAM name=TWO value=TOO>
</APPLET>

public class ParamApplet extends java.applet.Applet {
    public void init () {
        String param;
        float one;
        String two;
```

Example 14–1: Getting Parameters from an HTML File (continued)

```
            if ((param = getParameter ("ONE")) == null) {
                one = -1.0f;   // Not present
            } else {
                one = Float.valueOf (param).longValue();
            }
            if ((param = getParameter ("two")) == null) {
                two = "two";
            } else {
                two = param.toUpperCase();
            }
            System.out.println ("One: " + one);
            System.out.println ("Two: " + two);
        }
    }


    One: 1
    Two: TOO
```

public String getAppletInfo ()

The getAppletInfo() method lets an applet provide a short descriptive string to the browser. This method is frequently overridden to return a string showing the applet's author and copyright information. How (or whether) to display this information is up to the browser. With *appletviewer*, this information is displayed when the user selects the Info choice under the Applet menu. Neither Netscape Navigator nor Internet Explorer currently display this information.

public String[][] getParameterInfo ()

The getParameterInfo() method lets an applet provide a two-dimensional array of strings describing the parameters it reads from <PARAM> tags. It returns an array of three strings for each parameter. In each array, the first String represents the parameter name, the second describes the data type, and the third is a brief description or range of values. Like getAppletInfo(), how (or whether) to display this information is up to the browser. With appletviewer, this information is displayed when the user selects the Info choice under the Applet menu. Neither Netscape Navigator nor Internet Explorer currently display this information. The following code shows how an applet might use get-ParameterInfo() and getAppletInfo():

```
public String getAppletInfo() {
    String whoami = "By John Zukowski (c) 1997";
    return whoami;
}
public String[][] getParameterInfo() {
    String[][] strings = {
        {"parameter1",    "String",    "Background Color name"},
        {"parameter2",    "URL",       "Image File"},
        {"parameter3",    "1-10",      "Number in Series"}
```

```
        };
        return strings;
    }
```

public void showStatus (String message)

   The showStatus() method displays message on the browser's status line, if it
   has one. Again, how to display this string is up to the browser, and the browser
   can overwrite it whenever it wants. You should only use showStatus() for messages that the user can afford to miss.

public boolean isActive ()

   The isActive() method returns the current state of the applet. While an
   applet is initializing, it is not active, and calls to isActive() return false. The
   system marks the applet active just prior to calling start(); after this point,
   calls to isActive() return true.

public Locale getLocale () ★

   The getLocale() method retrieves the current Locale of the applet, if it has
   one. Using a Locale allows you to write programs that can adapt themselves to
   different languages and different regional variants. If no Locale has been set,
   getLocale() returns the default Locale. The default Locale has a user language of English and no region. To change the default Locale, set the system
   properties user.language and user.region, or call Locale.setDefault()
   (setDefault() verifies access rights with the security manager).*

Applet life cycle

The browser calls four methods of the Applet class to execute the applet. These
methods constitute the applet's life cycle. The default versions don't do anything;
you must override at least one of them to create a useful applet.

public void init ()

   The init() method is called once when the applet is first loaded. It should be
   used for tasks that need to be done only once. init() is often used to load
   images or sound files, set up the screen, get parameters out of the HTML file,
   and create objects the applet will need later. You should not do anything that
   might "hang" or wait indefinitely. In a sense, init() does things that might
   otherwise be done in an applet's constructor.

public void start ()

   The start() method is called every time the browser displays the web page
   containing the applet. start() usually does the "work" of the applet. It often
   starts threads, plays sound files, or does computation. start() may also be
   called when the browser is de-iconified.

---

* For more on the Locale class, see *Java Fundamental Classes Reference*, by Mark Grand, from O'Reilly &
Associates.

public void stop ()

> The stop() method is called whenever the browser leaves the web page containing the applet. It should stop or suspend anything that the applet is doing. For example, it should suspend any threads that have been created and stop playing any sound files. stop() may also be called when the browser is iconified.

public void destroy ()

> The destroy() method is called when the browser determines that it no longer needs to keep the applet around—in practice, when the browser decides to remove the applet from its cache or the browser exits. After this point, if the browser needs to display the applet again, it will reload the applet and call the applet's init() method. destroy() gives the applet a final opportunity to release any resources it is using (for example, close any open sockets). Most applets don't need to implement destroy(). It is always a good idea to release resources as soon as they aren't needed, rather than waiting for destroy(). There are no guarantees about when destroy() will be called; if your browser has a sufficiently large cache, the applet may stay around for a very long time.

Applet-sizing methods

public void resize(int width, int height)

> The resize() method changes the size of the applet space to width × height. The browser must support changing the applet space or else the sizing does not change. Netscape Navigator does not allow an applet to change its size; the applet is sized to the region allocated by the <APPLET> tag, period.
>
> Because Applet is a subclass of Component, it inherits the Java 1.1 method setSize(), which has the same function.

public void resize (Dimension dim)

> This resize() method calls the previous version of resize() with a width of dim.width and a height of dim.height.

Images

We have discussed Image objects extensively in Chapter 2, *Simple Graphics*, and Chapter 12, *Image Processing*, and used them in many of our examples. When writing an applet, you can use the getImage() method directly. In applications, you must go through Toolkit (which the following methods call) to get images.

public Image getImage (URL url)

> The getImage() method loads the image file located at url. url must be a complete and valid URL. The method returns a system-specific object that sub-

classes `Image` and returns immediately. The `Image` is not loaded until needed, either by `prepareImage()`, `MediaTracker`, or `drawImage()`.

public Image getImage (URL url, String filename)

> The `getImage()` method loads the image file located at `url` in `filename`. The applet locates the file relative to the specified URL; that is, if the URL ends with a filename, the applet removes the filename and appends the `filename` argument to produce a new URL. `getImage()` returns a system-specific object that subclasses `Image` and returns immediately. The `Image` is not loaded until needed, either by `prepareImage()`, `MediaTracker`, or `drawImage()`.

> In most cases, the `url` argument is a call to `getDocumentBase()` or `getCode-Base()`; most often, image files are located in the same directory as the HTML file, the applet's Java class file, or their own subdirectory.

Audio

Every Java platform is guaranteed to understand Sun's AU file format, which contains a single channel of 8000 Hz µLaw encoded audio data.[*] Java applets do not require any helper applications to play audio; they use the browser's audio capabilities. You can use an independent application, like Sun's *audiotool*, to control the volume. Of course, the user's workstation or PC needs audio hardware, but these days, it's hard to buy a computer that isn't equipped for audio.

The Java Media Framework API is rumored to provide support for additional audio formats, like Microsoft's *.wav* files or Macintosh/SGI *.aiff* audio files. At present, if you want your Java program to play audio files in other formats, you must first convert the audio file to the *.au* format, using a utility like SOX (Sound Exchange).[†] Once converted, your Java program can play the resulting *.au* file normally. (If you are interested in more information about audio, look in the *alt.binaries.sounds.d* newsgroup.)

The `Applet` class provides two ways to play audio clips. The first mechanism provides a method to load and play an audio file once:

public void play (URL url)

> The `play()` method downloads and plays the audio file located at `url`. `url` must be a complete and valid URL. If `url` is invalid, no sound is played. Some environments throw an exception if the URL is invalid, but not all. Calling `play()` within an applet's `destroy()` method usually has no effect; the applet

---

[*] The AU format is explained in the Audio File Format FAQ (version 3.10) located at *ftp://ftp.cwi.nl/pub/audio/index.html* in files *AudioFormats.part1* and *AudioFormats.part2*.

[†] SOX is available at *http://www.spies.com/Sox*. The current version of SOX is 10; version 11 is in gamma release. The UNIX source is located in *sox10.tar.gz*, while the DOS executable is *sox10dos.zip*.

and its resources will probably be deallocated before play() has time to download the audio file.

public void play (URL url, String filename)

This version of play() downloads and plays the audio file located at url in the file filename. The applet locates the file relative to the specified URL; that is, if the URL ends with a filename, the applet removes the filename and appends the filename argument to produce a new URL. If the resulting URL is invalid, no sound is played. Some environments throw an exception if the URL is invalid, but not all.

In most cases, the url argument is a call to getDocumentBase() or getCode-Base(); most often, sound files are located in the same directory as the HTML file or the applet's Java class file. For some reason, you cannot have a double dot (..) in the URL of an audio file; you can in the URL of an image file. Putting a double dot in the URL of an audio file raises a security exception in an applet causing play() to fail.

The following applet plays an audio file located relative to the HTML file from which the applet was loaded:

```
import java.net.*;
import java.applet.*;
public class audioTest extends Applet {
    public void init () {
        System.out.println ("Before");
        play (getDocumentBase(), "audio/flintstones.au");
        System.out.println ("After");
    }
}
```

The second way to play audio files splits the process into two steps: you get an AudioClip object and then play it as necessary. This procedure eliminates a significant drawback to play(): if you call play() repeatedly, it reloads the audio file each time, making the applet much slower.

public AudioClip getAudioClip (URL url)

The getAudioClip() method loads the audio file located at url. url must be a complete and valid URL. Upon success, getAudioClip() returns an instance of a class that implements the AudioClip interface. You can then call methods in the AudioClip interface (see Section 14.2) to play the clip. If an error occurs during loading (e.g., because the file was not found or the URL was invalid), getAudioClip() returns null.

getAudioClip() sounds similar to getImage(), and it is. However, Java currently loads audio clips synchronously; it does not start a separate thread as it does for images. You may want to create a helper class that loads audio clips in a separate thread.

The actual class of the `AudioClip` object depends on the platform you are using; you shouldn't need to know it. If you are curious, the *appletviewer* uses the class `sun.applet.AppletAudioClip`; Netscape Navigator uses the class `netscape.applet.AppletAudioClip`.

public AudioClip getAudioClip (URL url , String filename)

This version of the `getAudioClip()` method loads the audio file located at `url` in the file `filename`. The applet locates the file relative to the specified URL; that is, if the URL ends with a filename, the applet removes the filename and appends the `filename` argument to produce a new URL. If the resulting URL is invalid, the file is not loaded. Upon success, `getAudioClip()` returns an instance of a class that implements the `AudioClip` interface. You can then call methods in the `AudioClip` interface (see Section 14.2) to play the clip. If an error occurs during loading (e.g., because the file was not found or the URL was invalid), `getAudioClip()` returns `null`.

In most cases, the `url` argument is a call to `getDocumentBase()` or `getCode-Base()`; most often, sound files are located in the same directory as the HTML file or the applet's Java class file.

14.2 AudioClip Interface

Once an audio file is loaded into memory with `getAudioClip()`, you use the `AudioClip` interface to work with it.

Methods

Three methods define the `AudioClip` interface. The class that implements these methods depends on the run-time environment; the class is probably `sun.applet.AppletAudioClip` or `netscape.applet.AppletAudioClip`.

If you play an audio clip anywhere within your `Applet`, you should call the `Audio-Clip stop()` method within the `stop()` method of the applet. This ensures that the audio file will stop playing when the user leaves your web page. Stopping audio clips is a must if you call `loop()` to play the sound continuously; if you don't stop an audio clip, the user will have to exit the browser to get the sound to stop playing.

Applets can play audio clips simultaneously. Based upon the user's actions, you may want to play a sound file in the background continuously, while playing other files.

void play ()

The `play()` method plays the audio clip once from the beginning.

void loop ()

The loop() method plays the audio clip continuously. When it gets to the end-of-file marker, it resets itself to the beginning.

void stop ()

The stop() method stops the applet from playing the audio clip.

14.2.1 Using an AudioClip

The applet in Example 14-2 loads three audio files in the init() method. The start() method plays Dino barking in the background as a continuous loop. Whenever the browser calls paint(), Fred yells "Wilma," and when you click the mouse anywhere, the call to mouseDown() plays Fred yelling, "Yabba-Dabba-Doo." If you try real hard, all three can play at once. Before playing any audio clip, the applet makes sure that the clip is not null—that is, that the clip loaded correctly. stop() stops all clips from playing; you should make sure that applets stop all audio clips before the viewer leaves the web page.

Example 14–2: AudioClip Usage

```
import java.net.*;
import java.awt.*;
import java.applet.*;
public class AudioTestExample extends Applet{
    AudioClip audio1, audio2, audio3;
    public void init () {
        audio1 = getAudioClip (getCodeBase(), "audio/flintstones.au");
        audio2 = getAudioClip (getCodeBase(), "audio/dino.au");
        audio3 = getAudioClip (getCodeBase(), "audio/wilma.au");
    }
    public boolean mouseDown (Event e, int x, int y) {
        if (audio1 != null)
            audio1.play();
        return true;
    }
    public void start () {
        if (audio2 != null)
            audio2.loop();
    }
    public void paint (Graphics g) {
        if (audio3 != null)
            audio3.play();
    }
    public void stop () {
        if (audio1 != null)
            audio1.stop();
        if (audio2 != null)
            audio2.stop();
```

Example 14–2: AudioClip Usage (continued)

```
        if (audio3 != null)
            audio3.stop();
    }
}
```

14.3 AppletContext Interface

The `AppletContext` interface provides the means to control the browser environment where the applet is running.

Methods

Some of these methods are so frequently used that they are also provided within the `Applet` class.

public abstract AudioClip getAudioClip (URL url)

The `getAudioClip()` method loads the audio file located at `url`. `url` must be a complete and valid URL. Upon success, `getAudioClip()` returns an instance of a class that implements the `AudioClip` interface. You can then call methods in the `AudioClip` interface (see Section 14.2) to play the clip. If an error occurs during loading (e.g., because the file was not found or the URL was invalid), `getAudioClip()` returns `null`.

public abstract Image getImage (URL url)

The `getImage()` method loads the image file located at `url`. `url` must be a complete and valid URL. The method returns a system-specific object that subclasses `Image` and returns immediately. The `Image` is not loaded until needed. A call to `prepareImage()`, `MediaTracker`, or `drawImage()` forces loading to start.

public abstract Applet getApplet (String name)

The `getApplet()` method fetches the `Applet` from the current HTML page named `name`, which can be the applet's class name or the name provided in the `NAME` parameter of the `<APPLET>` tag. `getApplet()` returns `null` if the applet does not exist in the current context. This method allows you to call methods of other applets within the same context, loaded by the same `Class-Loader`. For example:

```
MyApplet who = (MyApplet)getAppletContext().getApplet("hey");
who.method();
```

TIP   Netscape Navigator 3.0 restricts which applets can communicate
               with each other. Internet Explorer seems to have a similar
               restriction. For applets to communicate, they must:

               • Have the same CODEBASE.

               • Have the same or no ARCHIVES tag.

               • Have MAYSCRIPT tags and appear in the same frame; alterna-
                 tively, neither applet may have a MAYSCRIPT tag.

               If these conditions are not met and you try to cast the return
               value of getApplet() or getApplets() to the appropriate class,
               either the cast will throw a ClassCastException; or nothing will
               happen, and the method will not continue beyond the point of
               the failure.

public abstract Enumeration getApplets ()

The getApplets() method gathers all the Applets in the current context,
loaded by the same ClassLoader, into a collection and returns the Enumeration. You can then cycle through them to perform some operation collec-
tively. For example:

```
Enumeration e = getAppletContext().getApplets();
while (e.hasMoreElements()) {
    Object o = e.nextElement();
    if (o instance of MyApplet) {
        MyApplet a = (Object)o;
        a.MyAppletMethod();
    }
}
```

TIP   If you want communication between applets on one page, be
               aware that there is no guarantee which applet will start first.
               Communications must be synchronized by using a controlling
               class or continual polling.

public abstract void showDocument (URL url)

The showDocument() method shows url in the current browser window. The
browser may ignore the request if it so desires.

public abstract void showDocument (URL url, String frame)

The showDocument() method shows url in a browser window specified by
frame. Different frame values and the results are shown in Table 14-1. The
browser may ignore the request, as *appletviewer* does.

```
try {
    URL u = new URL (getDocumentBase(), (String) file);
    getAppletContext().showDocument (u, "_blank");
} catch (Exception e) {
}
```

Table 14–1: Target Values

Target String	Results
_blank	Show url new browser window with no name.
_parent	Show url in the parent frame of the current window.
_self	Replace current url with url (i.e., display in the current window).
_top	Show url in top-most frame.
name	Show url in new browser window named name.

public abstract void showStatus (String message)

> The showStatus() method displays message on the browser's status line, if it has one. How to display this string is up to the browser, and the browser can overwrite it whenever it wants. You should use showStatus() only for messages that the user can afford to miss.

14.4 AppletStub Interface

The AppletStub interface provides a way to get information from the run-time browser environment. The Applet class provides methods with similar names that call these methods.

Methods

public abstract boolean isActive ()

> The isActive() method returns the current state of the applet. While an applet is initializing, it is not active, and calls to isActive() return false. The system marks the applet active just prior to calling start(); after this point, calls to isActive() return true.

public abstract URL getDocumentBase ()

> The getDocumentBase() method returns the complete URL of the HTML file that loaded the applet. This method can be used with the getImage() or getAudioClip() methods to load an image or audio file relative to the HTML file.

public abstract URL getCodeBase ()

The getCodeBase() method returns the complete URL of the *.class* file that contains the applet. This method can be used with the getImage() method or the getAudioClip() method to load an image or audio file relative to the *.class* file.

public abstract String getParameter (String name)

The getParameter() method allows you to get parameters from <PARAM> tags within the <APPLET> tag of the HTML file that loaded the applet. The name parameter of getParameter() must match the name string of the <PARAM> tag; name is case insensitive. The return value of getParameter() is the value associated with name; it is always a String regardless of the type of data in the tag. If name is not found within the <PARAM> tags of the <APPLET>, getParameter() returns null.

public abstract AppletContext getAppletContext ()

The getAppletContext() method returns the current AppletContext of the applet. This is part of the stub that is set by the system when setStub() is called.

public abstract void appletResize (int width, int height)

The appletResize() method is called by the resize method of the Applet class. The method changes the size of the applet space to width × height. The browser must support changing the applet space; if it doesn't, the size remains unchanged.

14.5 Audio in Applications

The rest of this chapter describes how to use audio in your applications. Because the audio support discussed so far has been provided by the browser, applications that don't run in the context of a browser must use a different set of classes to work with audio. These classes are within the sun.audio package. Although the sun.* package hierarchy is not necessarily included by other vendors, the sun.audio classes discussed here are provided with Netscape Navigator 2.0/3.0 and Internet Explorer 3.0. Therefore, you can use these classes within applets, too. This section ends by developing a SunAudioClip class that has an interface similar to the applet's audio interface; you can use it to minimize coding differences between applets and applications.

14.5.1 AudioData

The AudioData class holds a clip of 8000 Hz μLaw audio data. This data can be used to construct an AudioDataStream or ContinuousAudioDataStream, which can then be played with the AudioPlayer.

Constructor

public AudioData (byte buffer[])

The AudioData constructor accepts a byte array buffer and creates an instance of AudioData. The buffer should contain 8000 Hz μLaw audio data.

Methods

There are no methods for AudioData.

14.5.2 AudioStream

AudioStream subclasses FilterInputStream, which extends InputStream. Using an InputStream lets you move back and forth (rewind and fast forward) within an audio file, in addition to playing the audio data from start to finish.

Constructors

public AudioStream (InputStream in) throws IOException

The AudioStream constructor has InputStream in as its parameter and can throw IOException on error. In the following code, we get an input stream by opening a *.au* file. Another common way to construct an AudioStream is to use the stream associated with a URL through the URL's openStream() method.

```
FileInputStream fis = new FileInputStream ("/usr/openwin/demo/sounds/1.au");
AudioStream audiostream = new AudioStream (fis);
```

or:

```
AudioStream audiostream = new AudioStream (savedUrl.openStream());
```

If you are constructing the audio data yourself, you would use a ByteArrayInputStream. Whatever the source of the data, the input stream should provide data in Sun's *.au* format.

Methods

public int read (byte buffer[], int offset, int length) throws IOException

The read() method for AudioStream reads an array of bytes into buffer. offset is the first element of buffer that is used. length is the maximum number of bytes to read. This method blocks until some input is available. read() returns the actual number of bytes read. If the end of stream is encountered and no bytes were read, read() returns -1. Ordinarily, you read() an AudioStream only if you want to modify the audio data in some way.

public int getLength()

The getLength() method returns the length of the audio data contained within the AudioStream, excluding any header information in the file.

public AudioData getData () throws IOException

The getData() method of AudioStream is the most important and most frequently used. It reads the data from the input stream and creates an AudioData instance. As the following code shows, you can create an AudioStream and get the AudioData with one statement.

```
AudioData audiodata = new AudioStream (aUrl.openStream()).getData();
```

14.5.3 AudioDataStream

Constructors

public AudioDataStream (AudioData data)

This constructor creates an AudioDataStream from an AudioData object data. The resulting AudioDataStream is a subclass of ByteArrayInputStream and can be played by the AudioPlayer.start() method.

Methods

There are no methods for AudioDataStream.

14.5.4 ContinuousAudioDataStream

Constructors

public ContinuousAudioDataStream (AudioData data)

This constructor creates a continuous stream of audio from data. The resulting ContinuousAudioDataStream is a subclass of AudioDataStream and, therefore, of ByteArrayInputStream. It can be played by AudioPlayer.start(); whenever the player reaches the end of the continuous audio data stream, it restarts from the beginning.

Methods

public int read ()

This read() method of ContinuousAudioDataStream overrides the read() method in ByteArrayInputStream to rewind back to the beginning of the stream when end-of-file is reached. This method is used by the system when it reads the InputStream; it is rarely called directly. read() never returns -1 since it loops back to the beginning on end-of-file.

public int read (byte buffer[], int offset, int length)

This read() method of ContinuousAudioDataStream overrides the read() method in ByteArrayInputStream to rewind back to the beginning of the stream when end-of-file is reached. This method is used by the system when it reads the InputStream; it is rarely called directly. read() returns the actual number of bytes read. read() never returns -1 since it loops back to the beginning on end-of-file.

14.5.5 AudioStreamSequence

Constructors

public AudioStreamSequence (Enumeration e)

The constructor for AudioStreamSequence accepts an Enumeration e(normally the elements of a Vector of AudioStreams) as its sole parameter. The constructor converts the sequence of audio streams into a single stream to be played in order. An example follows:

```
Vector v = new Vector ();
v.addElement (new AudioStream (url1.openStream ()));
v.addElement (new AudioStream (url2.openStream ()));
AudioStreamSequence audiostream = new AudioStreamSequence (v.elements ());
```

Methods

public int read ()

This read() method of AudioStreamSequence overrides the read() method in InputStream to start the next stream when end-of-file is reached. This method is used by the system when it reads the InputStream and is rarely called directly. If the end of all streams is encountered and no bytes were read, read() returns -1. Otherwise, read() returns the character read.

public int read (byte buffer[], int offset, int length)

This read() method of AudioStreamSequence overrides the read() method in InputStream to start the next stream when end-of-file is reached. This method is used by the system when it reads the InputStream and is rarely called directly. read() returns the actual number of bytes read. If the end of all streams is encountered and no bytes were read, read() returns -1.

14.5.6 AudioPlayer

The AudioPlayer class is the workhorse of the sun.audio package. It is used to play all the streams that were created with the other classes. There is no constructor for AudioPlayer; it just extends Thread and provides start() and stop() methods.

Variable

public final static AudioPlayer player

`player` is the default audio player. This audio player is initialized automatically when the class is loaded; you do not have to initialize it (in fact, you can't because it is final) or call the constructor yourself.

Methods

public synchronized void start (InputStream in)

The `start()` method starts a thread that plays the `InputStream in`. Stream in continues to play until there is no more data or it is stopped. If in is a ContinuousAudioDataStream, the playing continues until `stop()` (described next) is called.

public synchronized void stop (InputStream in)

The `stop()` method stops the player from playing `InputStream in`. Nothing happens if the stream in is no longer playing or was never started.

14.5.7 *SunAudioClip Class Definition*

The class in Example 14-3 is all you need to play audio files in applications. It implements the `java.applet.AudioClip` interface, so the methods and functionality will be familiar. The test program in `main()` demonstrates how to use the class. Although the class itself can be used in applets, provided your users have the `sun.audio` package available, it is geared towards application users.

Example 14–3: The SunAudioClip Class

```
import java.net.URL;
import java.io.FileInputStream;
import sun.audio.*;
public class SunAudioClip implements java.applet.AudioClip {
    private AudioData audiodata;
    private AudioDataStream audiostream;
    private ContinuousAudioDataStream continuousaudiostream;
    static int length;
    public SunAudioClip (URL url) throws java.io.IOException {
        audiodata = new AudioStream (url.openStream()).getData();
        audiostream = null;
        continuousaudiostream = null;
    }
    public SunAudioClip (String filename) throws java.io.IOException {
        FileInputStream fis = new FileInputStream (filename);
        AudioStream audioStream = new AudioStream (fis);
        audiodata = audioStream.getData();
        audiostream = null;
        continuousaudiostream = null;
    }
    public void play () {
```

Example 14–3: The SunAudioClip Class (continued)

```
            audiostream = new AudioDataStream (audiodata);
            AudioPlayer.player.start (audiostream);
    }
    public void loop () {
            continuousaudiostream = new ContinuousAudioDataStream (audiodata);
            AudioPlayer.player.start (continuousaudiostream);
    }
    public void stop () {
        if (audiostream != null)
            AudioPlayer.player.stop (audiostream);
        if (continuousaudiostream != null)
            AudioPlayer.player.stop (continuousaudiostream);
    }
    public static void main (String args[]) throws Exception {
        URL url1 = new URL ("http://localhost:8080/audio/1.au");
        URL url2 = new URL ("http://localhost:8080/audio/2.au");
        SunAudioClip sac1 = new SunAudioClip (url1);
        SunAudioClip sac2 = new SunAudioClip (url2);
        SunAudioClip sac3 = new SunAudioClip ("1.au");
        sac1.play ();
        sac2.loop ();
        sac3.play ();
        try {// Delay for loop
            Thread.sleep (2000);
        } catch (InterruptedException ie) {}
        sac2.stop();
    }
}
```

15

Toolkit and Peers

This chapter describes the Toolkit class and the purposes it serves. It also describes the java.awt.peer package of interfaces, along with how they fit in with the general scheme of things. The most important advice I can give you about the peer interfaces is not to worry about them. Unless you are porting Java to another platform, creating your own Toolkit, or adding any native component, you can ignore the peer interfaces.

15.1 Toolkit

The Toolkit object is an abstract class that provides an interface to platform-specific details like window size, available fonts, and printing. Every platform that supports Java must provide a concrete class that extends the Toolkit class. The Sun JDK provides a Toolkit for Windows NT/95 (sun.awt.win32.MToolkit [Java1.0] or sun.awt.windows.MToolkit [Java1.1]), Solaris/Motif (sun.awt.motif.MToolkit), and Macintosh (sun.awt.macos.MToolkit). Although the Toolkit is used frequently, both directly and behind the scenes, you would never create any of these objects directly. When you need a Toolkit, you ask for it with the static method getDefaultToolkit() or the Component.getToolkit() method.

You might use the Toolkit object if you need to fetch an image in an application (getImage()), get the font information provided with the Toolkit (getFontList() or getFontMetrics()), get the color model (getColorModel()), get the screen metrics (getScreenResolution() or getScreenSize()), get the system clipboard (getSystemClipboard()), get a print job (getPrintJob()), or ring the bell (beep()). The other methods of Toolkit are called for you by the system.

15.1.1 Toolkit Methods

Constructors

public Toolkit()—cannot be called by user

Because `Toolkit` is an abstract class, it has no usable constructor. To get a `Toolkit` object, ask for your environment's default toolkit by calling the static method `getDefaultToolkit()` or call `Component.getToolkit()` to get the toolkit of a component. When the actual `Toolkit` is created for the native environment, the `awt` package is loaded, the `AWT-Win32` and `AWT-Callback-Win32` or `AWT-Motif` and `AWT-Input` threads (or the appropriate threads for your environment) are created, and the threads go into infinite loops for screen maintenance and event handling.

Pseudo-Constructors

public static synchronized Toolkit getDefaultToolkit ()

The `getDefaultToolkit()` method returns the system's default `Toolkit` object. The default `Toolkit` is identified by the `System` property `awt.toolkit`, which defaults to an instance of the `sun.awt.motif.MToolkit` class. On the Windows NT/95 platforms, this is overridden by the Java environment to be `sun.awt.win32.MToolkit` (Java1.0) or `sun.awt.windows.MToolkit` (Java1.1). On the Macintosh platform, this is overridden by the environment to be `sun.awt.macos.MToolkit`. Most browsers don't let you change the system property `awt.toolkit`. Since this is a static method, you don't need to have a `Toolkit` object to call it; just call `Toolkit.getDefaultToolkit()`.

Currently, only one `Toolkit` can be associated with an environment. You are more than welcome to try to replace the one provided with the JDK. This permits you to create a whole new widget set, outside of Java, while maintaining the standard AWT API.

System information

public abstract ColorModel getColorModel ()

The `getColorModel()` method returns the current `ColorModel` used by the system. The default `ColorModel` is the standard RGB model, with 8 bits for each of red, green, and blue. There are an additional 8 bits for the alpha component, for pixel-level transparency.

public abstract String[] getFontList ()

The `getFontList()` method returns a `String` array of the set Java fonts available with this `Toolkit`. Normally, these fonts will be understood on all the Java platforms. The set provided with Sun's JDK 1.0 (with Netscape Navigator and Internet Explorer, on platforms other than the Macintosh) contains Times-Roman, Dialog, Helvetica, Courier (the only fixed-width font), DialogInput, and ZapfDingbat.

In Java 1.1, `getFont()` reports all the 1.0 font names. It also reports Serif, which is equivalent to TimesRoman; San Serif, which is equivalent to Helvetica; and Monospaced, which is equivalent to Courier. The names Times-Roman, Helvetica, and Courier are still supported but should be avoided. They have been deprecated and may disappear in a future release. Although the JDK 1.1 reports the existence of the ZapfDingbat font, you can't use it. The characters in this font have been remapped to Unicode characters in the range \u2700 to \u27ff.

public abstract FontMetrics getFontMetrics (Font font)

The `getFontMetrics()` method returns the `FontMetrics` for the given `Font` object. You can use this value to compute how much space would be required to display some text using this `font`. You can use this version of `getFontMetrics()` (unlike the similar method in the `Graphics` class) prior to drawing anything on the screen.

public int getMenuShortcutKeyMask() ★

The `getMenuShortcutKeyMask()` method identifies the accelerator key for menu shortcuts for the user's platform. The return value is one of the modifier masks in the `Event` class, like `Event.CTRL_MASK`. This method is used internally by the `MenuBar` class to help in handling menu selection events. See Chapter 10, *Would You Like to Choose from the Menu?* for more information about dealing with menu accelerators.

public abstract PrintJob getPrintJob (Frame frame, String jobtitle, Properties props) ★

The `getPrintJob()` method initiates a print operation, `PrintJob`, on the user's platform. After getting a `PrintJob` object, you can use it to print the current graphics context as follows:

```
// Java 1.1 only
PrintJob p = getToolkit().getPrintJob (aFrame, "hi", aProps);
Graphics pg = p.getGraphics();
printAll (pg);
pg.dispose();
p.end();
```

With somewhat more work, you can print arbitrary content. See Chapter 17,

Printing, for more information about printing. The `frame` parameter serves as the parent to any print dialog window, `jobtitle` serves as the identification string in the print queue, and `props` serves as a means to provide platform-specific properties (default printer, page order, orientation, etc.). If `props` is `(Properties)null`, no properties will be used. `props` is particularly interesting in that it is used both for input and for output. When the environment creates a print dialog, it can read default values for printing options from the properties sheet and use that to initialize the dialog. After `getPrintJob()` returns, the properties sheet is filled in with the actual printing options that the user requested. You can then use these option settings as the defaults for subsequent print jobs.

The actual property names are `Toolkit` specific and may be defined by the environment outside of Java. Furthermore, the environment is free to ignore the `props` parameter altogether; this appears to be the case with Windows NT/95 platforms. (It is difficult to see how Windows NT/95 would use the properties sheet, since these platforms don't even raise the print dialog until you call the method `getGraphics()`.) Table 15-1 shows some of the properties recognized on UNIX platforms; valid property values are shown in a fixed-width font.

Table 15–1: UNIX Printing Properties

Property Name	Meaning and Possible Values
`awt.print.printer`	The name of the printer on your system to send the job to.
`awt.print.fileName`	The name of the file to save the print job to.
`awt.print.numCopies`	The number of copies to be printed.
`awt.print.options`	Other options to be used for the run-time system's print command.
`awt.print.destination`	Whether the print job should be sent to a `printer` or saved in a `file`.
`awt.print.paperSize`	The size of the paper on which you want to print— usually, `letter`.
`awt.print.orientation`	Whether the job should be printed in `portrait` or `landscape` orientation.

public static String getProperty (String key, String defaultValue) ★

The `getProperty()` method retrieves the `key` property from the system's *awt.properties* file (located in the *lib* directory under the *java.home* directory). If `key` is not a valid property, `defaultValue` is returned. This file is used to provide localized names for various system resources.

public abstract int getScreenResolution ()

The `getScreenResolution()` method retrieves the resolution of the screen in dots per inch. The sharper the resolution of the screen, the greater number of dots per inch. Values vary depending on the system and graphics mode. The `PrintJob.getPageResolution()` method returns similar information for a printed page.

public abstract Dimension getScreenSize ()

The `getScreenSize()` method retrieves the dimensions of the user's screen in pixels for the current mode. For instance, a VGA system in standard mode will return 640 for the width and 480 for the height. This information is extremely helpful if you wish to manually size or position objects based upon the physical size of the user's screen. The `PrintJob.getPageDimension()` method returns similar information for a printed page.

public abstract Clipboard getSystemClipboard() ★

The `getSystemClipboard()` method returns a reference to the system's clipboard. The clipboard allows your Java programs to use cut and paste operations, either internally or as an interface between your program and objects outside of Java. For instance, the following code copies a `String` from a Java program to the system's clipboard:

```
// Java 1.1 only
Clipboard clipboard = getToolkit().getSystemClipboard();
StringSelection ss = new StringSelection("Hello");
clipboard.setContents(ss, this);
```

Once you have placed the string `"Hello"` on the clipboard, you can paste it anywhere. The details of `Clipboard`, `StringSelection`, and the rest of the `java.awt.datatransfer` package are described in Chapter 16, *Data Transfer.*

public final EventQueue getSystemEventQueue() ★

After checking whether the security manager allows access, this method returns a reference to the system's event queue.

protected abstract EventQueue getSystemEventQueueImpl() ★

`getSystemEventQueueImpl()` does the actual work of fetching the event queue. The toolkit provider implements this method; only subclasses of `Toolkit` can call it.

Images

The `Toolkit` provides a set of basic methods for working with images. These methods are similar to methods in the `Applet` class; `Toolkit` provides its own implementation for use by programs that don't have access to an `AppletContext` (i.e., applications or applets that are run as applications). Remember that you need an instance of Toolkit before you can call these methods; for example, to get an image, you might call Toolkit.getDefaultToolkit().getImage("myImage.gif").

public abstract Image getImage (String filename)

The getImage() method with a String parameter allows applications to get an image from the local filesystem. Its argument is either a relative or absolute filename for an image in a recognized image file format. The method returns immediately; the Image object that it returns is initially empty. When the image is needed, the system attempts to get filename and convert it to an image. To force the file to load immediately or to check for errors while loading, use the MediaTracker class.

NOTE   This version of getImage() is not usable within browsers since it will throw a security exception because the applet is trying to access the local filesystem.

---

public abstract Image getImage (URL url)

The getImage() method with the URL parameter can be used in either applets or applications. It allows you to provide a URL for an image in a recognized image file format. Like the other getImage() methods, this method returns immediately; the Image object that it returns is initially empty. When the image is needed, the system attempts to load the file specified by url and convert it to an image. You can use the MediaTracker class to monitor loading and check whether any errors occurred.

public abstract boolean prepareImage (Image image, int width, int height, ImageObserver observer)

The prepareImage() method is called by the system or a program to force image to start loading. This method can be used to force an image to begin loading before it is actually needed. The Image image will be scaled to be width × height. A width and height of -1 means image will be rendered unscaled (i.e., at the size specified by the image itself). The observer is the Component on which image will be rendered. As the image is loaded across the network, the observer's imageUpdate() method is called to inform the observer of the image's status.

public abstract int checkImage (Image image, int width, int height, ImageObserver observer)

The checkImage() method returns the status of the image that is being rendered on observer. Calling checkImage() only provides information about the image; it does not force the image to start loading. The image is being scaled to be width × height. Passing a width and height of –1 means the image will be displayed without scaling. The return value of checkImage() is some combination of ImageObserver flags describing the data that is now available. The ImageObserver flags are: WIDTH, HEIGHT, PROPERTIES, SOMEBITS, FRAMEBITS, ALLBITS, ERROR, and ABORT. Once ALLBITS is set, the image is completely loaded, and the return value of checkImage() will not change. For more information about these flags, see Chapter 12, *Image Processing*.

The following program loads an image; whenever paint() is called, it displays what information about that image is available. When the ALLBITS flag is set, checkingImages knows that the image is fully loaded, and that a call to drawImage() will display the entire image.

```
import java.awt.*;
import java.awt.image.*;
import java.applet.*;
public class checkingImages extends Applet {
    Image i;
    public void init () {
        i = getImage (getDocumentBase(), "ora-icon.gif");
    }
    public void displayChecks (int i) {
        if ((i & ImageObserver.WIDTH) != 0)
            System.out.print ("Width ");
        if ((i & ImageObserver.HEIGHT) != 0)
            System.out.print ("Height ");
        if ((i & ImageObserver.PROPERTIES) != 0)
            System.out.print ("Properties ");
        if ((i & ImageObserver.SOMEBITS) != 0)
            System.out.print ("Some-bits ");
        if ((i & ImageObserver.FRAMEBITS) != 0)
            System.out.print ("Frame-bits ");
        if ((i & ImageObserver.ALLBITS) != 0)
            System.out.print ("All-bits ");
        if ((i & ImageObserver.ERROR) != 0)
            System.out.print ("Error-loading ");
        if ((i & ImageObserver.ABORT) != 0)
            System.out.print ("Loading-Aborted ");
        System.out.println ();
    }
    public void paint (Graphics g) {
        displayChecks (Toolkit.getDefaultToolkit().checkImage(i, -1, -1, this));
        g.drawImage (i, 0, 0, this);
    }
}
```

Here's the output from running checkingImages under Java 1.0; it shows that the width and height of the image are loaded first, followed by the image properties and the image itself. Java 1.1 also displays Frame-bits once the image is loaded.

```
Width Height
Width Height Properties Some-bits
Width Height Properties Some-bits All-bits
```

```
Width Height Properties Some-bits All-bits
Width Height Properties Some-bits All-bits
... (Repeated Forever More)
```

public abstract Image createImage (ImageProducer producer)

This createImage() method creates an Image object from an ImageProducer. The producer parameter must be some class that implements the ImageProducer interface. Image producers in the java.awt.graphics package are FilteredImageSource (which, together with an ImageFilter, lets you modify an existing image) and MemoryImageSource (which lets you turn an array of pixel information into an image). The image filters provided with java.awt.image are CropImageFilter, RGBImageFilter, AreaAveragingScaleFilter, and ReplicateScaleFilter. You can also implement your own image producers and image filters. These classes are all covered in detail in Chapter 12.

The following code uses this version of createImage() to create a modified version of an original image:

```
Image i = Toolkit.getDefaultToolkit().getImage (u);
    TransparentImageFilter tf = new TransparentImageFilter (.5f);
Image j = Toolkit.getDefaultToolkit().createImage (
            new FilteredImageSource (i.getSource(), tf));
```

public Image createImage (byte[] imageData) ★

This createImage() method converts the entire byte array in imageData into an Image. This data must be in one of the formats understood by this AWT Toolkit (GIF, JPEG, or XBM) and relies on the "magic number" of the data to determine the image type.

public Image createImage (byte[] imageData, int offset, int length) ★

This createImage() method converts a subset of the byte data in imageData into an Image. Instead of starting at the beginning, this method starts at offset and goes to offset+length-1, for a total of length bytes. If offset is 0 and length is imageData.length, this method is equivalent to the previous method and converts the entire array.

The data in imageData must be in one of the formats understood by this AWT Toolkit (GIF, JPEG, or XBM) and relies on the "magic number" of the data to determine the image type.

NOTE   For those unfamiliar with magic numbers, most data files are uniquely identified by the first handful or so of bytes. For instance, the first three bytes of a GIF file are "GIF". This is what createImage() relies upon to do its magic.

Miscellaneous methods

public abstract void beep () ★

> The beep() method attempts to play an audio beep. You have no control over
> pitch, duration, or volume; it is like putting echo ^G in a UNIX shell script.

public abstract void sync ()

> The sync() method flushes the display of the underlying graphics context.
> Normally, this is done automatically, but there are times (particularly when
> doing animation) when you need to sync() the display yourself.

15.2 The Peer Interfaces

Each GUI component that AWT provides has a *peer*. The peer is the implementation of that component in the native environment. For example, the Choice component in AWT corresponds to some native object that lets the user select one or
more items from a list. As a Java developer, you need to worry only about the interface of the Choice object; when someone runs your program, the Choice object is
mapped to an appropriate native object, which is the Choice peer, that "does the
right thing." You don't really care what the peer is or how it's implemented; in fact,
the peer may look (and to some extent, behave) differently on each platform.

The glue that allows an AWT component and its peer to work together is called a
peer interface. A peer interface is simply an interface that defines the methods that
the peer is required to support. These interfaces are collected in the package
java.awt.peer. For example, this package contains the ButtonPeer interface,
which contains the single method setLabel(). This means that the native object
used to implement a Button must contain a method called setLabel() in order
for AWT to use it as a button peer. (It's not quite that simple; since a button is also
a Component, the button's peer must also implement the ComponentPeer interface,
which is much more complicated.)

With one exception, there is a one-to-one correspondence between Component
classes and peer interfaces: a Window has a WindowPeer, a Checkbox has a Checkbox-
Peer, and so on. The one exception is a new peer interface that appears in Java
1.1: the LightweightPeer, which doesn't have a corresponding component. The
LightweightPeer is used by components that exist purely in Java, don't have a
native peer, and are displayed and managed by another container. Lightweight-
Peer makes it easier to create new components or containers that can behave like
other components, but don't subclass Canvas or Panel and don't correspond to
anything in the native environment. The best usage I can think of is to subclass
Container to create a lightweight Panel. If you are only using a Panel to manage

layout, there is no need for a peer to be created to process events. This should result in substantial resource savings where multiple panels need to be created just to help with layout. The following code is all you need to create a LightWeight-Panel:

```
import java.awt.*;
public class LightWeightPanel extends Container {
}
```

There also tends to be a one-to-one relationship between the peer methods and the methods of the Java component. That is, each method in the peer interface corresponds to a method of the component. However, although a peer must implement each method in its peer interface, it doesn't necessarily have to do anything in that method. It's entirely possible for a platform to have a native button object that doesn't let you set the label. In this case, the button peer would implement the setLabel() method required by the ButtonPeer interface, but it wouldn't do anything. Of course, the component may also have many methods that don't correspond to the peer methods. Methods that don't correspond to anything in the peer are handled entirely within Java.

The ComponentPeer interface is the parent of all non-menu objects in the peer package. The MenuComponentPeer is the parent of all menu objects. The trees mirror the regular object hierarchies. Figure 15-1 shows the object hierarchy diagram.

Creating a Java component (e.g., Button b = new Button ("Foo")) does not create the peer. An object's peer is created when the object's addNotify() method is called. This is usually when the component's container is added to the screen. The call to a component's addNotify() method in turn calls the appropriate createxxxx() method of the Toolkit (for a Button, createButton()). Figure 15-2 shows the process.

When you remove a component from a container by calling remove(), the container calls the component's removeNotify() method. This usually results in a call to the peer's dispose() method. Depending on the particular component, removeNotify() may be overridden to perform additional work. Removing a Component from a Container does not destroy the Component. The next time the method addNotify() is called, the component must be recreated by the peer, with its previous characteristics. For instance, when a TextField is removed, the current text, plus the start and stop points for the current selection, are saved. These will be restored if you add the text field to its container again. For some components, like a Label, there is no need to retain any additional information.

A component's peer needs to exist only when the user is interacting with it. If you are developing resource-intensive programs, you might want to consider drawing the components manually when they do not have the focus and using the peer only when they actually have input focus. This technique can save a considerable

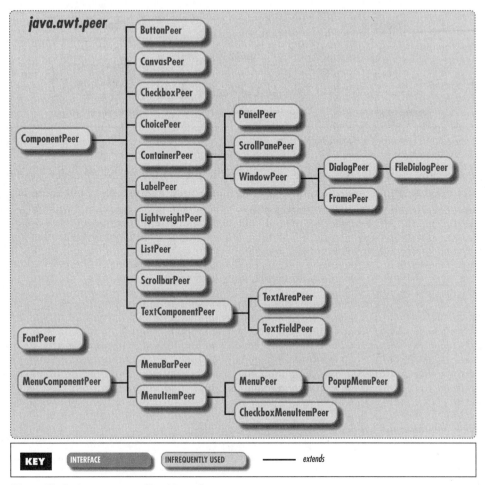

| KEY | INTERFACE | INFREQUENTLY USED | ——— extends |

Figure 15–1: java.awt.peer object hierarchy

amount of memory resources but requires extra work on your part as a developer and goes beyond the scope of this book. The LightweightPeer interface appears to be designed to make this process easier: you could create a dummy button that doesn't do anything and uses the LightweightPeer. Whenever the mouse enters the button's space, you could quickly remove the dummy button and add a real button.

The peer interfaces are listed in their entirety in the reference section. We won't list them here, primarily because you don't need to worry about them unless you're porting Java to a new platform. Each method in a peer interface corresponds exactly to the similarly named method in the matching component. LightweightPeer is the only exception, because it doesn't have a matching component, but that's easy to take care of: as you'd expect, LightweightPeer doesn't

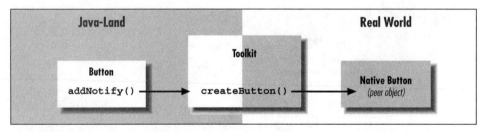

Figure 15–2: Creating a Button peer

define any methods. (Of course, a peer that implements LightweightPeer would still need to implement the methods inherited from ComponentPeer, but those are inherited when you subclass Component.)

16

Data Transfer

One feature that was missing from Java 1.0 was the ability to access the system clipboard. It was impossible to cut and paste data from one program into another. Java 1.1 includes a package called `java.awt.datatransfer` that supports clipboard operations. Using this package, you can cut an arbitrary object from one program and paste it into another. In theory, you can cut and paste almost anything; in practice, you usually want to cut and paste text strings, so the package provides special support for string operations. The current version allows only one object to be on the clipboard at a time.

`java.awt.datatransfer` consists of three classes, two interfaces, and one exception. Objects that can be transferred implement the `Transferable` interface. The `Transferable` interface defines methods for working with different *flavors* of an object. The concept of flavors is basic to Java's clipboard model. Essentially, a flavor is a MIME content type. Any object can be represented in several different ways, each corresponding to a different MIME type. For example, a text string could be represented by a Java `String` object, an array of Unicode character data, or some kind of rich text that contains font information. The object putting the string on the clipboard provides whatever flavors it is capable of; an object pasting the string from the clipboard takes whatever flavor it can handle. Flavors are represented by the `DataFlavor` class, and the `UnsupportedFlavorException` is used when an object asks for a `DataFlavor` that is not available.

The `Clipboard` class represents the clipboard itself. There is a single system clipboard, but you can create as many private clipboards as you want. The system clipboard lets you cut and paste between arbitrary applications (for example,

Microsoft Word and some Java programs). Private clipboards are useful within a single application, though you could probably figure out some way to export a clipboard to another application using RMI.

To put data on the clipboard, you must implement the `ClipboardOwner` interface, which provides a means for you to be notified when the data you write is removed from the clipboard. (There isn't any `ClipboardReader` interface; any object can read from the clipboard.) The final component of the `datatransfer` package is a special class called `StringSelection` that facilitates cutting and pasting text strings.

Cutting and pasting isn't the whole story; JavaSoft has also promised drag-and-drop capabilities, but this won't be in the initial release of Java 1.1.

16.1 DataFlavor

A `DataFlavor` represents a format in which data can be transferred. The `DataFlavor` class includes two common data flavors; you can create other flavors by extending this class. Flavors are essentially MIME content types and are represented by the standard MIME type strings. An additional content subtype has been added to represent Java classes; the content type of a Java object is:*

```
application/x-java-serialized-object
<classname>
```

For example, the content type of a `Vector` object would be:

```
application/x-java-serialized-object java.util.Vector
```

In addition to the content type, a `DataFlavor` also contains a *presentable name*. The presentable name is intended to be more comprehensible to humans than the MIME type. For example, the presentable name of a `VectorFlavor` object might just be "Vector", rather than the complex and lengthy MIME type given previously. Presentable names are useful when a program needs to ask the user which data flavor to use.

16.1.1 DataFlavor Methods

Variables

The `DataFlavor` class includes two public variables that hold "prebuilt" flavors representing different kinds of text objects. These flavors are used in conjunction with the `StringSelection` class. Although these flavors are variables for all practical purposes, they are used as constants.

---

* The type name changed to `x-java-serialized-object` in the 1.1.1 release.

public static DataFlavor stringFlavor ★

The `stringFlavor` variable is the data flavor for textual data represented as a Java `String` object. Its MIME type is `application/x-javaserializedobject String`.

public static DataFlavor plainTextFlavor ★

The `plainTextFlavor` variable is the data flavor for standard, Unicode-encoded text. Its MIME type is `text/plain; charset=unicode`.

Constructors

The `DataFlavor` class has two constructors. One creates a `DataFlavor` given a MIME content type; the other creates a `DataFlavor` given a Java class and builds the MIME type from the class name.

public DataFlavor(String mimeType, String humanPresentableName) ★

The first constructor creates an instance of `DataFlavor` for the `mimeType` flavor of data. The `humanPresentableName` parameter should be a more user-friendly name. It might be used in a menu to let the user select a flavor from several possibilities. It might also be used to generate an error message when the `UnsupportedFlavorException` occurs. The `plainTextFlavor` uses "Plain Text" as its presentable name.

To read data from the clipboard, a program calls the `Transferable.getTransferData()` method. If the data is represented by a `DataFlavor` that doesn't correspond to a Java class (for example, `plainTextFlavor`), `getTransferData()` returns an `InputStream` for you to read the data from.

public DataFlavor(Class representationClass, String humanPresentableName) ★

The other constructor creates an instance of `DataFlavor` for the specific Java class `representationClass`. Again, the `humanPresentableName` provides a more user-friendly name for use in menus, error messages, or other interactions with users. The `stringFlavor` uses "Unicode String" as its presentable name.

A program calls `Transferable.getTransferData()` to read data from the clipboard. If the data is represented by a Java class, `getTransferData()` returns an instance of the representation class itself. It does not return a `Class` object. For example, if the data flavor is `stringFlavor`, `getTransferData()` returns a `String`.

Presentations

public String getHumanPresentableName() ★

> The getHumanPresentableName() method returns the data flavor's presentable name; for example, stringFlavor.getHumanPresentableName() returns the string "Unicode String".

public void setHumanPresentableName(String humanPresentableName) ★

> The setHumanPresentableName() method changes the data flavor's presentable name to a new humanPresentableName. It is hard to imagine why you would want to change a flavor's name.

public String getMimeType() ★

> The getMimeType() method gets the MIME content type for the DataFlavor as a String.

public Class getRepresentationClass() ★

> The getRepresentationClass() method returns the Java type that is used to represent data of this flavor (i.e., the type that would be returned by the get-TransferData()method). It returns the type as a Class object, not an instance of the class itself. Note that all data flavors have a representation class, not just those for which the class is specified explicitly in the constructor. For example, the plainTextFlavor.getRepresentationClass() method returns the class java.io.StringReader.

public boolean isMimeTypeEqual(String mimeType) ★

> The isMimeTypeEqual() method checks for string equality between mimeType and the data flavor's MIME type string. For some MIME types, this comparison may be too simplistic because character sets may not be present on types like text/plain. Therefore, this method would tell you that the MIME type text/plain; charset=unicode is different from text/plain.

public final boolean isMimeTypeEqual(DataFlavor dataFlavor) ★

> The isMimeTypeEqual() method checks whether the MIME type of the dataFlavor parameter equals the current data flavor's MIME type. It calls the previous method, and therefore has the same weaknesses.

Protected methods

protected String normalizeMimeType(String mimeType) ★

> The normalizeMimeType() method is used to convert a MIME type string into a standard form. Its argument is a MIME type, as a String; it returns the new normalized MIME type. You would never call normalizeMimeType() directly, but you might want to override this method if you are creating a subclass of DataFlavor and want to change the default normalization process. For example, one thing you might do with this is add the string charset=US-ASCII to the text/plain MIME type if it appears without a character set.

protected String normalizeMimeTypeParameter(String parameterName, String parameter-Value) ★

The `normalizeMimeTypeParameter()` method is used to convert any parameters associated with MIME types into a standard form. Its arguments are a parameter name (for example, `charset`) and the parameter's value (for example, `unicode`). It returns `parameterValue` normalized. You would never call `normalizeMimeTypeParameter()` directly, but you might want to override this method if you are creating a subclass of `DataFlavor` and want to change the default normalization process. For example, parameter values may be case sensitive. You could write a method that would convert the value `Unicode` to the more appropriate form `unicode`.

While it may be more trouble than it's worth, carefully overriding these normalization methods might help you to get more predictable results from methods like `isMimeTypeEqual()`.

Miscellaneous methods

public boolean equals(DataFlavor dataFlavor) ★

The `equals()` method defines equality for flavors. Two `DataFlavor` objects are equal if their MIME type and representation class are equal.

16.2 Transferable Interface

Objects that can be placed on a clipboard must implement the `Transferable` interface. This interface defines a number of methods that let an object describe how it presents itself to clipboard readers. That sounds complex, but it isn't really; these methods let a clipboard reader find out what data flavors are available and what Java types they represent.

The significance of the `Transferable` interface is that it provides a way to get information about the object on the clipboard without knowing what the object actually is. When you read the clipboard, you don't necessarily know what kind of object is there. It might be some kind of text string, but it could just as likely be something bizarre. However, you shouldn't have to care. If you're looking for a `String`, you care only that the object exists in a `stringFlavor` representation. These methods let you ask the object what flavors it supports.

For text strings, the data transfer package provides a `StringSelection` class that implements `Transferable`. At this point, if you want to transfer other kinds of objects, you'll have to create a class that implements `Transferable` yourself. It wouldn't be unreasonable for JavaSoft to provide other "selection" classes (for example, `ImageSelection`) in the future.

Methods

public abstract DataFlavor[] getTransferDataFlavors() ★

> The `getTransferDataFlavors()` method should return a sorted array of `DataFlavors` that you support. The most descriptive flavor should be the first element in the array and the least descriptive, last. For example, a textual object would place `DataFlavor.plainTextFlavor` last, because it has less information than `DataFlavor.stringFlavor` (which includes information like the length of the string) and much less information than a hypothetical flavor like `DataFlavor.richTextFlavor`.

public abstract boolean isDataFlavorSupported(DataFlavor flavor) ★

> The `isDataFlavorSupported()` method should return `true` if the object supports the given `flavor` and `false` otherwise.

public abstract Object getTransferData(DataFlavor flavor)
throws UnsupportedFlavorException, IOException ★

> The `getTransferData()` method is the most complicated to implement. It should return an instance of the class representing the data in the given flavor. If flavor is not supported by this object, `getTransferData()` must throw the `UnsupportedFlavorException`. However, this method must be able to return a class for each flavor the object supports (i.e., each data flavor listed by `getTransferDataFlavors()`). The method could throw an `IOException` when returning with a `Reader` as the representation class. For example, if some data flavor required you to return a `FileReader` and the file doesn't exist, this method might throw an `IOException`.

16.3 ClipboardOwner Interface

Classes that need to place objects on a clipboard must implement the `Clipboard-Owner` interface. An object becomes the clipboard owner by placing something on a `Clipboard` and remains owner as long as that object stays on the clipboard; it loses ownership when someone else writes to the clipboard. The `ClipboardOwner` interface provides a way to receive notification when you lose ownership—that is, when the object you placed on the clipboard is replaced by something else.

Methods

public abstract void lostOwnership(Clipboard clipboard, Transferable contents) ★

> The `lostOwnership()` method tells the owner of `contents` that it is no longer on the given `clipboard`. It is usually implemented as an empty stub but is available for situations in which you have to know.

16.4 Clipboard

The Clipboard class is a repository for a Transferable object and can be used for cut, copy, and paste operations. You can work with a private clipboard by creating your own instance of Clipboard, or you can work with the system clipboard by asking the Toolkit for it:

```
Toolkit.getDefaultToolkit().getSystemClipboard()
```

When working with the system clipboard, native applications have access to information created within Java programs and vice versa. Access to the system clipboard is controlled by the SecurityManager and is restricted within applets.

16.4.1 Clipboard Methods

Variables

protected ClipboardOwner owner ★

> The owner instance variable represents the current owner of contents. When something new is placed on the clipboard, the previous owner is notified by a call to the lostOwnership() method. The owner usually ignores this notification. However, the clipboard's contents are passed back to owner in case some special processing or comparison needs to be done.

protected Transferable contents ★

> The contents instance variable is the object currently on the clipboard; it was placed on the clipboard by owner. To retrieve the current contents, use the getContents() method.

Constructors

public Clipboard(String name) ★

> The constructor for Clipboard allows you to create a private clipboard named name. This clipboard is not accessible outside of your program and has no security constraints placed upon it.

Miscellaneous methods

public String getName() ★

> The getName() method fetches the clipboard's name. For private clipboards, this is the name given in the constructor. The name of the system clipboard is "System".

public synchronized Transferable getContents(Object requester) ★

The getContents() method allows you to retrieve the current contents of the clipboard. This is the method you would call when the user selects Paste from a menu.

Once you have the Transferable data, you try to get the data in whatever flavor you want by calling the Transferable.getTransferData() method, possibly after calling Transferable.isDataFlavorSupported(). The requester represents the object that is requesting the clipboard's contents; it is usually just this, since the current object is making the request.

public synchronized void setContents(Transferable contents, ClipboardOwner owner) ★

The setContents() method changes the contents of the clipboard to contents and changes the clipboard's owner to owner. You would call this method when the user selects Cut or Copy from a menu. The owner parameter represents the object that owns contents. This object must implement the ClipboardOwner interface; it will be notified by a call to lostOwnership() when something else is placed on the clipboard.

16.5 StringSelection

StringSelection is a convenience class that can be used for copy and paste operations on Unicode text strings (String). It implements both the ClipboardOwner and Transferable interfaces, so it can be used both as the contents of the clipboard and as its owner. For example, if s is a StringSelection, you can call Clipboard.setContents(s,s). StringSelection supports both stringFlavor and plainTextFlavor and doesn't do anything when it loses clipboard ownership.

16.5.1 StringSelection Methods

Constructors

public StringSelection(String data) ★

The constructor creates an instance of StringSelection containing data. You can use this object to place the data on a clipboard.

Miscellaneous methods

public DataFlavor[] getTransferDataFlavors() ★

The getTransferDataFlavors() method returns a two-element DataFlavor array consisting of DataFlavor.stringFlavor and DataFlavor.plainTextFlavor. This means that you can paste a StringSelection as either a Java String or as plain text (i.e., the MIME type plain/text).

public boolean isDataFlavorSupported(DataFlavor flavor) ★

> The `isDataFlavorSupported()` method is returns `true` if flavor is either `DataFlavor.stringFlavor` or `DataFlavor.plainTextFlavor`; it returns `false` for any other flavor.

public Object getTransferData(DataFlavor flavor)
throws UnsupportedFlavorException, IOException ★

> The `getTransferData()` method returns an object from which you can get the data on the clipboard; the object's type is determined by the flavor parameter. This method returns a `String` containing the data on the clipboard if flavor is `DataFlavor.stringFlavor`; it returns a `StringBufferInputStream` from which you can read the data on the clipboard if you ask for `DataFlavor.plainTextFlavor`. Otherwise, `getTransferData()` throws an `UnsupportedFlavorException`.

public void lostOwnership(Clipboard clipboard, Transferable contents) ★

> The `lostOwnership()` method of `StringSelection` is an empty stub; it does nothing when you lose ownership. If you want to know when you've lost ownership of string data placed on the clipboard, write a subclass of `StringSelection` and override this method.

16.6 UnsupportedFlavorException

The `UnsupportedFlavorException` exception is thrown when you ask `Transferable.getTransferData()` to give you data in a flavor that isn't supported by the object on the clipboard. For example, if the clipboard currently holds an image and you ask for the data in the `stringFlavor`, you will almost certainly get an `UnsupportedFlavorException` because it is unlikely that an image object will be able to give you its data as a `String`. You can either ignore the exception or display an appropriate message to the user.

16.6.1 UnsupportedFlavorException Method

Constructor

public UnsupportedFlavorException (DataFlavor flavor)

> The sole constructor creates an `UnsupportedFlavorException` with a detail message containing the human presentable name of flavor. To retrieve this message, call `getMessage()`, which this exception inherits from the `Exception` superclass (and which is required by the `Throwable` interface).

16.7 Reading and Writing the Clipboard

Now that you know about the different java.awt.datatransfer classes required to use the clipboard, let's put them all together in an example. Example 16-1 creates a TextField for input (copying), a read-only TextArea for output (pasting), and a couple of buttons to control its operation. Figure 16-1 shows the program's user interface. When the user clicks on the Copy button or presses Return in the TextField, the text in the TextField is copied to the Clipboard. When the user clicks on the Paste button, the contents of the clipboard are drawn in the TextArea. Since the clipboard is not private, you can copy or paste from anywhere on your desktop, not just this program.

Example 16–1: Using the System Clipboard

```
// Java 1.1 only
import java.io.*;
import java.awt.*;
import java.awt.datatransfer.*;

public class ClipMe extends Frame {
    TextField tf;
    TextArea ta;
    Button copy, paste;
    Clipboard clipboard = null;
    ClipMe() {
        super ("Clipping Example");
        add (tf = new TextField("Welcome"), "North");
        add (ta = new TextArea(), "Center");
        ta.setEditable(false);
        Panel p = new Panel();
        p.add (copy = new Button ("Copy"));
        p.add (paste = new Button ("Paste"));
        add (p, "South");
        setSize (250, 250);
    }
    public static void main (String args[]) {
        new ClipMe().show();
    }
    public boolean handleEvent (Event e) {
        if (e.id == Event.WINDOW_DESTROY) {
            System.exit(0);
            return true;  // never gets here
        }
        return super.handleEvent (e);
    }
    public boolean action (Event e, Object o) {
        if (clipboard == null)
            clipboard = getToolkit().getSystemClipboard();
        if ((e.target == tf) || (e.target == copy)) {
            StringSelection data;
            data = new StringSelection (tf.getText());
```

Example 16–1: Using the System Clipboard (continued)

```
                clipboard.setContents (data, data);
        } else if (e.target == paste) {
            Transferable clipData = clipboard.getContents(this);
            String s;
            try {
                s = (String)(clipData.getTransferData(
                        DataFlavor.stringFlavor));
            } catch (Exception ee) {
                s = ee.toString();
            }
            ta.setText(s);
        }
        return true;
    }
}
```

Figure 16–1: Using the system clipboard

We won't say anything about how the display is set up; that should be familiar. All the interesting stuff happens in the `action` method, which is called in response to a button click. We check which button the user clicked; if the user clicked the Copy button, we read the text field `tf` and use it to create a new `StringSelection` named `data`. If the user clicked the Paste button, we retrieve the data from the clipboard by calling `getContents()`. This gives us an object about which (strictly speaking) we know nothing, except that it implements `Transferable`. In this case, we're pretty sure that we're getting text from the clipboard, so we call `getTransferData()` and ask for the data in the `stringFlavor` form. We catch the exception that might occur if we're wrong about the data flavor. This program has no way of placing anything but text on the clipboard, but there's no guarantee that the user didn't cut some other kind of object from a native application.

Once we have our `String`, we call the `setText()` method of the `TextArea` to tell it about the new string, and we are finished.

In this chapter:
- *PrintGraphics Interface*
- *PrintJob Class*
- *Component Methods*
- *Printing Example*
- *Printing Arbitrary Content*

17

Printing

Java 1.1 introduces the ability to print, a capability that was sadly missing in Java 1.0, even though the Component class had print() and printAll() methods. However, it is possible to print arbitrary content, including multipage documents. The printing facility in Java 1.1 is designed primarily to let a program print its display area or any of the components within its display.

Printing is implemented with the help of one public interface, PrintGraphics, and one public class, PrintJob, of AWT. The real work is hidden behind classes provided with the toolkit for your platform. On Windows NT/95 platforms, these classes are sun.awt.windows.WPrintGraphics and sun.awt.windows.WPrintJob. Other platforms have similarly named classes.

Printing from an applet has security implications and is restricted by the SecurityManager. It is reasonable to suppose that a browser will make it possible to print a page containing an applet; in fact, Netscape has done so ever since Navigator 3.0. However, this ability might not take advantage of Java's printing facility. It isn't reasonable to suppose that an applet will be able to initiate a print job on its own. You might allow a signed applet coming from a trusted source to do so, but you wouldn't want to give any random applet access to your printer. (If you don't understand why, imagine the potential for abuse.)

17.1 PrintGraphics Interface

Printing is similar to drawing an object on the screen. Just as you draw onto a graphics context to display something on the screen, you draw onto a "printing context" to create an image for printing. Furthermore, the printing context and graphics context are very closely related. The graphics context is an instance of the class Graphics. The printing context is also an instance of Graphics, with the additional requirement that it implement the PrintGraphics interface. Therefore, any methods that you use to draw graphics can also be used for printing. Furthermore, the paint() method (which a component uses to draw itself on the screen) is also called when a component must draw itself for printing.

In short, to print, you get a special Graphics object that implements the Print-Graphics interface by calling the getGraphics() method of PrintJob (discussed later in this chapter) through Toolkit. You then call a component's print() or printAll() method or a container's printComponents() method, with this object as the argument. These methods arrange for a call to paint(), which can draw on the printing context to its heart's content. In the simple case where you're just rendering the component on paper, you shouldn't have to change paint() at all. Of course, if you are doing something more complex (that is, printing something that doesn't look exactly like your component), you'll have to modify paint() to determine whether it's painting on screen or on paper, and act accordingly. The code would look something like this:

```
public void paint(Graphics g) {
    if (g instanceof PrintGraphics) {
        // Printing
    }else {
        // Painting
    }
}
```

If the graphics object you receive is an instance of PrintGraphics, you know that paint() has been called for a print request and can do anything specific to printing. As I said earlier, you can use all the methods of Graphics to draw on g. If you're printing, though, you might do anything from making sure that you print in black and white to drawing something completely different. (This might be the trick you use to print the contents of a component rather than the component itself. However, as of Java 1.1, it's impossible to prevent the component from drawing itself. Remember that your paint() method was never responsible for drawing the component; it only drew additions to the basic component. For the time being, it's the same with printing.)

When you call printComponents() on a Container, all the components within the container will be printed. Early beta versions of 1.1 only painted the outline of components within the container. The component should print as it appears on the screen.

17.1.1 Methods

public abstract PrintJob getPrintJob () ★

> The getPrintJob() method returns the PrintJob instance that created this PrintGraphics instance.

> This seems like circular logic: you need a PrintJob to create a PrintGraphics object, but you can get a PrintJob only from a PrintGraphics object. To break the circle, you can get an initial PrintJob by calling the getPrintJob() method of Toolkit. getPrintJob() looks like it will be useful primarily within paint(), where you don't have access to the original PrintJob object and need to get it from the graphics context.

System-provided PrintGraphics objects inherit their other methods from the Graphics class, which is discussed in Chapter 2, *Simple Graphics.** The one method that's worth noting here is dispose(). In a regular Graphics object, calling dispose() frees any system resources the object requires. For a PrintGraphics object, dispose() sends the current object to the printer prior to deallocating its resources. Calling dispose() is therefore equivalent to sending a form feed to eject the current page.

17.2 PrintJob Class

The abstract PrintJob class provides the basis for the platform-specific printing subclasses. Through PrintJob, you have access to properties like page size and resolution.

17.2.1 Constructor and Pseudo-Constructor

public PrintJob () ★

> The PrintJob() constructor is public; however, the class is abstract, so you would never create a PrintJob instance directly.

Since you can't call the PrintJob constructor directly, you need some other way of getting a print job to work with. The proper way to get an instance of PrintJob is to ask the Toolkit, which is described in Chapter 15, *Toolkit and Peers.* The getPrintJob() method requires a Frame as the first parameter, a String as the second parameter, and a Properties set as the third parameter. Here's how you might call it:

---

* Anything can implement the PrintGraphics interface, not just subclasses of Graphics. However, in order for paint() and print() to work, it must be a subclass of Graphics.

```
PrintJob pjob = getToolkit().getPrintJob(aFrame, "Job Title",
                                (Properties)null);
```

The `Frame` is used to hold a print dialog box, asking the user to confirm or cancel the print job. (Whether or not you get the print dialog may be platform specific, but your programs should always assume that the dialog may appear.) The `String` is the job's title; it will be used to identify the job in the print queue and on the job's header page, if there is one.

The `Properties` parameter is used to request printing options, like page reversal. The property names, and whether the requested properties are honored at all, are platform specific. UNIX systems use the following properties:

```
awt.print.printer
awt.print.paperSize
awt.print.destination
awt.print.orientation
awt.print.options
awt.print.fileName
awt.print.numCopies
```

Windows NT/95 ignores the properties sheet. If the properties sheet is `null`, as in the previous example, you get the system's default printing options. If the properties sheet is non-`null`, `getPrintJob()` modifies it to show the actual options used to print the job. You can use the modified properties sheet to find out what properties are recognized on your system and to save a set of printing options for use on a later print job.

If you are printing multiple pages, each page should originate from the same print job.

According to Sun's documentation, `getPrintJob()` ought to return `null` if the user cancels the print job. However, this is a problem. On some platforms (notably Windows NT/95), the print dialog box doesn't even appear until you call the `get-Graphics()` method. In this case, `getPrintJob()` still returns a print job and never returns `null`. If the user cancels the job, `getGraphics()` returns `null`.

17.2.2 Methods

public abstract Graphics getGraphics () ★

> The `getGraphics()` method returns an instance of `Graphics` that also implements `PrintGraphics`. This graphics context can then be used as the parameter to methods like `paint()`, `print()`, `update()`, or `printAll()` to print a single page. (All of these methods result in calls to `paint()`; in `paint()`, you draw whatever you want to print on the `Graphics` object.)

On Windows NT/95 platforms, getGraphics() returns null if the user cancels the print job.

public abstract Dimension getPageDimension () ★

The getPageDimension() method returns the dimensions of the page in pixels, as a Dimension object. Since getGraphics() returns a graphics context only for a single page, it is the programmer's responsibility to decide when the current page is full, print the current page, and start a new page with a new Graphics object. The page size is chosen to roughly represent a screen but has no relationship to the page size or orientation.

public abstract int getPageResolution () ★

The getPageResolution() method returns the number of pixels per inch for drawing on the page. It is completely unclear what this means, since the number returned has no relationship to the printer resolution. It appears to be similar to the screen resolution.

public abstract boolean lastPageFirst () ★

The lastPageFirst() method lets you know if the user configured the printer to print pages in reverse order. If this returns true, you need to generate the last page first. If false, you should print the first page first. This is relevant only if you are trying to print a multipage document.

public abstract void end () ★

The end() method terminates the print job. This is the last method you should call when printing; it does any cleaning up that's necessary.

public void finalize () ★

The finalize() method is called by the garbage collector. In the event you forget to call end(), finalize() calls it for you. However, it is best to call end() as soon as you know you have finished printing; don't rely on finalize().

17.3 Component Methods

The methods that start the printing process come from either the Component or Container class and are inherited by all their children. All components inherit the printAll() and print() methods. Containers also inherit the printComponents() method, in addition to printAll() and print(). A container should call print-Components() to print itself if it contains any components. Otherwise, it is sufficient to call printAll().

These methods end up calling paint(), which does the actual drawing.

17.4 Printing Example

Now that you know about the different classes necessary to print, let's put it all together. Printing takes four steps:

1. Get the `PrintJob`:

    ```
    PrintJob pjob = getToolkit().getPrintJob(this, "Job Title", (Properties)null);
    ```

2. Get the graphics context from the `PrintJob`:

    ```
    Graphics pg = pjob.getGraphics();
    ```

3. Print by calling `printAll()` or `print()`. When this method returns, you can call `dispose()` to send the page to the printer:

    ```
    printAll(pg);
    pg.dispose(); // This is like sending a form feed
    ```

4. Clean up after yourself:

    ```
    pjob.end();
    ```

The following code summarizes how to print:

```
// Java 1.1 only
PrintJob pjob = getToolkit().getPrintJob(this, "Print?", (Properties)null);
if (pjob != null) {
        Graphics pg = pjob.getGraphics();
        if (pg != null) {
            printAll(pg);
            pg.dispose();
        }
    pjob.end();
}
```

This code prints the current component: what you get from the printer should be a reasonable rendition of what you see on the screen. Note that we didn't need to modify `paint()` at all. That should always be the case if you want your printer output to look like your onscreen component.

17.5 Printing Arbitrary Content

Of course, in many situations, you want to do more than print the appearance of a component. You often want to print the contents of some component, rather than the component itself. For example, you may want to print the text the user has typed into a text area, rather than the text area itself. Or you may want to print the contents of a spreadsheet, rather than the collection of components that compose the spreadsheet.

Java 1.1 lets you print arbitrary content, which may include multipage documents. You aren't restricted to printing your components' appearance. In many ways, the steps required to print arbitrary content are similar to those we outlined previously. However, a few tricks are involved:

1. Get the `PrintJob`:

   ```
   PrintJob pjob = getToolkit().getPrintJob(this, "Job Title", (Properties)null);
   ```

2. Get the graphics context from the `PrintJob`:

   ```
   Graphics pg = pjob.getGraphics();
   ```

3. Don't call `printAll()` or `print()`. These methods will try to draw your component on the page, which you don't want. Instead, get the dimensions of the page by calling `getPageDimension()`:

   ```
   pjob.getPageDimension();
   ```

4. Set the font for your graphics context; then get the font metrics from your graphics context.

   ```
   Font times = new Font ("SansSerif", Font.PLAIN, 12);
   pg.setFont(times);
   FontMetrics tm = pg.getFontMetrics(times);
   ```

5. Draw whatever you want into the graphics context, using the methods of the `Graphics` class. If you are drawing text, it's your responsibility to do all the positioning, making sure that your text falls within the page boundaries. By the time you're through with this, you'll have the `FontMetrics` class memorized.

6. When you've finished drawing the current page, call `dispose()`; this sends the page to the printer and releases the resources tied up by the `PrintGraphics` object.

   ```
   pg.dispose(); // This is like sending a form feed
   ```

7. If you want to print more pages, return to step 2.

8. Clean up after yourself:

   ```
   pjob.end();
   ```

Remember to set a font for the `PrintGraphics` object explicitly! It doesn't have a default font.

An example that loads and prints a text file is available from this book's Web page.

18

java.applet Reference

Introduction to the Reference Chapters

The preceding seventeen chapters cover just about all there is to know about AWT. We have tried to organize them logically, and provide all the information that you would expect in a reference manual—plus much more in the way of examples and practical information about how to do things effectively. However, there are many times when you just need a reference book, pure and simple: one that's organized alphabetically, and where you can find any method if you know the class and package that it belongs to, without having to second guess the author's organizational approach. That's what the rest of this book provides. It's designed to help you if you need to look something up quickly, and find a brief but accurate summary of what it does. In these sections, the emphasis is on *brief*; if you want a longer description, look in the body of the book.

The reference sections describe the following packages:

- java.applet (Chapter 18, *java.applet Reference*)
- java.awt (Chapter 19, *java.awt Reference*)
- java.awt.datatransfer (Chapter 20, *java.awt.datatransfer Reference*)
- java.awt.event (Chapter 21, *java.awt.event Reference*)
- java.awt.image (Chapter 22, *java.awt.image Reference*)
- java.awt.peer (Chapter 23, *java.awt.peer Reference*)

Within each package, classes and interfaces are listed alphabetically. There is a description and a pseudo-code definition for each class or interface. Each variable and method is listed and described. New Java 1.1 classes are marked with a black star (★), as are new methods and new variables. Of course, if a class is new, all its methods are new. We didn't mark individual methods in new classes. Methods that are deprecated in Java 1.1 are marked with a white star (☆).

Inheritance presents a significant problem with documenting object-oriented libraries, because the bulk of a class's methods tend to be hiding in the super-classes. Even if you're very familiar with object-oriented software development, when you're trying to look up a method under the pressure of some deadline, it's easy to forget that you need to look at the superclasses in addition to the class you're interested in itself. Nowhere is this problem worse than in AWT, where some classes (in particular, components and containers) inherit well over 100 methods, and provide few methods of their own. For example, the Button class contains seven public methods, none of which happens to be setFont(). The font used to display a button's label is certainly settable—but to find it, you have to look in the superclass Component.

So far, we haven't found a way around this problem. The description of each class has an abbreviated class hierarchy diagram, showing superclasses (all the way back to Object), immediate subclasses, and the interfaces that the class implements. Ideally, it would be nice to have a list of all the inherited methods—and in other parts of Java, that's possible. For AWT, the lists would be longer than the rest of this book, much too long to be practical, or even genuinely useful. Someday, electronic documentation may be able to solve this problem, but we're not there yet.

Package diagrams

The following figures provide a visual representation of the relationships between the classes in the AWT packages.

java.awt, as the mother of all AWT packages, is better represented by two diagrams, one for the graphics classes and one for the component and layout classes.

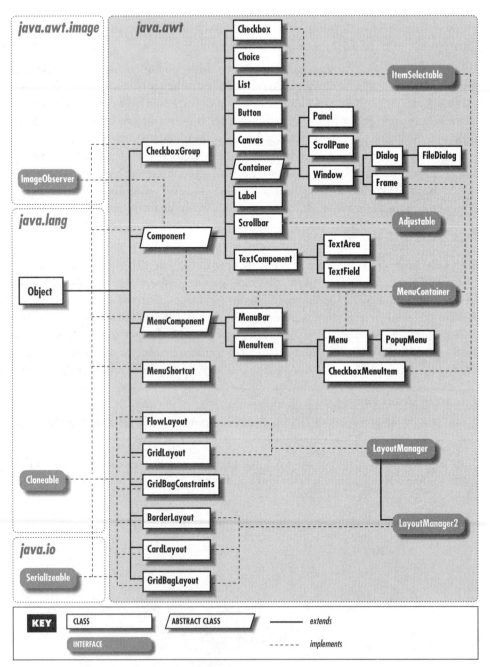

Figure 18–1: Component and Layout classes of the java.awt package.

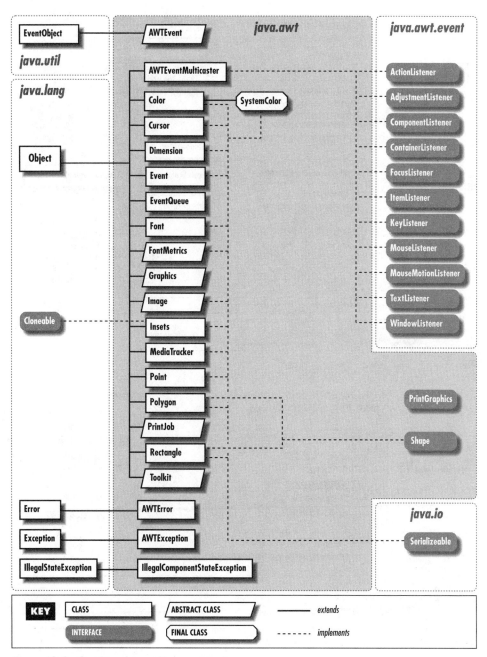

Figure 18–2: Graphics classes of java.awt package

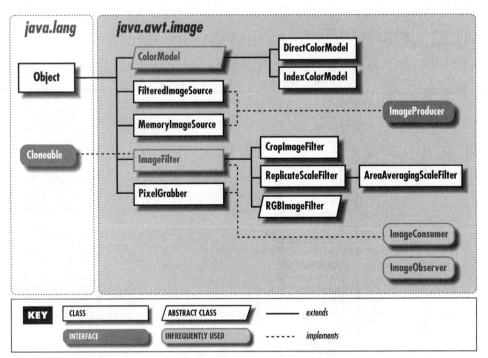

Figure 18–3: The java.awt.image package

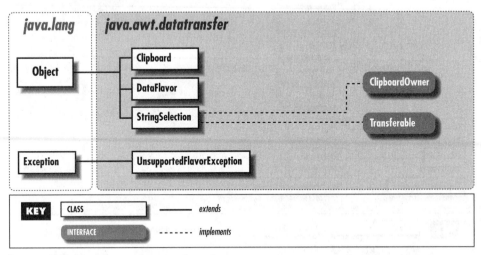

Figure 18–4: The java.awt.datatransfer package

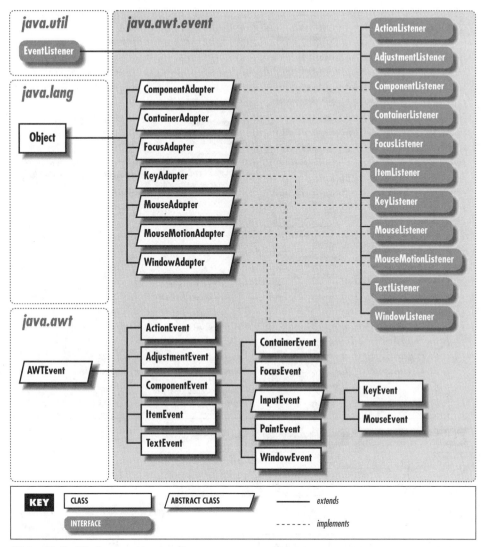

Figure 18–5: The java.awt.event package

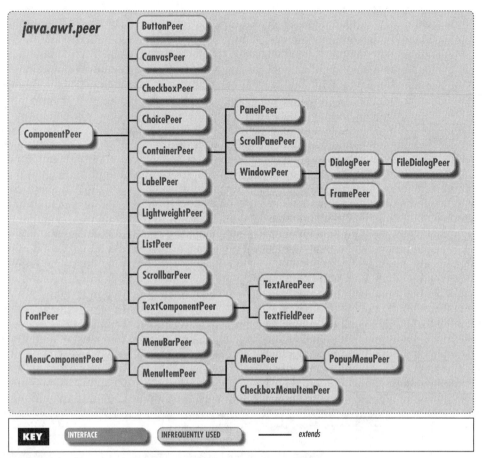

Figure 18–6: The java.awt.peer package

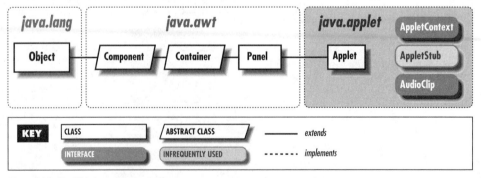

Figure 18–7: The java.applet package

18.1 Applet

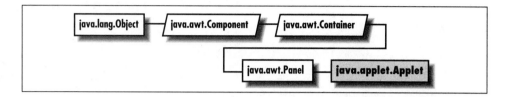

Description

The Applet class provides the framework for delivering Java programs within web pages.

Class Definition

```
public class java.applet.Applet
    extends java.awt.Panel {
// Constructors
public Applet();

// Instance Methods
public void destroy();
public AppletContext getAppletContext();
public String getAppletInfo();
public AudioClip getAudioClip (URL url);
public AudioClip getAudioClip (URL url, String filename);
public URL getCodeBase();
public URL getDocumentBase();
public Image getImage (URL url);
public Image getImage (URL url, String filename);
public Locale getLocale(); ★
public String getParameter (String name);
public String[][] getParameterInfo();
public void init();
public boolean isActive();
public void play (URL url);
public void play (URL url, String filename);
public void resize (int width, int height);
public void resize (Dimension dim);
public final void setStub (AppletStub stub);
public void showStatus (String message);
```

```
    public void start();
    public void stop();
}
```

Constructors

Applet

```
public Applet()
```

Description   Constructs an Applet object.

Instance Methods

destroy

```
public void destroy()
```

Description   Called when the browser determines that it doesn't need to keep the applet around anymore.

getAppletContext

```
public AppletContext getAppletContext()
```

Returns   The current AppletContext of the applet.

getAppletInfo

```
public String getAppletInfo()
```

Returns   A short information string about the applet to be shown to the user.

getAudioClip

```
public AudioClip getAudioClip (URL url)
```

Parameters   url   URL of an audio file.
Returns   Object that implements the AudioClip interface for playing audio files.
Description   Fetches an audio file to play with the AudioClip interface.

```
public AudioClip getAudioClip (URL url , String filename)
```

Parameters   url   Base URL of an audio file.
                      filename   Specific file, relative to url, that contains an audio file.
Returns   Object that implements AudioClip interface for playing audio file.

Description   Fetches an audio file to play with the `AudioClip` interface.

getCodeBase

`public URL getCodeBase()`

Returns   The complete URL of the *.class* file that contains the applet.

getDocumentBase

`public URL getDocumentBase()`

Returns   The complete URL of the *.html* file that loaded the applet.

getImage

`public Image getImage (URL url)`

Parameters   *url*   .   URL of an image file.
Returns   Image to be displayed.
Description   Initiates the image loading process for the file located at the specified location.

`public Image getImage (URL url, String filename)`

Parameters   *url*   Base URL of an image file.
             filename   Specific file, relative to `url`, that contains an image file.
Returns   Image to be displayed.
Description   Initiates the image loading process for the file located at the specified location.

getLocale

`public Locale getLocale() ★`

Returns   Applet's locale.
Overrides   `Component.getLocale()`
Description   Used for internationalization support.

getParameter

`public String getParameter (String name)`

Parameters   *name*   Name of parameter to get.
Returns   The value associated with the given parameter in the HTML file, or `null`.
Description   Allows you to get parameters from within the <APPLET> tag of the *.html* file that loaded the applet.

getParameterInfo

```
public String[][] getParameterInfo()
```

Returns   Overridden to provide a series of three-string arrays that describes the parameters this applet reads.

init

```
public void init()
```

Description   Called by the system when the applet is first loaded.

isActive

```
public boolean isActive()
```

Returns   true if the applet is active, false otherwise.

play

```
public void play (URL url)
```

Parameters   *url*   URL of an audio file .
Description   Plays an audio file once.

```
public void play (URL url, String filename)
```

Parameters   *url*   Base URL of an audio file .

                filename   Specific file, relative to url, that contains an audio file.
Description   Plays an audio file once.

resize

```
public void resize(int width, int height)
```

Parameters   *width*   New width for the Applet.

                height   New height for the Applet.
Description   Changes the size of the applet.

```
public void resize (Dimension dim)
```

Parameters   *dim*   New dimensions for the applet.
Description   Changes the size of the applet.

setStub

```
public final void setStub (AppletStub stub)
```

Parameters   *stub*   Platform specific stubfor environment.
Description   Called by the system to setup `AppletStub`.

showStatus

```
public void showStatus (String message)
```

Parameters   *message*   Message to display to user.
Description   Displays a message on the status line of the browser.

start

```
public void start()
```

Description   Called by the system every time the applet is displayed.

stop

```
public void stop()
```

Description   Called by the system when it wants the applet to stop execution;
               typically, every time the user leaves the page that includes the
               applet.

See Also

AppletContext, AppletStub, AudioClip, Container, Dimension, Image, Locale,
Panel, String, URL

18.2   AppletContext

```
java.applet.AppletContext
```

Description

AppletContext is an interface that provides the means to control the browser environment in which the applet is running.

Interface Definition

```
public abstract interface java.applet.AppletContext {

    // Interface Methods
    public abstract Applet getApplet (String name);
```

```
public abstract Enumeration getApplets();
public abstract AudioClip getAudioClip (URL url);
public abstract Image getImage (URL url);
public abstract void showDocument (URL url);
public abstract void showDocument (URL url, String frame);
public abstract void showStatus (String message);
}
```

Interface Methods

getApplet

```
public abstract Applet getApplet (String name)
```

Parameters	*name*	Name of applet to locate.
Returns	Applet fetched.	
Description	Gets a reference to another executing applet.	

getApplets

```
public abstract Enumeration getApplets()
```

Returns	List of applets executing.
Description	Gets references to all executing applets.

getAudioClip

```
public abstract AudioClip getAudioClip (URL url)
```

Parameters	*url*	Location of an audio file.
Returns	AudioClip fetched.	
Description	Loads an audio file.	

getImage

```
public abstract Image getImage (URL url)
```

Parameters	*url*	Location of an image file.
Returns	Image fetched.	
Description	Loads an image file.	

showDocument

```
public abstract void showDocument (URL url)
```

Parameters	*url*	New web page to display.
Description	Changes the displayed web page.	

```
public abstract void showDocument (URL url, String frame)
```

Parameters   *url*   New web page to display.

                   frame   Name of the frame in which to display the new page.

Description   Displays a web page in another frame.

showStatus

```
public abstract void showStatus (String message)
```

Parameters   *message*   Message to display.

Description   Displays a message on the status line of the browser.

See Also

Applet, AudioClip, Enumeration, Image, Object, String, URL

18.3 AppletStub

java.applet.AppletStub

Description

AppletStub is an interface that provides the means to get information from the run-time browser environment.

Interface Definition

```
public abstract interface java.applet.AppletStub {

    // Interface Methods
    public abstract void appletResize (int width, int height);
    public abstract AppletContext getAppletContext();
    public abstract URL getCodeBase();
    public abstract URL getDocumentBase();
    public abstract String getParameter (String name);
    public abstract boolean isActive();
}
```

Interface Methods

appletResize

```
public abstract void appletResize (int width, int height)
```

Parameters   *width*   Requested new width for applet.

              height   Requested new height for applet.

Description   Changes the size of the applet.

getAppletContext

```
public abstract AppletContext getAppletContext()
```

Returns   Current AppletContext of the applet.

getCodeBase

```
public abstract URL getCodeBase()
```

Returns   Complete URL for the applet's *.class* file.

getDocumentBase

```
public abstract URL getDocumentBase()
```

Returns   Complete URL for the applet's *.html* file.

getParameter

```
public abstract String getParameter (String name)
```

Parameters   *name*   Name of a <PARAM> tag.

Returns   Value associated with the parameter.

Description   Gets a parameter value from the <PARAM> tag(s) of the applet.

isActive

```
public abstract boolean isActive()
```

Returns   true if the applet is active, false otherwise

Description   Returns current state of the applet.

See Also

AppletContext, Object, String, URL

18.4   AudioClip

---

java.applet.AudioClip

Description

AudioClip is an interface for playing audio files.

Interface Definition

```
public abstract interface java.applet.AudioClip {

    // Interface Methods
    public abstract void loop();
    public abstract void play();
    public abstract void stop();
}
```

Interface Methods

loop

public abstract void loop()

Description   Plays an audio clip continuously.

play

public abstract void play()

Description   Plays an audio clip once from the beginning.

stop

public abstract void stop()

Description   Stops playing an audio clip.

See Also

Object

19

java.awt Reference

19.1 AWTError

Description

An AWTError; thrown to indicate a serious runtime error.

Class Definition

```
public class java.awt.AWTError
    extends java.lang.Error {

    // Constructors
    public AWTError (String message);
}
```

Constructors

AWTError

```
public AWTError (String message)
```

Parameters   *message*   Detail message

See Also

Error, String

19.2   AWTEvent ★

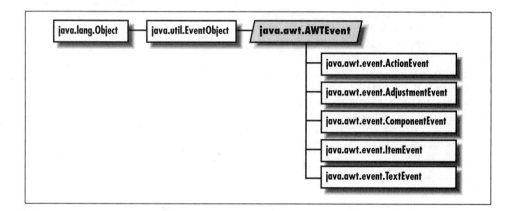

Description

The root class of all AWT events. Subclasses of this class are the replacement for java.awt.Event, which is only used for the Java 1.0.2 event model. In Java 1.1, event objects are passed from event source components to objects implementing a corresponding listener interface. Some event sources have a corresponding interface, too. For example, AdjustmentEvents are passed from Adjustable objects to AdjustmentListeners. Some event types do not have corresponding interfaces; for example, ActionEvents are passed from Buttons to ActionListeners, but there is no "Actionable" interface that Button implements.

Class Definition

```
public abstract class java.awt.AWTEvent
    extends java.util.EventObject {

    // Constants
    public final static long ACTION_EVENT_MASK;
    public final static long ADJUSTMENT_EVENT_MASK;
    public final static long COMPONENT_EVENT_MASK;
```

```
    public final static long CONTAINER_EVENT_MASK;
    public final static long FOCUS_EVENT_MASK;
    public final static long ITEM_EVENT_MASK;
    public final static long KEY_EVENT_MASK;
    public final static long MOUSE_EVENT_MASK;
    public final static long MOUSE_MOTION_EVENT_MASK;
    public final static long RESERVED_ID_MAX;
    public final static long TEXT_EVENT_MASK;
    public final static long WINDOW_EVENT_MASK;

    // Variables
    protected boolean consumed;
    protected int id;

    // Constructors
    public AWTEvent (Event event);
    public AWTEvent (Object source, int id);

    // Instance Methods
    public int getID();
    public String paramString();
    public String toString();

    // Protected Instance Methods
    protected void consume();
    protected boolean isConsumed();
}
```

Constants

ACTION_EVENT_MASK

```
    public static final long ACTION_EVENT_MASK
```

The mask for action events.

ADJUSTMENT_EVENT_MASK

```
    public static final long ADJUSTMENT_EVENT_MASK
```

The mask for adjustment events.

COMPONENT_EVENT_MASK

```
    public static final long COMPONENT_EVENT_MASK
```

The mask for component events.

CONTAINER_EVENT_MASK

public static final long CONTAINER_EVENT_MASK

The mask for container events.

FOCUS_EVENT_MASK

public static final long FOCUS_EVENT_MASK

The mask for focus events.

ITEM_EVENT_MASK

public static final long ITEM_EVENT_MASK

The mask for item events.

KEY_EVENT_MASK

public static final long KEY_EVENT_MASK

The mask for key events.

MOUSE_EVENT_MASK

public static final long MOUSE_EVENT_MASK

The mask for mouse events.

MOUSE_MOTION_EVENT_MASK

public static final long MOUSE_MOTION_EVENT_MASK

The mask for mouse motion events.

RESERVED_ID_MAX

public static final int

The maximum reserved event id.

TEXT_EVENT_MASK

public static final long TEXT_EVENT_MASK

The mask for text events.

WINDOW_EVENT_MASK

public static final long WINDOW_EVENT_MASK

The mask for window events.

Variables

consumed

`protected boolean consumed`

If consumed is true, the event will not be sent back to the peer. Semantic events will never be sent back to a peer; thus consumed is always true for semantic events.

id

`protected int id`

The type ID of this event.

Constructors

AWTEvent

`public AWTEvent (Event event)`

Parameters	*event*	A version 1.0.2 java.awt.Event object.
Description		Constructs a 1.1 java.awt.AWTEvent derived from a 1.0.2 java.awt.Event object.

`public AWTEvent (Object source, int id)`

Parameters	*source*	The object that the event originated from.
	id	An event type ID.
Description		Constructs an AWTEvent object.

Instance Methods

getID

`public int getID()`

Returns	The type ID of the event.

paramString

`public String paramString()`

Returns	A string with the current settings of AWTEvent.
Description	Helper method for toString() that generates a string of current settings.

toString

public String toString()

Returns   A string representation of the AWTEvent object.
Overrides   Object.toString()

Protected Instance Methods

consume

protected void consume()

Description   Consumes the event so it is not sent back to its source.

isConsumed

public boolean isConsumed()

Returns   A flag indicating whether this event has been consumed.

See Also

ActionEvent, AdjustmentEvent, ComponentEvent, Event, EventObject, FocusEvent,
ItemEvent, KeyEvent, MouseEvent, WindowEvent

19.3   AWTEventMulticaster ★

Description

This class multicasts events to event listeners. Each multicaster has two listeners,
cunningly named a and b. When an event source calls one of the listener methods
of the multicaster, the multicaster calls the same listener method on both a and b.
Multicasters are built into trees using the static add() and remove() methods. In
this way a single event can be sent to many listeners.

Static methods make it easy to implement event multicasting in component subclasses. Each time an add<type>Listener() function is called in the component
subclass, call the corresponding AWTEventMulticaster.add() method to chain
together (or "tree up") listeners. Similarly, when a remove<type>Listener() function is called, AWTEventMulticaster.remove() can be called to remove a chained
listener.

Class Definition

```
public class java.awt.AWTEventMulticaster
    extends java.lang.Object
    implements java.awt.event.ActionListener, java.awt.event.AdjustmentListener,
            java.awt.event.ComponentListener, java.awt.event.ContainerListener,
            java.awt.event.FocusListener, java.awt.event.ItemListener,
            java.awt.event.KeyListener, java.awt.event.MouseListener,
```

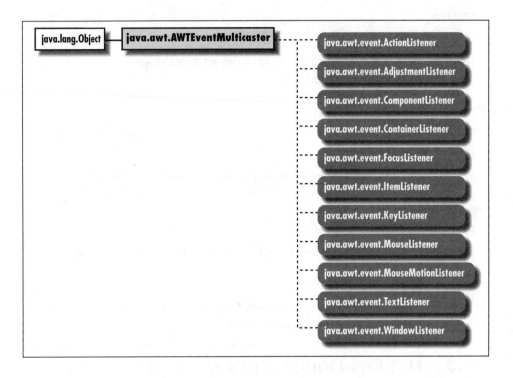

```
                java.awt.event.MouseMotionListener, java.awt.event.TextListener,
                java.awt.event.WindowListener {

// Variables
protected EventListener a;
protected EventListener b;

// Constructors
protected AWTEventMulticaster(EventListener a, EventListener b);

// Class Methods
public static ActionListener add(ActionListener a, ActionListener b);
public static AdjustmentListener add(AdjustmentListener a,
    AdjustmentListener b);
public static ComponentListener add(ComponentListener a,
    ComponentListener b);
public static ContainerListener add(ContainerListener a,
    ContainerListener b);
public static FocusListener add(FocusListener a, FocusListener b);
public static ItemListener add(ItemListener a, ItemListener b);
public static KeyListener add(KeyListener a, KeyListener b);
public static MouseListener add(MouseListener a, MouseListener b);
public static MouseMotionListener add(MouseMotionListener a,
    MouseMotionListener b);
```

```
public static TextListener add(TextListener a, TextListener b);
public static WindowListener add(WindowListener a, WindowListener b);
protected static EventListener addInternal(EventListener a, EventListener b);
public static ActionListener remove(ActionListener l, ActionListener oldl);
public static AdjustmentListener remove(AdjustmentListener l,
    AdjustmentListener oldl);
public static ComponentListener remove(ComponentListener l,
    ComponentListener oldl);
public static ContainerListener remove(ContainerListener l,
    ContainerListener oldl);
public static FocusListener remove(FocusListener l, FocusListener oldl);
public static ItemListener remove(ItemListener l, ItemListener oldl);
public static KeyListener remove(KeyListener l, KeyListener oldl);
public static MouseListener remove(MouseListener l, MouseListener oldl);
public static MouseMotionListener remove(MouseMotionListener l,
    MouseMotionListener oldl);
public static TextListener remove(TextListener l, TextListener oldl);
public static WindowListener remove(WindowListener l, WindowListener;
protected static EventListener removeInternal(EventListener l,
    EventListener oldl);

// Instance Methods
public void actionPerformed(ActionEvent e);
public void adjustmentValueChanged(AdjustmentEvent e);
public void componentAdded(ContainerEvent e);
public void componentHidden(ComponentEvent e);
public void componentMoved(ComponentEvent e);
public void componentRemoved(ContainerEvent e);
public void componentResized(ComponentEvent e);
public void componentShown(ComponentEvent e);
public void focusGained(FocusEvent e);
public void focusLost(FocusEvent e);
public void itemStateChanged(ItemEvent e);
public void keyPressed(KeyEvent e);
public void keyReleased(KeyEvent e);
public void keyTyped(KeyEvent e);
public void mouseClicked(MouseEvent e);
public void mouseDragged(MouseEvent e);
public void mouseEntered(MouseEvent e);
public void mouseExited(MouseEvent e);
public void mouseMoved(MouseEvent e);
public void mousePressed(MouseEvent e);
public void mouseReleased(MouseEvent e);
public void textValueChanged(TextEvent e);
public void windowActivated(WindowEvent e);
public void windowClosed(WindowEvent e);
public void windowClosing(WindowEvent e);
public void windowDeactivated(WindowEvent e);
public void windowDeiconified(WindowEvent e);
```

```
    public void windowIconified(WindowEvent e);
    public void windowOpened(WindowEvent e);
    // Protected Instance Methods
    protected EventListener remove(EventListener oldl);
    protected void saveInternal(ObjectOutputStream s, String k) throws IOException;
}
```

Variables

a

protected EventListener a

One of the EventListeners this AWTEventMulticaster sends events to.

b

protected EventListener b

One of the EventListeners this AWTEventMulticaster sends events to.

Constructors

AWTEventMulticaster

protected AWTEventMulticaster (EventListener a, EventListener b)

Parameters	*a*	A listener that receives events.
	b	A listener that receives events.
Description		Constructs an AWTEventMulticaster that sends events it receives to the supplied listeners. The constructor is protected because it is only the class methods of AWTEventMulticaster that ever instantiate this class.

Class Methods

add

public static ActionListener add (ActionListener a, ActionListener b)

Parameters	*a*	An event listener.
	b	An event listener.
Returns		A listener object that passes events to a and b.

public static AdjustmentListener add (AdjustmentListener a, AdjustmentListener b)

Parameters	*a*	An event listener.
	b	An event listener.

Returns   A listener object that passes events to a and b.

```
public static ComponentListener add (ComponentListener a,
ComponentListener b)
```

Parameters   *a*   An event listener.
              b   An event listener.
Returns   A listener object that passes events to a and b.

```
public static ContainerListener add (ContainerListener a,
ContainerListener b)
```

Parameters   *a*   An event listener.
              b   An event listener.
Returns   A listener object that passes events to a and b.

```
public static FocusListener add (FocusListener a, FocusListener b)
```

Parameters   *a*   An event listener.
              b   An event listener.
Returns   A listener object that passes events to a and b.

```
public static ItemListener add (ItemListener a, ItemListener b)
```

Parameters   *a*   An event listener.
              b   An event listener.
Returns   A listener object that passes events to a and b.

```
public static KeyListener add (KeyListener a, KeyListener b)
```

Parameters   *a*   An event listener.
              b   An event listener.
Returns   A listener object that passes events to a and b.

```
public static MouseListener add (MouseListener a, MouseListener b)
```

Parameters   *a*   An event listener.
              b   An event listener.
Returns   A listener object that passes events to a and b.

```
public static MouseMotionListener add (MouseMotionListener a,
MouseMotionListener b)
```

Parameters   *a*   An event listener.
              b   An event listener.
Returns   A listener object that passes events to a and b.

```
public static TextListener add (TextListener a, TextListener b)
```

Parameters	*a*	An event listener.
	b	An event listener.
Returns	A listener object that passes events to a and b.	

```
public static WindowListener add (WindowListener a, WindowListener
b)
```

Parameters	*a*	An event listener.
	b	An event listener.
Returns	A listener object that passes events to a and b.	

addInternal

```
public static EventListener addInternal (EventListener a,
EventListener b)
```

Parameters	*a*	An event listener.
	b	An event listener.
Returns	A listener object that passes events to a and b.	
Description	This method is a helper for the add() methods.	

remove

```
public static ActionListener remove (ActionListener l,
ActionListener oldl)
```

Parameters	*l*	An event listener.
	oldl	An event listener.
Returns	A listener object that multicasts to l but not oldl.	

```
public static AdjustmentListener remove (AdjustmentListener l,
AdjustmentListener oldl)
```

Parameters	*l*	An event listener.
	oldl	An event listener.
Returns	A listener object that multicasts to l but not oldl.	

```
public static ComponentListener remove (ComponentListener l,
ComponentListener oldl)
```

Parameters	*l*	An event listener.
	oldl	An event listener.
Returns	A listener object that multicasts to l but not oldl.	

```
public static ContainerListener remove (ContainerListener l,
ContainerListener oldl)
```

Parameters　　*l*　　　　　　An event listener.

　　　　　　　　oldl　　　　　　An event listener.

Returns　　　　A listener object that multicasts to l but not oldl.

```
public static FocusListener remove (FocusListener l, FocusListener
oldl)
```

Parameters　　*l*　　　　　　An event listener.

　　　　　　　　oldl　　　　　　An event listener.

Returns　　　　A listener object that multicasts to l but not oldl.

```
public static ItemListener remove (ItemListener l, ItemListener
oldl)
```

Parameters　　*l*　　　　　　An event listener.

　　　　　　　　oldl　　　　　　An event listener.

Returns　　　　A listener object that multicasts to l but not oldl.

```
public static KeyListener remove (KeyListener l, KeyListener oldl)
```

Parameters　　*l*　　　　　　An event listener.

　　　　　　　　oldl　　　　　　An event listener.

Returns　　　　A listener object that multicasts to l but not oldl.

```
public static MouseListener remove (MouseListener l, MouseListener
oldl)
```

Parameters　　*l*　　　　　　An event listener.

　　　　　　　　oldl　　　　　　An event listener.

Returns　　　　A listener object that multicasts to l but not oldl.

```
public static MouseMotionListener remove (MouseMotionListener l,
MouseMotionListener oldl)
```

Parameters　　*l*　　　　　　An event listener.

　　　　　　　　oldl　　　　　　An event listener.

Returns　　　　A listener object that multicasts to l but not oldl.

```
public static TextListener remove (TextListener l, TextListener
oldl)
```

Parameters　　*l*　　　　　　An event listener.

　　　　　　　　oldl　　　　　　An event listener.

Returns　　　　A listener object that multicasts to l but not oldl.

```
public static WindowListener remove (WindowListener l,
WindowListener oldl)
```

Parameters   *l*   An event listener.
                  oldl   An event listener.
Returns   A listener object that multicasts to l but not oldl.

```
public static WindowListener remove (WindowListener l,
WindowListener oldl)
```

Parameters   *l*   An event listener.
                  oldl   An event listener.
Returns   A listener object that multicasts to l but not oldl.

removeInternal

```
public static EventListener removeInternal (EventListener l,
EventListener oldl)
```

Parameters   *l*   An event listener.
                  oldl   An event listener.
Returns   A listener object that multicasts to l but not oldl.
Description   This method is a helper for the remove() methods.

Instance Methods

actionPerformed

```
public void actionPerformed (ActionEvent e)
```

Parameters   *e*   The action event that occurred.
Description   Handles the event by passing it on to listeners a and b.

adjustmentValueChanged

```
public void adjustmentValueChanged (AdjustmentEvent e)
```

Parameters   *e*   The adjustment event that occurred.
Description   Handles the event by passing it on to listeners a and b.

componentAdded

```
public void componentAdded (ContainerEvent e)
```

Parameters   *e*   The container event that occurred.
Description   Handles the event by passing it on to listeners a and b.

componentHidden

```
public void componentHidden (ComponentEvent e)
```

Parameters   *e*   The component event that occurred.

Description   Handles the event by passing it on to listeners a and b.

componentMoved

```
public void componentMoved (ComponentEvent e)
```

Parameters   *e*   The component event that occurred.

Description   Handles the event by passing it on to listeners a and b.

componentRemoved

```
public void componentRemoved (ContainerEvent e)
```

Parameters   *e*   The container event that occurred.

Description   Handles the event by passing it on to listeners a and b.

componentResized

```
public void componentResized (ComponentEvent e)
```

Parameters   *e*   The component event that occurred.

Description   Handles the event by passing it on to listeners a and b.

componentShown

```
public void componentShown (ComponentEvent e)
```

Parameters   *e*   The component event that occurred.

Description   Handles the event by passing it on to listeners a and b.

focusGained

```
public void focusGained (FocusEvent e)
```

Parameters   *e*   The focus event that occurred.

Description   Handles the event by passing it on to listeners a and b.

focusLost

```
public void focusLost (FocusEvent e)
```

Parameters   *e*   The focus event that occurred.

Description   Handles the event by passing it on to listeners a and b.

itemStateChanged

```
public void itemStateChanged (ItemEvent e)
```

Parameters	*e*	The item event that occurred.
Description	Handles the event by passing it on to listeners a and b.	

keyPressed

```
public void keyPressed (KeyEvent e)
```

Parameters	*e*	The key event that occurred.
Description	Handles the event by passing it on to listeners a and b.	

keyReleased

```
public void keyReleased (KeyEvent e)
```

Parameters	*e*	The key event that occurred.
Description	Handles the event by passing it on to listeners a and b.	

keyTyped

```
public void keyTyped (KeyEvent e)
```

Parameters	*e*	The key event that occurred.
Description	Handles the event by passing it on to listeners a and b.	

mouseClicked

```
public void mouseClicked (MouseEvent e)
```

Parameters	*e*	The mouse event that occurred.
Description	Handles the event by passing it on to listeners a and b.	

mouseDragged

```
public void mouseDragged (MouseEvent e)
```

Parameters	*e*	The mouse event that occurred.
Description	Handles the event by passing it on to listeners a and b.	

mouseEntered

```
public void mouseEntered (MouseEvent e)
```

Parameters	*e*	The mouse event that occurred.
Description	Handles the event by passing it on to listeners a and b.	

mouseExited

```
public void mouseExited (MouseEvent e)
```

Parameters   *e*   The mouse event that occurred.

Description   Handles the event by passing it on to listeners a and b.

mouseMoved

```
public void mouseMoved (MouseEvent e)
```

Parameters   *e*   The mouse event that occurred.

Description   Handles the event by passing it on to listeners a and b.

mousePressed

```
public void mousePressed (MouseEvent e)
```

Parameters   *e*   The mouse event that occurred.

Description   Handles the event by passing it on to listeners a and b.

mouseReleased

```
public void mouseReleased (MouseEvent e)
```

Parameters   *e*   The mouse event that occurred.

Description   Handles the event by passing it on to listeners a and b.

textValueChanged

```
public void textValueChanged (TextEvent e)
```

Parameters   *e*   The text event that occurred.

Description   Handles the event by passing it on to listeners a and b.

windowActivated

```
public void windowActivated (WindowEvent e)
```

Parameters   *e*   The window event that occurred.

Description   Handles the event by passing it on to listeners a and b.

windowClosed

```
public void windowClosed (WindowEvent e)
```

Parameters   *e*   The window event that occurred.

Description   Handles the event by passing it on to listeners a and b.

windowClosing

```
public void windowClosing (WindowEvent e)
```

Parameters	*e*	The window event that occurred.
Description	Handles the event by passing it on to listeners a and b.	

windowDeactivated

```
public void windowDeactivated (WindowEvent e)
```

Parameters	*e*	The window event that occurred.
Description	Handles the event by passing it on to listeners a and b.	

windowDeiconified

```
public void windowDeiconified (WindowEvent e)
```

Parameters	*e*	The window event that occurred.
Description	Handles the event by passing it on to listeners a and b.	

windowIconified

```
public void windowIconified (WindowEvent e)
```

Parameters	*e*	The window event that occurred.
Description	Handles the event by passing it on to listeners a and b.	

windowOpened

```
public void windowOpened (WindowEvent e)
```

Parameters	*e*	The window event that occurred.
Description	Handles the event by passing it on to listeners a and b.	

Protected Instance Methods

remove

```
protected EventListener remove(EventListener oldl)
```

Parameters	*oldl*	The listener to remove.
Returns	The resulting EventListener.	
Description	This method removes oldl from the AWTEventMulticaster and returns the resulting listener.	

See Also

ActionEvent, AdjustmentEvent, ComponentEvent, Event, EventListener, EventObject, FocusEvent, ItemEvent, KeyEvent, MouseEvent, WindowEvent

19.4   AWTException

Description

An AWTException; thrown to indicate an exceptional condition; must be caught or declared in a throws clause.

Class Definition

```
public class java.awt.AWTException
    extends java.lang.Exception {

    // Constructors
    public AWTException (String message);
}
```

Constructors

AWTException

```
public AWTException (String message)
```

Parameters   *message*   Detailed message.

See Also

Exception, String

19.5   Adjustable ★

Description

The Adjustable interface is useful for scrollbars, sliders, dials, and other components that have an adjustable numeric value. Classes that implement the Adjustable interface should send AdjustmentEvent objects to listeners that have registered via addAdjustmentListener(AdjustmentListener).

Interface Definition

```
public abstract interface java.awt.Adjustable {

  // Constants
  public final static int HORIZONTAL = 0;
  public final static int VERTICAL = 1;

  // Interface Methods
  public abstract void addAdjustmentListener (AdjustmentListener l);
  public abstract int getBlockIncrement();
  public abstract int getMaximum();
  public abstract int getMinimum();
  public abstract int getOrientation();
  public abstract int getUnitIncrement();
  public abstract int getValue();
  public abstract int getVisibleAmount();
  public abstract void removeAdjustmentListener (AdjustmentListener l);
  public abstract void setBlockIncrement (int b);
  public abstract void setMaximum (int max);
  public abstract void setMinimum (int min);
  public abstract void setUnitIncrement (int u);
  public abstract void setValue (int v);
  public abstract void setVisibleAmount (int v);
}
```

Constants

HORIZONTAL

```
public static final int HORIZONTAL
```

A constant representing horizontal orientation.

VERTICAL

```
public static final int VERTICAL
```

A constant representing vertical orientation.

Interface Methods

addAdjustmentListener

```
public abstract void addAdjustmentListener (ActionListener l)
```

Parameters   *l*   An object that implements the AdjustmentLis-
                                 tener interface.

Description   Add a listener for adjustment event.

getBlockIncrement

```
public abstract int getBlockIncrement()
```

Returns   The amount to scroll when a paging area is selected.

getMaximum

```
public abstract int getMaximum()
```

Returns   The maximum value that the Adjustable object can take.

getMinimum

```
public abstract int getMinimum()
```

Returns   The minimum value that the Adjustable object can take.

getOrientation

```
public abstract int getOrientation()
```

Returns   A value representing the direction of the Adjustable object.

getUnitIncrement

```
public abstract int getUnitIncrement()
```

Returns   The unit amount to scroll.

getValue

```
public abstract int getValue()
```

Returns   The current setting for the Adjustable object.

getVisibleAmount

```
public abstract int getVisibleAmount()
```

Returns   The current visible setting (i.e., size) for the Adjustable object.

removeAdjustmentListener

```
public abstract void removeAdjustmentListener (AdjustmentListener
l)
```

Parameters   *l*   One of the object's AdjustmentListeners.
Description   Remove an adjustment event listener.

setBlockIncrement

public abstract void setBlockIncrement (int b)

Parameters   *b*   New block increment amount.
Description   Changes the block increment amount for the Adjustable object.

setMaximum

public abstract void setMaximum (int max)

Parameters   *max*   New maximum value.
Description   Changes the maximum value for the Adjustable object.

setMinimum

public abstract void setMinimum (int min)

Parameters   *min*   New minimum value.
Description   Changes the minimum value for the Adjustable object.

setUnitIncrement

public abstract void setUnitIncrement (int u)

Parameters   *u*   New unit increment amount.
Description   Changes the unit increment amount for the Adjustable object.

setValue

public abstract void setValue (int v)

Parameters   *v*   New value.
Description   Changes the current value of the Adjustable object.

setVisibleAmount

public abstract void setVisibleAmount (int v)

Parameters   *v*   New amount visible.
Description   Changes the current visible amount of the Adjustable object.

See Also

AdjustmentEvent, AdjustmentListener, Scrollbar

19.6   *BorderLayout*

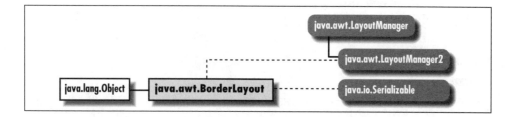

Description

BorderLayout is a LayoutManager that provides the means to lay out components along the edges of a container. It divides the container into five regions, named North, East, South, West, and Center. Normally you won't call the LayoutManager's methods yourself. When you add() a Component to a Container, the Container calls the addLayoutComponent() method of its LayoutManager.

Class Definition

```
public class java.awt.BorderLayout
    extends java.lang.Object
    implements java.awt.LayoutManager2, java.io.Serializable {

    // Constants
    public final static String CENTER; ★
    public final static String EAST; ★
    public final static String NORTH; ★
    public final static String SOUTH; ★
    public final static String WEST; ★


    // Constructors
    public BorderLayout();
    public BorderLayout (int hgap, int vgap);

    // Instance Methods
    public void addLayoutComponent (Component comp, Object constraints); ★
    public void addLayoutComponent (String name, Component component); ☆
    public int getHgap(); ★
    public abstract float getLayoutAlignmentX(Container target); ★
    public abstract float getLayoutAlignmentY(Container target); ★
    public int getVgap(); ★
    public abstract void invalidateLayout(Container target); ★

    public void layoutContainer (Container target);
    public abstract Dimension maximumLayoutSize(Container target); ★
    public Dimension minimumLayoutSize (Container target);
    public Dimension preferredLayoutSize (Container target);
```

```
    public void removeLayoutComponent (Component component);
    public void setHgap (int hgap);  ★
    public void setVgap (int vgap);  ★
    public String toString();
}
```

Constants

CENTER

```
public final static String CENTER
```

A constant representing center orientation.

EAST

```
public final static String EAST
```

A constant representing east orientation.

NORTH

```
public final static String NORTH
```

A constant representing north orientation.

SOUTH

```
public final static String SOUTH
```

A constant representing south orientation.

WEST

```
public final static String WEST
```

A constant representing west orientation.

Constructors

BorderLayout

```
public BorderLayout()
```

Description   Constructs a BorderLayout object.

```
public BorderLayout (int hgap, int vgap)
```

Parameters   *hgap*   Horizontal space between each component in the container.

              vgap   Vertical space between each component in the container.

Description   Constructs a BorderLayout object with the values specified as the gaps between each component in the container managed by this instance of BorderLayout.

Instance Methods

addLayoutComponent

public void addLayoutComponent (Component comp,
Object constraints) ★

Parameters   *comp*   The component being added.

                 constraints   An object describing the constraints on this component.

Implements   LayoutManager2.addLayoutComponent()

Description   Adds the component comp to a container subject to the given constraints. This is a more general version of addLayoutComponent(String, Component) method. It corresponds to java.awt.Container's add(Component, Object) method. In practice, it is used the same in version 1.1 as in Java 1.0.2, except with the parameters swapped:

```
Panel p = new Panel(new BorderLayout());
p.add(new Button("OK"), BorderLayout.SOUTH);
```

addLayoutComponent

public void addLayoutComponent (String name,
Component component) ☆

Parameters   *name*   Name of region to add component to.

                 component   Actual component being added.

Implements   LayoutManager.addLayoutComponent()

Description   Adds a component to a container in region name. This has been replaced in version 1.1 with the more general addLayoutComponent(Component, Object).

getHgap

public int getHgap() ★

Returns   The horizontal gap for this BorderLayout instance.

getLayoutAlignmentX

public abstract float getLayoutAlignmentX (Container target) ★

Parameters   *target*   The container to inspect.

Returns   The value .5 for all containers.

Description   This method returns the preferred alignment of the given container target. A return value of 0 is left aligned, .5 is centered, and 1 is right aligned.

getLayoutAlignmentY

public abstract float getLayoutAlignmentY (Container target) ★

Parameters	*target*	The container to inspect.
Returns		The value .5 for all containers.
Description		This method returns the preferred alignment of the given container target. A return value of 0 is top aligned, .5 is centered, and 1 is bottom aligned.

getVgap

public int getVgap() ★

Returns	The vertical gap for this BorderLayout instance.

invalidateLayout

public abstract void invalidateLayout (Container target) ★

Parameters	*target*	The container to invalidate.
Description		Does nothing.

layoutContainer

public void layoutContainer (Container target)

Parameters	*target*	The container that needs to be redrawn.
Implements		LayoutManager.layoutContainer()
Description		Draws components contained within target.

maximumLayoutSize

public abstract Dimension maximumLayoutSize (Container target) ★

Parameters	*target*	The container to inspect.
	Returns	A Dimension whose horizontal and vertical components are Integer.MAX_VALUE.
Description		For BorderLayout, a maximal Dimension is always returned.

minimumLayoutSize

public Dimension minimumLayoutSize (Container target)

Parameters	*target*	The container whose size needs to be calculated.
Returns		Minimum Dimension of the container target.
Implements		LayoutManager.minimumLayoutSize()
Description		Calculates minimum size of target. container.

preferredLayoutSize

```
public Dimension preferredLayoutSize (Container target)
```

Parameters   *target*   The container whose size needs to be calculated.
Returns   Preferred Dimension of the container target.
Implements   LayoutManager.preferredLayoutSize()
Description   Calculates preferred size of target container.

removeLayoutComponent

```
public void removeLayoutComponent (Component component)
```

Parameters   *component*   Component to stop tracking.
Implements   LayoutManager.removeLayoutComponent()
Description   Removes component from any internal tracking systems.

setHgap

```
public void setHgap (int hgap) ★
```

Parameters   *hgap*   The horizontal gap value.
Description   Sets the horizontal gap between components.

setVgap

```
public void setVgap (int vgap) ★
```

Parameters   *vgap*   The vertical gap value.
Description   Sets the vertical gap between components.

toString

```
public String toString()
```

Returns   A string representation of the BorderLayout object.
Overrides   Object.toString()

See Also

Component, Container, Dimension, LayoutManager, LayoutManager2, Object, String

19.7 Button

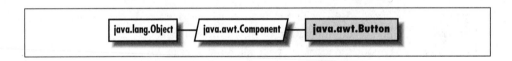

Description

The Button is the familiar labeled button object. It inherits most of its functionality from Component. For example, to change the font of the Button, you would use Component's setFont() method. The Button sends java.awt.event.ActionEvent objects to its listeners when it is pressed.

Class Definition

```
public class java.awt.Button
    extends java.awt.Component {

  // Constructors
  public Button();
  public Button (String label);

  // Instance Methods
  public void addActionListener (ActionListener l); ★
  public void addNotify();
  public String getActionCommand(); ★
  public String getLabel();
  public void removeActionListener (ActionListener l); ★
  public void setActionCommand (String command); ★
  public synchronized void setLabel (String label);

  // Protected Instance Methods
  protected String paramString();
  protected void processActionEvent (ActionEvent e); ★
  protected void processEvent (AWTEvent e); ★
}
```

Constructors

Button

```
public Button()
```

Description   Constructs a Button object with no label.

```
public Button (String label)
```

Parameters   *label*   The text for the label on the button
Description   Constructs a Button object with text of label.

Instance Methods

addActionListener

```
public void addActionListener (ActionListener l) ★
```

Parameters   *l*   An object that implements the ActionListener
                                       interface.
Description   Add a listener for the action event.

addNotify

```
public void addNotify()
```

Overrides   Component.addNotify()
Description   Creates Button's peer.

getActionCommand

```
public String getActionCommand() ★
```

Returns   Current action command string.
Description   Returns the string used for the action command.

getLabel

```
public String getLabel()
```

Returns   Text of the Button's label.

removeActionListener

```
public void removeActionListener (ActionListener l) ★
```

Parameters   *l*   One of this Button's ActionListeners.
Description   Remove an action event listener.

setActionCommand

```
public void setActionCommand (String command) ★
```

Parameters   *command*   New action command string.
Description   Specify the string used for the action command.

setLabel

```
public synchronized void setLabel (String label)
```

Parameters	*label*	New text for label of Button.
Description		Changes the Button's label to label.

Protected Instance Methods

paramString

```
protected String paramString()
```

Returns	String with current settings of Button.
Overrides	Component.paramString()
Description	Helper method for toString() used to generate a string of current settings.

processActionEvent

```
protected void processActionEvent (ActionEvent e) ★
```

Parameters	*e*	The action event to process.
Description		Action events are passed to this method for processing. Normally, this method is called by processEvent().

processEvent

```
protected void processEvent (AWTEvent e) ★
```

Parameters	*e*	The event to process.
Description		Low level AWTEvents are passed to this method for processing.

See Also

ActionListener, Component, String

19.8   Canvas

Description

Canvas is a Component that provides a drawing area and is often used as a base class for new components.

Class Definition

```
public class java.awt.Canvas
    extends java.awt.Component {

    // Constructors
    public Canvas();

    // Instance Methods
    public void addNotify();
    public void paint (Graphics g);
}
```

Constructors

Canvas

```
public Canvas()
```

Description   Constructs a Canvas object.

Instance Methods

addNotify

```
public void addNotify()
```

Overrides   Component.addNotify()
Description   Creates Canvas's peer.

paint

```
public void paint (Graphics g)
```

Parameters   *g*   Graphics context of component.
Description   Empty method to be overridden in order to draw something in graphics context.

See Also

Component, Graphics

19.9   CardLayout

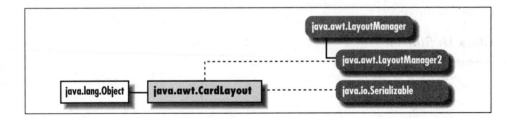

Description

The CardLayout LayoutManager provides the means to manage multiple components, displaying one at a time. Components are displayed in the order in which they are added to the layout, or in an arbitrary order by using an assignable name.

Class Definition

```
public class java.awt.CardLayout
    extends java.lang.Object
    implements java.awt.LayoutManager2, java.io.Serializable {

// Constructors
public CardLayout();
public CardLayout (int hgap, int vgap);

// Instance Methods
public void addLayoutComponent (Component comp,
    Object constraints); ★
public void addLayoutComponent (String name, Component component); ☆
public void first (Container parent);
public int getHgap(); ★
public abstract float getLayoutAlignmentX(Container target); ★
public abstract float getLayoutAlignmentY(Container target); ★
public int getVgap(); ★
public abstract void invalidateLayout(Container target); ★
public void last (Container parent);
public void layoutContainer (Container target);
public abstract Dimension maximumLayoutSize(Container target); ★
public Dimension minimumLayoutSize (Container target);
public void next (Container parent);
public Dimension preferredLayoutSize (Container target);
public void previous (Container parent);
public void removeLayoutComponent (Component component);
public void setHgap (int hgap); ★
public void setVgap (int vgap); ★
```

```
    public void show (Container parent, String name);
    public String toString();
}
```

Constructors

CardLayout

public CardLayout()

Description   Constructs a CardLayout object.

public CardLayout (int hgap, int vgap)

Parameters   *hgap*   Horizontal space around left and right of container

              vgap   Vertical space around top and bottom of container

Description   Constructs a CardLayout object with the values specified as the gaps around the container managed by this instance of Card-Layout.

Instance Methods

addLayoutComponent

public void addLayoutComponent (Component comp, Object constraints) ★

Parameters   *comp*   The component being added.

              constraints   An object describing the constraints on this component.

Implements   LayoutManager2.addLayoutComponent()

Description   Adds the component comp to a container subject to the given constraints. This is a more generalized version of addLayout-Component(String, Component). It corresponds to java.awt.Container's add(Component, Object). In practice, it is used the same in Java 1.1 as in Java 1.0.2, except with the parameters swapped:

```
    Panel p = new Panel();
    p.setLayoutManager(new CardLayout());
    p.add(new Button("OK"), "Don Julio");
```

addLayoutComponent

public void addLayoutComponent (String name,
Component component) ☆

Parameters	*name*	Name of the component to add.
	component	The actual component being added.
Implements	LayoutManager.addLayoutComponent()	
Description	Places component under the layout's management, assigning it the given name. This has been replaced in version 1.1 with the more general addLayoutComponent(Component, Object).	

first

public void first (Container parent)

Parameters	*parent*	The container whose displayed component is changing.
Throws	IllegalArgumentException	
		If the LayoutManager of parent is not CardLayout.
Description	Sets the container to display the first component in parent.	

getHgap

public int getHgap() ★

| Returns | The horizontal gap for this CardLayout instance. |

getLayoutAlignmentX

public abstract float getLayoutAlignmentX (Container target) ★

Parameters	*target*	The container to inspect.
Returns	The value .5 for all containers.	
Description	This method returns the preferred alignment of the given container target. A return value of 0 is left aligned, .5 is centered, and 1 is right aligned.	

getLayoutAlignmentY

public abstract float getLayoutAlignmentY (Container target) ★

Parameters	*target*	The container to inspect.
Returns	The value .5 for all containers.	
Description	This method returns the preferred alignment of the given container target. A return value of 0 is top aligned, .5 is centered, and 1 is bottom aligned.	

getVgap

    public int getVgap() ★

Returns   The vertical gap for this CardLayout instance.

invalidateLayout

    public abstract void invalidateLayout (Container target) ★

Parameters   *target*   The container to invalidate.
Description   Does nothing.

last

    public void last (Container parent)

Parameters   *parent*   The container whose displayed component is
                                   changing.
Throws   IllegalArgumentException
                                   If the LayoutManager of parent is not CardLay-
                                   out.
Description   Sets the container to display the final component in parent.

layoutContainer

    public void layoutContainer (Container target)

Parameters   *target*   The container that needs to be redrawn.
Implements   LayoutManager.layoutContainer()
Description   Displays the currently selected component contained within
                  target.

maximumLayoutSize

    public abstract Dimension maximumLayoutSize .hw Container
    (Container target) ★

Parameters   *target*   The container to inspect.
Returns   A Dimension whose horizontal and vertical components are
                  Integer.MAX_VALUE.
Description   For CardLayout, a maximal Dimension is always returned.

minimumLayoutSize

```
public Dimension minimumLayoutSize (Container target)
```

Parameters   *target*   The container whose size needs to be calculated.

Returns   Minimum Dimension of the container target.

Implements   LayoutManager.minimumLayoutSize()

Description   Calculates minimum size of the target container.

next

```
public void next (Container parent)
```

Parameters   *parent*   The container whose displayed component is changing.

Throws   IllegalArgumentException

                If the LayoutManager of parent is not CardLayout.

Description   Sets the container to display the following component in the parent.

preferredLayoutSize

```
public Dimension preferredLayoutSize (Container target)
```

Parameters   *target*   The container whose size needs to be calculated.

Returns   Preferred Dimension of the container target.

Implements   LayoutManager.preferredLayoutSize()

Description   Calculates preferred size of the target container.

previous

```
public void previous (Container parent)
```

Parameters   *parent*   The container whose displayed component is changing.

Throws   IllegalArgumentException

                If the LayoutManager of parent is not CardLayout.

Description   Sets the container to display the prior component in parent.

removeLayoutComponent

```
public void removeLayoutComponent (Component component)
```

Parameters   *component*   Component to stop tracking.

Implements   LayoutManager.removeLayoutComponent()

Description   Removes component from the layout manager's internal tables.

setHgap

public void setHgap (int hgap) ★

Parameters   *hgap*   The horizontal gap value.

Description   Sets the horizontal gap for the left and right of the container.

setVgap

public void setVgap (int vgap) ★

Parameters   *vgap*   The vertical gap value.

Description   Sets the vertical gap for the top and bottom of the container.

show

public void show (Container parent, String name)

Parameters   *parent*   The container whose displayed component is changing.

              name   Name of component to display.

Throws   IllegalArgumentException

                             If LayoutManager of parent is not CardLayout.

Description   Sets the container to display the component name in parent.

toString

public String toString()

Returns   A string representation of the CardLayout object.

Overrides   Object.toString()

See Also

Component, Container, Dimension, LayoutManager, LayoutManager2, Object, String

19.10   Checkbox

Description

The Checkbox is a Component that provides a true or false toggle switch for user input.

Class Definition

```
public class java.awt.Checkbox
    extends java.awt.Component
    implements java.awt.ItemSelectable {

    // Constructors
    public Checkbox();
    public Checkbox (String label);
    public Checkbox (String label, boolean state); ★
    public Checkbox (String label, boolean state, CheckboxGroup group); ★
    public Checkbox (String label, CheckboxGroup group, boolean state);

    // Instance Methods
    public void addItemListener (ItemListener l); ★
    public void addNotify();
    public CheckboxGroup getCheckboxGroup();
    public String getLabel();
    public Object[] getSelectedObjects(); ★
    public boolean getState();
    public void removeItemListener (ItemListener l); ★
    public void setCheckboxGroup (CheckboxGroup group);
    public synchronized void setLabel (String label);
    public void setState (boolean state);

    // Protected Instance Methods
    protected String paramString();
    protected void processEvent (AWTEvent e); ★
    protected void processItemEvent (ItemEvent e); ★
}
```

Constructors

Checkbox

```
public Checkbox()
```

Description   Constructs a Checkbox object with no label that is initially false.

```
public Checkbox (String label)
```

Parameters	*label*	Text to display with the Checkbox.
Description		Constructs a Checkbox object with the given label that is initially false.

```
public Checkbox (String label, boolean state) ★
```

Parameters	*label*	Text to display with the Checkbox.
	state	Intial value of the Checkbox.
Description		Constructs a Checkbox with the given label, initialized to the given state.

```
public Checkbox (String label, boolean state,
CheckboxGroup group) ★
```

Parameters	*label*	Text to display with the Checkbox.
	state	Intial value of the Checkbox.
	group	The CheckboxGroup this Checkbox should belong to.
Description		Constructs a Checkbox with the given label, initialized to the given state and belonging to group.

```
public Checkbox (String label, CheckboxGroup group, boolean state)
```

Parameters	*label*	Text to display with the Checkbox.
	group	The CheckboxGroup this Checkbox should belong to.
	state	Intial value of the Checkbox.
Description		Constructs a Checkbox object with the given settings.

Instance Methods

addItemListener

```
public void addItemListener (ItemListener l) ★
```

Parameters	*l*	The listener to be added.
Implements		ItemSelectable.addItemListener(ItemListener l)
Description		Adds a listener for the ItemEvent objects this Checkbox generates.

addNotify

```
public void addNotify()
```

Overrides	Component.addNotify()

Description   Creates Checkbox peer.

getCheckboxGroup

```
public CheckboxGroup getCheckboxGroup()
```

Returns   The current CheckboxGroup associated with the Checkbox, if any.

getLabel

```
public String getLabel()
```

Returns   The text associated with the Checkbox.

getSelectedObjects

```
public Object[] getSelectedObjects() ★
```

Implements   ItemSelectable.getSelectedObjects()
Description   If the Checkbox is checked, returns an array with length 1 containing the label of the Checkbox; otherwise returns null.

getState

```
public boolean getState()
```

Returns   The current state of the Checkbox.

removeItemListener

```
public void removeItemListener (ItemListener l) ★
```

Parameters   *l*   The listener to be removed.
Implements   ItemSelectable.removeItemListener (ItemListener l)
Description   Removes the specified ItemListener so it will not receive ItemEvent objects from this Checkbox.

setCheckboxGroup

```
public void setCheckboxGroup (CheckboxGroup group)
```

Parameters   *group*   New group in which to place the Checkbox.
Description   Associates the Checkbox with a different CheckboxGroup.

setLabel

    public synchronized void setLabel (String label)

Parameters   *label*   New text to associate with Checkbox.
Description   Changes the text associated with the Checkbox.

setState

    public void setState (boolean state)

Parameters   *state*   New state for the Checkbox.
Description   Changes the state of the Checkbox.

Protected Instance Methods

paramString

    protected String paramString()

Returns   String with current settings of Checkbox.
Overrides   Component.paramString()
Description   Helper method for toString() to generate string of current
              settings.

processEvent

    protected void processEvent(AWTEvent e) ★

Parameters   *e*   The event to process.
Description   Low level AWTEvents are passed to this method for processing.

processItemEvent

    protected void processItemEvent(ItemEvent e) ★

Parameters   *e*   The item event to process.
Description   Item events are passed to this method for processing. Normally,
              this method is called by processEvent().

See Also

CheckboxGroup, Component, ItemEvent, ItemSelectable, String

19.11   CheckboxGroup

Description

The CheckboxGroup class provides the means to group multiple Checkbox items into a mutual exclusion set, so that only one checkbox in the set has the value true at any time. The checkbox with the value true is the currently selected checkbox. Mutually exclusive checkboxes usually have a different appearance from regular checkboxes and are also called "radio buttons."

Class Definition

```
public class java.awt.CheckboxGroup
    extends java.lang.Object
    implements java.io.Serializable {

  // Constructors
  public CheckboxGroup();

  // Instance Methods
  public Checkbox getCurrent(); ☆
  public Checkbox getSelectedCheckbox() ★
  public synchronized void setCurrent (Checkbox checkbox); ☆
  public synchronized void setSelectedCheckbox (Checkbox checkbox); ★
  public String toString();
}
```

Constructors

CheckboxGroup

```
public CheckboxGroup()
```

Description   Constructs a CheckboxGroup object.

Instance Methods

getCurrent

```
public Checkbox getCurrent() ☆
```

Returns   The currently selected Checkbox within the CheckboxGroup.
Description   Replaced by the more aptly named getSelectedCheckbox().

getSelectedCheckbox

`public Checkbox getSelectedCheckbox()` ★

Returns   The currently selected Checkbox within the CheckboxGroup.

setCurrent

`public synchronized void setCurrent (Checkbox checkbox)` ☆

Parameters   *checkbox*   The Checkbox to select.
Description   Changes the currently selected Checkbox within the Checkbox-
               Group.
Description   Replaced by setSelectedCheckbox(Checkbox).

setSelectedCheckbox

`public synchronized void setSelectedCheckbox (Checkbox checkbox)`
★

Parameters   *checkbox*   The Checkbox to select.
Description   Changes the currently selected Checkbox within the Checkbox-
               Group.

toString

`public String toString()`

Returns   A string representation of the CheckboxGroup object.
Overrides   Object.toString()

See Also

Checkbox, Object, String

19.12   *CheckboxMenuItem*

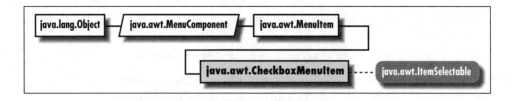

Description

The CheckboxMenuItem class represents a menu item with a boolean state.

Class Definition

```
public class java.awt.CheckboxMenuItem
    extends java.awt.MenuItem
    implements java.awt.ItemSelectable {

  // Constructors
  public CheckboxMenuItem(); ★
  public CheckboxMenuItem (String label);
  public CheckboxMenuItem (String label, boolean state); ★

  // Instance Methods
  public void addItemListener (ItemListener l); ★
  public void addNotify();
  public Object[] getSelectedObjects(); ★
  public boolean getState();
  public String paramString();
  public void removeItemListener (ItemListener l); ★
  public synchronized void setState (boolean condition);

  // Protected Instance Methods
  protected void processEvent (AWTEvent e); ★
  protected void processItemEvent (ItemEvent e); ★
}
```

Constructors

CheckboxMenuItem

```
public CheckboxMenuItem() ★
```

Description   Constructs a CheckboxMenuItem object with no label.

```
public CheckboxMenuItem (String label)
```

Parameters   *label*   Text that appears on CheckboxMenuItem.
Description   Constructs a CheckboxMenuItem object whose value is initially false.

```
public CheckboxMenuItem (String label, boolean state) ★
```

Parameters   *label*   Text that appears on CheckboxMenuItem.
              state   The initial state of the menu item.
Description   Constructs a CheckboxMenuItem object with the specified label and state.

Instance Methods

addItemListener

public void addItemListener (ItemListener l) ★

Parameters	*l*	The listener to be added.
Implements	ItemSelectable.addItemListener(ItemListener l)	
Description	Adds a listener for the ItemEvent objects this CheckboxMenu-Item fires off.	

addNotify

public void addNotify()

Overrides	MenuItem.addNotify()
Description	Creates CheckboxMenuItem's peer.

getSelectedObjects

public Object[] getSelectedObjects() ★

Implements	ItemSelectable.getSelectedObjects()
Description	If the CheckboxMenuItem is checked, returns an array with length 1 containing the label of the CheckboxMenuItem; otherwise returns null.

getState

public boolean getState()

Returns	The current state of the CheckboxMenuItem.

paramString

public String paramString()

Returns	A string with current settings of CheckboxMenuItem.
Overrides	MenuItem.paramString()
Description	Helper method for toString() to generate string of current settings.

removeItemListener

public void removeItemListener (ItemListener l) ★

Parameters	*l*	The listener to be removed.
Implements	ItemSelectable.removeItemListener (ItemListener l)	
Description	Removes the specified ItemListener so it will not receive Item-Event objects from this CheckboxMenuItem.	

setState

    public synchronized void setState (boolean condition)

Parameters   *condition*   New state for the CheckboxMenuItem.
Description   Changes the state of the CheckboxMenuItem.

Protected Instance Methods

processEvent

    protected void processEvent(AWTEvent e) ★

Parameters   *e*   The event to process.
Overrides   MenuItem.processEvent(AWTEvent)
Description   Low level AWTEvents are passed to this method for processing.

processItemEvent

    protected void processItemEvent(ItemEvent e) ★

Parameters   *e*   The item event to process.
Description   Item events are passed to this method for processing. Normally,
              this method is called by processEvent().

See Also

ItemEvent, ItemSelectable, MenuItem, String

19.13   Choice

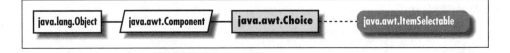

Description

The Choice is a Component that provides a drop-down list of choices to choose
from.

Class Definition

    public class java.awt.Choice
        extends java.awt.Component
        implements java.awt.ItemSelectable {

      // Constructors
      public Choice();

      // Instance Methods

```
    public synchronized void add (String item); ★
    public synchronized void addItem (String item); ☆
    public void addItemListener (ItemListener l); ★
    public void addNotify();
    public int countItems();   ☆
    public String getItem (int index);
    public int getItemCount(); ★
    public int getSelectedIndex();
    public synchronized String getSelectedItem();
    public synchronized Object[] getSelectedObjects(); ★
    public synchronized void insert (String item, int index); ★
    public synchronized void remove (int position); ★
    public synchronized void remove (String item); ★
    public synchronized void removeAll(); ★
    public void removeItemListener (ItemListener l); ★
    public synchronized void select (int pos);
    public synchronized void select (String str);

    // Protected Instance Methods
    protected String paramString();
    protected void processEvent (AWTEvent e);   ★
    protected void processItemEvent (ItemEvent e); ★
}
```

Constructors

Choice

```
public Choice()
```

Description   Constructs a Choice object.

Instance Methods

add

```
public synchronized void add (String item) ★
```

Parameters	*item*	Text for new entry.
Throws	NullPointerException	
		If item is null.
Description	Adds a new entry to the available choices.	

addItem

```
public synchronized void addItem (String item) ☆
```

Parameters	*item*	Text for new entry.
Throws	NullPointerException	
		If item is null.

Description   Replaced by add(String).

addItemListener

public void addItemListener (ItemListener l) ★

Parameters   *l*   The listener to be added.
Implements   ItemSelectable.addItemListener(ItemListener l)
Description   Adds a listener for the ItemEvent objects this Choice generates.

addNotify

public void addNotify()

Overrides   Component.addNotify()
Description   Creates Choice's peer.

countItems

public int countItems() ☆

Returns   Number of items in the Choice.
Description   Replaced by getItemCount().

getItem

public String getItem (int index)

Parameters   *index*   Position of entry.
Returns   A string for an entry at a given position.
Throws   ArrayIndexOutOfBoundsException
                               If index is invalid; indices start at zero.

getItemCount

public int getItemCount() ★

Returns   Number of items in the Choice.

getSelectedIndex

public int getSelectedIndex()

Returns   Position of currently selected entry.

getSelectedItem

```
public synchronized String getSelectedItem()
```

Returns   Currently selected entry as a String.

getSelectedObjects

```
public synchronized Object[] getSelectedObjects() ★
```

Implements   ItemSelectable.getSelectedObjects()
Description   A single-item array containing the current selection.

insert

```
public synchronized void insert (String item, int index) ★
```

Parameters   *item*   The string to add.
               index   The position for the new string.
Throws   IllegalArgumentException
                                   If index is less than zero.
Description   Inserts item in the given position.

remove

```
public synchronized void remove (int position) ★
```

Parameters   *position*   The index of an entry in the Choice component.
Description   Removes the entry in the given position.

```
public synchronized void remove (String string) ★
```

Parameters   *string*   Text of an entry within the Choice component.
Throws   IllegalArgumentException
                                   If string is not in the Choice.
Description   Makes the first entry that matches string the selected item.

removeAll

```
public synchronized void removeAll() ★
```

Description   Removes all the entries from the Choice.

removeItemListener

```
public void removeItemListener (ItemListener l) ★
```

Parameters   *l*   The listener to be removed.
Implements   ItemSelectable.removeItemListener (ItemListener l)

Description   Removes the specified ItemListener so it will not receive Item-
              Event objects from this Choice.

select

```
public synchronized void select (int pos)
```

Parameters   *pos*   The index of an entry in the Choice component.
Throws   IllegalArgumentException
                                 If the position is not valid.
Description   Makes the entry in the given position.

```
public synchronized void select (String str)
```

Parameters   *str*   Text of an entry within the Choice component.
Description   Makes the first entry that matches str the selected item for the
              Choice.

Protected Instance Methods

paramString

```
protected String paramString()
```

Returns   A string with current settings of Choice.
Overrides   Component.paramString()
Description   Helper method for toString() to generate string of current
              settings.

processEvent

```
protected void processEvent (AWTEvent e)  ★
```

Parameters   *e*   The event to process.
Description   Low level AWTEvents are passed to this method for processing.

processItemEvent

```
protected void processItemEvent (ItemEvent e)  ★
```

Parameters   *e*   The item event to process.
Description   Item events are passed to this method for processing. Normally,
              this method is called by processEvent().

See Also

Component, ItemSelectable, String

19.14   Color

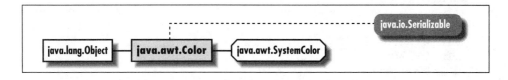

Description

The Color class represents a specific color to the system.

Class Definition

```
public final class java.awt.Color
    extends java.lang.Object
    implements java.io.Serializable {

    // Constants
    public static final Color black;
    public static final Color blue;
    public static final Color cyan;
    public static final Color darkGray;
    public static final Color gray;
    public static final Color green;
    public static final Color lightGray;
    public static final Color magenta;
    public static final Color orange;
    public static final Color pink;
    public static final Color red;
    public static final Color white;
    public static final Color yellow;

    // Constructors
    public Color (int rgb);
    public Color (int red, int green, int blue);
    public Color (float red, float green, float blue);

    // Class Methods
    public static Color decode (String name); ★
    public static Color getColor (String name);
    public static Color getColor (String name, Color defaultColor);
    public static Color getColor (String name, int defaultColor);
    public static Color getHSBColor (float hue, float saturation,
        float brightness);
    public static int HSBtoRGB (float hue, float saturation, float brightness);
    public static float[] RGBtoHSB (int red, int green, int blue,
        float hsbvalues[]);
```

```
// Instance Methods
public Color brighter();
public Color darker();
public boolean equals (Object object);
public int getBlue();
public int getGreen();
public int getRed();
public int getRGB();
public int hashCode();
public String toString();
}
```

Constants

black

```
public static final Color black
```

The color black.

blue

```
public static final Color blue
```

The color blue.

cyan

```
public static final Color cyan
```

The color cyan.

darkGray

```
public static final Color darkGray
```

The color dark gray.

gray

```
public static final Color gray
```

The color gray.

green

```
public static final Color green
```

The color green.

lightGray

public static final Color lightGray

The color light gray.

magenta

public static final Color magenta

The color magenta.

orange

public static final Color orange

The color orange.

pink

public static final Color pink

The color pink.

red

public static final Color red

The color red.

white

public static final Color white

The color white.

yellow

public static final Color yellow

The color yellow.

Constructors

Color

public Color (int rgb)

Parameters	*rgb*	Composite color value
Description		Constructs a Color object with the given rgb value.

public Color (int red, int green, int blue)

Parameters	*red*	Red component of color in the range [0, 255]

	green	Green component of color in the range[0, 255]
	blue	Blue component of color in the range[0, 255]

Description   Constructs a `Color` object with the given `red`, `green`, and `blue` values.

`public Color (float red, float green, float blue)`

Parameters	red	Red component of color in the range[0.0, 1.0]
	green	Green component of color in the range[0.0, 1.0]
	blue	Blue component of color in the range[0.0, 1.0]

Description   Constructs a `Color` object with the given `red`, `green`, and `blue` values.

Class Methods

decode

`public static Color decode (String nm)` ★

Parameters   *nm*   A `String` representing a color as a 24-bit integer.

Returns   The color requested.

Throws   `NumberFormatException`
          If `nm` cannot be converted to a number.

Description   Gets color specified by the given string.

getColor

`public static Color getColor (String name)`

Parameters   *name*   The name of a system property indicating which color to fetch.

Returns   Color instance of `name` requested, or `null` if the `name` is invalid.

Description   Gets color specified by the system property name.

`public static Color getColor (String name, Color defaultColor)`

Parameters   *name*   The `name` of a system property indicating which color to fetch.

              defaultColor   Color to return if `name` is not found in properties, or invalid.

Returns   Color instance of `name` requested, or `defaultColor` if the `name` is invalid.

Description   Gets color specified by the system property name.

```
public static Color getColor (String name, int defaultColor)
```

Parameters	*name*	The name of a system property indicating which color to fetch.
	defaultColor	Color to return if name is not found in properties, or invalid.
Returns		Color instance of name requested, or defaultColor if the name is invalid.
Description		Gets color specified by the system property name. The default color is specified as a 32-bit RGB value.

getHSBColor

```
public static Color getHSBColor (float hue, float saturation,
float brightness)
```

Parameters	*hue*	Hue component of Color to create, in the range[0.0, 1.0].
	saturation	Saturation component of Color to create, in the range[0.0, 1.0].
	brightness	Brightness component of Color to create, in the range[0.0, 1.0].
Returns		Color instance for values provided.
Description		Create an instance of Color by using hue, saturation, and brightness instead of red, green, and blue values.

HSBtoRGB

```
public static int HSBtoRGB (float hue, float saturation,
float brightness)
```

Parameters	*hue*	Hue component of Color to convert, in the range[0.0, 1.0].
	saturation	Saturation component of Color to convert, in the range[0.0, 1.0].
	brightness	Brightness component of Color to convert, in the range[0.0, 1.0].
Returns		Color value for hue, saturation, and brightness provided.
Description		Converts a specific hue, saturation, and brightness to a Color and returns the red, green, and blue values in a composite integer value.

RGBtoHSB

```
public static float[] RGBtoHSB (int red, int green, int blue,
float[] hsbvalues)
```

Parameters	*red*	Red component of Color to convert, in the range[0, 255].
	green	Green component of Color to convert, in the range[0, 255].
	blue	Blue component of Color to convert, in the range[0, 255].
	hsbvalues	Three element array in which to put the result. This array is used as the method's return object. If null, a new array is allocated.
Returns		Hue, saturation, and brightness values for Color provided, in elements 0, 1, and 2 (respectively) of the returned array.
Description		Allows you to convert specific red, green, blue value to the hue, saturation, and brightness equivalent.

Instance Methods

brighter

```
public Color brighter()
```

Returns	Brighter version of current color.
Description	Creates new Color that is somewhat brighter than current.

darker

```
public Color darker()
```

Returns	Darker version of current color.
Description	Creates new Color that is somewhat darker than current.

equals

```
public boolean equals (Object object)
```

Parameters	*object*	The object to compare.
Returns		true if object represents the same color, false otherwise.
Overrides		Object.equals(Object)
Description		Compares two different Color instances for equivalence.

getBlue

public int getBlue()

Returns   Blue component of current color.

getGreen

public int getGreen()

Returns   Green component of current color.

getRed

public int getRed()

Returns   Red component of current color.

getRGB

public int getRGB()

Returns   Current color as a composite value.
Description   Gets integer value of current color.

hashCode

public int hashCode()

Returns   A hashcode to use when storing Color in a Hashtable.
Overrides   Object.hashCode()
Description   Generates a hashcode for the Color.

toString

public String toString()

Returns   A string representation of the Color object.
Overrides   Object.toString()

See Also

Object, Properties, Serializable, String

19.15 Component

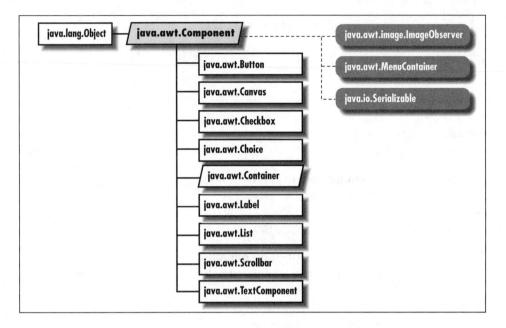

Description

The Component class is the parent of all non-menu GUI components.

Class Definition

```
public abstract class java.awt.Component
    extends java.lang.Object
    implements java.awt.image.ImageObserver
    implements java.awt.MenuContainer
    implements java.io.Serializable {

    // Constants
    public final static float BOTTOM_ALIGNMENT; ★
    public final static float CENTER_ALIGNMENT; ★
    public final static float LEFT_ALIGNMENT; ★
    public final static float RIGHT_ALIGNMENT; ★
    public final static float TOP_ALIGNMENT; ★

    // Variables
    protected Locale locale; ★

    // Constructors
    protected Component(); ★

    // Instance Methods
```

```
public boolean action (Event e, Object o); ☆
public synchronized void add (PopupMenu popup); ★
public synchronized void addComponentListener
    (ComponentListener l); ★
public synchronized void addFocusListener (FocusListener l); ★
public synchronized void addKeyListener (KeyListener l); ★
public synchronized void addMouseListener (MouseListener l); ★
public synchronized void addMouseMotionListener
    (MouseMotionListener l); ★
public void addNotify();
public Rectangle bounds(); ☆
public int checkImage (Image image, ImageObserver observer);
public int checkImage (Image image, int width, int height,
    ImageObserver observer);
public boolean contains (int x, int y); ★
public boolean contains (Point p); ★
public Image createImage (ImageProducer producer);
public Image createImage (int width, int height);
public void deliverEvent (Event e); ☆
public void disable(); ☆
public final void dispatchEvent (AWTEvent e) ★
public void doLayout(); ★
public void enable(); ☆
public void enable (boolean condition); ☆
public float getAlignmentX(); ★
public float getAlignmentY(); ★
public Color getBackground();
public Rectangle getBounds(); ★
public synchronized ColorModel getColorModel();
public Component getComponentAt (int x, int y); ★
public Component getComponentAt (Point p); ★
public Cursor getCursor(); ★
public Font getFont();
public FontMetrics getFontMetrics (Font f);
public Color getForeground();
public Graphics getGraphics();
public Locale getLocale(); ★
public Point getLocation(); ★
public Point getLocationOnScreen(); ★
public Dimension getMaximumSize(); ★
public Dimension getMinimumSize(); ★
public String getName(); ★
public Container getParent();
public ComponentPeer getPeer(); ☆
public Dimension getPreferredSize(); ★
public Dimension getSize(); ★
public Toolkit getToolkit();
public final Object getTreeLock(); ★
public boolean gotFocus (Event e, Object o); ☆
```

```
public boolean handleEvent (Event e); ☆
public void hide(); ☆
public boolean imageUpdate (Image image, int infoflags, int x, int y,
    int width, int height);
public boolean inside (int x, int y); ☆
public void invalidate();
public boolean isEnabled();
public boolean isFocusTraversable(); ★
public boolean isShowing();
public boolean isValid();
public boolean isVisible();
public boolean keyDown (Event e, int key); ☆
public boolean keyUp (Event e, int key); ☆
public void layout(); ☆
public void list();
public void list (PrintStream out);
public void list (PrintStream out, int indentation);
public void list (PrintWriter out); ★
public void list (PrintWriter out, int indentation); ★
public Component locate (int x, int y); ☆
public Point location(); ☆
public boolean lostFocus (Event e, Object o); ☆
public Dimension minimumSize(); ☆
public boolean mouseDown (Event e, int x, int y); ☆
public boolean mouseDrag (Event e, int x, int y); ☆
public boolean mouseEnter (Event e, int x, int y); ☆
public boolean mouseExit (Event e, int x, int y); ☆
public boolean mouseMove (Event e, int x, int y); ☆
public boolean mouseUp (Event e, int x, int y); ☆
public void move (int x, int y); ☆
public void nextFocus(); ☆
public void paint (Graphics g);
public void paintAll (Graphics g);
public boolean postEvent (Event e); ☆
public Dimension preferredSize(); ☆
public boolean prepareImage (Image image, ImageObserver observer);
public boolean prepareImage (Image image, int width, int height,
    ImageObserver observer);
public void print (Graphics g);
public void printAll (Graphics g);
public synchronized void remove (MenuComponent popup); ★
public synchronized void removeComponentListener
    (ComponentListener l); ★
public synchronized void removeFocusListener (FocusListener l); ★
public synchronized void removeKeyListener (KeyListener l); ★
public synchronized void removeMouseListener (MouseListener l); ★
public synchronized void removeMouseMotionListener
    (MouseMotionListener l); ★
public void removeNotify();
```

```
    public void repaint();
    public void repaint (long tm);
    public void repaint (int x, int y, int width, int height);
    public void repaint (long tm, int x, int y, int width, int height);
    public void requestFocus();
    public void reshape (int x, int y, int width, int height); ☆
    public void resize (Dimension d); ☆
    public void resize (int width, int height); ☆
    public void setBackground (Color c);
    public void setBounds (int x, int y, int width, int height); ★
    public void setBounds (Rectangle r); ★
    public synchronized void setCursor (Cursor cursor); ★
    public void setEnabled (boolean b); ★
    public synchronized void setFont (Font f);
    public void setForeground (Color c);
    public void setLocale (Locale l); ★
    public void setLocation (int x, int y); ★
    public void setLocation (Point p); ★
    public void setName (String name); ★
    public void setSize (int width, int height); ★
    public void setSize (Dimension d); ★
    public void setVisible (boolean b); ★
    public void show(); ☆
    public void show (boolean condition); ☆
    public Dimension size(); ☆
    public String toString();
    public void transferFocus(); ★
    public void update (Graphics g);
    public void validate();

    // Protected Instance Methods
    protected final void disableEvents (long eventsToDisable); ★
    protected final void enableEvents (long eventsToEnable); ★
    protected String paramString();
    protected void processComponentEvent (ComponentEvent e); ★
    protected void processEvent (AWTEvent e); ★
    protected void processFocusEvent (FocusEvent e); ★
    protected void processKeyEvent (KeyEvent e); ★
    protected void processMouseEvent (MouseEvent e); ★
    protected void processMouseMotionEvent (MouseEvent e); ★
}
```

Constants

BOTTOM_ALIGNMENT

public final static float BOTTOM_ALIGNMENT ★

Constant representing bottom alignment in getAlignmentY().

CENTER_ALIGNMENT

public final static float CENTER_ALIGNMENT ★

Constant representing center alignment in getAlignmentX() and getAlignmentY().

LEFT_ALIGNMENT

public final static float LEFT_ALIGNMENT ★

Constant representing left alignment in getAlignmentX().

RIGHT_ALIGNMENT

public final static float RIGHT_ALIGNMENT ★

Constant representing right alignment in getAlignmentX().

TOP_ALIGNMENT

public final static float TOP_ALIGNMENT ★

Constant representing top alignment in getAlignmentY().

Variables

locale

protected Locale locale ★

Description   The locale for the component. Used for internationalization support.

Constructors

Component

protected Component() ★

Description   This constructor creates a "lightweight" component. This constructor allows Component to be directly subclassed using code written entirely in Java.

Instance Methods

action

public boolean action (Event e, Object o) ☆

Parameters	*e*	Event instance identifying what triggered the call to this method.
	o	Argument specific to the component subclass that generated the event.
Returns		true if event handled, false to propagate it to parent container.
Description		Method called when user performs some action in Component. This method is a relic of the old 1.0.2 event model and is replaced by the process . . . Event() methods.

add

public synchronized void add (PopupMenu popup) ★

| Parameters | *popup* | The menu to add. |
| Description | | After the PopupMenu is added to a component, it can be shown in the component's coordinate space. |

addComponentListener

public void addComponentListener (ComponentListener l) ★

| Description | Adds a listener for the ComponentEvent objects this Component generates. |

addFocusListener

public void addFocusListener (FocusListener l) ★

| Description | Adds a listener for the FocusEvent objects this Component generates. |

addKeyListener

public void addKeyListener (KeyListener l) ★

| Description | Adds a listener for the KeyEvent objects this Component generates. |

addMouseListener

public void addMouseListener (MouseListener l) ★

Description   Adds a listener for the MouseEvent objects this Component generates.

addMouseMotionListener

public void addMouseMotionListener (MouseMotionListener l) ★

Description   Adds a listener for the motion MouseEvent objects this Component generates.

addNotify

public void addNotify()

Description   Creates peer of Component's subclass.

bounds

public Rectangle bounds() ☆

Returns   Gets bounding rectangle of Component.
Description   A Rectangle that returns the outer limits of the Component. Replaced by getBounds() in 1.1.

checkImage

public int checkImage (Image image, ImageObserver observer)

Parameters   *image*   Image to check.
              observer   The object an image will be rendered onto.
Returns   ImageObserver Flags ORed together indicating the image's status.
Description   Checks status of image construction.

public int checkImage (Image image, int width, int height, ImageObserver observer)

Parameters   *image*   Image to check.
              width   Horizontal size image will be scaled to.
              height   Vertical size image will be scaled to.
              observer   Object image will be rendered onto.
Returns   ImageObserver flags ORed together indicating the image's status.
Description   Checks status of image construction.

contains

public boolean contains (int x, int y) ★

Parameters	*x*	The x coordinate, in this Component's coordinate system.
	y	The y coordinate, in this Component's coordinate system.
Returns		true if the Component contains the point; false otherwise.

public boolean contains (Point p) ★

| Parameters | *p* | The point to be tested, in this Component's coordinate system. |
| Returns | | true if the Component contains the point; false otherwise. |

createImage

public Image createImage (ImageProducer producer)

Parameters	*producer*	Class that implements ImageProducer interface to create the new image.
Returns		Newly created image instance.
Description		Creates an Image based upon an ImageProducer.

public Image createImage (int width, int height)

Parameters	*width*	Horizontal size for in-memory Image.
	height	Vertical size for in-memory Image.
Returns		Newly created image instance.
Description		Creates an empty in-memory Image for double buffering; to draw on the image, use its graphics context.

deliverEvent

public void deliverEvent (Event e) ☆

| Parameters | *e* | Event instance to deliver. |
| Description | | Delivers event to the component for processing. |

disable

public void disable() ☆

| Description | Disables component so that it is unresponsive to user interactions. Replaced by setEnabled(false). |

dispatchEvent

```
public final void dispatchEvent (AWTEvent e) ★
```

Parameters   *e*   The AWTEvent to process.
Description   Tells the component to deal with the AWTEvent e.

doLayout

```
public void doLayout() ★
```

Description   Lays out component. This method is a replacement for lay-
                 out().

enable

```
public void enable() ☆
```

Description   Enables component so that it is responsive to user interactions.
                 Use setEnabled(true) instead.

```
public void enable (boolean condition) ☆
```

Parameters   *condition*   true to enable the component; false to disable
                                  it.
Description   Enables or disables the component based upon condition.
                 Use setEnabled(boolean) instead.

getAlignmentX

```
public float getAlignmentX() ★
```

Returns   A number between 0 and 1 representing the horizontal align-
                 ment of this component.
Description   One of the constants LEFT_ALIGNMENT, CENTER_ALIGNMENT, or
                 RIGHT_ALIGNMENT may be returned. CENTER_ALIGNMENT is
                 returned by default.

getAlignmentY

```
public float getAlignmentY() ★
```

Returns   A number between 0 and 1 representing the vertical alignment
                 of this component.
Description   One of the constants TOP_ALIGNMENT, CENTER_ALIGNMENT, or
                 BOTTOM_ALIGNMENT may be returned. CENTER_ALIGNMENT is
                 returned by default.

getBackground

```
public Color getBackground()
```

Returns   Background color of the component.

getBounds

```
public Rectangle getBounds() ★
```

Returns   Gets bounding rectangle of Component.

Description   Returns a Rectangle that returns the outer limits of the Component.

getColorModel

```
public synchronized ColorModel getColorModel()
```

Returns   ColorModel used to display the current component.

getComponentAt

```
public Component getComponentAt (int x, int y) ★
```

Parameters   *x*   The x coordinate, in this Component's coordinate system.

              y   The y coordinate, in this Component's coordinate system.

Returns   Returns the Component containing the given point.

```
public Component getComponentAt (Point p) ★
```

Parameters   *p*   The point to be tested, in this Component's coordinate system.

Returns   Returns the Component containing the given point.

getCursor

```
public Cursor getCursor() ★
```

Returns   Current cursor of the component.

getFont

```
public Font getFont()
```

Returns   Current font of the component.

getFontMetrics

`public FontMetrics getFontMetrics (Font f)`

| Parameters | f | A Font object, whose platform specific information is desired. |
| Returns | | Size information for the given Font. |

getForeground

`public Color getForeground()`

Returns   Foreground color of component.

getGraphics

`public Graphics getGraphics()`

Throws	InternalException
	If acquiring graphics context is unsupported.
Returns	Component's graphics context.

getLocale

`public Locale getLocale() ★`

Throws	IllegalComponentStateException
	If the component does not have a locale or it has not been added to a hierarchy that does.
Returns	Component's locale.

getLocation

`public Point getLocation() ★`

| Returns | Position of component. |
| Description | Gets the current position of this Component in its parent's coordinate space. |

getLocationOnScreen

`public Point getLocationOnScreen() ★`

| Returns | Position of component. |
| Description | Gets the current position of this Component in the screen's coordinate space. |

getMaximumSize

public Dimension getMaximumSize() ★

Returns   The maximum dimensions of the component.
Description   By default, a maximal Dimension is returned.

getMinimumSize

public Dimension getMinimumSize() ★

Returns   The minimum dimensions of the component.

getName

public String getName() ★

Returns   This component's name.

getParent

public Container getParent()

Returns   Parent Container of Component.
Description   Gets container that this Component is held in.

getPeer

public ComponentPeer getPeer() ☆

Returns   Peer of Component.

getPreferredSize

public Dimension getPreferredSize() ★

Returns   The preferred dimensions of the component.

getSize

public Dimension getSize() ★

Returns   Dimensions of component.
Description   Gets width and height of component.

getToolkit

public Toolkit getToolkit()

Returns   Toolkit of Component.

getTreeLock

public final Object getTreeLock() ★

Returns   The AWT tree locking object.

Description Returns the object used for tree locking and layout operations.

gotFocus

public boolean gotFocus (Event e, Object o) ☆

Parameters *e*   Event instance identifying what triggered the
                     call to this method.

            o   Argument specific to the component subclass
                     that generated the event.

Returns   true if event handled, false to propagate it to parent con-
            tainer.

Description Called when Component gets input focus. This method is not
             used in the 1.1 event model.

handleEvent

public boolean handleEvent (Event e) ☆

Parameters *e*   Event instance identifying what triggered the
                     call to this method.

Returns   true if event handled, false to propagate it to parent con-
            tainer.

Description High-level event handling routine that calls helper routines.
             Replaced by processEvent(AWTEvent).

hide

public void hide() ☆

Description Hides component from view. Replaced by setVisible(false).

imageUpdate

public boolean imageUpdate (Image image, int infoflags, int x,
int y, int width, int height)

Parameters *image*   Image being loaded.

            infoflags ImageObserver flags ORed together of available
                        information.

            x   x coordinate of upper-left corner of Image.

            y   y coordinate of upper-left corner of Image.

	width	Horizontal dimension of Image.
	height	Vertical dimension of Image.
Returns		true if Image fully loaded, false otherwise.
Implements		ImageObserver.imageUpdate()
Description		An asynchronous update interface for receiving notifications about Image information as it is loaded. Meaning of parameters changes with values of flags.

inside

```
public boolean inside (int x, int y) ☆
```

Parameters	*x*	Horizontal position.
	y	Vertical position.
Returns		true if the point (x, y) falls within the component's bounds, false otherwise.
Description		Checks if coordinates are within bounding box of Component. Replaced by contains(int, int).

invalidate

```
public void invalidate()
```

Description	Sets the component's valid state to false.

isEnabled

```
public boolean isEnabled()
```

Returns	true if enabled, false otherwise.
Description	Checks to see if the Component is currently enabled.

isFocusTraversable

```
public boolean isFocusTraversable() ★
```

Returns	true if this Component can be traversed using Tab and Shift-Tab, false otherwise.
Description	Checks to see if the Component is navigable using the keyboard.

isShowing

```
public boolean isShowing()
```

Returns	true if showing, false otherwise.
Description	Checks to see if the Component is currently showing.

isValid

```
public boolean isValid()
```

Returns   true if valid, false otherwise.

Description   Checks to see if the Component is currently valid.

isVisible

```
public boolean isVisible()
```

Returns   true if visible, false otherwise.

Description   Checks to see if the Component is currently visible.

keyDown

```
public boolean keyDown (Event e, int key)  ☆
```

Parameters   *e*   Event instance identifying what triggered the call to this method.

             key   Integer representation of key pressed.

Returns   true if event handled, false to propagate it to parent container.

Description   Method called whenever the user presses a key. Replaced by processKeyEvent(KeyEvent).

keyUp

```
public boolean keyUp (Event e, int key)  ☆
```

Parameters   *e*   Event instance identifying what triggered the call to this method.

             key   Integer representation of key released.

Returns   true if event handled, false to propagate it to parent container.

Description   Method called whenever the user releases a key. Replaced by processKeyEvent(KeyEvent).

layout

```
public void layout()  ☆
```

Description   Lays out component. Replaced by doLayout().

list

`public void list()`

Description   Prints the contents of the Component to System.out.

`public void list (PrintStream out)`

Parameters   *out*   Output stream to send results to.
Description   Prints the contents of the Component to a PrintStream.

`public void list (PrintStream out, int indentation)`

Parameters   *out*   Output stream to send results to.
              indentation   Indentation to use when printing.
Description   Prints the contents of the Component indented to a PrintStream.

`public void list (PrintWriter out)`

Parameters   *out*   Output stream to send results to.
Description   Prints the contents of the Component to a PrintWriter.

`public void list (PrintWriter out, int indentation)`

Parameters   *out*   Output stream to send results to.
              indentation   Indentation to use when printing.
Description   Prints the contents of the Component indented to a Print-Writer.

locate

`public Component locate (int x, int y)` ☆

Parameters   *x*   Horizontal position.
              y   Vertical position.
Returns   Component if the point (x, y) falls within the component, null otherwise.
Description   Replaced by getComponentAt(int, int).

location

`public Point location()` ☆

Returns   Position of component.
Description   Gets the current position of this Component in its parent's coordinate space. Replaced by getLocation().

lostFocus

`public boolean lostFocus (Event e, Object o)` ☆

Parameters	*e*	Event instance identifying what triggered the call to this method.
	o	Argument specific to the component subclass that generated the event.
Returns		true if event handled, false to propagate it to parent container.
Description		Method called when Component loses input focus. Replaced by processFocusEvent(FocusEvent).

minimizeSize

`public Dimension minimumSize()` ☆

Returns	The minimum dimensions of the component. Replaced by getMinimumSize().

mouseDown

`public boolean mouseDown (Event e, int x, int y)` ☆

Parameters	*e*	Event instance identifying what triggered the call to this method.
	x	Horizontal position of the mouse within Component when Event initiated
	y	Vertical position of the mouse within Component when Event initiated
Returns		true if event handled, false to propagate it to parent container.
Description		Method called when the user presses a mouse button over Component. Replaced by processMouseEvent(MouseEvent).

mouseDrag

`public boolean mouseDrag (Event e, int x, int y)` ☆

Parameters	*e*	Event instance identifying what triggered the call to this method.
	x	Horizontal position of the mouse within Component when Event initiated
	y	Vertical position of the mouse within Component when Event initiated

Returns   true if event handled, `false` to propagate it to parent con-
                tainer.

Description   Method called when the user is pressing a mouse button and
                moves the mouse. Replaced by `processMouseMotion-`
                `Event(MouseEvent)`.

mouseEnter

`public boolean mouseEnter (Event e, int x, int y)` ☆

Parameters   *e*   Event instance identifying what triggered the
                                call to this method.

                x   Horizontal position of the mouse within Compo-
                                nent when Event initiated

                y   Vertical position of the mouse within Component
                                when Event initiated

Returns   true if event handled, `false` to propagate it to parent con-
                tainer.

Description   Method called when the mouse enters Component. Replaced by
                `processMouseEvent(MouseEvent)`.

mouseExit

`public boolean mouseExit (Event e, int x, int y)` ☆

Parameters   *e*   Event instance identifying what triggered the
                                call to this method.

                x   Horizontal position of the mouse within Compo-
                                nent when Event initiated

                y   Vertical position of the mouse within Component
                                when Event initiated

Returns   true if event handled, `false` to propagate it to parent con-
                tainer.

Description   Method called when the mouse exits Component. Replaced by
                `processMouseEvent(MouseEvent)`.

mouseMove

`public boolean mouseMove (Event e, int x, int y)` ☆

Parameters   *e*   Event instance identifying what triggered the
                                call to this method.

                x   Horizontal position of the mouse within Compo-
                                nent when Event initiated

	y	Vertical position of the mouse within Component when Event initiated
Returns		true if event handled, false to propagate it to parent container.
Description		Method called when the user is not pressing a mouse button and moves the mouse. Replaced by processMouseMotionEvent(MouseEvent).

mouseUp

```
public boolean mouseUp (Event e, int x, int y) ☆
```

Parameters	e	Event instance identifying what triggered the call to this method.
	x	Horizontal position of the mouse within Component when Event initiated
	y	Vertical position of the mouse within Component when Event initiated
Returns		true if event is handled, false to propagate it to the parent container.
Description		Method called when user releases mouse button over Component. Replaced by processMouseEvent(MouseEvent).

move

```
public void move (int x, int y) ☆
```

Parameters	x	New horizontal position for component.
	y	New vertical position for component.
Description		Relocates component. Replaced by setLocation(int, int).

nextFocus

```
public void nextFocus() ☆
```

Description	Moves focus from current component to next one in parent container. Replaced by transferFocus().

paint

```
public void paint (Graphics g)
```

Parameters	g	Graphics context of component.
Description		Empty method to be overridden to draw something in the graphics context.

paintAll

public void paintAll (Graphics g)

Parameters   *g*   Graphics context of component.

Description   Method to validate component and paint its peer if it is visible.

postEvent

public boolean postEvent (Event e) ☆

Parameters   *e*   Event instance to post to component

Returns   If Event is handled, true is returned. Otherwise, false is returned.

Description   Tells Component to deal with Event.

preferredSize

public Dimension preferredSize() ☆

Returns   The preferred dimensions of the component. Replaced by getPreferredSize().

prepareImage

public boolean prepareImage (Image image, ImageObserver observer)

Parameters   *image*   Image to start loading.

observer   Component on which image will be rendered.

Returns   true if Image is fully loaded, false otherwise.

Description   Forces Image to start loading.

public boolean prepareImage (Image image, int width, int height, ImageObserver observer)

Parameters   *image*   Image to start loading.

width   Horizontal size of the Image after scaling.

height   Vertical size of the Image after scaling.

observer   Component on which image will be rendered.

Returns   true if Image is fully loaded, false otherwise.

Description   Forces Image to start loading.

print

public void print (Graphics g)

Parameters   *g*   Graphics context.

Description   Empty method to be overridden to print something into the graphics context.

printAll

```
public void printAll (Graphics g)
```

Parameters   *g*   Graphics context.

Description   Method to print this component and its children.

remove

```
public void remove (MenuComponent popup) ★
```

Parameters   *popup*   The menu to remove.

Description   After adding a PopupMenu, you can use this method to remove
               it.

removeComponentListener

```
public void removeComponentListener (ComponentListener 1) ★
```

Description   Removes the specified ComponentListener from this Component.

removeFocusListener

```
public void removeFocusListener (FocusListener 1) ★
```

Description   Removes the specified FocusListener from this Component.

removeKeyListener

```
public void removeKeyListener (KeyListener 1) ★
```

Description   Removes the specified KeyListener from this Component.

removeMouseListener

```
public void removeMouseListener (MouseListener 1) ★
```

Description   Removes the specified MouseListener from this Component.

removeMouseMotionListener

```
public void removeMouseMotionListener (MouseMotionListener 1) ★
```

Description   Removes the specified MouseMotionListener from this Compo-
               nent.

removeNotify

`public void removeNotify()`

Description   Removes peer of Component's subclass.

repaint

`public void repaint()`

Description   Requests scheduler to redraw the component as soon as possible.

`public void repaint (long tm)`

Parameters   *tm*   Millisecond delay allowed before repaint.

Description   Requests scheduler to redraw the component within a time period.

`public void repaint (int x, int y, int width, int height)`

Parameters   *x*   Horizontal origin of bounding box to redraw.

              y   Vertical origin of bounding box to redraw.

              width   Width of bounding box to redraw.

              height   Height of bounding box to redraw.

Description   Requests scheduler to redraw a portion of component as soon as possible.

`public void repaint (long tm, int x, int y, int width, int height)`

Parameters   *tm*   Millisecond delay allowed before repaint.

              x   Horizontal origin of bounding box to redraw.

              y   Vertical origin of bounding box to redraw.

              width   Width of bounding box to redraw.

              height   Height of bounding box to redraw.

Description   Requests scheduler to redraw a portion of component within a time period.

requestFocus

`public void requestFocus()`

Description   Requests the input focus for this Component.

reshape

`public void reshape (int x, int y, int width, int height)` ☆

Parameters	*x*	New horizontal position for component.
	y	New vertical position for component.
	width	New width for component.
	height	New height for component.
Description	Relocates and resizes component. Replaced by `setBounds(int, int, int, int)`.	

resize

`public void resize (Dimension d)` ☆

Parameters	*d*	New dimensions for the component.
Description	Resizes component. Replaced by `setSize(Dimension)`.	

`public void resize (int width, int height)` ☆

Parameters	*width*	New width for component.
	height	New height for component.
Description	Resizes component. Replaced by `setSize(int, int)`.	

setBackground

`public void setBackground (Color c)`

Parameters	*c*	New background color.
Description	Changes the component's background color.	

setBounds

`public void setBounds (int x, int y, int width, int height)` ★

Parameters	*x*	New horizontal position for component.
	y	New vertical position for component.
	width	New width for component.
	height	New height for component.
Description	Relocates and resizes the component.	

`public void setBounds (Rectangle r)` ★

Parameters	*r*	New coordinates for component.
Description	Relocates and resizes component.	

setCursor

```
public synchronized void setCursor (Cursor cursor) ★
```

Parameters   *cursor*   The new cursor for the component.

Description   Changes the component's cursor.

setEnabled

```
public void setEnabled (boolean b) ★
```

Parameters   *b*   true to enable the component, false to disable
                                 it.

Description   Enables or disables the component. Replaces enable(),
               enable(boolean), and disable().

setFont

```
public synchronized void setFont (Font f)
```

Parameters   *f*   Font to change component to.

Description   Changes the font of the component.

setForeground

```
public void setForeground (Color c)
```

Parameters   *c*   New foreground color.

Description   Changes the foreground color of component's area.

setLocale

```
public void setLocale (Locale l) ★
```

Parameters   *l*   The locale object for the component.

Description   Sets the Component's locale.

setLocation

```
public void setLocation (int x, int y) ★
```

Parameters   *x*   New horizontal position for component.

               y   New vertical position for component.

Description   Relocates the component.

```
public void setLocation (Point p) ★
```

Parameters   *p*   New position for component.

Description   Relocates the component.

setName

```
public void setName (String name) ★
```

Parameters   *name*   New name for component.
Description   Sets the component's name.

setSize

```
public void setSize (int width, int height) ★
```

Parameters   *width*   New width for component.
              height   New height for component.
Description   Resizes the component.

```
public void setSize (Dimension d) ★
```

Parameters   *d*   New dimensions for the component.
Description   Resizes the component.

setVisible

```
public void setVisible (boolean b) ★
```

Parameters   *b*   true to show component, false to hide it.
Description   Shows or hides the component based on the b parameter.

show

```
public void show() ☆
```

Description   Replaced by setVisible(true).

```
public void show (boolean condition) ☆
```

Parameters   *condition*   true to show the component, false to hide it.
Description   Replaced by setVisible(boolean).

size

```
public Dimension size() ☆
```

Returns   Dimensions of the component.
Description   Gets width and height of the component. Replaced by get-
              Size().

toString

```
public String toString()
```

Returns   A string representation of the Component object.
Overrides   Object.toString()

transferFocus

```
public void transferFocus() ★
```

Description   Transfers focus to the next component in the container hierarchy.

update

```
public void update (Graphics g)
```

Parameters   *g*   Graphics context of component.
Description   Called to update the component's display area.

validate

```
public void validate()
```

Description   Sets the component's valid state to true.

Protected Instance Methods

disableEvents

```
protected final void disableEvents (long eventsToDisable) ★
```

Parameters   *eventsToDisable*

A value representing certain kinds of events. This can be constructed by ORing the event mask constants defined in java.awt.AWTEvent.

Description   By default, a component receives events corresponding to the event listeners that have registered. If a component should not receive events of a certain type, even if there is a listener registered for that type of event, this method can be used to disable that event type.

enableEvents

protected final void enableEvents (long eventsToEnable) ★

Parameters	*eventsToEnable* A value representing certain kinds of events. This can be constructed by ORing the event mask constants defined in java.awt.AWTEvent.
Description	By default, a component receives events corresponding to the event listeners that have registered. If a component should receive other types of events as well, this method can be used to request them.

paramString

protected String paramString()

Returns	A String with the current settings of the Component.
Description	Helper method for toString() to generate a string of current settings.

processComponentEvent

protected void processComponentEvent(ComponentEvent e) ★

Parameters	*e* The event to process.
Description	Component events are passed to this method for processing. Normally, this method is called by processEvent().

processEvent

protected void processEvent(AWTEvent e) ★

Parameters	*e* The event to process.
Description	Low level AWTEvents are passed to this method for processing.

processFocusEvent

protected void processFocusEvent(FocusEvent e) ★

Parameters	*e* The event to process.
Description	Focus events are passed to this method for processing. Normally, this method is called by processEvent().

processKeyEvent

protected void processKeyEvent(KeyEvent e) ★

Parameters   *e*   The event to process.
Description   Key events are passed to this method for processing. Normally,
                this method is called by processEvent().

processMouseEvent

protected void processMouseEvent(MouseEvent e) ★

Parameters   *e*   The event to process.
Description   Mouse events are passed to this method for processing. Nor-
                mally, this method is called by processEvent().

processMouseMotionEvent

protected void processMouseMotionEvent(MouseEvent e) ★

Parameters   *e*   The event to process.
Description   Mouse motion events are passed to this method for processing.
                Normally, this method is called by processEvent().

See Also

Button, Canvas, Checkbox, Choice, Color, ColorModel, ComponentPeer, Container,
Dimension, Event, Font, FontMetrics, Graphics, ImageObserver, ImageProducer,
Label, List, MenuContainer, Object, Point, PrintStream, Rectangle, Scrollbar,
Serializable, String, TextComponent, Toolkit

19.16   Container

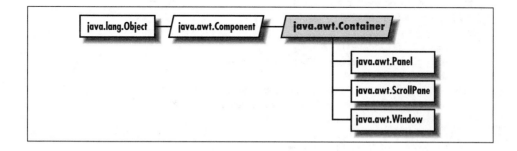

Description

The Container class serves as a general purpose holder of other Component objects.

Class Definition

```
public abstract class java.awt.Container
    extends java.awt.Component {

    // Constructors
    protected Container(); ★

    // Instance Methods
    public Component add (Component component);
    public Component add (Component component, int position);
    public void add (Component comp, Object constraints); ★
    public void add (Component comp, Object constraints,
        int position); ★
    public Component add (String name, Component component); ☆
    public synchronized void addContainerListener (ContainerListener l); ★
    public void addNotify();
    public int countComponents();
    public void deliverEvent (Event e); ★
    public void doLayout(); ★
    public float getAlignmentX(); ★
    public float getAlignmentY(); ★
    public Component getComponent (int n);
    public Component getComponentAt (int x, int y); ★
    public Component getComponentAt (Point p); ★
    public int getComponentCount(); ★
    public Component[] getComponents();
    public Insets getInsets(); ★
    public LayoutManager getLayout();
    public Dimension getMaximumSize(); ★
    public Dimension getMinimumSize(); ★
    public Dimension getPreferredSize(); ★
    public Insets insets();
    public void invalidate(); ★
    public boolean isAncestorOf (Component c); ★
    public void layout(); ☆
    public void list (PrintStream out, int indentation);
    public void list (PrintWriter out, int indentation); ★
    public Component locate (int x, int y); ☆
    public Dimension minimumSize(); ☆
    public void paint (Graphics g); ★
    public void paintComponents (Graphics g);
    public Dimension preferredSize(); ☆
    public void print (Graphics g); ★
    public void printComponents (Graphics g);
    public void remove (int index); ★
```

```
public void remove (Component component);
public void removeAll();
public void removeContainerListener (ContainerListener l); ★
public void removeNotify();
public void setLayout (LayoutManager manager);
public void validate();

// Protected Instance Methods
protected void addImpl (Component comp, Object constraints,
    int index); ★
protected String paramString();
protected void processContainerEvent (ContainerEvent e); ★
protected void processEvent (AWTEvent e); ★
protected void validateTree(); ★
}
```

Constructors

Container

protected Container() ★

Description   This constructor creates a "lightweight" container. This constructor allows Container to be subclassed using code written entirely in Java.

Instance Methods

add

public Component add (Component component)

Parameters   *component*   Component to add to container.
Returns   Component just added.
Throws   IllegalArgumentException if you add component to itself.
Description   Adds component as the last component in the container.

public Component add (Component component, int position)

Parameters   *component*   Component to add to container.
              position   Position of component; -1 adds the component as the last in the container.
Returns   Component just added.
Throws   ArrayIndexOutOfBoundsException
                              If position invalid.
              IllegalArgumentException
                              If you add Component to itself.

Description   Adds component to container at a certain position.

`public void add (Component component, Object constraints)` ★

Parameters   *component*   Component to add to container.
              constraints An object describing constraints on the compo-
                            nent being added.

Description   Adds component to container subject to contraints.

`public void add (Component component, Object constraints,`
`int index)` ★

Parameters   *component*   Component to add to container.
              constraints An object describing constraints on the compo-
                            nent being added.
              index   The position of the component in the con-
                            tainer's list.

Description   Adds component to container subject to contraints at position
              index.

`public Component add (String name, Component component)` ☆

Parameters   *name*   Name of component being added. This parame-
                            ter is often significant to the layout manager of
                            the container (e.g "North", "Center").
              component   Component to add to container.
Returns   Component just added.
Throws   *IllegalArgumentException*
                            If you add component to itself.
Description   Adds the component to the container with the given name.
              Replaced by the more general add(Component, Object).

addContainerListener

`public synchronized void addContainerListener (ContainerListener l)` ★

Parameters   *l*   An object that implements the ContainerLis-
                            tener interface.
Description   Add a listener for the container events.

addNotify

`public void addNotify()`

Overrides   Component.addNotify()
Description   Creates Container's peer and peers of contained components.

countComponents

`public int countComponents()`

Returns   Number of components within `Container`.

deliverEvent

`public void deliverEvent (Event e)` ☆

Parameters   *e*   `Event` instance to deliver.
Overrides   `Component.deliverEvent(Event)`
Description   Tries to locate the component contained in the container that should receive the event.

doLayout

`public void doLayout()` ★

Description   Lays out the container. This method is a replacement for `layout()`.

getAlignmentX

`public float getAlignmentX()` ★

Returns   A number between 0 and 1 representing the horizontal alignment of this component.
Overrides   `Component.getAlignmentX()`
Description   If the container's layout manager implements `LayoutManager2`, this method returns the `getLayoutAlignmentX()` value of the layout manager. Otherwise the `getAlignmentX()` value of `Component` is returned.

getAlignmentY

`public float getAlignmentY()` ★

Returns   A number between 0 and 1 representing the vertical alignment of this component.
Overrides   `Component.getAlignmentY()`
Description   If the container's layout manager implements `LayoutManager2`, this method returns the `getLayoutAlignmentY()` value of the layout manager. Otherwise the `getAlignmentY()` value of `Component` is returned.

getComponent

```
public synchronized Component getComponent (int position)
```

Parameters   *position*   Position of component to get.

Throws   ArrayIndexOutOfBoundsException
                                   If position is invalid.

Returns   Component at designated position within Container.

getComponentAt

```
public Component getComponentAt (int x, int y) ★
```

Parameters   *x*   The x coordinate, in this Container's coordinate
                                   system.

               y   The y coordinate, in this Container's coordinate
                                   system.

Returns   Returns the Component containing the give point.

```
public Component getComponentAt (Point p) ★
```

Parameters   *p*   The point to be tested, in this Container's coor-
                                   dinate system.

Returns   Returns the Component containing the give point.

getComponentCount

```
public int getComponentCount() ★
```

Returns   Returns the number of components in the container.

getComponents

```
public Component[] getComponents()
```

Returns   Array of components within the container.

getInsets

```
public Insets getInsets()
```

Returns   The insets of the container.

getLayout

```
public LayoutManager getLayout()
```

Returns   LayoutManager of Container.

getMaximumSize

```
public Dimension getMaximumSize() ★
```

Overrides   Component.getMaximumSize()

Returns   The maximum dimensions of the component.

getMinimumSize

```
public Dimension getMinimumSize() ★
```

Overrides   Component.getMinimumSize()

Returns   The minimum dimensions of the component.

getPreferredSize

```
public Dimension getPreferredSize() ★
```

Returns   The preferred dimensions of the component.

insets

```
public Insets insets() ☆
```

Returns   Current Insets of Container. Replaced by getInsets().

invalidate

```
public void invalidate()
```

Overrides   Component.invalidate()

Description   Sets the container's valid state to false.

isAncestorOf

```
public boolean isAncestorOf (Component c) ★
```

Parameters   *c*   The component in question.

Returns   If c is contained in the container's hierarchy, returns true; oth-
               erwise false.

layout

```
public void layout() ☆
```

Overrides   Component.layout()

Description   Replaced by doLayout().

list

`public void list (PrintStream out, int indentation)`

Parameters	*out*	Output Stream to send results to.
	indentation	Indentation to use when printing.
Overrides	Component.list(PrintStream, int)	
Description	Recursively lists all components in Container.	

`public void list (PrintWriter out, int indentation)`

Parameters	*out*	Output Writer to send results to.
	indentation	Indentation to use when printing.
Overrides	Component.list(PrintWriter, int)	
Description	Recursively lists all components in Container.	

locate

`public Component locate (int x, int y)` ☆

Parameters	*x*	Horizontal position to check.
	y	Vertical position to check.
Returns	Component within Container at given coordinates, or Container.	
Overrides	Component.locate(int, int)	
Description	Replaced by getComponentAt(int, int).	

minimizeSize

`public Dimension minimumSize()` ☆

Returns	Minimum dimensions of contained objects.
Overrides	Component.minimumSize()
Description	Replaced by getMinimumSize().

paint

`public void paint (Graphics g)`

Parameters	*g*	Graphics context of container.
Overrides	Component.paint()	
Description	This method tells any lightweight components that are children of this container to paint themselves.	

paintComponents

```
public void paintComponents (Graphics g)
```

Parameters	*g*	Graphics context of Container.
Description	Paints the different components in Container.	

preferredSize

```
public Dimension preferredSize() ☆
```

Returns	Preferred dimensions of contained objects.
Overrides	Component.preferredSize()
Description	Replaced by getPreferredSize().

print

```
public void print (Graphics g)
```

Parameters	*g*	Graphics context of container.
Overrides	Component.print()	
Description	This method tells any lightweight components that are children of this container to print themselves.	

printComponents

```
public void printComponents (Graphics g)
```

Parameters	*g*	Graphics context of Container.
Description	Prints the different components in Container.	

remove

```
public void remove (int index) ★
```

Parameters	*index*	Index of the component to remove.
Description	Removes the component in position index from Container.	

```
public void remove (Component component)
```

Parameters	*component*	Component to remove.
Description	Removes component from Container.	

removeAll

```
public void removeAll()
```

Description	Removes all components from Container.

removeContainerListener

```
public void removeContainerListener (ContainerListener l) ★
```

Parameters   *l*   One of this Container's ContainerListeners.
Description   Remove a container event listener.

removeNotify

```
public void removeNotify()
```

Overrides   Component.removeNotify()
Description   Removes Container's peer and peers of contained components.

setLayout

```
public void setLayout (LayoutManager manager)
```

Parameters   *manager*   New LayoutManager for Container.
Description   Changes LayoutManager of Container.

validate

```
public void validate()
```

Overrides   Component.validate()
Description   Sets Container's valid state to true and recursively validates its
               children.

Protected Instance Methods

addImpl

```
protected void addImpl (Component comp, Object constraints, int
index) ★
```

Parameters   *comp*   The component to add.
                 constraints   Constraints on the component.
                 index   Position at which to add this component. Pass -1
                                    to add the component at the end.
Description   This method adds a component subject to the given constraints
               at a specific position in the container's list of components. It is
               a helper method for the various overrides of add().

paramString

protected String paramString()

Returns   String with current settings of Container.
Overrides   Component.paramString()
Description   Helper method for toString() to generate string of current
              settings.

processContainerEvent

protected void processContainerEvent (ContainerEvent e) ★

Parameters   *e*   The event to process.
Description   Container events are passed to this method for processing. Nor-
              mally, this method is called by processEvent().

processEvent

protected void processEvent (AWTEvent e) ★

Parameters   *e*   The event to process.
Overrides   Component.processEvent()
Description   Low level AWTEvents are passed to this method for processing.

validateTree

protected void validateTree() ★

Description   Descends recursively into the Container's components and
              recalculates layout for any subtrees that are marked invalid.

See Also

Component, Dimension, Event, Graphics, Insets, LayoutManager, Panel,
PrintStream, String, Window

19.17   Cursor ★

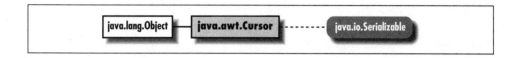

Description

The Cursor class represents the mouse pointer. It encapsulates information that used to be in java.awt.Frame in the 1.0.2 release.

Class Definition

```
public class java.awt.Cursor
    extends java.lang.Object
    implements java.io.Serializable {

    // Constants
    public final static int CROSSHAIR_CURSOR;
    public final static int DEFAULT_CURSOR;
    public final static int E_RESIZE_CURSOR;
    public final static int HAND_CURSOR;
    public final static int MOVE_CURSOR;
    public final static int N_RESIZE_CURSOR;
    public final static int NE_RESIZE_CURSOR;
    public final static int NW_RESIZE_CURSOR;
    public final static int S_RESIZE_CURSOR;
    public final static int SE_RESIZE_CURSOR;
    public final static int SW_RESIZE_CURSOR;
    public final static int TEXT_CURSOR;
    public final static int W_RESIZE_CURSOR;
    public final static int WAIT_CURSOR;

    // Class Variables
    protected static Cursor[] predefined;

    // Class Methods
    public static Cursor getDefaultCursor();
    public static Cursor getPredefinedCursor (int type);

    // Constructors
    public Cursor (int type);

    // Instance Methods
    public int getType();
}
```

Constants

CROSSHAIR_CURSOR

```
public final static int CROSSHAIR_CURSOR
```

Constant representing a cursor that looks like a crosshair.

DEFAULT_CURSOR

```
public final static int DEFAULT_CURSOR
```

Constant representing the platform's default cursor.

E_RESIZE_CURSOR

```
public final static int E_RESIZE_CURSOR
```

Constant representing the cursor for resizing an object on the left.

HAND_CURSOR

```
public final static int HAND_CURSOR
```

Constant representing a cursor that looks like a hand.

MOVE_CURSOR

```
public final static int MOVE_CURSOR
```

Constant representing a cursor used to move an object.

N_RESIZE_CURSOR

```
public final static int N_RESIZE_CURSOR
```

Constant representing a cursor for resizing an object on the top.

NE_RESIZE_CURSOR

```
public final static int NE_RESIZE_CURSOR
```

Constant representing a cursor for resizing an object on the top left corner.

NW_RESIZE_CURSOR

```
public final static int NW_RESIZE_CURSOR
```

Constant representing a cursor for resizing an object on the top right corner.

S_RESIZE_CURSOR

`public final static int S_RESIZE_CURSOR`

Constant representing a cursor for resizing an object on the bottom.

SE_RESIZE_CURSOR

`public final static int SE_RESIZE_CURSOR`

Constant representing a cursor for resizing an object on the bottom left corner.

SW_RESIZE_CURSOR

`public final static int SW_RESIZE_CURSOR`

Constant representing a cursor for resizing an object on the bottom right corner.

TEXT_CURSOR

`public final static int TEXT_CURSOR`

Constant representing a cursor used within text.

W_RESIZE_CURSOR

`public final static int W_RESIZE_CURSOR`

Constant representing a cursor for resizing an object on the right side.

WAIT_CURSOR

`public final static int WAIT_CURSOR`

Constant representing a cursor that indicates the program is busy.

Class Variables

predefined

`protected static Cursor[] predefined`

An array of cursor instances corresponding to the predefined cursor types.

Class Methods

getDefaultCursor

`public static Cursor getDefaultCursor()`

Returns   The default system cursor.

getPredefinedCursor

    public static Cursor getPredefinedCursor (int type)

Parameters   *type*   One of the type constants defined in this class.
Returns   A Cursor object with the specified type.

Constructors

Cursor

    public Cursor (int type)

Parameters   *type*   One of the type constants defined in this class.
Description   Constructs a Cursor object with the specified type.

Instance Methods

getType

    public int getType()

Returns   The type of cursor.

See Also

Frame

19.18   Dialog

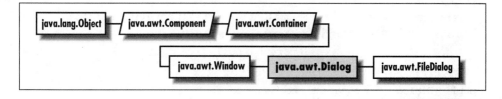

Description

The Dialog class provides a special type of display window that is used for pop-up messages and acquiring input from the user. Unlike most other components, dialogs are hidden by default; you must call show() to display them. Dialogs are always associated with a parent Frame. A Dialog may be either modal or non-modal; a modal dialog attracts all input typed by the user. The default layout for a Dialog is BorderLayout.

Class Definition

```
public class java.awt.Dialog
    extends java.awt.Window {

  // Constructors
  public Dialog (Frame parent);  ★
  public Dialog (Frame parent, boolean modal);
  public Dialog (Frame parent, String title);  ★
  public Dialog (Frame parent, String title, boolean modal);

  // Instance Methods
  public void addNotify();
  public String getTitle();
  public boolean isModal();
  public boolean isResizable();
  public void setModal (boolean b);  ★
  public synchronized void setResizable (boolean resizable);
  public synchronized void setTitle (String title);
  public void show();   ★

  // Protected Instance Methods
  protected String paramString();
}
```

Constructors

Dialog

`public Dialog (Frame parent)` ★

Parameters	*parent*	Frame that is to act as the parent of Dialog.
Throws	IllegalArgumentException	
		If parent is null.
Description	Constructs a Dialog object.	

`public Dialog (Frame parent, boolean modal)`

Parameters	*parent*	Frame that is to act as the parent of Dialog.
	modal	true if the Dialog is modal; false otherwise.
Throws	IllegalArgumentException	
		If parent is null.
Description	Replaced with Dialog(Frame, String, boolean).	

`public Dialog (Frame parent, String title)` ★

Parameters	*parent*	Frame that is to act as parent of Dialog.
	title	Initial title to use for Dialog.

Throws	IllegalArgumentException
	If parent is null.
Description	Constructs a Dialog object with given characteristics.

public Dialog (Frame parent, String title, boolean modal)

Parameters	*parent*	Frame that is to act as parent of Dialog.
	title	Initial title to use for Dialog.
	modal	true if the Dialog is modal; false otherwise.
Throws	IllegalArgumentException	
	If parent is null.	
Description	Constructs a Dialog object with given characteristics.	

Instance Methods

addNotify

public void addNotify()

Overrides	Window.addNotify()
Description	Creates Dialog's peer and peers of contained components.

getTitle

public String getTitle()

Returns	The current title for the Dialog.

isModal

public boolean isModal()

Returns	true if modal, false otherwise.

isResizable

public boolean isResizable()

Returns	true if resizable, false otherwise.

setModal

public void setModal (boolean b) ★

Parameters	*b*	true makes the Dialog modal; false if the Dialog should be modeless.
Description	Changes the modal state of the Dialog.	

setResizable

```
public synchronized void setResizable (boolean resizable)
```

Parameters   *resizable*   true makes the Dialog resizable; false if the
                               Dialog cannot be resized.
Description   Changes the resize state of the Dialog.

setTitle

```
public synchronized void setTitle (String title)
```

Parameters   *title*   New title for the Dialog.
Description   Changes the title of the Dialog.

show

```
public void show() ★
```

Overrides   Window.show()
Description   If the dialog is hidden, this method shows it. If the dialog is
                already visible, this method brings it to the front.

Protected Instance Methods

paramString

```
protected String paramString()
```

Returns   String with current settings of Dialog.
Overrides   Container.paramString()
Description   Helper method for toString() to generate string of current
                settings.

See Also

FileDialog, Frame, String, Window, WindowEvent, WindowListener

---

19.19   Dimension

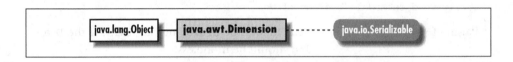

Description

The Dimension class encapsulates width and height in a single object.

Class Definition

```
public class java.awt.Dimension
    extends java.lang.Object
    implements java.io.Serializable {

  // Variables
  public int height;
  public int width;

  // Constructors
  public Dimension();
  public Dimension (int width, int height);
  public Dimension (Dimension d);

  // Instance Methods
  public boolean equals (Object obj);  ★
  public Dimension getSize();  ★
  public void setSize (Dimension d);  ★
  public void setSize (int width, int height);  ★
  public String toString();
}
```

Variables

height

```
public int height
```

The height of the Dimension.

width

```
public int width
```

The width of the Dimension.

Constructors

Dimension

```
public Dimension()
```

Description   Constructs an empty Dimension object.

```
public Dimension (int width, int height)
```

Parameters   *width*   Initial width of the object
               height   Initial height of the object
Description   Constructs a `Dimension` object with an initial dimension of width x height.

```
public Dimension (Dimension d)
```

Parameters   *d*   Initial dimensions of the object
Description   Constructs a `Dimension` object that is a clone of d.

Instance Methods

equals

```
public boolean equals (Object obj)  ★
```

Parameters   *obj*   The object to compare.
Returns   true if this `Dimension` is equivalent to obj; false otherwise.
Overrides   `Object.equals(Object)`
Description   Compares two `Dimension` instances.

getSize

```
public Dimension getSize ()  ★
```

Returns   The size of the `Dimension`.

setSize

```
public void setSize (Dimension d)  ★
```

Parameters   *d*   The new size.
Description   Changes the size of the `Dimension`.

```
public void setSize (int width, int height)  ★
```

Parameters   *width*   The new width.
               height   The new height.
Description   Changes the size of the `Dimension`.

toString

```
public String toString ()
```

Returns   A string representation of the `Dimension` object.
Overrides   `Object.toString()`

See Also

Object, String, Serializable

19.20   Event

Description

The Event class represents events that happen within the Java environment in a platform independent way. Events typically represent user actions, like typing a key or clicking the mouse. Although this class has been updated for the 1.1 release, it is only used for the 1.0 event model. When using the 1.1 event model, all events are represented by subclasses of java.awt.AWTEvent.

Class Definition

```
public class java.awt.Event
    extends java.lang.Object
    implements java.io.Serializable {

// Constants
public static final int ACTION_EVENT;
public static final int ALT_MASK;
public static final int BACK_SPACE; ★
public static final int CAPS_LOCK; ★
public static final int CTRL_MASK;
public static final int DELETE; ★
public static final int DOWN;
public static final int END;
public static final int ENTER; ★
public static final int ESCAPE; ★
public static final int F1;
public static final int F2;
public static final int F3;
public static final int F4;
public static final int F5;
public static final int F6;
public static final int F7;
public static final int F8;
public static final int F9;
public static final int F10;
public static final int F11;
public static final int F12;
```

```
public static final int GOT_FOCUS;
public static final int HOME;
public static final int INSERT; ★
public static final int KEY_ACTION;
public static final int KEY_ACTION_RELEASE;
public static final int KEY_PRESS;
public static final int KEY_RELEASE;
public static final int LEFT;
public static final int LIST_DESELECT;
public static final int LIST_SELECT;
public static final int LOAD_FILE;
public static final int LOST_FOCUS;
public static final int META_MASK;
public static final int MOUSE_DOWN;
public static final int MOUSE_DRAG;
public static final int MOUSE_ENTER;
public static final int MOUSE_EXIT;
public static final int MOUSE_MOVE;
public static final int MOUSE_UP;
public static final int NUM_LOCK; ★
public static final int PAUSE; ★
public static final int PGDN;
public static final int PGUP;
public static final int PRINT_SCREEN; ★
public static final int RIGHT;
public static final int SAVE_FILE;
public static final int SCROLL_ABSOLUTE;
public static final int SCROLL_BEGIN; ★
public static final int SCROLL_END; ★
public static final int SCROLL_LINE_DOWN;
public static final int SCROLL_LINE_UP;
public static final int SCROLL_LOCK; ★
public static final int SCROLL_PAGE_DOWN;
public static final int SCROLL_PAGE_UP;
public static final int SHIFT_MASK;
public static final int TAB; ★
public static final int UP;
public static final int WINDOW_DEICONIFY;
public static final int WINDOW_DESTROY;
public static final int WINDOW_EXPOSE;
public static final int WINDOW_ICONIFY;
public static final int WINDOW_MOVED;

// Variables
public Object arg;
public int clickCount;
public Event evt;
public int id;
public int key;
```

```
    public int modifiers;
    public Object target;
    public long when;
    public int x;
    public int y;

    // Constructors
    public Event (Object target, int id, Object arg);
    public Event (Object target, long when, int id, int x, int y,
        int key, int modifiers);
    public Event (Object target, long when, int id, int x, int y,
        int key, int modifiers, Object arg);

    // Instance Methods
    public boolean controlDown();
    public boolean metaDown();
    public boolean shiftDown();
    public String toString();
    public void translate (int x, int y);

    // Protected Instance Methods
    protected String paramString();
}
```

Constants

ACTION_EVENT

  public static final int ACTION_EVENT

  ID constant for Action Event.

ALT_MASK

  public static final int ALT_MASK

  Mask for ALT key.

BACK_SPACE

  public static final int BACK_SPACE ★

  ID constant for Backspace.

CAPS_LOCK

  public static final int CAPS_LOCK ★

  ID constant for Caps Lock key.

CTRL_MASK

`public static final int CTRL_MASK`

Mask for Control key.

DELETE

`public static final int DELETE` ★

ID constant for Delete.

DOWN

`public static final int DOWN`

ID constant for the down arrow key.

END

`public static final int END`

ID constant for End key.

ENTER

`public static final int ENTER` ★

ID constant for Enter key.

ESCAPE

`public static final int ESCAPE` ★

ID constant for Escape key.

F1

`public static final int F1`

ID constant for F1 key.

F2

`public static final int F2`

ID constant for F2 key.

F3

`public static final int F3`

ID constant for F3 key.

F4

    public static final int F4

    ID constant for F4 key.

F5

    public static final int F5

    ID constant for F5 key.

F6

    public static final int F6

    ID constant for F6 key.

F7

    public static final int F7

    ID constant for F7 key.

F8

    public static final int F8

    ID constant for F8 key.

F9

    public static final int F9

    ID constant for F9 key.

F10

    public static final int F10

    ID constant for F10 key.

F11

    public static final int F11

    ID constant for F11 key.

F12

    public static final int F12

    ID constant for F12 key.

GOT_FOCUS

> public static final int GOT_FOCUS
>
> ID constant for getting input focus Event.

HOME

> public static final int HOME
>
> ID constant for Home key.

INSERT

> public static final int INSERT ★
>
> ID constant for Insert key.

KEY_ACTION

> public static final int KEY_ACTION
>
> ID constant for Special Key Down Event.

KEY_ACTION_RELEASE

> public static final int KEY_ACTION_RELEASE
>
> ID constant for Special Key Up Event.

KEY_PRESS

> public static final int KEY_PRESS
>
> ID constant for Key Down Event.

KEY_RELEASE

> public static final int KEY_RELEASE
>
> ID constant for Key Up Event.

LEFT

> public static final int LEFT
>
> ID constant for the left arrow key.

LIST_DESELECT

> public static final int LIST_DESELECT
>
> ID constant for List DeSelect Event.

LIST_SELECT

public static final int LIST_SELECT

ID constant for List Select Event.

LOAD_FILE

public static final int LOAD_FILE

ID constant for File Load Event.

LOST_FOCUS

public static final int LOST_FOCUS

ID constant for losing input focus Event.

META_MASK

public static final int META_MASK

Mask for ALT key.

MOUSE_DOWN

public static final int MOUSE_DOWN

ID constant for Mouse Down Event.

MOUSE_DRAG

public static final int MOUSE_DRAG

ID constant for Mouse Drag Event.

MOUSE_ENTER

public static final int MOUSE_ENTER

ID constant for Mouse Enter Event.

MOUSE_EXIT

public static final int MOUSE_EXIT

ID constant for Mouse Exit Event.

MOUSE_MOVE

public static final int MOUSE_MOVE

ID constant for Mouse Move Event.

MOUSE_UP

    public static final int MOUSE_UP

ID constant for Mouse Up Event.

NUM_LOCK

    public static final int NUM_LOCK ★

ID constant for Num Lock key.

PAUSE

    public static final int PAUSE ★

ID constant for Pause key.

PGDN

    public static final int PGDN

ID constant for PageDown key.

PGUP

    public static final int PGUP

ID constant for PageUp key.

PRINT_SCREEN

    public static final int PRINT_SCREEN ★

ID constant for Print Screen key.

RIGHT

    public static final int RIGHT

ID constant for the right arrow key.

SAVE_FILE

    public static final int SAVE_FILE

ID constant for File Save Event.

SCROLL_ABSOLUTE

    public static final int SCROLL_ABSOLUTE

ID constant for Absolute Scroll Event.

SCROLL_BEGIN

    `public static final int SCROLL_ BEGIN` ★

    ID constant for Begin Scroll Event.

SCROLL_END

    `public static final int SCROLL_ END` ★

    ID constant for End Scroll Event.

SCROLL_LINE_DOWN

    `public static final int SCROLL_LINE_DOWN`

    ID constant for Line Down Scroll Event.

SCROLL_LINE_UP

    `public static final int SCROLL_LINE_UP`

    ID constant for Line Up Scroll Event.

SCROLL_LOCK

    `public static final int SCROLL_LOCK` ★

    Mask for Scroll Lock key.

SCROLL_PAGE_DOWN

    `public static final int SCROLL_PAGE_DOWN`

    ID constant for Page Down Scroll Event.

SCROLL_PAGE_UP

    `public static final int SCROLL_PAGE_UP`

    ID constant for Page Up Scroll Event.

SHIFT_MASK

    `public static final int SHIFT_MASK`

    Mask for SHIFT key.

TAB

    `public static final int TAB` ★

    ID constant for Tab key.

UP

    public static final int UP

ID constant for the up arrow key.

WINDOW_DEICONIFY

    public static final int WINDOW_DEICONIFY

ID constant for Window DeIconify Event.

WINDOW_DESTROY

    public static final int WINDOW_DESTROY

ID constant for Window Destroy Event.

WINDOW_EXPOSE

    public static final int WINDOW_EXPOSE

ID constant for Window Expose Event.

WINDOW_ICONIFY

    public static final int WINDOW_ICONIFY

ID constant for Window Iconify Event.

WINDOW_MOVED

    public static final int WINDOW_MOVED

ID constant for Window Move Event.

Variables

arg

    public Object arg

A variable argument that is specific to the event type.

clickCount

    public int clickCount

The number of consecutive MOUSE_DOWN events.

evt

   public Event evt

A means of passing a linked list of events as one.

id

   public int id

The ID constant that identifies the Event type.

key

   public int key

Integer value of key pressed, or ID constant identifying a special key.

modifiers

   public int modifiers

The state of the shift/alt/control/meta keys, formed by ORing the masks for the appropriate keys.

target

   public Object target

The Object that generated the event.

when

   public long when

The time the event happened.

x

   public int x

The x position at which the event happened.

y

   public int y

The y position at which the event happened.

Constructors

Event

```
public Event (Object target, int id, Object arg)
```

Parameters	*target*	The component to which the Event should be delivered
	id	The identifier of Event
	arg	The Object that is the cause of the event
Description		Constructs an Event object with the given values.

```
public Event (Object target, long when, int id, int x, int y, int
key, int modifiers)
```

Parameters	*target*	The component to which the Event should be delivered
	when	The time the event happened
	id	The identifier of Event
	x	The x position at which the event happened
	y	The y position at which the event happened
	key	Integer value of key pressed, or a constant identifying a special key
	modifiers	The state of the shift/alt/control/meta keys
Description		Constructs an Event object with the given values.

```
public Event (Object target, long when, int id, int x, int y, int
key, int modifiers, Object arg)
```

Parameters	*target*	The component to which the Event should be delivered
	when	The time the event happened
	id	The identifier of Event
	x	The x position at which the event happened
	y	The y position at which the event happened
	key	Integer value of key pressed, or a constant identifying a special key
	modifiers	The state of the shift/alt/control/meta keys
	arg	The Object that is the cause of the event
Description		Constructs an Event object with the given values.

Instance Methods

controlDown

```
public boolean controlDown()
```

Returns   true if the control key was down when the event was triggered,
                 false otherwise.

Description   Checks current settings for modifiers of the Event.

metaDown

```
public boolean metaDown()
```

Returns   true if the meta key was down when the event was triggered,
                 false otherwise.

Description   Checks current settings for modifiers of the Event.

shiftDown

```
public boolean shiftDown()
```

Returns   true if the shift key was down when the event was triggered,
                 false otherwise.

Description   Checks current settings for modifiers of the Event.

toString

```
public String toString()
```

Returns   A string representation of the Event object.

Overrides   Object.toString()

translate

```
public void translate (int x, int y)
```

Parameters   *x*   Amount to move Event in horizontal direction.
                 y   Amount to move Event in vertical direction.

Description   Translates x and y coordinates of Event instance by x and y.

Protected Instance Methods

paramString

```
protected String paramString()
```

Returns   String with current settings of Event.

Description   Helper method for toString() to generate string of current
                 settings.

See Also

AWTEvent, Component, Object, String

19.21 EventQueue ★

Description

The EventQueue class is a facility for queuing Java 1.1 AWT events, either for the system or for some other purpose. You rarely need to create your own event queue; for most purposes, you will want to work with the system's event queue, which you acquire using the Toolkit.

Class Definition

```
public class EventQueue extends Object {

    // Constructor
    public EventQueue();

    // Instance Methods
    public synchronized AWTEvent getNextEvent() throws InterruptedException;
    public synchronized AWTEvent peekEvent();
    public synchronized AWTEvent peekEvent (int id);
    public synchronized void postEvent (AWTEvent theEvent);
}
```

Constructor

EventQueue

   public EventQueue()

   Description   Creates an EventQueue for your own use.

Instance Methods

getNextEvent

   public synchronized AWTEvent getNextEvent() throws
   InterruptedException

   Throws   InterruptedException

                         If the thread is interrupted before an event is
                         posted to the queue.

Returns	AWTEvent taken from the event queue.
Description	Removes the next event from the event queue and returns it. If there are no events in the queue, this method will block until another thread posts one.

peekEvent

```
public synchronized AWTEvent peekEvent()
```

Returns	Next AWTEvent on the event queue.
Description	Returns a reference to the next event on the queue without removing it from the queue.

```
public synchronized AWTEvent peekEvent (int id)
```

Parameters	*id*	Type of event to find.
Returns	AWTEvent with the given type id; null if no event with the given type is currently in the queue.	
Description	Returns an event with the given type if one exists, but doesn't remove the event from the queue.	

See Also

AWTEvent, Event

19.22   FileDialog

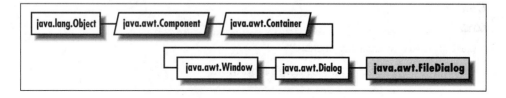

Description

The FileDialog class provides file selection capabilities for opening or saving files. Because FileDialog is a subclass of Dialog, a FileDialog is always associated with a Frame and is hidden by default. FileDialogs are always modal (i.e., they always attract all user input). In addition, FileDialogs have a load/save mode; the LOAD mode is for selecting files for an application to load, SAVE is for selecting a filename to save.

Class Definition

```
public class java.awt.FileDialog
    extends java.awt.Dialog {

  // Constants
  public final static int LOAD;
  public final static int SAVE;

  // Constructors
  public FileDialog (Frame parent); ★
  public FileDialog (Frame parent, String title);
  public FileDialog (Frame parent, String title, int mode);

  // Instance Methods
  public void addNotify();
  public String getDirectory();
  public String getFile();
  public FilenameFilter getFilenameFilter();
  public int getMode();
  public synchronized void setDirectory (String directory);
  public synchronized void setFile (String file);
  public synchronized void setFilenameFilter (FilenameFilter filter);
  public void setMode(int mode); ★

  // Protected Instance Methods
  protected String paramString();
}
```

Constants

LOAD

```
public final static int LOAD
```

Constant to specify the FileDialog's load mode.

SAVE

```
public final static int SAVE
```

Constant to specify the FileDialog's save mode.

Constructors

FileDialog

```
public FileDialog (Frame parent) ★
```

Parameters   *parent*   Frame that is to act as parent of FileDialog.

Description   Constructs a `FileDialog` object in LOAD mode.

`public FileDialog (Frame parent, String title)`

Parameters   *parent*   Frame that is to act as parent of `FileDialog`.
              title   Title to use for `FileDialog`.
Description   Constructs a `FileDialog` object in LOAD mode.

`public FileDialog (Frame parent, String title, int mode)`

Parameters   *parent*   Frame that is to act as parent of `Dialog`.
              title   Title to use for `FileDialog`.
              mode   The constant LOAD or SAVE, specifying the dia-
                          log's mode.
Description   Constructs a `FileDialog` object in the given mode.

Instance Methods

addNotify

`public void addNotify()`

Overrides   `Dialog.addNotify()`
Description   Creates `FileDialog`'s peer for the native platform.

getDirectory

`public String getDirectory()`

Returns   The current directory for the `FileDialog`.

getFile

`public String getFile()`

Returns   The current file selected by the `FileDialog`.

getFilenameFilter

`public FilenameFilter getFilenameFilter()`

Returns   The current filename filter for the `FileDialog`.

getMode

`public int getMode()`

Returns   The current mode of the `FileDialog`.

setDirectory

```
public synchronized void setDirectory (String directory)
```

Parameters	*directory*	Directory to be displayed by the FileDialog.
Description		Changes the directory displayed in the FileDialog.

setFile

```
public synchronized void setFile (String file)
```

Parameters	*file*	Initial file string for FileDialog.
Description		Change the default file selected by the FileDialog.

setFilenameFilter

```
public synchronized void setFilenameFilter (FilenameFilter filter)
```

Parameters	*filter*	Initial filter for FileDialog.
Description		Changes the current filename filter of the FileDialog.

setMode

```
public void setMode (int mode)  ★
```

Parameters	*mode*	The constant LOAD or SAVE, specifying the dialog's mode.
Description		Change the mode of the file dialog.

Protected Instance Methods

paramString

```
protected String paramString()
```

Returns		String with current settings of FileDialog.
Overrides		Dialog.paramString()
Description		Helper method for toString() to generate string of current settings.

See Also

Dialog, FilenameFilter, String

19.23   FlowLayout

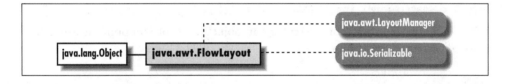

Description

The FlowLayout LayoutManager provides the means to lay out components in a
row by row fashion. As each row fills up, the components continue on the next
row.

Class Definition

```
public class java.awt.FlowLayout
    extends java.lang.Object
    implements java.awt.LayoutManager, java.io.Serializable {

    // Constants
    public static final int CENTER;
    public static final int LEFT;
    public static final int RIGHT;

    // Constructors
    public FlowLayout();
    public FlowLayout (int alignment);
    public FlowLayout (int alignment, int hgap, int vgap);

    // Instance Methods
    public void addLayoutComponent (String name, Component component);
    public int getAlignment(); ★
    public int getHgap(); ★
    public int getVgap(); ★
    public void layoutContainer (Container target);
    public Dimension minimumLayoutSize (Container target);
    public Dimension preferredLayoutSize (Container target);
    public void removeLayoutComponent (Component component);
    public void setAlignment (int align); ★
    public void setHgap (int hgap); ★
    public void setVgap (int vgap); ★
    public String toString();
}
```

Constants

CENTER

```
public static final int CENTER
```

The default alignment for a FlowLayout object; rows of components are centered within the container.

LEFT

```
public static final int LEFT
```

An alignment for a FlowLayout object; rows of components start on the left side of the container.

RIGHT

```
public static final int RIGHT
```

An alignment for a FlowLayout object; rows of components start on the right side of the container.

Constructors

FlowLayout

```
public FlowLayout()
```

Description   Constructs a FlowLayout object with CENTER alignment.

```
public FlowLayout (int alignment)
```

| Parameters | *alignment* | Alignment of components within the container. |
| Description | | Constructs a FlowLayout object with the given alignment. |

```
public FlowLayout (int alignment, int hgap, int vgap)
```

Parameters	*alignment*	Alignment of components within container
	hgap	Horizontal space between each component in a row
	vgap	Vertical space between each row
Description		Constructs a FlowLayout object with the given alignment and the values specified as the gaps between each component in the container managed by this instance of FlowLayout.

Instance Methods

addLayoutComponent

`public void addLayoutComponent (String name, Component component)`

Parameters	*name*	Name of component to add.
	component	Actual component being added.
Implements	`LayoutManager.addLayoutComponent()`	
Description	Does nothing.	

getAlignment

`public int getAlignment() ★`

Returns	The alignment constant for this `FlowLayout`.

getHgap

`public int getHgap() ★`

Returns	The horizontal gap between components.

getVgap

`public int getVgap() ★`

Returns	The vertical gap between components.

layoutContainer

`public void layoutContainer (Container target)`

Parameters	*target*	The container that needs to be redrawn.
Implements	`LayoutManager.layoutContainer()`	
Description	Draws the components contained within the `target` container.	

minimumLayoutSize

`public Dimension minimumLayoutSize (Container target)`

Parameters	*target*	The container whose size needs to be calculated.
Returns	Minimum `Dimension` of container `target`	
Implements	`LayoutManager.minimumLayoutSize()`	
Description	Calculates minimum size of `target` container.	

preferredLayoutSize

`public Dimension preferredLayoutSize (Container target)`

Parameters	*target*	The container whose size needs to be calculated.
Returns		Preferred `Dimension` of container `target`
Implements		`LayoutManager.preferredLayoutSize()`
Description		Calculates preferred size of `target` container.

removeLayoutComponent

`public void removeLayoutComponent (Component component)`

Parameters	*component*	Component to stop tracking.
Implements		`LayoutManager.removeLayoutComponent()`
Description		Does nothing.

setAlignment

`public void setAlignment(int align)` ★

Parameters	*alignment*	Alignment of components within container
Description		Sets the alignment for the `FlowLayout`.

setHgap

`public void setHgap(int hgap)` ★

Parameters	*hgap*	The horizontal gap value.
Description		Sets the horizontal gap between components.

setVgap

`public void setVgap(int vgap)` ★

Parameters	*vgap*	The vertical gap value.
Description		Sets the vertical gap between components.

toString

`public String toString()`

Returns	A string representation of the `FlowLayout` object.
Overrides	`Object.toString()`

See Also

`Component`, `Container`, `Dimension`, `LayoutManager`, `Object`, `Serializable`, `String`

19.24   Font

Description

The Font class represents a specific font to the system.

Class Definition

```
public class java.awt.Font
    extends java.lang.Object
    implements java.io.Serializable {

    // Constants
    public static final int BOLD;
    public static final int ITALIC;
    public static final int PLAIN;

    // Variables
    protected String name;
    protected int size;
    protected int style;

    // Constructors
    public Font (String name, int style, int size);

    // Class Methods
    public static Font decode (String str); ★
    public static Font getFont (String name)
    public static Font getFont (String name, Font defaultFont)

    // Instance Methods
    public boolean equals (Object object);
    public String getFamily();
    public String getName();
    public FontPeer getPeer(); ★
    public int getSize();
    public int getStyle();
    public int hashCode();
    public boolean isBold();
    public boolean isItalic();
    public boolean isPlain();
    public String toString();
}
```

Constants

BOLD

```
public static final int BOLD
```

Constant for specifying bold fonts.

ITALIC

```
public static final int ITALIC
```

Constant for specifying fonts.

PLAIN

```
public static final int PLAIN
```

Constant for specifying plain fonts.

Variables

name

```
protected String name
```

The font's logical name.

size

```
protected int size
```

The font size; allegedly in points, though probably not true typographer's points.

style

```
protected int style
```

The font style, e.g., bold or italic or a combination thereof.

Constructors

Font

```
public Font (String name, int style, int size)
```

Parameters	*name*	The name of the desired font.
	style	One of the style flags (PLAIN, BOLD, or ITALIC) or a combination.
	size	The size of the font to create.
Description		Constructs a Font object with the given characteristics.

Class Methods

decode

```
public static Font decode (String str) ★
```

Parameters	*str*	The string describing the font.
Returns		Font instance requested, or default if str is invalid.
Description		Gets font specified by str.

getFont

```
public static Font getFont (String name)
```

Parameters	*name*	The name of a system property specifying a font to fetch.
Returns		Font instance for name requested, or null if name is invalid.
Description		Gets font specified by the system property name.

```
public static Font getFont (String name, Font defaultFont)
```

Parameters	*name*	The name of a system property specifying a font to fetch.
	defaultFont	Font to return if name not found in properties.
Returns		Font instance of name requested, or defaultFont if name is invalid
Description		Gets font specified by the system property name.

Instance Methods

equals

```
public boolean equals (Object object)
```

Parameters	*object*	The object to compare.
Returns		true if the objects are equivalent fonts (same name, style, and point size), false otherwise.
Overrides		Object.equals(Object)
Description		Compares two different Font instances for equivalence.

getFamily

```
public String getFamily()
```

Returns		Retrieves the actual name of the font.

getName

```
public String getName()
```

Returns   Retrieves the logical name of the font.

getPeer

```
public FontPeer getPeer()  ★
```

Returns   The font's peer.

getSize

```
public int getSize()
```

Returns   Retrieves the size parameter from creation

getStyle

```
public int getStyle()
```

Returns   Retrieves the style parameter from creation.

hashCode

```
public int hashCode()
```

Returns   A hashcode to use when using the Font as a key in a Hashtable.
Overrides   Object.hashCode()
Description   Generates a hashcode for the Font.

isBold

```
public boolean isBold()
```

Returns   true if Font style is bold, false otherwise.

isItalic

```
public boolean isItalic()
```

Returns   true if Font style is italic, false otherwise.

isPlain

```
public boolean isPlain()
```

Returns   true if Font style is neither bold nor italic, false otherwise.

toString

```
public String toString()
```

Returns   A string representation of the Font object.
Overrides   Object.toString()

See Also

FontMetrics, Object, Properties, String

19.25   FontMetrics

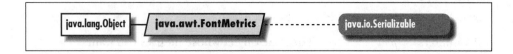

Description

The FontMetrics class provides the means to calculate actual width and height of text if drawn on the screen.

Class Definition

```
public abstract class java.awt.FontMetrics
    extends java.lang.Object
    implements java.io.Serializable {

  // Variables
  protected Font font;

  // Constructors
  protected FontMetrics (Font font);

  // Instance Methods
  public int bytesWidth (byte data[], int offset, int length);
  public int charsWidth (char data[], int offset, int length);
  public int charWidth (char character);
  public int charWidth (int character);
  public int getAscent();
  public int getDescent();
  public Font getFont();
  public int getHeight();
  public int getLeading();
  public int getMaxAdvance();
  public int getMaxAscent();
  public int getMaxDecent();
  public int getMaxDescent();
```

```
    public int[] getWidths();
    public int stringWidth (String string);
    public String toString();
}
```

Variables

font

protected Font font

The Font object whose metrics are represented by this object.

Constructors

FontMetrics

protected FontMetrics (Font font)

Parameters	*font*	The Font object whose metrics you want.
Description		Constructs a platform specific FontMetrics object for the given font.

Instance Methods

bytesWidth

public int bytesWidth (byte data[], int offset, int length)

Parameters	*data[]*	Array of characters to lookup.
	offset	Initial character position.
	length	Number of characters to lookup.
Returns		Advance width of characters in the array, starting with offset and ending with offset+length, in pixels.
Throws		*ArrayIndexOutOfBoundsException*
		If offset or length is invalid.

charsWidth

public int charsWidth (char data[], int offset, int length)

Parameters	*data[]*	Array of characters to lookup.
	offset	Initial character position.
	length	Number of characters to lookup.
Returns		Advance width of characters in the array, starting with offset and ending with offset+length-1, in pixels.
Throws		*ArrayIndexOutOfBoundsException*
		If offset or length is invalid.

charWidth

`public int charWidth (char character)`

Parameters   *character*   character to lookup
Returns   Advanced pixel width of character.

`public int charWidth (int character)`

Parameters   *character*   int value of character to lookup
Returns   Advanced pixel width of character.

getAscent

`public int getAscent ()`

Returns   Amount of space above the baseline required for the tallest character in the font.

getDescent

`public int getDescent ()`

Returns   Amount of space below the baseline required for the lowest descender (e.g., the tail on "p") in the font.

getFont

`public Font getFont ()`

Returns   The Font whose metrics are represented by this object.

getHeight

`public int getHeight ()`

Returns   The sum of getDescent(), getAscent(), and getLeading(); recommended total space between baselines.

getLeading

`public int getLeading ()`

Returns   Retrieves recommended amount of space between lines of text.

getMaxAdvance

`public int getMaxAdvance ()`

Returns   Retrieves advance pixel width of widest character in the font.

getMaxAscent

public int getMaxAscent()

Returns   Retrieves maximum amount of space above the baseline required for the tallest character within the font's FontMetrics. May differ from getAscent() for characters with diacritical marks.

getMaxDecent

public int getMaxDecent()

Returns   Retrieves the maximum amount of space below the baseline required for the deepest character for the font.

Description   A misspelling of getMaxDescent().

getMaxDescent

public int getMaxDescent()

Returns   Retrieves the maximum amount of space below the baseline required for the deepest character for the font.

getWidths

public int[] getWidths()

Returns   255 element array of character widths.

Description   Retrieves an integer array of the advance widths of the first 255 characters in the FontMetrics' font.

stringWidth

public int stringWidth (String string)

Parameters   *string*   Character string to lookup.

Returns   Advance pixel width of string.

toString

public String toString()

Returns   A string representation of the FontMetrics object.

Overrides   Object.toString()

See Also

Font, Object, String

19.26 Frame

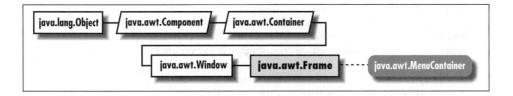

Description

The Frame class is a special type of Window that will appear like other high-level programs in your windowing environment. It adds a MenuBar, window title, and window gadgets (like resize, maximize, minimize, window menu) to the basic Window
object. Frames are initially invisible; call show() to display them. Frames may also
be associated with an Image to be used as an icon. The Frame class includes many
constants to represent different cursor styles. All styles aren't necessarily available
on any platform. In 1.1, these constants are defined in java.awt.Cursor.

Class Definition

```
public class java.awt.Frame
    extends java.awt.Window
    implements java.awt.MenuContainer {

    // Constants
    public final static int CROSSHAIR_CURSOR;
    public final static int DEFAULT_CURSOR;
    public final static int E_RESIZE_CURSOR;
    public final static int HAND_CURSOR;
    public final static int MOVE_CURSOR;
    public final static int N_RESIZE_CURSOR;
    public final static int NE_RESIZE_CURSOR;
    public final static int NW_RESIZE_CURSOR;
    public final static int S_RESIZE_CURSOR;
    public final static int SE_RESIZE_CURSOR;
    public final static int SW_RESIZE_CURSOR;
    public final static int TEXT_CURSOR;
    public final static int W_RESIZE_CURSOR;
    public final static int WAIT_CURSOR;

    // Constructors
    public Frame();
```

```
    public Frame (String title);

    // Instance Methods
    public void addNotify();
    public synchronized void dispose();
    public int getCursorType(); ☆
    public Image getIconImage();
    public MenuBar getMenuBar();
    public String getTitle();
    public boolean isResizable();
    public synchronized void remove (MenuComponent component);
    public synchronized void setCursor (int cursorType); ☆
    public synchronized void setIconImage (Image image);
    public synchronized void setMenuBar (MenuBar bar);
    public synchronized void setResizable (boolean resizable);
    public synchronized void setTitle (String title);

    // Protected Instance Methods
    protected String paramString();
}
```

Constants

CROSSHAIR_CURSOR

   `public final static int CROSSHAIR_CURSOR`

   Constant representing a cursor that looks like a crosshair.

DEFAULT_CURSOR

   `public final static int DEFAULT_CURSOR`

   Constant representing the platform's default cursor.

E_RESIZE_CURSOR

   `public final static int E_RESIZE_CURSOR`

   Constant representing the cursor for resizing an object on the left.

HAND_CURSOR

   `public final static int HAND_CURSOR`

   Constant representing a cursor that looks like a hand.

MOVE_CURSOR

    public final static int MOVE_CURSOR

Constant representing a cursor used to move an object.

N_RESIZE_CURSOR

    public final static int N_RESIZE_CURSOR

Constant representing a cursor for resizing an object on the top.

NE_RESIZE_CURSOR

    public final static int NE_RESIZE_CURSOR

Constant representing a cursor for resizing an object on the top left corner.

NW_RESIZE_CURSOR

    public final static int NW_RESIZE_CURSOR

Constant representing a cursor for resizing an object on the top right corner.

S_RESIZE_CURSOR

    public final static int S_RESIZE_CURSOR

Constant representing a cursor for resizing an object on the bottom.

SE_RESIZE_CURSOR

    public final static int SE_RESIZE_CURSOR

Constant representing a cursor for resizing an object on the bottom left corner.

SW_RESIZE_CURSOR

    public final static int SW_RESIZE_CURSOR

Constant representing a cursor for resizing an object on the bottom right corner.

TEXT_CURSOR

    public final static int TEXT_CURSOR

Constant representing a cursor used within text.

W_RESIZE_CURSOR

public final static int W_RESIZE_CURSOR

Constant representing a cursor for resizing an object on the right side.

WAIT_CURSOR

public final static int WAIT_CURSOR

Constant representing a cursor that indicates the program is busy.

Constructors

Frame

public Frame()

Description   Constructs a Frame object, with no title.

public Frame (String title)

Parameters   *title*   Initial title to use for Frame.
Description   Constructs a Frame object, with the given title.

Instance Methods

addNotify

public void addNotify()

Overrides   Window.addNotify()
Description   Creates Frame's peer and peers of contained components.

dispose

public synchronized void dispose()

Overrides   Window.dispose()
Description   Releases the resources of the Frame.

getCursorType

public int getCursorType() ☆

Returns   The constant for the current cursor. Replaced by Component.getCursor()

getIconImage

public Image getIconImage()

Returns   The image used as the icon, or null if there is no icon for this frame.

getMenuBar

public MenuBar getMenuBar()

Returns   The Frame's current menu bar, or null if there is no menu bar for this frame.

getTitle

public String getTitle()

Returns   The current title for the Frame, or null if there is no title for this frame.

isResizable

public boolean isResizable()

Returns   true if resizable, false otherwise.

remove

public synchronized void remove (MenuComponent component)

Parameters   *component*   MenuBar to remove from Frame.
Implements   MenuContainer.remove()
Description   Removes component from Frame if component is the Frame's menu bar.

setCursor

public synchronized void setCursor (int cursorType) ☆

Parameters   *cursorType*   One of Frame's cursor constants.
Throws   *IllegalArgumentException*
                    If cursorType invalid.
Description   Changes the cursor of the Frame. Replaced by Component.setCursor(Cursor).

setIconImage

public synchronized void setIconImage (Image image)

Parameters   *image*   New image to use for the Frame's icon.

Description   Changes the icon's image for the Frame.

setMenuBar

public synchronized void setMenuBar (MenuBar bar)

Parameters   *bar*   New MenuBar to use for the Frame.

Description   Changes the menu bar of the Frame.

setResizable

public synchronized void setResizable (boolean resizable)

Parameters   *resizable*   true to make the frame resizable, false to prevent resizing.

Description   Changes the resize state of the Frame.

setTitle

public synchronized void setTitle (String title)

Parameters   *title*   New title to use for the Frame.

Description   Changes the title of the Frame.

Protected Instance Methods

paramString

protected String paramString()

Returns   String with current settings of Frame.

Overrides   Container.paramString()

Description   Helper method for toString() to generate a string of current settings.

See Also

Container, Image, MenuBar, MenuContainer, String, Window

19.27   Graphics

Description

The Graphics class is an abstract class that represents an object on which you can draw. The concrete classes that are actually used to represent graphics objects are platform dependent, but because they extend the Graphics class, must implement the methods here.

Class Definition

```
public abstract class java.awt.Graphics
    extends java.lang.Object {

  // Constructors
  protected Graphics();

  // Instance Methods
  public abstract void clearRect (int x, int y, int width, int height);
  public abstract void clipRect (int x, int y, int width, int height);
  public abstract void copyArea (int x, int y, int width, int height,
      int deltax, int deltay);
  public abstract Graphics create();
  public Graphics create (int x, int y, int width, int height);
  public abstract void dispose();
  public void draw3DRect (int x, int y, int width, int height,
      boolean raised);
  public abstract void drawArc (int x, int y, int width, int height,
      int startAngle, int arcAngle);
  public void drawBytes (byte text[], int offset, int length,
      int x, int y);
  public void drawChars (char text[], int offset, int length,
      int x, int y);
  public abstract boolean drawImage (Image image, int x, int y,
      ImageObserver observer);
  public abstract boolean drawImage (Image image, int x, int y,
      int width, int height, ImageObserver observer);
  public abstract boolean drawImage (Image image, int x, int y,
      Color backgroundColor, ImageObserver observer);
  public abstract boolean drawImage (Image image, int x, int y,
      int width, int height, Color backgroundColor, ImageObserver observer);
  public abstract boolean drawImage(Image img, int dx1, int dy1,
      int dx2, int dy2, int sx1, int sy1, int sx2, int sy2, ImageObserver
      observer); ★
```

```
    public abstract boolean drawImage(Image img, int dx1, int dy1,
        int dx2, int dy2, int sx1, int sy1, int sx2, int sy2, Color bgcolor,
        ImageObserver observer); ★
    public abstract void drawLine (int x1, int y1, int x2, int y2);
    public abstract void drawOval (int x, int y, int width, int height);
    public abstract void drawPolygon (int xPoints[], int yPoints[],
        int numPoints);
    public void drawPolygon (Polygon p);
    public abstract void drawPolyline(int[ ] xPoints, int[ ] yPoints,
        int nPoints); ★
    public void drawRect (int x, int y, int width, int height);
    public abstract void drawRoundRect (int x, int y, int width,
        int height, int arcWidth, int arcHeight);
    public abstract void drawString (String text, int x, int y);
    public void fill3DRect (int x, int y, int width, int height,
        boolean raised);
    public abstract void fillArc (int x, int y, int width, int height,
        int startAngle, int arcAngle);
    public abstract void fillOval (int x, int y, int width, int height);
    public abstract void fillPolygon (int xPoints[], int yPoints[],
        int numPoints);
    public void fillPolygon (Polygon p);
    public abstract void fillRect (int x, int y, int width, int height);
    public abstract void fillRoundRect (int x, int y, int width,
        int height, int arcWidth, int arcHeight);
    public void finalize();
    public abstract Shape getClip(); ★
    public abstract Rectangle getClipBounds(); ★
    public abstract Rectangle getClipRect();
    public abstract Color getColor();
    public abstract Font getFont();
    public FontMetrics getFontMetrics();
    public abstract FontMetrics getFontMetrics (Font font);
    public abstract void setClip (int x, int y, int width, int height); ★
    public abstract void setClip (Shape clip); ★
    public abstract void setColor (Color color);
    public abstract void setFont (Font font);
    public abstract void setPaintMode();
    public abstract void setXORMode (Color xorColor);
    public String toString();
    public abstract void translate (int x, int y);
}
```

Constructors

Graphics

```
protected Graphics()
```

Description   Called by constructors of platform specific subclasses.

Instance Methods

clearRect

```
public abstract void clearRect (int x, int y, int width, int
height)
```

Parameters   *x*   x coordinate of origin of area to clear.

y   y coordinate of origin of area to clear.

width   size in horizontal direction to clear.

height   size in vertical direction to clear.

Description   Resets a rectangular area to the background color.

clipRect

```
public abstract void clipRect (int x, int y, int width, int
height)
```

Parameters   *x*   x coordinate of origin of clipped area.

y   y coordinate of origin of clipped area.

width   size in horizontal direction to clip.

height   size in vertical direction to clip.

Description   Reduces the drawing area to the intersection of the current
drawing area and the rectangular area defined by x, y, width,
and height.

copyArea

```
public abstract void copyArea (int x, int y, int width, int
height, int deltax, int deltay)
```

Parameters   *x*   x coordinate of origin of area to copy.

y   y coordinate of origin of area to copy.

width   size in horizontal direction to copy.

height   size in vertical direction to copy.

deltax   offset in horizontal direction to copy area to.

deltay   offset in vertical direction to copy area to.

Description   Copies a rectangular area to a new area, whose top left corner is
(x+deltax, y+deltay).

create

```
public abstract Graphics create()
```

Returns   New graphics context.

Description   Creates a second reference to the same graphics context.

```
public Graphics create (int x, int y, int width, int height)
```

Parameters	*x*	x coordinate of origin of new graphics context.
	y	y coordinate of origin of new graphics context.
	width	size in horizontal direction.
	height	size in vertical direction.

Returns   New graphics context

Description   Creates a second reference to a subset of the same graphics context.

dispose

```
public abstract void dispose()
```

Description   Frees system resources used by graphics context.

draw3DRect

```
public void draw3DRect (int x, int y, int width, int height,
boolean raised)
```

Parameters	*x*	x coordinate of the rectangle origin.
	y	y coordinate of the rectangle origin
	width	Width of the rectangle to draw.
	height	Height of the rectangle to draw.
	raised	Determines if rectangle drawn is raised or not; true for a raised rectangle.

Description   Draws an unfilled 3-D rectangle from (x, y) of size width x height.

drawArc

```
public abstract void drawArc (int x, int y, int width, int height,
int startAngle, int arcAngle)
```

Parameters	*x*	x coordinate of the bounding rectangle's origin.
	y	y coordinate of the bounding rectangle's origin
	width	Width of the bounding rectangle for the arc.
	height	Height of the bounding rectangle for the arc.

	startAngle	Angle at which arc begins, in degrees
	arcAngle	length of arc, in degrees
Description		Draws an unfilled arc from startAngle to arcAngle within bounding rectangle from (x, y) of size width x height. Zero degrees is at three o'clock; positive angles are counter clockwise.

drawBytes

```
public void drawBytes (byte text[], int offset, int length, int x,
int y)
```

Parameters	text	Text to draw, as a byte array.
	offset	Starting position within text to draw.
	length	Number of bytes to draw.
	x	x coordinate of baseline origin.
	y	y coordinate of baseline origin.
Throws	ArrayIndexOutOfBoundsException	
		If offset or length is invalid.
Description		Draws text on screen, starting with text[offset] and ending with text[offset+length-1].

drawChars

```
public void drawChars (char text[], int offset, int length, int x,
int y)
```

Parameters	text	Text to draw, as a char array.
	offset	Starting position within text to draw.
	length	Number of bytes to draw.
	x	x coordinate of baseline origin.
	y	y coordinate of baseline origin.
Throws	ArrayIndexOutOfBoundsException	
		If offset or length is invalid.
Description		Draws text on screen, starting with text[offset] and ending with text[offset+length-1].

drawImage

```
public abstract boolean drawImage (Image image, int x, int y,
ImageObserver observer)
```

Parameters	image	Image to draw.
	x	x coordinate of image origin.

	y	y coordinate of image origin.
	observer	Object that watches for image information; almost always this.
Returns		true if the image has fully loaded when the method returns, false otherwise.
Description		Draws image to screen at (x, y), at its original size. Drawing may be asynchronous. If image is not fully loaded when the method returns, observer is notified when additional information made available.

```
public abstract boolean drawImage (Image image, int x, int y, int
width, int height, ImageObserver observer)
```

Parameters	*image*	Image to draw.
	x	x coordinate of image origin.
	y	y coordinate of image origin.
	width	New image size in horizontal direction.
	height	New image size in vertical direction.
	observer	Object that watches for image information; almost always this.
Returns		true if the image has fully loaded when the method returns, false otherwise.
Description		Draws image to screen at (x, y), scaled to width x height. Drawing may be asynchronous. If image is not fully loaded when the method returns, observer is notified when additional information made available.

```
public abstract boolean drawImage (Image image, int x, int y,
Color backgroundColor, ImageObserver observer)
```

Parameters	*image*	Image to draw.
	x	x coordinate of image origin.
	y	y coordinate of image origin.
	backgroundColor	
		Color to show through image where transparent.
	observer	Object that watches for image information; almost always this.
Returns		true if the image has fully loaded when the method returns, false otherwise.
Description		Draws image to screen at (x, y), at its original size. Drawing may be asynchronous. If image is not fully loaded when the method returns, observer is notified when additional information made available. The background color is visible through any transparent pixels.

```
public abstract boolean drawImage (Image image, int x, int y, int
width, int height, Color backgroundColor, ImageObserver observer)
```

Parameters	*image*	Image to draw.
	x	x coordinate of image origin.
	y	y coordinate of image origin.
	width	New image size in horizontal direction.
	height	New image size in vertical direction.
	backgroundColor	
		Color to show through image where transparent.
	observer	Object that watches for image information; almost always this.
Returns		true if the image has fully loaded when the method returns, false otherwise.
Description		Draws image to screen at (x, y), scaled to width x height. Drawing may be asynchronous. If image is not fully loaded when the method returns, observer is notified when additional information made available. The background color is visible through any transparent pixels.

```
public abstract boolean drawImage (Image image, int dx1, int dy1,
int dx2, int dy2, int sx1, int sy1, int sx2, int sy2,
ImageObserver observer) ★
```

Parameters	*image*	Image to draw.
	dx1	x coordinate of one corner of destination (device) rectangle.
	dy1	y coordinate of one corner of destination (device) rectangle.
	dx2	x coordinate of the opposite corner of destination (device) rectangle.
	dy2	y coordinate of the opposite corner of destination (device) rectangle.
	sx1	x coordinate of one corner of source (image) rectangle.
	sy1	y coordinate of one corner of source (image) rectangle.
	sx2	x coordinate of the opposite corner of source (image) rectangle.
	sy2	y coordinate of the opposite corner of source (image) rectangle.

	observer	Object that watches for image information; almost always this.
Returns		true if the image has fully loaded when the method returns, false otherwise.
Description		Draws the part of image described by dx1, dy1, dx2, and dy2 to the screen into the rectangle described by sx1, sy1, sx2, and sy2. Drawing may be asynchronous. If image is not fully loaded when the method returns, observer is notified when additional information is made available.

```
public abstract boolean drawImage (Image image, int dx1, int dy1,
int dx2, int dy2, int sx1, int sy1, int sx2, int sy2, Color
backgroundColor, ImageObserver observer) ★
```

Parameters	*image*	Image to draw.
	dx1	x coordinate of one corner of destination (device) rectangle.
	dy1	y coordinate of one corner of destination (device) rectangle.
	dx2	x coordinate of the opposite corner of destination (device) rectangle.
	dy2	y coordinate of the opposite corner of destination (device) rectangle.
	sx1	x coordinate of one corner of source (image) rectangle.
	sy1	y coordinate of one corner of source (image) rectangle.
	sx2	x coordinate of the opposite corner of source (image) rectangle.
	sy2	y coordinate of the opposite corner of source (image) rectangle.
	backgroundColor	
		Color to show through image where transparent.
	observer	Object that watches for image information; almost always this.
Returns		true if the image has fully loaded when the method returns, false otherwise.
Description		Draws the part of image described by dx1, dy1, dx2, and dy2 to the screen into the rectangle described by sx1, sy1, sx2, and sy2. Drawing may be asynchronous. If image is not fully loaded when the method returns, observer is notified when additional information made available. The background color is visible through any transparent pixels.

drawLine

```
public abstract void drawLine (int x1, int y1, int x2, int y2)
```

Parameters   *x1*   x coordinate of one point on line.
             y1   y coordinate of one point on line.
             x2   x coordinate of the opposite point on line.
             y2   y coordinate of the opposite point on line.
Description Draws a line connecting (x1, y1) and (x2, y2).

drawOval

```
public abstract void drawOval (int x, int y, int width, int
height)
```

Parameters   *x*   x coordinate of bounding rectangle origin.
             y   y coordinate of bounding rectangle origin
             width   Width of bounding rectangle to draw in.
             height   Height of bounding rectangle to draw in.
Description Draws an unfilled oval within bounding rectangle from (x, y) of
             size width x height.

drawPolygon

```
public abstract void drawPolygon (int xPoints[], int yPoints[],
int numPoints)
```

Parameters   *xPoints[]*   The array of x coordinates for each point.
             yPoints[]   The array of y coordinates for each point.
             numPoints   The number of elements in both xPoints and
                            yPoints arrays to use.
Description Draws an unfilled polygon based on first numPoints elements in
             xPoints and yPoints.

```
public void drawPolygon (Polygon p)
```

Parameters   *p*   Points of object to draw.
Description Draws an unfilled polygon based on points within the Polygon
             p.

drawPolyline

```
public abstract void drawPolyline (int xPoints[], int yPoints[],
int nPoints) ★
```

Parameters   *xPoints[]*   The array of x coordinates for each point.

yPoints[]	The array of y coordinates for each point.
nPoints	The number of elements in both xPoints and yPoints arrays to use.
Description	Draws a series of line segments based on first numPoints elements in xPoints and yPoints.

drawRect

public void drawRect (int x, int y, int width, int height)

Parameters	*x*	x coordinate of rectangle origin.
	y	y coordinate of rectangle origin
	width	Width of rectangle to draw.
	height	Height of rectangle to draw.
Description		Draws an unfilled rectangle from (x, y) of size width x height.

drawRoundRect

public abstract void drawRoundRect (int x, int y, int width, int height, int arcWidth, int arcHeight)

Parameters	*x*	x coordinate of bounding rectangle origin.
	y	y coordinate of bounding rectangle origin
	width	Width of rectangle to draw.
	height	Height of rectangle to draw.
	arcWidth	Width of arc of rectangle corner.
	arcHeight	Height of arc of rectangle corner.
Description		Draws an unfilled rectangle from (x, y) of size width x height with rounded corners.

drawString

public abstract void drawString (String text, int x, int y)

Parameters	*text*	Text to draw.
	x	x coordinate of baseline origin.
	y	y coordinate of baseline origin.
Description		Draws text on screen.

fill3DRect

public void fill3DRect (int x, int y, int width, int height, boolean raised)

Parameters	*x*	x coordinate of rectangle origin.

	y	y coordinate of rectangle origin
	width	Width of rectangle to draw.
	height	Height of rectangle to draw.
	raised	true to draw a rectangle that appears raised; false to draw a rectangle that appears depressed.
Description		Draws a filled 3-D rectangle from (x, y) of size width x height.

fillArc

public abstract void fillArc (int x, int y, int width, int height, int startAngle, int arcAngle)

Parameters	*x*	x coordinate of bounding rectangle origin.
	y	y coordinate of bounding rectangle origin
	width	Width of bounding rectangle to draw in.
	height	Height of bounding rectangle to draw in.
	startAngle	Starting angle of arc.
	arcAngle	The extent of the arc, measured from startAngle
Description		Draws a filled arc from startAngle to arcAngle within bounding rectangle from (x, y) of size width x height. Zero degrees is at three o'clock; positive angles are counter clockwise.

fillOval

public abstract void fillOval (int x, int y, int width, int height)

Parameters	*x*	x coordinate of bounding rectangle origin.
	y	y coordinate of bounding rectangle origin
	width	Width of bounding rectangle to draw in.
	height	Height of bounding rectangle to draw in.
Description		Draws filled oval within bounding rectangle from (x, y) of size width x height.

fillPolygon

public abstract void fillPolygon (int xPoints[], int yPoints[], int numPoints)

Parameters	*xPoints[]*	The array of x coordinates for each point.
	yPoints[]	The array of y coordinates for each point.
	numPoints	The number of elements in both xPoints and yPoints arrays to use.

Throws   *ArrayIndexOutOfBoundsException*

  If numPoints > xPoints.length or numPoints > yPoints.length.

Description   Draws filled polygon based on first numPoints elements in xPoints and yPoints.

public void fillPolygon (Polygon p)

Parameters   *p*   Points of object to draw.

Description   Draws filled polygon based on points within the Polygon p.

fillRect

public abstract void fillRect (int x, int y, int width, int height)

Parameters   *x*   x coordinate of rectangle origin.

  y   y coordinate of rectangle origin

  width   Width of rectangle to draw.

  height   Height of rectangle to draw.

Description   Draws filled rectangle from (x, y) of size width x height.

fillRoundRect

public abstract void fillRoundRect (int x, int y, int width, int height, int arcWidth, int arcHeight)

Parameters   *x*   x coordinate of bounding rectangle origin.

  y   y coordinate of bounding rectangle origin

  width   Width of rectangle to draw.

  height   Height of rectangle to draw.

  arcWidth   Width of arc of rectangle corner.

  arcHeight   Height of arc of rectangle corner.

Description   Draws a filled rectangle from (x, y) of size width x height with rounded corners.

finalize

public void finalize()

Overrides   Object.finalize()

Description   Tells the garbage collector to dispose of graphics context.

getClip

`public abstract Shape getClip () ` ★

Returns   Shape describing the clipping are of the graphics context.

getClipBounds

`public abstract Rectangle getClipBounds() ` ★

Returns   Rectangle describing the clipping area of the graphics context.

getClipRect

`public abstract Rectangle getClipRect() ` ☆

Returns   Replaced by `getClipBounds()`.

getColor

`public abstract Color getColor()`

Returns   The current drawing `Color` of the graphics context.

getFont

`public abstract Font getFont()`

Returns   The current `Font` of the graphics context.

getFontMetrics

`public FontMetrics getFontMetrics()`

Returns   The `FontMetrics` of the current font of the graphics context.

`public abstract FontMetrics getFontMetrics (Font font)`

Parameters   *font*   Font to get metrics for.
Returns   The `FontMetrics` of the given font for the graphics context.

setClip

`public abstract void setClip (int x, int y, int width,`
`int height) ` ★

Parameters   *x*   x coordinate of rectangle
               y   y coordinate of rectangle
               width   width of rectangle
               height   height of rectangle
Description   Changes current clipping region to the specified rectangle.

```
public abstract void setClip (Shape clip) ★
```

Parameters   *clip*   The new clipping shape.
Description   Changes current clipping region to the specified shape.

setColor

```
public abstract void setColor (Color color)
```

Parameters   *color*   New color.
Description   Changes current drawing color of graphics context.

setFont

```
public abstract void setFont (Font font)
```

Parameters   *font*   New font.
Description   Changes current font of graphics context.

setPaintMode

```
public abstract void setPaintMode()
```

Description   Changes painting mode to normal mode.

setXORMode

```
public abstract void setXORMode (Color xorColor)
```

Parameters   *xorColor*   XOR mode drawing color.
Description   Changes painting mode to XOR mode; in this mode, drawing
              the same object in the same color at the same location twice has
              no net effect.

toString

```
public String toString()
```

Returns   A string representation of the Graphics object.
Overrides   Object.toString()

translate

```
public void translate (int x, int y)
```

Parameters   *x*   x coordinate of new drawing origin.
              y   y coordinate of new drawing origin.
Description   Moves the origin of drawing operations to (x, y).

See Also

Color, Font, FontMetrics, Image, ImageObserver, Object, Polygon, Rectangle, Shape, String

19.28   GridBagConstraints

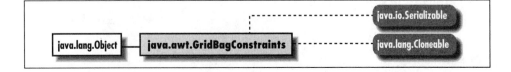

Description

The GridBagConstraints class provides the means to control the layout of components within a Container whose LayoutManager is GridBagLayout.

Class Definition

```
public class java.awt.GridBagConstraints
    extends java.lang.Object
    implements java.lang.Cloneable, java.io.Serializable {

// Constants
public final static int BOTH;
public final static int CENTER;
public final static int EAST;
public final static int HORIZONTAL;
public final static int NONE;
public final static int NORTH;
public final static int NORTHEAST;
public final static int NORTHWEST;
public final static int RELATIVE;
public final static int REMAINDER;
public final static int SOUTH;
public final static int SOUTHEAST;
public final static int SOUTHWEST;
public final static int VERTICAL;
public final static int WEST;

// Variables
public int anchor;
public int fill;
public int gridheight;
public int gridwidth;
public int gridx;
public int gridy;
public Insets insets;
```

```
public int ipadx;
public int ipady;
public double weightx
public double weighty

// Constructors
public GridBagConstraints();

// Instance Methods
public Object clone();
}
```

Constants

BOTH

```
public final static int BOTH
```

Constant for possible `fill` value.

CENTER

```
public final static int CENTER
```

Constant for possible anchor value.

EAST

```
public final static int EAST
```

Constant for possible anchor value.

HORIZONTAL

```
public final static int HORIZONTAL
```

Constant for possible `fill` value.

NONE

```
public final static int NONE
```

Constant for possible `fill` value.

NORTH

```
public final static int NORTH
```

Constant for possible anchor value.

NORTHEAST

public final static int NORTHEAST

Constant for possible anchor value.

NORTHWEST

public final static int NORTHWEST

Constant for possible anchor value.

RELATIVE

public final static int RELATIVE

Constant for possible gridx, gridy, gridwidth, or gridheight value.

REMAINDER

public final static int REMAINDER

Constant for possible gridwidth or gridheight value.

SOUTH

public final static int SOUTH

Constant for possible anchor value.

SOUTHEAST

public final static int SOUTHEAST

Constant for possible anchor value.

SOUTHWEST

public final static int SOUTHWEST

Constant for possible anchor value.

VERTICAL

public final static int VERTICAL

Constant for possible fill value.

WEST

public final static int WEST

Constant for possible anchor value.

Variables

anchor

```
public int anchor
```

Specifies the alignment of the component in the event that it is smaller than the space allotted for it by the layout manager; e.g., CENTER centers the object within the region.

fill

```
public int fill
```

The component's resize policy if additional space available.

gridheight

```
public int gridheight
```

Number of columns a component occupies.

gridwidth

```
public int gridwidth
```

Number of rows a component occupies.

gridx

```
public int gridx
```

Horizontal grid position at which to add component.

gridy

```
public int gridy
```

Vertical grid position at which to add component.

insets

```
public Insets insets
```

Specifies the outer padding around the component.

ipadx

```
public int ipadx
```

Serves as the internal padding within the component in both the right and left directions.

ipady

```
public int ipady
```

Serves as the internal padding within the component in both the top and bottom directions.

weightx

```
public double weightx
```

Represents the percentage of extra horizontal space that will be given to this component if there is additional space available within the container.

weighty

```
public double weighty
```

Represents the percentage of extra vertical space that will be given to this component if there is additional space available within the container.

Constructors

GridBagConstraints

```
public GridBagConstraints()
```

Description   Constructs a GridBagConstraints object.

Instance Methods

clone

```
public Object clone()
```

Returns   A new instance of GridBagConstraints with same values for constraints.

Overrides   Object.clone()

See Also

Cloneable, GridBagLayout, Insets, Object, Serializable

19.29 GridBagLayout

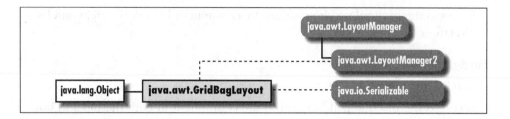

Description

The GridBagLayout LayoutManager provides the means to layout components in a flexible grid-based display model.

Class Definition

```
public class java.awt.GridBagLayout
    extends java.lang.Object
    implements java.awt.LayoutManager2, java.io.Serializable {

  // Protected Constants
  protected static final MAXGRIDSIZE;
  protected static final MINSIZE;
  protected static final PREFERREDSIZE;

  // Variables
  public double columnWeights[];
  public int columnWidths[];
  public int rowHeights[];
  public double rowWeights[];

  // Protected Variables
  protected Hashtable comptable;
  protected GridBagConstraints defaultConstraints;
  protected GridBagLayoutInfo layoutInfo;

  // Constructors
  public GridBagLayout();

  // Instance Methods
  public void addLayoutComponent (Component comp, Object constraints); ★
  public void addLayoutComponent (String name, Component component);
  public GridBagConstraints getConstraints (Component component);
  public abstract float getLayoutAlignmentX(Container target); ★
  public abstract float getLayoutAlignmentY(Container target); ★
  public int[][] getLayoutDimensions();
  public Point getLayoutOrigin();
  public double[][] getLayoutWeights();
```

```
    public abstract void invalidateLayout(Container target); ★
    public void layoutContainer (Container target);
    public Point location (int x, int y);
    public abstract Dimension maximumLayoutSize(Container target); ★
    public Dimension minimumLayoutSize (Container target);
    public Dimension preferredLayoutSize (Container target);
    public void removeLayoutComponent (Component component);
    public void setConstraints (Component component,
        GridBagConstraints constraints);
    public String toString();

    // Protected Instance Methods
    protected void AdjustForGravity (GridBagConstraints constraints,
        Rectangle r);
    protected void ArrangeGrid (Container target);
    protected GridBagLayoutInfo GetLayoutInfo (Container target,
        int sizeFlag);
    protected Dimension GetMinSize (Container target,
        GridBagLayoutInfo info);
    protected GridBagConstraints lookupConstraints (Component comp);
}
```

Protected Constants

MAXGRIDSIZE

```
    protected static final MAXGRIDSIZE
```

Maximum number of rows and columns within container managed by Grid-BagLayout.

MINSIZE

```
    protected static final MINSIZE
```

Used for internal sizing purposes.

PREFERREDSIZE

```
    protected static final PREFERREDSIZE
```

Used for internal sizing purposes.

Variables

columnWeights

```
    public double[] columnWeights
```

The weightx values of the components in the row with the most elements.

columnWidths

    public int[] columnWidths

The width values of the components in the row with the most elements.

rowHeights

    public int[] rowHeights

The height values of the components in the column with the most elements.

rowWeights

    public double[] rowWeights

The weighty values of the components in the column with the most elements.

Protected Variables

comptable

    protected Hashtable comptable

Internal table to manage components.

defaultConstraints

    protected GridBagConstraints defaultConstraints

Constraints to use for Components that have none.

layoutInfo

    protected GridBagLayoutInfo layoutInfo

Internal information about the GridBagLayout.

Constructors

GridBagLayout

    public GridBagLayout()

Description   Constructs a GridBagLayout object.

Instance Methods

addLayoutComponent

    public void addLayoutComponent (Component comp, Object
    constraints) ★

Parameters   *comp*   The component being added.
              constraints   An object describing the constraints on this com-
                              ponent.

Implements   LayoutManager2.addLayoutComponent()

Description   Adds the component comp to container subject to the given constraints. This is a more generalized version of addLayout-Component(String, Component). It corresponds to java.awt.Container's add(Component, Object).

public void addLayoutComponent (String name, Component component)

Parameters   *name*   Name of component to add.

              component   Actual component being added.

Implements   LayoutManager.addLayoutComponent()

Description   Does nothing.

getConstraints

public GridBagConstraints getConstraints (Component component)

Parameters   *component*   Component whose constraints are desired

Returns   GridBagConstraints for component requested.

getLayoutAlignmentX

public abstract float getLayoutAlignmentX (Container target) ★

Parameters   *target*   The container to inspect.

Returns   The value .5 for all containers.

Description   This method returns the preferred alignment of the given container target. A return value of 0 is left aligned, .5 is centered, and 1 is right aligned.

getLayoutAlignmentY

public abstract float getLayoutAlignmentY (Container target) ★

Parameters   *target*   The container to inspect.

Returns   The value .5 for all containers.

Description   This method returns the preferred alignment of the given container target. A return value of 0 is top aligned, .5 is centered, and 1 is bottom aligned.

getLayoutDimensions

public int[][] getLayoutDimensions()

Returns   Returns two single dimension arrays as a multi-dimensional array. Index 0 is an array of widths (columnWidths instance variable), while index 1 is an array of heights (rowHeights instance variable).

getLayoutOrigin

`public Point getLayoutOrigin()`

Returns   Returns the origin of the components within the `Container` whose `LayoutManager` is `GridBagLayout`.

getLayoutWeights

`public double[][] getLayoutWeights()`

Returns   Returns two single dimension arrays as a multi-dimensional array. Index 0 is an array of columns weights (`columnWeights` instance variable), while index 1 is an array of row weights (`rowWeights` instance variable).

invalidateLayout

`public abstract void invalidateLayout (Container target)` ★

Parameters   *target*   The container to invalidate.
Description   Does nothing.

layoutContainer

`public void layoutContainer (Container target)`

Parameters   *target*   The container that needs to be redrawn.
Implements   `LayoutManager.layoutContainer()`
Description   Draws components contained within `target`.

location

`public Point location (int x, int y)`

Parameters   *x*   The x coordinate of the grid position to find.
              y   The y coordinate of the grid position to find.
Returns   Returns the grid element under the location provided at position (x, y) in pixels. Note that the returned Point uses the `GridBagLayout`'s grid for its coordinate space.
Description   Locates the grid position in the `Container` under the given location.

maximumLayoutSize

public abstract Dimension maximumLayoutSize (Container target) ★

Parameters	*target*	The container to inspect.
Returns		A Dimension whose horizontal and vertical components are Integer.MAX_VALUE.
Description		For GridBagLayout, a maximal Dimension is always returned.

minimumLayoutSize

public Dimension minimumLayoutSize (Container target)

Parameters	*target*	The container whose size needs to be calculated.
Returns		Minimum Dimension of container target.
Implements		LayoutManager.minimumLayoutSize()
Description		Calculates minimum size of target container.

preferredLayoutSize

public Dimension preferredLayoutSize (Container target)

Parameters	*target*	The container whose size needs to be calculated.
Returns		Preferred Dimension of container target
Implements		LayoutManager.preferredLayoutSize()
Description		Calculates preferred size of target container.

removeLayoutComponent

public void removeLayoutComponent (Component component)

Parameters	*component*	Component to stop tracking.
Implements		LayoutManager.removeLayoutComponent()
Description		Does nothing.

setConstraints

public void setConstraints (Component component,
GridBagConstraints constraints)

Parameters	*component*	Component to set constraints for
	constraints	Constraints for component
Description		Changes the GridBagConstraints on component to those provided.

toString

```
public String toString()
```

Returns   A string representation of the GridBagLayout object.
Overrides   Object.toString()

Protected Instance Methods

AdjustForGravity

```
protected void AdjustForGravity (GridBagConstraints constraints,
Rectangle r)
```

Parameters   *constraints*   Constraints to use for adjustment of Rectangle.
                r   Rectangular area that needs to be adjusted.
Description   Helper routine for laying out a cell of the grid. The routine
                adjusts the values for r based upon the constraints.

ArrangeGrid

```
protected void ArrangeGrid (Container target)
```

Parameters   *target*   Container to layout.
Description   Helper routine that does the actual arrangement of compo-
                nents in target.

GetLayoutInfo

```
protected GridBagLayoutInfo GetLayoutInfo (Container target, int
sizeFlag)
```

Parameters   *target*   Container to get information about.
                sizeFlag   One of the constants MINSIZE or PREFERREDSIZE.
Returns   Returns an internal class used to help size the container.

GetMinSize

```
protected Dimension GetMinSize (Container target,
GridBagLayoutInfo info)
```

Parameters   *target*   Container to calculate size.
                info   Specifics about the container's constraints.
Returns   Minimum Dimension of container target based on info.
Description   Helper routine for calculating size of container.

lookupConstraints

protected GridBagConstraints lookupConstraints (Component comp)

Parameters   *comp*   Component in question.

Returns   A reference to the GridBagConstraints object for this compo-
              nent.

Description   Helper routine for calculating size of container.

See Also

Component, Container, Dimension, GridBagConstraints, Hashtable, LayoutManager, LayoutManager2, Object, Point, Rectangle, String

19.30   GridLayout

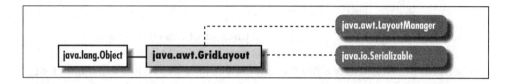

Description

The GridLayout LayoutManager provides the means to layout components in a
grid of rows and columns.

Class Definition

```
public class java.awt.GridLayout
        extends java.lang.Object
        implements java.awt.LayoutManager, java.io.Serializable
  {

// Constructors
  public GridLayout (); ★
  public GridLayout (int rows, int cols);
  public GridLayout (int rows, int cols, int hgap, int vgap);

// Instance Methods
  public void addLayoutComponent (String name, Component component);
  public int getColumns (); ★
  public int getHgap (); ★
  public int getRows (); ★

  public int getVgap (); ★
  public void layoutContainer (Container target);
  public Dimension minimumLayoutSize (Container target);
```

```
    public Dimension preferredLayoutSize (Container target);
    public void removeLayoutComponent (Component component);
    public int setColumns(int cols); ★
    public int setHgap(int hgap); ★
    public int setRows(int rows); ★

    public int setVgap(int vgap); ★
    public String toString();
}
```

Constructors

GridLayout

public GridLayout() ★

Description   Constructs a GridLayout object with a default single row and one column per component.

public GridLayout (int rows, int cols)

Parameters   *rows*   Requested number of rows in container.
              cols   Requested number of columns in container.

Description   Constructs a GridLayout object with the requested number of rows and columns. Note that the actual number of rows and columns depends on the number of objects in the layout, not the constructor's parameters.

public GridLayout (int rows, int cols, int hgap, int vgap)

Parameters   *rows*   Requested number of rows in container.
              cols   Requested number of columns in container.
              hgap   Horizontal space between each component in a row.
              vgap   Vertical space between each row.

Description   Constructs a GridLayout object with the requested number of rows and columns and the values specified as the gaps between each component. Note that the actual number of rows and columns depends on the number of objects in the layout, not the constructor's parameters.

Instance Methods

addLayoutComponent

public void addLayoutComponent (String name, Component component)

Parameters   *name*   Name of component to add.

               component   Actual component being added.

Implements   LayoutManager.addLayoutComponent()

Description   Does nothing.

getColumns

public int getColumns () ★

Returns   The number of columns.

getHgap

public int getHgap () ★

Returns   The horizontal gap for this GridLayout instance.

getRows

public int getRows () ★

Returns   The number of rows.

getVgap

public int getVgap () ★

Returns   The vertical gap for this GridLayout instance.

layoutContainer

public void layoutContainer (Container target)

Parameters   *target*   The container that needs to be redrawn.

Implements   LayoutManager.layoutContainer()

Description   Draws the components contained within the target.

minimumLayoutSize

public Dimension minimumLayoutSize (Container target)

Parameters   *target*   The container whose size needs to be calculated.

Returns   Minimum Dimension of the container target.

Implements   LayoutManager.minimumLayoutSize()

Description   Calculates the minimum size of the `target` container.

preferredLayoutSize

`public Dimension preferredLayoutSize (Container target)`

Parameters   *target*   The container whose size needs to be calculated.
Returns   Preferred `Dimension` of the container `target`.
Implements   `LayoutManager.preferredLayoutSize()`
Description   Calculates the preferred size of the `target` container.

removeLayoutComponent

`public void removeLayoutComponent (Component component)`

Parameters   *component*   Component to stop tracking.
Implements   `LayoutManager.removeLayoutComponent()`
Description   Does nothing.

setColumns

`public void setColumns(int cols)` ★

Parameters   *cols*   The new number of columns.
Description   Sets the number of columns.

setHgap

`public void setHgap(int hgap)` ★

Parameters   *hgap*   The horizontal gap value.
Description   Sets the horizontal gap between components.

setRows

`public void setRows(int rows)` ★

Parameters   *rows*   The new number of rows.
Description   Sets the number of rows.

setVgap

`public void setVgap(int vgap)` ★

Parameters   *vgap*   The vertical gap value.
Description   Sets the vertical gap between components.

toString

    public String toString()

Returns   A string representation of the GridLayout object.
Overrides   Object.toString()

See Also

Component, Container, Dimension, LayoutManager, Object, String

---

19.31   *IllegalComponentStateException* ★

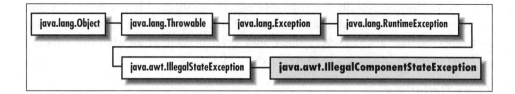

Description

An Exception indicating that a Component was not in an appropriate state to perform a requested action.

Class Definition

    public class java.awt.IllegalComponentStateException
        extends java.lang.IllegalStateException {

      // Constructors
      public IllegalComponentStateException();
      public IllegalComponentStateException (String s);
    }

Constructors

IllegalComponentStateException

    public IllegalComponentStateException()

Description   Constructs the exception object with no detail message.

    public IllegalComponentStateException (String s)

Parameters   *s*   Detail message
Description   Constructs the exception object with the given detail message.

See Also

Exception, String

19.32   Image

Description

The Image class represents a displayable object maintained in memory. Because Image is an abstract class, you never work with the Image class itself, but with a platform specific subclass. However, you should never need to know what that subclass is. To draw on an Image, get its graphics context.

Class Definition

```
public abstract class java.awt.Image
    extends java.lang.Object
    implements java.io.Serializable {

    // Constants
    public final static int SCALE_AREA_AVERAGING; ★
    public final static int SCALE_DEFAULT; ★
    public final static int SCALE_FAST; ★
    public final static int SCALE_REPLICATE; ★
    public final static int SCALE_SMOOTH; ★
    public final static Object UndefinedProperty;

    // Instance Methods
    public abstract void flush();
    public abstract Graphics getGraphics();
    public abstract int getHeight (ImageObserver observer);
    public abstract Object getProperty (String name, ImageObserver observer);
    public Image getScaledInstance (int width, int height, int hints); ★
    public abstract ImageProducer getSource();
    public abstract int getWidth (ImageObserver observer);
}
```

Constants

SCALE_AREA_AVERAGING

    public final static int SCALE_AREA_AVERAGING ★

Flag that requests use of `AreaAveragingScaleFilter`.

SCALE_DEFAULT

    public final static int SCALE_DEFAULT ★

Flag that requests use of the default image scaling algorithm.

SCALE_FAST

    public final static int SCALE_FAST ★

Flag that requests use of an image scaling algorithm that is faster rather than smoother.

SCALE_REPLICATE

    public final static int SCALE_REPLICATE ★

Flag that requests use of ReplicateScaleFilter.

SCALE_SMOOTH

    public final static int SCALE_SMOOTH ★

Flag that requests use of an image scaling algorithm that is smoother rather than faster.

UndefinedProperty

    public final static Object UndefinedProperty

Possible return object from `getProperty()`.

Instance Methods

flush

    public abstract void flush()

Description   Resets image to initial state.

getGraphics

    public abstract Graphics getGraphics()

Throws   *ClassCastException*

                                If image created from file or URL.

Returns   The graphics context of the image.

Description   Gets the graphics context of the image for drawing.

getHeight

```
public abstract int getHeight (ImageObserver observer)
```

Parameters   *observer*   An image observer; usually the Component on which the image is rendered.

Returns   Image height, or -1 if the height is not yet available.

getProperty

```
public abstract Object getProperty (String name, ImageObserver observer)
```

Parameters   *name*   Name of the property to fetch.

              observer   An image observer; usually the Component on which the image is rendered.

Returns   Object representing the requested property, null, or UndefinedProperty.

Throws   *ArrayIndexOutOfBoundsException*

                            If offset or length is invalid.

Description   Retrieves a property from the image's private property list.

getScaledInstance

```
public Image getScaledInstance (int width, int height,
int hints) ★
```

Parameters   *width*   The width for the scaled image. Use -1 to preserve the aspect ratio with reference to height.

              height   The height for the scaled image. Use -1 to preserve the aspect ratio with reference to width.

              hints   One or more of the SCALE_ constants.

Returns   The scaled image. It may be loaded asynchronously, even if the original image was fully loaded.

Description   Creates a copy of an image, scaled to width x height and using an algorithm chosen based on the hints given.

getSource

    public abstract ImageProducer getSource()

    Returns   The ImageProducer of the image.

getWidth

    public abstract int getWidth (ImageObserver observer)

    Parameters   *observer*   An image observer; usually the Component on which the image is rendered.

    Returns   Image width, or -1 if the width is not yet available.

See Also

Graphics, ImageObserver, ImageProducer, Object, Properties, String

19.33   Insets

Description

The Insets class provides a way to encapsulate the layout margins of the four different sides of a Container.

Class Definition

```
public class java.awt.Insets
    extends java.lang.Object
    implements java.io.Serializable, java.lang.Cloneable {

  // Variables
  public int bottom;
  public int left;
  public int right;
  public int top;

  // Constructors
  public Insets (int top, int left, int bottom, int right);
```

```
// Instance Methods
public Object clone();
public boolean equals (Object obj); ★
public String toString();
}
```

Variables

bottom

```
public int bottom
```

The border width for the bottom of a Container.

left

```
public int left
```

The border width for the left side of a Container.

right

```
public int right
```

The border width for the right side of a Container.

top

```
public int top
```

The border width for the top of a Container.

Constructors

Insets

```
public Insets (int top, int left, int bottom, int right)
```

Parameters	*top*	The border width for the top of a Container.
	left	The border width for the left side of a Container.
	bottom	The border width for the bottom of a Container.
	right	The border width for the right side of a Container.
Description		Constructs an Insets object with the appropriate border settings.

Instance Methods

clone

    public Object clone()

Returns	Clone of original object.
Overrides	Object.clone()
Description	Creates a copy of the original instance of an object.

equals

    public boolean equals (Object obj) ★

Parameters	*obj*	The object to be tested.
Returns	true if the objects are equal; false otherwise.	
Overrides	Object.equals(Object)	
Description	Tests two Insets objects for equality.	

toString

    public String toString()

Returns	A string representation of the Insets object.
Overrides	Object.toString()

See Also

Cloneable, Container, Object, Serializable, String

19.34   ItemSelectable ★

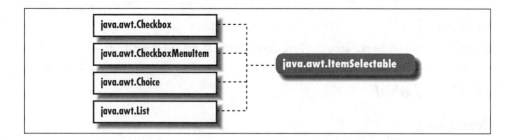

Description

An interface that describes an object that has one or more items that can be selected.

Interface Definition

```
public abstract interface ItemSelectable {

    // Instance Methods
    public abstract void addItemListener (ItemListener l);
    public abstract Object[] getSelectedObjects();
    public abstract void removeItemListener (ItemListener l);
}
```

Interface Methods

addItemListener

```
public abstract void addItemListener (ItemListener l)
```

| Parameters | *l* | The listener to be added. |
| Description | | Adds a listener for ItemEvent objects. |

getSelectedObjects

```
public abstract Object[] getSelectedObjects()
```

| Description | This method returns an array containing Objects representing the items that are currently selected. If no items are selected, null is returned. |

removeItemListener

```
public abstract void removeItemListener (ItemListener l)
```

| Parameters | *l* | The listener to be removed. |
| Description | | Removes the specified ItemListener so it will not receive Item-Event objects. |

See Also

Checkbox, CheckboxMenuItem, Choice, ItemEvent, ItemListener, List

---

19.35 Label

Description

The Label is a Component that displays a single line of static text.

Class Definition

```
public class java.awt.Label
    extends java.awt.Component {

    // Constants
    public static final int CENTER;
```

```
    public static final int LEFT;
    public static final int RIGHT;

    // Constructors
    public Label();
    public Label (String label);
    public Label (String label, int alignment);

    // Instance Methods
    public void addNotify();
    public int getAlignment();
    public String getText();
    public synchronized void setAlignment (int alignment);
    public synchronized void setText (String label);

    // Protected Instance Methods
    protected String paramString();
}
```

Constants

CENTER

```
public static final int CENTER
```

Description   Constant to center text within the label.

LEFT

```
public static final int LEFT
```

Description   Constant to left justify text within the label.

RIGHT

```
public static final int RIGHT
```

Description   Constant to right justify text within the label.

Constructors

Label

```
public Label()
```

Description   Constructs a Label object with the text centered within the label.

```
public Label (String label)
```

Parameters   *label*   The text for the label

Description   Constructs a Label object with the text label centered within the label.

```
public Label (String label, int alignment)
```

Parameters   *label*   The text for the label

              alignment   The alignment for the label; one of the constants CENTER, LEFT, or RIGHT.

Throws   *IllegalArgumentException*

                             If alignment is not one of CENTER, LEFT, or RIGHT.

Description   Constructs a Label object, with a given alignment and text of label.

Instance Methods

addNotify

```
public void addNotify()
```

Overrides   Component.addNotify()

Description   Creates Label's peer.

getAlignment

```
public int getAlignment()
```

Returns   Current alignment.

getText

```
public String getText()
```

Returns   Current text of Label.

setAlignment

public synchronized void setAlignment (int alignment)

Parameters   *alignment*   New alignment for Label; CENTER, LEFT, or RIGHT.

Throws   *IllegalArgumentException*
                            If alignment is not one of CENTER, LEFT, or RIGHT.

Description   Changes the current alignment of Label.

setText

public synchronized void setText (String label)

Parameters   *label*   New text for Label.

Description   Changes the current text of Label.

Protected Instance Methods

paramString

protected String paramString()

Returns   String with current settings of Label.

Overrides   Component.paramString()

Description   Helper method for toString() to generate string of current settings.

See Also

Component, String

19.36 *LayoutManager*

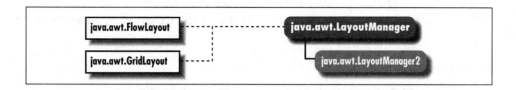

Description

LayoutManager is an interface that defines the responsibilities of an object that wants to lay out Components to the display in a Container.

Interface Definition

```
public abstract interface java.awt.LayoutManager {

  // Interface Methods
  public abstract void addLayoutComponent (String name,
      Component component);
  public abstract void layoutContainer (Container target);
  public abstract Dimension minimumLayoutSize (Container target);
  public abstract Dimension preferredLayoutSize (Container target);
  public abstract void removeLayoutComponent (Component component);
}
```

Interface Methods

addLayoutComponent

public abstract void addLayoutComponent (String name, Component component)

Parameters	*name*	Name of component to add.
	component	Actual component being added.
Description	Called when you call `Container.add(String, Component)` to add an object to a container.	

layoutContainer

public abstract void layoutContainer (Container target)

Parameters	*target*	The container who needs to be redrawn.
Description	Called when target needs to be redrawn.	

minimumLayoutSize

public abstract Dimension minimumLayoutSize (Container target)

Parameters	*target*	The container whose size needs to be calculated.
Returns	Minimum Dimension of the container target	
Description	Called when the minimum size of the target container needs to be calculated.	

preferredLayoutSize

public abstract Dimension preferredLayoutSize (Container target)

Parameters	*target*	The container whose size needs to be calculated.
Returns	Preferred Dimension of the container target	
Description	Called when the preferred size of the target container needs to be calculated.	

removeLayoutComponent

```
public abstract void removeLayoutComponent (Component component)
```

Parameters   *component*   Component to no longer track.

Description   Called when you call `Container.remove(Component)` to remove a component from the layout.

See Also

Component, Container, FlowLayout, GridLayout, Object, String

19.37 *LayoutManager2* ★

Description

LayoutManager2 is an extension of LayoutManager. It provides a more generalized way to add components to a container, as well as more sizing and alignment methods.

Interface Definition

```
public abstract interface java.awt.LayoutManager2
    extends java.awt.LayoutManager {

  // Interface Methods
  public abstract void addLayoutComponent (Component comp,
      Object constraints);
  public abstract float getLayoutAlignmentX(Container target);
  public abstract float getLayoutAlignmentY(Container target);
  public abstract void invalidateLayout(Container target);
  public abstract Dimension maximumLayoutSize(Container target);
}
```

Interface Methods

addLayoutComponent

public abstract void addLayoutComponent (Component comp, Object constraints)

Parameters   *comp*   Component to add.

             constraints   Constraints on the component.

Description   Called to add an object to a container. This is slightly more generic than LayoutManager's addLayoutComponent(String, Component).

getLayoutAlignmentX

public abstract float getLayoutAlignmentX (Container target)

Parameters   *target*   The container to inspect.

Returns   A value between 0 and 1.

Description   This method returns the preferred alignment of the given container target. A return value of 0 is left aligned, .5 is centered, and 1 is right aligned.

getLayoutAlignmentY

public abstract float getLayoutAlignmentY (Container target)

Parameters   *target*   The container to inspect.

Returns   A value between 0 and 1.

Description   This method returns the preferred alignment of the given container target. A return value of 0 is top aligned, .5 is centered, and 1 is bottom aligned.

invalidateLayout

public abstract void invalidateLayout (Container target)

Parameters   *target*   The container to invalidate.

Description   Sophisticated layout managers may cache information to improve performance. This method can be used to signal the manager to discard any cached information and start fresh.

maximumLayoutSize

public abstract Dimension maximumLayoutSize (Container target)

Returns   The maximum size of target.

Parameters   *target*   The container to inspect.
Description   This method returns the maximum size of `target` using this lay-
              out manager.

See Also

BorderLayout, CardLayout, Component, Container, GridBagLayout, Object, String

---

19.38   List

Description

The `List` is a `Component` that provides a scrollable list of choices to select from. A
`List` can be in one of two modes: single selection mode, in which only one item
may be selected at a time; and multiple selection mode, in which several items may
be selected at one time. A list does not necessarily display all of the choices at one
time; one of the constructors lets you specify the number of choices to display
simultaneously. Although the changes in 1.1 are extensive, almost all of them can
be boiled down to (1) using the 1.1 event model, and (2) standardizing method
names (e.g. set/get pairs).

Class Definition

```
public class java.awt.List
    extends java.awt.Component
    implements java.awt.ItemSelectable {

    // Constructors
    public List();
    public List (int rows); ★
    public List (int rows, boolean multipleSelections);

    // Instance Methods
    public void add (String item); ★
    public synchronized void add (String item, int index); ★
    public void addActionListener (ActionListener l); ★
    public void addItem (String item);
    public synchronized void addItem (String item, int index); ☆
    public void addItemListener (ItemListener l); ★
    public void addNotify();
    public boolean allowsMultipleSelections(); ☆
    public synchronized void clear(); ☆
```

```
    public int countItems(); ☆
    public synchronized void delItem (int position);
    public synchronized void delItems (int start, int end); ☆
    public synchronized void deselect (int index);
    public String getItem (int index);
    public int getItemCount(); ★
    public synchronized String[] getItems(); ★
    public Dimension getMinimumSize(); ★
    public Dimension getMinimumSize (int rows); ★
    public Dimension getPreferredSize(); ★
    public Dimension getPreferredSize (int rows); ★
    public int getRows();
    public synchronized int getSelectedIndex();
    public synchronized int[] getSelectedIndexes();
    public synchronized String getSelectedItem();
    public synchronized String[] getSelectedItems();
    public Object[] getSelectedObjects(); ★
    public int getVisibleIndex();
    public boolean isIndexSelected(int index); ★
    public boolean isMultipleMode(); ★
    public boolean isSelected (int index); ☆
    public synchronized void makeVisible (int index);
    public Dimension minimumSize(); ☆
    public Dimension minimumSize (int rows); ☆
    public Dimension preferredSize(); ☆
    public Dimension preferredSize (int rows); ☆
    public synchronized void remove (int position); ★
    public synchronized void remove (String item); ★
    public void removeActionListener (ActionListener l); ★
    public synchronized void removeAll(); ★
    public void removeItemListener (ItemListener l); ★
    public void removeNotify();
    public synchronized void replaceItem (String newItem, int index);
    public synchronized void select (int position);
    public synchronized void setMultipleMode (boolean b); ★
    public synchronized void setMultipleSelections (boolean value); ☆

    // Protected Instance Methods
    protected String paramString();
    protected void processActionEvent (ActionEvent e); ★
    protected void processEvent (AWTEvent e); ★
    protected void processItemEvent (ItemEvent e); ★
}
```

Constructors

List

```
public List()
```

Description   Constructs a List object in single-selection mode.

```
public List (int rows) ★
```

Parameters   *rows*   Requested number of rows to display.
Description   Constructs a List object with the specified number of rows, in single-selection mode.

```
public List (int rows, boolean multipleSelections)
```

Parameters   *rows*   Requested number of rows to display.
              multipleSelections
                               true to allow multiple selections; false to select one item at a time.
Description   Constructs a List object.

Instance Methods

add

```
public void add (String item) ★
```

Parameters   *item*   Text for entry to add.
Description   Adds a new entry to the available choices.

```
public synchronized void add (String item, int index) ★
```

Parameters   *item*   Text for entry to add.
              index   Position at which to add entry; the first entry has an index of zero.
Description   Adds a new entry to the available choices at the designated position.

addActionListener

```
public void addActionListener (ActionListener l) ★
```

Parameters   *l*   An object that implements the ActionListener interface.
Description   Add a listener for the action event.

addItem

```
public void addItem (String item)
```

Parameters   *item*   Text for entry to add.

Description   Replaced by add(String).

```
public synchronized void addItem (String item, int index) ☆
```

Parameters   *item*   Text for entry to add.

               index   Position at which to add entry; the first entry has an index of zero.

Description   Replaced by add(String, int).

addItemListener

```
public void addItemListener (ItemListener 1) ★
```

Parameters   *l*   The listener to be added.

Implements   ItemSelectable.addItemListener(ItemListener 1)

Description   Adds a listener for the ItemEvent objects this List fires off.

addNotify

```
public void addNotify()
```

Overrides   Component.addNotify()

Description   Creates List's peer.

allowsMultipleSelections

```
public boolean allowsMultipleSelections() ☆
```

Returns   true if multi-selection active, false otherwise. Replaced by isMultipleMode().

clear

```
public synchronized void clear() ☆
```

Description   Clears all the entries out of the List. Replaced by removeAll().

countItems

```
public int countItems() ☆
```

Returns   Number of items in the List. Replaced by getItemCount().

delItem

```
public synchronized void delItem (int position)
```

Parameters	*position*	Position of item to delete.
Description		Removes a single entry from the List. Replaced by remove(int) and remove(String).

delItems

```
public synchronized void delItems (int start, int end) ☆
```

Parameters	*start*	Starting position of entries to delete.
	end	Ending position of entries to delete.
Description		Removes a set of entries from the List.

deselect

```
public synchronized void deselect (int index)
```

Parameters	*index*	Position to deselect.
Description		Deselects the entry at the designated position, if selected.

getItem

```
public String getItem (int index)
```

Parameters	*index*	Position of entry to get.
Throws	*ArrayIndexOutOfBoundsException*	
		If index is invalid.
Returns		String for entry at given position.

getItemCount

```
public int getItemCount() ★
```

Returns	Number of items in the List.

getItems

```
public String[] getItems() ★
```

Returns	The string items in the List.

getMinimumSize

```
public Dimension getMinimumSize() ★
```

Returns	The minimum dimensions of the List.

```
public Dimension getMinimumSize (int rows) ★
```

Parameters   *rows*   Number of rows within List to size.

Returns   The minimum dimensions of a List of the given size.

getPreferredSize

```
public Dimension getPreferredSize() ★
```

Returns   The preferred dimensions of the List.

```
public Dimension getPreferredSize (int rows) ★
```

Parameters   *rows*   Number of rows within List to size.

Returns   The preferred dimensions of a List of the given size.

getRows

```
public int getRows()
```

Returns   Returns number of rows requested to be displayed in List.

getSelectedIndex

```
public synchronized int getSelectedIndex()
```

Returns   Position of currently selected entry, or -1 if nothing is selected, or if multiple entries are selected.

getSelectedIndexes

```
public synchronized int[] getSelectedIndexes()
```

Returns   An array whose elements are the indices of the currently selected entries.

getSelectedItem

```
public synchronized String getSelectedItem()
```

Returns   Currently selected entry as a String, or null if nothing is selected, or if multiple entries are selected.

getSelectedItems

```
public synchronized String[] getSelectedItems()
```

Returns   An array of strings whose elements are the labels of the currently selected entries.

getSelectedObjects

`public Object[] getSelectedObjects()` ★

Implements   `ItemSelectable.getSelectedObjects()`
Returns   An array of strings whose elements are the labels of the currently selected entries.

getVisibleIndex

`public int getVisibleIndex()`

Returns   The last index from a call to `makeVisible()`.

isIndexSelected

`public boolean isIndexSelected (int index)` ★

Parameters   *index*   Position to check.
Returns   true if index selected, false otherwise.
Description   Checks to see if a particular entry is currently selected.

isMultipleMode

`public boolean isMultipleMode()` ★

Returns   true if multiple selection is allowed, false otherwise.

isSelected

`public boolean isSelected (int index)` ☆

Parameters   *index*   Position to check.
Returns   true if index selected, false otherwise.
Description   Checks to see if a particular entry is currently selected. Replaced by `isIndexSelected(int)`.

makeVisible

`public synchronized void makeVisible (int index)`

Parameters   *index*   Position to make visible on screen.
Description   Ensures an item is displayed on the screen.

minimumSize

`public Dimension minimumSize()` ☆

Returns   The minimum dimensions of the List. Replaced by `getMinimumSize()`.

```
public Dimension minimumSize (int rows)  ☆
```

Parameters   *rows*   Number of rows within List to size.
Returns   The minimum dimensions of a List of the given size. Replaced
                by getMinimumSize(int).

preferredSize

```
public Dimension preferredSize ()  ☆
```

Returns   The preferred dimensions of the List. Replaced by getPre-
                ferredSize().

```
public Dimension preferredSize (int rows)  ☆
```

Parameters   *rows*   Number of rows within List to size.
Returns   The preferred dimensions of a List of the given size. Replaced
                by getPreferredSize(int).

remove

```
public synchronized void remove (int position)  ★
```

Parameters   *position*   Position of item to remove.
Description   Removes a single entry from the List.

```
public synchronized void remove (String item)  ★
```

Parameters   *item*   Item to remove.
Throws   *IllegalArgumentException*
                                 If item is not in the List.
Description   Removes a single entry from the List.

removeActionListener

```
public void removeActionListener (ActionListener l)  ★
```

Parameters   *l*   One of this List's ActionListeners.
Description   Remove an action event listener.

removeAll

```
public synchronized removeAll ()  ★
```

Description   Removes all items from the List.

removeItemListener

`public void removeItemListener (ItemListener l)` ★

Parameters	*l*	The listener to be removed.
Implements	`ItemSelectable.removeItemListener (ItemListener l)`	
Description	Removes the specified `ItemListener` so it will not receive `ItemEvent` objects from this `List`.	

removeNotify

`public void removeNotify()`

Description	Destroys the peer of the `List`.

replaceItem

`public synchronized void replaceItem (String newItem, int index)`

Parameters	*newItem*	Label for entry to add.
	index	Position of entry to replace.
Description	Replaces the contents at a particular position with a new entry.	

select

`public synchronized void select (int position)`

Parameters	*position*	Position to make selected entry.
Description	Makes the given entry the selected one for the `List`.	

setMultipleMode

`public synchronized void setMultipleMode (boolean b)` ★

Parameters	*b*	true to enable multiple selections; false to disable multiple selections.
Description	Changes `List`'s selection mode based upon flag.	

setMultipleSelections

`public synchronized void setMultipleSelections (boolean value)` ☆

Parameters	*value*	true to enable multiple selections; false to disable multiple selections.
Description	Changes `List`'s selection mode based upon flag. Replaced by `setMultipleMode(boolean)`.	

Protected Instance Methods

paramString

```
protected String paramString()
```

Returns	String with current settings of List.
Overrides	Component.paramString()
Description	Helper method for toString() to generate string of current settings.

processActionEvent

```
protected void processActionEvent (ActionEvent e) ★
```

Parameters	*e* The action event to process.
Description	Action events are passed to this method for processing. Normally, this method is called by processEvent().

processEvent

```
protected void processEvent (AWTEvent e) ★
```

Parameters	*e* The event to process.
Description	Low-level AWTEvents are passed to this method for processing.

processItemEvent

```
protected void processItemEvent(ItemEvent e) ★
```

Parameters	*e* The item event to process.
Description	Item events are passed to this method for processing. Normally, this method is called by processEvent().

See Also

Component, Dimension, ItemSelectable, String

19.39 MediaTracker

Description

The MediaTracker class assists in the loading of multimedia objects across the network. It can be used to wait until an object (or group of objects) has been loaded completely. Tracked objects are assigned to groups; if there is more than one object in a group, you can only track the behavior of the group as a whole (i.e., it isn't possible to track an individual object unless it is the only object in its group). Currently (1.0.2 and 1.1) MediaTracker only works for Image objects; future releases may extend MediaTracker to other multi-media types.

Class Definition

```
public abstract class java.awt.MediaTracker
    extends java.lang.Object
    implements java.io.Serializable {

// Constants
public static final int ABORTED;
public static final int COMPLETE;
public static final int ERRORED;
public static final int LOADING;


// Constructors
public MediaTracker (Component component);


// Instance Methods
public void addImage (Image image, int id);
public synchronized void addImage (Image image, int id, int width, int height);
public boolean checkAll();
public synchronized boolean checkAll (boolean load);
public boolean checkID (int id);
public synchronized boolean checkID (int id, boolean load);
public synchronized Object[] getErrorsAny();
public synchronized Object[] getErrorsID (int id);
public synchronized boolean isErrorAny();
public synchronized boolean isErrorID (int id);
public synchronized void removeImage(Image image); ★
public synchronized void removeImage(Image image, int id); ★
public synchronized void removeImage(Image image, int id, int width, int height); ★
public synchronized int statusAll (boolean load);
public synchronized int statusID (int id, boolean load);
public void waitForAll() throws InterruptedException;
public synchronized boolean waitForAll (long ms) throws InterruptedException;
public void waitForID (int id) throws InterruptedException;
public synchronized boolean waitForID (int id, long ms) throws InterruptedException;
}
```

Constants

ABORTED

```
public static final int ABORTED
```

Flag that indicates that the loading process aborted while loading a particular image.

COMPLETE

```
public static final int COMPLETE
```

Flag that indicates a particular image loaded successfully.

ERRORED

```
public static final int ERRORED
```

Flag that indicates an error occurred while a particular image was loading.

LOADING

```
public static final int LOADING
```

Flag that indicates a particular image is still loading.

Constructors

MediaTracker

```
public MediaTracker (Component component)
```

Parameters	*component*	Component that eventually renders objects being tracked.
Description	Constructs an MediaTracker object.	

Instance Methods

addImage

```
public void addImage (Image image, int id)
```

Parameters	*image*	Image to track.
	id	ID of a group.
Description	Tells a MediaTracker to track the loading of image, placing the image in the group identified by id.	

```
public synchronized void addImage (Image image, int id, int width,
int height)
```

Parameters	*image*	Image to track.
	id	ID of a group.

	width	Eventual rendering width.
	height	Eventual rendering height.

Description   Tells a MediaTracker to track the loading of `image`, which will be scaled to the given `height` and `width`, placing the image in the group identified by `id`.

checkAll

`public boolean checkAll()`

Returns   true if images completed loading (successfully or unsuccessfully), `false` otherwise.

Description   Determines if all images have finished loading.

`public synchronized boolean checkAll (boolean load)`

Parameters   *load*   Flag to force image loading to start.

Returns   true if all images have completed loading (successfully or unsuccessfully), `false` otherwise.

Description   Determines if all images have finished loading; the `load` parameter may be used to force images to start loading.

checkID

`public boolean checkID (int id)`

Parameters   *id*   ID of a group.

Returns   true if all images have completed loading (successfully or unsuccessfully), `false` otherwise.

Description   Determines if all images with the given ID tag have finished loading.

`public synchronized boolean checkID (int id, boolean load)`

Parameters   *id*   ID of a group.

load   Flag to force image loading to start.

Returns   true if all images have completed loading (successfully or unsuccessfully), `false` otherwise.

Description   Determines if all images with the given ID tag have finished loading; the `load` parameter may be used to force images to start loading.

getErrorsAny

```
public synchronized Object[] getErrorsAny()
```

Returns   An array of objects managed by this media tracker that encountered a loading error.

Description   Checks to see if any media encountered an error while loading.

getErrorsID

```
public synchronized Object[] getErrorsID (int id)
```

Parameters   *id*   ID of a group.

Returns   An array of objects that encountered a loading error.

Description   Checks to see if any media with the given ID tag encountered an error while loading.

isErrorAny

```
public synchronized boolean isErrorAny()
```

Returns   true if an error occurred, false otherwise.

Description   Checks to see if any media monitored by this media tracker encountered an error while loading.

isErrorID

```
public synchronized boolean isErrorID (int id)
```

Parameters   *id*   ID of a group.

Returns   true if error happened, false otherwise.

Description   Checks to see if any media in the given group encountered an error while loading.

removeImage

```
public synchronized void removeImage (Image image) ★
```

Parameters   *image*   The image to remove.

Description   Removes the specified image from this MediaTracker.

```
public synchronized void removeImage (Image image, int id) ★
```

Parameters   *image*   The image to remove.
               id   ID of a group.

Description   Removes the specified image from this MediaTracker. Only instances matching the given id will be removed.

```
public synchronized void removeImage (Image image, int id, int
width, int height) ★
```

Parameters	*image*	The image to remove.
	id	ID of a group.
	width	Width of the scaled image, or -1 for unscaled.
	height	Height of the scaled image, or -1 for unscaled.
Description		Removes the specified image from this `MediaTracker`. Only instances matching the given `id` and scale sizes will be removed.

statusAll

```
public synchronized int statusAll (boolean load)
```

Parameters	*load*	Flag to force image loading to start.
Returns		`MediaTracker` status flags ORed together.
Description		Checks load status of all the images monitored by this media tracker; the `load` parameter may be used to force images to start loading.

statusID

```
public synchronized int statusID (int id, boolean load)
```

Parameters	*id*	ID of a group.
	load	Flag to force image loading to start.
Returns		`MediaTracker` status flags ORed together.
Description		Checks load status of all the images in the given group; the `load` parameter may be used to force images to start loading.

waitForAll

```
public void waitForAll() throws InterruptedException
```

Throws	*InterruptedException*	
		If waiting interrupted.
Description		Waits for all the images monitored by this media tracker to load.

```
public synchronized boolean waitForAll (long ms) throws
InterruptedException
```

Parameters	*ms*	Time to wait for loading.
Throws	*InterruptedException*	
		If waiting interrupted.
Returns		`true` if images fully loaded, `false` otherwise.

Description   Waits at most ms milliseconds for all images monitored by this media tracker to load.

waitForID

public void waitForID (int id) throws InterruptedException

Parameters   *id*   ID of a group.
Throws   *InterruptedException*
                          If waiting interrupted.
Description   Waits for images in the given group to load.

public synchronized boolean waitForID (int id, long ms) throws InterruptedException

Parameters   *id*   ID of a group.
               ms   Maximum time to wait for loading.
Throws   *InterruptedException*
                          If waiting interrupted.
Returns   true if images fully loaded, false otherwise.
Description   Waits at most ms milliseconds for the images in the given group to load.

See Also

Component, Image, Object

19.40   Menu

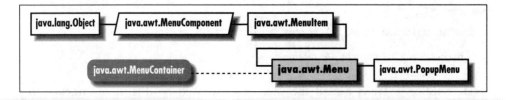

Description

The Menu class represents a group of MenuItem objects. Menus themselves are menu items, allowing you to build multi-level menus. Menus are always attached to MenuBars, which currently can only belong to frames.

Class Definition

```
public class java.awt.Menu
    extends java.awt.MenuItem
    implements java.awt.MenuContainer {

    // Constructors
    public Menu(); ★
    public Menu (String label);
    public Menu (String label, boolean tearOff);

    // Instance Methods
    public synchronized MenuItem add (MenuItem item);
    public void add (String label);
    public void addNotify();
    public void addSeparator();
    public int countItems(); ☆
    public MenuItem getItem (int index);
    public int getItemCount(); ★
    public void insert (String label, int index); ★
    public synchronized void insert (MenuItem menuitem, int index); ★
    public void insertSeparator (int index); ★
    public boolean isTearOff();
    public String paramString();  ★
    public synchronized void remove (int index);
    public synchronized void remove (MenuComponent component);
    public synchronized void removeAll(); ★
    public void removeNotify();
}
```

Constructors

Menu

   public Menu() ★

Description	Constructs a Menu object.

   public Menu (String label)

Parameters	*label* Text that appears on Menu.
Description	Constructs a Menu object with the given label.

   public Menu (String label, boolean tearOff)

Parameters	*label* Text that appears on Menu.
	tearOff true to create a tear-off menu, false otherwise.
Description	Constructs a Menu object; this will be a tear-off menu if tearOff is set to true.

Instance Methods

add

```
public synchronized MenuItem add (MenuItem item)
```

Parameters	*item*	A MenuItem to add to the Menu.
Returns	Item just added.	
Description	Adds a new item to a Menu.	

```
public void add (String label)
```

Parameters	*label*	Text for a MenuItem
Description	Constructs a new MenuItem object with the given label, and adds it to a Menu.	

addNotify

```
public void addNotify()
```

Overrides	MenuItem.addNotify()
Description	Creates a Menu peer, and peers for all MenuItem objects that appear on it.

addSeparator

```
public void addSeparator()
```

Description	Adds a separator bar to the Menu.

countItems

```
public int countItems() ☆
```

Returns	The number of items on the menu. Replaced by getItem-Count().

getItem

```
public MenuItem getItem (int index)
```

Parameters	*index* The position of the MenuItem to fetch; the first item has index 0.
Returns	The MenuItem at the designated position.

getItemCount

```
public int getItemCount() ★
```

Returns	The number of items on the menu.

insert

```
public void insert (String label, int index) ★
```

Parameters   *label*   The label for the new item.

                           index   The position for the new item.

Description   Adds a new item to this menu.

```
public synchronized void insert (MenuItem menuitem, int index) ★
```

Parameters   *menuitem*   The item to add.

                           index   The position for the new item.

Throws   *IllegalArgumentException*

                           If index is less than zero.

Description   Adds a new item to this menu.

insertSeparator

```
public void insertSeparator (int index) ★
```

Parameters   *index*   The position for the separator.

Throws   *IllegalArgumentException*

                           If index is less than zero.

Description   Adds a separator to this menu.

isTearOff

```
public boolean isTearOff()
```

Returns   true if the menu is a tear-off menu, false otherwise.

paramString

```
public String paramString() ★
```

Returns   String with current settings of Menu.

Overrides   MenuItem.paramString()

Description   Helper method for toString() to generate string of current
               settings.

remove

```
public synchronized void remove (int index)
```

Parameters   *index*   The position of the MenuItem to remove.

Description   Removes an item from the Menu.

```
public synchronized void remove (MenuComponent component)
```

Parameters   *component*   The element to remove.
Implements   `MenuContainer.remove()`
Description   Removes an item from the Menu.

removeAll

```
public synchronized void removeAll() ★
```

Description   Removes all items from the `Menu`.

removeNotify

```
public void removeNotify()
```

Description   Destroys `Menu` peer, and peers for all `MenuItem` objects that appear on it.

See Also

Frame, MenuComponent, MenuContainer, MenuItem, String

19.41 *MenuBar*

Description

A `MenuBar` holds menus. `MenuBars` are always attached to frames, and displayed on the top line of the `Frame`. One menu in a `MenuBar` may be designated a "help" menu.

Class Definition

```
public class java.awt.MenuBar
    extends java.awt.MenuComponent
    implements java.awt.MenuContainer {

  // Constructors
  public MenuBar();

  // Instance Methods
  public synchronized Menu add (Menu m);
  public void addNotify();
  public int countMenus(); ☆
  public void deleteShortcut (MenuShortcut s); ★
```

```
    public Menu getHelpMenu();
    public Menu getMenu (int index);
    public int getMenuCount(); ★
    public MenuItem getShortcutMenuItem (MenuShortcut s); ★
    public synchronized void remove (int index);
    public synchronized void remove (MenuComponent component);
    public void removeNotify();
    public synchronized void setHelpMenu (Menu m);
    public synchronized Enumeration shortcuts(); ★
}
```

Constructors

MenuBar

  public MenuBar()

  Description   Constructs a MenuBar object.

Instance Methods

add

  public synchronized Menu add (Menu m)

  Parameters   *m*   A Menu to add to MenuBar.
  Returns   Item just added.
  Description   Adds a new menu to the MenuBar.

addNotify

  public void addNotify()

  Description   Creates MenuBar's peer and peers of contained menus.

countMenus

  public int countMenus() ☆

  Returns   The number of menus on the menu bar. Replaced by getMenu-
                Count().

deleteShortcut

  public void deleteShortcut (MenuShortcut s) ★

  Parameters   *s*   The shortcut to remove.
  Description   Removes a menu shortcut.

getHelpMenu

```
public Menu getHelpMenu()
```

Returns   The menu that was designated the help menu.

getMenu

```
public Menu getMenu (int index)
```

Parameters   *index*   The position of the Menu to fetch.
Returns   The Menu at the designated position.

getMenuCount

```
public int getMenuCount() ★
```

Returns   The number of menus on the menu bar.

getShortcutMenuItem

```
public MenuItem getShortcutMenuItem (MenuShortcut s) ★
```

Parameters   *s*   A menu shortcut.
Returns   The corresponding menu item.
Description   Finds the MenuItem corresponding to the given MenuShortcut,
              or null if no match is found.

remove

```
public synchronized void remove (int index)
```

Parameters   *index*   The position of the Menu to remove.
Description   Removes a Menu from the MenuBar.

```
public synchronized void remove (MenuComponent component)
```

Parameters   *component*   The element of the MenuBar to remove.
Implements   MenuContainer.remove()
Description   Removes a Menu from the MenuBar.

removeNotify

```
public void removeNotify()
```

Description   Destroys the MenuBar peer, and peers for all Menu objects that
              appear on it.

setHelpMenu

public synchronized void setHelpMenu (Menu m)

Parameters	*m*	Menu to designate as the help menu.
Description		Designates a Menu as the MenuBar's help menu.

shortcuts

public synchronized Enumeration shortcuts() ★

Returns	An Enumeration of MenuShortcut objects.
Description	Returns an Enumeration of all MenuShortcut objects managed by this MenuBar.

See Also

Frame, Menu, MenuComponent, MenuContainer

19.42   MenuComponent

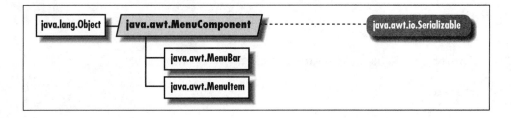

Description

The abstract MenuComponent class represents the parent of all menu GUI components.

Class Definition

```
public abstract class java.awt.MenuComponent
    extends java.lang.Object
    implements java.io.Serializable {

    // Instance Methods
    public final void dispatchEvent (AWTEvent e); ★
    public Font getFont();
    public String getName(); ★
    public MenuContainer getParent();
    public MenuComponentPeer getPeer(); ☆
    public boolean postEvent (Event e); ☆
    public void removeNotify();
    public void setFont (Font f);
```

```
public void setName (String name); ★
public String toString();

// Protected Instance Methods
protected String paramString(); ★
protected void processEvent (AWTEvent e); ★
}
```

Instance Methods

dispatchEvent

public final void dispatchEvent (AWTEvent e)

Parameters   *e*   The AWTEvent to process.

Description   Tells the menu component to deal with the AWTEvent e.

getFont

public Font getFont()

Returns   The font for the current MenuComponent.

getName

public Font getName() ★

Returns   The name for the current MenuComponent.

getParent

public MenuContainer getParent()

Returns   The parent MenuContainer for the MenuComponent.

getPeer

public MenuComponentPeer getPeer() ★

Returns   A reference to the MenuComponent's peer.

postEvent

public boolean postEvent (Event e) ☆

Parameters   *e*   Event instance to post to component.
Returns   Ignored for menus.
Description   Tells the Frame that contains the MenuBar containing the Menu-
               Component to deal with Event.

removeNotify

   public void removeNotify()

   Description   Removes peer of MenuComponent's subclass.

setFont

   public void setFont (Font f)

   Parameters   *f*   New font for MenuComponent.
   Description   Changes the font of the label of the MenuComponent.

setName

   public void setName (String name) ★

   Parameters   *name*   New name for MenuComponent.
   Description   Changes the name of the MenuComponent.

toString

   public String toString()

   Returns   A string representation of the MenuComponent object.

             Overrides   Object.toString()

Protected Instance Methods

paramString

   protected String paramString() ★

   Returns   String with current settings of MenuComponent.
   Overrides   Component.paramString()
   Description   Helper method for toString() to generate string of current settings.

processEvent

   protected void processEvent (AWTEvent e) ★

   Parameters   *e*   The event to process.
   Description   Low-level AWTEvents are passed to this method for processing.

See Also

Event, Font, MenuBar, MenuComponentPeer, MenuContainer, MenuItem, Object, Serializable, String

19.43   *MenuContainer*

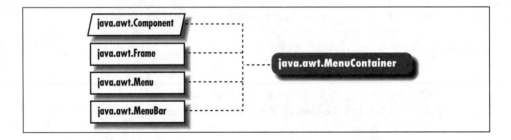

Description

MenuContainer is an interface that defines the responsibilities for objects that can have a menu.

Interface Definition

```
public abstract interface java.awt.MenuContainer
    extends java.lang.Object {

  // Interface Methods
  public abstract Font getFont();
  public abstract boolean postEvent (Event e);   ☆
  public abstract void remove (MenuComponent component);
}
```

Interface Methods

getFont

public abstract Font getFont()

Returns   Current font of the object implementing this method.

postEvent

public abstract boolean postEvent (Event e) ☆

Parameters   *e*   Event to post.
Returns   Ignores return value.
Description   Posts event to the object implementing this method.

remove

```
public abstract void remove (MenuComponent component)
```

Parameters   *component*   Menu object to remove

Description   Tells the object implementing this method to remove a menu component.

See Also

Event, Font, Frame, Menu, MenuBar, MenuComponent, Object

19.44 MenuItem

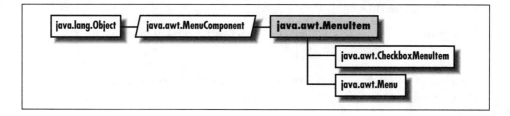

Description

The MenuItem class represents a selectable item on a menu.

Class Definition

```
public class java.awt.MenuItem
    extends java.awt.MenuComponent {

    // Constructors
    public MenuItem (); ★
    public MenuItem (String label);
    public MenuItem (String label, MenuShortcut s); ★

    // Instance Methods
    public void addActionListener (ActionListener l); ★
    public void addNotify ();
    public void deleteShortcut (); ★
    public synchronized void disable (); ☆
    public synchronized void enable (); ☆
    public void enable (boolean condition); ☆
    public String getActionCommand (); ★
    public String getLabel ();
    public MenuShortcut getShortcut (); ★
    public boolean isEnabled ();
    public String paramString ();
    public void removeActionListener (ActionListener l); ★
```

```
    public void setActionCommand (String command);  ★
    public synchronized void setEnabled (boolean b);  ★
    public synchronized void setLabel (String label);
    public void setShortcut (MenuShortcut s);  ★

    // Protected Instance Methods
    protected final void disableEvents (long eventsToDisable);  ★
    protected final void enableEvents (long eventsToEnable);  ★
    protected void processActionEvent (ActionEvent e);  ★
    protected void processEvent (AWTEvent e);  ★
}
```

Constructors

MenuItem

```
    public MenuItem ()  ★
```

Description   Constructs a MenuItem object with no label or shortcut.

```
    public MenuItem (String label)
```

Parameters   *label*   Text that appears on the MenuItem.
Description   Constructs a MenuItem object.

```
    public MenuItem (String label, MenuShortcut s)  ★
```

Parameters   *label*   Text that appears on the MenuItem.
              s   Shortcut for the MenuItem.
Description   Constructs a MenuItem object with the given shortcut.

Instance Methods

addActionListener

```
    public void addActionListener (ActionListener l)  ★
```

Parameters   *l*   An object that implements the ActionListener
                               interface.
Description   Add a listener for the action event.

addNotify

```
    public void addNotify ()
```

Description   Creates the MenuItem's peer.

deleteShortcut

> public void deleteShortcut() ★

Description   Removes the shortcut associated with this item.

disable

> public synchronized void disable() ☆

Description   Disables the menu component so that it is unresponsive to user interactions. Replaced by setEnabled(false).

enable

> public synchronized void enable() ☆

Description   Enables the menu component so that it is responsive to user interactions. Replaced by setEnabled(true).

> public void enable (boolean condition) ☆

Parameters   *condition*   true to enable the menu component; false to disable it.

Description   Enables or disables the menu component, depending on the condition parameter. Replaced by setEnabled(boolean).

getActionCommand

> public String getActionCommand() ★

Returns   Current action command string.

Description   Returns the string used for the action command.

getLabel

> public String getLabel()

Returns   The current text associated with the MenuItem.

getShortcut

> public MenuShortcut getShortcut() ★

Returns   The current shortcut for this item, or null if there is none.

isEnabled

public boolean isEnabled()

Returns   true if the menu item is enabled, false otherwise.

paramString

public String paramString()

Returns   String with current settings of MenuItem.

Description   Helper method for toString() to generate string of current
               settings.

removeActionListener

public void removeActionListener(ActionListener l) ★

Parameters   *l*   One of this Button's ActionListeners.

Description   Remove an action event listener.

setActionCommand

public void setActionCommand(String command) ★

Parameters   *command*   New action command string.

Description   Specify the string used for the action command.

setEnabled

public synchronized void setEnabled (boolean b) ★

Parameters   *b*   true to enable the item, false to disable it.

Description   Enables   or   disables   the   item.   Replaces   enable(),
               enable(boolean), and disable().

setLabel

public synchronized void setLabel (String label)

Parameters   *label*   New text to appear on MenuItem.

Description   Changes the label of the MenuItem.

setShortcut

public void setShortcut (MenuShortcut s) ★

Parameters   *s*   New shortcut for the MenuItem.

Description   Changes the shortcut of the MenuItem.

Protected Instance Methods

disableEvents

```
protected final void disableEvents (long eventsToDisable) ★
```

Parameters   *eventsToDisable*

A value representing certain kinds of events. This can be constructed by ORing the event mask constants defined in java.awt.AWTEvent.

Description   By default, a menu item receives events corresponding to the event listeners that have registered. If a menu item should not receive events of a certain type, even if there is a listener registered for that type of event, this method can be used to disable that event type.

enableEvents

```
protected final void enableEvents (long eventsToEnable) ★
```

Parameters   *eventsToDisable*

A value representing certain kinds of events. This can be constructed by ORing the event mask constants defined in java.awt.AWTEvent.

Description   By default, a menu item receives events corresponding to the event listeners that have registered. If a menu item should receive other types of events as well, this method can be used to get them.

processActionEvent

```
protected void processActionEvent (ActionEvent e) ★
```

Parameters   *e*   The action event to process.

Description   Action events are passed to this method for processing. Normally, this method is called by processEvent().

processEvent

```
protected void processEvent (AWTEvent e) ★
```

Parameters   *e*   The event to process.

Description   Low-level AWTEvents are passed to this method for processing.

See Also

CheckboxMenuItem, Menu, MenuComponent, MenuShortcut, String

19.45 MenuShortcut ★

Description

A MenuShortcut is used to associate a keystroke with a menu item. MenuShortcuts are constructed using their corresponding key; they are associated with menu items via MenuItem.setShortcut(MenuShortcut).

Class Definition

```
public class java.awt.MenuShortcut
    extends java.awt.Event {

    // Constructors
    public MenuShortcut (int key);
    public MenuShortcut (int key, boolean useShiftModifier);

    // Instance Methods
    public boolean equals (MenuShortcut s);
    public int getKey();
    public String toString();
    public boolean usesShiftModifier();

    // Protected Instance Methods
    protected String paramString();
}
```

Constructors

MenuShortcut

public MenuShortcut (int key)

Parameters *key*   A keycode like those returned with key press
                            Event objects.
Description Constructs a MenuShortcut object for the given key.

```
public MenuShortcut (int key, boolean useShiftModifier)
```

Parameters   *key*   A keycode like those returned with key press
                                   Event objects.

              useShiftModifier

                                   true if the Shift key must be used, false other-
                                   wise.

Description   Constructs a MenuShortcut object with the given values.

Instance Methods

equals

```
public boolean equals (MenuShortcut s)
```

Parameters   *s*   The MenuShortcut to compare.

Returns   true if s is equal to this MenuShortcut, false otherwise.

getKey

```
public int getKey()
```

Returns   The key for this MenuShortcut.

toString

```
public String toString()
```

Returns   A string representation of the MenuShortcut object.

Overrides   Event.toString()

usesShiftModifier

```
public boolean usesShiftModifier()
```

Returns   true if this MenuShortcut must be invoked with the Shift key
               pressed, false otherwise.

Protected Instance Methods

paramString

```
protected String paramString()
```

Returns   String with current settings of MenuShortcut.

Overrides   Event.paramString()

Description   Helper method for toString() to generate string of current
               settings.

See Also

Event, MenuItem

19.46 Panel

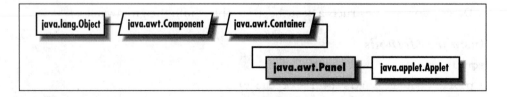

Description

The Panel class provides a generic Container within an existing display area.

Class Definition

```
public class java.awt.Panel
    extends java.awt.Container {

    // Constructors
    public Panel();
    public Panel(LayoutManager layout);  ★

    // Instance Methods
    public void addNotify();
}
```

Constructors

Panel

public Panel()

Description   Constructs a Panel object.

public Panel (LayoutManager layout) ★

Description   Constructs a Panel object with the specified layout manager.

Instance Methods

addNotify

```
public void addNotify()
```

Overrides   Container.addNotify()
Description   Creates Panel's peer and peers of contained components.

See Also

Applet, Container

19.47   Point

Description

The Point class encapsulates a pair of x and y coordinates within a single object.

Class Definition

```
public class java.awt.Point
    extends java.lang.Object
    implements java.io.Serializable {

  // Variables
  public int x;
  public int y;

  // Constructors
  public Point(); ★
  public Point (int width, int height);
  public Point (Point p); ★

  // Instance Methods
  public boolean equals (Object object);
  public Point getLocation(); ★
  public int hashCode();
  public void move (int x, int y);
  public void setLocation (int x, int y); ★
  public void setLocation (Point p); ★
  public String toString();
  public void translate (int deltax, int deltay);
}
```

Variables

x

```
public int x
```

The coordinate that represents the horizontal position.

y

```
public int y
```

The coordinate that represents the vertical position.

Constructors

Point

```
public Point() ★
```

Description   Constructs a Point object initialized to (0, 0).

```
public Point (int x, int y)
```

| Parameters | *x* | Coordinate that represents the horizontal position. |
| | *y* | Coordinate that represents the vertical position. |

Description   Constructs a Point object with an initial position of (x, y).

```
public Point (Point p) ★
```

| Parameters | *p* | Initial position. |

Description   Constructs a Point object with the same position as p.

Instance Methods

equals

```
public boolean equals (Object object)
```

Parameters	*object*	The object to compare.
Returns		true if both points have the same x and y coordinates, false otherwise.
Overrides		Object.equals()
Description		Compares two different Point instances for equivalence.

getLocation

```
public Point getLocation() ★
```

| Returns | Position of this point. |
| Description | Gets the current position of this Point. |

hashCode

```
public int hashCode()
```

Returns   A hashcode to use the Point is used as a key in a Hashtable.
Overrides   Object.hashCode()
Description   Generates a hashcode for the Point.

move

```
public void move (int x, int y)
```

Parameters   *x*   The new x coordinate.
               y   The new y coordinate.
Description   Changes the Point's location to (x, y).

setLocation

```
public void setLocation (int x, int y) ★
```

Parameters   *x*   The new x coordinate.
               y   The new y coordinate.
Description   Changes the Point's location to (x, y).

```
public void setLocation (Point p) ★
```

Parameters   *p*   The new location.
Description   Changes the Point's location to p.

toString

```
public String toString()
```

Returns   A string representation of the Point object.
Overrides   Object.toString()

translate

```
public void translate (int deltax, int deltay)
```

Parameters   *deltax*   Amount to move horizontally.
               deltay   Amount to move vertically.
Description   Moves the Point to the location (x+deltax, y+deltay).

See Also

Object, String

19.48   Polygon

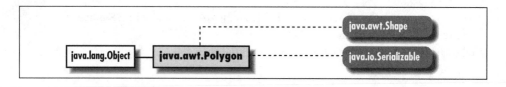

Description

The Polygon class encapsulates a collection of points used to create a series of line segments.

Class Definition

```
public class java.awt.Polygon
    extends java.lang.Object
    implements java.awt.Shape, java.io.Serializable {

  // Variables
  protected Rectangle bounds; ★
  public int npoints;
  public int xpoints[];
  public int ypoints[];

  // Constructors
  public Polygon();
  public Polygon (int xpoints[], int ypoints, int npoints);

  // Instance Methods
  public void addPoint (int x, int y);
  public boolean contains (int x, int y); ★
  public boolean contains (Point p); ★
  public Rectangle getBoundingBox(); ☆
  public Rectangle getBounds(); ★
  public boolean inside (int x,int y); ☆
  public void translate (int deltaX, int deltaY); ★
}
```

Variables

bounds

```
protected Rectangle bounds  ★
```

The rectangle that describes the boundaries of the Polygon.

npoints

```
public int npoints
```

The number of elements to use in the xpoints and ypoints arrays.

xpoints

```
public int xpoints[]
```

The array of x coordinates for each point.

ypoints

```
public int ypoints[]
```

The array of y coordinates for each point.

Constructors

Polygon

```
public Polygon()
```

Description   Constructs an empty Polygon object with no points.

```
public Polygon (int xPoints[], int yPoints[], int numPoints)
```

Parameters   *xPoints[]*   The initial array of x coordinates for each point.
              yPoints[]   The initial array of y coordinates for each point.
              numPoints   The number of elements in both xPoints and
                              yPoints arrays to use.

Throws   ArrayIndexOutOfBoundsException
                              If numPoints > xPoints.length or numPoints >
                              yPoints.length.

Description   Constructs a Polygon object with the set of points provided.

Instance Methods

addPoint

```
public void addPoint (int x, int y)
```

Parameters	*x*	The x coordinate of the point to be added.
	y	The y coordinate of the point to be added.
Description		Adds the point (x, y) to the end of the list of points for the Polygon.

contains

```
public boolean contains (int x, int y) ★
```

Parameters	*x*	The x coordinate to test.
	y	The y coordinate to test.
Returns		true if the Polygon contains the point; false otherwise.

```
public boolean contains (Point p) ★
```

| Parameters | *p* | The point to be tested. |
| Returns | | true if the Polygon contains the point; false otherwise. |

getBoundingBox

```
public Rectangle getBoundingBox() ☆
```

| Returns | Bounding Rectangle of the points within the Polygon. |
| Description | Returns the smallest Rectangle that contains all the points within the Polygon. Replaced by getBounds(). |

getBounds

```
public Rectangle getBounds() ★
```

Implements	Shape.getBounds()
Returns	Bounding Rectangle of the points within the Polygon.
Description	Returns the smallest Rectangle that contains all the points within the Polygon.

inside

```
public boolean inside (int x, int y) ☆
```

Parameters	*x*	The x coordinate of the point to be checked.
	y	The y coordinate of the point to be checked.
Returns		true if (x, y) within Polygon, false otherwise.
Description		Checks to see if the (x, y) point is within an area that would be filled if the Polygon was drawn with Graphics.fillPolygon(). Replaced by contains(int, int).

translate

public void translate (int deltaX, int deltaY) ★

Parameters   *deltaX*   Amount to move horizontally.
              deltaY   Amount to move vertically.
Description   Moves the Polygon to the location (x+deltaX, y+deltaY).

See Also

Graphics, Object, Rectangle

19.49   *PopupMenu* ★

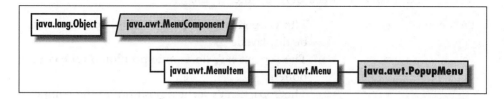

Description

A PopupMenu is a menu that can be popped up on a Component.

Class Definition

```
public class java.awt.PopupMenu
    extends java.awt.Menu {

    // Constructors
    public PopupMenu();
    public PopupMenu (String label);

    // Instance Methods
    public synchronized void addNotify();
    public void show (Component origin, int x, int y);
}
```

Constructors

PopupMenu

public PopupMenu()

Description   Constructs a PopupMenu object.

```
public PopupMenu (String label)
```

Parameters   *label*   Text that appears on Menu.
Description   Constructs a PopupMenu object with the given label.

Instance Methods

addNotify

```
public synchronized void addNotify()
```

Overrides   Menu.addNotify()
Description   Creates a PopupMenu peer.

show

```
public void show (Component origin, int x, int y)
```

Parameters   *origin*   The Component upon which the PopupMenu will
                              be displayed.
              x   The PopupMenu's horizontal position on the com-
                              ponent.
              y   The PopupMenu's vertical position on the compo-
                              nent.
Description   Shows the menu on the given Component. The origin specified
              must be contained in the hierarchy of the PopupMenu's parent
              component, which is determined by the call to Compo-
              nent.add(PopupMenu).

19.50   *PrintGraphics* ★

java.awt.PrintGraphics

Description

PrintGraphics is an interface for classes that provide a printing graphics context.

Interface Definition

```
public abstract interface java.awt.PrintGraphics {

  // Interface Methods
  public abstract PrintJob getPrintJob();
}
```

Interface Methods

getPrintJob

```
public abstract PrintJob getPrintJob()
```

Returns   The PrintJob from which the PrintGraphics object originated.

See Also

PrintJob

19.51   PrintJob ★

Description

PrintJob encapsulates printing information. When you call Toolkit.getPrintJob(), this is the object that is returned. From the PrintJob, you can access a Graphics object, which can be used for drawing to the printer.

Class Definition

```
public abstract class jav.awt.PrintJob
    extends java.lang.Object {

  // Instance Methods
  public abstract void end();
  public void finalize();
  public abstract Graphics getGraphics();
  public abstract Dimension getPageDimension();
  public abstract int getPageResolution();
  public abstract boolean lastPageFirst();
}
```

Instance Methods

end

```
public abstract void end()
```

Description   Ends printing and cleans up.

finalize

```
public void finalize()
```

Overrides   Object.finalize()
Description   Cleans up when this object is garbage collected.

getGraphics

```
public abstract Graphics getGraphics()
```

Returns   A Graphics object representing the next page. The object
                returned will also implement the PrintGraphics interface.
Description   Returns a Graphics object for printing.

getPageDimension

```
public abstract Dimension getPageDimension()
```

Returns   The page dimensions in pixels.

getPageResolution

```
public abstract int getPageResolution
```

Returns   The page resolution, in pixels per inch.

lastPageFirst

```
public abstract boolean lastPageFirst()
```

Returns   true if pages are printed in reverse order; false otherwise.

See Also

Dimension, Graphics, PrintGraphics, Toolkit

19.52   *Rectangle*

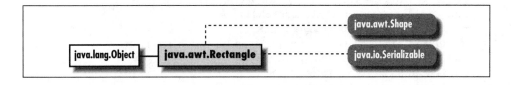

Description

The Rectangle class represents a rectangle by combining its origin (a pair of x and
y coordinates) with its size (a width and a height).

Class Definition

```
public class java.awt.Rectangle
    extends java.lang.Object
    implements java.awt.Shape, java.io.Serializable {

    // Variables
    pubic int height;
    public int width;
    public int x;
    public int y;

    // Constructors
    public Rectangle();
    public Rectangle (int width, int height);
    public Rectangle (int x, int y, int width, int height);
    public Rectangle (Dimension d);
    public Rectangle (Point p);
    public Rectangle (Point p, Dimension d);
    public Rectangle (Rectangle r); ★

    // Instance Methods
    public void add (int newX, int newY);
    public void add (Point p);
    public void add (Rectangle r);
    public boolean contains (int x, int y); ★
    public boolean contains (Point p); ★
    public boolean equals (Object object);
    public Rectangle getBounds(); ★
    public Point getLocation(); ★
    public Dimension getSize(); ★
    public void grow (int horizontal, int vertical);
    public int hashCode();
    public boolean inside (int x, int y); ☆
    public Rectangle intersection (Rectangle r);
    public boolean intersects (Rectangle r);
```

```
    public boolean isEmpty();
    public void move (int x, int y); ☆
    public void reshape (int x, int y, int width, int height); ☆
    public void resize (int width, int height); ☆
    public void setBounds (Rectangle r); ★
    public void setBounds (int x, int y, int width, int height); ★
    public void setLocation (int x, int y); ★
    public void setLocation (Point p); ★
    public void setSize (int width, int height); ★
    public void setSize (Dimension d); ★
    public String toString();
    public void translate (int x, int y);
    public Rectangle union (Rectangle r);
}
```

Variables

height

public int height

The height of the Rectangle.

width

public int width

The width of the Rectangle.

x

public int x

The x coordinate of the Rectangle's upper left corner (its origin).

y

public int y

The y coordinate of the Rectangle's upper left corner (its origin).

Constructors

Rectangle

public Rectangle()

Description   Constructs an empty Rectangle object with an origin of (0, 0) and dimensions of 0 x 0.

```
public Rectangle (int width, int height)
```

Parameters   *width*   width of `Rectangle`

                       height   height of `Rectangle`

Description   Constructs a `Rectangle` object with an origin of (0, 0) and dimensions of width x height.

```
public Rectangle (int x, int y, int width, int height)
```

Parameters   *x*   x coordinate of the `Rectangle`'s origin

                       y   y coordinate of the `Rectangle`'s origin

                       width   width of `Rectangle`

                       height   height of `Rectangle`

Description   Constructs a `Rectangle` object with an origin of (x, y) and dimensions of width x height.

```
public Rectangle (Dimension d)
```

Parameters   *d*   dimensions of `Rectangle`

Description   Constructs a `Rectangle` object with an origin of (0, 0) and dimensions of d.width x d.height.

```
public Rectangle (Point p)
```

Parameters   *p*   origin of `Rectangle`

Description   Constructs an empty `Rectangle` object with an origin of (p.x, p.y) and dimensions of 0 x 0.

```
public Rectangle (Point p, Dimension d)
```

Parameters   *p*   origin of `Rectangle`

                       d   dimensions of `Rectangle`

Description   Constructs a `Rectangle` object with an origin of (p.x, p.y) and dimensions of d.width x d.height.

```
public Rectangle (Rectangle r)  ★
```

Parameters   *r*   original `Rectangle`

Description   Constructs copy of the given `Rectangle`.

Instance Methods

add

```
public void add (int newX, int newY)
```

Parameters   *newX*   The x-coordinate of a point to incorporate within the `Rectangle`.

| *newY* | The y-coordinate of a point to incorporate within the `Rectangle`. |

Description   Extends the `Rectangle` so that the point (`newX`, `newY`) is within it.

`public void add (Point p)`

| Parameters | *p* | The new `Point` to add to the `Rectangle`. |

Description   Extends the `Rectangle` so that the point p is within it.

`public void add (Rectangle r)`

| Parameters | *r* | The `Rectangle` being added to the current `Rectangle`. |

Description   Extends the `Rectangle` to include the `Rectangle` r.

contains

`public boolean contains (int x, int y)` ★

| Parameters | *x* | The x coordinate to test. |
| | *y* | The y coordinate to test. |

Returns   true if the `Rectangle` contains the point; false otherwise.

`public boolean contains (Point p)` ★

| Parameters | *p* | The point to be tested. |

Returns   true if the `Rectangle` contains the point; false otherwise.

equals

`public boolean equals (Object object)`

| Parameters | *object* | The object to compare. |

Returns   true if both `Rectangles` have the same origin, width, and height; false otherwise.

Overrides   `Object.equals(Object)`

Description   Compares two different `Rectangle` instances for equivalence.

getBounds

`public Rectangle getBounds()` ★

Implements   `Shape.getBounds()`

Returns   Bounding `Rectangle`.

getLocation

```
public Point getLocation() ★
```

Returns	Position of the rectangle.
Description	Gets the current position of this Rectangle.

getSize

```
public Dimension getSize() ★
```

Returns	Dimensions of the rectangle.
Description	Gets width and height of the rectangle.

grow

```
public void grow (int horizontal, int vertical)
```

Parameters	*horizontal*	Amount to extend Rectangle in horizontal direction on both the left and right sides.
	vertical	Amount to extend Rectangle in vertical direction on both the top and the bottom.
Description	Increases the rectangle's dimensions.	

hashCode

```
public int hashCode()
```

Returns	A hashcode to use when using the Rectangle as a key in a Hashtable.
Overrides	Object.hashCode()
Description	Generates a hashcode for the Rectangle.

inside

```
public boolean inside (int x, int y) ☆
```

Parameters	*x*	The x coordinate to check.
	y	The y coordinate to check.
Returns	true if (x, y) falls within the Rectangle, false otherwise.	
Description	Checks to see if the point (x, y) is within the Rectangle. Replaced by contains(int, int).	

intersection

```
public Rectangle intersection (Rectangle r)
```

Parameters	*r*	Rectangle to add to the current Rectangle.
Returns		A new Rectangle consisting of all points in both the current Rectangle and r.
Description		Generates a new Rectangle that is the intersection of r and the current Rectangle.

intersects

```
public boolean intersects (Rectangle r)
```

Parameters	*r*	Rectangle to check.
Returns		true if any points in r are also in the current Rectangle, false otherwise.
Description		Checks to see if r crosses the Rectangle.

isEmpty

```
public boolean isEmpty()
```

Returns	true if the Rectangle is empty, false otherwise.
Description	Determines if the rectangle is dimensionless (i.e., width or height are less than or equal to 0).

move

```
public void move (int x, int y) ☆
```

Parameters	*x*	The new x coordinate of the Rectangle's upper left corner.
	y	The new y coordinate of the Rectangle's upper left corner.
Description		Changes the Rectangle's origin to (x, y). Replaced by setLocation(int, int).

reshape

```
public void reshape (int x, int y, int width, int height) ☆
```

Parameters	*x*	The new x coordinate of the Rectangle's upper left corner.
	y	The new y coordinate of the Rectangle's upper left corner.

	width	The new width.
	height	The new height.
Description		Changes `Rectangle`'s origin and dimensions. Replaced by set-Bounds(int, int, int, int).

resize

public void resize (int width, int height) ☆

Parameters	*width*	The new width.
	height	The new height.
Description		Changes `Rectangle`'s dimensions. Replaced by setSize(int, int).

setBounds

public void setBounds (Rectangle r) ★

Parameters	*r*	A `Rectangle` describing the new bounds.
Description		Changes `Rectangle`'s location and size.

public void setBounds (int x, int y, int width, int height) [New in 1.1]

Parameters	*x*	The new x coordinate of the `Rectangle`'s upper left corner.
	y	The new y coordinate of the `Rectangle`'s upper left corner.
	width	The new width.
	height	The new height.
Description		Changes `Rectangle`'s location and size.

setLocation

public void setLocation (int x, int y) ★

Parameters	*x*	New horizontal position.
	y	New vertical position.
Description		Relocates the rectangle.

public void setLocation (Point p) ★

Parameters	*p*	New position for component.
Description		Relocates the rectangle.

setSize

public void setSize (int width, int height) ★

Parameters	*width*	New width.
	height	New height.
Description	Resizes the rectangle.	

public void setSize (Dimension d) ★

Parameters	*d*	New dimensions.
Description	Resizes the rectangle.	

toString

public String toString()

Returns	A string representation of the Rectangle object.
Overrides	Object.toString()

translate

public void translate (int deltax, int deltay)

Parameters	*deltax*	Amount to move Rectangle horizontally.
	deltay	Amount to move Rectangle vertically.
Description	Moves the Rectangle's origin to (x+deltax, y+deltay).	

union

public Rectangle union (Rectangle r)

Parameters	*r*	Rectangle to determine union with.
Returns	The smallest Rectangle containing both r and the current Rectangle.
Description	Generates a new Rectangle by combining r and the current Rectangle.

See Also

Dimension, Object, Point, String

19.53   ScrollPane ★

Description

The ScrollPane class provides automatic scrolling of a child component.

Class Definition

```
public class java.awt.ScrollPane
    extends java.awt.Container {

    // Constants
    public final static int SCROLLBARS_ALWAYS;
    public final static int SCROLLBARS_AS_NEEDED;
    public final static int SCROLLBARS_NEVER;

    // Constructors
    public ScrollPane();
    public ScrollPane (int scrollbarDisplayPolicy);

    // Public Instance Methods
    public void addNotify();
    public void doLayout();
    public Adjustable getHAdjustable();
    public int getHScrollbarHeight();
    public Point getScrollPosition();
    public int getScrollbarDisplayPolicy();
    public Adjustable getVAdjustable();
    public int getVScrollbarWidth();
    public Dimension getViewportSize();
    public void layout(); ☆
    public String paramString();
    public void printComponents (Graphics g);
    public final void setLayout (LayoutManager mgr);
    public void setScrollPosition (int x, int y);
    public void setScrollPosition (Point p);

    //Protected Instance Methods
    protected final void addImpl (Component comp, Object constraints,
        int index);
}
```

Constants

SCROLLBARS_ALWAYS

```
public final static int SCROLLBARS_ALWAYS
```

Always show the scrollbars.

SCROLLBARS_AS_NEEDED

```
public final static int SCROLLBARS_AS_NEEDED
```

Only show the scrollbars if the contents of the `ScrollPane` are larger than what is visible.

SCROLLBARS_NEVER

```
public final static int SCROLLBARS_NEVER
```

Don't ever show the scrollbars. The `ScrollPane` can still be scrolled programmatically.

Constructors

ScrollPane

```
public ScrollPane()
```

Description   Constructs a `ScrollPane` object with `SCROLLBARS_AS_NEEDED`.

```
public ScrollPane (int scrollbarDisplayPolicy)
```

Parameters   *scrollbarDisplayPolicy*

                    One of the `SCROLLBARS_` constants.

Description   Constructs a `ScrollPane` object with the specified scrollbar display policy.

Instance Methods

addImpl

```
protected final void addImpl (Component comp, Object constraints,
int index)
```

Parameters	*comp*	The component to add to the `Scrollpane`.
	constraints	Layout constraints; ignored.
	index	The position at which to add the component; should always be less than or equal to 0.
Returns		The component that was added.
Overrides		`Container.addImpl (Component, Object, int)`
Throws		*IllegalArgumentException*
		If pos is greater than 0.

Description   Adds a child component to the Scrollpane. If there already was
a child component, it is replaced by the new component.

addNotify

`public void addNotify()`

Overrides   `Container.addNotify()`
Description   Creates ScrollPane's peer.

doLayout

`public void doLayout()`

Overrides   `Container.doLayout()`
Description   Lays out the ScrollPane. Resizes the child component to its
preferred size.

getHAdjustable

`public Adjustable getHAdjustable()`

Returns   The object implementing the Adjustable interface that is used
to adjust the ScrollPane horizontally. Usually this is a Scrollbar.

getHScrollbarHeight

`public int getHScrollbarHeight()`

Returns   The height a horizontal scrollbar would occupy, regardless of
whether it's shown or not.

getScrollPosition

`public Point getScrollPosition()`

Returns   Returns the position within the child component that is displayed at 0, 0 in the ScrollPane.

getScrollbarDisplayPolicy

`public int getScrollbarDisplayPolicy()`

Returns   The display policy for the scrollbars (one of the SCROLLBARS_
constants).

getVAdjustable

public Adjustable getVAdjustable()

Returns   The object implementing the Adjustable interface that is used to adjust the ScrollPane vertically. Usually this is a Scrollbar.

getVScrollbarWidth

public int getVScrollbarWidth()

Returns   The width a vertical scrollbar would occupy, regardless of whether it's shown or not.

getViewportSize

public Dimension getViewportSize()

Returns   The size of the ScrollPane's port (the area of the child component that is shown).

layout

public void layout() ☆

Overrides   Container.layout()
Description   Lays out component. Replaced by doLayout().

paramString

public String paramString()

Returns   String with current settings of ScrollPane.
Overrides   Container.paramString()
Description   Helper method for toString() to generate string of current settings.

printComponents

public void printComponents (Graphics g)

Parameters   g   Graphics context.
Overrides   Container.printComponents(Graphics)
Description   Prints the ScrollPane's child component.

setLayout

public void setLayout (LayoutManager manager)

Parameters	*manager*	Ignored.
Overrides	Container.setLayout(LayoutManager)	
Description	Does nothing. No layout manager is needed because there is only one child component.	

setScrollPosition

public void setScrollPosition (int x, int y)

Parameters	*x*	New horizontal position.
	y	New vertical position.
Throws	*IllegalArgumentException*	
	If the point given is not valid.	
Description	Scroll to the given position in the child component.	

public void setScrollPosition (Point p)

Parameters	*p*	New position.
Throws	*IllegalArgumentException*	
	If the point given is not valid.	
Description	Scroll to the given position in the child component.	

See Also

Adjustable, Container, Point, Scrollbar

19.54   Scrollbar

Description

The Scrollbar is a Component that provides the means to get and set values within a predetermined range. For example, a scrollbar could be used for a volume control. Scrollbars are most frequently used to help users manipulate areas too large to be displayed on the screen (pre version 1.1) or to set a value within an integer range.

Class Definition

```
public class java.awt.Scrollbar
    extends java.awt.Component
    implements java.awt.Adjustable {

// Constants
public final static int HORIZONTAL;
public final static int VERTICAL;

// Constructors
public Scrollbar();
public Scrollbar (int orientation);
public Scrollbar (int orientation, int value, int visible, int minimum,
    int maximum);

// Instance Methods
public void addAdjustmentListener (AdjustmentListener l); ★
public void addNotify();
public int getBlockIncrement(); ★
public int getLineIncrement(); ☆
public int getMaximum();
public int getMinimum();
public int getOrientation();
public int getPageIncrement(); ☆
public int getUnitIncrement(); ★
public int getValue();
public int getVisible(); ☆
public int getVisibleAmount(); ★
public void removeAdjustmentListener (AdjustmentListener l); ★
public synchronized void setBlockIncrement (int v); ★
public void setLineIncrement (int amount); ☆
public synchronized void setMaximum (int newMaximum); ★
public synchronized void setMinimum (int newMinimum); ★
public synchronized void setOrientation (int orientation); ★
public void setPageIncrement (int amount); ☆
public synchronized void setUnitIncrement(int v); ★
public synchronized void setValue (int value);
public synchronized void setValues (int value, int visible,
    int minimum, int maximum);
public synchronized void setVisibleAmount (int newAmount); ★

// Protected Instance Methods
protected String paramString();
protected void processAdjustmentEvent (AdjustmentEvent e); ★
protected void processEvent (AWTEvent e); ★
}
```

Constants

HORIZONTAL

public final static int HORIZONTAL

Constant used for a Scrollbar with a horizontal orientation.

VERTICAL

public final static int VERTICAL

Constant used for a Scrollbar with a vertical orientation.

Constructors

Scrollbar

public Scrollbar()

Description	Constructs a vertical Scrollbar object; slider size, minimum value, maximum value, and initial value are all zero.

public Scrollbar (int orientation)

Parameters	*orientation*	Scrollbar constant designating direction.
Throws	*IllegalArgumentException*	
		If orientation is invalid.
Description	Constructs a Scrollbar object, in the designated direction; slider size, minimum value, maximum value, and initial value are all zero.	

public Scrollbar (int orientation, int value, int visible, int minimum, int maximum)

Parameters	*orientation*	Scrollbar constant designating direction.
	value	Initial value of Scrollbar.
	visible	Initial slider size.
	minimum	Initial minimum value.
	maximum	Initial maximum value.
Throws	*IllegalArgumentException*	
		If orientation is invalid.
Description	Constructs a Scrollbar object with the given values.	

Instance Methods

addAdjustmentListener

```
public void addAdjustmentListener (AdjustmentListener l) ★
```

Parameters	*l*	An object that implements the AdjustmentListener interface.
Implements	Adjustable.addAdjustmentListener()	
Description	Add a listener for adjustment event.	

addNotify

```
public void addNotify()
```

Overrides	Component.addNotify()
Description	Creates Scrollbar's peer.

getBlockIncrement

```
public int getBlockIncrement() ★
```

Implements	Adjustable.getBlockIncrement()
Returns	The amount to scroll when a paging area is selected.

getLineIncrement

```
public int getLineIncrement() ☆
```

Returns	The amount to scroll when one of the arrows at the ends of the scrollbar is selected. Replaced by getUnitIncrement().

getMaximum

```
public int getMaximum()
```

Implements	Adjustable.getMaximum()
Returns	The maximum value that the Scrollbar can take.

getMinimum

```
public int getMinimum()
```

Implements	Adjustable.getMinimum()
Returns	The minimum value that the Scrollbar can take.

getOrientation

```
public int getOrientation()
```

Implements   `Adjustable.getOrientation()`

Returns   A constant representing the direction of the `Scrollbar`.

getPageIncrement

```
public int getPageIncrement() ☆
```

Returns   The amount to scroll when a paging area is selected. Replaced with `getBlockIncrement()`.

getUnitIncrement

```
public int getUnitIncrement() ★
```

Implements   `Adjustable.getUnitIncrement()`

Returns   The amount to scroll when one of the arrows at the ends of the scrollbar is selected.

getValue

```
public int getValue()
```

Implements   `Adjustable.getValue()`

Returns   The current setting for the `Scrollbar`.

getVisible

```
public int getVisible() ☆
```

Returns   The current visible setting (i.e., size) for the slider. Replaced by `getVisibleAmount()`.

getVisibleAmount

```
public int getVisibleAmount() ★
```

Implements   `Adjustable.getVisibleAmount()`

Returns   The current visible setting (i.e., size) for the slider.

removeAdjustmentListener

```
public void removeAdjustmentListener (AdjustmentListener l) ★
```

Parameters   *l*   One of this `Scrollbar`'s `AdjustmentListeners`.

Implements   `Adjustable.removeAdjustmentListener()`

Description   Remove an adjustment event listener.

setBlockIncrement

public synchronized void setBlockIncrement (int amount) ★

Parameters   *amount*   New paging increment amount.
Implements   Adjustable.setBlockIncrement()
Description   Changes the block increment amount for the Scrollbar; the
               default block increment is 10.

setLineIncrement

public void setLineIncrement (int amount) ☆

Parameters   *amount*   New line increment amount.
Description   Changes the line increment amount for the Scrollbar. The
               default line increment is 1. Replaced by setUnitIncre-
               ment(int).

setMaximum

public synchronized void setMaximum (int newMaximum) ★

Parameters   *newMaximum*   New maximum value.
Implements   Adjustable.setMaximum()
Description   Changes the maximum value for the Scrollbar.

setMinimum

public synchronized void setMinimum (int newMinimum) ★

Parameters   *newMinimum*   New minimum value.
Implements   Adjustable.setMinimum()
Description   Changes the minimum value for the Scrollbar.

setOrientation

public synchronized void setOrientation (int orientation) ★

Parameters   *orientation*   One of the orientation constants HORIZONTAL or
                                 VERTICAL.
Description   Changes the orientation of the Scrollbar.

setPageIncrement

public void setPageIncrement (int amount) ☆

Parameters   *amount*   New paging increment amount.
Description   Changes the paging increment amount for the Scrollbar; the
               default page increment is 10. Replaced by setBlockIncre-
               ment(int).

setUnitIncrement

public synchronized void setUnitIncrement (int amount) ★

Parameters	*amount*	New line increment amount.
Implements	Adjustable.setUnitIncrement()	
Description	Changes the unit increment amount for the Scrollbar. The default unit increment is 1.	

setValue

public synchronized void setValue (int value)

Parameters	*value*	New Scrollbar value.
Implements	Adjustable.setValue()	
Description	Changes the current value of the Scrollbar.	

setValues

public synchronized void setValues (int value, int visible, int minimum, int maximum)

Parameters	*value*	New Scrollbar value.
	visible	New slider width.
	minimum	New minimum value for Scrollbar.
	maximum	New maximum value for Scrollbar.
Description	Changes the settings of the Scrollbar to the given amounts.	

setVisibleAmount

public synchronized void setVisibleAmount (int newAmount) ★

Parameters	*newAmount*	New amount visible.
Implements	Adjustable.setVisibleAmount()	
Description	Changes the current visible amount of the Scrollbar.	

Protected Instance Methods

paramString

protected String paramString()

Returns	String with current settings of Scrollbar.
Overrides	Component.paramString()
Description	Helper method for toString() to generate string of current settings.

processAdjustmentEvent

protected void processAdjustmentEvent (AdjustmentEvent e) ★

Parameters   *e*   The adjustment event to process.
Description   Adjustment events are passed to this method for processing.
                 Normally, this method is called by processEvent().

processEvent

protected void processEvent (AWTEvent e) ★

Parameters   *e*   The event to process.
Description   Low level AWTEvents are passed to this method for processing.

See Also

Adjustable, Component, String

19.55   *Shape* ★

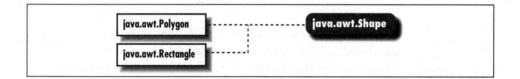

Description

Shape is an interface describing a two-dimensional geometric shape.

Interface Definition

```
public abstract interface java.awt.Shape {

  // Interface Methods
  public abstract Rectangle getBounds();
}
```

Interface Methods

getBounds

public abstract Rectangle getBounds()

Returns   A Rectangle that completely encloses the shape.

See Also

Polygon, Rectangle

19.56   *SystemColor* ★

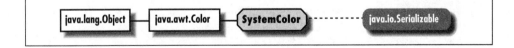

Description

SystemColor provides information on the colors that the windowing system uses to display windows and other graphic components. Most windowing systems allow the user to choose different color schemes; SystemColor enables programs to find out what colors are in use in order to paint themselves in a consistent manner.

Class Definition

```
public final class java.awt.SystemColor
    extends java.awt.Color
    implements java.io.Serializable {

// Constants
public final static int ACTIVE_CAPTION;
public final static int ACTIVE_CAPTION_BORDER;
public final static int ACTIVE_CAPTION_TEXT;
public final static int CONTROL;
public final static int CONTROL_DK_SHADOW;
public final static int CONTROL_HIGHLIGHT;
public final static int CONTROL_LT_HIGHLIGHT;
public final static int CONTROL_SHADOW;
public final static int CONTROL_TEXT;
public final static int DESKTOP;
public final static int INACTIVE_CAPTION;
public final static int INACTIVE_CAPTION_BORDER;
public final static int INACTIVE_CAPTION_TEXT;
public final static int INFO;
public final static int INFO_TEXT;
public final static int MENU;
public final static int MENU_TEXT;
public final static int NUM_COLORS;
public final static int SCROLLBAR;
public final static int TEXT;
public final static int TEXT_HIGHLIGHT;
public final static int TEXT_HIGHLIGHT_TEXT;
public final static int TEXT_INACTIVE_TEXT;
public final static int TEXT_TEXT;
```

```
    public final static int WINDOW;
    public final static int WINDOW_BORDER;
    public final static int WINDOW_TEXT;
    public final static SystemColor activeCaption;
    public final static SystemColor activeCaptionBorder;
    public final static SystemColor activeCaptionText;
    public final static SystemColor control;
    public final static SystemColor controlDkShadow;
    public final static SystemColor controlHighlight;
    public final static SystemColor controlLtHighlight;
    public final static SystemColor controlShadow;
    public final static SystemColor controlText;
    public final static SystemColor desktop;
    public final static SystemColor inactiveCaption;
    public final static SystemColor inactiveCaptionBorder;
    public final static SystemColor inactiveCaptionText;
    public final static SystemColor info;
    public final static SystemColor infoText;
    public final static SystemColor menu;
    public final static SystemColor menuText;
    public final static SystemColor scrollbar;
    public final static SystemColor text;
    public final static SystemColor textHighlight;
    public final static SystemColor textHighlightText;
    public final static SystemColor textInactiveText;
    public final static SystemColor textText;
    public final static SystemColor window;
    public final static SystemColor windowBorder;
    public final static SystemColor windowText;

    // Public Instance Methods
    public int getRGB();
    public String toString();
}
```

Constants

ACTIVE_CAPTION

```
public static final int ACTIVE_CAPTION
```

ACTIVE_CAPTION_BORDER

```
public static final int ACTIVE_CAPTION_BORDER
```

ACTIVE_CAPTION_TEXT

public static final int ACTIVE_CAPTION_TEXT

CONTROL

public static final int CONTROL

CONTROL_DK_SHADOW

public static final int CONTROL_DK_SHADOW

CONTROL_HIGHLIGHT

public static final int CONTROL_HIGHLIGHT

CONTROL_LT_HIGHLIGHT

public static final int CONTROL_LT_HIGHLIGHT

CONTROL_SHADOW

public static final int CONTROL_SHADOW

CONTROL_TEXT

public static final int CONTROL_TEXT

DESKTOP

public static final int DESKTOP

INACTIVE_CAPTION

public static final int INACTIVE_CAPTION

INACTIVE_CAPTION_BORDER

public static final int INACTIVE_CAPTION_BORDER

INACTIVE_CAPTION_TEXT

public static final int INACTIVE_CAPTION_TEXT

INFO

```
public static final int INFO
```

INFO_TEXT

```
public static final int INFO_TEXT
```

MENU

```
public static final int MENU
```

MENU_TEXT

```
public static final int MENU_TEXT
```

NUM_COLORS

```
public static final int NUM_COLORS
```

SCROLLBAR

```
public static final int SCROLLBAR
```

TEXT

```
public static final int TEXT
```

TEXT_HIGHLIGHT

```
public static final int TEXT_HIGHLIGHT
```

TEXT_HIGHLIGHT_TEXT

```
public static final int TEXT_HIGHLIGHT_TEXT
```

TEXT_INACTIVE_TEXT

```
public static final int TEXT_INACTIVE_TEXT
```

TEXT_TEXT

```
public static final int TEXT_TEXT
```

WINDOW

    public static final int WINDOW

WINDOW_BORDER

    public static final int WINDOW_BORDER

WINDOW_TEXT

    public static final int WINDOW_TEXT

activeCaption

    public static final SystemColor activeCaption

Background color for captions in window borders.

activeCaptionBorder

    public static final SystemColor activeCaptionBorder

Border color for captions in window borders.

activeCaptionText

    public static final SystemColor activeCaptionText

Text color for captions in window borders.

control

    public static final SystemColor control

Background color for controls.

controlDkShadow

    public static final SystemColor controlDkShadow

Dark shadow color for controls.

controlHighlight

    public static final SystemColor controlHighlight

Highlight color for controls.

controlLtHighlight

public static final SystemColor controlLtHighlight

Light highlight color for controls.

controlShadow

public static final SystemColor controlShadow

Shadow color for controls.

controlText

public static final SystemColor controlText

Text color for controls.

desktop

public static final SystemColor desktop

Desktop background color.

inactiveCaption

public static final SystemColor inactiveCaption

Background color for inactive captions in window borders.

inactiveCaptionBorder

public static final SystemColor inactiveCaptionBorder

Border color for inactive captions in window borders.

inactiveCaptionText

public static final SystemColor inactiveCaptionText

Text color for inactive captions in window borders.

info

public static final SystemColor info

Background color for informational text.

infoText

public static final SystemColor infoText

Text color for informational text.

menu

    public static final SystemColor menu

    Background color for menus.

menuText

    public static final SystemColor menuText

    Text color for menus.

scrollbar

    public static final SystemColor scrollbar

    Background color for scrollbars.

text

    public static final SystemColor text

    Background color for text components.

textHighlight

    public static final SystemColor textHighlight

    Background color for highlighted text.

textHighlightText

    public static final SystemColor textHighlightText

    Text color for highlighted text.

textInactiveText

    public static final SystemColor textInactiveText

    Text color for inactive text.

textText

    public static final SystemColor textText

    Text color for text components.

window

    public static final SystemColor window

    Background color for windows.

windowBorder

   public static final SystemColor windowBorder

Border color for windows.

windowText

   public static final SystemColor windowText

Text color for windows.

Instance Methods

getRGB

   public int getRGB()

Returns	Current color as a composite value
Overrides	Color.getRGB()
Description	Gets integer value of current system color.

toString

   public String toString()

Returns	A string representation of the SystemColor object.
Overrides	Color.toString()

See Also

Color, Serializable, String

19.57   TextArea

Description

The TextArea class provides a multi-line Component for textual user input.

Class Definition

```
public class java.awt.TextArea
    extends java.awt.TextComponent {

    // Constants
    public final static int SCROLLBARS_BOTH;  ★
    public final static int SCROLLBARS_HORIZONTAL_ONLY;  ★
    public final static int SCROLLBARS_NONE;  ★
```

```
public final static int SCROLLBARS_VERTICAL_ONLY; ★

// Constructors
public TextArea ();
public TextArea (int rows, int columns);
public TextArea (String text);
public TextArea (String text, int rows, int columns);
public TextArea (String text, int rows, int columns, int scrollbars); ★

// Instance Methods
public void addNotify();
public synchronized void append (String string); ★
public void appendText (String string); ☆
public int getColumns();
public Dimension getMinimumSize(); ★
public Dimension getMinimumSize (int rows, int columns); ★
public Dimension getPreferredSize(); ★
public Dimension getPreferredSize (int rows, int columns); ★
public int getRows();
public int getScrollbarVisibility(); ★
public synchronized void insert (String string, int position); ★
public void insertText (String string, int position); ☆
public Dimension minimumSize(); ☆
public Dimension minimumSize (int rows, int columns); ☆
public Dimension preferredSize(); ☆
public Dimension preferredSize (int rows, int columns); ☆
public synchronized void replaceRange (String str, int start, int end); ★
public void replaceText (String string, int startPosition, int endPosition); ☆
public void setColumns (int columns); ★
public void setRows (int rows); ★

// Protected Instance Methods
protected String paramString();
}
```

Constants

SCROLLBARS_BOTH

public final static int SCROLLBARS_BOTH ★

Show both the horizontal and vertical scrollbars.

SCROLLBARS_HORIZONTAL_ONLY

public final static int SCROLLBARS_HORIZONTAL_ONLY ★

Show the horizontal scrollbar.

SCROLLBARS_NONE

public final static int SCROLLBARS_NONE ★

Show no scrollbars.

SCROLLBARS_VERTICAL_ONLY

public final static int SCROLLBARS_VERTICAL_ONLY ★

Show the vertical scrollbar.

Constructors

TextArea

public TextArea()

Description	Constructs a TextArea object with the default size and no initial content. The default size of a text area varies widely from platform to platform, so it's best to avoid this constructor.

public TextArea (int rows, int columns)

Parameters	*rows*	Requested number of displayed rows.
	columns	Requested number of displayed columns.
Description		Constructs a TextArea object of the given size and no initial content.

public TextArea (String text)

Parameters	*text*	Initial text for TextArea.
Description		Constructs a TextArea object with the given initial content.

public TextArea (String text, int rows, int columns)

Parameters	*text*	Initial text for TextArea.
	rows	Requested number of displayed rows.
	columns	Requested number of displayed columns.
Description		Constructs a TextArea object with the given content and size.

public TextArea (String text, int rows, int columns, int scrollbars) ★

Parameters	*text*	Initial text for TextArea.
	rows	Requested number of displayed rows.
	columns	Requested number of displayed columns.
	scrollbars	Requested scrollbar visibility. Use one of the constants defined.
Description		Constructs a TextArea object with the given content, size, and scrollbar visibility.

Instance Methods

addNotify

```
public void addNotify()
```

Overrides   Component.addNotify()
Description   Creates TextArea's peer.

append

```
public synchronized void append (String string) ★
```

Parameters   *string*   Content to append to the end of the TextArea.
Description   Appends the given text string to the text already displayed in
                  the TextArea.

appendText

```
public void appendText (String string) ☆
```

Parameters   *string*   Content to append to end of TextArea.
Description   Replaced by append(String).

getColumns

```
public int getColumns()
```

Returns   The width of the TextArea in columns.

getMinimumSize

```
public Dimension getMinimumSize() ★
```

Returns   The minimum dimensions of the TextArea.

```
public Dimension getMinimumSize (int rows, int columns) ★
```

Parameters   *rows*   Number of rows within TextArea to size.
                 columns   Number of columns within TextArea to size.
Returns   The minimum dimensions of a TextArea of the given size.

getPreferredSize

```
public Dimension getPreferredSize() ★
```

Returns   The preferred dimensions of the TextArea.

```
public Dimension getPreferredSize (int rows, int columns) ★
```

Parameters   *rows*   Number of rows within TextArea to size.

          columns   Number of columns within `TextArea` to size.

Returns   The preferred dimensions of a `TextArea` of the given size.

getRows

```
public int getRows()
```

Returns   The height of the `TextArea` in rows.

getScrollbarVisibility

```
public int getScrollbarVisibility() ★
```

Returns   One of the `SCROLLBAR_` constants indicating which scrollbars are visible.

insert

```
public synchronized void insert (String string, int position) ★
```

Parameters   *string*   Content to place within `TextArea` content.
                    position   Location to insert content.
Description   Places additional text within the `TextArea` at the given position.

insertText

```
public void insertText (String string, int position) ☆
```

Parameters   *string*   Content to place within `TextArea` content.
                    position   Location to insert content.
Description   Places additional text within the `TextArea` at the given position. Replaced by `insert(String, int)`.

minimumSize

```
public Dimension minimumSize() ☆
```

Returns   The minimum dimensions of the `TextArea`. Replaced by `get-MinimumSize()`.

```
public Dimension minimumSize (int rows, int columns) ☆
```

Parameters   *rows*   Number of rows within `TextArea` to size.
                    columns   Number of columns within `TextArea` to size.
Returns   The minimum dimensions of a `TextArea` of the given size. Replaced by `getMinimumSize(int, int)`.

preferredSize

public Dimension preferredSize() ☆

Returns   The preferred dimensions of the TextArea. Replaced by get-
                 PreferredSize().

public Dimension preferredSize (int rows, int columns) ☆

Parameters   *rows*   Number of rows within TextArea to size.
              columns   Number of columns within TextArea to size.
Returns   The preferred dimensions of a TextArea of the given size.
                 Replaced by getPreferredSize(int, int).

replaceRange

public synchronized void replaceRange (String str, int start, int
end) ★

Parameters   *str*   New content to place in TextArea.
              start   Starting position of content to replace.
              end   Ending position of content to replace.
Description   Replaces a portion of the TextArea's content with the given
                 text.

replaceText

public void replaceText (String string, int startPosition, int
endPosition) ☆

Parameters   *string*   New content to place in TextArea.
              startPosition Starting position of content to replace.
              endPosition   Ending position of content to replace.
Description   Replaces a portion of the TextArea's content with the given
                 text. Replaced by replaceRange(String, int, int).

setColumns

public void setColumns (int columns) ★

Parameters   *columns*   New number of columns.
Throws   *IllegalArgumentException*
                              If columns is less than zero.
Description   Changes the number of columns.

setRows

    public void setRows (int rows) ★

Parameters	*rows*	New number of columns.
Throws	*IllegalArgumentException*	
		If rows is less than zero.
Description	Changes the number of rows.	

Protected Instance Methods

paramString

    protected String paramString()

Returns	String with current settings of TextArea.
Overrides	TextComponent.paramString()
Description	Helper method for toString() to generate string of current settings.

See Also

Dimension, TextComponent, String

19.58   TextComponent

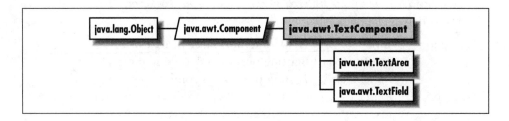

Description

The abstract TextComponent class provides the base class for the text input components, TextArea and TextField.

Class Definition

```
public abstract class java.awt.TextComponent
    extends java.awt.Component {

  // Instance Methods
  public synchronized void addTextListener (TextListener l); ★
  public int getCaretPosition(); ★
  public synchronized String getSelectedText();
  public synchronized int getSelectionEnd();
```

```
    public synchronized int getSelectionStart();
    public synchronized String getText();
    public boolean isEditable();
    public void removeNotify();
    public void removeTextListener (TextListener l); ★
    public synchronized void select (int selectionStart, int selectionEnd);
    public synchronized void selectAll();
    public void setCaretPosition (int position); ★
    public synchronized void setEditable (boolean state);
    public synchronized void setSelectionEnd (int selectionEnd); ★
    public synchronized void setSelectionStart (int selectionStart); ★
    public synchronized void setText (String text);

    // Protected Instance Methods
    protected String paramString();
    protected void processEvent (AWTEvent e); ★
    protected void processTextEvent (TextEvent e); ★
}
```

Instance Methods

addTextListener

public synchronized void addTextListener (TextListener l) ★

Parameters   *l*   An object that implements the TextListener
                               interface.

Description   Add a listener for the text events.

getCaretPosition

public int getCaretPosition() ★

Returns   The position, in characters, of the caret (text cursor).

getSelectedText

public synchronized String getSelectedText()

Returns   The currently selected text of the TextComponent.

getSelectionEnd

public synchronized int getSelectionEnd()

Returns   The ending cursor position of any selected text.

getSelectionStart

`public synchronized int getSelectionStart()`

Returns   The initial position of any selected text.

getText

`public synchronized String getText()`

Returns   Current contents of the TextComponent.

isEditable

`public boolean isEditable()`

Returns   true if editable, false otherwise.

removeNotify

`public void removeNotify()`

Description   Destroys the peer of the TextComponent.

removeTextListener

`public void removeTextListener (TextListener l)` ★

Parameters   *l*   One of this TextComponent's TextListeners.
Description   Remove a text event listener.

select

`public synchronized void select (int selectionStart, int selectionEnd)`

Parameters   *selectionStart*   Beginning position of text to select.
              selectionEnd   Ending position of text to select.
Description   Selects text in the TextComponent.

selectAll

`public synchronized void selectAll()`

Description   Selects all the text in the TextComponent.

setCaretPosition

`public void setCaretPosition (int position)` ★

Parameters   *position*   The new character position for the caret.

Throws   *IllegalArgumentException*
                      If position is less than zero.
Description   Allows you to change the location of the caret.

setEditable

```
public synchronized void setEditable (boolean state)
```

Parameters   *state*   true to allow the user to edit the text in the
                                 TextComponent; false to prevent editing.
Description   Allows you to make the TextComponent editable or read-only.

setSelectionEnd

```
public synchronized void setSelectionEnd (int selectionEnd) ★
```

Parameters   *selectionEnd*   The character position of the end of the selec-
                                 tion.
Description   Allows you to change the location of the end of the selected
              text.

setSelectionStart

```
public synchronized void setSelectionStart (int selectionStart) ★
```

Parameters   *selectionStart* The character position of the start of the selec-
                                 tion.
Description   Allows you to change the location of the start of the selected
              text.

setText

```
public synchronized void setText (String text)
```

Parameters   *text*   New text for TextComponent.
Description   Sets the content of the TextComponent.

Protected Instance Methods

paramString

```
protected String paramString()
```

Returns   String with current settings of TextComponent.
Overrides   Component.paramString()
Description   Helper method for toString() to generate string of current
              settings.

processEvent

> protected void processEvent (AWTEvent e) ★

Parameters	*e*	The event to process.
Description		Low-level AWTEvents are passed to this method for processing.

processTextEvent

> protected void processTextEvent (TextEvent e) ★

Parameters	*e*	The event to process.
Description		Text events are passed to this method for processing. Normally, this method is called by processEvent().

See Also

Component, TextArea, TextField, String

19.59   *TextField*

Description

The TextField class provides a single line Component for user input.

Class Definition

```
public class java.awt.TextField
    extends java.awt.TextComponent {

    // Constructors
    public TextField();
    public TextField (int columns);
    public TextField (String text);
    public TextField (String text, int columns);

    // Instance Methods
    public void addActionListener (ActionListener l); ★
    public void addNotify();
    public boolean echoCharIsSet();
    public int getColumns();
    public char getEchoChar();
    public Dimension getMinimumSize(); ★
    public Dimension getMinimumSize (int columns); ★
    public Dimension getPreferredSize(); ★
```

```
    public Dimension getPreferredSize (int columns); ★
    public Dimension minimumSize(); ☆
    public Dimension minimumSize (int columns); ☆
    public Dimension preferredSize(); ☆
    public Dimension preferredSize (int columns); ☆
    public void removeActionListener (ActionListener l); ★
    public void setColumns(int columns); ★
    public void setEchoChar(char c); ★
    public void setEchoCharacter (char c); ☆

    // Protected Instance Methods
    protected String paramString();
    protected void processActionEvent (ActionEvent e); ★
    protected void processEvent (AWTEvent e); ★
}
```

Constructors

TextField

public TextField()

Description   Constructs a TextField object of the default size.

public TextField (int columns)

Parameters   *columns*   Requested number of displayed columns.
Description   Constructs a TextField object of the given size.

public TextField (String text)

Parameters   *text*   Initial text for TextField.
Description   Constructs a TextField object with the given content.

public TextField (String text, int columns)

Parameters   *text*   Initial text for TextField.
              columns   Requested number of displayed columns.
Description   Constructs a TextField object with the given content and size.

Instance Methods

addActionListener

public void addActionListener (ActionListener l) ★

Parameters   *l*   An object that implements the ActionListener
                     interface.
Description   Add a listener for the action event.

addNotify

`public synchronized void addNotify()`

Overrides   `Component.addNotify()`

Description   Creates `TextField`'s peer.

echoCharIsSet

`public boolean echoCharIsSet()`

Returns   true if the `TextField` has an echo character used as a response to any input character; `false` otherwise. An echo character can be used to create a `TextField` for hidden input, like a password; the same character (e.g., "x") is used to echo all input.

getColumns

`public int getColumns()`

Returns   The width of the `TextField` in columns.

getEchoChar

`public char getEchoChar()`

Returns   The current echo character.

getMinimumSize

`public Dimension getMinimumSize() ★`

Returns   The minimum dimensions of the `TextField`.

`public Dimension getMinimumSize (int columns) ★`

Parameters   columns   Number of columns within `TextField` to size.

Returns   The minimum dimensions of a `TextField` of the given size.

getPreferredSize

`public Dimension getPreferredSize() ★`

Returns   The preferred dimensions of the `TextField`.

`public Dimension getPreferredSize (int columns) ★`

Parameters   columns   Number of columns within `TextField` to size.

Returns   The preferred dimensions of a `TextField` of the given size.

minimumSize

public Dimension minimumSize() ☆

Returns	The minimum dimensions of the TextField. Replaced by get-MinimumSize().

public Dimension minimumSize (int columns) ☆

Parameters	*columns*	Number of columns within TextField to size.
Returns		The minimum dimensions of a TextField of the given size. Replaced by getMinimumSize(int).

preferredSize

public Dimension preferredSize() ☆

Returns	The preferred dimensions of the TextField. Replaced by get-PreferredSize().

public Dimension preferredSize (int columns) ☆

Parameters	*columns*	Number of columns within TextField to size.
Returns		The preferred dimensions of a TextField of the given size. Replaced by getPreferredSize(int).

removeActionListener

public void removeActionListener (ActionListener l) ★

Parameters	*l*	One of this TextField's ActionListeners.
Description		Remove an action event listener.

setColumns

public void setColumns (int columns) ★

Parameters	*columns*	New number of columns.
Throws	*IllegalArgumentException*	
		If columns is less than zero.
Description		Changes the number of columns.

setEchoChar

public void setEchoChar (char c) ★

Parameters	*c*	The character to echo for all input. To echo the characters that the user types (the default), set the echo character to 0 (zero).

Description   Changes the character that is used to echo all user input in the
                TextField.

setEchoCharacter

public void setEchoCharacter (char c) ☆

Parameters   *c*   The character to echo for all input. To echo the
                                characters that the user types (the default), set
                                the echo character to 0 (zero).
Description   Replaced by setEchoChar(char) for consistency with getEcho-
                Char().

Protected Instance Methods

paramString

protected String paramString()

Returns   String with current settings of TextField.
Overrides   TextComponent.paramString()
Description   Helper method for toString() to generate string of current
                settings.

processActionEvent

protected void processActionEvent (ActionEvent e) ★

Parameters   *e*   The action event to process.
Description   Action events are passed to this method for processing. Nor-
                mally, this method is called by processEvent().

processEvent

protected void processEvent (AWTEvent e) ★

Parameters   *e*   The event to process.
Description   Low-level AWTEvents are passed to this method for processing.

See Also

Dimension, TextComponent, String

19.60   Toolkit

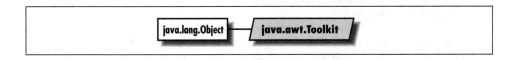

Description

The abstract Toolkit class provides access to platform-specific details like window size and available fonts. It also deals with creating all the components' peer objects when you call addNotify().

Class Definition

```
public abstract class java.awt.Toolkit
    extends java.lang.Object {

// Class Methods
public static synchronized Toolkit getDefaultToolkit();
protected static Container getNativeContainer (Component c); ★
public static String getProperty (String key, String defaultValue); ★

// Instance Methods
public abstract void beep(); ★
public abstract int checkImage (Image image, int width, int height,
  ImageObserver observer);
public abstract Image createImage (ImageProducer producer);
public Image createImage (byte[] imagedata); ★
public abstract Image createImage (byte[ ] imagedata, int imageoffset,
    int imagelength); ★
public abstract ColorModel getColorModel();
public abstract String[] getFontList();
public abstract FontMetrics getFontMetrics (Font font);
public abstract Image getImage (String filename);
public abstract Image getImage (URL url);
public int getMenuShortcutKeyMask(); ★
public abstract PrintJob getPrintJob (Frame frame, String jobtitle,
  Properties props); ★
public abstract int getScreenResolution();
public abstract Dimension getScreenSize();
public abstract Clipboard getSystemClipboard(); ★
public final EventQueue getSystemEventQueue(); ★
public abstract boolean prepareImage (Image image, int width, int height,
  ImageObserver observer);
public abstract void sync();

// Protected Instance Methods
protected abstract ButtonPeer createButton (Button b);
```

```
    protected abstract CanvasPeer createCanvas (Canvas c);
    protected abstract CheckboxPeer createCheckbox (Checkbox cb);
    protected abstract CheckboxMenuItemPeer createCheckboxMenuItem
      (CheckboxMenuItem cmi);
    protected abstract ChoicePeer createChoice (Choice c);
    protected LightweightPeer createComponent(Component target); ★
    protected abstract DialogPeer createDialog (Dialog d);
    protected abstract FileDialogPeer createFileDialog (FileDialog fd);
    protected abstract FramePeer createFrame (Frame f);
    protected abstract LabelPeer createLabel (Label l);
    protected abstract ListPeer createList (List l);
    protected abstract MenuPeer createMenu (Menu m);
    protected abstract MenuBarPeer createMenuBar (MenuBar mb);
    protected abstract MenuItemPeer createMenuItem (MenuItem mi);
    protected abstract PanelPeer createPanel (Panel p);
    protected abstract PopupMenuPeer createPopupMenu (PopupMenu target); ★
    protected abstract ScrollPanePeer createScrollPane (ScrollPane target);  ★
    protected abstract ScrollbarPeer createScrollbar (Scrollbar sb);
    protected abstract TextAreaPeer createTextArea (TextArea ta);
    protected abstract TextFieldPeer createTextField (TextField tf);
    protected abstract WindowPeer createWindow (Window w);
    protected abstract FontPeer getFontPeer (String name, int style); ★
    protected abstract EventQueue getSystemEventQueueImpl(); ★
    protected void loadSystemColors (int[] systemColors);  ★
}
```

Class Methods

getDefaultToolkit

public static synchronized Toolkit getDefaultToolkit()

Throws	*AWTError*	If the toolkit for the current platform cannot be found.
Returns		The system's default Toolkit.

getNativeContainer

protected static Container getNativeContainer (Component c) ★

Returns	The native container for the given component. The component's immediate parent may be a lightweight component.

getProperty

public static String getProperty (String key,
String defaultValue) ★

Parameters	*key*	The name of a property.
	defaultValue	A default value to return if the property is not found.
Returns		The value of the property described by key, or defaultValue if it is not found.

Instance Methods

beep

```
public abstract void beep() ★
```

Description   Produces an audible beep.

checkImage

```
public abstract int checkImage (Image image, int width, int
height, ImageObserver observer)
```

Parameters	*image*	Image to check.
	width	Width of the scaled image; -1 if image will be rendered unscaled.
	height	Height of the scaled image; -1 if image will be rendered unscaled.
	observer	The Component that image will be rendered on.
Returns		The ImageObserver flags ORed together for the data that is now available.
Description		Checks on the status of the construction of a screen representation of image on observer.

createImage

```
public abstract Image createImage (ImageProducer producer)
```

Parameters	*producer*	An ImageProducer that generates data for the desired image.
Returns		Newly created Image.
Description		Creates a new Image from an ImageProducer.

```
public abstract Image createImage (byte[] imagedata) ★
```

Parameters	*imagedata*	Raw data representing an image.
Returns		Newly created Image.
Description		Creates a new Image from the imagedata provided.

```
public abstract Image createImage (byte[] imagedata,
int imageoffset, int imagelength) ★
```

Parameters *imagedata* Raw data representing one or more images.
      imageoffset An offset into the data given.
      imagelength The length of data to use.
Returns   Newly created `Image`.
Description Creates a new `Image` from the `imagedata` provided, starting at `imageoffset` bytes and reading `imagelength` bytes.

getColorModel

```
public abstract ColorModel getColorModel()
```

Returns   The current `ColorModel` used by the system.

getFontList

```
public abstract String[] getFontList()
```

Returns   A `String` array of the set of Java fonts available with this Toolkit.

getFontMetrics

```
public abstract FontMetrics getFontMetrics (Font font)
```

Parameters *font*   A `Font` whose metrics are desired
Returns   The current `FontMetrics` for the font on the user's system.

getImage

```
public abstract Image getImage (String filename)
```

Parameters *filename* Location of `Image` on local filesystem
Returns   The `Image` that needs to be fetched.
Description Fetches an image from the local file system.

```
public abstract Image getImage (URL url)
```

Parameters *url*   Location of `Image`.
Returns   The `Image` that needs to be fetched.
Description Fetches an image from a URL.

getMenuShortcutKeyMask

```
public int getMenuShortcutKeyMask() ★
```

Returns   The modifier key mask used for menu shortcuts. This will be one of the mask constants defined in `java.awt.Event`.

getPrintJob

```
public abstract PrintJob getPrintJob (Frame frame,
String jobtitle, Properties props) ★
```

Parameters   *frame*   The `frame` to be used as the parent of a platform-specific printing dialog.

                jobtitle   The name of the job.

                props   Properties for this print job.

Returns   A `PrintJob` object. If the user canceled the printing operation, `null` is returned.

getScreenResolution

```
public abstract int getScreenResolution()
```

Returns   The current resolution of the user's screen, in dots-per-inch.

getScreenSize

```
public abstract Dimension getScreenSize()
```

Returns   The size of the screen available to the `Toolkit`, in pixels, as a `Dimension` object.

getSystemClipboard

```
public abstract Clipboard getSystemClipboard() ★
```

Returns   A `Clipboard` object that can be used for cut, copy, and paste operations.

getSystemEventQueue

```
public final EventQueue getSystemEventQueue() ★
```

Returns   A reference to the system's event queue, allowing the program to post new events or inspect the queue.

prepareImage

```
public abstract boolean prepareImage (Image image, int width, int
height, ImageObserver observer)
```

Parameters	*image*	Image to check.
	width	Width of the scaled image; -1 if image will be rendered unscaled.
	height	Height of the scaled image; -1 if image will be rendered unscaled.
	observer	The Component that image will be rendered on.
Returns		true if image fully loaded, false otherwise.
Description		Forces the system to start loading the image.

sync

```
public abstract void sync()
```

| Description | Flushes the display of the underlying graphics context. |

Protected Instance Methods

createButton

```
protected abstract ButtonPeer createButton (Button b)
```

Parameters	*b*	Component whose peer needs to be created.
Returns		Newly created peer.
Description		Creates a peer for the Button.

createCanvas

```
protected abstract CanvasPeer createCanvas (Canvas c)
```

Parameters	*c*	Component whose peer needs to be created.
Returns		Newly created peer.
Description		Creates a peer for the Canvas.

createCheckbox

```
protected abstract CheckboxPeer createCheckbox (Checkbox cb)
```

Parameters	*cb*	Component whose peer needs to be created.
Returns		Newly created peer.
Description		Creates a peer for the Checkbox.

createCheckboxMenuItem

protected abstract CheckboxMenuItemPeer createCheckboxMenuItem
(CheckboxMenuItem cmi)

Parameters	*cmi*	Component whose peer needs to be created.
Returns		Newly created peer.
Description		Creates a peer for the CheckboxMenuItem.

createChoice

protected abstract ChoicePeer createChoice (Choice c)

Parameters	*c*	Component whose peer needs to be created.
Returns		Newly created peer.
Description		Creates a peer for the Choice.

createComponent

protected LightweightPeer createComponent (Component target) ★

Parameters	*target*	Component whose peer needs to be created.
Returns		Newly created peer.
Description		Creates a peer for the Component.

createDialog

protected abstract DialogPeer createDialog (Dialog d)

Parameters	*d*	Component whose peer needs to be created.
Returns		Newly created peer.
Description		Creates a peer for the Dialog.

createFileDialog

protected abstract FileDialogPeer createFileDialog (FileDialog fd)

Parameters	*fd*	Component whose peer needs to be created.
Returns		Newly created peer.
Description		Creates a peer for the FileDialog.

createFrame

protected abstract FramePeer createFrame (Frame f)

Parameters	*f*	Component whose peer needs to be created.
Returns		Newly created peer.
Description		Creates a peer for the Frame.

createLabel

protected abstract LabelPeer createLabel (Label l)

Parameters	*l*	Component whose peer needs to be created.
Returns	Newly created peer.	
Description	Creates a peer for the Label.	

createList

protected abstract ListPeer createList (List l)

Parameters	*l*	Component whose peer needs to be created.
Returns	Newly created peer.	
Description	Creates a peer for the List.	

createMenu

protected abstract MenuPeer createMenu (Menu m)

Parameters	*m*	Menu whose peer needs to be created.
Returns	Newly created peer.	
Description	Creates a peer for the given Menu.	

createMenuBar

protected abstract MenuBarPeer createMenuBar (MenuBar mb)

Parameters	*mb*	MenuBar whose peer needs to be created.
Returns	Newly created peer.	
Description	Creates a peer for the MenuBar.	

createMenuItem

protected abstract MenuItemPeer createMenuItem (MenuItem mi)

Parameters	*mi*	MenuItem whose peer needs to be created.
Returns	Newly created peer.	
Description	Creates a peer for the MenuItem.	

createPanel

protected abstract PanelPeer createPanel (Panel p)

Parameters	*p*	Component whose peer needs to be created.
Returns	Newly created peer.	
Description	Creates a peer for the Panel.	

createPopupMenu

protected abstract PopupMenuPeer createPopupMenu
(PopupMenu target) ★

Parameters	*target*	Component whose peer needs to be created.
Returns		Newly created peer.
Description		Creates a peer for the PopupMenu.

createScrollPane

protected abstract ScrollPanePeer createScrollPane
(ScrollPane target) ★

Parameters	*target*	Component whose peer needs to be created.
Returns		Newly created peer.
Description		Creates a peer for the ScrollPane.

createScrollbar

protected abstract ScrollbarPeer createScrollbar (Scrollbar sb)

Parameters	*sb*	Component whose peer needs to be created.
Returns		Newly created peer.
Description		Creates a peer for the Scrollbar.

createTextArea

protected abstract TextAreaPeer createTextArea (TextArea ta)

Parameters	*ta*	Component whose peer needs to be created.
Returns		Newly created peer.
Description		Creates a peer for the TextArea.

createTextField

protected abstract TextFieldPeer createTextField (TextField tf)

Parameters	*tf*	Component whose peer needs to be created.
Returns		Newly created peer.
Description		Creates a peer for the TextField.

createWindow

```
protected abstract WindowPeer createWindow (Window w)
```

Parameters	*w*	Component whose peer needs to be created.
Returns		Newly created peer.
Description		Creates a peer for the Window.

getFontPeer

```
protected abstract FontPeer getFontPeer (String name,
int style) ★
```

Parameters	*name*	Name of the font to be created.
	style	Style of the font to be created.
Returns		Newly created peer.
Description		Creates a FontPeer.

getSystemEventQueueImpl

```
protected abstract getSystemEventQueueImpl()★
```

Returns	A toolkit-specific EventQueue object.

loadSystemColors

```
protected abstract void loadSystemColors (int[] systemColors) ★
```

Description	Fills the given integer array with the current system colors.

See Also

Button, ButtonPeer, Canvas, CanvasPeer, Checkbox, CheckboxMenuItem, Checkbox-
MenuItemPeer, CheckboxPeer, Choice, ChoicePeer, Clipboard, ColorModel, Compo-
nent, Container, Dialog, DialogPeer, Dimension, FileDialog, FileDialogPeer,
Font, FontMetrics, FontPeer, Frame, FramePeer, Image, ImageObserver, ImagePro-
ducer, Label, LabelPeer, LightweightPeer, List, ListPeer, Menu, MenuBar,
MenuBarPeer, MenuItem, MenuItemPeer, MenuPeer, Panel, PanelPeer, PrintJob,
Scrollbar, ScrollbarPeer, ScrollPane, ScrollPanePeer, String, TextArea,
TextAreaPeer, TextField, TextFieldPeer, Window, WindowPeer

19.61   Window

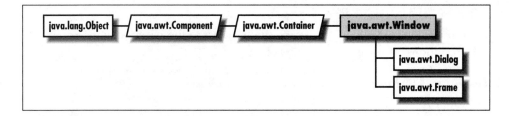

Description

The Window class serves as a top-level display area that exists outside the browser or applet area you may be working in. A window must have a parent Frame.

Class Definition

```
public class java.awt.Window
    extends java.awt.Container {

  // Constructors
  public Window (Frame parent);

  // Instance Methods
  public void addNotify();
  public synchronized void addWindowListener (WindowListener l); ★
  public void dispose();
  public Component getFocusOwner(); ★
  public Locale getLocale(); ★
  public Toolkit getToolkit();
  public final String getWarningString();
  public boolean isShowing(); ★
  public void pack();
  public boolean postEvent (Event e); ☆
  public synchronized void remove WindowListener (WindowListener l); ★
  public void show();
  public void toBack();
  public void toFront();
//Protected Instance Methods
  protected void processEvent (AWTEvent e); ★
  protected void processWindowEvent (WindowEvent e); ★
}
```

Constructors

Window

```
public Window (Frame parent)
```

Parameters   *parent*   Frame that is to act as the parent of Window.

Description   Constructs a Window object.

Instance Methods

addNotify

```
public void addNotify()
```

Overrides   Container.addNotify()

Description   Creates Window's peer and peers of contained components.

removeWindowListener

```
public synchronized void removeWindowListener
(WindowListener l) ★
```

Parameters   *l*   One of this Frame's WindowListeners.

Description   Remove an event listener.

addWindowListener

```
public synchronized void addWindowListener (WindowListener l) ★
```

Parameters   *l*   An object that implements the WindowListener
                            interface.

Description   Add a listener for windowing events.

dispose

```
public void dispose()
```

Returns   Releases the resources of the Window.

getFocusOwner

```
public Component getFocusOwner() ★
```

Returns   The child component that currently has the input focus.

getLocale

```
public Locale getLocale() ★
```

Returns   The locale for this Window.

Overrides   Window.getLocale()

getToolkit

```
public Toolkit getToolkit()
```

Returns   Toolkit of Window.

Overrides   Component.getToolkit()

getWarningString

```
public final String getWarningString()
```

Returns   String that will be displayed on the bottom of insecure Window
             instances.

isShowing

```
public boolean isShowing()
```

Returns   true if the Window is showing on the screen, false otherwise.

pack

```
public void pack()
```

Description Resizes Window to getPreferredSize() of contained compo-
             nents.

postEvent

```
public boolean postEvent (Event e) ☆
```

Parameters   e   Event instance to post to window.

Returns   If Event is handled, true is returned. Otherwise, false is
             returned.

Description Tells the Window to deal with Event.

removeWindowListener

```
public synchronized void removeWindowListener (WindowListener l)
★
```

Parameters   l   One of this Frame's WindowListeners.

Description Remove an event listener.

show

    public void show()

Description	Show the Window and validate its components.
Overrides	Component.show()

toBack

    public void toBack()

Description	Puts the Window in the background of the display.

toFront

    public void toFront()

Description	Brings the Window to the foreground of the display.

Protected Instance Methods

processEvent

    protected void processEvent (AWTEvent e) ★

Parameters	*e*	The event to process.
Description	Low level AWTEvents are passed to this method for processing.	

processWindowEvent

    protected void processWindowEvent (WindowEvent e) ★

Parameters	*e*	The event to process.
Description	Window events are passed to this method for processing. Normally, this method is called by processEvent().	

See Also

Component, Container, Dialog, Frame, String, Toolkit

20

java.awt.datatransfer Reference

20.1 *Clipboard* ★

Description

The Clipboard class is a repository for a Transferable object and can be used for cut, copy, and paste operations. The system clipboard can be accessed by calling Toolkit.getDefaultToolkit().getSystemClipboard(). You can use this technique if you are interested in exchanging data between your application and other applications (Java or non-Java) running on the system. In addition, Clipboard can be instantiated directly, if "private" clipboards are needed.

Class Definition

```
public class java.awt.datatransfer.Clipboard
   extends java.lang.Object {

  // Variables
  protected Transferable contents;
  protected ClipboardOwner owner;

  // Constructors
  public Clipboard (String name);
```

```
// Instance Methods
public synchronized Transferable getContents (Object requestor);
public String getName();
public synchronized void setContents (Transferable contents, ClipboardOwner owner);
}
```

Variables

contents

`protected Transferable contents`

The object that the Clipboard contains, i.e., the object that has been cut or copied.

owner

`protected ClipboardOwner owner`

The object that owns the contents. When something else is placed on the clipboard, owner is notified via lostOwnership().

Constructors

Clipboard

`public Clipboard (String name)`

Parameters	*name*	The name for this Clipboard.
Description		Constructs a Clipboard object with the given name.

Instance Methods

getContents

`public synchronized Transferable getContents (Object requestor)`

Parameters	*requestor*	The object asking for the contents.
Returns		An object that implements the Transferable interface.
Description		Returns the current contents of the Clipboard. You could use this method to paste data from the clipboard into your application.

getName

`public String getName()`

Returns		Clipboard's name.
Description		Returns the name used when this clipboard was constructed. Toolkit.getSystemClipboard() returns a Clipboard named "System".

setContents

```
public synchronized void setContents (Transferable contents,
ClipboardOwner owner)
```

Parameters   *contents*   New contents.

              owner   Owner of the new contents.

Description   Changes the contents of the Clipboard. You could use this
               method to cut or copy data from your application to the clip-
               board.

See Also

ClipboardOwner, Toolkit, Transferable

20.2   *ClipboardOwner* ★

Description

ClipboardOwner is implemented by classes that want to be notified when someone
else sets the contents of a clipboard.

Interface Definition

```
public abstract interface java.awt.datatransfer.ClipboardOwner {

  // Interface Methods
  public abstract void lostOwnership (Clipboard clipboard, Transferable contents);
}
```

Interface Methods

lostOwnership

```
public abstract void lostOwnership (Clipboard clipboard,
Transferable contents)
```

Parameters   *clipboard*   The clipboard whose contents have changed.

              contents   The contents that this owner originally put on
                                the clipboard.

Description   Tells the ClipboardOwner that the contents it placed on the given clipboard are no longer there.

See Also

Clipboard, StringSelection, Transferable

20.3   DataFlavor ★

Description

The DataFlavor class encapsulates information about data formats.

Class Definition

```
public class java.awt.datatransfer.DataFlavor
   extends java.lang.Object {

// Class Variables
public static DataFlavor plainTextFlavor;
public static DataFlavor stringFlavor;

// Constructors
public DataFlavor (Class representationClass,
   String humanPresentableName);
public DataFlavor (String MIMEType, String humanPresentableName);

// Instance Methods
public boolean equals (DataFlavor dataFlavor);
public String getHumanPresentableName();
public String getMIMEType();
public Class getRepresentationClass();
public boolean isMIMETypeEqual (String MIMEType);
public final boolean isMIMETypeEqual (DataFlavor dataFlavor);
public void setHumanPresentableName (String humanPresentableName);

// Protected Instance Methods
protected String normalizeMIMEType (String MIMEType);
protected String normalizeMIMETypeParameter (String parameterName,
   String parameterValue);
}
```

Class Variables

plainTextFlavor

public static DataFlavor plainTextFlavor

A preset DataFlavor object representing plain text.

stringFlavor

public static DataFlavor stringFlavor

A preset DataFlavor object representing a Java String.

Constructors

DataFlavor

public DataFlavor (Class representationClass, String humanPresentableName)

Parameters	*representationClass*	
		The Java class that represents data in this flavor.
	humanPresentableName	
		A name for this flavor that humans will recognize.
Description		Constructs a DataFlavor object with the given characteristics. The MIME type for this DataFlavor is application/x-java-serialized-object <Java ClassName>.[*]

public DataFlavor (String MIMEType, String humanPresentableName)

Parameters	*MIMEType*	The MIME type string this DataFlavor represents.
	humanPresentableName	
		A name for this flavor that humans will recognize.
Description		Constructs a DataFlavor object with the given characteristics. The representation class used for this DataFlavor is java.io.InputStream.

---

[*] The type name changed to x-java-serialized-object in the 1.1.1 release.

Instance Methods

equals

```
public boolean equals (DataFlavor dataFlavor)
```

Parameters   *dataFlavor*   The flavor to compare.

Returns   true if dataFlavor is equivalent to this DataFlavor, false otherwise.

Description   Compares two different DataFlavor instances for equivalence.

getHumanPresentableName

```
public String getHumanPresentableName()
```

Returns   The name of this flavor.

getMIMEType

```
public String getMIMEType()
```

Returns   The MIME type string for this flavor.

getRepresentationClass

```
public Class getRepresentationClass()
```

Returns   The Java class that will be used to represent data in this flavor.

isMIMETypeEqual

```
public boolean isMIMETypeEqual (String MIMEType)
```

Parameters   *MIMEType*   The type to compare.

Returns   true if the given MIME type is the same as this DataFlavor's MIME type; false otherwise.

Description   Compares two different DataFlavor MIME types for equivalence.

```
public final boolean isMIMETypeEqual (DataFlavor dataFlavor)
```

Parameters   *dataFlavor*   The flavor to compare.

Returns   true if DataFlavor's MIME type is the same as this DataFlavor's MIME type; false otherwise.

Description   Compares two different DataFlavor MIME types for equivalence.

setHumanPresentableName

```
public void setHumanPresentableName (String humanPresentableName)
```

Parameters   *humanPresentableName*

> A name for this flavor that humans will recognize.

Description   Changes the name of the `DataFlavor`.

Protected Instance Methods

normalizeMIMEType

```
protected String normalizeMIMEType (String MIMEType)
```

Parameters   *MIMEType*   The MIME type string to normalize.
Returns   Normalized MIME type string.
Description This method is called for each MIME type string. Subclasses can override this method to add default parameter/value pairs to MIME strings.

normalizeMIMETypeParameter

```
protected String normalizeMIMETypeParameter (String parameterName,
String parameterValue)
```

Parameters   *parameterName*

> The MIME type parameter to normalize.

> *parameterValue*

> The corresponding value.

Returns   Normalized MIME type parameter string.
Description This method is called for each MIME type parameter string. Subclasses can override this method to handle special parameters, such as those that are case-insensitive.

See Also

`Class`, `String`

20.4   StringSelection ★

Description

`StringSelection` is a "convenience" class that can be used for copy and paste operations on Unicode text strings. For example, you could place a string on the system's clipboard with the following code:

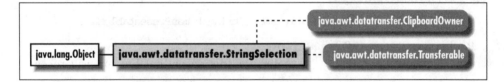

```
Clipboard c =
  Toolkit.getDefaultToolkit().getSystemClipboard();
StringSelection s = new StringSelection(

  "Be safe when you cut and paste.");
c.setContents(s, s);
```

Class Definition

```
public class java.awt.datatransfer.StringSelection
   extends java.lang.Object
   implements java.awt.datatransfer.ClipboardOwner,
         java.awt.datatransfer.Transferable {

  // Constructor
  public StringSelection(String data);

  // Instance Methods
  public synchronized Object getTransferData (DataFlavor flavor)
     throws UnsupportedFlavorException, IOException;
  public synchronized DataFlavor[] getTransferDataFlavors();
  public boolean isDataFlavorSupported (DataFlavor flavor);
  public void lostOwnership (Clipboard clipboard, Transferable contents);
}
```

Constructors

StringSelection

```
public StringSelection (String data)
```

Parameters   *data*   The string to be placed in a clipboard.
Description   Constructs a StringSelection object from the given string.

Instance Methods

getTransferData

```
public synchronized Object getTransferData (DataFlavor flavor)
throws UnsupportedFlavorException, IOException
```

Parameters	*flavor*	The requested flavor for the returned data, which can be either DataFlavor.stringFlavor or DataFlavor.plainTextFlavor.
Returns		The string that the StringSelection was constructed with. This is returned either as a String object or a Reader object, depending on the flavor requested.
Throws	*UnsupportedFlavorException*	If the requested flavor is not supported.
	IOException	If a Reader representing the string could not be created.
Implements		Transferable.getTransferData(DataFlavor)
Description		Returns the string this StringSelection represents. This is returned either as a String object or a Reader object, depending on the flavor requested.

getTransferDataFlavors

public synchronized DataFlavor[] getTransferDataFlavors()

Returns	An array of the data flavors the StringSelection supports.
Implements	Transferable.getTransferDataFlavors()
Description	DataFlavor.stringFlavor and DataFlavor.plainTextFlavor are returned.

isDataFlavorSupported

public boolean isDataFlavorSupported (DataFlavor flavor)

Parameters	*flavor*	The flavor in question.
Returns		true if flavor is supported; false otherwise.
Implements		Transferable.isDataFlavorSupported(DataFlavor)

lostOwnership

public void lostOwnership (Clipboard clipboard, Transferable contents)

Parameters	*clipboard*	The clipboard whose contents are changing.
	contents	The contents that were on the clipboard.
Implements		ClipboardOwner.lostOwnership(Clipboard, Transferable)
Description		Does nothing.

See Also

Clipboard, ClipboardOwner, DataFlavor, String, Transferable

20.5   Transferable ★

Description

The Transferable interface is implemented by objects that can be placed on Clipboards.

Interface Definition

```
public abstract interface Transferable {

  // Instance Methods
  public abstract Object getTransferData (DataFlavor flavor)
    throws UnsupportedFlavorException, IOException;
  public abstract DataFlavor[] getTransferDataFlavors();
  public abstract boolean isDataFlavorSupported (DataFlavor flavor);
}
```

Interface Methods

getTransferData

public abstract Object getTransferData (DataFlavor flavor) throws UnsupportedFlavorException, IOException

Parameters	*flavor*	The requested flavor for the returned data.
Returns		The data represented by this Transferable object, in the requested flavor.
Throws	*UnsupportedFlavorException*	
		If the requested flavor is not supported.
	IOException	If a Reader representing the data could not be created.
Description		Returns the data this Transferable object represents. The class of object returned depends on the flavor requested.

getTransferDataFlavors

```
public abstract DataFlavor[] getTransferDataFlavors()
```

Returns   An array of the supported data flavors.

Description   The data flavors should be returned in order, sorted from most to least descriptive.

isDataFlavorSupported

```
public abstract boolean isDataFlavorSupported (DataFlavor flavor)
```

Parameters   *flavor*   The flavor in question.

Returns   true if flavor is supported; false otherwise.

See Also

Clipboard, DataFlavor, Reader, StringSelection, Transferable

20.6   *UnsupportedFlavorException* ★

Description

This exception is thrown from Transferable.getTransferData(DataFlavor) to indicate that the DataFlavor requested is not available.

Class Definition

```
public class java.awt.datatransfer.UnsupportedFlavorException
   extends java.lang.Exception {

  // Constructor
  public UnsupportedFlavorException (DataFlavor flavor);
}
```

Constructors

UnsupportedFlavorException

```
public UnsupportedFlavorException (DataFlavor flavor)
```

Parameters   *flavor*   The flavor that caused the exception.

See Also

DataFlavor, Exception, Transferable

21

java.awt.event Reference

21.1 ActionEvent ★

Description

Action events are fired off when the user performs an action on a component, such as pushing a button, double-clicking on a list item, or selecting a menu item. There is only one action event type, `ACTION_PERFORMED`.

Class Definition

```
public class java.awt.event.ActionEvent
   extends java.awt.AWTEvent {

   // Constants
   public final static int ACTION_FIRST;
   public final static int ACTION_LAST;
   public final static int ACTION_PERFORMED;
   public final static int ALT_MASK;
   public final static int CTRL_MASK;
   public final static int META_MASK;
   public final static int SHIFT_MASK;

   // Constructors
   public ActionEvent (Object source, int id, String command);
```

```
    public ActionEvent (Object source, int id, String command, int modifiers);

    // Instance Methods
    public String getActionCommand();
    public int getModifiers();
    public String paramString();
}
```

Constants

ACTION_FIRST

public final static int ACTION_FIRST

Specifies the beginning range of action event ID values.

ACTION_LAST

public final static int ACTION_LAST

Specifies the ending range of action event ID values.

ACTION_PERFORMED

public final static int ACTION_PERFORMED

The only action event type; it indicates that the user has performed an action.

ALT_MASK

public final static int ALT_MASK

A constant representing the ALT key. ORed with other masks to form modifiers setting of an AWTEvent.

CTRL_MASK

public final static int CTRL_MASK

A constant representing the Control key. ORed with other masks to form modifiers setting of an AWTEvent.

META_MASK

public final static int META_MASK

A constant representing the META key. ORed with other masks to form modifiers setting of an AWTEvent.

SHIFT_MASK

public final static int SHIFT_MASK

A constant representing the Shift key. ORed with other masks to form modifiers setting of an AWTEvent.

Constructors

ActionEvent

public ActionEvent (Object source, int id, String command)

Parameters   *source*   The object that generated the event.
              id   The type ID of the event.
              command   The action command string.

Description   Constructs an ActionEvent with the given characteristics.

public ActionEvent (Object source, int id, String command, int modifiers)

Parameters   *source*   The object that generated the event.
              id   The type ID of the event.
              command   The action command string.
              modifiers   A combination of the key mask constants.

Description   Constructs an ActionEvent with the given characteristics.

Instance Methods

getActionCommand

public String getActionCommand()

Returns   The action command string for this ActionEvent.
Description   Generally the action command string is the label of the component that generated the event. Also, when localization is necessary, the action command string can provide a setting that does not get localized.

getModifiers

public int getModifiers()

Returns   A combination of the key mask constants.
Description   Returns the modifier keys that were held down when this action was performed. This enables you to perform special processing if, for example, the user holds down Shift while pushing a button.

paramString

   public String paramString()

Returns	String with current settings of ActionEvent.
Overrides	AWTEvent.paramString()
Description	Helper method for toString() to generate string of current settings.

See Also

ActionListener, AWTEvent, String

21.2 ActionListener ★

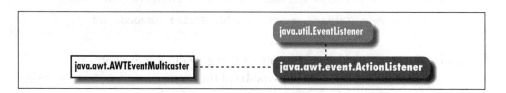

Description

Objects that implement the ActionListener interface can receive ActionEvent objects. Listeners must first register themselves with objects that produce events. When events occur, they are then automatically propagated to all registered listeners.

Interface Definition

```
public abstract interface java.awt.event.ActionListener
   extends java.util.EventListener {

  // Interface Methods
  public abstract void actionPerformed (ActionEvent e);
}
```

Interface Methods

actionPerformed

   public abstract void actionPerformed (ActionEvent e)

Parameters	*e*	The action event that occurred.

Description	Notifies the ActionListener that an event occurred.

See Also

ActionEvent, AWTEventMulticaster, EventListener

21.3   *AdjustmentEvent* ★

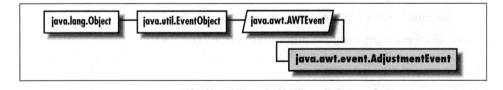

Description

AdjustmentEvents are generated by objects that implement the Adjustable inter-face. Scrollbar is one example of such an object.

Class Definition

```
public class java.awt.event.AdjustmentEvent
   extends java.awt.AWTEvent {

   // Constants
   public final static int ADJUSTMENT_FIRST;
   public final static int ADJUSTMENT_LAST;
   public final static int ADJUSTMENT_VALUE_CHANGED;
   public final static int BLOCK_DECREMENT;
   public final static int BLOCK_INCREMENT;
   public final static int TRACK;
   public final static int UNIT_DECREMENT;
   public final static int UNIT_INCREMENT;

   // Constructors
   public AdjustmentEvent (Adjustable source, int id, int type, int value);

   // Instance Methods
   public Adjustable getAdjustable();
   public int getAdjustmentType();
   public int getValue();
   public String paramString();
}
```

Constants

ADJUSTMENT_FIRST

    public final static int ADJUSTMENT_FIRST

Specifies the beginning range of adjustment event ID values.

ADJUSTMENT_LAST

    public final static int ADJUSTMENT_LAST

Specifies the ending range of adjustment event ID values.

ADJUSTMENT_VALUE_CHANGED

    public final static int ADJUSTMENT_VALUE_CHANGED

Event type ID for value changed.

BLOCK_DECREMENT

    public final static int BLOCK_DECREMENT

Adjustment type for block decrement.

BLOCK_INCREMENT

    public final static int BLOCK_INCREMENT

Adjustment type for block increment.

TRACK

    public final static int TRACK

Adjustment type for tracking.

UNIT_DECREMENT

    public final static int UNIT_DECREMENT

Adjustment type for unit decrement.

UNIT_INCREMENT

    public final static int UNIT_INCREMENT

Adjustment type for unit increment.

Constructors

AdjustmentEvent

public AdjustmentEvent (Adjustable source, int id, int type, int value)

Parameters	source	The object that generated the event.
	id	The event type ID of the event.
	type	The type of adjustment event.
	value	The value of the Adjustable object.

Description   Constructs an AdjustmentEvent with the given characteristics.

Instance Methods

getAdjustable

public Adjustable getAdjustable()

Returns   The source of this event.

getAdjustmentType

public int getAdjustmentType()

Returns   One of the adjustment type constants.

Description   The type will be BLOCK_DECREMENT, BLOCK_INCREMENT, TRACK, UNIT_DECREMENT, or UNIT_INCREMENT.

getValue

public int getValue()

Returns   The new value of the Adjustable object.

paramString

public String paramString()

Returns   String with current settings of the AdjustmentEvent.

Overrides   AWTEvent.paramString()

Description   Helper method for toString() to generate string of current settings.

See Also

Adjustable, AdjustmentListener, AWTEvent, Scrollbar

21.4 AdjustmentListener ★

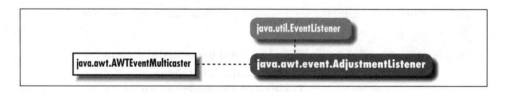

Description

Objects that implement the AdjustmentListener interface can receive Adjust-mentEvent objects. Listeners must first register themselves with objects that produce events. When events occur, they are then automatically propagated to all registered listeners.

Interface Definition

```
public abstract interface java.awt.event.AdjustmentListener
   extends java.util.Eventlistener {

 // Interface Methods
 public abstract void adjustmentValueChanged (AdjustmentEvent e);
}
```

Interface Methods

adjustmentPerformed

public abstract void adjustmentValueChanged (AdjustmentEvent e)

Parameters   *e*   The adjustment event that occurred.

Description   Notifies the AdjustmentListener that an event occurred.

See Also

AdjustmentEvent, AWTEventMulticaster, EventListener

21.5 ComponentAdapter ★

Description

ComponentAdapter is a class that implements the methods of ComponentListener with empty functions. It may be easier for you to extend ComponentAdapter, overriding only those methods you are interested in, than to implement ComponentListener and provide the empty functions yourself.

Class Definition

```
public abstract class java.awt.event.ComponentAdapter
    extends java.lang.Object
    implements java.awt.event.ComponentListener {

    // Instance Methods
    public void componentHidden (ComponentEvent e);
    public void componentMoved (ComponentEvent e);
    public void componentResized (ComponentEvent e);
    public void componentShown (ComponentEvent e);
}
```

Instance Methods

componentHidden

```
public void componentHidden (ComponentEvent e)
```

Parameters   *e*   The event that has occurred.

Description   Does nothing. Override this function to be notified when a component is hidden.

componentMoved

```
public void componentMoved (ComponentEvent e)
```

Parameters   *e*   The event that has occurred.

Description   Does nothing. Override this function to be notified when a component is moved.

componentResized

```
public void componentResized (ComponentEvent e)
```

Parameters   *e*   The event that has occurred.

Description   Does nothing. Override this function to be notified when a component is resized.

componentShown

  public void componentShown (ComponentEvent e)

  Parameters   *e*   The event that has occurred.

  Description   Does nothing. Override this function to be notified when a
                component is shown.

See Also

Component, ComponentEvent, ComponentListener

21.6   *ComponentEvent* ★

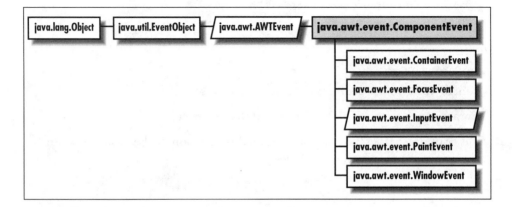

Description

Component events are generated when a component is shown, hidden, moved, or resized. AWT automatically deals with component moves and resizing; these events are provided only for notification. Subclasses of ComponentEvent deal with other specific component-level events.

Class Definition

```
public class java.awt.event.ComponentEvent
   extends java.awt.AWTEvent {

   // Constants
   public final static int COMPONENT_FIRST;
   public final static int COMPONENT_HIDDEN;
   public final static int COMPONENT_LAST;
   public final static int COMPONENT_MOVED;
   public final static int COMPONENT_RESIZED;
   public final static int COMPONENT_SHOWN;
```

```
    // Constructors
    public ComponentEvent (Component source, int id);

    // Instance Methods
    public Component getComponent();
    public String paramString();
}
```

Constants

COMPONENT_FIRST

```
public final static int COMPONENT_FIRST
```

Specifies the beginning range of component event ID values.

COMPONENT_HIDDEN

```
public final static int COMPONENT_HIDDEN
```

Event type ID indicating that the component was hidden.

COMPONENT_LAST

```
public final static int COMPONENT_LAST
```

Specifies the ending range of component event ID values.

COMPONENT_MOVED

```
public final static int COMPONENT_MOVED
```

Event type ID indicating that the component was moved.

COMPONENT_RESIZED

```
public final static int COMPONENT_RESIZED
```

Event type ID indicating that the component was resized.

COMPONENT_SHOWN

```
public final static int COMPONENT_SHOWN
```

Event type ID indicating that the component was shown.

Constructors

ComponentEvent

```
public ComponentEvent (Component source, int id)
```

Parameters   *source*   The object that generated the event.

id   The event type ID of the event.

Description   Constructs a ComponentEvent with the given characteristics.

Instance Methods

getComponent

public Component getComponent()

Returns   The source of this event.

paramString

public String paramString()

Returns   String with current settings of the ComponentEvent.
Overrides   AWTEvent.paramString()
Description   Helper method for toString() to generate string of current
               settings.

See Also

AWTEvent, Component, ComponentAdapter, ComponentListener, ContainerEvent,
FocusEvent, InputEvent, PaintEvent, WindowEvent

21.7   ComponentListener ★

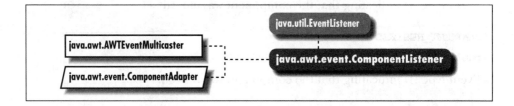

Description

Objects that implement the ComponentListener interface can receive Component-
Event objects. Listeners must first register themselves with objects that produce
events. When events occur, they are then automatically propagated to all registered listeners.

Interface Definition

```
public abstract interface java.awt.event.ComponentListener
    extends java.util.EventListener {

    // Instance Methods
    public abstract void componentHidden (ComponentEvent e);
```

```
    public abstract void componentMoved (ComponentEvent e);
    public abstract void componentResized (ComponentEvent e);
    public abstract void componentShown (ComponentEvent e);
}
```

Interface Methods

componentHidden

public abstract void componentHidden (ComponentEvent e)

Parameters   *e*   The component event that occurred.

Description   Notifies the ComponentListener that a component was hidden.

componentMoved

public abstract void componentMoved (ComponentEvent e)

Parameters   *e*   The component event that occurred.

Description   Notifies the ComponentListener that a component was moved.

componentResized

public abstract void componentResized (ComponentEvent e)

Parameters   *e*   The component event that occurred.

Description   Notifies the ComponentListener that a component was resized.

componentShown

public abstract void componentShown (ComponentEvent e)

Parameters   *e*   The component event that occurred.

Description   Notifies the ComponentListener that a component was shown.

See Also

AWTEventMulticaster, ComponentAdapter, ComponentEvent, EventListener

---

21.8   ContainerAdapter ★

Description

The ContainerAdapter class implements the methods of ContainerListener with empty functions. It may be easier for you to extend ContainerAdapter, overriding only those methods you are interested in, than to implement ContainerListener and provide the empty functions yourself.

Class Definition

```
public abstract class java.awt.event.ContainerAdapter
    extends java.lang.Object
    implements java.awt.event.ContainerListener {

    // Instance Methods
    public void componentAdded (ContainerEvent e);
    public void componentRemoved (ContainerEvent e);
}
```

Instance Methods

componentAdded

```
public void componentAdded (ComponentEvent e)
```

Parameters   *e*   The event that has occurred.

Description   Does nothing. Override this function to be notified when a component is added to a container.

componentRemoved

```
public void componentRemoved (ComponentEvent e)
```

Parameters   *e*   The event that has occurred.

Description   Does nothing. Override this function to be notified when a component is removed from a container.

See Also

ContainerEvent, ContainerListener

21.9   ContainerEvent ★

Description

Container events are fired off when a component is added to or removed from a container. The AWT automatically deals with adding components to containers; these events are provided only for notification.

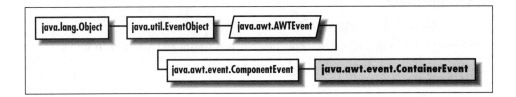

Class Definition

```
public class java.awt.event.ContainerEvent
    extends java.awt.event.ComponentEvent {

    // Constants
    public final static int COMPONENT_ADDED;
    public final static int COMPONENT_REMOVED;
    public final static int CONTAINER_FIRST;
    public final static int CONTAINER_LAST;

    // Constructors
    public ContainerEvent (Component source, int id, Component child);

    // Instance Methods
    public Component getChild();
    public Container getContainer();
    public String paramString();
}
```

Constants

COMPONENT_ADDED

```
public final static int COMPONENT_ADDED
```

Event type ID indicating that a component was added to a container.

CONTAINER_FIRST

```
public final static int CONTAINER_FIRST
```

Specifies the beginning range of container event ID values.

CONTAINER_LAST

```
public final static int CONTAINER_LAST
```

Specifies the ending range of container event ID values.

COMPONENT_REMOVED

> `public final static int COMPONENT_REMOVED`

Event type ID indicating that a component was removed from a container.

Constructors

ContainerEvent

> `public ContainerEvent (Component source, int id, Component child)`

Parameters	*source*	The object that generated the event.
	id	The event type ID of the event.
	child	The component that was added or removed.

Description   Constructs a `ContainerEvent` with the given characteristics.

Instance Methods

getChild

> `public Component getChild()`

Returns   The component that is being added or removed.

getContainer

> `public Container getContainer()`

Returns   The container for this event.

paramString

> `public String paramString()`

Returns	String with current settings of the `ContainerEvent`.
Overrides	`ComponentEvent.paramString()`
Description	Helper method for `toString()` to generate string of current settings.

See Also

Component, ComponentEvent, Container, ContainerAdapter, ContainerListener

21.10   *ContainerListener* ★

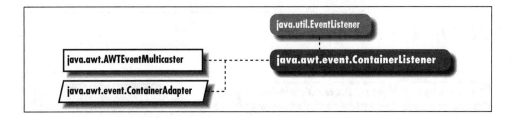

Description

Objects that implement the ContainerListener interface can receive ContainerEvent objects. Listeners must first register themselves with objects that produce events. When events occur, they are then automatically propagated to all registered listeners.

Interface Definition

```
public abstract interface java.awt.event.ContainerListener
    extends java.util.EventListener {

    // Instance Methods
    public abstract void componentAdded (ContainerEvent e);
    public abstract void componentRemoved (ContainerEvent e);
}
```

Interface Methods

componentAdded

public abstract void componentAdded (ContainerEvent e)

Parameters	*e*	The event that occurred.
Description		Notifies the ContainerListener that a component has been added to the container.

componentRemoved

public abstract void componentRemoved (ContainerEvent e)

Parameters	*e*	The event that occurred.
Description		Notifies the ContainerListener that a component has been removed from the container.

See Also

ContainerAdapter, ContainerEvent, EventListener

21.11   *FocusAdapter* ★

Description

The FocusAdapter class implements the methods of FocusListener with empty functions. It may be easier for you to extend FocusAdapter, overriding only those methods you are interested in, than to implement FocusListener and provide the empty functions yourself.

Class Definition

```
public abstract class java.awt.event.FocusAdapter
   extends java.lang.Object
   implements java.awt.event.FocusListener {

  // Instance Methods
  public void focusGained (FocusEvent e);
  public void focusLost (FocusEvent e);
}
```

Instance Methods

focusGained

public void focusGained (FocusEvent e)

Parameters   *e*   The event that has occurred.

Description   Does nothing. Override this function to be notified when a component gains focus.

focusLost

public void focusLost (FocusEvent e)

Parameters   *e*   The event that has occurred.

Description   Does nothing. Override this function to be notified when a component loses focus.

See Also

FocusEvent, FocusListener

21.12   FocusEvent ★

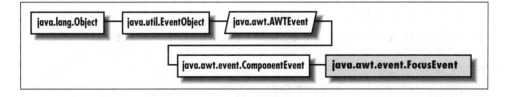

Description

Focus events are generated when a component gets or loses input focus. Focus events come in two flavors, permanent and temporary. Permanent focus events occur with explicit focus changes. For example, when the user tabs through components, this causes permanent focus events. An example of a temporary focus event is when a component loses focus as its containing window is deactivated.

Class Definition

```
public class java.awt.event.FocusEvent
    extends java.awt.event.ComponentEvent {

  // Constants
  public final static int FOCUS_FIRST;
  public final static int FOCUS_GAINED;
  public final static int FOCUS_LAST;
  public final static int FOCUS_LOST;

  // Constructors
  public FocusEvent (Component source, int id);
  public FocusEvent (Component source, int id, boolean temporary);

  // Instance Methods
  public boolean isTemporary();
  public String paramString();
}
```

Constants

FOCUS_FIRST

```
public final static int FOCUS_FIRST
```

Specifies the beginning range of focus event ID values.

FOCUS_GAINED

```
public final static int FOCUS_GAINED
```

Event type ID indicating that the component gained the input focus.

FOCUS_LAST

```
public final static int FOCUS_LAST
```

Specifies the ending range of focus event ID values.

FOCUS_LOST

```
public final static int FOCUS_LOST
```

Event type ID indicating that the component lost the input focus.

Constructors

FocusEvent

```
public FocusEvent (Component source, int id)
```

Parameters	*source*	The object that generated the event.
	id	The event type ID of the event.
Description	Constructs a non-temporary FocusEvent with the given characteristics.	

```
public FocusEvent (Component source, int id, boolean temporary)
```

Parameters	*source*	The object that generated the event.
	id	The event type ID of the event.
	temporary	A flag indicating whether this is a temporary focus event.
Description	Constructs a FocusEvent with the given characteristics.	

Instance Methods

isTemporary

```
public boolean isTemporary()
```

Returns   true if this is a temporary focus event; false otherwise.

paramString

```
public String paramString()
```

Returns   String with current settings of the FocusEvent.
Overrides   ComponentEvent.paramString()
Description   Helper method for toString() to generate string of current
               settings.

See Also

Component, ComponentEvent, FocusAdapter, FocusListener

21.13   FocusListener ★

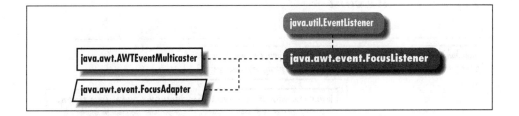

Description

Objects that implement the FocusListener interface can receive FocusEvent
objects. Listeners must first register themselves with objects that produce events.
When events occur, they are then automatically propagated to all registered listeners.

Interface Definition

```
public abstract interface java.awt.event.FocusListener
    extends java.util.EventListener {

    // Instance Methods
    public abstract void focusGained (FocusEvent e);
    public abstract void focusLost (FocusEvent e);
}
```

Interface Methods

focusGained

```
public abstract void focusGained (FocusEvent e)
```

Parameters   *e*   The component event that occurred.

Description   Notifies the FocusListener that a component gained the input
                 focus.

focusLost

```
public abstract void focusLost (FocusEvent e)
```

Parameters   *e*   The component event that occurred.

Description   Notifies the FocusListener that a component lost the input
                 focus.

See Also

AWTEventMulticaster, EventListener, FocusAdapter, FocusEvent

21.14   InputEvent ★

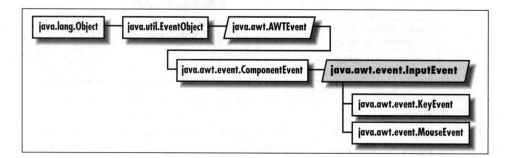

Description

InputEvent is the root class for representing user input events. Input events are
passed to listeners before the event source processes them. If one of the listeners
consumes an event by using consume(), the event will not be processed by the
event source peer.

Class Definition

```
public abstract class java.awt.event.InputEvent
    extends java.awt.event.ComponentEvent {

    // Constants
```

```
    public final static int ALT_MASK;
    public final static int BUTTON1_MASK;
    public final static int BUTTON2_MASK;
    public final static int BUTTON3_MASK;
    public final static int CTRL_MASK;
    public final static int META_MASK;
    public final static int SHIFT_MASK;

    // Instance Methods
    public void consume();
    public int getModifiers();
    public long getWhen();
    public boolean isAltDown();
    public boolean isConsumed();
    public boolean isControlDown();
    public boolean isMetaDown();
    public boolean isShiftDown();
}
```

Constants

ALT_MASK

```
public final static int ALT_MASK
```

The ALT key mask. ORed with other masks to form modifiers setting of event.

BUTTON1_MASK

```
public final static int BUTTON1_MASK
```

The mouse button 1 key mask. ORed with other masks to form modifiers setting of event.

BUTTON2_MASK

```
public final static int BUTTON2_MASK
```

The mouse button 2 key mask. ORed with other masks to form modifiers setting of event. This constant is identical to ALT_MASK.

BUTTON3_MASK

```
public final static int BUTTON3_MASK
```

The mouse button 3 key mask. ORed with other masks to form modifiers setting of event. This constant is identical to ALT_MASK.

CTRL_MASK

```
public final static int CTRL_MASK
```

The Control key mask. ORed with other masks to form modifiers setting of event.

META_MASK

```
public final static int META_MASK
```

The Meta key mask. ORed with other masks to form modifiers setting of event.

SHIFT_MASK

```
public final static int SHIFT_MASK
```

The Shift key mask. ORed with other masks to form modifiers setting of event.

Instance Methods

consume

```
public void consume()
```

Description   A consumed event will not be delivered to its source for default processing.

getModifiers

```
public int getModifiers()
```

Returns   The modifier flags, a combination of the _MASK constants.
Description   Use this method to find out what modifier keys were pressed when an input event occurred.

getWhen

```
public long getWhen()
```

Returns   The time at which this event occurred.
Description   The time of the event is returned as the number of milliseconds since the epoch (00:00:00 UTC, January 1, 1970). Conveniently, java.util.Date has a constructor that accepts such values.

isAltDown

```
public boolean isAltDown()
```

Returns   true if the Alt key was pressed; false otherwise.

isConsumed

```
public boolean isConsumed()
```

Returns   true if the event has been consumed; false otherwise.

isControlDown

```
public boolean isControlDown()
```

Returns   true if the Control key was pressed; false otherwise.

isMetaDown

```
public boolean isMetaDown()
```

Returns   true if the Meta key was pressed; false otherwise.

isShiftDown

```
public boolean isShiftDown()
```

Returns   true if the Shift key was pressed; false otherwise.

See Also

ComponentEvent, KeyEvent, MouseEvent

21.15   ItemEvent ★

Description

ItemEvents are generated by objects that implement the ItemSelectable interface. Choice is one example of such an object.

Class Definition

```
public class java.awt.event.ItemEvent
   extends java.awt.AWTEvent {

   // Constants
   public final static int DESELECTED;
```

```
    public final static int ITEM_FIRST;
    public final static int ITEM_LAST;
    public final static int ITEM_STATE_CHANGED;
    public final static int SELECTED;

    // Constructors
    public ItemEvent (ItemSelectable source, int id, Object item, int stateChange);

  // Instance Methods
    public Object getItem();
    public ItemSelectable getItemSelectable();
    public int getStateChange();
    public String paramString();
  }
```

Constants

DESELECTED

```
    public final static int DESELECTED
```

Indicates that an item was deselected.

ITEM_FIRST

```
    public final static int ITEM_FIRST
```

Specifies the beginning range of item event ID values.

ITEM_LAST

```
    public final static int ITEM_LAST
```

Specifies the ending range of item event ID values.

ITEM_STATE_CHANGED

```
    public final static int ITEM_STATE_CHANGED
```

An event type indicating that an item was selected or deselected.

SELECTED

```
    public final static int SELECTED
```

Indicates that an item was selected.

Constructors

ItemEvent

```
public ItemEvent (ItemSelectable source, int id, Object item, int
stateChange)
```

Parameters	*source*	The object that generated the event.
	id	The type ID of the event.
	item	The item whose state is changing.
	stateChange	Either SELECTED or DESELECTED.

Description   Constructs an ItemEvent with the given characteristics.

Instance Methods

getItem

```
public Object getItem()
```

Returns   The item pertaining to this event.

Description   Returns the item whose changed state triggered this event.

getItemSelectable

```
public ItemSelectable getItemSelectable()
```

Returns   The source of this event.

Description   Returns an object that implements the ItemSelectable interface.

getStateChange

```
public int getStateChange()
```

Returns   The change in state that triggered this event. The new state is returned.

Description   This method will return SELECTED or DESELECTED.

paramString

```
public String paramString()
```

Returns   String with current settings of ItemEvent.

Overrides   AWTEvent.paramString()

Description   Helper method for toString() to generate string of current settings.

See Also

AWTEvent, ItemSelectable, ItemListener

21.16   ItemListener ★

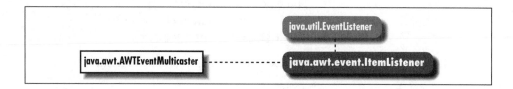

Description

Objects that implement the ItemListener interface can receive ItemEvent objects. Listeners must first register themselves with objects that produce events. When events occur, they are then automatically propagated to all registered listeners.

Interface Definition

```
public abstract interface java.awt.event.ItemListener
    extends java.util.EventListener {

  // Interface Methods
  public abstract void itemStateChanged (ItemEvent e);
}
```

Interface Methods

itemStateChanged

public abstract void itemStateChanged (ItemEvent e)

Parameters   *e*   The item event that occurred.

Description   Notifies the ItemListener that an event occurred.

See Also

AWTEventMulticaster, EventListener, ItemEvent

21.17   KeyAdapter ★

Description

The KeyAdapter class implements the methods of KeyListener with empty functions. It may be easier for you to extend KeyAdapter, overriding only those methods you are interested in, than to implement KeyListener and provide the empty functions yourself.

Class Definition

```
public abstract class java.awt.event.KeyAdapter
    extends java.lang.Object
    implements java.awt.event.KeyListener {

// Instance Methods
public void keyPressed (KeyEvent e);
public void keyReleased (KeyEvent e);
public void keyTyped (KeyEvent e);
}
```

Instance Methods

keyPressed

```
public void keyPressed (KeyEvent e)
```

Parameters   *e*   The event that has occurred.

Description   Does nothing. Override this function to be notified when a key
                  is pressed.

keyReleased

```
public void keyReleased (KeyEvent e)
```

Parameters   *e*   The event that has occurred.

Description   Does nothing. Override this function to be notified when a
                  pressed key is released.

keyTyped

public void keyTyped (KeyEvent e)

Parameters   *e*   The event that has occurred.

Description   Does nothing. Override this function to be notified when a key has been pressed and released.

See Also

KeyEvent, KeyListener

21.18 KeyEvent ★

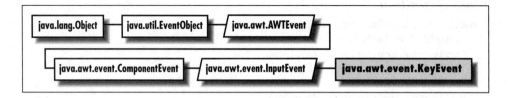

Description

Key events are generated when the user types on the keyboard.

Class Definition

```
public class java.awt.event.KeyEvent
    extends java.awt.event.InputEvent {

// Constants
public final static int CHAR_UNDEFINED;
public final static int KEY_FIRST;
public final static int KEY_LAST;
public final static int KEY_PRESSED;
public final static int KEY_RELEASED;
public final static int KEY_TYPED;
public final static int VK_0;
public final static int VK_1;
public final static int VK_2;
public final static int VK_3;
public final static int VK_4;
public final static int VK_5;
public final static int VK_6;
public final static int VK_7;
public final static int VK_8;
public final static int VK_9;
public final static int VK_A;
```

```
public final static int VK_ACCEPT;
public final static int VK_ADD;
public final static int VK_ALT;
public final static int VK_B;
public final static int VK_BACK_QUOTE;
public final static int VK_BACK_SLASH;
public final static int VK_BACK_SPACE;
public final static int VK_C;
public final static int VK_CANCEL;
public final static int VK_CAPS_LOCK;
public final static int VK_CLEAR;
public final static int VK_CLOSE_BRACKET;
public final static int VK_COMMA;
public final static int VK_CONTROL;
public final static int VK_CONVERT;
public final static int VK_D;
public final static int VK_DECIMAL;
public final static int VK_DELETE;
public final static int VK_DIVIDE;
public final static int VK_DOWN;
public final static int VK_E;
public final static int VK_END;
public final static int VK_ENTER;
public final static int VK_EQUALS;
public final static int VK_ESCAPE;
public final static int VK_F;
public final static int VK_F1;
public final static int VK_F2;
public final static int VK_F3;
public final static int VK_F4;
public final static int VK_F5;
public final static int VK_F6;
public final static int VK_F7;
public final static int VK_F8;
public final static int VK_F9;
public final static int VK_F10;
public final static int VK_F11;
public final static int VK_F12;
public final static int VK_FINAL;
public final static int VK_G;
public final static int VK_H;
public final static int VK_HELP;
public final static int VK_HOME;
public final static int VK_I;
public final static int VK_INSERT;
public final static int VK_J;
public final static int VK_K;
public final static int VK_KANA;
public final static int VK_KANJI;
```

```
public final static int VK_L;
public final static int VK_LEFT;
public final static int VK_M;
public final static int VK_META;
public final static int VK_MODECHANGE;
public final static int VK_MULTIPLY;
public final static int VK_N;
public final static int VK_NONCONVERT;
public final static int VK_NUM_LOCK;
public final static int VK_NUMPAD0;
public final static int VK_NUMPAD1;
public final static int VK_NUMPAD2;
public final static int VK_NUMPAD3;
public final static int VK_NUMPAD4;
public final static int VK_NUMPAD5;
public final static int VK_NUMPAD6;
public final static int VK_NUMPAD7;
public final static int VK_NUMPAD8;
public final static int VK_NUMPAD9;
public final static int VK_O;
public final static int VK_OPEN_BRACKET;
public final static int VK_P;
public final static int VK_PAGE_DOWN;
public final static int VK_PAGE_UP;
public final static int VK_PAUSE;
public final static int VK_PERIOD;
public final static int VK_PRINTSCREEN;
public final static int VK_Q;
public final static int VK_QUOTE;
public final static int VK_R;
public final static int VK_RIGHT;
public final static int VK_S;
public final static int VK_SCROLL_LOCK;
public final static int VK_SEMICOLON;
public final static int VK_SEPARATER;
public final static int VK_SHIFT;
public final static int VK_SLASH;
public final static int VK_SPACE;
public final static int VK_SUBTRACT;
public final static int VK_T;
public final static int VK_TAB;
public final static int VK_U;
public final static int VK_UNDEFINED;
public final static int VK_UP;
public final static int VK_V;
public final static int VK_W;
public final static int VK_X;
public final static int VK_Y;
public final static int VK_Z;
```

```
// Constructors
public KeyEvent (Component source, int id, long when, int modifiers,
  int keyCode, char keyChar);

// Class Methods
public static String getKeyModifiersText(int modifiers);
public static String getKeyText(int keyCode);

// Instance Methods
public char getKeyChar();
public int getKeyCode();
public boolean isActionKey();
public String paramString();
public void setKeyChar (char keyChar);
public void setKeyCode (int keyCode);
public void setModifiers (int modifiers);
}
```

Constants

CHAR_UNDEFINED

public final static int CHAR_UNDEFINED

This constant is used for key presses have that no associated character.

KEY_FIRST

public final static int KEY_FIRST

Specifies the beginning range of key event ID values.

KEY_LAST

public final static int KEY_LAST

Specifies the ending range of key event ID values.

KEY_PRESSED

public final static int KEY_PRESSED

An event ID type for a key press.

KEY_RELEASED

public final static int KEY_RELEASED

An event ID type for a key release.

KEY_TYPED

public final static int KEY_TYPED

An event ID type for a typed key (a press and a release).

VK_0

public final static int VK_0

The 0 key.

VK_1

public final static int VK_1

The 1 key.

VK_2

public final static int VK_2

The 2 key.

VK_3

public final static int VK_3

The 3 key.

VK_4

public final static int VK_4

The 4 key.

VK_5

public final static int VK_5

The 5 key.

VK_6

public final static int VK_6

The 6 key.

VK_7

public final static int VK_7

The 7 key.

VK_8

> public final static int VK_8
>
> The 8 key.

VK_9

> public final static int VK_9
>
> The 9 key.

VK_A

> public final static int VK_A
>
> The 'a' key.

VK_ACCEPT

> public final static int VK_ACCEPT
>
> This constant is used for Asian keyboards.

VK_ADD

> public final static int VK_ADD
>
> The plus (+) key on the numeric keypad.

VK_ALT

> public final static int VK_ALT
>
> The Alt key.

VK_B

> public final static int VK_B
>
> The 'b' key.

VK_BACK_QUOTE

> public final static int VK_BACK_QUOTE
>
> The backquote (') key.

VK_BACK_SLASH

> public final static int VK_BACK_SLASH
>
> The backslash key.

VK_BACK_SPACE

    public final static int VK_BACK_SPACE

The Backspace key.

VK_C

    public final static int VK_C

The 'c' key.

VK_CANCEL

    public final static int VK_CANCEL

The Cancel key.

VK_CAPS_LOCK

    public final static int VK_CAPS_LOCK

The Caps Lock key.

VK_CLEAR

    public final static int VK_CLEAR

The Clear key.

VK_CLOSE_BRACKET

    public final static int VK_CLOSE_BRACKET

The close bracket ']' key.

VK_COMMA

    public final static int VK_COMMA

The comma (,) key.

VK_CONTROL

    public final static int VK_CONTROL

The Control key.

VK_CONVERT

    public final static int VK_CONVERT

This constant is used for Asian keyboards.

VK_D

    public final static int VK_D

The 'd' key.

VK_DECIMAL

    public final static int VK_DECIMAL

The decimal (.) key on the numeric keypad.

VK_DELETE

    public final static int VK_DELETE

The Delete key.

VK_DIVIDE

    public final static int VK_DIVIDE

The divide (/) key on the numeric keypad.

VK_DOWN

    public final static int VK_DOWN

The Down arrow key.

VK_E

    public final static int VK_E

The 'e' key.

VK_END

    public final static int VK_END

The End key.

VK_ENTER

    public final static int VK_ENTER

The Enter key.

VK_EQUALS

    public final static int VK_ EQUALS

The equals (=) key.

VK_ESCAPE

```
public final static int VK_ESCAPE
```

The Escape key.

VK_F

```
public final static int VK_F
```

The 'f' key.

VK_F1

```
public final static int VK_F1
```

The F1 key.

VK_F2

```
public final static int VK_F2
```

The F2 key.

VK_F3

```
public final static int VK_F3
```

The F3 key.

VK_F4

```
public final static int VK_F4
```

The F4 key.

VK_F5

```
public final static int VK_F5
```

The F5 key.

VK_F6

```
public final static int VK_F6
```

The F6 key.

VK_F7

```
public final static int VK_F7
```

The F7 key.

VK_F8

public final static int VK_F8

The F8 key.

VK_F9

public final static int VK_F9

The F9 key.

VK_F10

public final static int VK_F10

The F10 key.

VK_F11

public final static int VK_F11

The F11 key.

VK_F12

public final static int VK_F12

The F12 key.

VK_FINAL

public final static int VK_FINAL

This constant is used for Asian keyboards.

VK_G

public final static int VK_G

The 'g' key.

VK_H

public final static int VK_H

The 'h' key.

VK_HELP

public final static int VK_HELP

The Help key.

VK_HOME

```
public final static int VK_HOME
```

The Home key.

VK_I

```
public final static int VK_I
```

The 'i' key.

VK_INSERT

```
public final static int VK_INSERT
```

The Insert key.

VK_J

```
public final static int VK_J
```

The 'j' key.

VK_K

```
public final static int VK_K
```

The 'k' key.

VK_KANA

```
public final static int VK_KANA
```

This constant is used for Asian keyboards.

VK_KANJI

```
public final static int VK_KANJI
```

This constant is used for Asian keyboards.

VK_L

```
public final static int VK_L
```

The 'l' key.

VK_LEFT

```
public final static int VK_LEFT
```

The Left arrow key.

VK_M

   public final static int VK_M

   The 'm' key.

VK_MODECHANGE

   public final static int VK_MODECHANGE

   This constant is used for Asian keyboards.

VK_META

   public final static int VK_META

   The Meta key.

VK_MULTIPLY

   public final static int VK_MULTIPLY

   The * key on the numeric keypad.

VK_N

   public final static int VK_N

   The 'n' key.

VK_NONCONVERT

   public final static int VK_NONCONVERT

   This constant is used for Asian keyboards.

VK_NUM_LOCK

   public final static int VK_NUM_LOCK

   The Num Lock key.

VK_NUMPAD0

   public final static int VK_NUMPAD0

   The 0 key on the numeric keypad.

VK_NUMPAD1

   public final static int VK_NUMPAD1

   The 1 key on the numeric keypad.

VK_NUMPAD2

    `public final static int VK_NUMPAD2`

    The 2 key on the numeric keypad.

VK_NUMPAD3

    `public final static int VK_NUMPAD3`

    The 3 key on the numeric keypad.

VK_NUMPAD4

    `public final static int VK_NUMPAD4`

    The 4 key on the numeric keypad.

VK_NUMPAD5

    `public final static int VK_NUMPAD5`

    The 5 key on the numeric keypad.

VK_NUMPAD6

    `public final static int VK_NUMPAD6`

    The 6 key on the numeric keypad.

VK_NUMPAD7

    `public final static int VK_NUMPAD7`

    The 7 key on the numeric keypad.

VK_NUMPAD8

    `public final static int VK_NUMPAD8`

    The 8 key on the numeric keypad.

VK_NUMPAD9

    `public final static int VK_NUMPAD9`

    The 9 key on the numeric keypad.

VK_O

    `public final static int VK_O`

    The 'o' key.

VK_OPEN_BRACKET

> public final static int VK_OPEN_BRACKET

> The open bracket '[' key.

VK_P

> public final static int VK_P

> The 'p' key.

VK_PAGE_DOWN

> public final static int VK_PAGE_DOWN

> The Page Down key.

VK_PAGE_UP

> public final static int VK_PAGE_UP

> The Page Up key.

VK_PAUSE

> public final static int VK_PAUSE

> The Pause key.

VK_PERIOD

> public final static int VK_PERIOD

> The period (.) key.

VK_PRINTSCREEN

> public final static int VK_PRINTSCREEN

> The Print Screen key.

VK_Q

> public final static int VK_Q

> The 'q' key.

VK_QUOTE

> public final static int VK_QUOTE

> The quotation mark (") key.

VK_R

```
public final static int VK_R
```

The 'r' key.

VK_RIGHT

```
public final static int VK_RIGHT
```

The Right arrow key.

VK_S

```
public final static int VK_S
```

The 's' key.

VK_SCROLL_LOCK

```
public final static int VK_SCROLL_LOCK
```

The Scroll Lock key.

VK_SEMICOLON

```
public final static int VK_SEMICOLON
```

The semicolon (;) key.

VK_SEPARATER

```
public final static int VK_SEPARATER
```

The numeric separator key on the numeric keypad (i.e., the locale-dependent key used to separate groups of digits). A misspelling of VK_SEPARATOR.

VK_SHIFT

```
public final static int VK_SHIFT
```

The Shift key.

VK_SLASH

```
public final static int VK_SLASH
```

The slash (/) key.

VK_SPACE

> public final static int VK_SPACE

> The space key.

VK_SUBTRACT

> public final static int VK_SUBTRACT

> The subtract (−) key on the numeric keypad.

VK_T

> public final static int VK_T

> The 't' key.

VK_TAB

> public final static int VK_TAB

> The Tab key.

VK_U

> public final static int VK_U

> The 'u' key.

VK_UNDEFINED

> public final static int VK_UNDEFINED

> An undefined key.

VK_UP

> public final static int VK_UP

> The Up arrow key.

VK_V

> public final static int VK_V

> The 'v' key.

VK_W

> public final static int VK_W

> The 'w' key.

VK_X

public final static int VK_X

The 'x' key.

VK_Y

public final static int VK_Y

The 'y' key.

VK_Z

public final static int VK_Z

The 'z' key.

Constructors

KeyEvent

public KeyEvent (Component source, int id, long when, int modifiers, int keyCode, char keyChar)

Parameters	*source*	The object that generated the event.
	id	The event type ID of the event.
	when	When the event occurred, in milliseconds from the epoch.
	modifiers	What modifier keys were pressed with this key.
	keyCode	The code of the key.
	keyChar	The character for this key.
Description		Constructs a KeyEvent with the given characteristics.

Class Methods

getKeyModifiersText

public static String getKeyModifiersText(int modifiers)

| Parameters | *modifiers* | One or more modifier keys. |
| Returns | | A string describing the modifiers. |

getKeyText

public static String getKeyText(int keyCode)

| Parameters | *keyCode* | One of the key codes. |
| Returns | | A string describing the given key. |

Instance Methods

getKeyChar

`public char getKeyChar()`

Returns   The character corresponding to this event. KEY_TYPED events have characters.

getKeyCode

`public int getKeyCode()`

Returns   The integer key code corresponding to this event. This will be one of the constants defined above. KEY_PRESSED and KEY_RELEASED events have codes. Key codes are virtual keys, not actual. Pressing the 'a' key is identical to 'A', but has different modifiers. Same for '/' and '?' on a standard keyboard.

isActionKey

`public boolean isActionKey()`

Returns   true if this event is for one of the action keys; false otherwise.

Description   In general, an action key is a key that causes an action but has no printing equivalent. The action keys are the function keys, the arrow keys, Caps Lock, End, Home, Insert, Num Lock, Pause, Page Down, Page Up, Print Screen, and Scroll Lock. They do not generate a KEY_TYPED event, only KEY_PRESSED and KEY_RELEASED.

paramString

`public String paramString()`

Returns   A string with current settings of the KeyEvent.

Overrides   ComponentEvent.paramString()

Description   Helper method for toString() to generate string of current settings.

setKeyChar

`public void setKeyChar(char keyChar)`

Parameters   *keyChar*   The new key character.

Description   Sets the character code of this KeyEvent.

setKeyCode

```
public void setKeyCode (int keyCode)
```

Parameters   *keyCode*   The new key code.

Description   Sets the key code of this KeyEvent.

setModifiers

```
public void setModifiers (int modifiers)
```

Parameters   *modifiers*   The new modifiers.

Description   This is a combination of the mask constants defined in
                java.awt.event.InputEvent.

See Also

Component, ComponentEvent, InputEvent, KeyAdapter, KeyListener

21.19   *KeyListener* ★

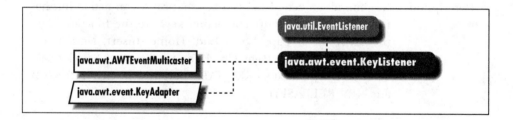

Description

Objects that implement the KeyListener interface can receive KeyEvent objects.
Listeners must first register themselves with objects that produce events. When
events occur, they are then automatically propagated to all registered listeners.

Interface Definition

```
public abstract interface java.awt.event.KeyListener
    extends java.util.EventListener {

  // Instance Methods
  public abstract void keyPressed (KeyEvent e);
  public abstract void keyReleased (KeyEvent e);
  public abstract void keyTyped (KeyEvent e);
}
```

Interface Methods

keyPressed

    public abstract void keyPressed (KeyEvent e)

Parameters   *e*   The key event that occurred.

Description   Notifies the KeyListener that a key was pressed.

keyReleased

    public abstract void keyReleased (KeyEvent e)

Parameters   *e*   The key event that occurred.

Description   Notifies the KeyListener that a key was released.

keyTyped

    public abstract void keyTyped (KeyEvent e)

Parameters   *e*   The key event that occurred.

Description   Notifies the KeyListener that a key was typed (pressed and
               released).

See Also

AWTEventMulticaster, EventListener, KeyEvent, KeyListener

21.20   *MouseAdapter* ★

Description

The MouseAdapter class implements the methods of MouseListener with empty
functions. It may be easier for you to extend MouseAdapter, overriding only those
methods you are interested in, than to implement MouseListener and provide the
empty functions yourself.

Class Definition

    public abstract class java.awt.event.MouseAdapter
        extends java.lang.Object
        implements java.awt.event.MouseListener {

    // Instance Methods

```
  public void mouseClicked (MouseEvent e);
  public void mouseEntered (MouseEvent e);
  public void mouseExited (MouseEvent e);
  public void mousePressed (MouseEvent e);
  public void mouseReleased (MouseEvent e);
}
```

Instance Methods

mouseClicked

```
public void mouseClicked (MouseEvent e)
```

Parameters   *e*   The event that has occurred.

Description   Does nothing. Override this function to be notified when the mouse button is clicked (pressed and released).

mouseEntered

```
public void mouseEntered (MouseEvent e)
```

Parameters   *e*   The event that has occurred.

Description   Does nothing. Override this function to be notified when the user moves the mouse cursor into a component.

mouseExited

```
public void mouseExited (MouseEvent e)
```

Parameters   *e*   The event that has occurred.

Description   Does nothing. Override this function to be notified when the moves the mouse cursor out of a component.

mousePressed

```
public void mousePressed (MouseEvent e)
```

Parameters   *e*   The event that has occurred.

Description   Does nothing. Override this function to be notified when the mouse button is pressed.

mouseReleased

```
public void mouseReleased (MouseEvent e)
```

Parameters   *e*   The event that has occurred.

Description   Does nothing. Override this function to be notified when the
              mouse button is released.

See Also

MouseEvent, MouseListener

21.21   MouseEvent ★

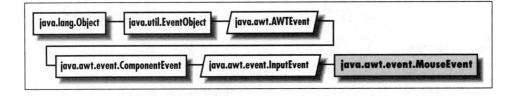

Description

Mouse events are generated when the user moves and clicks the mouse.

Class Definition

```
public class java.awt.event.MouseEvent
   extends java.awt.event.InputEvent {

   // Constants
   public final static int MOUSE_CLICKED;
   public final static int MOUSE_DRAGGED;
   public final static int MOUSE_ENTERED;
   public final static int MOUSE_EXITED;
   public final static int MOUSE_FIRST;
   public final static int MOUSE_LAST;
   public final static int MOUSE_MOVED;
   public final static int MOUSE_PRESSED;
   public final static int MOUSE_RELEASED;

   // Constructors
   public MouseEvent (Component source, int id, long when, int modifiers, int x,
      int y, int clickCount, boolean popupTrigger);

   // Instance Methods
   public int getClickCount();
   public synchronized Point getPoint();
   public int getX();
   public int getY();
   public boolean isPopupTrigger();
   public String paramString();
   public synchronized void translatePoint (int x, int y);
```

```
}
```

Constants

MOUSE_CLICKED

```
public final static int MOUSE_CLICKED
```

An event type ID indicating a mouse click.

MOUSE_DRAGGED

```
public final static int MOUSE_DRAGGED
```

An event type ID indicating a mouse move with the button held down.

MOUSE_ENTERED

```
public final static int MOUSE_ENTERED
```

An event type ID indicating that a mouse entered a component.

MOUSE_EXITED

```
public final static int MOUSE_EXITED
```

An event type ID indicating that a mouse left a component.

MOUSE_FIRST

```
public final static int MOUSE_FIRST
```

Specifies the beginning range of mouse event ID values.

MOUSE_LAST

```
public final static int MOUSE_LAST
```

Specifies the ending range of mouse event ID values.

MOUSE_MOVED

```
public final static int MOUSE_MOVED
```

An event type ID indicating a mouse move.

MOUSE_PRESSED

```
public final static int MOUSE_PRESSED
```

An event type ID indicating a mouse button press.

MOUSE_RELEASED

    public final static int MOUSE_RELEASED

An event type ID indicating a mouse button release.

Constructors

MouseEvent

    public MouseEvent (Component source, int id, long when, int
    modifiers, int x, int y, int clickCount, boolean popupTrigger)

Parameters	*source*	The object that generated the event.
	id	The event type ID of the event.
	when	When the event occurred, in milliseconds from the epoch.
	modifiers	What modifier keys were pressed with this key.
	x	The horizontal location of the event.
	y	The vertical location of the event.
	clickCount	The number of times the mouse button has been clicked.
	popupTrigger	A flag indicating if this event is a popup trigger event.
Description		Constructs a MouseEvent with the given characteristics.

Instance Methods

getClickCount

    public int getClickCount()

Returns	The number of consecutive mouse button clicks for this event.

getPoint

    public synchronized Point getPoint()

Returns	The location where the event happened.

getX

    public int getX()

Returns	The horizontal location where the event happened.

getY

```
public int getY()
```

Returns   The vertical location where the event happened.

isPopupTrigger

```
public boolean isPopupTrigger()
```

Returns   Returns true if this event is the popup menu event for the run-
time system.

paramString

```
public String paramString()
```

Returns   String with current settings of the MouseEvent.
Overrides   ComponentEvent.paramString()
Description   Helper method for toString() to generate string of current
settings.

translatePoint

```
public synchronized void translatePoint (int x, int y)
```

Parameters   *x*   The horizontal amount of translation.
                 y   The vertical amount of translation.

Description   Translates the location of the event by the given amounts.

See Also

Component, ComponentEvent, InputEvent, MouseAdapter, MouseListener, Point

21.22   MouseListener ★

Description

Objects that implement the MouseListener interface can receive non-motion oriented MouseEvent objects. Listeners must first register themselves with objects that
produce events. When events occur, they are then automatically propagated to all
registered listeners.

Interface Definition

```
public abstract interface java.awt.event.MouseListener
    extends java.util.EventListener {

  // Instance Methods
  public abstract void mouseClicked (MouseEvent e);
```

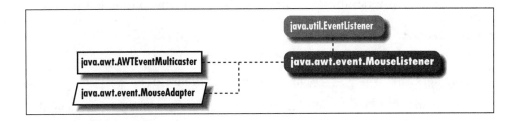

```
    public abstract void mouseEntered (MouseEvent e);
    public abstract void mouseExited (MouseEvent e);
    public abstract void mousePressed (MouseEvent e);
    public abstract void mouseReleased (MouseEvent e);
}
```

Interface Methods

mouseClicked

public abstract void mouseClicked (MouseEvent e)

| Parameters | *e* | The key event that occurred. |

Description   Notifies the MouseListener that the mouse button was clicked (pressed and released).

mouseEntered

public abstract void mouseEntered (MouseEvent e)

| Parameters | *e* | The key event that occurred. |

Description   Notifies the MouseListener that the mouse cursor has been moved into a component's coordinate space.

mouseExited

public abstract void mouseExited (MouseEvent e)

| Parameters | *e* | The key event that occurred. |

Description   Notifies the MouseListener that the mouse cursor has been moved out of a component's coordinate space.

mousePressed

public abstract void mousePressed (MouseEvent e)

| Parameters | *e* | The key event that occurred. |

Description   Notifies the MouseListener that the mouse button was pressed.

mouseReleased

    public abstract void mouseReleased (MouseEvent e)

Parameters   *e*   The key event that occurred.

Description   Notifies the MouseListener that the mouse button was released.

See Also

EventListener, MouseAdapter, MouseEvent

21.23   *MouseMotionAdapter* ★

Description

The MouseMotionAdapter class implements the methods of MouseMotionListener
with empty functions. It may be easier for you to extend MouseMotionAdapter,
overriding only those methods you are interested in, than to implement MouseMotionListener and provide the empty functions yourself.

Class Definition

```
public abstract class java.awt.event.MouseMotionAdapter
    extends java.lang.Object
    implements java.awt.event.MouseMotionListener {

// Instance Methods
public void mouseDragged (MouseEvent e);
public void mouseMoved (MouseEvent e);
}
```

Instance Methods

mouseDragged

```
public void mouseDragged (MouseEvent e)
```

Parameters   *e*   The event that has occurred.

Description   Does nothing. Override this function to be notified when the mouse is dragged.

mouseMoved

```
public void mouseEntered (MouseEvent e)
```

Parameters   *e*   The event that has occurred.

Description   Does nothing. Override this function to be notified when the mouse moves.

See Also

MouseEvent, MouseMotionListener

21.24   MouseMotionListener ★

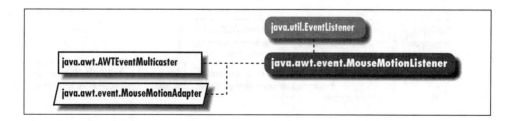

Description

Objects that implement the MouseMotionListener interface can receive motion-oriented MouseEvent objects. Listeners must first register themselves with objects that produce events. When events occur, they are automatically propagated to all registered listeners.

Interface Definition

```
public abstract interface java.awt.event.MouseMotionListener
   extends java.util.EventListener {

  // Instance Methods
  public abstract void mouseDragged (MouseEvent e);
  public abstract void mouseMoved (MouseEvent e);
}
```

Interface Methods

mouseDragged

```
public abstract void mouseDragged (MouseEvent e)
```

Parameters   *e*   The key event that occurred.

Description   Notifies the `MouseMotionListener` that the mouse has been dragged.

mouseMoved

```
public abstract void mouseMoved (MouseEvent e)
```

Parameters   *e*   The key event that occurred.

Description   Notifies the `MouseMotionListener` that the mouse has been moved.

See Also

`AWTEventMulticaster, EventListener, MouseEvent, MouseMotionAdapter`

21.25   PaintEvent ★

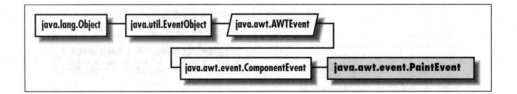

Description

The `PaintEvent` class represents the paint and update operations that the AWT performs on components. There is no `PaintListener` interface, so the only way to catch these events is to override `paint(Graphics)` and `update(Graphics)` in `Component`. This class exists so that paint events will get serialized properly.

Class Definition

```
public class java.awt.event.PaintEvent
    extends java.awt.event.ComponentEvent {

    // Constants
    public final static int PAINT;
    public final static int PAINT_FIRST;
    public final static int PAINT_LAST;
    public final static int UPDATE;
```

```
// Constructor
public PaintEvent (Component source, int id, Rectangle updateRect);

// Instance Methods
public Rectangle getUpdateRect();
public String paramString();
public void setUpdateRect (Rectangle updateRect);
}
```

Class Definition

```
public class java.awt.event.PaintEvent
        extends java.awt.event.ComponentEvent {

    // Constants
    public final static int PAINT;
    public final static int PAINT_FIRST;
    public final static int PAINT_LAST;
    public final static int UPDATE;

    //Constructor
    public PaintEvent (Component source, int id, Rectangle updateRect);

    // Instance Methods
    public Rectangle getUpdateRect();
    public String paramString();
    public void setUpdateRect (Rectangle updateRect);
}
```

Constants

PAINT

public final static int PAINT

The paint event type.

PAINT_FIRST

public final static int PAINT_FIRST

Specifies the beginning range of paint event ID values.

PAINT_LAST

public final static int PAINT_LAST

Specifies the ending range of paint event ID values.

UPDATE

> public final static int UPDATE

The update event type.

Constructor

PaintEvent

> public PaintEvent (Component source, ind id, Rectangle updateRect)

Parameters	*source*	The source of the event.
	id	The event type ID.
	g	The rectangular area to paint.

Description	Constructs a PaintEvent with the given characteristics.

Instance Methods

getUpdateRect

> public Rectangle getUpdateRect()

Returns	The rectangular area that needs painting.

paramString

> public String paramString()

Returns	String with current settings of the PaintEvent.
Overrides	ComponentEvent.paramString()
Description	Helper method for toString() to generate string of current settings.

setUpdateRect

> public void setUpdateRect (Rectangle updateRect)

Parameters	*updateRect*	The rectangular area to paint.

Description	Changes the rectangular area that this PaintEvent will paint.

See Also

Component, ComponentEvent, Graphics

21.26   *TextEvent* ★

Description

Text events are generated by text components when their contents change, either programmatically or by a user typing.

Class Definition

```
public class java.awt.event.TextEvent
    extends java.awt.AWTEvent {

    // Constants
    public final static int TEXT_FIRST;
    public final static int TEXT_LAST;
    public final static int TEXT_VALUE_CHANGED;

    // Constructors
    public TextEvent (Object source, int id);

    // Instance Methods
    public String paramString();
}
```

Constants

TEXT_FIRST

   public final static int TEXT_FIRST

   Specifies the beginning range of text event ID values.

TEXT_LAST

   public final static int TEXT_LAST

   Specifies the ending range of text event ID values.

TEXT_VALUE_CHANGED

   public final static int TEXT_VALUE_CHANGED

   The only text event type; it indicates that the contents of something have changed.

Constructors

TextEvent

```
public TextEvent (Object source, int id)
```

Parameters   *source*   The object that generated the event.
             id   The type ID of the event.

Description   Constructs a TextEvent with the given characteristics.

Instance Methods

paramString

```
public String paramString()
```

Returns   String with current settings of the TextEvent.
Overrides   AWTEvent.paramString()
Description   Helper method for toString() to generate string of current
              settings.

See Also

AWTEvent, TextListener

21.27   TextListener ★

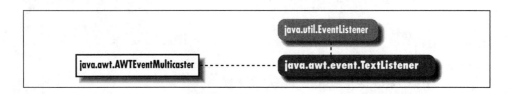

Description

Objects that implement the TextListener interface can receive TextEvent objects.
Listeners must first register themselves with objects that produce events. When
events occur, they are then automatically propagated to all registered listeners.

Interface Definition

```
public abstract interface java.awt.event.TextListener
   extends java.util.EventListener {

 // Interface Methods
 public abstract void textValueChanged (TextEvent e);
}
```

Interface Methods

textValueChanged

  public abstract void textValueChanged (TextEvent e)

  Parameters   *e*   The text event that occurred.

  Description   Notifies the TextListener that an event occurred.

See Also

AWTEventMulticaster, EventListener, TextEvent

21.28   WindowAdapter ★

Description

The WindowAdapter class implements the methods of WindowListener with empty functions. It may be easier for you to extend WindowAdapter, overriding only those methods you are interested in, than to implement WindowListener and provide the empty functions yourself.

Class Definition

```
public abstract class java.awt.event.WindowAdapter
   extends java.lang.Object
   implements java.awt.event.WindowListener {

   // Instance Methods
   public void windowActivated (WindowEvent e);
   public void windowClosed (WindowEvent e);
   public void windowClosing (WindowEvent e);
   public void windowDeactivated (WindowEvent e);
   public void windowDeiconified (WindowEvent e);
   public void windowIconified (WindowEvent e);
   public void windowOpened (WindowEvent e);
}
```

Instance Methods

windowActivated

```
public void windowActivated (WindowEvent e)
```

Parameters   *e*   The event that has occurred.

Description   Does nothing. Override this function to be notified when a window is activated.

windowClosed

```
public void windowClosed (WindowEvent e)
```

Parameters   *e*   The event that has occurred.

Description   Does nothing. Override this function to be notified when a window is closed.

windowClosing

```
public void windowClosing (WindowEvent e)
```

Parameters   *e*   The event that has occurred.

Description   Does nothing. Override this function to be notified when a window is in the process of closing.

windowDeactivated

```
public void windowDeactivated (WindowEvent e)
```

Parameters   *e*   The event that has occurred.

Description   Does nothing. Override this function to be notified when a window is deactivated.

windowDeiconified

```
public void windowDeiconified (WindowEvent e)
```

Parameters   *e*   The event that has occurred.

Description   Does nothing. Override this function to be notified when an iconified window is restored.

windowIconified

```
public void windowIconified (WindowEvent e)
```

Parameters   *e*   The event that has occurred.

Description   Does nothing. Override this function to be notified when a window is iconified (minimized).

windowOpened

```
public void windowOpened (WindowEvent e)
```

Parameters   *e*   The event that has occurred.

Description   Does nothing. Override this function to be notified when a window is opened.

See Also

WindowEvent, WindowListener

21.29   *WindowEvent* ★

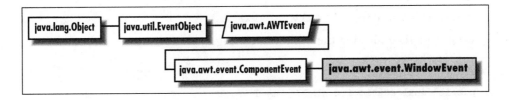

Description

Window events are generated when a window is opened, closed, iconified, or deiconified.

Class Definition

```
public class java.awt.event.WindowEvent
    extends java.awt.event.ComponentEvent {

    // Constants
    public final static int WINDOW_ACTIVATED;
    public final static int WINDOW_CLOSED;
    public final static int WINDOW_CLOSING;
    public final static int WINDOW_DEACTIVATED;
    public final static int WINDOW_DEICONIFIED;
    public final static int WINDOW_FIRST;
    public final static int WINDOW_ICONIFIED;
    public final static int WINDOW_LAST;
```

```
public final static int WINDOW_OPENED;

// Constructors
public WindowEvent (Window source, int id);

// Instance Methods
public Window getWindow();
public String paramString();
}
```

Constants

WINDOW_ACTIVATED

`public final static int WINDOW_ACTIVATED`

Event type ID indicating the window has been activated, brought to the foreground.

WINDOW_CLOSED

`public final static int WINDOW_CLOSED`

Event type ID indicating the window has closed.

WINDOW_CLOSING

`public final static int WINDOW_CLOSING`

Event type ID indicating the window is closing.

WINDOW_DEACTIVATED

`public final static int WINDOW_DEACTIVATED`

Event type ID indicating the window has been deactivated, placed in the background.

WINDOW_DEICONIFIED

`public final static int WINDOW_DEICONIFIED`

Event type ID indicating the window has been restored from an iconified state.

WINDOW_FIRST

`public final static int WINDOW_FIRST`

Specifies the beginning range of window event ID values.

WINDOW_ICONIFIED

public final static int WINDOW_ICONIFIED

Event type ID indicating the window has been iconified (minimized).

WINDOW_LAST

public final static int WINDOW_LAST

Specifies the ending range of window event ID values.

WINDOW_OPENED

public final static int WINDOW_OPENED

Event type ID indicating the window has opened.

Constructors

WindowEvent

public WindowEvent (Window source, int id)

Parameters	*source*	The object that generated the event.
	id	The event type ID of the event.
Description		Constructs a WindowEvent with the given characteristics.

Instance Methods

getWindow

public Window getWindow()

| Returns | The window that generated this event. |

paramString

public String paramString()

Returns	String with current settings of the WindowEvent.
Overrides	ComponentEvent.paramString()
Description	Helper method for toString() to generate string of current settings.

See Also

ComponentEvent, Window, WindowAdapter, WindowListener

21.30 *WindowListener* ★

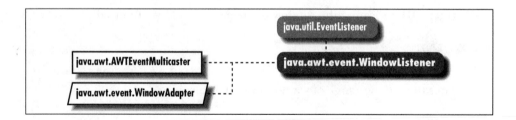

Description

Objects that implement the WindowListener interface can receive WindowEvent objects. Listeners must first register themselves with objects that produce events. When events occur, they are then automatically propagated to all registered listeners.

Interface Definition

```
public abstract interface java.awt.event.WindowListener
    extends java.util.EventListener {

  // Instance Methods
  public abstract void windowActivated (WindowEvent e);
  public abstract void windowClosed (WindowEvent e);
  public abstract void windowClosing (WindowEvent e);
  public abstract void windowDeactivated (WindowEvent e);
  public abstract void windowDeiconified (WindowEvent e);
  public abstract void windowIconified (WindowEvent e);
  public abstract void windowOpened (WindowEvent e);
}
```

Interface Methods

windowActivated

public abstract void windowActivated (WindowEvent e)

Parameters   *e*   The event that occurred.

Description   Notifies the WindowListener that a window has been activated.

windowClosed

public abstract void windowClosed (WindowEvent e)

Parameters   *e*   The event that occurred.

Description   Notifies the WindowListener that a window has closed.

windowClosing

public abstract void windowClosing (WindowEvent e)

Parameters   *e*   The event that occurred.

Description   Notifies the WindowListener that a window is closing.

windowDeactivated

public abstract void windowDeactivated (WindowEvent e)

Parameters   *e*   The event that occurred.

Description   Notifies the WindowListener that a window has been deactivated.

windowDeiconified

public abstract void windowDeiconified (WindowEvent e)

Parameters   *e*   The event that occurred.

Description   Notifies the WindowListener that a window has been restored from an iconified state.

windowIconified

public abstract void windowIconified (WindowEvent e)

Parameters   *e*   The event that occurred.

Description   Notifies the WindowListener that a window has iconified (minimized).

windowOpened

public abstract void windowOpened (WindowEvent e)

Parameters   *e*   The event that occurred.

Description   Notifies the WindowListener that a window has opened.

See Also

AWTEventMulticaster, EventListener, Window, WindowAdapter, WindowEvent

22

java.awt.image Reference

22.1   AreaAveragingScaleFilter ★

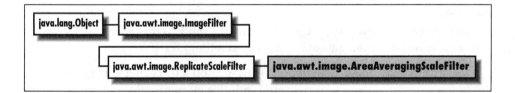

Description

The AreaAveragingScaleFilter class scales an image using a simple smoothing algorithm.

Class Definition

```
public class java.awt.image.AreaAveragingScaleFilter
    extends java.awt.image.ReplicateScaleFilter {

  // Constructor
  public AreaAveragingScaleFilter (int width, int height);

  // Instance Methods
  public void setHints (int hints);
  public void setPixels (int x, int y, int w, int h, ColorModel model,
    byte[] pixels, int off, int scansize);
```

```
    public void setPixels (int x, int y, int w, int h, ColorModel model,
      int[] pixels, int off, int scansize);
}
```

Constructor

AreaAveragingScaleFilter

public AreaAveragingScaleFilter (int width, int height)

Parameters	*width*	Width of scaled image.
	height	Height of scaled image.
Description	Constructs an AverageScaleFilter that scales the original image to the specified size.	

Instance Methods

setHints

public void setHints (int hints)

Parameters	*hints*	Flags indicating how data will be delivered.
Overrides	ImageFilter.setHints(int)	
Description	Gives this filter hints about how data will be delivered.	

setPixels

public void setPixels (int x, int y, int w, int h, ColorModel model, byte[] pixels, int off, int scansize)

Parameters	*x*	x-coordinate of top-left corner of pixel data delivered with this method call.
	y	y-coordinate of top-left corner of pixel data delivered with this method call.
	w	Width of the rectangle of pixel data delivered with this method call.
	h	Height of the rectangle of pixel data delivered with this method call.
	model	Color model of image data.
	pixels	Image data.
	off	Offset from beginning of the pixels array.
	scansize	Size of each line of data in pixels array.
Overrides	ReplicateScaleFilter.setPixels(int, int, int, int, ColorModel, byte[], int, int)	
Description	Receives a rectangle of image data from the ImageProducer; scales these pixels and delivers them to any ImageConsumers.	

```
public void setPixels (int x, int y, int w, int h, ColorModel
model, int[] pixels, int off, int scansize)
```

Parameters	*x*	x-coordinate of top-left corner of pixel data delivered with this method call.
	y	y-coordinate of top-left corner of pixel data delivered with this method call.
	w	Width of the rectangle of pixel data delivered with this method call.
	h	Height of the rectangle of pixel data delivered with this method call.
	model	Color model of image data.
	pixels	Image data.
	off	Offset from beginning of the pixels array.
	scansize	Size of each line of data in pixels array.
Overrides	ReplicateScaleFilter.setPixels(int, int, int, int, ColorModel, int[], int, int)	
Description	Receives a rectangle of image data from the ImageProducer; scales these pixels and delivers them to any ImageConsumers.	

See Also

ColorModel, ReplicateScaleFilter

22.2   ColorModel

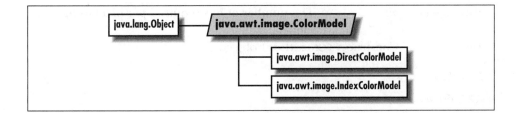

Description

The abstract ColorModel class defines the way a Java program represents colors. It provides methods for extracting different color components from a pixel.

Class Definition

```
public class java.awt.image.ColorModel
    extends java.lang.Object {

    // Variables
```

```
    protected int pixel_bits;

    // Constructors
    public ColorModel (int bits);

    // Class Methods
    public static ColorModel getRGBdefault();

    // Instance Methods
    public void finalize();  ★
    public abstract int getAlpha (int pixel);
    public abstract int getBlue (int pixel);
    public abstract int getGreen (int pixel);
    public int getPixelSize();
    public abstract int getRed (int pixel);
    public int getRGB (int pixel);
}
```

ProtectedVariables

pixel_bits

protected int pixel_bits

The pixel_bits variable saves the ColorModel's bits setting (the total number of bits per pixel).

Constructors

ColorModel

public ColorModel (int bits)

Parameters	*bits*	The number of bits required per pixel using this model.
Description		Constructs a ColorModel object.

Class Methods

getRGBdefault

public static ColorModel getRGBdefault()

Returns	The default ColorModel format, which uses 8 bits for each of a pixel's color components: alpha (transparency), red, green, and blue.

Instance Methods

finalize

```
public void finalize() ★
```

Overrides   Object.finalize()

Description   Cleans up when this object is garbage collected.

getAlpha

```
public abstract int getAlpha (int pixel)
```

Parameters   *pixel*   A pixel encoded with this ColorModel.

Returns   The current alpha setting of the pixel.

getBlue

```
public abstract int getBlue (int pixel)
```

Parameters   *pixel*   A pixel encoded with this ColorModel.

Returns   The current blue setting of the pixel.

getGreen

```
public abstract int getGreen (int pixel)
```

Parameters   *pixel*   A pixel encoded with this ColorModel.

Returns   The current green setting of the pixel.

getPixelSize

```
public int getPixelSize()
```

Returns   The current pixel size for the color model.

getRed

```
public abstract int getRed (int pixel)
```

Parameters   *pixel*   A pixel encoded with this ColorModel.

Returns   The current red setting of the pixel.

getRGB

```
public int getRGB (int pixel)
```

Parameters   *pixel*   A pixel encoded with this ColorModel.

Returns   The current combined red, green, and blue settings of the pixel.

Description   Gets the color of `pixel` in the default RGB color model.

See Also

`DirectColorModel`, `IndexColorModel`, `Object`

22.3   *CropImageFilter*

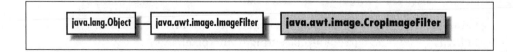

Description

The `CropImageFilter` class creates a smaller image by cropping (i.e., extracting a rectangular region from) a larger image.

Class Definition

```
public class java.awt.image.CropImageFilter
    extends java.awt.image.ImageFilter {

// Constructors
public CropImageFilter (int x, int y, int width, int height);

// Instance Methods
public void setDimensions (int width, int height);
public void setPixels (int x, int y, int width, int height, ColorModel model,
   byte[] pixels, int offset, int scansize);
public void setPixels (int x, int y, int width, int height, ColorModel model,
   int[] pixels, int offset, int scansize);
public void setProperties (Hashtable properties);
}
```

Constructors

CropImageFilter

`public CropImageFilter (int x, int y, int width, int height)`

Parameters	*x*	x-coordinate of top-left corner of piece to crop.
	y	y-coordinate of top-left corner of piece to crop.
	width	Width of image to crop.
	height	Height of image to crop.
Description		Constructs a `CropImageFilter` that crops the specified region from the original image.

Instance Methods

setDimensions

```
public void setDimensions (int width, int height)
```

Parameters	*width*	Ignored parameter.
	height	Ignored parameter.
Overrides		`ImageFilter.setDimensions(int, int)`
Description		Called with the original image's dimensions; these dimensions are ignored. The method in turn calls the `ImageConsumer` with the dimensions of the cropped image.

setPixels

```
public void setPixels (int x, int y, int width, int height,
ColorModel model, byte[] pixels, int offset, int scansize)
```

Parameters	*x*	x-coordinate of top-left corner of pixel data delivered with this method call.
	y	y-coordinate of top-left corner of pixel data delivered with this method call.
	width	Width of the rectangle of pixel data delivered with this method call.
	height	Height of the rectangle of pixel data delivered with this method call.
	model	Color model of image data.
	pixels	Image data.
	offset	Offset from beginning of the pixels array.
	scansize	Size of each line of data in pixels array.
Overrides		`ImageFilter.setPixels(int, int, int, int, ColorModel, byte[], int, int)`
Description		Receives a rectangle of image data from the `ImageProducer`; crops these pixels and delivers them to any `ImageConsumers`.

```
public void setPixels (int x, int y, int width, int height,
ColorModel model, int[] pixels, int offset, int scansize)
```

Parameters	*x*	x-coordinate of top-left corner of pixel data delivered with this method call.
	y	y-coordinate of top-left corner of pixel data delivered with this method call.
	width	Width of the rectangle of pixel data delivered with this method call.

	height	Height of the rectangle of pixel data delivered with this method call.
	model	Color model of image data.
	pixels	Image data.
	offset	Offset from beginning of the pixels array.
	scansize	Size of each line of data in pixels array.

Overrides   `ImageFilter.setPixels(int, int, int, int, ColorModel, int[], int, int)`

Description   Receives a rectangle of image data from the `ImageProducer`; crops these pixels and delivers them to any `ImageConsumers`.

setProperties

`public void setProperties (Hashtable properties)`

Parameters   *properties*   The properties for the image.

Overrides   `ImageFilter.setProperties(Hashtable)`

Description   Adds the "croprect" image property to the properties list.

See Also

`ColorModel`, `Hashtable`, `ImageFilter`

22.4   DirectColorModel

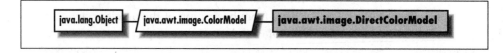

Description

The `DirectColorModel` class provides a `ColorModel` that specifies a translation between pixels and alpha, red, green, and blue component values, where the color values are embedded directly within the pixel.

Class Definition

```
public class java.awt.image.DirectColorModel
    extends java.awt.image.ColorModel {

  // Constructors
  public DirectColorModel (int bits, int redMask, int greenMask,
    int blueMask);
  public DirectColorModel (int bits, int redMask, int greenMask,
    int blueMask,
    int alphaMask);
```

```
// Instance Methods
public final int getAlpha (int pixel);
public final int getAlphaMask();
public final int getBlue (int pixel);
public final int getBlueMask();
public final int getGreen (int pixel);
public final int getGreenMask()
public final int getRed (int pixel);
public final int getRedMask();
public final int getRGB (int pixel);
}
```

Constructors

DirectColorModel

public DirectColorModel (int bits, int redMask, int greenMask, int blueMask)

Parameters	*bits*	The number of bits required per pixel of an image using this model.
	redMask	The location of the red component of a pixel.
	greenMask	The location of the green component of a pixel.
	blueMask	The location of the blue component of a pixel.
Throws	IllegalArgumentException	
		If the mask bits are not contiguous or overlap.
Description		Constructs a DirectColorModel object with the given size and color masks; the alpha (transparency) component is not used.

public DirectColorModel (int bits, int redMask, int greenMask, int blueMask, int alphaMask)

Parameters	*bits*	The number of bits required per pixel of an image using this model.
	redMask	The location of the red component of a pixel.
	greenMask	The location of the green component of a pixel.
	blueMask	The location of the blue component of a pixel.
	alphaMask	The location of the alpha component of a pixel.
Throws	IllegalArgumentException	
		If the mask bits are not contiguous or overlap.
Description		Constructs a DirectColorModel object with the given size and color masks.

Instance Methods

getAlpha

```
public final int getAlpha (int pixel)
```

Parameters	*pixel*	A pixel encoded with this ColorModel.
Returns		The current alpha setting of the pixel.
Overrides		ColorModel.getAlpha(int)

getAlphaMask

```
public final int getAlphaMask()
```

Returns	The current alpha mask setting of the color model.

getBlue

```
public final int getBlue (int pixel)
```

Parameters	*pixel*	A pixel encoded with this ColorModel.
Returns		The current blue setting of the pixel.
Overrides		ColorModel.getBlue(int)

getBlueMask

```
public final int getBlueMask()
```

Returns	The current blue mask setting of the color model.

getGreen

```
public final int getGreen (int pixel)
```

Parameters	*pixel*	A pixel encoded with this ColorModel.
Returns		The current green setting of the pixel.
Overrides		ColorModel.getGreen(int)

getGreenMask

```
public final int getGreenMask()
```

Returns	The current green mask setting of the color model.

getRed

```
public final int getRed (int pixel)
```

Parameters	*pixel*	A pixel encoded with this ColorModel.
Returns		The current red setting of the pixel.

Overrides   ColorModel.getRed(int)

getRedMask

public final int getRedMask()

Returns   The current red mask setting of the color model.

getRGB

public final int getRGB (int pixel)

Parameters   *pixel*   A pixel encoded with this ColorModel.
Returns   The current combined red, green, and blue settings of the
                 pixel.
Overrides   ColorModel.getRGB(int)
Description   Gets the color of pixel in the default RGB color model.

See Also

ColorModel

22.5   FilteredImageSource

Description

The FilteredImageSource class acts as glue to put an original ImageProducer and
ImageFilter together to create a new image. As the ImageProducer for the new
image, FilteredImageSource is responsible for registering image consumers for
the new image.

Class Definition

```
public class java.awt.image.FilteredImageSource
    extends java.lang.Object
    implements java.awt.image.ImageProducer {

  // Constructors
  public FilteredImageSource (ImageProducer original,
     ImageFilter filter);

  // Instance Methods
  public synchronized void addConsumer (ImageConsumer ic);
  public synchronized boolean isConsumer (ImageConsumer ic);
```

```
    public synchronized void removeConsumer (ImageConsumer ic);
    public void requestTopDownLeftRightResend (ImageConsumer ic);
    public void startProduction (ImageConsumer ic);
}
```

Constructors

FilteredImageSource

public FilteredImageSource (ImageProducer original, ImageFilter filter)

Parameters	*original*	An ImageProducer that generates the image to be filtered.
	filter	The ImageFilter to use to process image data delivered by original.
Description		Constructs a FilteredImageSource object to filter an image generated by an ImageProducer.

Class Methods

addConsumer

public synchronized void addConsumer (ImageConsumer ic)

Parameters	*ic*	ImageConsumer interested in receiving the new image.
Implements		ImageProducer.addConsumer(ImageConsumer)
Description		Registers an ImageConsumer as interested in Image information.

isConsumer

public synchronized boolean isConsumer (ImageConsumer ic)

Parameters	*ic*	ImageConsumer to check.
Returns		true if ImageConsumer is registered with this ImageProducer, false otherwise.
Implements		ImageProducer.isConsumer(ImageConsumer)

removeConsumer

public synchronized void removeConsumer (ImageConsumer ic)

Parameters	*ic*	ImageConsumer to remove.
Implements	ImageProducer.removeConsumer(ImageConsumer)	
Description	Removes an ImageConsumer from the registered consumers for this ImageProducer.	

requestTopDownLeftRightResend

public void requestTopDownLeftRightResend (ImageConsumer ic)

Parameters	*ic*	ImageConsumer to communicate with.
Implements	ImageProducer.requestTopDownLeftRightResend()	
Description	Requests the retransmission of the Image data in top-down, left-to-right order.	

startProduction

public void startProduction (ImageConsumer ic)

Parameters	*ic*	ImageConsumer to communicate with.
Implements	ImageProducer.startProduction(ImageConsumer)	
Description	Registers ImageConsumer as interested in Image information and tells ImageProducer to start creating the filtered Image data immediately.	

See Also

ImageFilter, ImageConsumer, ImageProducer, Object

22.6   ImageConsumer

Description

ImageConsumer is an interface that provides the means to consume pixel data and render it for display.

Interface Definition

```
public abstract interface java.awt.image.ImageConsumer {

    // Constants
    public final static int COMPLETESCANLINES;
    public final static int IMAGEABORTED;
    public final static int IMAGEERROR;
    public final static int RANDOMPIXELORDER;
    public final static int SINGLEFRAME;
    public final static int SINGLEFRAMEDONE;
    public final static int SINGLEPASS;
    public final static int STATICIMAGEDONE;
    public final static int TOPDOWNLEFTRIGHT;


    // Interface Methods
    public abstract void imageComplete (int status);
    public abstract void setColorModel (ColorModel model);
    public abstract void setDimensions (int width, int height);
    public abstract void setHints (int hints);
    public abstract void setPixels (int x, int y, int width, int height,
        ColorModel model, byte[] pixels, int offset, int scansize);
    public abstract void setPixels (int x, int y, int width, int height,
        ColorModel model, int[] pixels, int offset, int scansize);
    public abstract void setProperties (Hashtable properties);
}
```

Constants

COMPLETESCANLINES

```
public final static int COMPLETESCANLINES
```

Hint flag for the setHints(int) method; indicates that the image will be delivered one or more scanlines at a time.

IMAGEABORTED

```
public final static int IMAGEABORTED
```

Status flag for the imageComplete(int) method indicating that the loading process for the image aborted.

IMAGEERROR

```
public final static int IMAGEERROR
```

Status flag for the imageComplete(int) method indicating that an error happened during image loading.

RANDOMPIXELORDER

```
public final static int RANDOMPIXELORDER
```

Hint flag for the setHints(int) method; indicates that the pixels will be delivered in no particular order.

SINGLEFRAME

```
public final static int SINGLEFRAME
```

Hint flag for the setHints(int) method; indicates that the image consists of a single frame.

SINGLEFRAMEDONE

```
public final static int SINGLEFRAMEDONE
```

Status flag for the imageComplete(int) method indicating a single frame of the image has loaded.

SINGLEPASS

```
public final static int SINGLEPASS
```

Hint flag for the setHints(int) method; indicates that each pixel will be delivered once (i.e., the producer will not make multiple passes over the image).

STATICIMAGEDONE

```
public final static int STATICIMAGEDONE
```

Status flag for the imageComplete(int) method indicating that the image has fully and successfully loaded, and that there are no additional frames.

TOPDOWNLEFTRIGHT

```
public final static int TOPDOWNLEFTRIGHT
```

Hint flag for the setHints(int) method; indicates that pixels will be delivered in a top to bottom, left to right order.

Interface Methods

imageComplete

```
public abstract void imageComplete (int status)
```

Parameters   *status*   Image loading status flags.
Description   Called when the image, or a frame of an image sequence, is complete to report the completion status.

setColorModel

```
public abstract void setColorModel (ColorModel model)
```

Parameters   *model*   The color model for the image.

Description   Tells the ImageConsumer the color model used for most of the
               pixels in the image.

setDimensions

```
public abstract void setDimensions (int width, int height)
```

Parameters   *width*   Width for image.

               height   Height for image.

Description   Tells the consumer the image's dimensions.

setHints

```
public abstract void setHints (int hints)
```

Parameters   *hints*   Image consumption hints.

Description   Gives the consumer information about how pixels will be deliv-
               ered.

setPixels

```
public abstract void setPixels (int x, int y, int width,
int height, ColorModel model, byte[] pixels, int offset,
int scansize)
```

Parameters   *x*   x-coordinate of top-left corner of pixel data
                                delivered with this method call.

               y   y-coordinate of top-left corner of pixel data
                                delivered with this method call.

               width   Width of the rectangle of pixel data delivered
                                with this method call.

               height   Height of the rectangle of pixel data delivered
                                with this method call.

               model   Color model of image data.

               pixels   Image data.

               offset   Offset from beginning of the pixels array.

               scansize   Size of each line of data in pixels array.

Description   Delivers a rectangular block of pixels to the image consumer.

```
public abstract void setPixels (int x, int y, int width,
int height, ColorModel model, int[] pixels, int offset,
int scansize)
```

Parameters	*x*	x-coordinate of top-left corner of pixel data delivered with this method call.
	y	y-coordinate of top-left corner of pixel data delivered with this method call.
	width	Width of the rectangle of pixel data delivered with this method call.
	height	Height of the rectangle of pixel data delivered with this method call.
	model	Color model of image data.
	pixels	Image data.
	offset	Offset from beginning of the pixels array.
	scansize	Size of each line of data in pixels array.
Description		Delivers a rectangular block of pixels to the image consumer.

setProperties

```
public abstract void setProperties (Hashtable properties)
```

Parameters	*properties*	The properties for the image.
Description		Delivers a Hashtable that contains the image's properties.

See Also

ColorModel, Hashtable, ImageFilter, PixelGrabber, Object

22.7   ImageFilter

Description

The ImageFilter class sits between the ImageProducer and ImageConsumer as an image is being created to provide a filtered version of that image. Image filters are always used in conjunction with a FilteredImageSource. As an implementer of the ImageConsumer interface, an image filter receives pixel data from the original image's source and delivers it to another image consumer. The ImageFilter class implements a null filter (i.e., the new image is the same as the original); to produce a filter that modifies an image, create a subclass of ImageFilter.

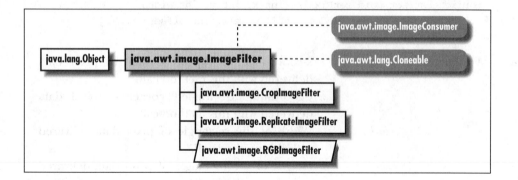

Class Definition

```
public class java.awt.image.ImageFilter
    extends java.lang.Object
    implements java.awt.image.ImageConsumer, java.lang.Cloneable {

// Variables
protected ImageConsumer consumer;

// Constructors
public ImageFilter();

// Instance Methods
public Object clone();
public ImageFilter getFilterInstance (ImageConsumer ic);
public void imageComplete (int status);
public void resendTopDownLeftRight (ImageProducer ip);
public void setColorModel (ColorModel model);
public void setDimensions (int width, int height);
public void setHints (int hints);
public void setPixels (int x, int y, int width, int height,
    ColorModel model, byte[] pixels, int offset, int scansize);
public void setPixels (int x, int y, int width, int height,
    ColorModel model, int[] pixels, int offset, int scansize);
public void setProperties (Hashtable properties);
}
```

Protected Variables

consumer

```
protected ImageConsumer consumer
```

The consumer variable is a reference to the actual ImageConsumer for the
Image.

Constructors

ImageFilter

`public ImageFilter()`

Description   Constructs an empty `ImageFilter` instance.

Instance Methods

clone

`public Object clone()`

Overrides   `Object.clone()`
Returns   A copy of the `ImageFilter` instance.

getFilterInstance

`public ImageFilter getFilterInstance (ImageConsumer ic)`

Parameters   *ic*   The consumer in question.
Returns   A copy of the `ImageFilter` instance.
Description   Returns the filter that will do the filtering for ic.

imageComplete

`void imageComplete (int status)`

Parameters   *status*   Image loading completion status flags.
Implements   `ImageConsumer.imageComplete(int)`
Description   Called by the `ImageProducer` to indicate an image's completion status. `ImageFilter` passes these flags to the consumer unchanged.

resendTopDownLeftRight

`public void resendTopDownLeftRight (ImageProducer ip)`

Parameters   *ip*   The `ImageProducer` generating the original image.
Description   Called by the `ImageConsumer` to ask the filter to resend the image data in the top-down, left-to-right order. In `ImageFilter`, this method calls the same method in the `ImageProducer`, thus relaying the request.

setColorModel

```
void setColorModel (ColorModel model)
```

Parameters	*model*	The color model for the image.
Implements	`ImageConsumer.setColorModel(ColorModel)`	
Description	Sets the image's color model.	

setDimensions

```
void setDimensions (int width, int height)
```

Parameters	*width*	Width for image.
	height	Height for image.
Implements	`ImageConsumer.setDimensions(int, int)`	
Description	Sets the image's dimensions.	

setHints

```
void setHints (int hints)
```

Parameters	*hints*	Image consumption hints.
Implements	`ImageConsumer.setHints(int)`	
Description	Called by the `ImageProducer` to deliver hints about how the image data will be delivered. `ImageFilter` passes these hints on to the `ImageConsumer`.	

setPixels

```
void setPixels (int x, int y, int width, int height, ColorModel
model, byte[] pixels, int offset, int scansize)
```

Parameters	*x*	x-coordinate of top-left corner of pixel data delivered with this method call.
	y	y-coordinate of top-left corner of pixel data delivered with this method call.
	width	Width of the rectangle of pixel data delivered with this method call.
	height	Height of the rectangle of pixel data delivered with this method call.
	model	Color model of image data.
	pixels	Image data.
	offset	Offset from beginning of the pixels array.
	scansize	Size of each line of data in pixels array.
Implements	`ImageConsumer.setPixels(int, int, int, int, ColorModel, byte[], int, int)`	

Description   Delivers a rectangular block of pixels to the ImageFilter. ImageFilter passes these pixels on to the consumer unchanged.

```
void setPixels (int x, int y, int width, int height, ColorModel
model, int[] pixels, int offset, int scansize)
```

Parameters   *x*   x-coordinate of top-left corner of pixel data delivered with this method call.

y   y-coordinate of top-left corner of pixel data delivered with this method call.

width   Width of the rectangle of pixel data delivered with this method call.

height   Height of the rectangle of pixel data delivered with this method call.

model   Color model of image data.

pixels   Image data.

offset   Offset from beginning of the pixels array.

scansize Size of each line of data in pixels array.

Implements   ImageConsumer.setPixels(int, int, int, int, ColorModel, int[], int, int)

Description   Delivers a rectangular block of pixels to the ImageFilter. ImageFilter passes these pixels on to the consumer unchanged.

setProperties

```
void setProperties (Hashtable properties)
```

Parameters   *properties*   The properties for the image.

Implements   ImageConsumer.setProperties(Hashtable)

Description   Initializes the image's properties. ImageFilter adds the property "filter" to the Hashtable, and passes the result on to the image consumer; the value of the property is the string returned by the filter's toString() method. If the property "filter" is already in the Hashtable, ImageFilter adds the string returned by its toString() method to the value already associated with that property.

See Also

Cloneable, ColorModel, CropImageFilter, Hashtable, ImageConsumer, ImageProducer, Object, ReplicateImageFilter, RGBImageFilter

22.8   *ImageObserver*

Description

ImageObserver is an interface that provides constants and the callback mechanism to receive asynchronous information about the status of an image as it loads.

Interface Definition

```
public abstract interface java.awt.image.ImageObserver {

    // Constants
    public static final int ABORT;
    public static final int ALLBITS;
    public static final int ERROR;
    public static final int FRAMEBITS;
    public static final int HEIGHT;
    public static final int PROPERTIES;
    public static final int SOMEBITS;
    public static final int WIDTH;

    // Interface Methods
    public abstract boolean imageUpdate (Image image, int infoflags,
        int x, int y, int width, int height);
}
```

Constants

ABORT

```
public static final int ABORT
```

The ABORT flag indicates that the image aborted during loading. An attempt to reload the image may succeed, unless ERROR is also set.

ALLBITS

```
public static final int ALLBITS
```

The ALLBITS flag indicates that the image has completely loaded successfully. The x, y, width, and height arguments to imageUpdate() should be ignored.

ERROR

```
public static final int ERROR
```

The ERROR flag indicates that an error happened during the image loading process. An attempt to reload the image will fail.

FRAMEBITS

```
public static final int FRAMEBITS
```

The FRAMEBITS flag indicates that a complete frame of a multi-frame image has loaded. The x, y, width, and height arguments to imageUpdate() should be ignored.

HEIGHT

```
public static final int HEIGHT
```

The HEIGHT flag indicates that the height information is available for an image; the image's height is in the height argument to imageUpdate().

PROPERTIES

```
public static final int PROPERTIES
```

The PROPERTIES flag indicates that the properties information is available for an image.

SOMEBITS

```
public static final int SOMEBITS
```

The SOMEBITS flag indicates that the image has started loading and some pixels are available. The bounding rectangle for the pixels that have been delivered so far is indicated by the x, y, width, and height arguments to imageUpdate().

WIDTH

```
public static final int WIDTH
```

The WIDTH flag indicates that the width information is available for an image; the image's width is in the width argument to imageUpdate().

Interface Methods

imageUpdate

```
public abstract boolean imageUpdate (Image image, int infoflags,
int x, int y, int width, int height)
```

Parameters	*image*	Image that is being loaded.
	infoflags	The ImageObserver flags for the information that is currently available.
	x	Meaning depends on infoflags that are set.
	y	Meaning depends on infoflags that are set.
	width	Meaning depends on infoflags that are set.
	height	Meaning depends on infoflags that are set.
Returns		true if image has completed loading (successfully or unsuccessfully), false if additional information needs to be loaded.
Description		Provides the callback mechanism for the asynchronous loading of images.

See Also

Component, Image, Object

22.9   *ImageProducer*

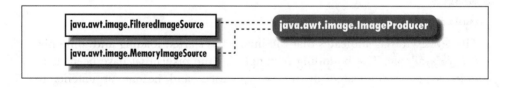

Description

ImageProducer is an interface that provides the methods necessary for the production of images and the communication with classes that implement the ImageConsumer interface.

Interface Definition

```
public abstract interface java.awt.image.ImageProducer {

  // Interface Methods
  public abstract void addConsumer (ImageConsumer ic);
  public abstract boolean isConsumer (ImageConsumer ic);
  public abstract void removeConsumer (ImageConsumer ic);
  public abstract void requestTopDownLeftRightResend (ImageConsumer ic);
  public abstract void startProduction (ImageConsumer ic);
}
```

Interface Methods

addConsumer

```
public abstract void addConsumer (ImageConsumer ic)
```

Parameters   *ic*   An `ImageConsumer` that wants to receive image data.

Description   Registers an `ImageConsumer` as interested in image information.

isConsumer

```
public abstract boolean isConsumer (ImageConsumer ic)
```

Parameters   *ic*   `ImageConsumer` to check.

Returns   true if `ImageConsumer` has registered with the `ImageProducer`, false otherwise.

removeConsumer

```
public abstract void removeConsumer (ImageConsumer ic)
```

Parameters   *ic*   `ImageConsumer` to remove.

Description   Removes an `ImageConsumer` from registered consumers for this `ImageProducer`.

requestTopDownLeftRightResend

```
public abstract void requestTopDownLeftRightResend
(ImageConsumer ic)
```

Parameters   *ic*   `ImageConsumer` to communicate with.

Description   Requests the retransmission of the image data in top-down, left-to-right order.

startProduction

```
public abstract void startProduction (ImageConsumer ic)
```

Parameters   *ic*   ImageConsumer to communicate with.

Description   Registers `ImageConsumer` as interested in image information and tells `ImageProducer` to start sending the image data immediately.

See Also

`FilteredImageSource`, `Image`, `ImageConsumer`, `ImageFilter`, `MemoryImageSource`, `Object`

22.10 IndexColorModel

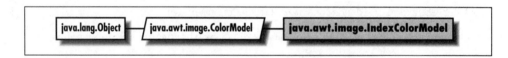

Description

The IndexColorModel class is a ColorModel that uses a color map lookup table (with a maximum size of 256) to convert pixel values into their alpha, red, green, and blue component parts.

Class Definition

```
public class java.awt.image.IndexColorModel
    extends java.awt.image.ColorModel {

// Constructors
public IndexColorModel (int bits, int size,
    byte[] colorMap, int start, boolean hasalpha);
public IndexColorModel (int bits, int size,
    byte[] colorMap, int start, boolean hasalpha, int transparent);
public IndexColorModel (int bits, int size,
    byte[] red, byte[] green, byte[] blue);
public IndexColorModel (int bits, int size,
    byte[] red, byte[] green, byte[] blue, byte[] alpha);
public IndexColorModel (int bits, int size,
    byte[] red, byte[] green, byte[] blue, int transparent);

// Instance Methods
public final int getAlpha (int pixel);
public final void getAlphas (byte[] alphas);
public final int getBlue (int pixel);
public final void getBlues (byte[] blues);
public final int getGreen (int pixel);
public final void getGreens (byte[] greens);
public final int getMapSize ();
public final int getRed (int pixel);
public final void getReds (byte[] reds);
public final int getRGB (int pixel);
public final int getTransparentPixel ();
}
```

Constructors

IndexColorModel

public IndexColorModel (int bits, int size, byte[] colorMap, int start, boolean hasalpha)

Parameters	*bits*	The number of bits in a pixel.
	size	The number of entries in the color map. Note: this is not the size of the colorMap parameter.
	colorMap	Color component values in red, green, blue, alpha order; the alpha component is optional, and may not be present.
	start	The starting position in colorMap array.
	hasalpha	If hasalpha is true, alpha components are present in colorMap array.
Throws	ArrayIndexOutOfBoundsException	
		If size is invalid.
Description		Constructs an IndexColorModel object with the given component settings. The size of colorMap must be at least 3*size+start, if hasalpha is false; if hasalpha is true, colorMap.length must be at least 4*size+start.

public IndexColorModel (int bits, int size, byte[] colorMap, int start, boolean hasalpha, int transparent)

Parameters	*bits*	The number of bits in a pixel.
	size	The number of entries in the color map. Note: this is not the size of the colorMap parameter.
	colorMap	Color component values in red, green, blue, alpha order; the alpha component is optional, and may not be present.
	start	The starting position in colorMap array.
	hasalpha	If hasalpha is true, alpha components are present in colorMap array.
	transparent	Position of colorMap entry for transparent pixel entry.
Throws	ArrayIndexOutOfBoundsException	
		If size invalid.
Description		Constructs an IndexColorModel object with the given component settings. The size of colorMap must be at least 3*size+start, if hasalpha is false; if hasalpha is true, colorMap.length must be at least 4*size+start. The color map has a transparent pixel; its location is given by transparent.

```
public IndexColorModel (int bits, int size, byte[] red, byte[]
green, byte[] blue)
```

Parameters	*bits*	The number of bits in a pixel.
	size	The number of entries in the color map.
	red	Red color component values.
	green	Green color component values.
	blue	Blue color component values.
Throws	ArrayIndexOutOfBoundsException	
		If size invalid.
Description	Constructs an IndexColorModel object with the given compo-	
	nent settings. There is no alpha component. The length of the	
	red, green, and blue arrays must be greater than size.	

```
public IndexColorModel (int bits, int size, byte[] red, byte[]
green, byte[] blue, byte[] alpha)
```

Parameters	*bits*	The number of bits in a pixel.
	size	The number of entries in the color map.
	red	Red color component values.
	green	Green color component values.
	blue	Blue color component values.
	alpha	Alpha component values.
Throws	ArrayIndexOutOfBoundsException	
		If size is invalid.
	NullPointerException	
		If size is positive and alpha array is null.
Description	Constructs an IndexColorModel object with the given compo-	
	nent settings. The length of the red, green, blue, and alpha	
	arrays must be greater than size.	

```
public IndexColorModel (int bits, int size, byte[] red, byte[]
green, byte[] blue, int transparent)
```

Parameters	*bits*	The number of bits in a pixel.
	size	The number of entries in the color map.
	red	Red color component values.
	green	Green color component values.
	blue	Blue color component values.
	transparent	Position of transparent pixel entry.
Throws	ArrayIndexOutOfBoundsException	
		If size is invalid.

Description   Constructs an IndexColorModel object with the given compo-
                nent settings. The length of the red, green, blue, and alpha
                arrays must be greater than size. The color map has a transpar-
                ent pixel; its location is given by transparent.

Instance Methods

getAlpha

```
public final int getAlpha (int pixel)
```

Parameters   *pixel*   A pixel encoded with this ColorModel.
Returns   The current alpha setting of the pixel.
Overrides   ColorModel.getAlpha(int)

getAlphas

```
public final void getAlphas (byte[] alphas)
```

Parameters   *alphas*   The alpha values of the pixels in the color
                                 model.
Description   Copies the alpha values from the color map into the array
                 alphas[].

getBlue

```
public final int getBlue (int pixel)
```

Parameters   *pixel*   A pixel encoded with this ColorModel.
Returns   The current blue setting of the pixel.
Overrides   ColorModel.getBlue(int)

getBlues

```
public final void getBlues (byte[] blues)
```

Parameters   *blues*   The blue values of the pixels in the color model.
Description   Copies the blue values from the color map into the array
                 blues[].

getGreen

```
public final int getGreen (int pixel)
```

Parameters   *pixel*   A pixel encoded with this ColorModel.
Returns   The current green setting of the pixel.
Overrides   ColorModel.getGreen(int)

getGreens

```
public final void getGreens (byte[] greens)
```

Parameters   *greens*   The green values of the pixels in the color model.

Description   Copies the green values from the color map into the array greens[].

getMapSize

```
public final int getMapSize()
```

Returns   The current size of the color map table.

getRed

```
public final int getRed (int pixel)
```

Parameters   *pixel*   A pixel encoded with this ColorModel.

Returns   The current red setting of the pixel.

Overrides   ColorModel.getRed(int)

getReds

```
public final void getReds (byte[] reds)
```

Parameters   *reds*   The red values of the pixels in the color model.

Description   Copies the red values from the color map into the array reds[].

getRGB

```
public final int getRGB (int pixel)
```

Parameters   *pixel*   A pixel encoded with this ColorModel.

Returns   The current combined red, green, and blue settings of the pixel.

Overrides   ColorModel.getRGB(int)

Description   Gets the color of pixel in the default RGB color model.

getTransparentPixel

```
public final int getTransparentPixel()
```

Returns   The array index for the transparent pixel in the color model.

See Also

ColorModel

22.11   *MemoryImageSource*

Description

The MemoryImageSource class allows you to create images completely in memory. You provide an array of data; it serves as an image producer for that data. In the 1.1 release, new methods support using this class for animation (notably setAnimated() and the various overrides of newPixels()).

Class Definition

```
public class java.awt.image.MemoryImageSource
    extends java.lang.Object
    implements java.awt.image.ImageProducer {

// Constructors
public MemoryImageSource (int w, int h, ColorModel cm,
    byte[] pix, int off, int scan);
public MemoryImageSource (int w, int h, ColorModel cm,
    byte[] pix, int off, int scan, Hashtable props);
public MemoryImageSource (int w, int h, ColorModel cm,
    int[] pix, int off, int scan);
public MemoryImageSource (int w, int h, ColorModel cm,
    int[] pix, int off, int scan, Hashtable props);
public MemoryImageSource (int w, int h, int[] pix,
    int off, int scan);
public MemoryImageSource (int w, int h, int[] pix,
    int off, int scan, Hashtable props);

// Instance Methods
public synchronized void addConsumer (ImageConsumer ic);
public synchronized boolean isConsumer (ImageConsumer ic);
public void newPixels (); ★
public synchronized void newPixels (int x, int y,
    int w, int h); ★
public synchronized void newPixels (int x, int y,
    int w, int h, boolean framenotify); ★
public synchronized void newPixels (byte[] newpix,
    ColorModel newmodel, int offset, int scansize); ★
public synchronized void newPixels (int[] newpix,
    ColorModel newmodel, int offset, int scansize); ★
public synchronized void removeConsumer (ImageConsumer ic);
public void requestTopDownLeftRightResend (ImageConsumer ic);
public synchronized void setAnimated (boolean animated); ★
```

```
    public synchronized void setFullBufferUpdates
        (boolean fullbuffers); ★
    public void startProduction (ImageConsumer ic);
}
```

Constructors

MemoryImageSource

public MemoryImageSource (int w, int h, ColorModel cm, byte[] pix, int off, int scan)

Parameters	*w*	Width of the image being created.
	h	Height of the image being created.
	cm	ColorModel of the image being created.
	pix	Array of pixel information.
	off	The offset of the first pixel in the array; elements prior to this pixel are ignored.
	scan	The number of pixels per scan line in the array.
Description		Constructs a MemoryImageSource object with the given parameters to serve as an ImageProducer for a new image.

public MemoryImageSource (int w, int h, ColorModel cm, byte[] pix, int off, int scan, Hashtable props)

Parameters	*w*	Width of the image being created.
	h	Height of the image being created.
	cm	ColorModel of the image being created.
	pix	Array of pixel information.
	off	The offset of the first pixel in the array; elements prior to this pixel are ignored.
	scan	The number of pixels per scan line in the array.
	props	Hashtable of properties associated with image.
Description		Constructs a MemoryImageSource object with the given parameters to serve as an ImageProducer for a new image.

public MemoryImageSource (int w, int h, ColorModel cm, int[] pix, int off, int scan)

Parameters	*w*	Width of the image being created.
	h	Height of the image being created.
	cm	ColorModel of the image being created.
	pix	Array of pixel information.
	off	The offset of the first pixel in the array; elements prior to this pixel are ignored.

	scan	The number of pixels per scan line in the array.
Description		Constructs a `MemoryImageSource` object with the given parameters to serve as an `ImageProducer` for a new image.

```
public MemoryImageSource (int w, int h, ColorModel cm, int[] pix,
int off, int scan, Hashtable props)
```

Parameters	*w*	Width of the image being created.
	h	Height of the image being created.
	cm	`ColorModel` of the image being created.
	pix	Array of pixel information.
	off	The offset of the first pixel in the array; elements prior to this pixel are ignored.
	scan	The number of pixels per scan line in the array.
	props	`Hashtable` of properties associated with image.
Description		Constructs a `MemoryImageSource` object with the given parameters to serve as an `ImageProducer` for a new image.

```
public MemoryImageSource (int w, int h, int[] pix, int off, int
scan)
```

Parameters	*w*	Width of the image being created.
	h	Height of the image being created.
	pix	Array of pixel information.
	off	The offset of the first pixel in the array; elements prior to this pixel are ignored.
	scan	The number of pixels per scan line in the array.
Description		Constructs a `MemoryImageSource` object with the given parameters to serve as an `ImageProducer` for a new image.

```
public MemoryImageSource (int w, int h, int[] pix, int off, int
scan, Hashtable props)
```

Parameters	*w*	Width of the image being created.
	h	Height of the image being created.
	pix	Array of pixel information.
	off	The offset of the first pixel in the array; elements prior to this pixel are ignored.
	scan	The number of pixels per scan line in the array.
	props	`Hashtable` of properties associated with image.
Description		Constructs a `MemoryImageSource` object with the given parameters to serve as an `ImageProducer` for a new image.

Class Methods

addConsumer

```
public synchronized void addConsumer (ImageConsumer ic)
```

Parameters   *ic*   ImageConsumer requesting image data.

Implements   ImageProducer.addConsumer(ImageConsumer)

Description   Registers an ImageConsumer as interested in Image information.

isConsumer

```
public synchronized boolean isConsumer (ImageConsumer ic)
```

Parameters   *ic*   ImageConsumer to check.

Returns   true if ImageConsumer is registered with this ImageProducer, false otherwise.

Implements   ImageProducer.isConsumer(ImageConsumer)

newPixels

```
public synchronized void newPixels() ★
```

Description   Notifies the MemoryImageSource that there is new data available. The MemoryImageSource notifies all ImageConsumers that there is new data, sending the full rectangle and notifying the consumers that the frame is complete.

```
public synchronized void newPixels (int x, int y, int w,  int h,
boolean framenotify) ★
```

Parameters   *x*   x coordinate of the top left corner of the new image data.

                 y   y coordinate of the top left corner of the new image data.

                 w   Width of the new image data.

                 h   Height of the new image data.

Description   Notifies the MemoryImageSource that there is new data available. The MemoryImageSource notifies all ImageConsumers that there is new data in the rectangle described by x, y, w, and h. The consumers are notified that the frame is complete.

```
public synchronized void newPixels (int x, int y, int w, int h,
boolean framenotify) ★
```

Parameters   *x*   x coordinate of the top left corner of the new image data.

y		y coordinate of the top left corner of the new image data.
w		Width of the new image data.
h		Height of the new image data.
framenotify		Determines whether this is a complete frame or not.

Description   Notifies the MemoryImageSource that there is new data available. The MemoryImageSource notifies all ImageConsumers that there is new data in the rectangle described by x, y, w, and h. If framenotify is true, the consumers will also be notified that a frame is complete.

```
public synchronized void newPixels (byte[] newpix, ColorModel
newmodel, int offset, int scansize) ★
```

Parameters	*newpix*	New array of image data.
	newmodel	The color model to use for the new data.
	offset	Offset into the data array
	scansize	Size of each line.

Description   Changes the image data for this MemoryImageSource and notifies its ImageConsumers that new data is available.

```
public synchronized void newPixels (int[] newpix, ColorModel
newmodel, int offset, int scansize) ★
```

Parameters	*newpix*	New array of image data.
	newmodel	The color model to use for the new data.
	offset	Offset into the data array
	scansize	Size of each line.

Description   Changes the image data for this MemoryImageSource and notifies its ImageConsumers that new data is available.

removeConsumer

```
public void removeConsumer (ImageConsumer ic)
```

Parameters	*ic*	ImageConsumer to remove.
Implements		ImageProducer.removeConsumer(ImageConsumer)
Description		Removes an ImageConsumer from registered consumers for this ImageProducer.

requestTopDownLeftRightResend

public void requestTopDownLeftRightResend (ImageConsumer ic)

Parameters	*ic*	ImageConsumer requesting image data.
Implements	ImageProducer.requestTopDownLeftRightResend(ImageConsumer)	
Description	Requests the retransmission of the Image data in top-down, left-to-right order.	

setAnimated

public void setAnimated (boolean animated) ★

Parameters	*animated*	Flag indicating whether this image is animated.
Description	To use this MemoryImageSource for animation, call setAnimated(true). The newPixels() methods will not work otherwise.	

setFullBufferUpdates

public void setFullBufferUpdates (boolean fullbuffers) ★

Parameters	*fullbuffers*	true to send full buffers; false otherwise.
Description	This method is only important for animations; i.e., you should call setAnimated(true) before using this function. If you do request to send full buffers, then any rectangle parameters passed to newPixels() will be ignored and the entire image will be sent to the consumers.	

startProduction

public void startProduction (ImageConsumer ic)

Parameters	*ic*	ImageConsumer requesting image data.
Implements	ImageProducer.startProduction(ImageConsumer)	
Description	Registers ImageConsumer as interested in Image information and tells ImageProducer to start sending the image data immediately.	

See Also

ColorModel, Hashtable, ImageConsumer, ImageProducer, Object

22.12   PixelGrabber

Description

The PixelGrabber class is an ImageConsumer that captures the pixels from an image and saves them in an array.

Class Definition

```
public class java.awt.image.PixelGrabber
    extends java.lang.Object
    implements java.awt.image.ImageConsumer {

// Constructors
public PixelGrabber (Image img, int x, int y, int w, int h,
    boolean forceRGB); ★
public PixelGrabber (Image image, int x, int y, int width,
    int height, int[] pixels, int offset, int scansize);
public PixelGrabber (ImageProducer ip, int x, int y, int width,
    int height, int[] pixels, int offset, int scansize);

// Instance Methods
public synchronized void abortGrabbing (); ★
public synchronized ColorModel getColorModel (); ★
public synchronized int getHeight (); ★
public synchronized Object getPixels (); ★
public synchronized int getStatus (); ★
public synchronized int getWidth (); ★
public boolean grabPixels () throws InterruptedException;
public synchronized boolean grabPixels (long ms)
    throws InterruptedException;
public synchronized void imageComplete (int status);
public void setColorModel (ColorModel model);
public void setDimensions (int width, int height);
public void setHints (int hints);
public void setPixels (int x, int y, int width, int height,
    ColorModel model, byte[] pixels, int offset, int scansize);
public void setPixels (int x, int y, int width, int height,
    ColorModel model, int[] pixels, int offset, int scansize);
public void setProperties (Hashtable properties);
public synchronized void startGrabbing (); ★
public synchronized int status (); ☆
}
```

Constructors

PixelGrabber

public PixelGrabber (Image img, int x, int y, int w, int h,
boolean forceRGB) ★

Parameters	*img*	Image to use as source of pixel data.
	x	x-coordinate of top-left corner of pixel data.
	y	y-coordinate of top-left corner of pixel data.
	w	Width of pixel data.
	h	Height of pixel data.
	forceRGB	true to force the use of the RGB color model; false otherwise.
Description		Constructs a PixelGrabber instance to grab the specified area of the image.

public PixelGrabber (Image image, int x, int y, int width, int
height, int[] pixels, int offset, int scansize)

Parameters	*image*	Image to use as source of pixel data.
	x	x-coordinate of top-left corner of pixel data.
	y	y-coordinate of top-left corner of pixel data.
	width	Width of pixel data.
	height	Height of pixel data.
	pixels	Where to store pixel data when grabPixels() called.
	offset	Offset from beginning of each line in pixels array.
	scansize	Size of each line of data in pixels array.
Description		Constructs a PixelGrabber instance to grab the specified area of the image and store the pixel data from this area in the array pixels[].

public PixelGrabber (ImageProducer ip, int x, int y, int width,
int height, int[] pixels, int offset, int scansize)

Parameters	*ip*	ImageProducer to use as source of pixel data.
	x	x-coordinate of top-left corner of pixel data.
	y	y-coordinate of top-left corner of pixel data.
	width	Width of pixel data.
	height	Height of pixel data.
	pixels	Where to store pixel data when grabPixels() called.

offset	Offset from beginning of each line in pixels array.
scansize	Size of each line of data in pixels array.

Description   Constructs a `PixelGrabber` instance to grab data from the specified area of the image generated by an `ImageProducer` and store the pixel data from this area in the array `pixels[]`.

Instance Methods

abortGrabbing

`public synchronized void abortGrabbing() ★`

Description   Stops the `PixelGrabber`'s image-grabbing process.

getColorModel

`public synchronized ColorModel getColorModel() ★`

Returns   The color model the `PixelGrabber` is using for its array.

getHeight

`public synchronized int getHeight() ★`

Returns   The height of the grabbed image, or -1 if the height is not known.

getPixels

`public synchronized Object getPixels() ★`

Returns   The array of pixels.

Description   Either a byte array or an integer array is returned, or `null` if the size and format of the image are not yet known. Because the `PixelGrabber` may change its mind about what `ColorModel` it's using, different calls to this method may return different arrays until the image acquisition is complete.

getStatus

`public synchronized int getStatus() ★`

Returns   A combination of `ImageObserver` flags indicating what data is available.

getWidth

`public synchronized int getWidth()` ★

Returns   The width of the grabbed image, or -1 if the width is not known.

grabPixels

`public boolean grabPixels() throws InterruptedException`

Throws   `InterruptedException`
             If image grabbing is interrupted before completion.

Returns   `true` if the image has completed loading, `false` if the loading process aborted or an error occurred.

Description Starts the process of grabbing the pixel data from the source and storing it in the array `pixels[]` from constructor. Returns when the image is complete, loading aborts, or an error occurs.

`public synchronized boolean grabPixels (long ms) throws`
`InterruptedException`

Parameters   *ms*   Milliseconds to wait for completion.

Returns   `true` if image has completed loading, `false` if the loading process aborted, or an error or a timeout occurred.

Throws   `InterruptedException`
             If image grabbing is interrupted before completion.

Description Starts the process of grabbing the pixel data from the source and storing it in the array `pixels[]` from constructor. Returns when the image is complete, loading aborts, an error occurs, or a timeout occurs.

imageComplete

`public synchronized void imageComplete (int status)`

Parameters   *status*   Image loading completion status flags.

Implements   `ImageConsumer.imageComplete(int)`

Description Called by the `ImageProducer` to indicate that the image has been delivered.

setColorModel

void setColorModel (ColorModel model)

Parameters	*model*	The color model for the image.
Implements	ImageConsumer.setColorModel(ColorModel)	
Description	Does nothing.	

setDimensions

void setDimensions (int width, int height)

Parameters	*width*	Width for image.
	height	Height for image.
Implements	ImageConsumer.setDimensions(int, int)	
Description	Does nothing.	

setHints

void setHints (int hints)

Parameters	*hints*	Image consumption hints.
Implements	ImageConsumer.setHints(int)	
Description	Does nothing.	

setPixels

void setPixels (int x, int y, int width, int height, ColorModel
model, byte[] pixels, int offset, int scansize)

Parameters	*x*	x-coordinate of top-left corner of pixel data delivered with this method call.
	y	y-coordinate of top-left corner of pixel data delivered with this method call.
	width	Width of the rectangle of pixel data delivered with this method call.
	height	Height of the rectangle of pixel data delivered with this method call.
	model	Color model of image data.
	pixels	Image data.
	offset	Offset from beginning of the pixels array.
	scansize	Size of each line of data in pixels array.
Implements	ImageConsumer.setPixels(int, int, int, int, ColorModel, byte[], int, int)	
Description	Called by the ImageProducer to deliver pixel data from the image.	

```
void setPixels (int x, int y, int width, int height, ColorModel
model, int[] pixels, int offset, int scansize)
```

Parameters	*x*	x-coordinate of top-left corner of pixel data delivered with this method call.
y	y-coordinate of top-left corner of pixel data delivered with this method call.
width	Width of the rectangle of pixel data delivered with this method call.
height	Height of the rectangle of pixel data delivered with this method call.
model	Color model of image data.
pixels	Image data.
offset	Offset from beginning of the pixels array.
scansize	Size of each line of data in pixels array.
Implements	`ImageConsumer.setPixels(int, int, int, int, ColorModel, int[], int, int)`
Description	Called by the `ImageProducer` to deliver pixel data from the image.

setProperties

```
void setProperties (Hashtable properties)
```

Parameters	*properties*	The properties for the image.
Implements	`ImageConsumer.setProperties(Hashtable)`
Description	Does nothing.

startGrabbing

```
public synchronized void startGrabbing () ★
```

Description	Starts the `PixelGrabber`'s image-grabbing process.

status

```
public synchronized int status () ☆
```

Returns	The `ImageObserver` flags OR'ed together representing the available information about the image. Replaced by `getStatus()`.

See Also

`ColorModel`, `Hashtable`, `Image`, `ImageConsumer`, `ImageProducer`, `InterruptedException`, `MemoryImageSource`, `Object`

22.13   *ReplicateScaleFilter* ★

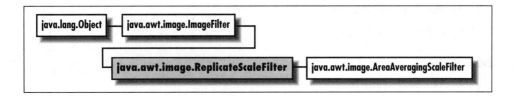

Description

The ReplicateScaleFilter class uses a simple-minded algorithm to scale an image. If the image is to be reduced, rows and columns of pixels are removed. If the image is to be expanded, rows and columns are duplicated (replicated).

Class Definition

```
public class ReplicateScaleFilter
    extends java.awt.image.ImageFilter {

  // Variables
  protected int destHeight;
  protected int destWidth;
  protected Object outpixbuf;
  protected int srcHeight;
  protected int srcWidth;
  protected int[] srccols;
  protected int[] srcrows;

  // Constructor
  public ReplicateScaleFilter(int width, int height);

  // Instance Methods
  public void setDimensions (int w, int h);
  public void setPixels(int x, int y, int w, int h, ColorModel model,
      byte[] pixels, int off, int scansize);
  public void setPixels(int x, int y, int w, int h, ColorModel model,
      int[] pixels, int off, int scansize);
  public void setProperties(Hashtable props);
}
```

Variables

destHeight

protected int destHeight

Height of the scaled image.

destWidth

protected int destWidth

Width of the scaled image.

outpixbuf

protected Object outpixbuf

An internal buffer.

srcHeight

protected int srcHeight

Height of the original image.

srcWidth

protected int srcWidth

Width of the original image.

srccols

protected int[] srccols

Internal array used to map incoming columns to outgoing columns.

srcrows

protected int[] srcrows

Internal array used to map incoming rows to outgoing rows.

Constructor

ReplicateScaleFilter

public ReplicateScaleFilter (int width, int height)

Parameters	*width*	Width of scaled image.
	height	Height of scaled image.
Description	Constructs a ReplicateScaleFilter that scales the original image to the specified size. If both width and height are -1, the destination image size will be set to the source image size. If either one of the parameters is -1, it will be set to preserve the aspect ratio of the original image.	

Instance Methods

setDimensions

```
public void setDimensions (int w, int h)
```

Parameters	*w*	Width of the source image.
	h	Height of the source image.
Overrides	ImageFilter.setDimensions(int, int)	
Description	Sets the size of the source image.	

setPixels

```
void setPixels (int x, int y, int w, int h, ColorModel model,
byte[] pixels, int off, int scansize)
```

Parameters	*x*	x-coordinate of top-left corner of pixel data delivered with this method call.
	y	y-coordinate of top-left corner of pixel data delivered with this method call.
	w	Width of the rectangle of pixel data delivered with this method call.
	h	Height of the rectangle of pixel data delivered with this method call.
	model	Color model of image data.
	pixels	Image data.
	off	Offset from beginning of the pixels array.
	scansize	Size of each line of data in pixels array.
Overrides	ImageFilter.setPixels(int, int, int, int, ColorModel, byte[], int, int)	
Description	Receives a rectangle of image data from the ImageProducer; scales these pixels and delivers them to any ImageConsumers.	

```
void setPixels (int x, int y, int w, int h, ColorModel model,
int[] pixels, int off, int scansize)
```

Parameters	*x*	x-coordinate of top-left corner of pixel data delivered with this method call.
	y	y-coordinate of top-left corner of pixel data delivered with this method call.
	w	Width of the rectangle of pixel data delivered with this method call.
	h	Height of the rectangle of pixel data delivered with this method call.

	model	Color model of image data.
	pixels	Image data.
	off	Offset from beginning of the pixels array.
	scansize	Size of each line of data in pixels array.
Overrides		`ImageFilter.setPixels(int, int, int, int, ColorModel, int[], int, int)`
Description		Receives a rectangle of image data from the `ImageProducer`; scales these pixels and delivers them to any `ImageConsumers`.

setProperties

```
public void setProperties (Hashtable props)
```

Parameters	*props*	The properties for the image.
Overrides		`ImageFilter.setProperties(Hashtable)`
Description		Adds the "rescale" image property to the properties list.

See Also

ColorModel, Hashtable, ImageConsumer, ImageFilter, ImageProducer

---

22.14 RGBImageFilter

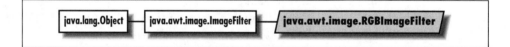

Description

RGBImageFilter is an abstract class that helps you filter images based on each pixel's color and position. In most cases, the only method you need to implement in subclasses is filterRGB(), which returns a new pixel value based on the old pixel's color and position. RGBImageFilter cannot be used to implement filters that depend on the value of neighboring pixels, or other factors aside from color and position.

Class Definition

```
public abstract class java.awt.image.RGBImageFilter
    extends java.awt.image.ImageFilter {

  // Variables
  protected boolean canFilterIndexColorModel;
  protected ColorModel newmodel;
  protected ColorModel oldmodel;
```

```
// Instance Methods
public IndexColorModel filterIndexColorModel (IndexColorModel icm);
public abstract int filterRGB (int x, int y, int rgb);
public void filterRGBPixels (int x, int y, int width,
    int height, int[] pixels, int off, int scansize);
public void setColorModel (ColorModel model);
public void setPixels (int x, int y, int width, int height,
    ColorModel model, byte[] pixels, int offset, int scansize);
public void setPixels (int x, int y, int width, int height,
    ColorModel model, int[] pixels, int offset, int scansize);
public void substituteColorModel (ColorModel oldModel,
    ColorModel newModel);
}
```

Variables

canFilterIndexColorModel

```
protected boolean canFilterIndexColorModel
```

Setting the canFilterIndexColorModel variable to true indicates the filter can filter IndexColorModel images. To filter an IndexColorModel, the filter must depend only on color, not on position.

newmodel

```
protected ColorModel newmodel
```

A place to store a new ColorModel.

origmodel

```
protected ColorModel origmodel
```

A place to store an old ColorModel.

Instance Methods

filterIndexColorModel

```
public IndexColorModel filterIndexColorModel (IndexColorModel icm)
```

Parameters	*icm*	Color model to filter.
Returns	Filtered color model.	
Description	Helper method for setColorModel() that runs the entire color table of icm through the filterRGB() method of the subclass. Used only if canFilterIndexColorModel is true, and the image uses an IndexColorModel.	

filterRGB

> public abstract int filterRGB (int x, int y, int rgb)

Parameters   *x*   x-coordinate of pixel data.

                y   y-coordinate of pixel data.

                rgb   Color value of pixel to filter.

Returns   New color value of pixel.

Description   Subclasses implement this method to provide a filtering function that generates new pixels.

filterRGBPixels

> public void filterRGBPixels (int x, int y, int width, int height, int[] pixels, int off, int scansize)

Parameters   *x*   x-coordinate of top-left corner of pixel data within entire image.

                y   y-coordinate of top-left corner of pixel data within entire image.

                width   Width of pixel data within entire image.

                height   Height of pixel data within entire image.

                pixels   Image data.

                off   Offset from beginning of each line in pixels array.

                scansize   Size of each line of data in pixels array.

Description   Helper method for setPixels() that filters each element of the pixels buffer through the subclass's filterRGB() method.

setColorModel

> public void setColorModel (ColorModel model)

Parameters   *model*   The color model for the image.

Overrides   ImageFilter.setColorModel(ColorModel)

Description   Sets the image's color model.

setPixels

> public void setPixels (int x, int y, int width, int height, ColorModel model, byte[] pixels, int offset, int scansize)

Parameters   *x*   x-coordinate of top-left corner of pixel data delivered with this method call.

                y   y-coordinate of top-left corner of pixel data delivered with this method call.

	width	Width of the rectangle of pixel data delivered with this method call.
	height	Height of the rectangle of pixel data delivered with this method call.
	model	Color model of image data.
	pixels	Image data.
	offset	Offset from beginning of the pixels array.
	scansize	Size of each line of data in pixels array.
Overrides		ImageFilter.setPixels(int, int, int, int, ColorModel, byte[], int, int)
Description		Called by the ImageProducer to deliver a rectangular block of pixels for filtering.

```
public void setPixels (int x, int y, int width, int height,
ColorModel model, int[] pixels, int offset, int scansize)
```

Parameters	*x*	x-coordinate of top-left corner of pixel data delivered with this method call.
	y	y-coordinate of top-left corner of pixel data delivered with this method call.
	width	Width of the rectangle of pixel data delivered with this method call.
	height	Height of the rectangle of pixel data delivered with this method call.
	model	Color model of image data.
	pixels	Image data.
	offset	Offset from beginning of the pixels array.
	scansize	Size of each line of data in pixels array.
Overrides		ImageFilter.setPixels(int, int, int, int, ColorModel, int[], int, int)
Description		Called by the ImageProducer to deliver a rectangular block of pixels for filtering.

substituteColorModel

```
public void substituteColorModel (ColorModel oldModel, ColorModel
newModel)
```

Parameters	*oldModel*	New value for origmodel variable.
	newModel	New value for newmodel variable.
Description		Helper method for setColorModel() to initialize the protected variables newmodel and origmodel.

See Also

ColorModel, ImageFilter

23

java.awt.peer Reference

23.1 *ButtonPeer*

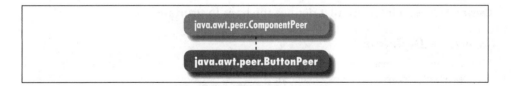

Description

ButtonPeer is an interface that defines the basis for buttons.

Interface Definition

```
public abstract interface java.awt.peer.ButtonPeer
extends java.awt.peer.ComponentPeer {

  // Interface Methods
  public abstract void setLabel (String label);
}
```

Interface Methods

setLabel

```
public abstract void setLabel (String label)
```

| Parameters | *label* | New text for label of button's peer. |
| Description | | Changes the text of the label of button's peer. |

See Also

ComponentPeer, String

23.2 CanvasPeer

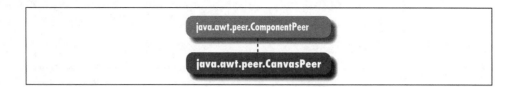

Description

CanvasPeer is an interface that defines the basis for canvases.

Interface Definition

```
public abstract interface java.awt.peer.CanvasPeer
    extends java.awt.peer.ComponentPeer {
}
```

See Also

ComponentPeer

23.3 CheckboxMenuItemPeer

Description

CheckboxMenuItemPeer is an interface that defines the basis for checkbox menu items.

Interface Definition

```
public abstract interface java.awt.peer.CheckboxMenuItemPeer
    extends java.awt.peer.MenuItemPeer {

    // Interface Methods
    public abstract void setState (boolean condition);
```

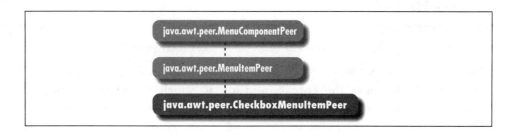

```
}
```

Interface Methods

setState

```
public abstract void setState (boolean condition)
```

Parameters   *condition*   New state for checkbox menu item's peer.
Description   Changes the state of checkbox menu item's peer.

See Also

MenuComponentPeer, MenuItemPeer

23.4   CheckboxPeer

Description

CheckboxPeer is an interface that defines the basis for checkbox components.

Interface Definition

```
public abstract interface java.awt.peer.CheckboxPeer
   extends java.awt.peer.ComponentPeer {

  // Interface Methods
  public abstract void setCheckboxGroup (CheckboxGroup group);
  public abstract void setLabel (String label);
  public abstract void setState (boolean state);
}
```

Interface Methods

setCheckboxGroup

```
public abstract void setCheckboxGroup (CheckboxGroup group)
```

Parameters   *group*   New group to put the checkbox peer in.
Description   Changes the checkbox group to which the checkbox peer belongs; implicitly removes the peer from its old group, if any.

setLabel

```
public abstract void setLabel (String label)
```

Parameters   *label*   New text for label of checkbox's peer.
Description   Changes the text of the label of the checkbox's peer.

setState

```
public abstract void setState (boolean state)
```

Parameters   *state*   New state for the checkbox's peer.
Description   Changes the state of the checkbox's peer.

See Also

CheckboxGroup, ComponentPeer, String

23.5   ChoicePeer

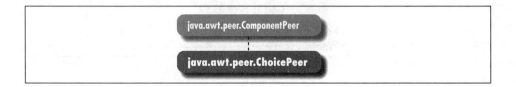

Description

ChoicePeer is an interface that defines the basis for choice components.

Interface Definition

```
public abstract interface java.awt.peer.ChoicePeer
    extends java.awt.peer.ComponentPeer {

  // Interface Methods
  public abstract void add (String item, int index); ★
  public abstract void addItem (String item, int position); ☆
```

```
    public abstract void remove (int index); ★
    public abstract void select (int position);
}
```

Interface Methods

add

```
public abstract void add (String item, int index) ★
```

Parameters   *item*   Text of the entry to add.

              index   Position in which to add the entry; position 0 is
                            the first entry in the list.

Description   Adds a new entry to the available choices at the designated posi-
               tion.

addItem

```
public abstract void addItem (String item, int position) ☆
```

Parameters   *item*   Text of the entry to add.

              position   Position in which to add the entry; position 0 is
                            the first entry in the list.

Description   Adds a new entry to the available choices at the designated posi-
               tion.

remove

```
public abstract void remove (int index) ★
```

Parameters   *index*   Position of the item to remove.
Description   Removes an entry at the given position.

select

```
public abstract void select (int position)
```

Parameters   *position*   Position to make selected entry.
Description   Makes the given entry the selected one for the choice's peer.

See Also

ComponentPeer, String

23.6 ComponentPeer

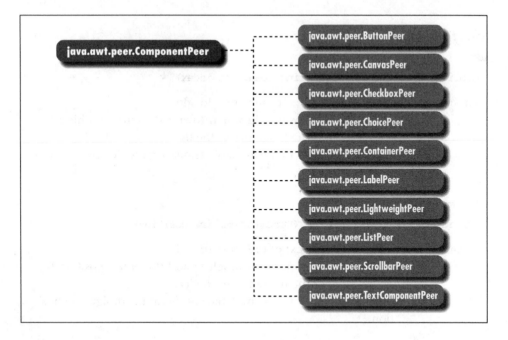

Description

ComponentPeer is an interface that defines the basis for all non-menu GUI peer interfaces.

Interface Definition

```
public abstract interface java.awt.peer.ComponentPeer {
  // Interface Methods
  public abstract int checkImage (Image image, int width, int height,
    ImageObserver observer);
  public abstract Image createImage (ImageProducer producer);
  public abstract Image createImage (int width, int height);
  public abstract void disable(); ☆
  public abstract void dispose();
  public abstract void enable(); ☆
  public abstract ColorModel getColorModel();
  public abstract FontMetrics getFontMetrics (Font f);
  public abstract Graphics getGraphics();
  public abstract Point getLocationOnScreen(); ★
  public abstract Dimension getMinimumSize(); ★
  public abstract Dimension getPreferredSize(); ★
  public abstract Toolkit getToolkit();
  public abstract boolean handleEvent (Event e);
  public abstract void hide(); ☆
```

```
    public abstract boolean isFocusTraversable();  ★
    public abstract Dimension minimumSize();  ☆
    public abstract void paint (Graphics g);
    public abstract Dimension preferredSize ();  ☆
    public abstract boolean prepareImage (Image image, int width, int height,
        ImageObserver observer);
    public abstract void print (Graphics g);
    public abstract void repaint (long tm, int x, int y, int width, int height);
    public abstract void requestFocus();
    public abstract void reshape (int x, int y, int width, int height);  ☆
    public abstract void setBackground (Color c);
    public abstract void setBounds (int x, int y, int width, int height);  ★
    public abstract void setCursor (Cursor cursor);  ★
    public abstract void setEnabled (boolean b);  ★
    public abstract void setFont (Font f);
    public abstract void setForeground (Color c);
    public abstract void setVisible (boolean b);  ★
    public abstract void show();  ☆
}
```

Interface Methods

checkImage

```
public abstract int checkImage (Image image, int width, int
height, ImageObserver observer)
```

Parameters	*image*	Image to check.
	width	Horizontal size to which the image will be scaled.
	height	Vertical size to which the image will be scaled.
	observer	An ImageObserver to monitor image loading; normally, the object on which the image will be rendered.
Returns		ImageObserver flags ORed together indicating status.
Description		Checks status of image construction.

createImage

```
public abstract Image createImage (ImageProducer producer)
```

Parameters	*producer*	An object that implements the ImageProducer interface to create a new image.
Returns		Newly created image instance.
Description		Creates an Image based upon an ImageProducer.

```
public abstract Image createImage (int width, int height)
```

Parameters	*width*	Horizontal size for in-memory Image.
	height	Vertical size for in-memory Image.
Returns		Newly created image instance.
Description		Creates an in-memory Image for double buffering.

disable

```
public abstract void disable ()  ☆
```

Description   Disables component so that it is unresponsive to user interactions. Replaced by setEnabled(false).

dispose

```
public abstract void dispose ()
```

Description   Releases resources used by peer.

enable

```
public abstract void enable ()  ☆
```

Description   Enables component so that it is responsive to user interactions. Replaced by setEnabled(true).

getColorModel

```
public abstract ColorModel getColorModel ()
```

Returns   ColorModel used to display the current component.

getFontMetrics

```
public abstract FontMetrics getFontMetrics (Font f)
```

| Parameters | *f* | A font whose metrics are desired. |
| Returns | | Font sizing information for the desired font. |

getGraphics

```
public abstract Graphics getGraphics ()
```

Throws   *InternalException*
                   If acquiring a graphics context is unsupported
Returns   Component's graphics context.

getLocationOnScreen

public abstract Point getLocationOnScreen() ★

Returns   The location of the component in the screen's coordinate space.

getMinimumSize

public abstract Dimension getMinimumSize() ★

Returns   The minimum dimensions of the component.

getPreferredSize

public abstract Dimension getPreferredSize() ★

Returns   The preferred dimensions of the component.

getToolkit

public abstract Toolkit getToolkit()

Returns   Toolkit of Component.

handleEvent

public abstract boolean handleEvent (Event e)

Parameters   *e*   Event instance identifying what caused the method to be called.

Returns   true if the peer handled the event, false to propagate the event to the parent container.

Description   High-level event handling routine.

hide

public abstract void hide() ☆

Description   Hides the component. Replaced by setVisible(false).

isFocusTraversable

public abstract boolean isFocusTraversable() ★

Returns   true if the peer can be tabbed onto, false otherwise.

Description   Determines if this peer is navigable using the keyboard.

minimumSize

    public abstract Dimension minimumSize() ☆

Returns   The minimum dimensions of the component. Replaced by get-
              MinimumSize().

paint

    public abstract void paint (Graphics g)

Parameters   *g*   Graphics context of the component.
Description   Draws something in graphics context.

preferredSize

    public abstract Dimension preferredSize() ☆

Returns   The preferred dimensions of the component. Replaced by get-
              PreferredSize().

prepareImage

    public abstract boolean prepareImage (Image image, int width,
    int height, ImageObserver observer)

Parameters   *image*   Image to load.
              width   Horizontal size to which the image will be
                             scaled.
              height   Vertical size to which the image will be scaled.
              observer   An ImageObserver to monitor image loading;
                             normally, the object on which the image will be
                             rendered.
Returns   true if the image has already loaded, false otherwise.
Description   Forces the image to start loading.

print

    public abstract void print (Graphics g)

Parameters   *g*   Graphics context of component.
Description   Print something from the graphics context.

repaint

    public abstract void repaint (long tm, int x, int y, int width,
    int height)

Parameters	*tm*	Millisecond delay allowed before repaint.
	x	Horizontal origin of bounding box to redraw.
	y	Vertical origin of bounding box to redraw.
	width	Width of bounding box to redraw.
	height	Height of bounding box to redraw.
Description		Requests scheduler to redraw portion of component within a time period.

requestFocus

    public abstract void requestFocus()

Description   Requests this Component gets the input focus.

reshape

    public abstract void reshape (int x, int y, int width,
    int height) ☆

Parameters	*x*	New horizontal position for component.
	y	New vertical position for component.
	width	New width for component.
	height	New height for component.
Description		Relocates and resizes the component's peer. Replaced by set-Bounds(int, int, int, int).

setBackground

    public abstract void setBackground (Color c)

| Parameters | *c* | New color for the background. |
| Description | | Changes the background color of the component. |

setBounds

    public abstract void setBounds (int x, int y, int width,
    int height) ★

Parameters	*x*	New horizontal position for component.
	y	New vertical position for component.
	width	New width for component.
	height	New height for component.

Description   Relocates and resizes the component's peer.

setCursor

```
public abstract void setCursor (Cursor cursor) ★
```

Parameters   *cursor*   New cursor.
Description   Changes the cursor of the component.

setEnabled

```
public abstract void setEnabled (boolean b) ★
```

Parameters   *b*   true to enable the peer; false to disable it.
Description   Enables or disables the peer.

setFont

```
public abstract void setFont (Font f)
```

Parameters   *f*   New font for the component.
Description   Changes the font used to display text in the component.

setForeground

```
public abstract void setForeground (Color c)
```

Parameters   *c*   New foreground color for the component.
Description   Changes the foreground color of the component.

setVisible

```
public abstract void setVisible (boolean b) ★
```

Parameters   *b*   true to show the peer; false to hide it.
Description   Shows or hides the peer.

show

```
public abstract void show() ☆
```

Description   Makes the peer visible. Replaced by setVisible(true).

See Also

ButtonPeer, CanvasPeer, CheckboxPeer, ChoicePeer, Color, ColorModel, ContainerPeer, Cursor, Dimension, Event, Font, FontMetrics, Graphics, Image, ImageObserver, ImageProducer, LabelPeer, ListPeer, ScrollbarPeer, TextComponentPeer, Toolkit

23.7   *ContainerPeer*

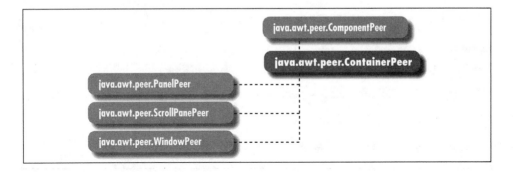

Description

ContainerPeer is an interface that defines the basis for containers.

Interface Definition

```
public abstract interface java.awt.peer.ContainerPeer
   extends java.awt.peer.ComponentPeer {

  // Interface Methods
  public abstract void beginValidate();  ★
  public abstract void endValidate();  ★
  public abstract Insets getInsets();  ★
  public abstract Insets insets();  ☆
}
```

Interface Methods

beginValidate

public abstract void beginValidate() ★

Description   Notifies the peer that the Container is going to validate its contents.

endValidate

public abstract void endValidate() ★

Description   Notifies the peer that the Container is finished validating its contents.

getInsets

public Insets getInsets() ★

Returns   Current Insets of container's peer.

insets

public Insets insets() ☆

Returns   Current Insets of container's peer. Replaced by getInsets().

See Also

ComponentPeer, Insets, PanelPeer, ScrollPanePeer, WindowPeer

23.8   DialogPeer

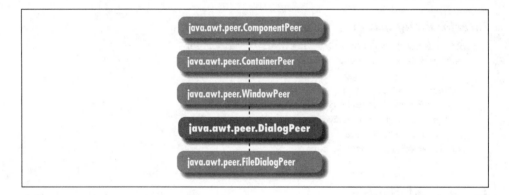

Description

DialogPeer is an interface that defines the basis for a dialog box.

Interface Definition

```
public abstract interface java.awt.peer.DialogPeer
   extends java.awt.peer.WindowPeer {

   // Interface Methods
   public abstract void setResizable (boolean resizable);
   public abstract void setTitle (String title);
}
```

Interface Methods

setResizable

```
public abstract void setResizable (boolean resizable)
```

Parameters	*resizable*	true if the dialog's peer should allow resizing; false to prevent resizing.
Description		Changes the resize state of the dialog's peer.

setTitle

```
public abstract void setTitle (String title)
```

Parameters	*title*	New title for the dialog's peer.
Description		Changes the title of the dialog's peer.

See Also

FileDialogPeer, String, WindowPeer

23.9   FileDialogPeer

Description

FileDialogPeer is an interface that defines the basis for a file dialog box.

Interface Definition

```
public abstract interface java.awt.peer.FileDialogPeer
   extends java.awt.peer.DialogPeer {

   // Interface Methods
   public abstract void setDirectory (String directory);
   public abstract void setFile (String file);
   public abstract void setFilenameFilter (FilenameFilter filter);
}
```

Interface Methods

setDirectory

```
public abstract void setDirectory (String directory)
```

Parameters	*directory*	Initial directory for file dialog's peer.
Description		Changes the directory displayed in the file dialog's peer.

setFile

```
public abstract void setFile (String file)
```

Parameters	*file*	Initial filename for the file dialog's peer.
Description		Changes the default file selection for the file dialog's peer.

setFilenameFilter

```
public abstract void setFilenameFilter (FilenameFilter filter)
```

Parameters	*filter*	Initial filter for file dialog's peer.
Description		Changes the current filename filter of the file dialog's peer.

See Also

DialogPeer, FilenameFilter, String

23.10   FontPeer ★

java.awt.peer.FontPeer

Description

FontPeer is an interface that defines the basis for fonts.

Interface Definition

```
public abstract interface java.awt.peer.FontPeer {
}
```

See Also

ComponentPeer

23.11   *FramePeer*

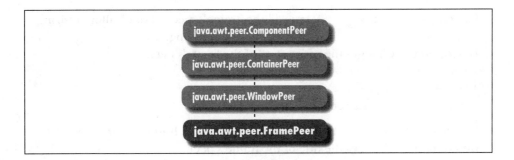

Description

FramePeer is an interface that defines the basis for a frame.

Interface Definition

```
public abstract interface java.awt.peer.FramePeer
   extends java.awt.peer.WindowPeer {

  // Interface Methods
  public abstract void setIconImage (Image image);
  public abstract void setMenuBar (MenuBar bar);
  public abstract void setResizable (boolean resizable);
  public abstract void setTitle (String title);
}
```

Interface Methods

setIconImage

public abstract void setIconImage (Image image)

| Parameters | *image* | New image to use for frame peer's icon. |
| Description | | Changes the icon associated with the frame's peer. |

setMenuBar

public abstract void setMenuBar (MenuBar bar)

| Parameters | *bar* | New MenuBar to use for the frame's peer. |
| Description | | Changes the menu bar of the frame. |

setResizable

   public abstract void setResizable (boolean resizable)

Parameters   *resizable*   true if the frame's peer should allow resizing, false to prevent resizing.

Description   Changes the resize state of the frame's peer.

setTitle

   public abstract void setTitle (String title)

Parameters   *title*   New title to use for the frame's peer.

Description   Changes the title of the frame's peer.

See Also

Image, MenuBar, String, WindowPeer

23.12   *LabelPeer*

Description

LabelPeer is an interface that defines the basis for label components.

Interface Definition

```
public abstract interface java.awt.peer.LabelPeer
   extends java.awt.peer.ComponentPeer {

   // Interface Methods
   public abstract void setAlignment (int alignment);
   public abstract void setText (String label);
}
```

Interface Methods

setAlignment

```
public abstract void setAlignment (int alignment)
```

Parameters   *alignment*   New alignment for label's peer.
Description   Changes the current alignment of label's peer.

setText

```
public abstract void setText (String label)
```

Parameters   *label*   New text for label's peer.
Description   Changes the current text of label's peer.

See Also

ComponentPeer, String

23.13   LightweightPeer ★

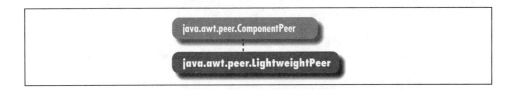

Description

LightweightPeer is an interface that defines the basis for components that don't have a visual representation. When you directly subclass Component or Container, a LightweightPeer is used.

Interface Definition

```
public abstract interface java.awt.peer.LightweightPeer
    extends java.awt.peer.ComponentPeer {
}
```

See Also

ComponentPeer

23.14   ListPeer

Description

ListPeer is an interface that defines the basis for list components.

Interface Definition

```
public abstract interface java.awt.peer.ListPeer
    extends java.awt.peer.ComponentPeer {

    // Interface Methods
    public abstract void add (String item, int index); ★
    public abstract void addItem (String item, int index); ☆
    public abstract void clear(); ☆
    public abstract void delItems (int start, int end);
    public abstract void deselect (int index);
    public abstract Dimension getMinimumSize (int rows); ★
    public abstract Dimension getPreferredSize (int rows); ★
    public abstract int[] getSelectedIndexes();
    public abstract void makeVisible (int index);
    public abstract Dimension minimumSize (int rows); ☆
    public abstract Dimension preferredSize (int rows); ☆
    public abstract void removeAll(); ★
    public abstract void select (int position);
    public abstract void setMultipleMode (boolean b); ★
    public abstract void setMultipleSelections (boolean value); ☆
}
```

Interface Methods

add

```
public abstract void add (String item, int index) ★
```

Parameters	*item*	Text of an entry to add to the list.
	index	Position in which to add the entry; position 0 is the first entry in the list.
Description		Adds a new entry to the available choices of the list's peer at the designated position.

addItem

public abstract void addItem (String item, int index) ☆

Parameters	*item*	Text of an entry to add to the list.
	index	Position in which to add the entry; position 0 is the first entry in the list.
Description		Adds a new entry to the available choices of the list's peer at the designated position. Replaced by add(String, int).

clear

public abstract void clear() ☆

| Description | Clears all the entries out of the list's peer. Replaced by removeAll(). |

delItems

public abstract void delItems (int start, int end)

Parameters	*start*	Starting position of entries to delete.
	end	Ending position of entries to delete.
Description		Removes a set of entries from the list's peer.

deselect

public abstract void deselect (int index)

| Parameters | *index* | Position to deselect. |
| Description | | Deselects entry at designated position, if selected. |

getMinimumSize

public abstract Dimension getMinimumSize (int rows) ★

| Parameters | *rows* | Number of rows within list's peer to size. |
| Returns | | The minimum dimensions of a list's peer of the given size. |

getPreferredSize

public abstract Dimension getPreferredSize (int rows) ★

| Parameters | *rows* | Number of rows within list's peer to size. |
| Returns | | The preferred dimensions of a list's peer of the given size. |

getSelectedIndexes

```
public abstract int[] getSelectedIndexes()
```

Returns   Array of positions of currently selected entries in list's peer.

makeVisible

```
public abstract void makeVisible (int index)
```

Parameters   *index*   Position to make visible on screen.
Description   Ensures an item is displayed on the screen in the list's peer.

minimumSize

```
public abstract Dimension minimumSize (int rows)  ☆
```

Parameters   *rows*   Number of rows within list's peer to size.
Returns   The minimum dimensions of a list's peer of the given size.
              Replaced by `getMinimumSize(int)`.

preferredSize

```
public abstract Dimension preferredSize (int rows)  ☆
```

Parameters   *rows*   Number of rows within list's peer to size.
Returns   The preferred dimensions of a list's peer of the given size.
              Replaced by `getPreferredSize(int)`.

removeAll

```
public abstract void removeAll()  ★
```

Description   Clears all the entries out of the list's peer.

select

```
public abstract void select (int position)
```

Parameters   *position*   Position to select; 0 indicates the first item in the
                            list.
Description   Makes the given entry the selected item for the list's peer; dese-
              lects other selected entries if multiple selections are not
              enabled.

setMultipleMode

```
public abstract void setMultipleMode (boolean value) ★
```

Parameters	*value*	true to allow multiple selections within the list's peer; false to disallow multiple selections.
Description		Changes list peer's selection mode.

setMultipleSelections

```
public abstract void setMultipleSelections (boolean value) ☆
```

Parameters	*value*	true to allow multiple selections within the list's peer; false to disallow multiple selections.
Description		Changes list peer's selection mode. Replaced by setMultiple-Mode(boolean).

See Also

ComponentPeer, Dimension, String

23.15   *MenuBarPeer*

Description

MenuBarPeer is an interface that defines the basis for menu bars.

Interface Definition

```
public abstract interface java.awt.peer.MenuBarPeer
   extends java.awt.peer.MenuComponentPeer {

  // Interface Methods
  public abstract void addHelpMenu (Menu m);
  public abstract void addMenu (Menu m);
  public abstract void delMenu (int index);
}
```

Interface Methods

addHelpMenu

```
public abstract void addHelpMenu (Menu m)
```

Parameters	*m*	Menu to designate as the help menu with the menu bar's peer.
Description		Sets a particular menu to be the help menu of the menu bar's peer.

addMenu

```
public abstract void addMenu (Menu m)
```

Parameters	*m*	Menu to add to the menu bar's peer
Description		Adds a menu to the menu bar's peer.

delMenu

```
public abstract void delMenu (int index)
```

Parameters	*index*	Menu position to delete from the menu bar's peer.
Description		Deletes a menu from the menu bar's peer.

See Also

Menu, MenuComponentPeer

23.16   *MenuComponentPeer*

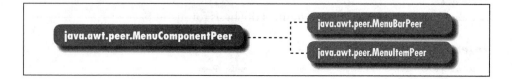

Description

MenuComponentPeer is an interface that defines the basis for all menu GUI peer interfaces.

Interface Definition

```
public abstract interface java.awt.peer.MenuComponentPeer {

   // Interface Methods
   public abstract void dispose();
}
```

Interface Methods

dispose

```
public abstract void dispose()
```

Description   Releases resources used by peer.

See Also

MenuBarPeer, MenuItemPeer

23.17 MenuItemPeer

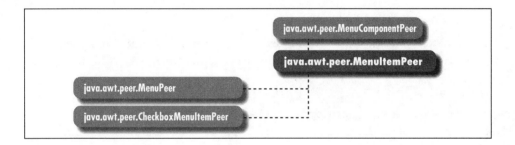

Description

MenuBarPeer is an interface that defines the basis for menu bars.

Interface Definition

```
public abstract interface java.awt.peer.MenuItemPeer
    extends java.awt.peer.MenuComponentPeer {

  // Interface Methods
  public abstract void disable(); ☆
  public abstract void enable(); ☆
  public abstract void setEnabled (boolean b); ★
  public abstract void setLabel (String label);
}
```

Interface Methods

disable

```
public abstract void disable() ☆
```

Description   Disables the menu item's peer so that it is unresponsive to user
                interactions. Replaced by setEnabled(false).

enable

public abstract void enable() ☆

Description   Enables the menu item's peer so that it is responsive to user interactions. Replaced by setEnabled(true).

setEnabled

public abstract void setEnabled (boolean b) ★

Parameters   *b*   true to enable the peer; false to disable it.
Description   Enables or disables the menu item's peer.

setLabel

public abstract void setLabel (String label)

Parameters   *label*   New text to appear on the menu item's peer.
Description   Changes the label of the menu item's peer.

See Also

CheckboxMenuItemPeer, MenuComponentPeer, MenuPeer, String

23.18   MenuPeer

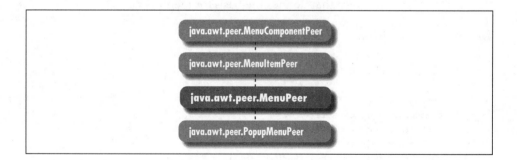

Description

MenuPeer is an interface that defines the basis for menus.

Interface Definition

```
public abstract interface java.awt.peer.MenuPeer
    extends java.awt.peer.MenuItemPeer {

    // Interface Methods
    public abstract void addItem (MenuItem item);
    public abstract void addSeparator();
```

```
   public abstract void delItem (int index);
}
```

Interface Methods

addItem

```
public abstract void addItem (MenuItem item)
```

Parameters   *item*   MenuItem to add to the menu's peer
Description   Adds a menu item to the menu's peer.

addSeparator

```
public abstract void addSeparator()
```

Description   Adds a menu separator to the menu's peer.

delItem

```
public abstract void delItem (int index)
```

Parameters   *index*   MenuItem position to delete from the menu's
                                  peer.
Description   Deletes a menu item from the menu's peer.

See Also

MenuItem, MenuItemPeer

23.19   PanelPeer

Description

PanelPeer is an interface that defines the basis for a panel.

Interface Definition

```
public abstract interface java.awt.peer.PanelPeer
    extends java.awt.peer.ContainerPeer {
}
```

See Also

ContainerPeer

23.20   PopupMenuPeer ★

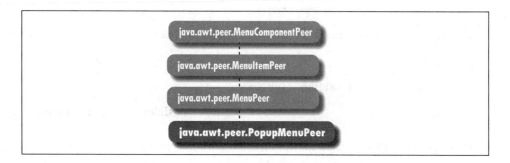

Description

PopupMenuPeer is an interface that defines the basis for a popup menu.

Interface Definition

```
public abstract interface java.awt.peer.PopupMenuPeer
    extends java.awt.peer.MenuPeer {

    // Interface Methods
    public abstract void show (Event e);
}
```

Interface Methods

show

```
public abstract void show (Event e)
```

Parameters *e* A mouse down event that begins the display of
the popup menu.

Description Shows the peer at the location encapsulated in e.

See Also

Event, MenuPeer

23.21   ScrollbarPeer

Description

ScrollbarPeer is an interface that defines the basis for scrollbar components.

Interface Definition

```
public abstract interface java.awt.peer.ScrollbarPeer
   extends java.awt.peer.ComponentPeer {

// Interface Methods
public abstract void setLineIncrement (int amount);
public abstract void setPageIncrement (int amount);
public abstract void setValues (int value, int visible, int minimum, int maximum);
}
```

Interface Methods

setLineIncrement

public abstract void setLineIncrement (int amount)

Parameters	*amount*	New line increment amount.
Description		Changes the line increment amount for the scrollbar's peer.

setPageIncrement

public abstract void setPageIncrement (int amount)

Parameters	*amount*	New paging increment amount.
Description		Changes the paging increment amount for the scrollbar's peer.

setValues

public abstract void setValues (int value, int visible, int
minimum, int maximum)

Parameters   *value*   New value for the scrollbar's peer.

                visible   New slider width.

                minimum   New minimum value for the scrollbar's peer.

                maximum New maximum value for the scrollbar's peer.

Description   Changes the settings of the scrollbar's peer to the given amounts.

See Also

ComponentPeer

23.22 *ScrollPanePeer* ★

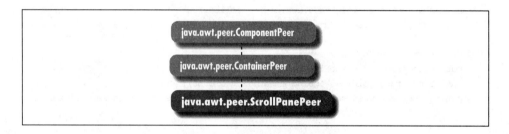

Description

ScrollPanePeer is an interface that defines the basis for a scrolling container.

Interface Definition

```
public abstract interface java.awt.peer.ScrollPanePeer
   extends java.awt.peer.ContainerPeer {

   // Interface Methods
   public abstract void childResized (int w, int h);
   public abstract int getHScrollbarHeight();
   public abstract int getVScrollbarWidth();
   public abstract void setScrollPosition (int x, int y);
   public abstract void setUnitIncrement (Adjustable adj, int u);
   public abstract void setValue (Adjustable adj, int v);
}
```

Interface Methods
childResized
public abstract void childResized (int w, int h)

Parameters   *w*   The new child width.
              h   The new child height.
Description   Tells the peer that the child has a new size.

getHScrollbarHeight
public abstract int getHScrollbarHeight()

Returns   Height that a horizontal scrollbar would occupy.
Description   The height is returned regardless of whether the scrollbar is showing or not.

getVScrollbarWidth
public abstract int getVScrollbarWidth()

Returns   Width that a vertical scrollbar would occupy.
Description   The width is returned regardless of whether the scrollbar is showing or not.

setScrollPosition
public abstract void setScrollPosition (int x, int y)

Parameters   *x*   The new horizontal position.
              y   The new vertical position.
Description   Changes the coordinate of the child component that is displayed at the origin of the ScrollPanePeer.

setUnitIncrement
public abstract void setUnitIncrement (Adjustable adj, int u)

Parameters   *adj*   The Adjustable object to change.
              u   The new value.
Description   Changes the unit increment of the given Adjustable object.

setValue
public abstract void setValue (Adjustable adj, int v)

Parameters   *adj*   The Adjustable object to change.
              v   The new value.

Description   Changes the value of the given `Adjustable` object.

See Also

`Adjustable`, `ContainerPeer`, `Scrollbar`

23.23   TextAreaPeer

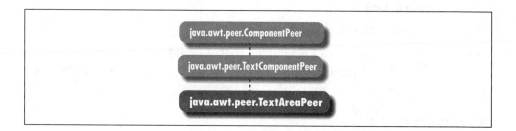

Description

TextAreaPeer is an interface that defines the basis for text areas.

Interface Definition

```
public abstract interface java.awt.peer.TextAreaPeer
   extends java.awt.peer.TextComponentPeer {

   // Interface Methods
   public abstract Dimension getMinimumSize (int rows, int columns); ★
   public abstract Dimension getPreferredSize (int rows, int columns); ★
   public abstract void insert (String string, int position); ★
   public abstract void insertText (String string, int position); ☆
   public abstract Dimension minimumSize (int rows, int columns); ☆
   public abstract Dimension preferredSize (int rows, int columns); ☆
   public abstract void replaceRange (String string, int startPosition, int endPosition); ★
   public abstract void replaceText (String string, int startPosition, int endPosition); ☆
}
```

Interface Methods

getMinimumSize

public abstract Dimension getMinimumSize
(int rows, int columns) ★

Parameters	*rows*	Number of rows within the text area's peer.
	columns	Number of columns within the text area's peer.
Returns		The minimum dimensions of a text area's peer of the given size.

getPreferredSize

public abstract Dimension getPreferredSize
(int rows, int columns) ★

Parameters	*rows*	Number of rows within the text area's peer.
	columns	Number of columns within the text area's peer.
Returns		The preferred dimensions of a text area's peer of the given size.

insert

public abstract void insert (String string, int position) ★

Parameters	*string*	Content to place within the text area's peer.
	position	Location at which to insert the content.
Description		Places additional text within the text area's peer.

insertText

public abstract void insertText (String string, int position) ☆

Parameters	*string*	Content to place within the text area's peer.
	position	Location at which to insert the content.
Description		Places additional text within the text area's peer. Replaced by insert(String, int).

minimumSize

public abstract Dimension minimumSize (int rows, int columns) ☆

Parameters	*rows*	Number of rows within the text area's peer.
	columns	Number of columns within the text area's peer.
Returns		The minimum dimensions of a text area's peer of the given size. Replaced by getMinimumSize(int, int).

preferredSize

public abstract Dimension preferredSize (int rows, int columns) ☆

Parameters	*rows*	Number of rows within the text area's peer.
	columns	Number of columns within the text area's peer.
Returns		The preferred dimensions of a text area's peer of the given size. Replaced by getPreferredSize(int, int).

replaceRange

public abstract void replaceRange (String string,
int startPosition, int endPosition) ★

Parameters	*string*	New content to place in the text area's peer.
	startPosition	Starting position of the content to replace.
	endPosition	Ending position of the content to replace.
Description		Replaces a portion of the text area peer's content with the given text.

replaceText

public abstract void replaceText (String string,
int startPosition, int endPosition) ☆

Parameters	*string*	New content to place in the text area's peer.
	startPosition	Starting position of the content to replace.
	endPosition	Ending position of the content to replace.
Description		Replaces a portion of the text area peer's content with the given text. Replaced by replaceRange(String, int, int).

See Also

Dimension, String, TextComponentPeer

23.24 TextComponentPeer

Description

TextComponentPeer is an interface that defines the basis for text components.

Interface Definition

```
public abstract interface java.awt.peer.TextComponentPeer
   extends java.awt.peer.ComponentPeer {

   // Interface Methods
   public abstract int getCaretPosition(); ★
   public abstract int getSelectionEnd();
   public abstract int getSelectionStart();
```

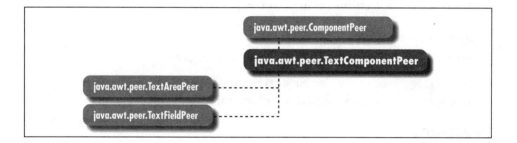

```
    public abstract String getText();
    public abstract void select (int selectionStart, int selectionEnd);
    public abstract void setCaretPosition (int pos); ★
    public abstract void setEditable (boolean state);
    public abstract void setText (String text);
}
```

Interface Methods

getCaretPosition

```
    public abstract int getCaretPosition() ★
```

Returns   The current position of the caret (text cursor).

getSelectionEnd

```
    public abstract int getSelectionEnd()
```

Returns   The ending cursor position of any selected text.

getSelectionStart

```
    public abstract int getSelectionStart()
```

Returns   The initial position of any selected text.

getText

```
    public abstract String getText()
```

Returns   The current contents of the text component's peer.

select

```
    public abstract void select (int selectionStart, int selectionEnd)
```

Parameters   *selectionStart*   Beginning position of the text to select.
               selectionEnd   Ending position of the text to select.

Description   Selects text in the text component's peer.

selectCaretPosition

public abstract void selectCaretPosition (int pos)

Parameters   *pos*   New caret position.
Description   Changes the position of the caret (text cursor).

setEditable

public abstract void setEditable (boolean state)

Parameters   *state*   true if the user can change the contents of the
                              text component's peer (i.e., true to make the
                              peer editable); false to make the peer read-
                              only.
Description   Allows you to change the current editable state of the text com-
              ponent's peer.

setText

public abstract void setText (String text)

Parameters   *text*   New text for the text component's peer .
Description   Sets the content of the text component's peer.

See Also

ComponentPeer, String, TextAreaPeer, TextFieldPeer

23.25   TextFieldPeer

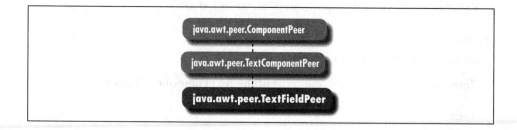

Description

TextFieldPeer is an interface that defines the basis for text fields.

Interface Definition

```
public abstract interface java.awt.peer.TextFieldPeer
    extends java.awt.peer.TextComponentPeer {

    // Interface Methods
    public abstract Dimension getMinimumSize (int rows, int columns); ★
    public abstract Dimension getPreferredSize (int rows, int columns); ★
    public abstract Dimension minimumSize (int rows, int columns); ☆
    public abstract Dimension preferredSize (int rows, int columns); ☆
    public abstract void setEchoChar (char echoChar); ★
    public abstract void setEchoCharacter (char c); ☆
}
```

Interface Methods

getMinimumSize

public abstract Dimension getMinimumSize (int rows) ★

Parameters	*rows*	Number of rows within the text field's peer.
Returns		The minimum dimensions of a text field's peer of the given size.

getPreferredSize

public abstract Dimension getPreferredSize (int rows) ★

Parameters	*rows*	Number of rows within the text field's peer.
Returns		The preferred dimensions of a text field's peer of the given size.

minimumSize

public abstract Dimension minimumSize (int rows) ☆

Parameters	*rows*	Number of rows within the text field's peer.
Returns		Replaced by getMinimumSize(int).

preferredSize

public abstract Dimension preferredSize (int rows) ☆

Parameters	*rows*	Number of rows within the text field's peer.
Returns		Replaced by getPreferredSize(int).

setEchoChar

```
public abstract void setEchoChar (char c) ★
```

Parameters	*c*	The character to display for all input.
Description		Changes the character that is displayed to the user for every character he or she types in the text field.

setEchoCharacter

```
public abstract void setEchoCharacter (char c) ☆
```

Parameters	*c*	The character to display for all input.
Description		Replaced by setEchoChar(char).

See Also

Dimension, TextComponentPeer

23.26   WindowPeer

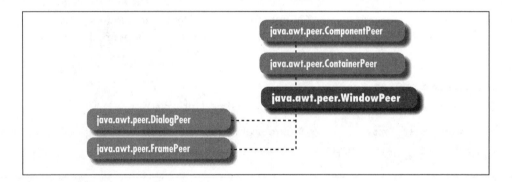

Description

WindowPeer is an interface that defines the basis for a window.

Interface Definition

```
public abstract interface java.awt.peer.WindowPeer
    extends java.awt.peer.ContainerPeer {

    // Interface Methods
    public abstract void toBack();
    public abstract void toFront();
}
```

Interface Methods

toBack

    public abstract void toBack()

Description   Puts the window's peer in the background of the display.

toFront

    public abstract void toFront()

Description   Brings the window's peer to the foreground of the display.

See Also

ContainerPeer, DialogPeer, FramePeer

Using Properties and Resources

Java provides "property lists" that are similar to Xdefaults in the X Window system. Programs can use properties to customize their behavior or find out information about the run-time environment; by reading a property list, a program can set defaults, choose colors and fonts, and more, without any changes to the code. Java 1.1 makes property lists much more general. Although the basic features of property lists did not change between Java 1.0 and 1.1, the way you access them did. Instead of providing specific locations for files, Java 1.1 provides access to these resource bundles in a more general scheme, described in Section A.3.

A.1 System Properties

Although Java applications can define property lists as conveniences, there is one special property list that is common to all applications and applets: System Properties. This list currently has 14 properties in Java 1.0 and 21 in Java 1.1, although you may add to it, and more standard properties may be added in the future. An application has access to all of them. Because of security restrictions, an applet has access only to 9. Among other things, these properties allow you to customize your code for different platforms if you want to provide workarounds for platform-specific deficiencies or load native methods if available.

Table A-1 contains the complete list of system properties. The last column specifies whether an applet can access each property; applications can access all properties. As a word of caution, different vendors may report different values for the same environment (for example, os.arch could be x86 or 80486). The values in the property list reflect the run-time environment, not the development environment.

Table A–1: System Properties

Name	Description	Sample Value	Applet
awt.toolkit ★	Toolkit vendor	sun.awt.window.Wtoolkit	No
file.encoding ★	File encoding	8859_1	No
file.encoding.pkg ★	File encoding package	sun.io	No
file.separator	File separator	"\" or "/"	Yes
java.class.path	Java's CLASSPATH	C:\JAVA\LIB;.; C:\JAVA\BIN\.\classes; C:\JAVA\BIN\.\lib\classes.zip	No
java.class.version	Java's class library version	45.3	Yes
java.home	Java's installation directory	C:\JAVA	No
java.vendor	Java's virtual machine vendor	Netscape Communications	Yes
java.vendor.url	Java vendor's URL	http://www.netscape.com	Yes
java.version	Java version	1.021	Yes
line.separator	Line separator	"\n"	Yes
os.arch	Operating system architecture	x86 or 80486	Yes
os.name	Operating system name	Windows NT	Yes
os.version ★	Operating system version	4.0	Yes
path.separator	Path separator	";" or ":"	Yes
user.dir	User's working directory	C:\JAZ\AWTCode\Chapter2	No
user.home	User's home directory	C:\JAVA	No
user.language ★	User's language	en	No
user.name ★	User's login name	JOHNZ	No
user.region ★	User's geographic region	US	No
user.timezone ★	User's time zone	EST	No

To read one of the system properties, use the getProperty() method of the System class:

```
System.getProperty (String s);     // for the property you want
```

If s is a valid property and is accessible by your program, the system retrieves the
current value as a String. If it is not, the return value is null. For example, the following line of code retrieves the vendor for the Java platform you are working
with:

```
String s = System.getProperty ("java.vendor");
```

If an applet tries to access a property it does not have permission to read, a security
exception is thrown.

For an application, the Java interpreter can add additional system properties at
run-time with the *-D* flag. The following command runs the program *className*,
adding the program.name property to the list of available properties; the value of
this property is the string Foo:

```
java -Dprogram.name=Foo className
```

An application can also modify its property list by calling various methods of the
Properties class. The following code duplicates the effect of the *-D* flag in the previous example:

```
Properties p = System.getProperties ();
p.put ("program.name", "Foo");  // To add a new one
p.put ("java.vendor", "O'Reilly");  // To replace the current one
System.setProperties(p);
```

An applet running within Netscape Navigator or Internet Explorer may not add or
change system properties since Netscape Navigator and Internet Explorer do not
let applets touch the local filesystem, and calls to getProperties() generate a
security violation. Version 1.0 of HotJava, the JDK, and the *appletviewer* allow you to
set properties with the *properties* file in the *.hotjava* directory. Other browsers may
or may not enable this option.

NOTE   The location of the system properties file depends on the run-time
             environment you are using. Ordinarily, the file will go into a subdi-
             rectory of the installation directory or, for environments where users
             have home directories, in a subdirectory for the user.

Users may add properties to the system property file by hand; of course, in this
case, it's the Java developer's responsibility to document what properties the program reads, and to provide reasonable defaults in case those properties aren't set.
The Color and Font classes have methods to read colors and fonts from the system

properties list. These are two areas in which it would be appropriate for a program to define its own properties, expecting the user to set an appropriate value. For example, a program might expect the property `myname.awt.drawingColor` to define a default color for drawing; it would be the user's responsibility to add a line defining this property in the property file:

```
myname.awt.drawingColor=0xe0e0e0    #default drawing color: light gray
```

A.2 Server Properties

Java programs can read properties from any file to which they have access. Applications, of course, can open files on the platform where they execute; applets cannot. However, applets can read certain files from the server. Example A-1 is an applet that reads a properties file from its server and uses those properties to customize itself. This is a useful technique for developers working on commercial applets: you can deliver an applet to a customer and let the customer customize the applet by providing a property sheet. The alternative, having the applet read all of its customizations from HTML parameter tags, is a bit more clumsy. Server properties let you distinguish between global customizations like company name (which would be the same on all instances of the applet) and situation-specific customizations, like the name of the animation the user wants to display (the user may use the same applet for many animation sequences). The company name should be configured through a style sheet; the animation filename should be configured by using a <PARAM> tag.

Example A-1 uses a properties list to read a message and font information. Following the source is the actual property file. The property file must be in the same directory as the HTML file because we use `getDocumentBase()` to build the property file's URL. Once we have loaded the property list, we can use `getProperty()` to read individual properties. Unfortunately, in Java 1.0, we cannot use the `Font` class's methods to read the font information directly; `getFont()` can only read properties from the system property list. Therefore, we need to read the font size, name, and type as strings, and call the `Font` constructor using the pieces as arguments. Java 1.1 does a lot to fix this problem; we'll see how in the next section.

Example A–1: Getting Properties from a Server File

```
import java.util.Properties;
import java.awt.*;
import java.io.IOException;
import java.io.InputStream;
import java.net.URL;
import java.net.MalformedURLException;

public class Prop extends java.applet.Applet {
    Properties p;
```

Example A–1:   Getting Properties from a Server File   (continued)

```
    String theMessage;
    public void init () {
        p = new Properties();
        try {
            URL propSource = new URL (getDocumentBase(), "prop.list");
            InputStream propIS = propSource.openStream();
            p.load(propIS);
            p.list(System.out);
            initFromProps(p);
            propIS.close();
        } catch (MalformedURLException e) {
            System.out.println ("Invalid URL");
        } catch (IOException e) {
            System.out.println ("Error loading properties");
        }
    }
    public void initFromProps (Properties p) {
        String fontsize = p.getProperty ("MyProg.font.size");
        String fontname = p.getProperty ("MyProg.font.name");
        String fonttype = p.getProperty ("MyProg.font.type");
        String message  = p.getProperty ("MyProg.message");
        int size;
        int type;
        if (fontsize == null) {
            size = 12;
        } else {
            size = Integer.parseInt (fontsize);
        }
        if (fontname == null) {
            fontname = "TimesRoman";
        }
        type = Font.PLAIN;
        if (fonttype != null) {
            fonttype.toLowerCase();
            boolean bold = (fonttype.indexOf ("bold") != -1);
            boolean italic = (fonttype.indexOf ("italic") != -1);
            if (bold) type |= Font.BOLD;
            if (italic) type |= Font.ITALIC;
        }
        if (message == null) {
            theMessage = "Welcome to Java";
        } else {
            theMessage = message;
        }
        setFont (new Font (fontname, type, size));
    }
    public void paint (Graphics g) {
        g.drawString (theMessage, 50, 50);
    }
}
```

The file *prop.list*:

```
MyProg.font.size=20
MyProg.font.type=italic-bold
MyProg.font.name=Helvetica
MyProg.message=Hello World
```

Figure A-1 results from using this applet with this property file.

Figure A–1: Reading server properties

A.3 Resource Bundles

Java 1.1 adds two new pieces to make its property lists more general and flexible. The first is the ability to use localized resource bundles; the second is the use of resource files.

Resource bundles let you write internationalized programs. The general idea is that any string you want to display (for example, a button label) shouldn't be specified as a literal constant. Instead, you want to look up the string in a table of equivalents—a "resource bundle"—that contains equivalent strings for different locales. For example, the string "yes" is equivalent to "ja", "si", "oui", and many other language-specific alternatives. A resource bundle lets your program look up the right alternative at run-time, depending on the user's locale. The list of alternatives must be implemented as a subclass of `ResourceBundle` or `ListResource-Bundle`, in which you provide a key value pair for each label. For each locale you support, a separate subclass and list must be provided. Then you look up the appropriate string through the `ResourceBundle.getString()` method. A complete example of how to use resource bundles could easily require an entire chapter; I hope this is enough information to get you started.[*]

Resource bundles have one important implication for more mundane programs. Resource bundles can be saved in files and read at run-time. To support them, Java 1.1 has added the ability to load arbitrary properties files. In Example A-1, we looked for the *prop.list* file on the applet server. What if we want to permit users to

---

[*] See the *Java Fundamental Classes Reference* for a more complete description.

modify the default font to be what they want, not what we think they want? With Java 1.0, that could not be done because there was no way for an applet to access the local filesystem. Now, with Java 1.1, you can access read-only resource files located in the CLASSPATH. To do so, you use the Class.getResource() method, which takes the name of a properties list file as an argument. This method returns the URL of the file requested, which could be available locally or on the applet server; where it actually looks depends on the ClassLoader. Once the file is found, treat it as a Properties file, as in Example A-1, or do anything you want with it. A similar method, Class.getResourceAsStream(), returns the InputStream to work with, instead of the URL.

Example A-2 is similar to Example A-1. The file *prop11.list* includes three properties: the font to use, a message, and an image. We need only a single property because we can use the new Font.decode() method to convert a complete font specification into a Font object: we don't need to load the font information in pieces, as we did in the earlier example. As an added bonus, this example displays an image. The name of the image is given by the property MyProg.image. Like the property file itself, the image file can be located anywhere. Here's the properties list, which should be placed in the file *prop11.list*:

```
MyProg.font=Helvetica-italic-30
MyProg.message=Hello World
MyProg.image=ora-icon.gif
```

And the code for the applet is in Example A-2.

Example A–2: Getting Properties from a Resource File

```
// Java 1.1 only
import java.io.*;
import java.net.*;
import java.awt.*;
import java.util.Properties;
import java.applet.Applet;
public class Prop11 extends Applet {
    Image im;
    Font f;
    String msg;
    public void paint (Graphics g) {
        g.setFont (f);
        if (im != null)
            g.drawImage (im, 50, 100, this);
        if (msg != null)
            g.drawString (msg, 50, 50);
    }
    public void init () {
        InputStream is = getClass().getResourceAsStream("prop11.list");
        Properties p = new Properties();
        try {
            p.load (is);
```

Example A–2: Getting Properties from a Resource File (continued)

```
            f = Font.decode(p.getProperty("MyProg.font"));
            msg = p.getProperty("MyProg.message");
            String name = p.getProperty("MyProg.image");
            URL url = getClass().getResource(name);
            im = getImage (url);
        } catch (IOException e) {
            System.out.println ("error loading props...");
        }
    }
}
```

B

HTML Markup For Applets

B.1 The Applet Tag

The introduction of Java created the need for additional HTML tags. In the alpha release of Java, the HotJava browser used the <APP> tag to include applets within HTML files. However, <APP> was unacceptable to the standards committee because it could have an infinite number of parameters. It was replaced by the <APPLET> tag, used in conjunction with the <PARAM> tag. Apparently, the standards folks did not like the <APPLET> tag either, so you can expect it to be replaced eventually, although at this point, there is no agreement about its successor, and it is highly unlikely that any production browser would stop supporting <APPLET>.

The syntax of the <APPLET> tag is shown below; the order of the parameters does not matter:

```
<APPLET
    [ALIGN = alignment]
    [ALT = alternate-text]
    CODE = applet-filename or OBJECT = serialized-applet
    [CODEBASE = applet-directory-url]
    [ARCHIVE = filename.zip/filename.jar]
    HEIGHT = applet-pixel-height
    [HSPACE = horizontal-pixel-margin]
    [MAYSCRIPT = true/false]
    [NAME = applet-name]
    [VSPACE = vertical-pixel-margin]
    WIDTH = applet-pixel-width
>
<PARAM NAME=parameter1 VALUE=value1>
<PARAM NAME=parameter2 VALUE=value2>
<PARAM NAME=parameter3 VALUE=value3>
...
[alternate-html]
</APPLET>
```

`<APPLET>`

The `<APPLET>` tag specifies where and how to display an applet within the HTML document. If the browser does not understand the `<APPLET>` and `<PARAM>` tags, it displays the alternate-html. (It displays the alternate-html because it doesn't understand the surrounding tags and ignores them. There's no magic to the alternate-html itself.) If a browser does understand `<APPLET>` but cannot run Java (for example, a browser on Windows 3.1) or Java has been disabled, the browser displays the alternate-html or the alternate-text specified by the optional ALT parameter. The CODE, WIDTH, and HEIGHT parameters are required. Parameters within the `<APPLET>` tag are separated by spaces, not by commas.

`</APPLET>`

Closes the `<APPLET>` tag. Anything prior to `</APPLET>` is considered alternate-html if it is not a `<PARAM>` tag. The alternate-html is displayed when Java is disabled, when Java cannot be run in the current browser, or when the browser does not understand the `<APPLET>` tag.

The following parameters may appear inside the `<APPLET>` tag.

ALIGN

alignment, optional. Specifies the applet's alignment on the Web page. Valid values are: left, right, top, texttop, middle, absmiddle, baseline, bottom, absbottom. Default: left. The alignment values have the same meanings as they do in the `<IMG>` tag.

ALT

alternate-text, optional. The alternate text is displayed when the browser understands the `<APPLET>` tag but is incapable of executing applets, either because Java is disabled or not supported on the platform. Support of this tag is browser dependent; most browsers just display the alternate-html since that is not restricted to text.

ARCHIVE

filename.zip/filename.jar, optional. Points to a comma-separated list of uncompressed ZIP or JAR files that contain one or more Java classes. Each file is downloaded once to the user's disk and searched for the class named in the CODE parameter, and any helper classes required to execute that class. JAR files may be signed to grant additional access. (JAR files are Java archives, a new archive format defined in Java 1.1. JAR files support features like digital signatures and compression. While they are not yet in wide use, they should become an important way of distributing sets of Java classes.)

CODE

> `applet-filename`. This parameter or the `OBJECT` parameter is required. Name of applet *.class* file. The *.class* extension is not required in the `<APPLET>` tag but is required in the class's actual filename. The filename has to be a quoted string only if it includes whitespace.

CODEBASE

> `applet-directory-url`, optional. Relative or absolute URL specifying the directory in which to locate the *.class* file or ZIP archive for the applet. Default: html directory.

HEIGHT

> `applet-pixel-height`, required. Initial height of applet in pixels. Many browsers do not allow applets to change their height.

HSPACE

> `horizontal-pixel-margin`, optional. Horizontal margin left and right of the applet, in pixels.

MAYSCRIPT

> Required for applets that wish to use LiveConnect and the `netscape.javascript` classes to interact with JavaScript. Set to `true` to communicate with JavaScript. Set to `false`, or omit this parameter to disable communication with JavaScript. Both Java and JavaScript must be enabled in the browser.

NAME

> `applet-name`, optional. Allows simultaneously running applets to communicate by this name. Default: the applet's class name.

OBJECT

> `serialized-applet`. This parameter or the `CODE` parameter is required. Name of applet saved to a file as a serialized object. When loaded, `init()` is not called again but `start()` is. Parameters for running the applet are taken from this `<APPLET>` tag, not the original.

VSPACE

> `vertical-pixel-margin`, optional. Vertical margin above and below the applet, in pixels.

WIDTH

> `applet-pixel-width`, required. Initial width of applet in pixels. Many browsers do not allow applets to change their width.

The `<PARAM>` tag may appear between the `<APPLET>` and `</APPLET>` tags:

<PARAM>

The <PARAM> tag allows the HTML author to provide run-time parameters to the applet as a series of NAME and VALUE pairs. The NAME is case insensitive, and each VALUE is passed as a String. See Chapter 14, *And Then There Were Applets* for a discussion of how to read parameters in an applet. Quotes are required around the parameter name or its value if there are any embedded spaces. There can be an infinite number of <PARAM> tags, and they all must appear between <APPLET> and </APPLET>

The special parameter name CABBASE is used for sending CAB files with Internet Explorer 3.0. CAB files are similar to ZIP files but are compressed into a CABinet file and can store audio and image files, in addition to classes. (For a full explanation see: http://207.68.137.43/workshop/java/overview.htm.) When *.class* files are placed within a CAB file, they are decompressed at the local end. Here's an example:

```
<APPLET CODE="oreilly.class" WIDTH=400 HEIGHT=400>
<PARAM NAME="cabbase" VALUE="ora.cab>
</APPLET>
```

The special parameter name ARCHIVES is reserved for sending JAR files. JAR files can also be specified using the ARCHIVES parameter to the <APPLET> tag.[*] Here's an example:

```
<APPLET CODE="oreilly.class" WIDTH=400 HEIGHT=400>
<PARAM NAME="archives" VALUE="ora.jar>
</APPLET>
```

---

[*] For a full explanation see http://www.javasoft.com/products/JDK/1.1/docs/guide/jar/index.html.

C

Platform-Specific Event Handling

My life with Java began in September of 1995. I started on a Sun Sparc20 and have since used Java on Windows 95, Windows NT (3.51/4.0), a PowerMac, and an early version of a Java terminal. At the time I started using Java, it was in its alpha 3 release. Even before the beta release, the Internet crowd was hailing Java as the programming language for the next millennium, and people were lining up to take Sun's Java training classes.

Although Java has many important features, probably the most important is platform independence: you can compile a program once and run it anywhere. At least, that was the goal; and Java came impressively close to meeting that goal. However, there are some problems, particularly in the area of event handling. Java programs just do not act the same, from platform to platform, environment to environment. Even if you stay within Sun's Java Developer's Kit, you cannot take a program created on one platform, move it to another, and be guaranteed that it will react the same way to the user's interactions. To make matters worse, Netscape, the makers of the first run-time environment for beta API applets, Netscape, decided to take matters into its own hands with Navigator version 3.0; its version of AWT behaves slightly differently than the JDK's. On top of that, Navigator itself differs from platform to platform. Version 1.1 of the JDK introduces more idiosyncrasies, even as it resolves some others.

With more Java environments available, HotJava, Internet Explorer, and Java terminals to name a few, and new official extensions to AWT coming out, the differences are expanding, instead of contracting. Hopefully, there will be a day when this appendix can go away, completely. Until that time, I've tried to document the behavior of different run-time systems, on different platforms. If the platform is not included in this appendix, the source for a test program is. If you run the program on your platform and send the results to me at *jaz@ora.com*, they will be included in a future printing or provided online. The test program requires user-interaction, so please follow directions carefully. Between printings, the book's Web site will maintain the latest information at *http://www.ora.com/catalog/javawt/*. Only the results from using the latest releases of each platform are included in Table C-1.

C.1 The Results

Table C-1 shows the events delivered to each component on the major platforms in Java 1.0. An ✓ in a particular entry means that the event is passed to Java from the component's peer; a dash means it is not.

Table C–1: Component Events in Java 1.0

Component/Events vs. Run-time/Platform	NN3.0 NT/ Win95	NN3.0 Mac	NN3.0 Sun	SDK NT/ Win95	JDK NT/ Win95	JDK Mac	JDK Sun Win95	IE3.0 NT/ Win95	HJ NT/	HJ Sun
Button										
KEY_PRESS	✓	—	✓	✓	✓	—	✓	✓	✓	✓
KEY_RELEASE	✓	—	✓	✓	✓	—	✓	✓	✓	✓
KEY_ACTION	✓	—	—	✓	✓	—	✓	✓	✓	✓
KEY_ACTION_RELEASE	✓	—	—	✓	✓	—	✓	✓	✓	✓
MOUSE_DOWN	✓	—	—	—	—	—	—	—	—	—
MOUSE_UP	✓	✓	—	—	—	—	—	—	—	—
MOUSE_MOVE	✓	✓	—	—	—	✓	—	—	—	—
MOUSE_ENTER	✓	✓	—	—	—	✓	—	—	—	—
MOUSE_EXIT	✓	✓	—	—	—	✓	—	—	—	—
MOUSE_DRAG	✓	✓	—	—	—	—	—	—	—	—
ACTION_EVENT	✓	✓	✓	✓	✓	✓	✓	✓	✓	✓
GOT_FOCUS	✓	—	—	—	—	—	✓	—	—	—
LOST_FOCUS	✓	—	—	—	—	—	✓	—	—	—
Canvas										
KEY_PRESS	✓	✓	✓	✓	✓	✓	—	✓	✓	—
KEY_RELEASE	✓	✓	✓	✓	✓	✓	—	✓	✓	—
KEY_ACTION	✓	✓	—	✓	✓	✓	—	✓	✓	—
KEY_ACTION_RELEASE	✓	✓	—	✓	✓	—	—	✓	✓	—
MOUSE_DOWN	✓	✓	✓	✓	✓	✓	✓	✓	✓	✓
MOUSE_UP	✓	✓	✓	✓	✓	✓	✓	✓	✓	✓

Table C–1: Component Events in Java 1.0 (continued)

Component/Events vs. Run-time/Platform	NN3.0 NT/Win95	NN3.0 Mac	NN3.0 Sun	SDK NT/Win95	JDK NT/Win95	JDK Mac	JDK Sun Win95	IE3.0 NT/Win95	HJ NT/	HJ Sun
MOUSE_MOVE	✓	✓	✓	✓	✓	✓	✓	✓	✓	✓
MOUSE_ENTER	✓	✓	✓	✓	✓	✓	✓	✓	✓	✓
MOUSE_EXIT	✓	✓	✓	✓	✓	✓	✓	✓	✓	✓
MOUSE_DRAG	✓	✓	✓	✓	✓	✓	✓	✓	✓	✓
ACTION_EVENT	—	—	—	—	—	—	—	—	—	—
GOT_FOCUS	✓	✓	—	✓	✓	✓	—	✓	✓	—
LOST_FOCUS	✓	✓	—	✓	✓	✓	—	✓	✓	—
Checkbox										
KEY_PRESS	✓	—	✓	✓	✓	—	✓	✓	✓	—
KEY_RELEASE	✓	—	✓	✓	✓	—	✓	✓	✓	—
KEY_ACTION	✓	—	—	✓	✓	—	✓	✓	✓	—
KEY_ACTION_RELEASE	✓	—	—	✓	✓	—	✓	✓	✓	—
MOUSE_DOWN	✓	—	—	—	—	—	—	—	—	—
MOUSE_UP	✓	✓	—	—	—	—	—	—	—	—
MOUSE_MOVE	✓	✓	—	—	—	✓	—	—	—	—
MOUSE_ENTER	✓	✓	—	—	—	✓	—	—	—	—
MOUSE_EXIT	✓	✓	—	—	—	✓	—	—	—	—
MOUSE_DRAG	✓	✓	—	—	—	—	—	—	—	—
ACTION_EVENT	✓	✓	✓	✓	✓	✓	✓	✓	✓	✓
GOT_FOCUS	✓	—	—	—	—	—	✓	—	—	—
LOST_FOCUS	✓	—	—	—	—	—	✓	—	—	—
Choice										
KEY_PRESS	✓	—	—	✓	✓	—	—	✓	✓	—
KEY_RELEASE	✓	—	—	✓	✓	—	—	✓	✓	—
KEY_ACTION	✓	—	—	✓	✓	—	—	✓	✓	—
KEY_ACTION_RELEASE	✓	—	—	✓	✓	—	—	✓	✓	—
MOUSE_DOWN	✓	—	—	—	—	—	—	—	—	—
MOUSE_UP	✓	—	✓	—	—	—	—	—	—	—
MOUSE_MOVE	✓	✓	✓	—	—	✓	—	—	—	—
MOUSE_ENTER	✓	✓	✓	—	—	✓	—	—	—	—
MOUSE_EXIT	✓	✓	✓	—	—	✓	—	—	—	—
MOUSE_DRAG	✓	✓	—	—	—	—	—	—	—	—
ACTION_EVENT	✓	✓	✓	✓	✓	✓	✓	✓	✓	✓

Table C–1: Component Events in Java 1.0 (continued)

Component/Events vs. Run-time/Platform	NN3.0 NT/ Win95	NN3.0 Mac	NN3.0 Sun	SDK NT/ Win95	JDK NT/ Win95	JDK Mac	JDK Sun Win95	IE3.0 NT/ Win95	HJ NT/	HJ Sun
GOT_FOCUS	✓	—	—	—	—	—	—	—	—	—
LOST_FOCUS	✓	—	—	—	—	—	—	—	—	—

Label

KEY_PRESS	✓	—	✓	—	—	—	✓	—	—	—
KEY_RELEASE	✓	—	✓	—	—	—	✓	—	—	—
KEY_ACTION	✓	—	—	—	—	—	✓	—	—	—
KEY_ACTION_RELEASE	✓	—	—	—	—	—	✓	—	—	—
MOUSE_DOWN	✓	—	—	—	—	—	—	—	—	—
MOUSE_UP	✓	✓	—	—	—	—	—	—	—	—
MOUSE_MOVE	✓	✓	—	—	—	✓	—	—	—	—
MOUSE_ENTER	✓	✓	—	—	—	✓	—	—	—	—
MOUSE_EXIT	✓	✓	—	—	—	✓	—	—	—	—
MOUSE_DRAG	✓	✓	—	—	—	—	—	—	—	—
ACTION_EVENT	—	—	—	—	—	—	—	—	—	—
GOT_FOCUS	✓	—	—	—	—	—	—	—	—	—
LOST_FOCUS	✓	—	—	—	—	—	—	—	—	—

List

KEY_PRESS	✓	—	—	✓	✓	—	✓	✓	✓	—
KEY_RELEASE	✓	—	—	✓	✓	—	✓	✓	✓	—
KEY_ACTION	✓	—	—	✓	✓	—	✓	✓	✓	—
KEY_ACTION_RELEASE	✓	—	—	✓	✓	—	✓	✓	✓	—
MOUSE_DOWN	✓	—	—	—	—	—	—	—	—	—
MOUSE_UP	✓	✓	—	—	—	—	—	—	—	—
MOUSE_MOVE	✓	✓	—	—	—	✓	—	—	—	—
MOUSE_ENTER	✓	✓	—	—	—	✓	—	—	—	—
MOUSE_EXIT	✓	✓	—	—	—	✓	—	—	—	—
MOUSE_DRAG	✓	✓	—	—	—	—	—	—	—	—
LIST_SELECT	✓	✓	✓	✓	✓	✓	✓	✓	✓	✓
LIST_DESELECT	✓	✓	✓	✓	✓	✓	✓	✓	✓	✓
ACTION_EVENT	✓	✓	✓	✓	✓	✓	✓	✓	✓	✓
GOT_FOCUS	✓	—	—	—	—	—	✓	—	—	—
LOST_FOCUS	✓	—	—	—	—	—	✓	—	—	—

Table C–1: Component Events in Java 1.0 (continued)

Component/Events vs. Run-time/Platform	NN3.0 NT/ Win95	NN3.0 Mac	NN3.0 Sun	SDK NT/ Win95	JDK NT/ Win95	JDK Mac	JDK Sun Win95	IE3.0 NT/ Win95	HJ NT/	HJ Sun
Scrollbar										
KEY_PRESS	—	—	✓	—	—	—	—	—	—	—
KEY_RELEASE	—	—	✓	—	—	—	—	—	—	—
KEY_ACTION	—	—	—	—	—	—	—	—	—	—
KEY_ACTION_RELEASE	—	—	—	—	—	—	—	—	—	—
MOUSE_DOWN	✓	—	—	—	—	—	—	—	—	—
MOUSE_UP	—	✓	—	—	—	—	—	—	—	—
MOUSE_MOVE	✓	✓	—	—	—	✓	—	—	—	—
MOUSE_ENTER	✓	✓	—	—	—	✓	—	—	—	—
MOUSE_EXIT	✓	✓	—	—	—	✓	—	—	—	—
MOUSE_DRAG	—	✓	—	—	—	—	—	—	—	—
SCROLL_LINE_UP	✓	✓	✓	✓	✓	✓	✓	✓	✓	✓
SCROLL_LINE_DOWN	✓	✓	✓	✓	✓	✓	✓	✓	✓	✓
SCROLL_PAGE_UP	✓	✓	✓	✓	✓	✓	✓	✓	✓	✓
SCROLL_PAGE_DOWN	✓	✓	✓	✓	✓	✓	✓	✓	✓	✓
SCROLL_ABSOLUTE	✓	✓	✓	✓	✓	✓	✓	✓	✓	✓
ACTION_EVENT	—	—	—	—	—	—	—	—	—	—
GOT_FOCUS	—	—	—	—	—	—	✓	—	—	—
LOST_FOCUS	—	—	—	—	—	—	✓	—	—	—
TextArea										
KEY_PRESS	✓	✓	—	✓	✓	✓	✓	✓	✓	✓
KEY_RELEASE	✓	✓	—	✓	✓	✓	✓	✓	✓	✓
KEY_ACTION	✓	—	—	✓	✓	✓	✓	✓	✓	✓
KEY_ACTION_RELEASE	✓	—	—	✓	✓	—	✓	✓	✓	✓
MOUSE_DOWN	✓	—	—	—	—	—	—	—	—	—
MOUSE_UP	✓	✓	—	—	—	—	—	—	—	—
MOUSE_MOVE	✓	✓	—	—	—	✓	—	—	—	—
MOUSE_ENTER	✓	✓	—	—	—	✓	—	—	—	—
MOUSE_EXIT	✓	✓	—	—	—	✓	—	—	—	—
MOUSE_DRAG	✓	✓	—	—	—	—	—	—	—	—
ACTION_EVENT	—	—	—	—	—	—	—	—	—	—
GOT_FOCUS	✓	✓	✓	—	—	✓	✓	—	—	✓
LOST_FOCUS	✓	✓	✓	—	—	✓	✓	—	—	✓

Table C–1: Component Events in Java 1.0 (continued)

Component/Events vs. Run-time/Platform	NN3.0 NT/ Win95	NN3.0 Mac	NN3.0 Sun	SDK NT/ Win95	JDK NT/ Win95	JDK Mac	JDK Sun Win95	IE3.0 NT/ Win95	HJ NT/	HJ Sun
TextField										
KEY_PRESS	✓	✓	✓	✓	✓	✓	✓	✓	✓	✓
KEY_RELEASE	✓	✓	✓	✓	✓	✓	✓	✓	✓	✓
KEY_ACTION	✓	✓	—	✓	✓	✓	✓	✓	✓	✓
KEY_ACTION_RELEASE	✓	✓	—	✓	✓	—	✓	✓	✓	✓
MOUSE_DOWN	✓	—	—	—	—	—	—	—	—	—
MOUSE_UP	✓	✓	—	—	—	—	—	—	—	—
MOUSE_MOVE	✓	✓	—	—	—	✓	—	—	—	—
MOUSE_ENTER	✓	✓	—	—	—	✓	—	—	—	—
MOUSE_EXIT	✓	✓	—	—	—	✓	—	—	—	—
MOUSE_DRAG	✓	✓	—	—	—	—	—	—	—	—
ACTION_EVENT	✓	✓	✓	✓	✓	✓	✓	✓	✓	✓
GOT_FOCUS	✓	✓	✓	—	—	✓	✓	—	—	✓
LOST_FOCUS	✓	✓	✓	—	—	✓	✓	—	—	✓

Key:

IE   Microsoft's Internet Explorer

HJ   Sun's Hot Java Prebeta 1

JDK
    Java Developer's Kit 1.0.2 (*appletviewer*/Java)

NN
    Netscape Navigator

SDK
    Microsoft SDK

Sun
    Solaris 2.x (UNIX/Motif)

Yes, things changed again with the 1.1 release. Table C-2 shows which Java 1.0 events are generated for each component in Java 1.1. Fortunately, there is one clear improvement: the Java 1.1 event model promises much more uniform event processing, since it's largely under your control. For example, you can attach a `MouseListener` to a `Label` and receive mouse events that would not be generated with the 1.0 event model.

Table C–2: Java 1.0 Component Events in Java 1.1

Component/Events vs. Run-time/Platform	HJ/JDK WinNT/95	HJ/JDK Sun
Button		
KEY_PRESS	✓	✓
KEY_RELEASE	✓	✓
KEY_ACTION	✓	✓
KEY_ACTION_RELEASE	✓	✓
MOUSE_DOWN	—	—
MOUSE_UP	—	—
MOUSE_MOVE	—	—
MOUSE_ENTER	—	—
MOUSE_EXIT	—	—
MOUSE_DRAG	—	—
ACTION_EVENT	✓	✓
GOT_FOCUS	✓	✓
LOST_FOCUS	✓	✓
Canvas		
KEY_PRESS	—	—
KEY_RELEASE	—	—
KEY_ACTION	—	—
KEY_ACTION_RELEASE	—	—
MOUSE_DOWN	✓	✓
MOUSE_UP	✓	✓
MOUSE_MOVE	✓	✓
MOUSE_ENTER	✓	✓
MOUSE_EXIT	✓	✓
MOUSE_DRAG	✓	✓
ACTION_EVENT	—	—
GOT_FOCUS	—	—
LOST_FOCUS	—	—
Checkbox		
KEY_PRESS	✓	✓
KEY_RELEASE	✓	✓
KEY_ACTION	✓	—
KEY_ACTION_RELEASE	✓	—
MOUSE_DOWN	—	—

Table C–2: Java 1.0 Component Events in Java 1.1 (continued)

Component/Events vs. Run-time/Platform	HJ/JDK WinNT/95	HJ/JDK Sun
MOUSE_UP	—	—
MOUSE_MOVE	—	—
MOUSE_ENTER	—	—
MOUSE_EXIT	—	—
MOUSE_DRAG	—	—
ACTION_EVENT	✓	✓
GOT_FOCUS	✓	✓
LOST_FOCUS	✓	✓
Choice		
KEY_PRESS	✓	—
KEY_RELEASE	✓	—
KEY_ACTION	✓	—
KEY_ACTION_RELEASE	✓	—
MOUSE_DOWN	—	—
MOUSE_UP	—	—
MOUSE_MOVE	—	—
MOUSE_ENTER	—	—
MOUSE_EXIT	—	—
MOUSE_DRAG	—	—
ACTION_EVENT	✓	✓
GOT_FOCUS	✓	—
LOST_FOCUS	✓	—
Label		
KEY_PRESS	—	—
KEY_RELEASE	—	—
KEY_ACTION	—	—
KEY_ACTION_RELEASE	—	—
MOUSE_DOWN	—	—
MOUSE_UP	—	—
MOUSE_MOVE	—	—
MOUSE_ENTER	—	—
MOUSE_EXIT	—	—
MOUSE_DRAG	—	—
ACTION_EVENT	—	—

Table C–2: Java 1.0 Component Events in Java 1.1   (continued)

Component/Events vs. Run-time/Platform	HJ/JDK WinNT/95	HJ/JDK Sun
GOT_FOCUS	—	—
LOST_FOCUS	—	—
List		
KEY_PRESS	✓	✓
KEY_RELEASE	✓	✓
KEY_ACTION	✓	✓
KEY_ACTION_RELEASE	✓	✓
MOUSE_DOWN	—	—
MOUSE_UP	—	—
MOUSE_MOVE	—	—
MOUSE_ENTER	—	—
MOUSE_EXIT	—	—
MOUSE_DRAG	—	—
LIST_SELECT	✓	✓
LIST_DESELECT	✓	✓
ACTION_EVENT	✓	✓
GOT_FOCUS	✓	✓
LOST_FOCUS	✓	✓
ScrollBar		
KEY_PRESS	—	—
KEY_RELEASE	—	—
KEY_ACTION	—	—
KEY_ACTION_RELEASE	—	—
MOUSE_DOWN	—	—
MOUSE_UP	—	—
MOUSE_MOVE	—	—
MOUSE_ENTER	—	—
MOUSE_EXIT	—	—
MOUSE_DRAG	—	—
SCROLL_LINE_UP	✓	✓
SCROLL_LINE_DOWN	✓	✓
SCROLL_PAGE_UP	✓	✓
SCROLL_PAGE_DOWN	✓	✓
SCROLL_ABSOLUTE	✓	✓

Table C–2: Java 1.0 Component Events in Java 1.1 (continued)

Component/Events vs. Run-time/Platform	HJ/JDK WinNT/95	HJ/JDK Sun
ACTION_EVENT	—	—
GOT_FOCUS	—	✓
LOST_FOCUS	—	✓
TextArea		
KEY_PRESS	✓	✓
KEY_RELEASE	✓	✓
KEY_ACTION	✓	✓
KEY_ACTION_RELEASE	✓	✓
MOUSE_DOWN	—	—
MOUSE_UP	—	—
MOUSE_MOVE	—	—
MOUSE_ENTER	—	—
MOUSE_EXIT	—	—
MOUSE_DRAG	—	—
ACTION_EVENT	—	—
GOT_FOCUS	✓	✓
LOST_FOCUS	✓	✓
TextField		
KEY_PRESS	✓	✓
KEY_RELEASE	✓	✓
KEY_ACTION	✓	✓
KEY_ACTION_RELEASE	✓	✓
MOUSE_DOWN	—	—
MOUSE_UP	—	—
MOUSE_MOVE	—	—
MOUSE_ENTER	—	—
MOUSE_EXIT	—	—
MOUSE_DRAG	—	—
ACTION_EVENT	✓	✓
GOT_FOCUS	✓	✓
LOST_FOCUS	✓	✓

Key:

HJ Sun's Hot Java Prebeta 2

JDK
   Java Developer's Kit 1.1 (*appletviewer*/Java)

Sun
   Solaris 2.x (UNIX/Motif)

C.2 Test Program

The test program, compList, listed in Section C.2.2 shows the events peers pass along to the Java run-time system. You can then examine the output to see how the run-time system reacts to the different events. When you run compList, the screen looks something like the one in Figure C-1.

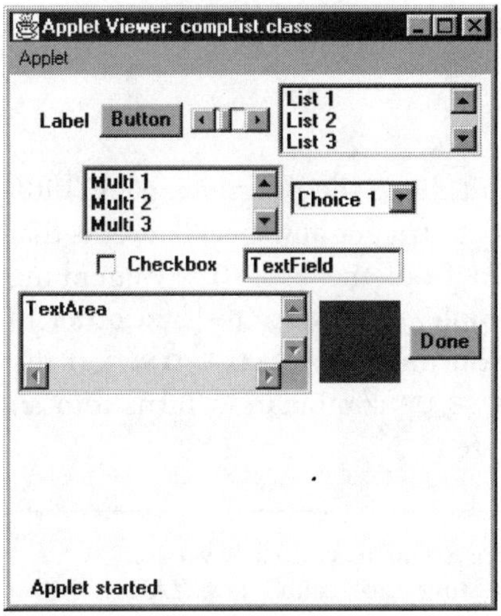

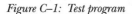

Figure C–1: Test program

C.2.1 How to Use the Program

Java does not have an automated record and playback feature, so the work is left for you to do. The program displays 10 components: Label, Button, Scrollbar, List, multiselection List, Choice, Checkbox, TextField, TextArea, and Canvas (the black box in Figure C-1). Basically, you must manually trigger every event for every component.

For *every* component on the screen (except Done), do the following:

With the mouse
> Move the cursor over the object, press the mouse button and release, and drag the cursor over the object.

With the keyboard
> Press and release an alphabetic key, press and release the Home and End keys, arrow keys, and function keys. Do this for every component, even for components like Button and Label that have no logical reason for using keyboard events.

For items with choices
> Select and deselect a few choices; double-click and single-click selections.

For the scrollbar
> Click on each arrow, drag the slider, and click in the paging area (the space between each arrow and the slider).

For the text field
> Press Enter.

When finished
> Press the Done button, and analyze the results. Run the program again (without exiting), and check the results again. Try to trigger any specific events that you expect but didn't appear in the output from the first pass. Generating some events requires a little work. For example, on a Macintosh, in order to get the MOUSE_UP and MOUSE_DRAG events, you must do a MOUSE_DOWN off the component; otherwise, the MOUSE_DOWN/MOUSE_UP combination turns into an ACTION_EVENT, if that component can generate it.

NOTE   The SunTest business unit of Sun Microsystems has an early version of a record and playback Java GUI testing tool called JavaSTAR. Information about it is available at *http://www.suntest.com/JavaSTAR/JavaSTAR.html.* In the future, it may be possible to use JavaSTAR to help automate this process.

C.2.2 Source Code

The following is the source code for the test program:

```
import java.awt.*;
import java.util.*;
import java.applet.*;
public class compList extends Applet {
    Button done = new Button ("Done");
    Hashtable values = new Hashtable();
```

```
public void init () {
    add (new Label ("Label"));
    add (new Button ("Button"));
    add (new Scrollbar (Scrollbar.HORIZONTAL, 50, 25, 0, 255));
    List l1 = new List (3, false);
    l1.addItem ("List 1");
    l1.addItem ("List 2");
    l1.addItem ("List 3");
    l1.addItem ("List 4");
    l1.addItem ("List 5");
    add (l1);
    List l2 = new List (3, true);
    l2.addItem ("Multi 1");
    l2.addItem ("Multi 2");
    l2.addItem ("Multi 3");
    l2.addItem ("Multi 4");
    l2.addItem ("Multi 5");
    add (l2);
    Choice c = new Choice ();
    c.addItem ("Choice 1");
    c.addItem ("Choice 2");
    c.addItem ("Choice 3");
    c.addItem ("Choice 4");
    c.addItem ("Choice 5");
    add (c);
    add (new Checkbox ("Checkbox"));
    add (new TextField ("TextField", 10));
    add (new TextArea ("TextArea", 3, 20));
    Canvas c1 = new Canvas ();
    c1.resize (50, 50);
    c1.setBackground (Color.blue);
    add (c1);
    add (done);
}
public boolean handleEvent (Event e) {
    if (e.target == done) {
        if (e.id == Event.ACTION_EVENT) {
            System.out.println (System.getProperty ("java.vendor"));
            System.out.println (System.getProperty ("java.version"));
            System.out.println (System.getProperty ("java.class.version"));
            System.out.println (System.getProperty ("os.name"));
            System.out.println (values);
        }
    }else {
        Vector v;
        Class c = e.target.getClass ();
        v = (Vector)values.get (c);
        if (v == null)
            v = new Vector();
        Integer i = new Integer (e.id);
        if (!v.contains (i)) {
            v.addElement (i);
            values.put (c, v);
        }
```

```
        }

    return super.handleEvent (e);
    }
}
```

An HTML document to display the applet in a browser should look something like the following:

```
<APPLET code="compList.class" height=300 width=300>
</APPLET>
```

C.2.3 Examining Results

The results of the program are sent to standard output when you click on the Done button. What happens to the output depends on the platform. It may be sent to a log file (Internet Explorer), the Java Console (Netscape Navigator), or the command line (appletviewer). The following is sample output from Internet Explorer 3.0 on a Windows 95 platform.

```
Microsoft Corp.
1.0.2
45.3
Windows 95
{class java.awt.Canvas=[504, 503, 1004, 501, 506, 502, 505, 1005,
401, 402, 403, 404], class java.awt.Choice=[1001, 401, 402, 403,
404], class java.awt.Checkbox=[1001, 402, 401, 403, 404], class
compList=[504, 503, 501, 506, 502, 505, 1004, 1005], class java.
awt.TextField=[401, 402, 403, 404], class java.awt.List=[701,
1001, 401, 402, 403, 404, 702], class java.awt.Scrollbar=[602,
605, 604, 603, 601], class java.awt.TextArea=[401, 402, 403, 404],
class java.awt.Button=[1001, 401, 402, 403, 404]}
```

In addition to some identifying information about the run-time environment, the program displays a list of classes and the events they passed. The integers represent the event constants of the Event class; for example, Canvas received events with identifiers 504, 503, etc. The events are not sorted, so you can see the order in which they were sent. Unfortunately, you have to look up these constants in the source code yourself. The class listed as compList is the applet itself and shows you the events that the Applet class receives.

In this appendix:
- *How Images are Loaded*
- *A Brief Tour of sun.awt.image*

D

Image Loading

D.1 *How Images are Loaded*

You have seen how easy it is to display an image on screen and have probably guessed that there's more going on behind the scenes. The getImage() and draw-Image() methods trigger a series of events that result in the image being available for display on the ImageObserver. The image is fetched asynchronously in another thread. The entire process* goes as follows:

1. The call to getImage() triggers Toolkit to call createImage() for the image's InputStreamImageSource (which is a URLImageSource in this case; it would be a FileImageSource if we were loading the image from a local file).

2. The Toolkit registers the image as being "desired." Desired just means that something will eventually want the image loaded. The system then waits until an ImageObserver registers its interest in the image.

3. The drawImage() method (use of MediaTracker or prepareImage()) registers an ImageObserver as interested.

4. Registering an ImageObserver kicks the image's ImageRepresentation into action; this is the start of the loading process, although image data isn't actually transferred until step 9. ImageRepresentation implements the ImageConsumer interface.

5. The start of production registers the image source (ImageProducer URLImage-Source) with the ImageFetcher and also registers the ImageRepresentation as an ImageConsumer for the image.

---

* This summary covers Sun's implementation (JDK). Implementations that don't derive from the JDK may behave completely differently.

6. The ImageFetcher creates a thread to get the image from its source.

7. The ImageFetcher reads data and passes it along to the InputStreamImage-Source, which is a URLImageSource.

8. The URLImageSource determines that JPEGImageDecoder is the proper ImageDecoder for converting the input stream into an Image. (Other ImageDecoders are used for other image types, like GIF.)

9. The ImageProducer starts reading the image data from the source; it calls the ImageConsumer (i.e., the ImageRepresentation) as it processes the image. The most important method in the ImageConsumer interface is setPixels(), which delivers pixel data to the consumer for rendering onscreen.

10. As the ImageConsumer (i.e., the ImageRepresentation) gets additional information, it notifies the ImageObserver via imageUpdate() calls.

11. When the image is fully acquired across the network, the thread started by the ImageFetcher stops.

As you see, there are a lot of unfamiliar moving pieces. Many of them are from the java.awt.image package and are discussed in Chapter 12, *Image Processing*. Others are from the sun.awt.image package; they are hidden in that you don't need to know anything about them to do image processing in Java. However, if you're curious, we'll briefly summarize these classes in the next section.

D.2 A Brief Tour of sun.awt.image

The classes in sun.awt.image do the behind-the-scenes work for rendering an image from a file or across the network. This information is purely for the curious; you should never have to work with these classes yourself.

Image

> The Image class in this package represents a concrete Image instance. It contains the basis for the Image class that is actually used on the run-time platform, which exists in the package for the specific environment. For instance, the sun.awt.win32 package includes the W32Image (Java 1.0), the sun.awt.windows package includes WImage (Java 1.1), while the sun.awt.motif package includes the X11Image, and the sun.awt.macos package includes the MacImage.

ImageRepresentation

> The ImageRepresentation is the ImageConsumer that watches the creation of the image and notifies the ImageObserver when it is time to update the display. It plays an important part in the overall control of the Image production process.

Image sources

A Java image can come from three different sources: memory (through `create-Image()`), local disk, or the network (through `getImage()`).

- `OffScreenImageSource` implements `ImageProducer` for a single framed image in memory. When an `Image` created from an `OffScreenImageSource` is drawn with `drawImage()`, the `ImageObserver` parameter can be `null` since all the image information is already in memory and there is no need for periodic updating as more is retrieved from disk. You can get the graphics context of `OffScreenImageSource` images and use the context to draw on the image area. This is how double buffering works.

- `InputStreamImageSource` implements `ImageProducer` for an image that comes from disk or across the network. When an `Image` created from an `InputStreamImageSource` is drawn with `drawImage()`, the `ImageObserver` parameter should be the component being drawn on (usually `this`) since the image information will be loaded periodically with the help of the `ImageObserver` interface). This class determines how to decode the image type and initializes the `ImageDecoder` to one of `GifImageDecoder`, `JPEGImageDecoder`, or `XbmImageDecoder`, although that can be overridden by a subclass. It can use a `ContentHandler` to work with unknown image types.

- `FileImageSource` is a subclass of `InputStreamImageSource` for images that come from the filesystem. It uses the filename to determine the type of image to decode and checks the security manager to ensure that access is allowed.

- `URLImageSource` is a subclass of `InputStreamImageSource` for images that are specified by a URL.

- `ByteArrayImageSource` (Java 1.1 only) is a subclass of `InputStreamImage-Source` for images that are created by calling `Toolkit.createImage(byte[])`.

Image decoders

An `ImageDecoder` is utilized to convert the image source to an image object. If there is no decoder for an image type, it can be read in with the help of a `ContentHandler` or your own class that implements `ImageProducer`, like the `PPMImageDecoder` shown in Chapter 12.

- `GifImageDecoder` reads in an image file in the GIF format.

- `JPEGImageDecoder` reads in an image file in the JPEG format.

- `XbmImageDecoder` reads in an image file in the XBM format. Although XBM support is not required by the language specification, support is provided with Netscape Navigator, Internet Explorer, HotJava, and the Java Developer's Kit from Sun.

ImageFetcher

The `ImageFetcher` class fetches the actual image from its source. This class creates a separate daemon thread to fetch each image. The thread is run at a higher priority than the default but not at the maximum priority.

Index

About the Author

John Zukowski is a consulting computer programmer, trainer, and speaker. John has been working with Java since the late alpha stages of the language. He has been a Java instructor since those early days, teaching a variety of Java classes of different lengths and styles. John founded the Mid-Atlantic Java User Group (MAJUG) and coordinated it until he moved out of the area. Pre-Java, John was a C/C++/X Windows/Database/Network programmer for Rapid Systems Solutions, a Maryland-based consulting firm. He has a computer science master's degree from The Johns Hopkins University, with undergraduate degrees in math and computer science from Northeastern University.

Colophon

Edie Freedman designed the cover of this book, using an image from the CMCD PhotoCD Collection that she manipulated in Adobe Photoshop. The cover layout was produced with Quark XPress 3.3 using the Bodoni Black font from URW Software and bt bodoni Bold Italic from Bitstream. The inside layout was designed by Nancy Priest.

Text was prepared by Erik Ray in SGML DocBook 2.4 DTD. The print version of this book was created by translating the SGML source into a set of gtroff macros using a filter developed at ORA by Norman Walsh. Steve Talbott designed and wrote the underlying macro set on the basis of the GNU troff -gs macros; Lenny Muellner adapted them to SGML and implemented the book design. The GNU groff text formatter version 1.09 was used to generate PostScript output. The heading font is Bodoni BT; the text font is New Baskerville. The illustrations that appear in the book were created in Macromedia Freehand 5.0 by Chris Reilley.

 # More Titles from O'Reilly

Java Programming

Exploring Java, Second Edition

By Patrick Niemeyer & Joshua Peck
2nd Edition June 1997 (est.)
500 pages (est.), ISBN 1-56592-271-9

The second edition of *Exploring Java*,
fully revised to cover Version 1.1 of the
JDK, introduces the basics of Java, the
object-oriented programming language for
networked applications. The ability to create animated World Wide Web pages sparked the rush to Java. But what also makes this language so important is that it's truly portable. The code runs on any machine that provides a Java interpreter, whether Windows 95, Windows NT, the Macintosh, or any flavor of UNIX.

Java in a Nutshell, Second Edition

By David Flanagan
2nd Edition May 1997
650 pages, ISBN 1-56592-262-X

The bestselling Java book just got better. Java programmers migrating to 1.1 find this second edition of Java in a Nutshell contains everything they need to get up to speed.

Newcomers find it still has all of the features that have made it the Java book most often recommended on the Internet. This complete quick reference contains descriptions of all of the classes in the core Java 1.1 API, making it the only quick reference that a Java programmer needs.

Java Virtual Machine

By Troy Downing & Jon Meyer
1st Edition March 1997
440 pages, ISBN 1-56592-194-1

This book is a comprehensive programming guide for the Java Virtual Machine (JVM). It gives readers a strong overview and reference of the JVM so that they may create their own implementations of the JVM or write their own compilers that create Java object code. A Java assembler is provided with the book, so the examples can all be compiled and executed.

Java Language Reference, Second Edition

By Mark Grand
2nd Edition July 1997 (est.)
448 pages, ISBN 1-56592-326-X

The second edition of the *Java Language Reference* is an invaluable tool for Java programmers, especially those who have migrated to Java 1.1. Part of O'Reilly's Java documentation series, this complete reference describes all aspects of the Java language plus new features in Version 1.1, such as inner classes, final local variables and method parameters, anonymous arrays, class literals, and instance initializers.

Java Fundamental Classes Reference

By Mark Grand
1st Edition May 1997
1152 pages, ISBN 1-56592-241-7

The *Java Fundamental Classes Reference* provides complete reference documentation for the Java fundamental classes.

This book takes you beyond what you'd expect from a standard reference manual. Classes and methods are, of course, described in detail. It offers tutorial-style explanations of the important classes in the Java Core API and includes lots of sample code to help you learn by example.

Java AWT Reference

By John Zukowski
1st Edition March 1997
1100 pages, ISBN 1-56592-240-9

With AWT, you can create windows, draw, work with images, and use components like buttons, scrollbars, and pulldown menus. *Java AWT Reference* covers the classes that comprise the java.awt, java.awt.image, and java.applet packages. These classes provide the functionality that allows a Java application to provide user interaction in a graphical environment. It offers a comprehensive explanation of how AWT components fit together with easy-to-use reference material on every AWT class and lots of sample code to help you learn by example.

O'REILLY™

TO ORDER: **800-998-9938** • *order@ora.com* • *http://www.ora.com/*
OUR PRODUCTS ARE AVAILABLE AT A BOOKSTORE OR SOFTWARE STORE NEAR YOU.
FOR INFORMATION: **800-998-9938** • **707-829-0515** • *info@ora.com*

Java Programming *continued*

Java Threads

By Scott Oaks and Henry Wong
1st Edition January 1997
252 pages, ISBN 1-56592-216-6

Java Threads is a comprehensive guide to the intricacies of threaded programming in Java, covering everything from the most basic synchronization techniques to advanced topics like writing your own thread scheduler.

Java Threads uncovers the one tricky but essential aspect of Java programming and provides techniques for avoiding deadlock, lock starvation, and other topics.

Java Network Programming

By Elliotte Rusty Harold
1st Edition February 1997
448 pages, ISBN 1-56592-227-1

Java Network Programming is a complete introduction to developing network programs, both applets and applications, using Java; covering everything from networking fundamentals to remote method invocation (RMI).

It also covers what you can do without explicitly writing network code, how you can accomplish your goals using URLs and the basic capabilities of applets.

Developing Java Beans

By Rob Englander
1st Edition June 1997 (est.)
300 pages (est.), ISBN 1-56592-289-1

With *Developing Java Beans,* you'll learn how to create components that can be manipulated by tools like Borland's Latte or Symantec's Visual Cafe, enabling others to build entire applications by using and reusing these building blocks. Beyond the basics, *Developing Java Beans* teaches you how to create Beans that can be saved and restored properly; how to take advantage of introspection to provide more information about a Bean's capabilities; how to provide property editors and customizers that manipulate a Bean in sophisticated ways; and how to integrate Java Beans into ActiveX projects.

Java in a Nutshell, DELUXE EDITION

By various authors
1st Edition June1997 (est.)
ISBN 1-56592-304-9
includes CD-ROM and books.

Java in a Nutshell, Deluxe Edition, is a Java programmer's dream come true in one small package. The heart of this Deluxe Edition is the Java reference library on CD-ROM, which brings together five indispensable volumes for Java developers and programmers, linking related info across books. It includes: *Exploring Java 2nd Edition*, *Java Language Reference, 2nd Edition*, *Java Fundamental Classes Reference*, *Java AWT Reference*, and *Java in a Nutshell, 2nd Edition*, included both on the CD-ROM and in a companion desktop edition. This deluxe library gives you everything you need to do serious programming with Java 1.1.

Database Programming with JDBC and Java

By George Reese
1st Edition July 1997 (est.)
300 pages (est.), ISBN 1-56592-270-0

Java and databases make a powerful combination. Getting the two sides to work together, however, takes some effort—largely because Java deals in objects while most databases do not.

This book describes the standard Java interfaces that make portable,object-oriented access to relational databases possible, and offers a robust model for writing applications that are easy to maintain. It introduces the JDBC and RMI packages and uses them to develop three-tier applications (applications divided into a user interface, an object-oriented logic component, and an information store). Covers Java 1.1.

Perl

Programming Perl, Second Edition

By Larry Wall, Tom Christiansen,
& Randal L. Schwartz
2nd Edition September 1996
676 pages, ISBN 1-56592-149-6

Programming Perl, Second Edition, is coauthored by Larry Wall, the creator of Perl. Perl is a language for easily manipulating text, files, and processes. It provides a more concise and readable way to do many jobs that were formerly accomplished (with difficulty) by programming with C or one of the shells. This heavily revised second edition contains a full explanation of Perl version 5.003.

Learning Perl, Second Edition

By Randal L. Schwartz
Foreword by Larry Wall
2nd Edition July 1997
400 pages, ISBN 1-56592-284-0

This second edition of *Learning Perl*, with a foreword by Perl author Larry Wall, fully covers Perl, Version 5. In this new edition, program examples and exercise answers have been radically updated to reflect typical usage under Perl 5, and numerous details have been added or modified. In addition, you'll find new sections introducing Perl references and CGI programming.

Learning Perl, Second Edition is ideal for system administrators, programmers, and anyone else wanting a down-to-earth introduction to this useful language. Written by a Perl trainer, its aim is to make a competent, hands-on Perl programmer out of the reader as quickly as possible. The book takes a tutorial approach and includes hundreds of short code examples, along with some lengthy ones. The relatively inexperienced programmer will find *Learning Perl* easily accessible. For a comprehensive and detailed guide to advanced programming with Perl, read O'Reilly's companion book, *Programming Perl, Second Edition*.

CGI Programming on the World Wide Web

By Shishir Gundavaram
1st Edition March 1996
450 pages, ISBN 1-56592-168-2

This book offers a comprehensive explanation of CGI and related techniques for people who hold on to the dream of providing their own information servers on the Web. It starts at the beginning, explaining the value of CGI and how it works, then moves swiftly into the subtle details of programming.

Perl 5 Desktop Reference

By Johan Vromans
1st Edition February 1996
44 pages, ISBN 1-56592-187-9

This is the standard quick-reference guide for the Perl programming language. It provides a complete overview of the language, from variables to input and output, from flow control to regular expressions, from functions to document formats—all packed into a convenient, carry-around booklet. Updated to cover Perl version 5.003.

Mastering Regular Expressions

By Jeffrey E. F. Friedl
1st Edition January 1997
368 pages, ISBN 1-56592-257-3

Regular expressions, a powerful tool for manipulating text and data, are found in scripting languages, editors, programming environments, and specialized tools. In this book, author Jeffrey Friedl leads you through the steps of crafting a regular expression that gets the job done. He examines a variety of tools and uses them in an extensive array of examples, dedicating an entire chapter to Perl.

How to stay in touch with O'Reilly

1. Visit Our Award-Winning Web Site
http://www.ora.com/

★ "Top 100 Sites on the Web" —*PC Magazine*
★ "Top 5% Web sites" —*Point Communications*
★ "3-Star site" —*The McKinley Group*

Our web site contains a library of comprehensiveproduct information (including book excerpts and tables of contents), downloadable software, background articles, interviews with technology leaders, links to relevant sites, book cover art, and more. File us in your Bookmarks or Hotlist!

2. Join Our Email Mailing Lists
New Product Releases
To receive automatic email with brief descriptions of all new O'Reilly products as they are released, send email to: **listproc@online.ora.com**
Put the following information in the first line of your message (*not* in the Subject field):
subscribe ora-news "Your Name" of "Your Organization" (for example: subscribe ora-news Kris Webber of Fine Enterprises)

O'Reilly Events
If you'd also like us to send information about trade show events, special promotions, and other O'Reilly events, send email to: **listproc@online.ora.com**
Put the following information in the first line of your message (*not* in the Subject field):
subscribe ora-events "Your Name" of "Your Organization"

3. Get Examples from Our Books via FTP
There are two ways to access an archive of example files from our books:

Regular FTP
* ftp to:
  ftp.ora.com
  (login: anonymous
  password: your email address)
* Point your web browser to:
  ftp://ftp.ora.com/

FTPMAIL
* Send an email message to:
  ftpmail@online.ora.com
  (Write "help" in the message body)

4. Visit Our Gopher Site
* Connect your gopher to:
  gopher.ora.com

* Point your web browser to:
  gopher://gopher.ora.com/

* Telnet to:
  gopher.ora.com
  login: gopher

5. Contact Us via Email
order@ora.com
To place a book or software order online. Good for North American and international customers.

subscriptions@ora.com
To place an order for any of our newsletters or periodicals.

books@ora.com
General questions about any of our books.

software@ora.com
For general questions and product information about our software. Check out O'Reilly Software Online at **http://software.ora.com/** for software and technical support information. Registered O'Reilly software users send your questions to: **website-support@ora.com**

cs@ora.com
For answers to problems regarding your order or our products.

booktech@ora.com
For book content technical questions or corrections.

proposals@ora.com
To submit new book or software proposals to our editors and product managers.

international@ora.com
For information about our international distributors or translation queries. For a list of our distributors outside of North America check out:
http://www.ora.com/www/order/country.html

O'Reilly & Associates, Inc.
101 Morris Street, Sebastopol, CA 95472 USA
TEL   707-829-0515 or 800-998-9938
          (6am to 5pm PST)
FAX   707-829-0104

O'REILLY™
TO ORDER: **800-998-9938** • **order@ora.com** • **http://www.ora.com/**
OUR PRODUCTS ARE AVAILABLE AT A BOOKSTORE OR SOFTWARE STORE NEAR YOU.
FOR INFORMATION: **800-998-9938** • **707-829-0515** • **info@ora.com**

Titles from O'Reilly

Please note that upcoming titles are displayed in italic.

International Distributors

UK, Europe, Middle East and Northern Africa (except France, Germany, Switzerland, & Austria)

INQUIRIES

International Thomson Publishing
Europe
Berkshire House
168-173 High Holborn
London WC1V 7AA, United Kingdom
Telephone: 44-171-497-1422
Fax: 44-171-497-1426
Email: itpint@itps.co.uk

ORDERS

International Thomson Publishing
Services, Ltd.
Cheriton House, North Way
Andover, Hampshire SP10 5BE,
United Kingdom
Telephone: 44-264-342-832
  (UK orders)
Telephone: 44-264-342-806
  (outside UK)
Fax: 44-264-364418 (UK orders)
Fax: 44-264-342761 (outside UK)
UK & Eire orders: itpuk@itps.co.uk
International orders: itpint@itps.co.uk

France

Editions Eyrolles
61 bd Saint-Germain
75240 Paris Cedex 05
France
Fax: 33-01-44-41-11-44

FRENCH LANGUAGE BOOKS

All countries except Canada
Phone: 33-01-44-41-46-16
Email: geodif@eyrolles.com

ENGLISH LANGUAGE BOOKS

Phone: 33-01-44-41-11-87
Email: distribution@eyrolles.com

Australia

WoodsLane Pty. Ltd.
7/5 Vuko Place, Warriewood NSW 2102
P.O. Box 935, Mona Vale NSW 2103
Australia
Telephone: 61-2-9970-5111
Fax: 61-2-9970-5002
Email: info@woodslane.com.au

Germany, Switzerland, and Austria

INQUIRIES

O'Reilly Verlag
Balthasarstr. 81
D-50670 Köln
Germany
Telephone: 49-221-97-31-60-0
Fax: 49-221-97-31-60-8
Email: anfragen@oreilly.de

ORDERS

International Thomson Publishing
Königswinterer Straße 418
53227 Bonn, Germany
Telephone: 49-228-97024 0
Fax: 49-228-441342
Email: order@oreilly.de

Asia (except Japan & India)

INQUIRIES

International Thomson Publishing Asia
60 Albert Street #15-01
Albert Complex
Singapore 189969
Telephone: 65-336-6411
Fax: 65-336-7411

ORDERS

Telephone: 65-336-6411
Fax: 65-334-1617
thomson@signet.com.sg

New Zealand

WoodsLane New Zealand Ltd.
21 Cooks Street (P.O. Box 575)
Wanganui, New Zealand
Telephone: 64-6-347-6543
Fax: 64-6-345-4840
Email: info@woodslane.com.au

Japan

O'Reilly Japan, Inc.
Kiyoshige Building 2F
12-Banchi, Sanei-cho
Shinjuku-ku
Tokyo 160 Japan
Telephone: 81-3-3356-5227
Fax: 81-3-3356-5261
Email: kenji@ora.com

India

Computer Bookshop (India) PVT. LTD.
190 Dr. D.N. Road, Fort
Bombay 400 001
India
Telephone: 91-22-207-0989
Fax: 91-22-262-3551
Email: cbsbom@giasbm01.vsnl.net.in

The Americas

O'Reilly & Associates, Inc.
101 Morris Street
Sebastopol, CA 95472 U.S.A.
Telephone: 707-829-0515
Telephone: 800-998-9938 (U.S. &
Canada)
Fax: 707-829-0104
Email: order@ora.com

Southern Africa

International Thomson Publishing
Southern Africa
Building 18, Constantia Park
138 Sixteenth Road
P.O. Box 2459
Halfway House, 1685 South Africa
Telephone: 27-11-805-4819
Fax: 27-11-805-3648

O'REILLY™

O'Reilly & Associates, Inc.
101 Morris Street
Sebastopol, CA 95472-9902
1-800-998-9938

Visit us online at:
http://www.ora.com/
orders@ora.com

O'REILLY WOULD LIKE TO HEAR FROM YOU

Which book did this card come from?

_____

Where did you buy this book?
- ❏ Bookstore
- ❏ Direct from O'Reilly
- ❏ Bundled with hardware/software
- ❏ Other _____

- ❏ Computer Store
- ❏ Class/seminar

What operating system do you use?
- ❏ UNIX
- ❏ Windows NT
- ❏ Other _____
- ❏ Macintosh
- ❏ PC(Windows/DOS)

What is your job description?
- ❏ System Administrator
- ❏ Network Administrator
- ❏ Web Developer
- ❏ Other _____
- ❏ Programmer
- ❏ Educator/Teacher

❏ Please send me O'Reilly's catalog, containing a complete listing of O'Reilly books and software.

Name _____   Company/Organization _____

Address _____

City _____   State _____   Zip/Postal Code _____   Country _____

Telephone _____   Internet or other email address (specify network) _____

Nineteenth century wood engraving
of a bear from the O'Reilly &
Associates Nutshell Handbook®
Using & Managing UUCP.

POST CARD

BUSINESS REPLY MAIL
FIRST CLASS MAIL   PERMIT NO. 80   SEBASTOPOL, CA

Postage will be paid by addressee

O'Reilly & Associates, Inc.
101 Morris Street
Sebastopol, CA 95472-9902